The handbook of psychothei

D0589087

Psychotherapy is a fast-growing profession, and *The Handbook of Psychotherapy* offers a unique and comprehensive overview of its many aspects. The editors and contributors are all highly experienced practitioners who articulate, singly or jointly, a particular viewpoint, approach or opinion to produce an overall perspective on psychotherapy today. Each brings a different emphasis to the relevant issues, and the creative tension of the dialogue between them contributes to a lively and well-informed picture of theory and practice.

Presented under five main headings – the nature of psychotherapy and its research, its culture, modalities, settings and issues – the book offers a rich source of information and reference.

The *Handbook* has been written for all health professionals, including nurses and general practitioners; for social workers; for psychotherapists in training; for anyone considering psychotherapy as a career or seeking psychotherapy; for voluntary organizations; in short, for all those who need or wish to know more about psychotherapy.

Petrūska Clarkson, MA, PhD, AFBPsS (BPS), is a chartered clinical and counselling psychologist, lecturer and supervisor, consultant integrative psychotherapist, founder director of **metanoia** Psychotherapy Training Institute and founder of the British Institute for Integrative Psychotherapy. She is the author of numerous papers and books in the field of psychotherapy, supervision, organisations and consultancy. She is past Chair of the British organisation of the Society for the Exploration of Psychotherapy Integration, and is also on the British Psychological Society Board of Examiners for the Diploma in Counselling Psychology.

Michael Pokorny, MB, ChB, DPM, FRCPsych., Member Brit. Psi.-An. Soc., is a psychoanalyst and psychoanalytic psychotherapist. He is a member of the Council of the London Centre for Psychotherapy and is current Chair of the Registration Board of the United Kingdom Council for Psychotherapy. He is past Chair of the United Kingdom Standing Conference for Psychotherapy.

The handbook of psychotherapy

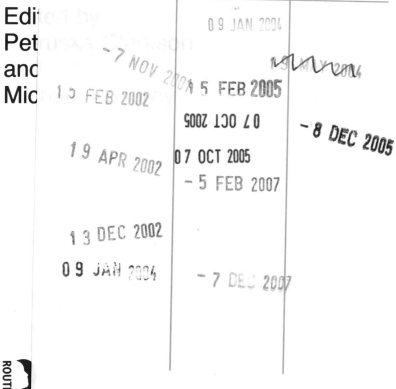
Edited by
Petruska Clarkson
and
Michael Pokorny

London and New York

First published 1994
by Routledge
11 New Fetter Lane, London EC4P 4EE

Simultaneously published in the USA and Canada
by Routledge
29 West 35th Street, New York, NY 10001

Reprinted 1995

Typeset in Times by J&L Composition Ltd, Filey, North Yorkshire
Printed and bound in Great Britain by
Biddles Ltd, Guildford and King's Lynn

British Library Cataloguing in Publication Data
A catalogue record for this book is available from the British Library

Library of Congress Cataloguing in Publication Data
A catalogue record for this book is available from the Library of Congress

ISBN 0-415-07722-2 (hbk)
ISBN 0-415-07723-0 (pbk)

8. 1. 97

Contents

Part III Modalities

Part IV Settings

Part V Issues

Illustrations

FIGURES

The dying and the bereaved

Appendix A

TABLES

Nature and range

Family

Communities

Sexual contact

Contributors

Nachman Alon, MA, is a Clinical Psychologist in private practice in Tel Aviv, Israel. His main therapeutic interest is the integration of several modes of psychotherapy, including hypnosis. He gained experience of PTSD patients during several years of military service both as a commander and as a psychologist.

Talia Levine Bar-Yoseph, MA (Hons Clin. Psych.) is a Clinical Psychologist and Psychotherapist and is currently Director of the Gestalt Programme at **metanoia** Psychotherapy Training Institute. She trained at the Gestalt Training Centre in San Diego and at the Gestalt Institute of Los Angeles, and is a consultant in Organisational Behaviour.

Michael Barkham, MA, MSc, PhD, is a Research Clinical Psychologist at the MRC/ESRC Social and Applied Psychology Unit, University of Sheffield, and has published scientific papers in the areas of psychotherapy, clinical psychology and counselling psychology. He is currently engaged in several major psychotherapy studies and has particular interests in the areas of research design and methodology, brief psychotherapies and service evaluation. He was the recipient of the British Psychological Society's May Davidson Award for 1991 in recognition of his contribution to clinical psychology, and is currently UK Vice-President of the International Society for Psychotherapy Research.

Arnon Bentovim, MB, BS, FRCPsych., DPM, is Consultant Psychiatrist in Child and Adolescent Psychiatry at the Hospital for Sick Children, Great Ormond Street, and the Tavistock Clinic, London, having trained in psychiatry and psychotherapy at the Maudsley Hospital. He trained as a psychoanalyst and has been interested in the development of family therapy approaches since the early 1970s. He was a founder and chair of both the Association and Institute of Family Therapy and was closely associated with the Group Analytic Society and Institute of Group Analysis where he helped found the first Family Therapy course with Dr Robin Skynner. He has been concerned with child protection matters for some years and helped to set up the first sexual abuse treatment project in the United Kingdom in 1980; he has written extensively in this field, most recently *Trauma-Organized Systems: Systemic Understanding of Family Violence* (Karnac, 1992).

Janet Bungener, MEd, MACP, is a Psychoanalytic Child Psychotherapist working in Wood Green Child and Family Consultation Centre and Haringey Child Development Centre. She has a special interest in psycho-dynamic work with children and families with learning and physical disabilities as well as autism. She is a visiting teacher at the Tavistock Clinic for various courses concerning learning disability.

Gillian Butler, PhD, CPsychol., after qualifying as a clinical psychologist, worked as a therapist in the NHS offering short-term psychological treatment to patients referred to a busy out-patient department. She then held a research post in Oxford University Department of Psychiatry for nine years, and specialised in the development and evaluation of treat-ments for the more complex and long-standing anxiety disorders. In addition, she has trained as a cognitive therapist and has always been interested in developing a wide range of clinical skills. She now works for the NHS again, and divides her time between therapy, supervision, training, teaching and writing.

Petrūska Clarkson, MA, PhD, is a Chartered Clinical Psychologist and practising psychotherapist, supervisor and organisational consultant. She is Principal Clinical Psychologist of the **metanoia** Psychotherapy Training Institute in London. She was Chair for the British Institute of Integrative Psychotherapy (BIIP), which is affiliated with the Society for Exploration of Psychotherapy Integration (SEPI International). She has written numerous papers in the field of psychotherapy, supervision, counselling and organisa-tions, and several books, amongst which are *Transactional Analysis Psychotherapy: An Integrated Approach* (Routledge, 1992), *Gestalt Counselling in Action* (Sage, 1989), *On Psychotherapy* (Whurr, 1993) and *The Therapeutic Relationship* (Wiley, in press).

Alan Cooklin, MB, ChB, FRCPsych., DPM, is Consultant in Family Psychiatry at the Marlborough Family Service and University College and the Middlesex Hospitals, and Honorary Senior Lecturer at University College London, and Birkbeck College, London. He was Chairman of the MSc degree course in Family Therapy between the Institute of Family Therapy and Birkbeck College. He is currently Chair of the Institute of Family Therapy and Clinical Director in the North-west London Mental Health NHS Trust.

Louise Embleton Tudor, Adv. Cert. Biodynamic Massage, Dip. Dram. Art, Dip. Ed., Dip. Psychotherapy, ITHP, is an Integrative Psychotherapist. She worked in further education and in the mental health field before training at the Minster Centre for Analytic and Humanistic Psychotherapy, and is a member of the Institute for Traditional and Humanistic Psychotherapy.

She has undertaken further training in Biodynamic Massage at the Chiron Centre for Holistic Psychotherapy and in the Supervision of Counsellors and Psychotherapists at **metanoia** Psychotherapy Training Institute, and has recently established herself in Sheffield as a freelance psychotherapist, supervisor, trainer and consultant.

Sheila Ernst, BA, CertEd, Member Inst. Group Analysis, has worked at the Women's Therapy Centre in London for many years. She is in private practice as a member of the Group Analytic Network and trains counsellors and psychotherapists. She is co-author (with Lucy Goodison) of *In Our Own Hands* (Women's Press, 1981) and co-editor (with Marie Maguire) of *Living with the Sphinx: Papers from the Women's Therapy Centre* (Women's Press, 1987).

Alexandra Fanning trained as a psychoanalytic psychotherapist with the Arbours Association and has held a number of posts within it. She founded and was first Chair of the Arbours Association of Psychotherapists. Having been for many years on the Arbours Training Committee, she is currently the Director of Training. She is also a delegate to the UKCP, having been delegate to the prior organisations, the UKSCP and the original Rugby Psychotherapy Conference, where she was a member of the Working Party and the first treasurer in the period leading up to the inauguration of the UK Standing Conference for Psychotherapy. She is in full-time private practice as a psychoanalytic psychotherapist with a special interest in conjoint marital psychotherapy.

Tanya Garrett, BA, MSc, CPsychol., AFBPsS, is a Chartered Clinical Psychologist and Associate Fellow of the British Psychological Society. She works as a Clinical Psychologist with Walsall Community Health Trust where she manages the Clinical Psychology Service to children, young people and families and provides a psychotherapy resource for the Clinical Psychology Department. She is currently undertaking PhD research at the University of Warwick in the field of sexual contact between psychotherapists and their patients.

Gill Gorell Barnes, MA, MSc, is Senior Clinical Lecturer in the Child and Family Department of the Tavistock Clinic, Consultant to the Training Department at the Institute of Family Therapy, and was previously Director of Training at the Institute for many years.

David Gowling, Dip. Soc. Stud. (Oxford), CQSW, initially worked in industry for twelve years. After qualifying as a social worker, he specialised in work with adolescents, with child abuse and in mental health. During this period he trained and qualified as a psychotherapist. Currently he has a private psychotherapy practice and is involved in both the training and supervision of counsellors and psychotherapists. He is a qualified

Transactional Analysis Clinician and a Provisional Teaching and Supervising Transactional Analyst (with Clinical Speciality).

Pat Grant, MSc (Counselling Psychology), BEd (Hons), RNT, DN, RMN, SCM, RGN, is a Senior Lecturer at the University of Greenwich, London, where she lectures in education and counselling psychology. She is a Counselling Psychologist involved in counselling and supervision. She is a black woman who has done a lot of work with black clients and black supervisees in England. One of her many interests in the field of counselling is working with bereaved clients.

Helena Hargaden, BA (Hons), PGCE, CTA, CIP, BAC Accredited Counsellor, has a psychotherapy and supervision practice in South-east London and is a Primary Tutor on the Diploma in Counselling course at **metanoia** Psychotherapy Training Institute. Previously she was a lecturer in communication studies.

Peter Harper, BSocSc, BA (Hons), MSc (Clinical Psychology), AFBPsS, is a Consultant Clinical Psychologist working in the Child Health Directorate, Northampton. He has a wide range of experience as a clinician, psychotherapist, trainer and supervisor, both in the United Kingdom and abroad. He is a member of several professional organisations and is on the Editorial Board of *The Child Care Worker*, a journal to which he has made a number of contributions on working therapeutically with children.

Judith Hassan, BSc (Hons), CQSW, Dip. App. Soc. Stud., began work at the Jewish Welfare Board in 1969. Since 1977 she has specialised in working with survivors of the Nazi Holocaust, and has chaired the Survivor Centre Steering Group. In 1990 she became Director of Shalvata (Jewish Care), a therapy centre for adults with emotional difficulties, and in 1992 Chair of the Management Committee of the new Centre for Holocaust Survivors in Hendon, and she maintains management responsibility for both centres. In 1992 she organised the European Conference for Professionals Working with Survivors. She has published numerous papers on survivors, presented work on radio and television, and teaches rabbis, hospital staff, social services and Jewish organisations.

Peter Hawkins, BA(Hons), MAHPP, PhD, is Organisational Consultant and founding Partner of Bath Consultancy Group, through whom he works with a wide variety of organisations. He is also a psychotherapist and founder of the Bath Centre for Psychotherapy and Counselling. He is co-author with Robin Shohet of *Supervision in the Helping Professions* (Open University Press, 1989).

Paul Hitchings, MSc, BSc, PGCE, Chartered Psychologist, Accredited Counsellor (BAC), is a practising counselling psychologist with over ten years' experience of working with clients individually, in couples and in group settings. His practice also includes training and supervision of counsellors, teaching counselling psychology in academic settings on undergraduate and postgraduate programs and consultancy work for staff teams in the helping professions.

Robert Jezzard, MA, MRCP, FRCPsych., is a Consultant Child and Adolescent Psychiatrist based at the Bloomfield Clinic, Guy's Hospital. He works in the context of a multidisciplinary team of mental health professionals, primarily with young people and their families from Southeast London. Although he is based in a hospital, he sees many of the young people in community settings in addition to the clinic.

Adele Kosviner, MSc, AFBPsS, CPsychol., is a Consultant Clinical Psychologist working within the National Health Service in Riverside Mental Health Trust, London. She is at present Chair of the British Psychological Society's Psychotherapy Section and representative of the Society to its Joint Standing Committee with the Royal College of Psychiatrists and to the United Kingdom Council for Psychotherapy.

Tom Leary is a priest in the Church of England. He trained in couples work with the National Marriage Guidance Council, St George's Hospital, and at the Tavistock Institute of Marital Studies. At present he is co-ordinator of family and marital work at Westminster Pastoral Foundation, and also works in private practice.

Christine Lister-Ford, BEd, Dip. Hum. Psych., Training and Supervising Transactional Analyst (ITAA), Recognised Supervisor (BAC), is a director of Stockton Psychotherapy Training Institute where she co-ordinates the four-year psychotherapy training in Transactional Analysis. She is Chairperson of the Training Standards Committee of the Institute of Transactional Analysis. She has maintained a private practice for thirteen years.

Sara Llewellin, BA (Hons), PGCE, is currently the Director of St Giles Trust – a voluntary sector agency providing services for homeless people in South London. She has been active in women's, lesbian and anti-racist politics. She is studying TA at **metanoia** Psychotherapy Training Institute.

James Low, PhD, works as a psychotherapist, supervisor and trainer at the Monroe Clinic, Guy's Hospital and in private practice.

Brendan McCormack, MB, BCh, LRCP & SI, MSc Clinical Psychotherapy, MRC Psych., trained in psychiatry at St Thomas and Guy's Hospitals in London. He is Clinical Director and Consultant Psychiatrist at Cheeverstown House, Templeogue in Dublin. He has worked as Consultant Psychiatrist (Mental Handicap) at the Harperbury Hospital and for Haringey Health Authority's Services for People with Learning Difficulties, at St Anne's Hospital in London, and was also a visiting teacher and member of the Mental Handicap Workshop at the Tavistock Clinic.

Oded Manor, BA, PhD, PGDip. App. Soc. Studies and CQSW Dip. Counselling Skills, is Principal Lecturer in Social Work at Middlesex University, London. Previously a Senior Practitioner for group and family work, he continues to supervise group workers and has published numerous papers on the subject. For over twenty years he has been engaged in lecturing and consultancy in various other countries as well.

David Millard, MA, MB, ChB, FRCPsych., is honorary Consultant Psychiatrist to Oxfordshire Health Authority and Emeritus Fellow of Green College, Oxford. He recently retired after twenty years as Lecturer in Applied Social Studies, University of Oxford and consultant at Warneford Hospital. He was previously editor of the *International Journal of Therapeutic Communities*.

Eric Miller, MA, PhD (Cantab), carried out anthropological fieldwork in India and Thailand and was an internal consultant to textile companies in the United States and India before joining the Tavistock Institute in 1958. His main field is organisational research and consultancy, combining systemic and psychodynamic perspectives, and he has worked with a wide variety of organisations in the United Kingdom and internationally. He has also been director of the Institute's Group Relations Programme since 1969. His published output includes numerous papers and six books.

Colin Murray Parkes, MD, FRCPsych., is Honorary Consultant Psychiatrist to the Royal London Hospital and to St Christopher's Hospice, Sydenham. He is author of *Bereavement: Studies of Grief in Adult Life* (Pelican/IUP, 1986), and of numerous papers on the psychological aspects of bereavement, crisis, amputation of a limb and terminal cancer care. He is President of Cruse (Bereavement Care), Scientific Editor of *Bereavement Care* and editorial advisor on numerous journals concerned with hospices and bereavement.

Haya Oakley, BA, PSW, UKCP Reg. Psy. Psychotherapist, was born and educated in Israel, where she graduated as a psychiatric social worker from the Hebrew University of Jerusalem. She is a training committee member of the Philadelphia Association and Chair of the Guild of Psychotherapists. She works as a Psychoanalytic Psychotherapist in private practice and has worked as a community therapist in PA Houses. She appeared on the Channel 4 series *A Change of Mind*, and BBC Radio 4's 'Room to Listen, Room to Talk', and has contributed to 'Thresholds between Philosophy and Psychoanalysis', FAB, London 1989. She was honorary secretary of the UKCP.

Miranda Passey, BA, CQSW, MACP, is Principal Clinical Psychotherapist on the Isle of Wight. She trained at the Tavistock Clinic and has a particular interest in developing awareness of the work of Child Psychotherapists in order to reach a greater number of children in difficulties than is at present possible. As well as her work in the Health Service, she works in a school for children with speech and language difficulties.

Michael Pokorny, MB, ChB, DPM, FRCPsych., Member Brit. Psi.-An. Soc., trained in medicine and psychiatry before training in psychoanalysis and psychoanalytic psychotherapy with adults: individual, group and marital. He was Chair of the Rugby Psychotherapy Conference Working Party from 1982 until the inauguration of the United Kingdom Standing Conference for Psychotherapy in 1989. He was elected Chair of UKSCP annually from 1989 until 1993, when he was appointed to be the first Chair of the Registration Board of the United Kingdom Council for Psychotherapy. He is in full-time private practice as a Psychoanalyst and Psychotherapist with a special interest in conjoint marital psychotherapy.

Charlotte Sills, MA, DipIntegrative Psychotherapy, TSTA (ITAA), is a UKCP registered psychotherapist in private practice and works as a trainer and consultant in a variety of settings, including the National Institute of Social Work and various counselling organisations. Her particular interest has been in bereavement and loss, and for four years she ran the Hounslow Social Services' Bereavement Project. She is also committed to the psychotherapeutic use of groups. She is a qualified Transactional Analysis clinician and a Teaching and Supervising Transactional Analyst (with Clinical Speciality). She is Director of the T.A. Psychotherapy Training Programme at **metanoia** Psychotherapy Training Institute.

Jonathan Smith, LLB, CQSW, Dip. App. Soc. Stud., Dip. Psychotherapy, studied law at Warwick University, then trained as a social worker and obtained a CQSW from Sheffield University. He worked for five years as a social worker for the London Borough of Hounslow, before training as a psychotherapist at the Institute of Psychotherapy and Social Studies. For a further five years he worked on a project to develop counselling and psychotherapy for social services clients in Hounslow, and now works full-time as a psychotherapist and supervisor, and as a tutor on a counselling course at Birkbeck College, University of London.

Kenneth Kirk Smith, MA (Oxon), Dip. App. Soc. Stud. (London), read law at Brasenose College, Oxford, and after two years Voluntary Service Overseas in India, trained to be a social worker at Bedford College, London. In 1967, he began to work with the London Probation Service at the Old Street Magistrates Court in Hackney. In 1970, he became a child-care worker in Barnet. After the local government re-organisation following the Seebohm Report, he spent a year at the Tavistock Clinic on the full-time social work course. After this, he worked for the Family Welfare Association for ten years, and for Wandsworth Social Services for a further eight. Facing another reorganisation, he took early retirement, and spent a year at the LSE as a social worker with a group of people researching new religious movements. He now works with the Church Army as a social worker, at the Marylebone Project which is in the forefront of the problem of homelessness. He is a member of BASW, and was chair of GAPS for six years. He is treasurer of the United Kingdom Council for Psychotherapy.

Keith Tudor, MA, CQSW, is a qualified social worker and has worked in the mental health field for a number of years. He has completed four years of clinical training as a Transactional Analysis psychotherapist and is studying on the Gestalt in Organisations programme; both at **metanoia** Psychotherapy Training Institute, where for the last three years he has been a primary tutor on the BAC-recognised Person-Centred Counselling Course, and is a BAC Accredited Counsellor. He is an Honorary Research Fellow at King's College, University of London. He has a private practice in Sheffield, offering counselling and psychotherapy as well as training, consultancy and research.

Marianne Tranter, BSc, CQSW, Psychiatric Social Worker, Family Therapist, trained in social work at the London School of Economics and had placements at the Maudsley Hospital, where she trained in family therapy initially with Dr Robin Skynner. She has worked in community mental health and child protection teams and was concerned with the founding of family therapy workshops in the community. She has worked at the Hospital for Sick Children for twelve years and has worked in a variety of teams, co-founding the Child Sexual Abuse Team with Arnon Bentovim. She is concerned with integrating individual and family approaches, and she and Arnon Bentovim have been involved with training throughout the United Kingdom and internationally. She also works in private practice.

Gillian Walton, MA, Dip. Ed., after careers in social work and teaching, trained as a marital therapist with the National Marriage Guidance Council and the Tavistock Institute for Marital Studies. She is Head of Training and Supervision at London Marriage Guidance, and works in private practice as a therapist and consultant.

Estela V. Welldon, MD, FRCPsych., is President of the International Association for Forensic Psychotherapy; Consultant Psychotherapist at the Portman Clinic; founding Director of the Forensic Psychotherapy Diploma Course; and an Honorary Lecturer in Forensic Psychotherapy at the British Postgraduate Medical Federation (University of London). She is the author of *Mother, Madonna, Whore: The Idealisation and Denigration of Motherhood* (1988). She has specialised in the application of group analysis to social and sexual deviancy and has written several papers on these subjects. She is a member of the Board of Directors of the International Association of Group Psychotherapy. She also works in private practice and is Consultant to professional women's groups.

Jenifer Elton Wilson, BA, MSc, is a Chartered Psychologist whose work as a psychotherapist has been focused on the recent establishment and provision of counselling psychology within the UK. Having both studied and taught counselling psychology at Master's level, she is currently Head of an expanded counselling service at the new University of the West of England, Bristol. She is Chair of the British Psychological Society Special Group in Counselling Psychology. Her main interest is in the interface between personal meanings and the impossible struggle for excellence in the practice of psychological therapy.

Preface

Petrūska Clarkson and Michael Pokorny

THE BACKGROUND

From our differing but complementary backgrounds, we have shared the idea of a *Handbook of Psychotherapy* for some time. As far back as 1990, Bob Hinshelwood was prescient by linking our two names together in working to push forward the frontiers of psychotherapy in our respective ways. In an editorial of the *British Journal of Psychotherapy*, he wrote:

> If the Standing Conference (UKSCP) shows signs of cohering into a proper professional organisation at last it is because of years of cool (though sometimes impatient) debate. The Conference has become a forum where those who would never normally feel inclined to speak to each other have sat down and shared passionate hopes together. Michael Pokorny's letter, as chairman of the Conference, marks steady progress in the political organisation of psychotherapy in this country and in Europe.
>
> Politics is one thing: perhaps, however, we are still a long way from a similar engagement over differences of theory and practice. However Petrūska Clarkson's careful analysis of the various levels of the psychotherapeutic relationship is an attempt to find a perspective from which an overview might become possible. She contends that all therapeutic relationships have five levels even though the different psychotherapies prioritise different levels. This offers a way of circumventing the inherent contradictions and incompatibilities that exist between different psychotherapies; instead of compatibilities we have different priorities and emphasis. And this leaves a way open for the beginnings of a possible integration of the psychotherapies.
>
> (Hinshelwood 1990: 119)

Although the idea for this book was first mooted by Routledge to Petrūska in 1989, it has taken several years to come to maturity. It was when Michael Pokorny joined as co-editor that a dialogic relationship was formed which provided the necessary impetus for carrying it to completion.

The original idea for the *Handbook* was to provide a reasonably comprehensive overview of the field of psychotherapy which was accessible
enough to the intelligent lay person; as well as useful enough for people
who may wish to use or refer in terms of these services (such as general
practitioners, social workers and employers), and serious enough to
be interesting to practitioners, trainers and supervisors in the field of
psychotherapy.

THE *HANDBOOK*: BACKGROUND

The *Handbook* is divided into five parts: Introductions, Culture, Modalities,
Settings and Issues. The three chapters in the introductions series constitute a scene-setting: first comes 'The nature and range of psychotherapy', which surveys (1) the different professions involved in this field
such as counsellors, psychotherapists and counselling psychologists (differentiating them from adjacent disciplines), (2) the three different ideological traditions or 'schools' in psychotherapy, and (3) presents a map
for conceptualising the different modalities of psychotherapy. The second
chapter is a version of the paper 'The multiplicity of psychotherapeutic
relationships'. It is this paper which first appeared in the *British Journal of
Psychotherapy*, and which Hinshelwood introduced above as having 'the
potential for the beginnings of a possible integration', or at the very least
a framework within which to begin to communicate across the inevitable
schisms, suspicions and territorial disputes of different schools. Even at
the end of this book it became clear that, throughout most of the chapters,
there was a constant implicit, if not explicit, awareness and exploration of
the importance of the therapeutic relationship.

Contrary to the usual procedure of putting the research chapter last, or
towards the end, we acceded to the request of Wilson and Barker to
position the research paper near the beginning as the third chapter. This
chapter could, in addition to the relationship paper, act as an initial prism
to highlight a perspective through which to view all the chapters that
follow, rather than being an afterthought.

We believe that cultural issues in psychotherapy have been significantly
neglected compared to theoretical disputations, and that the influence of
such factors is vastly underrated in many of the approaches to psychotherapy that tend to be Eurocentric, patriarchal and limiting. That is why
cultural issues are separately grouped in Part II of the book. Here, from
her vast experience, Grant explores some of the issues of psychotherapy
and race. Ernst and Gowling, from their different perspectives, address
the influence of gender on psychotherapy – the counter-transference issues
which are so enormous that none of us, however conscious, can consider
ourselves free from the pernicious influences of the sexism that has
pervaded the theory, practice and management of psychotherapy. In

Chapter 6, Hassan discusses her work – the result of another of our culture's most penetrating abuses. This is particularly relevant at the time of writing as we read reports, for example, about ethnic cleansing in Bosnia. Hitchings then offers a view of the issue of sexual orientation as it affects psychotherapy.

In Part III, Modalities, Pokorny and Lister-Ford survey the field of individual adult psychotherapy in Chapter 8, with a brief glance at some of the therapeutic orientations. It must be said that this book, contrary to some excellent others, has attempted to underplay the emphasis on difference between schools and to emphasise common themes and concerns across schools. Harper gives an overview of the spectrum of psychological therapies with children, and Passey surveys the field of analytical psychotherapy with children, while Jezzard gives another perspective on psychotherapy with adolescents culled from his own rich experience. Butler and Low give, jointly and severally, two of the many perspectives on short-term psychotherapy; Leary and Walton briefly but effectively discuss marital psychotherapy. Gorell Barnes and Cooklin skilfully review family psychotherapy, followed by Manor's contribution of a perspective on group psychotherapy of different orientations.

Part IV concerns settings. Psychotherapy in and with organisations brings together the work of Hawkins and Miller, whereas Kosviner expertly reviews the state of psychotherapy within the NHS, with additional material from Knowles. The two Smiths look at the place of psychotherapy in the social services, whereas Oakley and Millard contribute a wide-ranging theoretical perspective on psychotherapeutic communities. Llewellin uses the contributions of several colleagues to bring together her chapter on psychotherapy in the voluntary sector, while Pokorny and Fanning discuss some of the issues of psychotherapy in private practice, with additional material from Hargaden.

Part V concerns recurring and significant current issues in psychotherapy. Bungener and McCormack explore the relatively neglected area of psychotherapy and learning difficulties; Embleton and Tudor, some aspects of the roles of power and influence in psychotherapy – the subject of a number of current conferences. Bentovim and Tranter describe the very important sector of psychotherapy with adult survivors of sexual abuse. This is followed by a chapter on its professional corollary – sexual contact between psychotherapists and their patients, in which Garrett gives a preview of her research. Alon and Levine Bar-Yoseph draw on their experience of post-traumatic stress disorder, and Welldon surveys the less well-known but significant field of forensic psychotherapy. Finally, and fittingly, the book ends with the chapter by Parkes and Sills on psychotherapy with the dying and the bereaved. Two appendices follow – the structure of the United Kingdom Council for Psychotherapy and its member organisations, and the UKCP Code of Ethics.

It is definitely not expected that this book will be read from start to finish, but rather that it will become a useful resource for professionals and lay people alike, beginners and experts, in opening or re-opening doors to areas of interest, learning and professional growth.

With many of the chapters, the authors and/or editors have adduced sources, contact addresses and further reading lists in addition to the usual references. We apologise for no doubt numerous omissions, but wanted to indicate some rather than be exhaustive. For the interested inquirer just beginning a search into a particular area, contacting or reading a couple of sources can often act as a key to unlock the riches which are available but sometimes difficult to access. Information on training is also available from any one of the UKCP member organisations.

The authors in this *Handbook* are an unrepresentative cross-section of the field as it exists today, based on the response we elicited from practitioners able and willing to write within the time limits at our disposal. Each chapter should therefore not be seen as a definitive statement: the diversity of styles and approaches illustrates a sampling of the wide diversity of the voices in the field. Our aim was to have more than one author speak on each subject where possible; this way, the reader benefits not only from two expert perspectives, but from the creative tension that can emerge from all such dialogue. The final collection is not intended to be representative of all themes, modalities, settings and forms of psycho-therapy. In many cases we did ask colleagues to contribute and they could not join the project in time. The authors finally represented here are the outcome of a long and frequently fraught process of contacting authors who promised and did not deliver, who backed out at the last minute, who stepped into the breach, who delivered promptly and with good humour, who forgave our occasional mistakes with good grace, and those who showed some care and concern for our responsibilities and for us as people.

Diversity is an integral and important element of psychotherapy in the United Kingdom and we are proud to carry this flag into Europe and the wider world. It is an integral phenomenon of the English-speaking world to tolerate idiosyncrasy, celebrate difference *and* maintain professional standards. The diversity in this book, we hope, reflects and respects the multitudinous differences that exist among the human beings who come to us for help.

Where clinical material is used for illustration by any author, details have been changed to ensure anonymity. The responsibility for clinical material belongs to the author(s) who have written it, as does the responsibility for permission to reproduce material in the form of extended quotations or diagrams. Despite research showing that no single school has 'all the answers', as mentioned in several chapters (such as 2 and 3), most psychotherapists adhere to a particular orientation, even if it is their one version of the integrative psychotherapies. Authors will therefore refer to people who seek help from psychotherapists, sometimes as patients and sometimes as clients.

The views expressed in these chapters are the view of the authors and not necessarily of the editors. We have also used the terms 'he' and 'she' interchangeably for both the psychotherapist and client in order to try to maintain a balance.

We wish you *bon voyage*.

REFERENCE

Hinshelwood, R. D. (1990) 'Editorial', *British Journal of Psychotherapy* 7(2): 119–20.

Acknowledgements

Our gratitude is due to the many people who have collaborated on this project: in particular Bob Hinshelwood and Windy Dryden; also Ann Kearns for her sterling editorial help and valuable advice, Helena Hargaden for her material, and Camilla Sim, Rita Cremona and Barbara Kulesza. Our thanks go also to all other people who may not be named here but have assisted in various ways. The physical and administrative construction of this book is almost wholly thanks to the dedicated, encouraging and careful ministrations of Katherine Pierpoint, who navigated with patience, fortitude and imagination a task of enormous complexity, involving many authors who did or did not eventually participate and two editors, whose professional lives made constant counter-claims on their time and attention. Particular gratitude is due to our families, the local curry house and all those who have helped late at night, at the end of the project, and when times were difficult.

Edwina Welham, our editor, is especially thanked for her patience and foresight in waiting for the most propitious timing for this book to appear; and it is hoped that the support which has been given to the project by **metanoia** Education for Living Ltd (while Petrūska Clarkson was principal) will continue to bear fruit.

The editors gratefully acknowledge permission to reproduce material previously published elsewhere. Penguin Books granted permission to reproduce Figure 8.1 (Berne's original ego state model) from *Games People Play*. Whurr Publishers granted permission to reproduce Table 13.1 (Comparison between family group therapy, 'stranger' group therapy and individual therapy) from *An Outline for Trainee Psychiatrists, Medical Students and Practitioners*. Every effort has been made to obtain permission to reproduce copyright material throughout this book. If any acknowledgement has not yet been made, the copyright holder should contact the publisher.

Part I

Introduction

Chapter 1

The nature and range of psychotherapy*

Petrūska Clarkson

A chapter of this length cannot fully do justice to the ongoing debate about the nature and range of psychotherapy. It is a subject which continues to exercise some of the finest minds active in psychotherapy today, as witness both the mainstay texts in any training course in counselling and psychotherapy, and the current debate in specialist journals.

In the first instance, definitions of psychotherapy will be briefly reviewed. This will be followed by an attempted differentiation between the major professions engaged in counselling and psychotherapy, following closely the conventions of the main professional bodies involved. The third section will concern a review of the major traditions in psychology which have given rise to different approaches, and briefly review the significance of research in this field. Lastly, there is a diagram for differentiating between different modalities or arenas for counselling and for psychotherapy.

DEFINITIONS

Definitions of psychotherapy are legion, and none is entirely comprehensive nor entirely satisfactory.

> Legislators and courts of law have found it almost impossible to define 'psychotherapy' in such a way as to include, by universal agreement among therapists, that which *is* psychotherapy and to exclude that which *is not* psychotherapy.
>
> (Watkins 1965: 1142)

In their textbook of psychiatry, Henderson and Gillespie (1956) regard psychotherapy as any therapy of the mind, appearing to include talking treatment alongside insulin coma in their fifth edition of 1940 but, by their

* The author wishes to thank Michael Carroll for his valuable editorial input, and for providing the definition of counselling psychology; also Michael Pokorny for his additional material. A portion of this chapter is from 'Counselling, psychotherapy, psychology and applied psychology: the same and different', by P. Clarkson with M. Carroll, in P. Clarkson (1993) *On Psychotherapy*, London: Whurr.

eighth edition of 1956, psychotherapy has become specific to psycho-analysis and its derivatives. Mayer-Gross *et al.* (1954) do not offer a general definition of psychotherapy but use the term to cover a variety of talking treatments. They seem to distinguish it from psychoanalysis as well as from behaviour therapy. They regard all forms of physical treatments as quite separate and different. Merskey and Tonge (1965) clearly regard psychotherapy as talking treatment.

Holmes and Lindley offer a definition: 'The systematic use of a relation-ship between therapist and patient – as opposed to pharmacological or social methods – to produce changes in cognition, feelings and behaviour' (1989: 3). Notice that the use has to be systematic. Holmes and Lindley go on to consider forms of psychotherapy under the headings of structure, space and relationship. Another idea is that psychotherapy is the treatment of psychological conflicts no matter what the presenting symptoms are.

All these definitions rely on the idea of bringing about changes in the personality and manner of a person's relating by the use of essentially psychological techniques. If we are to cover all forms of psychotherapy, that seems to be about as definite as we can get. As soon as we try to be more specific, we begin to exclude some therapies. Of course we may wish to exclude some therapies. There is no agreement on the exact boundaries of psychotherapy. One result of this is that the political definition of psychotherapy has given rise to great argument and considerable tensions within the profession. I refer to the process by which the United Kingdom Council for Psychotherapy (UKCP) has come into being from the original Rugby Psychotherapy Conferences, via the intermediate stage of the UK Standing Conference for Psychotherapy. It is possible to define psycho-therapy as all those therapies that are recognised by the UKCP. That is a simple way of reaching some sort of agreement. The trouble is that there are always some who claim that some psychotherapy is excluded from the Council. This is merely another way of having the argument of what is, and what is not, psychotherapy. On the other hand we can recognise that other professions also have ill-defined borders, and we can stop worrying so much about our general definition or our political solution by recognising that the borders of psychotherapy are not fixed.

The time-span within which psychotherapy operates ranges from one interview to many years of treatment. The rise of brief psychotherapy (as discussed in Chapter 11) has shown that not only can important changes be made very quickly, such as in ten or fifteen sessions, but can also occur within just one interview. The time boundaries of group psychotherapy have proved to be very varied. From a start of once-weekly group meetings lasting one-and-a-half or one-and-a-quarter hours, groups have become marathon, intermittent, more than once a week; the variations that have been tried out seem endless. Once the psychotherapy is exported to the home setting, as can happen in some family therapy clinics, the time frame

changes altogether, lasting until something is achieved, or the team has to leave. Even in the psychoanalytic sphere there has been change. In some places analysis takes place five times per week, in others four or three times weekly. Even more radical, the revolutionary French psychoanalyst Lacan would end the session when some significant moment had been experienced. Thus sessions could last for ten minutes or two hours.

In many psychotherapies a contract for time and fees is made at the start, although it may have to be modified later. Even where the contract appears not to have been made overtly, as in psychoanalysis, in reality the contract is for as long as it takes, even if that is many years. Of course in a therapeutic community the time involved is twenty-four hours a day for many weeks, months or years.

The range of clients that are offered psychotherapy has varied from time to time and from place to place. There seems to be general agreement that neurotic symptoms are amenable to psychotherapy, and there is so far no clear evidence that the form of the psychotherapy makes a material difference to the outcome. Other diagnostic categories, or the psychotherapy from which they draw, produce very different reactions from different psychotherapists. There are therapeutic communities that specialise in treating psychosis, such as the Arbours Association and the Philadelphia Association, both being descendants of the original work of Laing. Some psychotherapy schools seem to specialise in certain types of client, so that, for instance, specific phobias have become largely the province of behaviour therapy, especially the implosion treatment for phobia of spiders (arachnophobia). Others have specialised in the treatment of psychopathy, especially the Henderson Hospital, and yet others in the treatment of offenders, such as the Portman Clinic for sexual offenders and Grendon Underwood prison which has an excellent record in the rehabilitation of recidivist criminals using a combination of community and group methods, including psychodrama. The validation of results, psychotherapy studies or outcome (as discussed in Chapter 3) is another matter of great concern to us all. It is hoped that the new moves towards psychotherapy audit will help on this front.

ALLIED DISCIPLINES

This section considers some of the factors involved in differentiating counselling, psychotherapy, psychology, psychiatry and several allied fields. It is written for several reasons. One is to help establish for counsellors, psychotherapists and counselling psychologists separate and valuable professional identities which have a place and domain of their own. Such an attempt can provide helpful guidelines for referral agencies, professionals and members of the public to distinguish between different kinds of service provision, so that needs and resources can be more

accurately aligned. Ignorance and confusion in themselves further perpetuate difficulties endemic to the most complex task of providing the best and most cost-effective help for individuals in emotional trouble, with the least long-term detrimental effects, and hopefully of most benefit in terms of improved psychological health. Secondly, the ability to know where helping modalities overlap and where they differ can be a tremendous help to professionals themselves. It can establish boundaries, acknowledge strengths and limitations and afford a working relationship between them that fosters mutual respect rather than distrust. Professionalisation, accreditation and ethical sanctions can go some way towards reducing potential damage: they can also provide the first step towards professional identity and the ability to relate to other professionals from similar and different helping backgrounds.

According to Carroll (1991, 1992b), there are three main approaches to considering the relationship between counselling, psychotherapy, psychology and psychiatry.

First, there are those who 'lump them together' and refuse to acknowledge any differences. They point dramatically to the client groups dealt with by each profession and hail the fact that counsellors see clients, psychotherapists see clients (but they may call them patients) and counselling psychologists see clients (they call them both clients and patients) and that these clients do not differ substantially from one another. Domains held sacred by one profession are invaded without apology by another. Psychotherapists see clients in long-term therapy, some of whom are very disturbed and difficult people who may even have psychiatric histories and they may work with transference and the unconscious. Such very disturbed clients traditionally have been the work of the psychiatrist, the clinical psychologist, or the psychotherapist. The counsellor, on the other hand, sometimes works in a college of higher education, can average six sessions a client and deals with crisis and developmental issues. The counselling psychologist (a new breed on the British scene) works in hospitals, organisations, mental health centres and all those areas once claimed by counsellors, psychotherapists and clinical psychologists. Why try to fabricate differences if all three approaches do much the same thing?

According to Carroll, a second group 'split' the groups and refuse to acknowledge many similarities. Counsellors, they claim, are low on theory, have no requirement for personal therapy in their training, work in the short term and with developmental issues. Counselling psychologists are psychologists who use counselling in their work, are high on theory and research and as yet seem unsure about where they will end up or in what client groups they will specialise. Psychotherapists concentrate on personal psychotherapy, use supervised client work, spend a long time as apprentices, and have deeply disturbed and long-term clients. However you view it, these are three different approaches to helping people and proponents

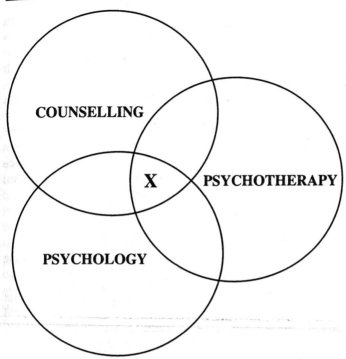

Figure 1.1 Venn diagram representing the three primary arenas of counselling, psychology and psychotherapy

of this view believe they must be kept separate. Some view the differences in terms of specialisation, others in terms of training. It is also true that issues of power, ideology, money, status, employability and snobbery play a significant part in such territorial anxieties.

A third group talk about 'overlap' between the three: areas of similarity and areas of difference. Duffy (1990: 11) recognises the areas in common and sees differences coming from 'intentionality'; that is, not what is done but how practitioners think of their work. This contribution of Carroll is supplemented here by a diagram (Figure 1.1), which I developed to illustrate the discussion. Figure 1.1 is offered as a potentially helpful tool in guiding and demarcating the discussion areas between the overlapping fields of counselling, psychology and psychotherapy and will form the basis for the discussion in the rest of this section.

Figure 1.1 shows each area as distinct in itself, but relating to each of the other two areas, and indicates the interrelationship between all three. The overlap area between counselling and psychotherapy represents the work of counselling professionals with advanced practice qualifications or the psychotherapist using counselling skills. The overlap area between psychotherapy and psychology represents psychotherapists with a psychology

qualification or psychologists trained as psychotherapists. The overlap area between counselling and psychology represents counselling psychologists – that is, psychology graduates with counselling qualifications, but no special training in psychotherapy. 'X' marks the area of work which involves the work of psychology graduates who have training and experience in both counselling and psychotherapy. This may be the appropriate area for the profession of counselling psychology.

We will look in detail at each of the above – namely, the counsellor, the psychotherapist and the counselling psychologist – and then note four areas where dialogue can take place between the three approaches. For each profession, people can be self-referred, or come via their general practitioners, friends or contacts.

Counsellor

The British Association for Counselling, founded in 1977, defines counselling as follows:

> Counselling is the skilled and principled use of relationship to facilitate self-knowledge, emotional acceptance and growth, and the optimal development of personal resources. The overall aim is to provide an opportunity to work towards living more satisfyingly and resourcefully. Counselling relationships will vary according to need but may be concerned with developmental issues, addressing and resolving specific problems, making decisions, coping with crisis, developing personal insights and knowledge, working through feelings of inner conflict or improving relationships with others.
>
> The counsellor's role is to facilitate the client's work in ways that respect the client's values, personal resources and capacity for self determination.
>
> (BAC 1989: 1)

Counsellors may bring special training, experience and expertise to the counselling relationship, to enable people to further their own growth and enhance their personal functioning. In this way, counsellors are enablers and facilitators, helping a client with a specific problem and focusing on evolutionary change. Counselling is largely a general field, but it can also be quite specific; for example, redundancy counselling, marital or sexual counselling, debt counselling, HIV, retirement and health counselling, or bereavement counselling.

The British Association of Counselling publishes a directory of counsellors throughout the United Kingdom. This body also has a Code of Ethics and Practice for Counsellors, whose aim 'is to establish and maintain standards for counsellors and to inform and protect members of the public seeking their services'. Also under this code, 'counsellors subscribe to

counselling, (2) issues of
(BAC 1984: 1).
ion through the BAC, which
as a Personal, Family, Sexual
ral Counselling, Counselling in
Medical Settings. Training in
irs, although some people who
alifications than experience and
ietimes with good reason, that they
erlap between the two areas. A well-
qual value to that of people in other
to remain with more short-term work,
nbers of the population, and with areas
vement or career counselling or crisis
solving rather than in-depth work on a
of counselling is to give the client an
and clarify ways of living more satisfyingly
is thus not a destructuring and restructuring
eate the conditions through the counselling
on can connect with their basic drive towards
n adjusting to changes of role situations and
ife. Counsellors usually do not have psychology
consciously use psychology as an academic disci-
their practice. Pastoral counselling centres (for
minster Pastoral Foundation) more usually train
iodynamic theory and practice.
s stage best to serve the two areas, counselling and
y concentrating on where they are most different; that is,
polar opposites, rather than getting stuck in a quagmire
ounselling can be seen to focus on evolutionary change,
hotherapy focuses on revolutionary change. Proctor (1989)
person-centred problem solving in the here-and-now. Diffi-
distinguishing between counselling and psychotherapy do not
is from responsibility to look at the poles. Issues become clearer
e look at the two poles; and just because the task is difficult does
an it shouldn't be done. Doing this, we can establish whether an
is closer to one 'end' or the other. This is easier and more effective
trying to make a boundary, because clearly there is considerable
erlap.

Counsellors help to oil the wheels of someone's experience so that they manage to function better. It is meant to alleviate suffering. It is for those whose life position is comfortable enough so that they could get through life very well without a 'metanoia' or a turnabout. Counselling seems most suited to a model of human growth in human beings, and indeed many

counselling courses are predicated on the work of Rogers, who emphasised that, through the creation of the necessary conditions of respect, empathy and genuineness, the human being will naturally learn

> to *be* more of his experience – to be the feelings of which he has been frightened as well as the feelings he has regarded as more acceptable. He becomes a more fluid, changing, learning person . . . the motivation for learning and change springs from the self-actualising tendency of life . . . to flow into all the differentiated channels of potential development, insofar as these are experienced as enhancing.
>
> (Rogers 1961: 285)

A characteristic of revolutionary change is that the starting conditions and basic components of the system have to be changed, and may even appear out of the regions of probable predictions. Evolutionary change, in contrast, suggests that the same starting conditions and basic components can conceivably lead to the accomplished outcomes; that is, one could predict the range of probable outcomes. The juxtaposition of evolutionary and revolutionary change emphasises different sets of skills, different goals and different methodologies. An individual's defensive structures can be left intact or strengthened in counselling, by using existing personality resources and the individual's potential for growth and self-healing.

Psychotherapy, on the other hand, focuses on discontinuous, revolutionary change. The justification for psychotherapy often needs to be that such an expensive and time-consuming intervention is necessitated because, unless discontinuous change is implemented, serious tragedy may result. In this case, the medical model may be appropriate in terms of diagnosis (or at least assessment) leading to treatment implementing or seeking for a 'cure'. A medical model may be more effective when there is actual structural damage to the organism which has to be reversed before the organism can start reconnecting with its own innate healing process. Psychotherapy, whether psychodynamic, behavioural or humanistic/existential, concerns the destructuring and restructuring of the personality, whether it is conceived of as belief-and-behaviour systems, ego states, or super-ego and self structures.

Sometimes counsellors lack the training and the facilities in screening, assessing and monitoring risks of suicide, homicide or psychosis which may only become apparent in the later stages of a helping relationship. Of course, this is not to suggest that all screening or assessment procedures, even when done by extremely experienced psychotherapists or psychiatrists, are always either effective or helpful. On the other hand, there are many reports of well-functioning individuals who set out to find someone to help them with a circumscribed problem such as a lack of interest in sex with a marital partner, and then end up several years later,

having entered (for example) three-times-weekly psychoanalysis, with a sense of having been misled or misinformed. The point here is not to suggest that there are absolute dividing lines between the work of the different professions, but to engage others (in and outside these professions) to continue to question and articulate what differences there may be; not so much in the overlap areas, but in the areas which are more distinctly differentiated.

Loughley (1985), during a conference on training in counselling and psychotherapy, put it this way:

> Counselling and psychotherapy are not the same process, although I know there are some of you who would disagree with that statement. For me the difference between them is one of history. Counselling focuses on that which belongs to the now-here. It can be achieved through care and cognition, it is possible to think about it. Psychotherapy on the other hand, is to take the now as a living history: that the things learnt then are happening now but in a different context.

Counselling therefore can be seen to focus on *enabling* and *facilitating*, whereas psychotherapy can be seen to emphasise *intervention*, *treatment* and *reconstruction*. Given that in evolutionary change the organism is striving, naturally and probably successfully, towards its fulfilment, the helper needs to be supportive, enabling and facilitating of this self-generated and self-directed process. In revolutionary change the focus is on interpretation, confrontation, destructuring and reconstruction. The risk of systemic disintegration is naturally lesser in evolutionary change than in revolutionary change, and therefore the skills and experience involved in the latter are naturally of a different order; but not necessarily better or worse than the skills of enabling or facilitation. Goal-setting and the educational task will therefore be more important in counselling training, and diagnosis of pathology more important in the training of psychotherapists.

It is less differentiating but, practically, still the case that counselling assists people in finding the solution to a particular problem, or dealing with a particular crisis, whereas psychotherapy helps people to develop new ways of solving problems which can become generalised to new situations. There is also sometimes, as with Loughly above, a differentiation drawn between counselling as dealing with a current situation contrasted with psychotherapy as dealing with a past situation.

Psychotherapist

Psychotherapy can also be defined as:

> a form of treatment for mental illness and behavioural disturbances in which a trained person establishes a professional contact with the

patient and through definite therapeutic communication, both verbal and non-verbal, attempts to alleviate the emotional disturbance, reverse or change maladaptive patterns of behaviour, and encourage personality growth and development. Psychotherapy is distinguished from such other forms of psychiatric treatment as the use of drugs, surgery, electric shock treatment and insulin coma treatment.

(Freedman *et al*. 1975: 2601)

Psychotherapy is the treatment by psychological means of problems of an emotional nature in which a trained person deliberately establishes a professional relationship with a patient with the object of removing, modifying or retarding existing symptoms, of mediating disturbed patterns of behavior and of promoting positive personal growth and development.

(Wolberg 1954: 118)

Previously, anybody could set up as a psychotherapist: that is, prior to the formation of the UKCP, whose aim is to create a profession and a register so that the public can identify appropriately trained practitioners who are subject to an enforceable Code of Ethics. It was founded as the UKSCP in 1989, is now the UKCP and has seventy-three member organisations grouped into eight sections, each containing a distinct kind of psychotherapy (see Appendix A for details). The voluntary Register, which appeared in May 1993, will form the foundation of a Statutory Register of psychotherapists. A national audit of psychotherapy is in preparation and a variety of initiatives are under way, including co-operation with the development of national vocational qualifications at the higher levels, research into and management of the overlap between psychotherapy, counselling and counselling psychology.

There is now usually a minimum of three years' training, and most psychotherapy training institutions involved in the UKCP require most of their trainees to be in extended personal psychotherapy so that professionals who graduate from these training programmes have personal experience of the process and uses of psychotherapy themselves. Thus, personal psychotherapy is considered to be a vital part of most training. The personal psychotherapy of trainees usually is of a similar duration, type and frequency as that which they would be offering their clients.

Psychotherapists would expect to deal with more serious problems, such as clinical aspects; clients are seen frequently, in regular sessions at least once a week, perhaps more frequently. Clients (or patients) may want to go deep and far back into their past; repetitive patterns of behaviour are identified, worked on and cleared if they are having a negative effect upon the client's present life. Psychotherapists will usually have a wider range and greater flexibility in their working methods than counsellors or psychoanalysts. Psychotherapists may or may not be psychoanalysts.

Psychoanalyst

Freud gave several definitions of psychoanalysis. One of the most explicit is to be found at the beginning of an encyclopaedia article written in 1922:

> Psycho-analysis is the name (i) of a procedure for the investigation of mental processes which are almost inaccessible in any other way, (ii) of a method (based on that investigation) for the treatment of neurotic disorders and (iii) of a collection of psychological information obtained along those lines, which is gradually being accumulated into a new scientific discipline.
>
> (Laplanche and Pontalis 1988: 367)

> The word 'psychoanalysis' refers to a theoretical viewpoint concerning personality structure and function, in the application of this theory to other branches of knowledge and also to a specific psycho-therapeutic technique. Although much developed since his time this body of knowledge is based upon the discoveries of Sigmund Freud.
>
> (British Psycho-Analytical Society 1990: 37)

Psychoanalysts may or may not be medical doctors; but all psychiatrists are medically qualified. Psychoanalysts have recently organised themselves into a body called the British Confederation of Psychotherapists.

Psychiatrist

The Shorter Oxford Dictionary defines psychiatry as 'healing, medical treatment. . . . The medical treatment of diseases of the mind' (Onions 1968: 1700). The relevant professional body is the Royal College of Psychiatrists. Psychiatrists have a medical degree, then undergo further specialist training in psychiatry. Many psychiatrists are not trained in psychotherapy, but they can prescribe drugs. There is a clear difference between child and adult psychiatry. Psychiatrists are specialists in the treatment and management of serious disturbances such as psychosis, schizophrenia, manic-depressive disorders and so on. They tend to work in hospital or psychiatric settings, unless they work in private practice settings.

Psychologist and applied psychologist

Psychologists and applied psychologists are another category to be distinguished. Psychologists are professionals with at least one degree in psychology. Many move on to further postgraduate studies in applied psychology, one of which, these days, is counselling psychology.

The dictionary definition of 'psychology' as 'the science of the nature, functions and phenomena of the human soul or mind' (Onions 1968: 1700) is somewhat restrictive in its view. Psychology is not only the 'science of the mind' but also the science of human behaviour in all its aspects. Psychology interprets the person (Carroll and Pickard 1993) and results in a number of theories of personality and research methods for understanding the person. Its questions are person-related: why do people behave the way they do? What motivates the individual? How do people grow and begin to think and use language? Can we isolate stages of life as individuals progress towards old age? From its academic base, psychology is divided into a number of subsections, such as development psychology, cognitive, personality theory, biological basis of behaviour, abnormal psychology psychological assessment. From this academic basis, psychologists move to apply their subject to the world.

The British Psychological Society is an amalgamation of the various applied psychologies. There are approximately thirteen Divisions, Sections and Special Interest Groups within the Society, ranging through developmental psychology, educational, occupational, clinical, counselling, clinical neuropsychology and so on. It can be difficult at times to differentiate between the three: the occupational psychologist, the clinical psychologist and the counselling psychologist.

Occupational psychologist

An occupational psychologist will have knowledge in relation to the following eight areas: 'Human-machine interaction, design of environments and of work, personnel selection and assessment, performance appraisal and career development, training (including identification of needs and evaluation), employee relations and motivation and organization development' (Fitzgibbon 1990).

Not many occupational psychologists train to do psychotherapy. Occupational psychologists are usually better paid than clinical psychologists, since they usually work in industry (as opposed to the NHS), and they may, for example, work on computers to make software programs.

Clinical psychologist

'The key tasks of clinical psychologists are: Assessment, Treatment, Training/teaching and Research (both patient and service related) as well as Management' (BPS 1988b: 4).

All clinical psychologists must belong to their professional body, the British Psychological Society, and they will then be on the Register of Chartered Psychologists. This document is available from the BPS, and it contains the names, qualifications and contact addresses of all the chartered psychologists in the United Kingdom. The BPS distinguishes between members who are prohibited from using MBPsS on publicity (BPS

1991: 26–27), and chartered psychologists who have done additional training in psychology in addition to holding a psychology degree.

A clinical psychologist will have studied psychology for a long time (usually a bachelor's and often a master's degree in psychology), and will have trained in clinical settings; for example hospitals, with clinical focus, or made special study of mental retardation, or management of phobias or behaviour disorders. Not all chartered clinical psychologists are trained in psychotherapy; many have not been in psychotherapy themselves. They do not prescribe drugs, but they are usually trained to do psychodiagnostics, such as the use of tests such as the Rorschach, Myers Briggs, MMPI or Wechsler.

> The range of treatment techniques has grown considerably during the last twenty years, from the previously limited range of essentially educational or psychodynamic techniques. . . . Examples are the treatment of elimination disorders in children, phobic conditions in adults and the remediation of cognitive difficulties following different types of brain injury. Some of these treatments now offer positive alternatives to drug treatments (such as anxiety-management procedures), and supplement medical treatments in people with long-term-disabling conditions.
>
> Behavioural methods (such as desensitisation), methods based on social learning principles (such as social skills training) and cognitive methods, used especially for altered mood states, are now widely used. In addition, a wider range of psychotherapeutic approaches has been developed, based on theories that are not essentially psychodynamic (such as personal construct theory). It has become apparent that there are a number of non-specific factors which are relevant to many apparently different techniques. A number of these approaches are used by counsellors and other non-psychologists to help people with less serious conditions.
>
> (BPS 1988a: 5)

As said before, 'the boundaries between clinical psychology as a discipline and other academic and health-care disciplines, are not fixed' (BPS 1988a: 1), and the development of the profession of counselling psychology demonstrates this further.

Counselling psychologist

Training as a Counselling Psychologist is already an avenue to chartered psychologist status and the group may soon become an independent Division of the BPS. At the time of writing it is a Special Group of the BPS, as Carroll makes clear:

counselling psychology moved from being a 'Section' in 1982 to becoming a 'Special Group' in 1988 with increasing aspirations to becoming a Division within BPS. Its membership . . . is still probably the fastest-growing section of the BPS. . . . Becoming a Division with BPS would bring with it major implications for training, training courses, career structure and pay levels, status, and supervision. A proposed new Diploma in Counselling has been outlined as the next step on the journey to Division status.

(1991: 74)

One important, if not the most important, difference between counsellors and counselling psychologists is the conscious use of academic psychology alongside practical counselling skills. Counselling psychologists have a basic degree in psychology, and then further training in counselling psychology (MSc). Counselling psychology is here conceptualised as the overlapping area between counselling and psychotherapy in the Venn diagram (see Figure 1.1 above) representing the three primary arenas of counselling, psychology and psychotherapy.

Counselling psychology is not considered identical with counselling (even when it is carried out by psychology graduates). In counselling psychology, there is an emphasis on the systemic application of distinctively psychological understanding, based on empirical research of the client and the counselling process, to the practice of counselling. The relevant psychological knowledge is partly concerned with the problems of presenting clients, and partly with the procedures and processes involved in counselling. It would be remembered that counselling psychology involves work in an organisational context as well as with individual clients, and synthesises elements of better-developed areas of professional work such as clinical and occupational psychology. Life-span developmental psychologies, and the social psychology of interpersonal processes are among the areas that supply the academic foundations of counselling psychology. Of central scientific relevance, of course, are empirical investigations of the processes and outcomes of counselling and of related methods of psychotherapy.

The psychological understanding of counselling derives not only from formal psychological enquiry but also from the *interpersonal relationships* between practitioners and their clients. The essence of such relationships is one of personal exploration and clarification in which psychological knowledge is utilized and shared in ways which enable clients to deal more effectively with their inter- and intra-personal concerns. The capacity to establish and maintain such relationships ultimately rests upon the personal qualities and maturity of the individual counselling psychologist. Personal qualities such as non-defensiveness and a capacity to experience and communicate empathic resonance, constitute essential resources which the counselling psychologist draws upon. Whilst these characteristics may be enhanced by skills training they derive primarily from a foundation of personal experience and integrative maturity.

(BPS 1989: 1; author's italics added)

Emerging issues

From the above, a number of interesting areas emerge as crucial to the ongoing dialogue of exploring, differentiating or ignoring professional disciplinary boundaries.

First, the concept of change and what it means. There are different kinds of change possible within therapeutic settings: problem-solving, environmental change, adjustment, renegotiation (as in a relationship), developmental change (evolutionary) and revolutionary change (personality restructuring). Is it possible to look at the professional approaches above to see if certain approaches are more appropriate for certain kinds of change within the person and his/her environment?

A second area of interest is the area of relationship within therapeutic settings. Clarkson (1991) and Gelso and Carter (1985) have outlined different kinds of relationships appropriate to different therapeutic approaches or more applicable to different client groups. It may well be that such relationships are also in keeping with the professions above.

The third area is that of training. Carroll (1991) has outlined ways of connecting training and education in counselling, psychotherapy and counselling psychology that connects rather than diversifies them. He suggests a three-stage model depicting pathways in which counselling is (1) integrated in an already existing profession, such as nursing or social work, (2) seen as the primary work of the practitioner, (3) a specialisation in a given area or field, like employee counselling, student counselling, working with eating disorders, marital counselling (psychotherapy training and practice would enter here). Further theory, practice and research that connects counselling and psychotherapy with psychology (or indeed another profession – counselling could be connected to sociology or education or politics) would add postgraduate qualifications to the above, leading to Advanced Diplomas, MA or MSc degrees. Carroll (1991) has also pointed out the problems emerging if the three main organisations to whom counsellors, psychotherapists, and counselling psychologists are affiliated (the BAC, UKCP and BPS) become too isolated and ally themselves to rigid training that refuses to recognise other expertise.

DIFFERENT APPROACHES

For lay persons, as well as helping professionals, it is not exactly easy to find one's way (in addition to disciplinary confusion) around the theories and psychotherapy prevalent at this time of the late twentieth century. In the professional literature, some 250 different schools or approaches to counselling and psychotherapy have been identified (Corsini 1986); Holmes and Lindley (1989) refer to the existence of over 300 types of psychotherapy. In addition to the difficulties attendant on differentiating professional boundaries, this task can be bedevilled by the incredible range of approaches, theories and schools which are all part of the vast ocean of work conducted by the different professionals in these fields. Karasu (1986) has talked of polling 450 models of counselling/psychotherapy nationwide in the United States alone.

It can be both difficult to identify where particular approaches come from historically, or where they share characteristics or belong *vis-à-vis* other approaches in terms of family resemblances. Dryden's book *Individual Therapy in Britain* (1984) can be extremely useful to help understand the differences between the approaches. Any attempt to map out psychotherapy is fraught with ambiguity and argument, because deep psychological as well as social, ideological and economic factors influence this profession as much as any other. However, many people have found it helpful to have some kind of overall location diagram of major thinkers in psychotherapy, at least to give them some initial starting points (see Table 1.1 below). It is thus not suggested that this table is the only way to do it, or that it does any more than provide the starting point for several debates. However, its usefulness over two decades with psychology students and interested lay people has acted as an encouragement to make it more available. Inevitably, where space and time is restricted, some important names have been omitted. It is hoped that the general notion is clear enough for readers to continue to fill in from their own reading, their inquiries and their own experience.

A brief overview follows of the underlying traditions of counselling and psychotherapy, with a look to the future and the goals of integrative psychotherapy as one of the ways forward.

THE THREE MAJOR TRADITIONS IN TWENTIETH-CENTURY PSYCHOTHERAPY

Three major streams of psychotherapy all originated around the turn of the twentieth century. Freud's (1915/1973) theory of psychoanalysis came to represent one major stream of psychological thinking and psychotherapy. His first major work, *The Interpretation of Dreams*, was published in 1900. Freudian and Kleinian psychoanalytic thinking tended to view human beings as biologically determined, and motivated primarily by sexual and aggressive drives. For Freud, the purpose of psychoanalysis was exploration and understanding or analysis, not necessarily change (1915/1973).

The second major stream derives its theoretical lineage from Pavlov (1927), the Russian psychophysiologist who studied conditioned reflexes and other learning behaviours. Theoreticians following in this tradition are usually referred to as learning theorists, behaviour modification specialists, or latterly, cognitive-behaviour therapists.

In 1968 Abraham Maslow coined the term 'third-force psychology' (1968: iii) to distinguish the third grouping shown below. This tradition did *not* originate from Freud or from Pavlovian ideas. The intellectual and ideological grandfather of this humanistic/existential tradition is Jacob Moreno. Moreno was arguably the first psychiatrist to put 'the patient' in a centrally responsible role in his own life drama. He worked with people to empower them to do their own healing. Moreno was applying group psychotherapy with children based on humanistic existential principles, and writing about it by 1908 (Greenberg 1975: 201).

Professionals and lay people familiar with the inter- and intra-disciplinary squabbles of different traditions will be able to use their own knowledge to augment or modify this presentation in Table 1.1 considerably for themselves. Such attempts at distinguishing between different kinds of service provision can provide basic guidelines for members of the public and trainees, so that needs and resources can be more accurately aligned. The task of providing the best and most cost-effective help for individuals in emotional trouble is complex in itself, and ignorance of the field can intensify the complexity for people already in trouble. For someone who may already be confused and simply in need of emotional help, it may not be easy to find that appropriate help (that holds the least long-term detrimental effects, and the most benefit in terms of improved psychological health). The person may need emergency help and may not have the leisure and rationality to sift through the huge variety of approaches available. Secondly, the ability to know where helping modalities overlap and where they differ can be a tremendous help to professionals themselves. It can establish boundaries, acknowledge strengths and limitations and afford a working relationship between them that fosters mutual respect rather than distrust.

There are some psychotherapists who are quite hard to place in Table 1.1 because they cross over in terms of values or according to their interpreters, or because they have become fundamentally integrated with others. For example, Reich (1945) was primarily from a psychoanalytic lineage, but his influence today is most clearly manifested in the humanistic/ existential grouping through the presence of the bio-energetic therapy of Lowen (1969). Further examples are Alice Miller (1979/83), originally a psychoanalyst who sounds very humanistic, and Geoffrey Kelly (1955), who developed a constructivist view. Whereas Masterson (1976) is clearly in the first group, despite his early protestations, Kohut's (1977) actual

Table 1.1 Map of major traditions of psychotherapy

School of therapy	Psychoanalytic	Behavioural	Humanistic/ existential
Founder	Freud	Pavlov	Moreno
Date when active	1893	1902	1908
Comments about philosophy, orientation and practice	Bio-psychological determinism. Analysand lying on couch. Psychotherapist is abstinent/opaque, makes interpretations from position of greater understanding. Centrality of unconscious process and transference relationship.	Behaviours seen as a result of learning and conditioning. Emphasis on experimental research and measurable variables. Stimulus/response chains. Cognitive processes. Working alliance essential.	Centrality of responsibility. Non-interpretative concern with here-and-now. Psychotherapist as person, plus transference in some approaches. Occasionally includes transpersonal. Dialogue and relationship. Real relationship emphasised.
Application	Used particularly for neurotic illness, usually modified approach for other disorders. Select client group.	Used particularly for phobias and obsessive behaviours, also depression. Wide client group.	Used for psychoses, personality disorders and neuroses, but also for growth and development. Self-motivated client group.
Aetiology	Sexual and aggressive drives. Early childhood experience.	Conditioned reflexes. Biology. Contingencies of reinforcement.	Biological, social and creative needs from child to adult.
Techniques	Analysis, free association, dream interpretation, parapraxes, etc. Resistance and transference. Interpretation. Catharsis.	Learning and conditioning. Flooding. Modelling. Desensitisation. Thought-stopping. Role rehearsal. Creation of reinforcement schedules. Other cognitive/behavioural techniques (Hawton *et al.* 1989).	Meaning and change. Feelings expressed. Wide and diverse. Active. Interventionist. Invitation to take responsibility. Creative.
Goal	Resignation to the depressive position (Hinshelwood, 1989: 153). Insight.	Adjustment or elimination.	Self-realisation. Self-responsibility.

Table 1.1 Continued

School of therapy	Psychoanalytic	Behavioural	Humanistic/ existential
Other workers	Bion (1962/84)	Beck *et al.* (1990)	Berne (1972/75)
	Bowlby (1952)	Dryden (1984)	Binswanger (1958)
	Anna Freud (1968)	Ellis (1962)	Boss (1979)
	Fairbairn (1952)	Eysenck (1968)	Egan (1975/1982)
	Federn (1977)	Hawton *et al.* (1989)	Frankl (1969)
	Jung (1953)	Lazarus (1981)	Laing (1960)
	Klein (1949)	Skinner (1953)	Maslow (1968)
	Lacan (Benvenuto 1986)		May (1969)
	Malan (1979)		Perls *et al.* (1969)
	Samuels (1985; 1989)		Rogers (1986)
	Symington (1986)		Rowan (1990)
	Winnicott (1958)		Yalom (1970)
Focus	Why?	What?	How?
	The past.	The present, including the immediate past.	The present, including past and future.

position can be ambiguous. Some of Berne's TA followers have remained linked to psychoanalytical developmental theory. Some approaches do not easily fit into this map at all. Hypnotherapy is originally Pavlovian, and systems theorists may be psychodynamic, cognitive-behavioural, humanistic, existential, or all of these in combination or integration (Beutler and Clarkin 1990).

Jung (1953), particularly when thoroughly infused with Kleinian developmental principles, is clearly within the psychoanalytic tradition; for example, in the work of Fordham (1958). However, when the focus is on the positive role of the unconscious, the interactive humanity of the psychotherapist and the person's self-realisation, his theories and approaches are very much more at home with the humanistic/existentialist group. Samuels (1985), in *Jung and the Post-Jungians*, explores some of the important issues of such a debate, and provides an excellent example of how, within the Jungian tradition, different schools have emerged. Also, the humanistic/ existentialist traditions have, more explicitly than the others, emphasised the importance of values, self-chosen meaning and the spiritual dimensions of human life and psychotherapy. This has led to the close liaison with approaches to psychotherapy like psychosynthesis, which emphasise a transpersonal view of the person. I believe this transpersonal relationship (however defined) forms an important dimension in all healing encounters. It has been suggested (Rowan 1990) that these transpersonal approaches may even constitute a fourth force in psychotherapy. The wider use of all three therapeutic approaches by counsellors has also blurred differences.

Of course, individual psychotherapists rarely fit into categories, particularly the more experienced they become. It has been found (Heine 1953) that it was not possible, from client descriptions of psychotherapist activity, to determine to which theoretical school a psychotherapist belongs. What differentiates between therapists appears to be, in fact, the names and labels clients attach to the 'fundamental causes' of their troubles. Ever since Fiedler's studies in the 1950s, it has become more accepted that differences in actual practice between more experienced people are considerably smaller than between beginners of different schools and their more senior colleagues. That is, it appears that which theory guides practice is much less important than experience gained in the field.

Internationally, there is now a discernible trend towards integrative or pluralistic psychotherapy which draws on many traditions and does not adhere to only one 'truth'. In the United States, most psychologists say they are integrative; and it is likely that this trend will become more established in the next few years in the United Kingdom (Dryden 1984). Psychotherapy 'after schoolism' is in view (Clarkson 1995a).

In this book we have brought together experienced psychotherapists from a large variety of approaches, ranging from the purist to the eclectic, from hypnotherapeutic approaches to behavioural, from group analysis to cultural perspectives, from orthodox psychoanalytic to humanistic and existential – with all shades in between – to exemplify the richness and diversity of the field.

THE FUTURE

Whatever the nature of psychotherapy in the future, we believe that certain issues will be crucial to the ongoing debate as to its core concerns. First, the concept of change and what it means. As discussed, there are different kinds of change possible within therapeutic settings: problem-solving, environmental change, adjustment, renegotiation (as in a relationship), developmental change (evolutionary) and personality restructuring (revolutionary change). Certain professional approaches may well be more appropriate than others for certain kinds of change within the person and his/her environment. A second area of great interest is that of relationship within therapeutic settings. Research (Norcross 1986) shows that theoretical differences between 'schools or approaches' is far less important in terms of successful outcome of counselling or psychotherapy, than the quality of the *relationship* between counsellor and client and certain client characteristics, including motivation for change and the willingness to take responsibility for their part in the process. Clarkson (1991, 1995b) and Gelso and Carter (1985) have outlined different relationships appropriate to different therapeutic approaches or client groups (also see Chapters 2 and 8 in this *Handbook*).

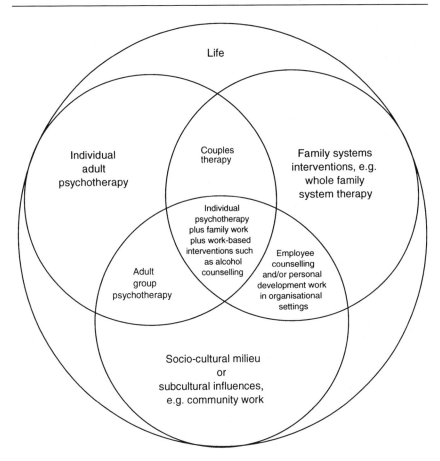

Figure 1.2 The different arenas and modalities of intervention

The third area is that of training. It has now been agreed by all the organisations of UKCP that entry to psychotherapy training must be at postgraduate level and have an academic content roughly equivalent to a master's degree, in addition to supervised clinical practice. It has also been agreed that each psychotherapy training must show that it has adequate arrangements for the trainee to become aware of and manage appropriately their own personal contribution to the kind of psychotherapy being practised. For the psychoanalytically based and humanistic/existential or integrative psychotherapies, these arrangements will continue to be the personal training psychotherapy or psychoanalysis. All require ongoing professional supervision. Further requirements of training courses are evolving gradually and will affect not only the form and content of the courses but are likely to introduce requirements for good educational practice and to establish the universality of external assessment. Moves are being made to link private psychotherapy trainings with academic units offering psychotherapy diplomas and degrees.

Finally, the question of different arenas and modalities of interventions emerges. Figure 1.2 maps out some of the possibilities. The indication or contra-indication for working with different modalities will be addressed in different chapters as the book progresses. The reader is invited to refer back to this diagram whenever it would prove useful to clarify options, complementary modalities and conceptualisations. Are there clients who could be designated as more appropriately the domain of one approach rather than another? This could be done in terms of the 'change' envisaged (or the degree of disturbance); it could be seen in terms of the training of the helper; it could be viewed from the assessed problem of the client. Or indeed, it might well be a combination of all three. *Systematic Treatment Selection* (Beutler and Clarkin 1990) is a good text with which to explore this.

As all these professions continue to develop as fully articulated disciplines, it is hoped that there would be a rich representation of both specialist and integrative approaches to the field, so that this endeavour of alleviating human distress and increasing human happiness can benefit from the uniqueness of classical exclusivity and purity, as well as from the complexity of pluralism, synthesis or even, occasionally, integration.

REFERENCES

Beck, A. T., Freeman, A. and associates (1990) *Cognitive Therapy of Personality Disorders*, New York: Guilford Press.

Benvenuto, B. and Kennedy, R. (1986) *The Works of Jacques Lacan: An Introduction*, London: Free Association Books.

Berne, E. (1975) *What Do You Say After You Say Hello?* London: Corgi (first published 1972).

Beutler, L. E. and Clarkin, J. F. (1990) *Systematic Treatment Selection: Toward Targeted Therapeutic Interventions*, New York: Brunner/Mazel.

Binswanger, L. (1958) 'The existential analysis school of thought' (E. Angel, trans.), pp. 191–213 in R. May, E. Angel and H. F. Ellenberger (eds), *Existence: A New Dimension in Psychiatry and Psychology*, New York: Clarion Books.

Bion, W. R. (1984) *Learning from Experience*, London: Karnac (first published 1962).

Boss, M. (1979) *Existential Foundations of Medicine and Psychology*, New York: Jason Aronson.

Bowlby, J. (1952) *Maternal Care and Mental Health*, Geneva: World Health Organisation.

British Association for Counselling (1984) *Code of Ethics and Practice for Counsellors* (Form no. 20, Sept.), BAC: Rugby.

—— (1989) *Invitation to Membership* (Form no. 1, Oct.), BAC: Rugby.

British Psycho-Analytical Society (1990) *UKSCP Member Organisations' General Information and Training Courses (Sept.)*, London: UKCP.

British Psychological Society, Division of Clinical Psychology (1988a) *MPAG*

Project on Clinical Psychology Services, Manpower and Training Issues: Key Tasks of Clinical Psychology Services (19 July), Leicester: BPS.

—— Division of Clinical Psychology (1988b) *The Representation of Clinical Psychologists: Interim Briefing Paper (Aug.)*, Leicester: BPS.

—— Membership and Qualifications Board (1989) *Report of the Working Party on the Diploma in Counselling Psychology (20 Nov.)*, Leicester: BPS.

—— (1991) *Code of Conduct, Ethical Principles and Guidelines (March)*, Leicester: BPS.

Carroll, M. (1991) 'Counsellor training or counsellor education? A response', *Counselling* 2(3) 104–5.

—— (1992a) *The Generic Tasks of Supervision*, private publication.

—— (1992b) Personal communication.

Carroll, M. and Pickard, E. (1993) 'Psychology and counselling', in B. Thorne and W. Dryden (eds) *Counselling: Interdisciplinary Perspectives*, Milton Keynes: Open University Press.

Clarkson, P. (1991) 'A multiplicity of psychotherapeutic relationships', *British Journal of Psychotherapy* 7(2) 148–63.

—— (1995a) 'After schoolism'. Unpublished paper.

—— (1995b) *The Therapeutic Relationship*, London: Whurr.

Corsini, R. (ed.) (1986) *Current Psychotherapies*, Itasca, IL: F. E. Peacock Publishers.

Dryden, W. (ed.) (1984) *Individual Therapy in Britain*, London: Harper & Row.

Duffy, M. (1990) 'Counselling psychology USA: patterns of continuity and change', *Counselling Psychology Review* 5(3) 9–18.

Egan, G. (1982) *The Skilled Helper: Models, Skills and Methods for Effective Helping*, Belmont, CA: Brooks/Cole (first published 1975).

Ellis, A. (1962) *Reason and Emotion in Psychotherapy*, Secaucus, NJ: Citadel Press.

Eysenck, H. J. (1968) *Handbook of Abnormal Psychology*, London: Pitman Medical.

Fairbairn, W. R. D. (1952) *Psycho-analytic Studies of the Personality*, London: Tavistock.

Federn, P. (1977) *Ego Psychology and the Psychoses*, London: Maresfield Reprints.

Fiedler, F. E. (1950) 'A comparison of therapeutic relationships in psychoanalytic, nondirective and Adlerian therapy', *Journal of Consulting Psychology* 14: 436–45.

Fitzgibbon, G. (1990) Personal communication.

Fordham, M. (1958) *The Objective Psyche*, London: Routledge & Kegan Paul.

Frankl, V. (1969) *Man's Search for Meaning*, London: Hodder & Stoughton.

Freedman, A. M., Kaplan, H. I. and Sadock, B. J. (1975) *Comprehensive Textbook of Psychiatry*, vol. 2, Baltimore: Williams & Wilkins Co.

Freud, A. (1968) 'The widening scope of indications for psychoanalysis: discussion', in *Indications for Child Analysis and Other Papers 1945–1956, the Writings of Anna Freud*, vol. 4, New York: International Universities Press.

Freud, S. (1915/1973) 'Introductory lectures on psychoanalysis', in A. Richards (ed.), J. Strachey (trans.), *The Pelican Freud Library*, vol. 1, Harmondsworth: Pelican (first published 1915–17).

Gelso, C. J. and Carter, J. A. (1985) 'The relationship in counselling and psychotherapy: components, consequences, and theoretical antecedents', *The Counselling Psychologist* 13(2) 155–243.

Greenberg, I. A. (ed.) (1975) *Psychodrama: Theory and Therapy*, London: Souvenir Press.

Hawton, K., Salkovskis, P. M., Kirk, J. and Clark, D. M. (eds). (1989) *Cognitive Behaviour Therapy for Psychiatric Problems: A Practical Guide*, Oxford: Oxford Medical Publications.

Heine, R. W. (1953) 'A comparison of patients' reports on psychotherapeutic experience with psychoanalytic, nondirective and Adlerian therapists', *American Journal of Psychotherapy* 7: 16–23.

Henderson, D. and Gillespie, R. D. (1956) *A Text-Book of Psychiatry*, Oxford: Oxford University Press (first published 1940).

Hinshelwood, R. D. (1989) *A Dictionary of Kleinian Thought*, London: Free Association Books.

Holmes, J. and Lindley, R. (1989) *The Values of Psychotherapy*, Oxford: Oxford University Press.

Jung, C. G. (1953) *Psychological Types*, London: Routledge & Kegan Paul; New York: Trench Trubner.

Karasu, T. B. (1986) 'The psychotherapies: benefits and limitations', *American Journal of Psychotherapy* 40(3) 324–43.

Kelly, G. (1955) *The Psychology of Personal Constructs*, vols 1 and 2: 75, 595, 600–1, New York: Norton.

Klein, M. (1949) *The Psychoanalysis of Children*, London: Hogarth Press.

Kohut, H. (1977) *The Restoration of the Self*, New York: International Universities Press.

Laing, R. D. (1960) *The Divided Self*, Harmondsworth: Penguin Books.

Laplanche, J. and Pontalis, J. B. (1988) *The Language of Psychoanalysis*, London: Karnac (first published 1973).

Lazarus, A. A. (1981) *The Practice of Multi-modal Therapy*, New York: McGraw-Hill.

Loughley, J. (1985) Personal communication at BPS Counselling Psychology Conference, London.

Lowen, A. (1969) *The Betrayal of the Body*, New York: Collier-Macmillan.

Malan, D. H. (1979) *Individual Psychotherapy and the Science of Psychodynamics*, London: Butterworth.

Maslow, A. H. (1968) *Toward a Psychology of Being* (2nd ed.), New York: D. Van Nostrand.

Masterson, J. F. (1976) *Psychotherapy of the Borderline Adult: A Developmental Approach*, New York: Brunner/Mazel.

May, R. (1969) *Love and Will*, New York: W. W. Norton.

Mayer-Gross, W., Slater, E. and Roth, M. (1954) *Clinical Psychiatry*, London: Cassell.

Merskey, H. and Tonge, W. L. (1965) *Psychiatric Illness*, London: Baillière, Tindall & Cox.

Miller, A. (1983) *The Drama of the Gifted Child and the Search for the True Self* (R. Ward, trans.), London: Faber & Faber (first published 1979).

Moreno, J. (1965) 'Therapeutic vehicles and the concept of surplus reality', *Group Psychotherapy* 18(4): 213.

Norcross, J. (ed.) (1986) *Handbook of Eclectic Psychotherapy*, New York: Brunner/Mazel.

Onions, C. T. (1968) *The Shorter Oxford English Dictionary*, Oxford: Clarendon/Oxford University Press.

Pavlov, I. P. (1927) *Conditioned Reflexes*, New York: Oxford University Press (first published 1908).

Perls, F. S., Hefferline, R. F. and Goodman, P. (1969) *Gestalt Therapy: Excitement and Growth in the Human Personality*, New York: Julian Press.

Proctor, B. (1989) Personal communication.

Reich, W. (1945) *Character Analysis*, New York: Simon & Schuster.

Roget, P. M. (1947) *Thesaurus of Words and Phrases*, New York: Grosset & Dunlap.

Rogers, C. R. (1961) *On Becoming a Person: A Therapist's View of Psych*
London: Constable.
—— (1986) *Client-centred Therapy*, London: Constable.
Rowan, J. (1990) *What is Humanistic Psychotherapy?* London, Routledge.
Samuels, A. (1985) *Jung and the Post-Jungians*, London: Routledge & Kegan P
—— (1989) *The Plural Psyche*, London: Routledge.
Skinner, B. F. (1953) *Science and Human Behaviour*, New York: Macmillan.
Symington, N. (1986) *The Analytic Experience*, London: Free Association Books.
Watkins, J. G. (1965) 'Psychotherapeutic Methods', pp. 1143–67 in B. B. Wolman
(ed.) *Handbook of Clinical Psychology*, New York: McGraw-Hill.
Winnicott, D. W. (1958) *Collected Papers*, London: Tavistock Publications.
Wolberg, L. R. (1954) *The Technique of Psychotherapy*, New York: Grune &
Stratton.
Wolman, B. B. (ed.) (1965) *Handbook of Clinical Psychology*, New York:
McGraw-Hill.
Yalom, I. D. (1970) *The Theory and Practice of Group Psychotherapy*, New York:
Basic Books.

In this chapter I want to present a theoretical and conceptual lens through which to view the many and varied contributions which follow in the rest of this book. Not every reader may find themselves in agreement with this, nor is it necessary to accept this perspective in its entirety in order to derive benefit from what follows. However, it is meant to provide a complete contribution in and of itself – a review of five different kinds of psycho-therapeutic relationship which may be potentially available for construc-tive use in psychotherapy. It is also an invitation to engage in, reflect on and view the contributions which follow. Most of the approaches discussed in the previous chapter can be considered in terms of which, or how many, of the five relationships I have identified, are foregrounded or emphasised in the work of the practitioners from that discipline or from that approach. As you read the following chapters, you may be aware of how implicitly or explicitly the relationship is dealt with, and how aspects of it are treated more fully. It is nevertheless my contention that all of these five relation-ships are available in every psychotherapeutic encounter, available for attention or not, according to the nature of the people involved, the context, the approach and the setting. For example, it may be more difficult to acknowledge transpersonal influences on the psychotherapeutic endeavour in a highly rationalist, experimentally orientated, cognitive-behavioural clinic. Similarly, the ideologies and cultural constraints of some forms of psychoanalysis may impede and inhibit the therapeutic use of, say, the provision of an educationally needed, enacted rehearsal for a job interview, or a longed-for touch on the shoulder when in deep distress. It is my belief that these five modalities of relationship exist in every psychotherapeutic relationship (whether it be with individuals, groups, families or larger systems). Like the keys on a piano, some of them may be played more frequently or more loudly than others, depending on the

* This chapter forms the basis of Petrūska Clarkson's *The Therapeutic Relationship* (London: Whurr).

nature of the music. But they are always potentially there in every therapeutic encounter whether or not the pianist uses them, whether or not the composer acknowledges their existence in the written score.

In this way, I think that the variety and nature of psychotherapeutic relationships is present implicitly or explicitly throughout the psychotherapeutic canon. In working with this material, experienced clinicians tend to recognise that in their own practices some aspects of these relationships are indeed more or less present. Novice psychotherapists have found it very helpful as a matrix from which to learn from many different traditions in psychotherapy and as a framework for integrating what they may still learn; helping them to order, categorise and prioritise the literature while developing precision and purpose in practice.

Relationship or the interconnectedness between two people has been significant in all healing since the time of Hippocrates and Galen. Relationship can be defined as 'the state of being related; a condition or character based upon this; kinship' (Onions 1973: 1786). Relationship is the first condition of being human. It circumscribes two or more individuals and creates a bond in the space between them which is more than the sum of the parts. It is so obvious that it is frequently taken for granted, and so mysterious that many of the world's greatest psychologists, novelists and philosophers have made it a lifetime's preoccupying passion. According to the received wisdom of the late twentieth century, of all the forces of nature it is our familial relationships which often serve to cause the most damage. Statistically you are more likely to be killed by a relation than by a stranger. According to Boss, the great existentialist, all illness and treatment develop out of the patient's disturbed human relationships: 'In focusing on the physician–patient relationship, Freud called attention to the true locus of all therapeutic efforts, whether they were surgical, internal or psychotherapeutic' (1979: 257).

It is the intention of this chapter to make explicit what is often implicit in psychotherapy literature regarding the variety and nature of psychotherapeutic relationships. This chapter reaches for an elucidation of relationship, the *betweenness* of people. It is common knowledge that ordinary human relationships can have therapeutic value. The old structures of religion, accepted moral order and extended family networks used to provide supportive relationships and healing matrices for many people. These appear to have started to crumble in the twentieth century. Indeed, it is possible that psychotherapy as an institutionalized profession became necessary as a consequence of such a decline in the society and quality of healing relationships which were available in previous centuries.

As discussed in Chapter 3 regarding research, one of the most important factors to emerge is the significance of the therapeutic relationship, which is thought to be common to all psychotherapies. 'A constant focus has been on what it is that therapists do which leads to client change' (Barkham and

Elton Wilson, p. 58 in this volume). As discussed in the previous chapter and as emerges from the research, it is very difficult if not impossible to establish with anything more than partisan preferences that any one psychotherapy is more effective than any other: 'All have won and all must have prizes' (Luborsky *et al.* 1975). However, there is a consensus of agreement of the crucial importance of the therapeutic relationship. This has led to a development of integrative psychotherapy on the one hand, and on the other to the broadening and deepening of the understanding of interventions, and to theoretical explorations of many of the unimodal approaches to psychotherapy.

Research, empirical studies and reviews have failed to demonstrate clear advantages differentially attributable to different psychotherapy systems. Research has focused on the identification of the common factor or common ingredients. It seems that success in psychotherapy can best be predicted by the properties of the psychotherapist, the client and their particular relationship. Frank (1979) and Hynan (1981) are two of the many researchers who have found that the client, the psychotherapist and the therapeutic relationship between them are repeatedly more closely related to outcome than whatever technique has been used.

> Most beginning clinicians understand that it is important to live by the basic ground rules of therapy. Confidentiality must be honored, and the boundaries of the therapeutic relationship must be respected, which means remembering every moment that our clients are neither friends nor lovers. Most therapists know these rules, but until one has grasped just how subtle and complex the relationship can be, and how important the therapist becomes to the client, one is likely to seriously under-estimate how easy it is to damage the therapy. The slightest breach of confidentiality can be magnified by the client into a major betrayal; a chance encounter with a client outside the consulting room can evolve into a problematic social situation and have serious repercussions. An off-hand remark or thoughtless joke can cause pain or confusion the client may not be able to acknowledge. . . . The second reason for attending to the relationship is that it gives one a major therapeutic advantage. This book will take the position that awareness of the subtleties and changes in the relationship provides the therapist with a powerful tool, perhaps the most powerful therapeutic tool of all. It will try to show why that is true and how that tool might be used in our work with clients.

> (Kahn 1991: 2–3)

It was after the publication of my paper that I came across Kahn's book, in which he introduces a perspective on using the relationship as a central factor in all of psychotherapy. Kahn's teacher said, 'The relationship *is* the therapy' (Kahn 1991: 1).

If indeed the therapeutic relationship is one of the most, if not *the* most, important factor in successful psychotherapy, one would expect much of the training in psychotherapy to be training in the intentional use of relationship. Some psychotherapists claim that psychotherapy requires use of only one kind of relationship, or at most two. Some specifically exclude the use of certain kinds of relationship. For example, Goulding and Goulding (1979), transactional analysts, minimise the use of transference, whereas Moiso (1985), also in transactional analysis, sees it as a central focal point of classical Bernian psychotherapy. Gestaltists Polster and Polster (1973) and the existentialist May (1969) focus on the existential nature of the therapeutic relationship. Some psychotherapeutic approaches pay hardly any theoretical attention to the nature of the relationship and they may attempt to be entirely free of content. For example, in some approaches to hypnotherapy or Neuro-Linguistic Programming (NLP), therapeutic changes are claimed to be made by the patient without the practitioner necessarily knowing what these changes may be.

Psychoanalysts, whether most influenced by Freud or Klein or Bion, consider the transference relationship to be the most important, if not the only, defining characteristic of the approach.

THE WORKING ALLIANCE

The working alliance is probably the most essential relationship modality operative in psychotherapy. Without such a working alliance psychotherapy is certainly limited in its goals and restricted in scope. This working alliance is represented by the client's or patient's willingness to engage in the psychotherapeutic relationship even when they at some archaic level may no longer wish to do so (see also Chapter 8 regarding individual adult psychotherapy).

In transactional analysis, the working alliance is conceptualised as a contract or agreement between the adult of the psychotherapist and adult of the client. In psychoanalysis it is 'the relatively non-neurotic, rational, and realistic attitudes of the patient toward the analyst. . . . It is this part of the patient–analyst relationship that enables the patient to identify with the analyst's point of view and to work with the analyst despite the neurotic transference reactions' (Greenson 1967: 29). The attitudes and character traits which further the development of the transference neurosis are basically antithetical to those which further the working alliance (Stone 1961; Greenson 1965, 1967). So it is unlikely that both can become operative at the same moment. Which one is allowed to become figure, or focus, must depend on the nature of the psychotherapeutic task at a particular time with each unique patient. Other modes of therapeutic relationship may also be present but may be more in the background at a particular time.

For many psychotherapists the working alliance is the crucial and necessary relationship for effective therapy (Dryden 1984). It certainly is the necessary co-operation that even the general practitioner requires in order to work effectively with patients, be it simply at the level that the patient takes the medication as prescribed. Anecdotal evidence and research have shown that this working alliance is frequently missing in general practice (Griffith 1990). 'The therapeutic alliance is the powerful joining of forces which energizes and supports the long, difficult, and frequently painful work of life-changing psychotherapy' (Bugental 1987: 49). Bordin (1979) differentiated goals, bonds and tasks – three aspects of the working alliance which seem to be required for any form of therapy to be successful. Several studies emphasise the importance of further common factors:

> Among the common factors most frequently studied have been those identified by the client-centred school as 'necessary and sufficient conditions' for patient personality to change; accurate empathy, positive regard, nonpossessive warmth, and congruence or genuineness. Virtually all schools of psychotherapy accept the notion that these or related therapist relationship variables are important for significant progress in psychotherapy and, in fact, fundamental in the formation of a working alliance.
>
> (Lambert 1986: 444–5)

Most forms of psychotherapy use this state of voluntary kinship or relationship more or less consciously and more or less in awareness. The Jungian Samuels states that 'the psychology of the soul turns out to be about people in relationship' (Samuels 1985: 21).

THE TRANSFERENTIAL/COUNTER-TRANSFERENTIAL RELATIONSHIP

This mode of therapeutic relationship is the one most extensively written about, for it is extremely well developed, articulated and effectively used within the theoretically rich psychoanalytic tradition and other approaches (Racker 1982; Heimann, 1950; Cashdan 1988; Langs 1976; Clarkson 1992). It is important to remember that Freud did not intend psychoanalysis to be a cure but rather a search for understanding, and he frowned upon people who wished to 'change' instead of analyse. So the transference relationship is an essential part of the analytic procedure since the analysis consists in inviting the transference and gradually dissolving it by means of interpretation (Greenson 1967).

Laplanche and Pontalis describe transference as follows:

> For psycho-analysis, a process of actualization of unconscious wishes. Transference uses specific objects and operates in the framework of a

specific relationship established with these objects. Its context *par excellence* is the analytic situation. In the transference, infantile prototypes re-emerge and are experienced with a strong sensation of immediacy. As a rule what psycho-analysts mean by the unqualified use of the term 'transference' is *transference during treatment*. Classically, the transference is acknowledged to be the terrain on which all the basic problems of a given analysis play themselves out: the establishment, modalities, interpretation and resolution of the transference are in fact what define the cure.

(1988: 455)

Freud (1912b) went so far at one point as to suggest that the analyst model himself on the surgeon, put aside his human sympathy and adopt an attitude of emotional coldness. 'This means that the analyst must have the ability to restrain his therapeutic intentions, must control his urge for closeness and must "blanket" his usual personality' (Stone 1961: 20). Freud advocated that the analyst should refrain from intruding his personality into the treatment, and he introduced the simile of the analyst being a 'mirror' for the analysand (Freud 1912b: 118). This may not in fact be an accurate picture of what Freud had in mind. Perhaps he emphasised certain 'unnatural' aspects of psychoanalytic technique because they were so foreign and artificial to the usual doctor–patient relationship and the customary psychotherapy of his day.

For example, in a paper written in the same year (1912) as the one in which he cites the recommendations for emotional coldness and the mirror-like attitude, Freud stated:

Thus the solution of the puzzle is that transference to the doctor is suitable for resistance to the treatment only in so far as it is a negative transference or a positive transference of repressed erotic impulses. If we 'remove' the transference by making it conscious, we are detaching only these two components of the emotional act from the person of the doctor; the other component, which is admissible to consciousness and unobjectionable, persists and is the vehicle of success in psycho-analysis exactly as it is in other methods of treatment.

(1912a: 105)

Alexander and French expressed the psychoanalytic principle as follows:

The old pattern was an attempt at adaptation on the part of the child to parental behavior . . . the analyst's objective and understanding attitudes allows the patient . . . to make a new settlement of the old problem. . . . While the patient continues to act according to outdated patterns, the analyst's reaction conforms strictly to the actual therapeutic situation.

(1946: 66–7)

Berne wrote:

> Transactionally, this means that when the patient's Child attempts to provoke the therapist's Parent, it is confronted instead with the therapist's Adult. The therapeutic effect arises from the disconcertion caused by this crossed transaction.
>
> (1961: 174)

The patient's question 'How are you?' may often be met with analytic silence. Alternatively the analyst may reply: 'I wonder what prompts your concern for me? It may be that you are anxious again, like you were with your mother, that I will not be able to withstand your envy towards me.'

This transferential psychotherapeutic relationship can be compared to that of stepparent or godparent. Negative transference connects with the former (the witch of many traditional fairy tales – for example, Hansel and Gretel) and idealising positive transference resonates with the godparent or fairy godmother relationship in that a putative family connection exists, but it lacks the immediacy of a real parent. Whether or not the psychotherapist identifies with such projections, and how he or she handles them, may destroy or facilitate the psychotherapy. Clearly, the nature and vicissitudes of the counter-transference are inextricably interwoven with the management of the transference relationship, and efficacy of the psychotherapy may well be determined by it.

A narcissistic, apparently generous but dynamically retentive patient whose mother over-fed him physically while never responding to his real feelings of isolation, abandonment or rage reports the following dream: 'I am at a sumptuous banquet which is presided over by you [the psychotherapist]. I take the food from the table, but I don't eat it. I put it in a plastic bag so that you won't see and I throw it in a wastepaper basket. I want to continue to be invited, but not to have to eat the food.'

> The great importance of the transference has often led to the mistaken idea that it is absolutely indispensable for a cure, that it must be demanded from the patient, so to speak. But a thing like that can no more be demanded than faith, which is only valuable when it is spontaneous. Enforced faith is nothing but spiritual cramp. Anyone who thinks that he must 'demand' a transference is forgetting that this is only one of the therapeutic factors.
>
> (Jung 1966: 172)

THE REPARATIVE/DEVELOPMENTALLY NEEDED RELATIONSHIP

The reparative/developmentally needed relationship is another relationship mode which can occasionally be differentiated from the others. This is the intentional provision by the psychotherapist of a corrective/reparative or replenishing parental relationship (or action) where the original parenting was deficient, abusive or over-protective. The following dream shows a client separating out a developmentally needed relationship (for the client's future) from the transferential relationship (based on the client's past).

He dreams about two psychotherapists, both with the same name as his psychotherapist. One psychotherapist says to him in the dream: 'How could you make such mistakes, this is terrible, you ought to be punished!'. In the dream the other psychotherapist says, 'Look, I myself received a D in this subject. I wasn't very interested in it, and you can see that you don't have to be perfect in all things.' The first psychotherapist responds with anger and accusations of unethical conduct, saying, 'How could you say such things, you are just encouraging him to make mistakes and setting a very bad example!' The client himself then steps in to arbitrate and explains to the first psychotherapist: 'Actually she is right. You have to understand what she is saying *in the right spirit.*' This is what the client needed to hear.

Dreams often act as unconscious communication about the progress of the psychotherapy from the unconscious of the client. In this dream the client is clearly telling the psychotherapist what he needs developmentally – what was absent in the original relationship where he veered between being the saintly, clean little boy who has to play without getting dirty and the disgusting child who causes embarrassment and shame to his family if he as much as gets his hands dirty. (In his adult life he veers between saintly self-sacrifice and secret addictions.) The client is also communicating a most significant fact – not only has he internalised the psychotherapist and distinguishes the two personifications of the person of the same name, but happily he is siding with the psychotherapist who has his best interests at heart, and least resembles the transferential parent who would 'write him off' for the smallest misdemeanour, or shame him for not getting the best marks in every subject regardless of his true interests (even the D is still a passing mark!).

The developmentally needed relationship as indicated in the cited dream refers to those aspects of relationship which may have been absent or traumatic for the client at particular periods of his or her childhood and which are supplied or repaired by the psychotherapist, usually in a contracted form (on request by or with agreement from the patient) during the psychotherapy. Ferenczi (1926/1980), one of Freud's early followers, attempted this early in the history of psychoanalysis. He departed from neutrality and impassivity in favour of giving nursery care, friendly hugs or management of regression to very sick patients, including one whom he saw any time, day or night, and took with him on his holidays. Ferenczi held that there needed to be a contrast between the original trauma in infancy and the analytic situation so that remembering can be facilitative instead of a renewed trauma for the patient.

The advocacy relationship proposed by Alice Miller (1983, 1985) can be seen to be the provision of the developmentally needed force in a child's life which should have been provided by a parent or other significant caretakers but which the psychotherapist ultimately has to provide. The holding environment of Winnicott (1958) is another example of such provision, as are the reparenting techniques of Schiff *et al.* (1975) in transactional analysis.

Freud (1912b) prescribed a mirror-like impassivity on the part of the analyst, who should him- or herself be analysed, who should not reciprocate the patient's confidences, nor try to educate, morally influence, or 'improve' the patient, and who should be tolerant of the patient's weakness. In practice, however, Freud conducted psychotherapy as no classical Freudian analyst would conduct it nowadays (Malcolm 1981); shouting at the patient, praising him, arguing, accepting flowers from him on his birthday, lending him money, visiting him at home and even gossiping with him about other patients!

The psychoanalyst Sechehaye (1951) was able to break through the unreal wall that hemmed in her patient Renée and bring her into some contact with life. In order to do this, Sechehaye not only took her on holiday to the seashore, as Ferenczi had done with one of his patients, but also took Renée into her home for extended periods. She allowed her to regress to the point where she felt she was re-entering her mother's body, thus becoming one of the first of those psychotherapists who have actually undertaken to 'reparent' schizophrenic clients. She allowed her to lean on her bosom and pretended to give milk from her breasts to the doll with whom Renée identified.

> That Sechehaye was far more involved personally than even the most humanistic of therapists usually are we can infer from the accounts of how she gave instructions for her meals, saw to her baths, and in general played for Renée the nourishing mother that she had been denied as an infant. That this took an emotional toll far beyond the ordinary is evident from Renée's own account that 'Mama was extremely upset' or that she regained consciousness and found Mama weeping over her.
>
> (Friedman, 1985: 188)

The psychotherapist's reply to a client who asks: 'How are you?' in this kind of relationship will be determined by the specific needs that were not appropriately responded to by their caretakers in childhood. In response to the adult who as a child was never allowed to show her care or love for the parent the therapist may reply: 'I'm fine, thank you, and I appreciate your caring.' Alternatively, in response to the adult who as a child was burdened with parental intimacies, a therapist may reply, 'It is not necessary for you to worry about me, right now I am here to take care of you and I am ready to do that.'

In the developmentally needed relationship, the metaphoric kinship relationship being established is clearly closer to a real parent-and-child relationship than any of the other forms of bonding in psychotherapy. In the words of J. Schiff:

> I am as much part of the symbiosis and as vulnerable as any parent. While my attachments don't occur at the same kind of depth with each youngster, they have not been selective in favor of those kids who were successful, and several times I have experienced tremendous loss and grief.
>
> (1977: 63)

In view of the regressive nature of this kind of work and the likely length of time involved, the professional and ethical responsibilities of the psychotherapists are also concomitantly greater and perhaps so awesome that many psychotherapists try to avoid them. It is certainly true that this depth of long-standing psychotherapeutic relationship as the primary therapeutic relationship modality is more frequently reported between psychotherapists and more severely damaged patients.

THE I–YOU RELATIONSHIP

Particularly within the humanistic/existential tradition, there is appreciation of the *person-to-person relationship* or *real relationship*. This therapeutic relationship modality shows most continuity with the healing relationships of ordinary life. Buber (1970) called this the I–Thou, or I–You relationship to differentiate it from the I–It relationship. The I–You relationship is referred to elsewhere in psychotherapeutic literature as the real relationship or the core relationship (Barr 1987). It is very likely that those ordinary relationships which human beings have experienced as particularly healing over the ages have been characterised by the qualities of the I–You relationship (Buber 1970). This has been retrieved and valued for its transformative potential in the psychotherapeutic arena *if* used skilfully and ethically (Rogers 1961; Laing 1965; Polster and Polster 1973). However, there has always been, and there is again, growing recognition within psychoanalytic practice that the real relationship between analyst and analysand – following Freud's own example – is a deeply significant, unavoidable and potentially profoundly healing force also within the psychoanalytic paradigm (Malcolm 1981; Klauber 1986; Archambeau 1979).

With Freud's discovery of the importance of the transference relationship came deep suspicion of the real relationship – the therapeutic relationship most similar to ordinary human relationships. Certainly for some decades psychoanalysts' emotional reactions to their patients were usually understood to be a manifestation of the analysts' unresolved conflicts. It is only comparatively recently that analyst feelings or counter-transference reactions have been seen as valid and important sources of information to be used effectively in the psychotherapy (Heimann 1950).

Object relations theorists have offered psychotherapy profoundly useful concepts and theoretical understandings, but the I–You therapeutic relationship is the opposite of an object relationship. For Buber, the other is a person, not an object.

> Whoever says You does not have something for his object. For wherever there is something there is also another something; every It borders on other Its; It is only by virtue of bordering on others. But where You is said, there is no something. You has no borders. Whoever says You does not have something; he has nothing. But he stands in relation.
>
> (Buber 1970: 55)

The emotional involvement in this relationship between psychotherapist and patient is that between *person and person* in the existential dilemma where both stand in a kind of mutuality to each other. Indeed, as Friedman (1985) points out, it is a kind of mutuality because the psychotherapist is also *in* role. However, in the immediacy of the existential encounter, the mutuality is almost complete and the Self of the therapist becomes the instrument through which the healing evolves.

An intuitive, introverted type of patient sadly remembers difficulty with differentiating right from left, along with physical discomfort in the real world and incomprehension when required to learn kinaesthetically. The psychotherapist bends down to show the scar on her leg which she used as a little girl to help her decide which side was left. The moment is unforgettable; the bonding, person to person. Yet it is enacted by a professional person who, at that very moment, has taken responsibility for that self-disclosure in the psychotherapy, judging it appropriate and timely to trust or delight the patient with a sense of shared personhood. The two then become siblings in incomprehension, siblings in discovery, and siblings in the quest for wholeness.

Such self-disclosure needs, of course, to be done with extreme care and, in its worst, abusive form, has been an excuse for inauthentic acting out of the psychotherapist's own need for display, hostility or seductiveness. Genuine, well-judged use of the I–You relationship is probably one of the most difficult forms of therapeutic relating. Doubtless this was the very good reason behind the early analysts' regarding it with extreme suspicion. It probably requires the most skill, the most self-knowledge and the greatest care, because its potential for careless or destructive use is so great. Yet there are only a few trainings – for example, in Gestalt – which specifically address this experientially and theoretically. Sometimes lip-service is paid to the I–You, person-to-person concept as if we know what it's about, or it is 'outlawed' in the analysis – as if this were possible.

'There can be no psychoanalysis without an existential bond between the analyst and the analysand', writes Boss (1963: 118). The I–You relationship is characterised by the *here-and-now existential encounter* between the two people. It involves mutual participation in the process and the recognition that each is changed by the other. Its field is not object relations, but subject relations. The real person of the psychotherapist can never be totally excluded from an interactional matrix of therapy. Existential psychotherapy (Boss 1963; Binswanger 1968; May 1969), specifically includes the I–You genuine encounter as a major therapeutic modality, but analysts are also addressing the issue.

> It is good for analyst and patient to have to admit some of the analyst's weaknesses as they are revealed in the interchange in the consulting room. The admission of deficiencies may help patient and analyst to let go of one another more easily when they have had enough. In other words, the somewhat freer admission of realities – but not too free – facilitates the process of mourning which enables an analysis to end satisfactorily. The end of analysis is in this way prepared from the beginning.
>
> (Klauber 1986: 213)

To Fromm-Reichmann (1950/1974), Sullivan's (1940) concept of the psychotherapist as 'participant observer' included spontaneous and genuine responses on the part of the psychotherapist and even, in some cases, reassuring touch and gestures of affection. This does *not* include transforming the professional relationship into a social one, nor seeking extraneous personal gratification from the dialogue with the patient. But it does include confirmation of patients as worthy of respect, and meeting them on the basis of mutual human equality.

Guntrip (1961) also rejected the traditional restriction of the functions of the psychotherapist to the dual one of a screen upon which the patient projects his fantasies and a colourless instrument of interpretative technique. Instead, he saw the real personal relationship between patient and analyst as the truly psychotherapeutic factor on which all others depend. For him, true psychotherapy only happens when the therapist and patient find the person behind each other's defences.

Deep insight, as Fairbairn (1952) points out, only develops inside a good therapeutic relationship. What is therapeutic, when it is achieved, is 'the moment of real meeting'. This experience is transforming for both psychotherapist and patient because it is not what happened before (that is transference) but what has never happened before, a genuine experience of relationship centred in the here-and-now.

What Freud calls 'transference' Boss (1979) describes as 'always a genuine relationship between the analysand and the analyst'. Despite the difference in their positions the partners disclose themselves to each other as human beings. It seems that Freud and Boss are describing different therapeutic relationship modalities which are intrinsically different in intent, in execution, and in effect; not merely a semantic blurring.

Of course, the humanistically orientated psychotherapies (such as Gestalt which emphasises here-and-now *contact* as a valid form of therapeutic relating) have greatly amplified the value and use of the person-to-person encounter in psychotherapy.

> The details of technique vary, but the strategy is always to keep a steady, gentle pressure toward the direct and responsible I–thou orientation, keeping the focus of awareness on the difficulties the patients experience in doing this, and helping them find their own ways through these difficulties.
>
> (Fagan and Shepherd 1971: 116)

For Rogers and Stevens (1967), too, the establishment of a relationship of genuineness, respect and empathy became the cornerstone conditions for facilitating human growth and development. In psychoanalysis, even Anna Freud called for the recognition that in analysis two real people of equal adult status stand in a real personal relationship to each other: 'There are differences in the ways in which we receive and send off patients, and in the degree to which we permit a real relationship to the patient to coexist with the transferred, fantasied one' (1968: 360). It is the neglect of this side of the relationship, and not just 'transference' that may cause the hostile reactions analysts get from their patients, according to Stone (1961). Stone expressed concern lest the analyst's unrelentingly analytic behaviour subvert the process by shaking the patient's faith in the analyst's benignity. He declared that a failure to show reasonable human response at a critical juncture can invalidate years of patient, skilful work.

According to Malcolm (1981), honesty and spontaneity can correct the patient's transference misperceptions, making the psychotherapist's responses unpredictable and therefore less likely to be manipulated by the patient. The patient's distrust may be relieved when the psychotherapist provides a model of authentic being with which he can identify. Such authenticity on the psychotherapist's part may mean that the therapeutic relationship changes the therapist as much as the patient. Both Jourard (1971) and Jung (1966) held this as a central truth in all healing endeavour. Searles (1975) also believed that the patient has a powerful innate striving to heal the analyst (as he or she may have desired to heal the parents), which can and does contribute to greater individuation and growth for the psychotherapist as they are *both* transformed in the therapeutic dialogue. 'What is confirmed most of all is the personal "realness" of the therapist that has arisen from and been brought into the therapeutic relationship'

(Archambeau 1979: 141–58). I also quote Greenson directly: 'A certain amount of compassion, friendliness, warmth, and respect for the patient's rights is indispensable. The analyst's office is a treatment room and not a research laboratory' (1967: 391).

Greenacre (1959) and Stone (1961) are clear that the analyst must be able to become emotionally involved with and committed to the patient. He must like the patient; prolonged dislike or disinterest as well as too strong a love will interfere with therapy. He must have a wish to help and cure the patient, and he must be concerned with the patient's welfare without losing sight of his long-range goals.

In all cases the person-to-person relationship will be honoured by truthfulness or authenticity – not at the expense of the client but in the spirit of mutuality. According to Buber, the genuine psychotherapist can only accomplish the true task of regenerating the stunted growth of a personal centre by entering as 'a partner into a person-to-person relationship, but never through the observation and investigation of an object' (1970: 179). Significantly, though, this does not mean injudicious honesty. Buber further acknowledges the limited nature of the psychotherapeutic person-to-person relationship: 'Every I–You relationship in a situation defined by the attempt of one partner to act on the other one so as to accomplish some goal depends on a mutuality that is condemned never to become complete' (1970: 179).

THE TRANSPERSONAL RELATIONSHIP

This refers to the spiritual dimension of relationship in psychotherapy. Within the Jungian tradition (Jung 1969) and also within the humanistic/ existential perspective (Rowan 1983), there is acknowledgement of the influence of the qualities which presently transcend the limits of our understanding (as expressed by Hamlet with 'There are more things on heaven and earth, Horatio, than are dreamt of in your philosophy' (Shakespeare, in Alexander 1951: 166). However defined, some implicit or explicit recognition of the possibility, if not the existence, of a *transpersonal relationship* between healer and healed as it unfolds within the psychotherapeutic *vas* (container) is gradually beginning to gain more acceptance (Clarkson 1990).

'If the analyst has been moved by his patient, then the patient is more aware of the analyst as a healing presence' (Samuels 1985: 189). The transpersonal relationship in psychotherapy is characterised by its timelessness, and in Jungian thought is conceived of as the relationship between the unconscious of the analyst and the unconscious of the patient not mediated by consciousness (Guggenbuhl-Craig 1971).

The psychotherapist and the client find themselves in a relationship built on mutual unconsciousness. The psychotherapist is led to a direct

confrontation of the unreconciled part of himself. The activated unconsciousness of both the client and the therapist causes both to become
involved in a transformation of the 'third'. Hence, the relationship itself
becomes transformed in the process.

(Archambeau 1979: 162)

There is surprisingly little documented about the transpersonal relationship in psychotherapy. Peck (1978) mentions the concept of 'grace', as has
Buber before him, as the ultimate factor which operates in the person-to-
person encounter and which may make the difference between whether a
patient gets better or not. Berne, too, was aware of it in 1966 when he
quoted: '"Je le pensay, et Dieu le guarit" . . . I treat him, but it is God
who cures him' (Agnew 1963: 75).

The nature of this transpersonal dimension is therefore quite difficult to
describe, because it is both rare and not easily accessible to the kind of
descriptions which can easily be used in discussing the other forms of
therapeutic relationships. 'The *numinosum* is either a quality belonging to
a visible object or the influence of an invisible presence that causes a
peculiar alternation of consciousness' (Jung 1969: 7). It is also possible that
there may be a certain amount of embarrassment in psychotherapists who
have to admit that after all the years of training and personal analysis and
supervision, ultimately we still don't know precisely what it is that we are
doing or whether it makes any difference at all. This is the kind of statement one can only be sure of being understood correctly by experienced
psychotherapists who have been faced repeatedly with incomprehensible
and unpredictable outcomes – the person of whom you despaired, suddenly
and sometimes apparently inexplicably, gets well, thrives and actualises
beyond all expectation. At the other polarity, the client for whom the
analyst had made an optimistic prognosis reaches plateaux from which in
effect they never move, and the analysis is abandoned with a lingering
sense of potential glimpsed but never to be reached.

The transpersonal relationship is also characterised paradoxically by a
kind of intimacy and by an 'emptying of the ego' at the same time. It is
rather as if the ego of even the personal unconscious of the psychotherapist
is 'emptied out' of the therapeutic space, leaving space for something
numinous to be created in the 'between' of the relationship. This space
can then become the 'temenos' or 'the *vas bene clausum* inside which the
transmutation takes place' (Adler 1979: 21). It implies a letting-go of
skills, of knowledge, of experience, of preconceptions, even of the desire
to heal, to be present. It is essentially allowing 'passivity' and receptiveness
for which preparation is always inadequate. But paradoxically you have
to be full in order to be empty. It cannot be made to happen, it can only
be encouraged in the same way that the inspirational muse of creativity
cannot be forced, but needs to have the ground prepared or seized in

the serendipitous moment of readiness. What can be prepared are the conditions conducive to the spontaneous or spiritual act.

A trainee reports:

> When I first started learning psychotherapy it was like trying to learn a new language, say French, but when I saw a very experienced psychotherapist working it appeared to me that she was speaking an entirely different language, such as Chinese. The more I have learnt the more I have come to realize that she does indeed speak French, she just speaks it very well. And sometimes she speaks Chinese.

This comment arose from the context of how he has perceived the supervisor at times intuitively to know facts, feelings or intentions of patients without there being any prior evidence to lead to the conclusions. It is these intuitive illuminations which seem to flourish the more the psychotherapist dissolves the individual ego from the therapeutic container, allowing wisdom and insight and transformation to occur as a self-manifesting process. The essence of the communication is in the heart of the shared silence of being-together in a dimension impossible to articulate exactly, too delicate to analyse and yet too pervasively present in psychotherapy to ignore.

Another trainee in supervision brought the following ethical problem. He had seen a particular client for several years, who was seriously disturbed and showed no sign of improvement. He had utilised all the major interpretations and strategies for such cases to no avail. Indeed, the client refused to form any working alliance in the shape of an agreed goal for her psychotherapy. It was exceedingly uncertain what benefit there could be for her, yet she continued coming because (we speculated) this was the only human relationship which was alive for her in a physically and emotionally impoverished life.

The psychotherapist responsibly questioned whether she should be referred to another treatment facility. Yet he feared that she would experience this as abandonment. In our supervision we explored the possibility that he let go of expectations that she should be different from the way she was. The psychotherapist was even willing and able to let go of the healer archetype, allowing himself to become an empty vessel, a container wherein healing could have space to manifest, or beingness could be validated without any expectation even of the acceptance. This needs to be truly done in good faith and not based on the trickery of paradoxical interventions where expectations are removed *in order* for the patient to change. The atmosphere is more a trance-like meditation, the quality of which is conveyed by the being-with of highly evolved psychotherapists with patients who are in acute psychosis, such as Gendlin (1967), who affirm the spiritual dimension in psychotherapy. (It is quite possible that psychotherapists may be deluding themselves in ways which may be dangerous for themselves and their clients if they mistakenly, prematurely or naïvely focus on the transpersonal and, for example, overlook or minimise transferential or personal phenomena.)

James and Savary contributed the notion of a third self created in such a dimension of betweenness when the inner core energies of the dialoguing partners merge. 'Third-self sharing, perhaps the most complete form of sharing, involves not only *self-awareness* (of the individual self) and *other-awareness* (of the relating self), but *together-awareness* (of the third self)' (1977: 325). Psychosynthesis also recognises the notion of a higher self (Hardy 1989).

This resembles the archetype of the Self which Jung refers to as the person's inherent and psychic disposition to experience centredness and meaning in life, sometimes conceived of as the God within ourselves. Buber was essentially concerned with the close association of the relation to God with the relation to one's fellow men, with the I–Thou which issues from the encounter with the *other in relationship*. This dimension in the psychotherapeutic relationship cannot be proved and can hardly be described, and Buber concludes: 'Nothing remains to me in the end but an appeal to the testimony of your own mysteries' (1970: 174).

CONCLUSION

This chapter has briefly described five kinds of psychotherapeutic relationship available as potential avenues for constructive use, and each will be expanded in following chapters. It has indicated some characteristics of each and begun an effort to clarify, specify and differentiate more acutely in theory and practice the nature and intentions of the multiplicity of psychotherapeutic relationships available in the consulting room. Different psychotherapies stress different relationships for different reasons. Whatever the orientation, the psychotherapeutic relationship is therefore a continuing theme throughout all the chapters in this *Handbook*.

It is perhaps time that psychotherapists acknowledged explicitly that these five forms of relationship are intentionally or unintentionally present in most approaches to psychotherapy. Which of these modes of psychotherapeutic relationships are used, and how explicitly and purposefully, may be one of the major ways in which some approaches resemble one another more and differ most from others.

It may need to be recognised in most psychotherapy trainings that experience and supervision are required in distinguishing between such different forms of psychotherapeutic relationship and assessing and evaluating the usefulness of each at different stages of psychotherapy. Equally, different modes may be indicated for individuals with different characteristic ways of relating so that there is not a slipshod vacillation due to error or neurotic counter-transference, nor a denial of the obvious.

Confusion and lack of clarity abound when types of psychotherapeutic relationship are confused with one other, or the validity of one is used as necessarily substituting for the other. It is possible that humans need all of these forms of relating, and that psychotherapists with flexibility and range can become skilful in the appropriate use of all of them, although not all are required in all psychotherapies or for all patients.

The far-ranging implications of this perspective for psychotherapy research, assessment and treatment need to be developed further. Integration of a multiplicity of therapeutic relationship modalities does not mean eclectic or unconscious use. Indeed, if such is the declared field, the responsibility is awesome. Freedom does not mean that we forgo discipline. Courage in actively embracing the fullest range of potentials of the self, theory or the *numinosum* needs to be accompanied by the severest form of testing, and forged anew with each client from moment to moment, no matter what the prescriptions or proscriptions of theoretical orthodoxy.

REFERENCES

Adler, G. (1979) *Dynamics of the Self*, London: Coventure (first published 1951).

Agnew, L. R. C. (1963) 'Notes and events: Paré's apophthegm', *Journal of the History of Medicine* 18: 75–7.

Alexander, F. and French, T. (1946) *Psychoanalytic Therapy*, New York: Ronald Press.

Archambeau, E. (1979) 'Beyond countertransference: the psychotherapist's experience of healing in the therapeutic relationship', Doctoral dissertation, San Diego: California School of Professional Psychology.

Barr, J. (1987) 'Therapeutic relationship model', *Transactional Analysis Journal* 17(4): 141.

Berne, E. (1961) *Transactional Analysis in Psychotherapy: A Systematic Individual and Social Psychiatry*, New York: Grove Press.

—— (1966) *Principles of Group Treatment*, New York: Grove Press.

Binswanger, L. (1968) *Being-in-the-World*, New York: Harper Torchbooks.

Bordin, E. S. (1979) 'The generalizability of the psychoanalytical concept of the working alliance', *Psychotherapy: Theory, Research and Practice* 16(3): 252–60.

Boss, M. (1963) *Psychoanalysis and Daseinanalysis* (L. B. Lefebre, trans.), New York: Basic Books.

—— (1979) *Existential Foundations of Medicine and Psychology*, New York: Jason Aronson.

Buber, M. (1970) *I and Thou* (W. Kaufmann, trans.), Edinburgh: T. & T. Clark (first published 1923).

Bugental, J. F. T. (1987) *The Art of the Psychotherapist*, New York: W. W. Norton.

Cashdan, S. (1988) *Interactional Psychotherapy: Stages and Strategies in Behavioural Change*, New York: Grune & Stratton.

Clarkson, P. (1990) 'A multiplicity of psychotherapeutic relationships', *British Journal of Psychotherapy* 7(2) 148–63.

—— (1992) *TA Psychotherapy: An Integrated Approach*, London: Routledge.

—— (1995) *The Therapeutic Relationship*, London: Whurr.

Dryden, W. (ed.) (1984) *Individual Therapy in Britain*, London: Harper & Row.

Fagan, J. and Shepherd, I. L. (eds) (1971) *Gestalt Therapy Now: Theory, Techniques, Applications*, New York: Harper & Row.

Fairbairn, W. R. D. (1952) *Psychoanalytic Studies of the Personality*, London: Tavistock Publications.

Ferenczi, S. (1980) *Further Contributions to the Theory and Technique of Psychoanalysis*, London: Maresfield Reprints/Karnac Books (first published 1926).

Frank, J. D. (1979) 'The present status of outcome studies', *Journal of Consulting and Clinical Psychology* 47: 310–16.

Freud, A. (1968) *Indications for Child Analysis and Other Papers 1945 to 1956: The Writings of Anna Freud*, vol. 4, New York: International Universities Press.

Freud, S. (1912a) 'The dynamics of transference', pp. 97–108 in J. Strachey (ed.), *The Standard Edition of the Complete Psychological Works of Sigmund Freud*, vol. 12, London: Hogarth Press.

—— (1912b) 'Recommendations to physicians practising psycho-analysis', pp. 109–20 in J. Strachey (ed.) *The Standard Edition of the Complete Psychological Works of Sigmund Freud*, vol. 12, London: Hogarth Press.

Friedman, M. (1985) *The Healing Dialogue in Psychotherapy*, New York: Jason Aronson.

Fromm-Reichmann, F. (1974) *Principles of Intensive Psychotherapy*, Chicago: University of Chicago Press (first published 1950).

Gendlin, E. (1967) 'Subverbal communication and therapist expressivity: trends in client-centred therapy with schizophrenics', pp. 119–49 in C. R. Rogers and B. Stevens (eds) *Person to Person – the Problem of Being a Human: A New Trend in Psychology*, Lafayette, CA: Real People Press.

Goulding, M. M. and Goulding, R. L. (1979) *Changing Lives through Redecision Therapy*, New York: Grove Press.

Greenacre, P. (1959) 'Certain technical problems in the transference relationship', *Journal of the American Psychoanalysis Association* 7: 484–502.

Greenson, R. R. (1965) 'The working alliance and the transference neurosis', *Psychoanalysis Quarterly* 34: 155–81.

—— (1967) *The Technique and Practice of Psychoanalysis*, vol. 1, New York: International Universities Press.

Griffith, S. (1990) 'A review of the factors associated with patient compliance and the taking of prescribed medicines', *British Journal of General Practice* 40: 114–16.

Guggenbuhl-Craig, A. (1971) *Power in the Helping Professions*, Dallas, TX: Spring Publications.

Guntrip, H. (1961) 'Personality structure and human interaction: the developing synthesis of psychodynamic theory', No. 56 in J. D. Sutherland (ed.) *The International Psycho-analytical Library*, London: Hogarth Press and the Institute of Psycho-Analysis.

Hardy, J. (1989) *A Psychology with a Soul*, London: Arkana.

Heimann, P. (1950) 'On countertransference', *International Journal of Psycho-Analysis* 31: 81–4.

Hynan, M. T. (1981) 'On the advantages of assuming that the techniques of psychotherapy are ineffective', *Psychotherapy: Theory, Research and Practice* 18: 11–3.

James, M. and Savary, L. (1977) *A New Self: Self-therapy with Transactional Analysis*, Reading, MA: Addison-Wesley.

Jourard, S. M. (1971) *The Transparent Self*, New York: Van Nostrand Reinhold.

Jung, C. G. (1966) 'The psychology of the transference', pp. 162–323 in *The*

Collected Works, vol. 16 (R. F. C. Hull, trans.), London: Routledge & Kegan Paul (first published 1946).

—— (1969) 'Psychology and religion', pp. 3–105 in *The Collected Works*, vol. 11 (R. F. C. Hull, trans.), London: Routledge & Kegan Paul (first published 1938).

Kahn, M. D. (1991) *Between the Therapist and Client: The New Relationship*, New York: W. H. Freeman.

Kidd, C. (1988) Personal communication.

Klauber, J. (1986) 'Elements of the psychoanalytic relationship and their therapeutic implications', pp. 200–13 in G. Kohon (ed.) *The British School of Psychoanalysis: The Independent Tradition*, London: Free Association Books.

Laing, R. D. (1965) *The Divided Self*, Harmondsworth: Penguin.

Lambert, M. J. (1983) 'Introduction to assessment of psychotherapy outcome: historical perspective and current issues', in M. J. Lambert, E. R. Christiansen and S. S. DeJulio (eds) *The Assessment of Psychotherapy Outcome*, New York: Wiley & Sons.

—— (1986) 'Implications of psychotherapy outcome research for eclectic psychotherapy', pp. 436–62 in J. C. Norcross (ed.) *Handbook of Eclectic Psychotherapy*, New York: Brunner/Mazel.

Langs, R. (1976) *The Bipersonal Field*, New York: Jason Aronson.

Laplanche, J. and Pontalis, J-B. (1988) *The Language of Psycho-analysis*, London: Karnac (first published 1973).

Luborsky, L., Singer, B. and Luborsky, L. (1975) 'Comparative studies of psychotherapies: is it true that "Everybody has won and all must have prizes"?', *Archives of General Psychiatry* 32: 995–1008.

Malcolm, J. (1981) *Psychoanalysis: The Impossible Profession*, New York: Knopf.

May, R. (1969) *Love and Will*, London: Collins.

Miller, A. (1983) *The Drama of the Gifted Child and the Search for the True Self* (R. Ward, trans.), London: Faber & Faber (first published 1979).

—— (1985) *Thou Shalt Not be Aware: Society's Betrayal of the Child* (H. and H. Hannum, trans.), London: Pluto (first published 1981).

Moiso, C. (1985) 'Ego states and transference', *Transactional Analysis Journal* 15(3) 194–201.

Norcross, J. C. (1986) *Handbook of Eclectic Psychotherapy*, New York: Brunner/Mazel.

Onions, C. T. (1973) *The Shorter Oxford English Dictionary: On Historical Principles*, vol. 2, Oxford: Clarendon Press.

Peck, S. (1978) *The Road Less Traveled: A New Psychology of Love, Traditional Values and Spiritual Growth*, New York: Simon & Schuster.

Polster, E. and Polster, M. (1973) *Gestalt Therapy Integrated*, New York: Random House.

Racker, H. (1982) *Transference and Countertransference*, London: Maresfield Reprints (first published 1968).

Rogers, C. R. (1967) *On Becoming a Person: A Therapist's View of Psychotherapy*, London: Constable (first published 1961).

Rogers, C. R. and Stevens, B. (1967) *Person to Person – the Problem of Being Human: A New Trend in Psychology*, Lafayette, CA: Real People Press.

Rowan, J. (1983) *The Reality Game: A Guide to Humanistic Counselling and Therapy*, London: Routledge & Kegan Paul.

Samuels, A. (1985) *Jung and the Post-Jungians*, London: Routledge & Kegan Paul.

Schiff, J. L., with Schiff, A. W., Mellor, K., Schiff, E., Schiff, S., Richman, D., Fishman, J., Wolz, L., Fishman, C. and Momb, D. (1975) *Transactional Analysis Treatment of Psychosis*, New York: Harper & Row.

Schiff, J. L. (1977) 'One hundred children generate a lot of TA', pp. 54–7 in G. Barnes (ed.) *Transactional Analysis after Eric Berne*, New York: Harper's College Press.

Searles, H. (1975) 'The patient as therapist to his analyst', pp. 95–151 in R. Langs (ed.) *Classics in Psycho-analytic Technique*, New York: Jason Aronson.

Sechehaye, M. (1951) *Reality Lost and Regained: Autobiography of a Schizophrenic Girl* (G. Urbin-Rabson, trans.), New York: Grune & Stratton.

Shakespeare, W. *The Complete Works* (P. Alexander, ed.), London: Collins (1951).

Stone, L. (1961) *The Psychoanalytic Situation*, New York: International Universities Press.

Sullivan, H. S. (1940) *Conception of Modern Psychiatry*, New York: Norton.

Winnicott, D. W. (1958) *Collected Papers: Through Paediatrics to Psycho-analysis*, London: Tavistock Publications.

Chapter 3

A practitioner-scientist approach to psychotherapy process and outcome research

Jenifer Elton Wilson and Michael Barkham

> Several recent lines of thinking . . . strongly suggest . . . the need for a science of human action that intensively studies individual life courses as a means of appropriately understanding (and intervening) with human beings.
>
> (Howard 1986: 73)

Psychotherapy practitioners are pragmatists, interested in the theory and research which 'fits' with their current belief system and with their observations of their own practice. It is commonplace to bemoan the lack of interest shown by most practitioners in reading or using research findings (Howarth 1988; Morrow-Bradley and Elliott 1986). Volumes purporting to be 'complete guides' of psychotherapy contain only cursory mention of research or evaluation (Corey 1986; Kovel 1976). This dismissive reaction usually stems from some previous encounter with the historical struggle to argue for and against the effectiveness of psychotherapy in general and any one therapeutic approach in particular.

Eysenck's (1952, 1966) relegation of the curative claims of psychotherapy, with the exception of behaviour therapy, to the results of spontaneous remission is remembered as hostile and partisan. The resulting claims and counter-claims (Lambert *et al.* 1986; Rachman and Wilson 1980), together with an over-reliance on the logic of the randomised clinical trial, seem distant and alien to the rich experience of psychotherapy. Many practitioners finally lost interest after the review of Luborsky *et al.* (1975) – 'Everyone has won and all must have prizes' – showing the positive but broadly equivalent outcomes of diverse psychotherapies, findings which were substantiated in later meta-analytic studies (Shapiro and Shapiro 1982; Smith and Glass 1977). The researchers could continue with their critiques as long as practitioners could continue with their own practices, supported by the literature of interesting case studies, novel approaches and theoretical propositions which engaged and challenged the imagination. Doubts remain about the absolute necessity for structured research as a 'means to test the accuracy and meaningfulness of our theories' (Ivey *et al.*, 1987: 380). However, the climate of increasing accountability has heightened the need for individual practitioners to monitor and evaluate the outcome of their own clinical work, a situation which is likely to become more urgent if renewable licences to practice are introduced. In addition, the development of innovative procedures for tapping the process of psychotherapy has rekindled interest in investigating within-session change.

In response to this developing situation, we aim in this chapter to provide a 'practitioner-scientist' perspective on research into the processes and outcomes of psychotherapy. Rather than provide a purely academic perspective on research findings, of which there are many accessible volumes (for example, Barkham 1990; Goldfried *et al.* 1990; Lambert *et al.* 1986), we have adopted the position that psychotherapy 'practitioners' are continuously employing, monitoring, evaluating and testing hypotheses at the moment-to-moment level with individual clients. From this position, we wish to extend and place this information within a 'research' or scientific paradigm such that the individual practitioner, as well as the discipline itself, is able to be reflexive and apply this knowledge base to increase our understanding about what is therapeutic about psychotherapy. To facilitate this procedure, we have made explicit reference to potential measures at both process and outcomes levels. However, to convert research 'fantasies' into action – see Waskow (1975b) for an account of this process – practitioners need to understand some of the basic assumptions of research and also be able to apply these assumptions in a practical setting. We therefore begin by setting out a range of choices in research approach and then address questions of research application and evidence in a sequential manner through three stages of psychotherapy: first, the precursors to psychotherapy – namely, what the client and psychotherapist bring to the psychotherapy; second, the process of psychotherapy itself – namely, what happens during psychotherapy; and third, the outcomes of psychotherapy – that is, the effectiveness or otherwise of these processes. Finally, we consider a number of guidelines for evaluating psychotherapy process and outcome.

SELECTING A RESEARCH DESIGN

Most practitioners can describe their own methods of evaluating their work. Some rely on purely subjective observation of their clients' progress and their own feelings of interest and satisfaction. Others use feedback from supervisors, consultants and the clients themselves. Those with a more structured strategy keep careful records of each client's initial aims, and the practitioner's planned approach, in order to check these against actual progress made. Almost all psychotherapy consists of an inquiry into the client's experience, although the focus and the application of this information varies between psychotherapists. Psychotherapists make notes and/or listen to audio-tapes of their work. They share their observations with colleagues, supervisors and consultants. Psychotherapists read about psychotherapeutic approaches, attend conferences and undertake retraining. From these activities, hypotheses are generated, theoretical constructs modified and clinical interventions planned. All these activities are potentially research enterprises. The data are already available and the necessary attitude of curiosity and investigation is not far distant. To make the shift from conscientious practice maintenance to a structured research project involves some consideration of the issues which influence any form of data collection. It is the aim of this section to outline and summarise four inter-linking issues: (1) purpose, (2) design and methodology, (3) values, and (4) resources.

1 Purpose – *what* does the practitioner wish to know?

To a large extent this will depend on the interests and views of the practitioner as inquirer. It has been suggested that there are distinct psychological styles that have created alternative forms of scientific inquiry (Mitroff and Kilmann 1978; Southgate and Randall 1981). It may be helpful to consult Reason and Rowan's (1981) review of Mitroff and Kilmann's (1978) scientific-style typology which is aligned with Jung's (1971) four psychological types as follows: (1) the 'Analytical Scientist' (that is, sensing-thinking); (2) the 'Conceptual Theorist' (that is, intuitive-thinking); (3) the 'Conceptual Humanist' (that is, intuitive-feeling); and (4) the 'Particular Humanist' (that is, sensing-feeling). Identifying and accepting one's own approach, and level of subjectivity, encourages the birth of a need to know. From this base, research questions are likely to arise which fit the prospective investigator's own field of talent and competence. The practitioner-scientist to whom we address this chapter is likely to be the 'Conceptual Theorist' or 'Conceptual Humanist' type. The more detached 'Theorist' may seek to find widely applicable answers to precisely defined questions in a nomothetic search for general laws. In this case a structured survey or the introduction of specific experimental interventions could be used by practitioners in collaboration with their clients. The more personally involved 'Humanist' may seek to arrive at a more precise ideographic understanding of extensive clinical experience which can be made relevant to individual experience. Process research, with its detailed observation of variables, and action research through which a series of experientially based hypotheses are explored with the client as co-researcher, are both suitable research designs for this type of practitioner.

2 Design and methodology – *how* will the practitioner find out?

The decisions made when arriving at a design are complex, and the requirements for a 'good' study as well as the possible criticisms which can be levelled at any 'well-designed' study are numerous (Barkham and Shapiro 1992; Kazdin 1986; Kline 1992). For the practitioner-scientist, as for the researcher, both psychological style and the nature of the research question are likely to influence choices made at this stage. Practitioners of psychotherapy are particularly encouraged to consider qualitative research as a complement to the quantitative experimental model. Reason and Rowan argue that much qualitative research is not 'new paradigm' research, retaining too strong an allegiance to the old ideal of an objective search to find answers to 'efficiency questions' (1981: xx). We suggest that the 'new paradigm' principle of objective subjectivity (Reason and Rowan 1981) is likely to inform most qualitative research undertaken by practitioner-scientists, especially those which emphasise the collaborative and the experiential. However, we do not wish to set up a contest between qualitative and quantitative methodologists. Our view is that the greatest gains will result from employing the most appropriate methodology for the research question being asked. To do so, practitioner-scientists need to adopt a position of methodological pluralism such that they can utilise the relative strengths of each approach rather than claim the superiority of a single method.

An ideographic approach, mentioned above, has considerable appeal to practitioners because of its being rooted in the client's experience. This approach, exemplified in the use of the Personal Questionnaire method (see Phillips 1986) and developed by M. B. Shapiro, utilises items chosen by clients as having personal significance for them. Clients compile statements (such as 'My difficulty in dealing with my dementing mother') which are personally meaningful to them in a way that items in standard measures are sometimes not. Whereas items may be unique to clients, the scale on which they are evaluated is standardised, thereby enabling comparisons both within and between clients. Such an approach has been further developed in the concept of 'moving targets' whereby new statements are introduced throughout psychotherapy as new or repressed issues surface, thereby reflecting the developmental nature of the therapeutic process.

In adopting a quantitative approach, the practitioner-scientist is selecting a paradigm in which the phenomenon under investigation is deemed to be amenable to summary in numerical format. In order to secure a sufficient degree of confidence that the phenomenon is being tapped, researchers employ a wide range of items and/or measures in order that sufficient data are collected such that the accumulated evidence will provide a reasonable approximation to the phenomenon under investigation. The aim of quantification has been to standardise the measurement procedure, and has been adopted in the comparative outcome trial which is based on the logic of the randomised clinical trial (Elkin *et al.* 1989; Shapiro *et al.* in press) where questions concerning the relative efficacy of one treatment compared with another are central. Nomothetic measures – that is, those which set an individual's score against some normative context – are important in making comparisons between any individual and a particular population. However, comparative outcome trials are rarely suited to individual practice unless carried out in collaboration with colleagues and a well-resourced research centre.

The adoption of a qualitative approach is sometimes taken as a reaction against the use of 'numbers' to summarise the therapeutic process. The danger is that it becomes anecdotal and, as a result, under-estimates the potency of the qualitative tradition. What is important is to appreciate that qualitative methods are no less rigorous than those employed in quantitative methodology. For example, there is a growing body of research espousing the use of task analytic procedures (Greenberg 1991, 1992; Safran *et al.* 1988). Task analysis is a research strategy in which the focus is on the individuals actually engaged in performing some therapeutic task rather than relating dependent and independent variables within an experimental design. The procedure involves testing a theoretical model of a 'perform-ance' (for instance, the resolution of an interpersonal conflict) against an experimental verification of that model, which in turn feeds back and adjusts the original assumption.

In addition, the single-case design, utilising a time-series methodology (that is, the collection of a series of measures on the same individual over a period of time), offers the practitioner-scientist a potentially powerful but manageable approach to carrying out process and outcome research. This methodology allows the practitioner to set up and test specific hypotheses for specific clients but also to replicate any component of the design with subsequent clients. Accordingly, it provides considerable flexibility and is a user-friendly way of introducing oneself to carrying out psychotherapy research. In this respect, McCullough (1984) has summarised some important principles for carrying out single-case 'investigatory' research based on the pioneering work of M. B. Shapiro. In addition, the single-case approach can be used as an initial step in a progressive strategy for carrying out further research with many individuals. However, single-case designs need not be confined to research where the number of clients is small. As Barlow *et al.* (1984) point out, this reflects a misunderstanding about single-case studies in that such strategies are applicable to the analysis of the *individual* and are not intended to *restrict* the numbers of individuals analysed.

In terms of adopting a research strategy, Horowitz (1982) has suggested that any psychotherapy research should progress through three distinct stages. First, descriptive studies in which much naturalistic information can be obtained about the phenomenon under investigation. Second, correlational studies in which associations between relevant variables are investigated through the literature. And third, only after the previous two stages have been employed, is the group contrast design employed. In response to this suggestion as well as what is seen as a disappointing yield from the traditional group contrast design, there is currently a strong move within psychotherapy research towards description and explanation (Greenberg 1986), in which the emphasis is upon understanding the therapeutic process: we need rigorous description and explanation to illuminate prediction – to define what it is that leads to positive outcomes in psychotherapy (Greenberg 1986: 708). In particular, there are increasing examples in the literature of researchers adopting a 'case formulation' approach to evaluate the process of outcome (for example Persons *et al.* 1991; Silberschatz *et al.* 1989). The case formulation approach proposes that treatment outcome is more related to the accuracy of the formulation than to the intervention strategies used. From a research perspective, this approach clearly has considerable utility for individual practitioner-scientists for whom the significance of the clinical material is paramount and who are willing to work collaboratively with colleagues.

3 Values – *which* approach is acceptable to the practitioner?

Whereas the direction of the research question may be dependent on the psychological style of the researcher, the choices made regarding methodology will depend on the researcher's own personal convictions. In the same way in which the role of psychotherapists' values are increasingly recognised as an important variable in psychotherapy (Kelly 1990), so the values of the practitioner-scientist are similarly important. All recorded observations are data, and reflect the values and beliefs of the observer. For example, the use of audio- or video-tapes of psychotherapy sessions is still debated. Many psychoanalytic practitioners contend that recording devices are *always* invasive, exploitative of the client, and damaging to the analytic endeavour (Casement 1991). Other psychotherapy practitioners argue that, without tapes, a dangerously subjective view of the therapeutic process is maintained and many eminent psychotherapists have strongly espoused their use both for clinical as well as research purposes (for example, Hobson 1985: 208). The range of issues arising from audio- and video-taping of psychotherapy sessions has been well documented (see Aveline 1992). This issue is only one illustration of a potential ethical dilemma in respect of methodological choices, which demonstrates the limitations likely to be imposed on any research design by the cultural and individual values of the scientist-practitioner.

4 Resources – *how much* time, money and support is available?

A defining constraint upon any research is that of resources, be it human, financial, space and so on. The guiding rule is to design the research within the limits of the resources available. Considerable effort can be expended on the logistics of implementation and equal consideration to practicalities is a hallmark of the proficient practitioner-scientist.

PRECURSORS TO PSYCHOTHERAPY – CLIENT AND PSYCHOTHERAPIST FACTORS

Having considered issues central to the research endeavour, we turn now to the content of the therapeutic enterprise first by addressing factors which are brought to the psychotherapy session (precursors) and then, in the following two sections, addressing issues of therapeutic process and outcome respectively. Addressing the first of these, there is general agreement between psychotherapists that the *person* of the practitioner has a major influence on the progress of psychotherapy. However, it has been stated that '[N]one of the professional, demographic or personal character-istics of psychotherapists studied have been consistently associated with therapeutic outcome' (Orlinsky 1989: 427). In general, psychotherapist activity and skilfulness appear possible candidates for enhancing therapeutic outcomes (Orlinsky and Howard 1986a) and these appear to be more prominent characteristics than the traditional demographic features. In summary, Orlinsky concludes: 'How much and how skilfully psycho-therapists do what they do seems to be more important than who they are, or which of many possible techniques they use' (1989: 427). Tangentially, it is likely that future research into psychotherapist effectiveness (that is, skilfulness) may show considerably more differentiation of outcomes than have comparisons between theoretical orientations.

A consideration which has been the subject of some controversy and research is the need for psychotherapy practitioners to have engaged in personal psychotherapy before commencing a professional practice. Norcross, who has explored this area exhaustively with colleagues (Norcross and Prochaska 1986; Norcross *et al.* 1988), concludes that the person of the psychotherapist is 'inextricably entwined' (Dryden 1991: 35) with the success or failure of any psychotherapeutic intervention. He argues that all practitioners should prioritise psychological health and recommends personal psychotherapy as the most efficacious means of ensuring this, although he stops short of making personal psychotherapy a requirement, even for the psychotherapist in training (Dryden 1991: 59). The require-ment for personal psychotherapy as the foundation for psychotherapeutic training and practice is grounded in the Freudian tradition and has been adopted by many other models of psychotherapy. The marked excep-tion to this legacy is the cognitive-behavioural paradigm, which has dominated clinical and academic psychology and been actively influential in psychotherapy research.

Most of the findings which question or oppose the need for the practitioners to engage in personal psychotherapy are linked to outcome research, with all the associated methodological difficulties of measurement and definition. Even the most usually quoted studies (for example, Grunebaum 1986) fail to show a clear relationship between professional ability and the use, misuse or absence of personal psychotherapy. Two major reviews of this debate, Clark (1986) and Herron (1988), comment on the difficulty in designing effective studies and find the evidence ambiguous. Herron (1988) concludes that there is some logic in the notion that psychotherapy is likely, at the very least, to provide a useful personal learning experience for most psychotherapy practitioners. More recent research (Guy et al. 1988; Liaboe et al. 1989; Norcross et al. 1988) has surveyed the taboo topic of the amount and type of psychotherapy actually used by psychotherapists in practice. The largest of these studies (Liaboe et al. 1989) found their predictions confounded. The majority of the psychotherapists interviewed had experienced psychotherapy since qualification and the most frequent reason given for this re-engagement was not professional stress but difficulties with intimate personal relationship.

The other primary factor to consider in practice-based research is the influence of the client's qualities and characteristics. The client's level of motivation and preparation for psychotherapy has been cited by Garfield (1986) as a major predictor of the level of engagement in psychotherapy. Lambert and Asay (1981) take account of a variety of client characteristics, including motivation, symptoms, expectations and intelligence. Orlinsky (1989) identified client 'openness' (that is, lack of defensiveness) and initial level of functioning to be client characteristics which have been consistently related to differential outcome. He concludes: 'The net impression is that patients who initially are psychologically stronger, less disturbed, and better prepared for psychotherapy derive more benefit from it' (1989: 427). In addition, cultural, demographic and environmental factors should be considered, since all of the client's experience is likely to affect the psychotherapy process. The practitioner-scientist, engaging in collaborative research, will need to consider all these variables for both psychotherapist and client.

There has been an ongoing interest in the match between client, psychotherapist and setting. Paul's (1967) difficult question as to 'What treatment, by whom, is most effective for this individual with that specific problem, and under which set of circumstances?' still haunts psychotherapy research, and disturbs the practitioner. It seems likely that the ideal of close client–psychotherapist matching on demographic and experiential variables is unlikely to be achieved by the majority of practitioners. The practitioner brings a set of theoretical expectations, a complex training in human relations and a relevant range of skills and experience. All but the most sophisticated clients are likely to have different expectations of the therapeutic encounter. Both parties bring along their own personal and demographic characteristics. Issues arising from attempts to progress client–therapy matching have been addressed by Beutler (for example, 1989). In particular, he advances the role of 'dispositional' assessment (that is, treatment response) rather than 'diagnostic' assessment (namely, syndromes) for matching clients to psychotherapy. Accordingly, directive interventions might match with external locus-of-control clients while more insight-orientated approaches might better suit more psychologically minded clients. In addition, practitioners bring to the research endeavour their own personal and demographic characteristics. A keen awareness of these variables is needed, perhaps leading to their use in creating a more meaningful dialogic interpretation of the process of psychotherapy within a research model.

For practitioners seeking to carry out research into their own practice, it may be imperative to select clients not only with respect to their suitability for the research envisaged, but also with regard to the likely effect of such involvement on their well-being and on the therapeutic alliance. Most often this selection is made by the psychotherapists themselves (Oldfield 1983), although the risk of their collusion, defensiveness and bias needs to be guarded against. Full participatory involvement in most practice-based research can be an empowering experience for clients and their resilience should not be under-estimated. The open disclosures of therapeutic and research intention, recommended here, are in contrast with the tradition of clinical observation and case-history write-up which has been widely used by psychotherapists from a variety of orientations.

Both Heron (1981) and Harré (1981) have been influential social scientists encouraging the shift towards participatory psychological engagement. Exemplars of an investigative approach can be seen in Malan's (1963) meticulous studies of brief psychotherapy, which provide a congenial model for client selection and psychotherapist matching. These studies take full account of situational variables and limitations but do not attempt to include the patients studied as full participants in the research project.

THE PROCESS OF PSYCHOTHERAPY AND HOW TO EVALUATE IT

Process research has traditionally been viewed as the analysis of what actually takes place *within* the psychotherapy session. Historically, process research has developed as a distinct area of inquiry when interest moved away from discovering *whether* psychotherapy was effective and towards discovering *what* was effective about the psychotherapeutic encounter. The central components of psychotherapy 'process' have been encapsulated within Orlinsky and Howard's (1987) generic model of psychotherapy: therapeutic contract, therapeutic intervention, therapeutic bond, patient self-relatedness and therapeutic realisation. Research findings pertaining to these particular areas have been well documented (Orlinsky and Howard 1986a), as have a range of areas central to carrying out research in the area of psychotherapy process (Greenberg and Pinsof 1986). These all relate to a central question asked by practitioners: what are the necessary *components* of effective psychotherapy? In a similar vein, psychotherapy process researchers are seeking to understand the mechanisms by which change is achieved.

In this respect, research interest focuses on two domains. One is termed 'specific' effects, which comprise behaviours such as psychotherapist interpretations, the role of which is theoretically identified with a therapeutic modality. The other is termed 'common' factors, and comprises process such as the *therapeutic relationship*, the importance of which is deemed to be common to all psychotherapies. The debate between the role of specific and common factors has continued unabated, with Lambert (1986) estimating that approximately 15 per cent of outcome variance is accounted for by specific factors while common factors account for twice that amount. As stated above, a constant focus has been on what it is that psychotherapists do which leads to client change. Fiedler's (1950) much-quoted observation that experienced psychotherapists have similar clinical behaviours, whatever their theoretical orientation, pointed the way to a continuing investigation and classification of these behaviours. Examples of instruments developed to code particular psychotherapist (and client) behaviours have been taxonomies of verbal response modes (VRMs: see Elliott *et al.* 1987), and core conflictual relationship themes (CCRTs) with a high correlation having been reported between the accuracy of interpretations (as derived from CCRTs) and outcome (Crits-Christoph *et al.* 1988).

The careful specifications of psychotherapist qualities made by Rogers (1957) have become part of the essential world view of psychotherapists and counsellors. Almost all would argue that the qualities of warmth, personal congruence, empathy, contact and positive regard are necessary if not sufficient components of any effective psychotherapeutic alliance. However, empirical research on these constructs has not resulted in a clear endorsement. For example, Orlinsky and Howard (1986a) report that 45 of 86 findings drawn from 40 studies showed no positive relationship between psychotherapist empathy and outcome. Indeed, the literature remains somewhat equivocal as to the specific role of, for example, empathy in psychotherapy outcome. More recently, the Rogerian components have become enshrined in work on the quality and nature of the client–psychotherapist relationship which has itself emerged as the crucial variable linked with outcome (Gaston 1990). Psychotherapists have an interest and a responsibility to explore this particular domain of their practice.

The function of the *therapeutic relationship* varies between the major orientations. Behaviour therapists seek to establish a positive reality-oriented working alliance so as to facilitate the client's experiments with behaviour change. Cognitive therapists are concerned to model authenticity, and offer personal warmth so as to enable clients to accept challenges to their established constructions of reality. Psychodynamic therapists seek to explore beyond the working alliance and to engage with the transferential elements of the relationship. Existential humanists, in addition, work towards a more genuine real relationship. All these are different theoretical concepts which reflect the expectations of the psychotherapist, and may or may not match the client's expectations and motivations. This potential is gaining research interest through the use of measures such as the California Psychotherapy Alliance Scales (CALPAS; for example, Gaston 1991) and the Working Alliance Inventory (WAI; for instance, Horvath and Greenberg 1989) with the latter identifying the distinct domains of tasks, goals and bonds, thereby providing the logic for investigating the development of different bonds as a function of differing therapeutic tasks and goals.

The consensus of agreement about the crucial importance of the *therapeutic relationship* has encouraged a more integrative approach to psychotherapy research. Seeking links between process and outcome has been a constant task for researchers. Kiesler (1981) argued that the comparison of different 'treatment packages', typical of conventional outcome research, was meaningless without some understanding of what goes on within the treatment. Research sought to verify the link between the psychotherapist's interventions and actual change, or lack of change, on the part of the client. Process analysis clarifies the correlation between client change within psychotherapy and client change external to psychotherapy. Kiesler (1981) concluded that 'scientific outcome research requires process analysis of both psychotherapists' and patients' interview behaviors'. However, the scientific yield from investigations into links between process and outcome (namely, the establishment of process–outcome correlations) has been disappointing. Indeed, attempts to establish direct links between process and outcome variables have been roundly criticised as being conceptually flawed (Stiles 1988; Stiles and Shapiro 1990).

Disquiet with this approach has provided support for the adoption of a more phenomenologically based approach termed the 'events paradigm' in which data are collected on specific classes of phenomenon which occur in psychotherapy (such as insight events, perceived-empathy and so on) and which are purported to be crucial to understanding the process of change. Elliott (1983) has elaborated the search for 'significant events' in the psychotherapy process and has developed a methodology producing highly detailed transcripts of taped sessions, which are subjected to multiple revisions, through the use of Interpersonal Process Recall (IPR: Elliott 1986; Kagan 1980) and a range of rating scales to produce a comprehensive qualitative analysis. Building upon these procedures, Elliott and Shapiro (1992) provide an account of the use of the Comprehensive Process Analysis method (CPA: Elliott 1989) in understanding a single event during psychotherapy. The aim of such work is to develop general models of particular kinds of significant events which can then be used to improve the practice of psychotherapy (Elliott and Shapiro 1992: 165). Such an approach, rather than relying upon a pool of independent raters, depends upon the collaboration between client and psychotherapist in these analytic procedures.

A different, but complementary, approach to evaluating the process of psychotherapy can be seen in work evaluating models of stages of change (Prochaska and DiClemente 1986) and the assimilation of problematic experiences (Stiles *et al.* 1990). The Stages of Change model identifies four stages which categorise the level at which *clients* are ready to work therapeutically: pre-contemplation, contemplation, action and maintenance. The Assimilation model articulates eight stages through which a particular *problematic experience* may be progressively resolved: warded off, unwanted thoughts, vague awareness, problem clarification, insight, application of understanding, problem solution and mastery. Clearly, not all problems originate from the same stage nor do they progress to the same point of resolution. However, both models provide the practitioner-scientist with frameworks for describing their therapeutic work and contributing to our understanding about the factors which bring about effective client change.

For the novice practitioner-scientist, these developments in the field of psychotherapy research are exciting and accessible. Focus on process is part of the psychotherapist's repertoire. The research task is to structure and systematise this focus. Modern technology has made possible minutely detailed observation of the psychotherapy session through frame-by-frame video analysis. Recall procedures, for example using brief structured recall (a variant of IPR), would enable psychotherapists to work as co-researchers in which one would act as the observer for the other. Once again, this methodology may be uncongenial to psychoanalytic practitioners for the reasons given above. One possible solution to this quandary is the use of structured case notes in combination with post-session rating scales for practitioner and client. Another opportunity to observe process is the use of the one-way screen, which has been accepted by many psychoanalytically trained psychotherapists and is widely used in family psychotherapy. All these methods provide access to the therapeutic arena to a wider range of observers, although needing to be balanced with concerns for professional containment and confidentiality.

Howard (1986) argues cogently and extensively for the integration of practice and research. He takes a broad view of process research, encouraging practitioners to use the model of historical research to explore personal patterns with their clients in conjunction with carefully structured phenomenological interventions. His view is that a highly individualised experimental approach, which takes account of each client's role as active agent in their own life course, can still yield information about the 'lawlike regularities' (Howard 1986: 72) of the human situation which condition human endeavours. This type of mini-research project will be familiar to many psychotherapists whose approach is existential humanist, with Gestalt psychotherapy being particularly accessible to this research application. We give below a suggested research design for the type of individualised study which practitioners might carry out within their own practice, following Howard's (1986) model of the single case study which includes experiments carried out with client as co-researcher.

Research question

What has been the client's chosen strategy for survival in the past and how is this maintained by problematic behaviours and distressed feelings in the present?

Research design

We suggest using specific experimental interventions within the psychotherapy session, planned in advance with the client's co-operation, and using 'experimental' and 'control' recorded sessions to monitor the responses of client and psychotherapist. These constructed 'significant events' (Elliott 1983) can then be submitted to multiple revisions through the use of IPR (Interpersonal Process Recall) by the two participants as well as external analysis by observers.

Kagan's (1980) IPR technique represents a phenomenological approach to process research with its structured attempt to elicit from memory the moment-by-moment details of experience. McLeod (1990a; 1990b), in his reviews of the literature regarding client and practitioner experience of the therapeutic encounter, comments on the reliance on external observations demonstrated by the majority of process studies in contrast with the comparatively sparse research which utilises the experience of clients and practitioners, as actually *reported*.

When asked to give an account of their own experiences of psychotherapy, clients emphasise *the importance of positive relationship* factors and clear contractual agreements as to the structure and aims of psychotherapy (Maluccio 1979; Rennie 1987). Some of these findings make uncomfortable reading for most psychotherapists. Clients describe feelings of confused ambivalence between the need to be fully understood and the wish to avoid conflict and discomfort (Orlinsky and Howard 1986b). In particular, clients are shown as highly motivated to defer to and please their psychotherapists (Rennie 1987), and preferring advice and reassurance (Llewelyn 1988; Murphy *et al.* 1984).

Orlinsky and Howard's (1977: 585) post-session questionnaires also explored the practitioners' experiences of psychotherapy and arrived at a categorisation of sessions as '*smooth sailing, coasting, heavy going or foundering*'. 'Heavy going' sessions, during which the client was perceived to be in distress and the psychotherapist highly effective, seemed to be the experience most highly prized by practitioners. Studies in this area have utilised the Session Evaluation Questionnaire (SEQ: Stiles 1980), and have replicated psychotherapists' preference for 'deep and rough' sessions (Stiles and Snow 1984) and contrasts with most clients' endorsement of safe, warm and encouraging sessions. However, it is important to grasp that people having different roles will undoubtedly have differing perspectives on the psychotherapeutic process. For example, Stiles *et al.* (1988) found psychotherapists, in line with theoretical predictions, to rate sessions in which a *relationship-orientated psychotherapy* was utilised as significantly 'deeper' than sessions of cognitive-behavioural psychotherapy. In contrast, clients rated neither orientation as significantly deeper than the other. For clients, psychotherapy sessions *per se* were deep (as compared with their experiences of other everyday interactions during their period of depression). What is both obvious but at the same time important to appreciate, is that many of the concepts which researchers investigate, although having theoretical salience for them, simply do not have 'psychological significance' for clients. This mismatch of values and objectives between client and psychotherapist is one of the interesting issues uncovered by research into the experiences of psychotherapy which are not usually disclosed within the *therapeutic relationship*.

The literature reflects several developing interests which appear to have potential implications for our understanding of psychotherapy. The study of 'therapists' dilemmas' (Dryden 1985) and difficulties (Davis *et al.* 1987) is likely to engage the interest of many practitioners with the courage to explore their own experience of impasse. Similarly, there is a slow but increasing recognition of clients', and indeed psychotherapists', inter-session experiences and the need to take account of them in understanding the change process (Tarragona and Orlinsky 1988). A striking feature of both these areas is their amenability to investigation at the clinically descriptive level.

These studies all accept, celebrate and employ subjectivity within a research format. The methodology used offers a choice or combination of the following: rating scales, IPR interviews, journals, structured questionnaires, open-ended questionnaires (rich in material but difficult to analyse). More recently, there has been a conceptual *rapprochement* between process and outcome research in that it is recognised that within sessions there are mini-outcomes (small o's) which influence processes within subsequent sessions, all of which ultimately lead, at the end of psycho-therapy, to a final outcome (the big O). Accordingly, within-session events comprise both process and mini-outcomes which have implications for carrying out research.

OUTCOMES OF PSYCHOTHERAPY AND HOW TO EVALUATE THEM

Outcome research attempts to examine the validity of any theory of change. Research into outcomes of psychotherapy has been shadowed by arguments regarding the effectiveness of psychotherapy in general or of one psychotherapeutic approach over another. Practitioners, critical of this research, complain about the lack of agreement as to *what* constitutes a satisfactory outcome. There are philosophical and moral differences between social adjustment and self-realisation goals. There are questions of *whose* judgement is sought, *how* the outcome is measured, and for *how long* after termination of the psychotherapy contract. Even more complex are the arguments for and against the plausibility of assigning a causal effect to any psychotherapeutic intervention. Bohart and Todd (1988) point out the dangers of over-reliance on the psychotherapist's own experience as sufficient validation for any theory of change. They state that therapy sessions are an important source of ideas but do not provide empirically validated *truth* (1988: 292). It is our view that practitioners remain very interested in *appropriate* research into effectiveness, particu-larly findings which compare different theoretical approaches and which comment on the results obtained by approaches similar to their own.

The flood of outcome studies generated by Eysenck's (1952) challenge have been extensively reviewed, summarised and meta-analysed (Glass and Kliegl 1983; Meltzoff and Kornreich 1970; Nietzel *et al.* 1987; Robinson *et al.* 1990; Smith and Glass 1977; Shapiro and Shapiro 1982). In general, they uphold the effectiveness of psychotherapy such that the average client receiving psychotherapy is better off than 80 per cent of a control population, and comment on the possibility of an average 8 per cent of clients being 'harmed' by psychotherapy (Lambert *et al.* 1986). Most interestingly, they fail to identify any one therapeutic approach as significantly more effective than any other (Luborsky *et al.* 1975; Sloane *et al.* 1975). This 'outcome' has been termed the 'equivalence paradox', in which psychotherapies which are technically diverse in their content have been shown to be *broadly* equivalent in their outcomes (Stiles *et al.* 1986).

However, the desirability of matching particular problem areas to specific treatment approaches is not well supported (Parloff 1979). For example, systematic desensitisation is acknowledged as effective with simple phobias, cognitive-behavioural techniques with anxiety and depression, and the verbal psychotherapies with self-esteem difficulties (Smith *et al.* 1980). Matching clients' presenting problems with specific therapeutic orientations has not produced the clinical yield which was once expected, but it has provided some basis for the move towards eclecticism among some psychotherapists. Although the risks of hasty and inappropriate incorporation of techniques is recognised by most practitioners, a more considered integration might be achieved by means of the practice-based mini-research projects we have recommended in this chapter.

Practitioner-scientists, in researching the effectiveness of their own interventions, are encouraged to shift from a limited range of explanations, based on the practitioner's current belief system, to an open-minded search to understand the multiplicity of variables and processes which contribute to client change. The tendency for psychotherapy practitioners to over-emphasise the influence of the psychotherapy session can be curbed by taking account of situational and environmental factors, as well as the healthy human drive towards 'spontaneous recovery' (Eysenck 1952). In addition, a focus on inter-session change is much needed in order to further our understanding of how clients work on issues and problematic experiences between sessions. Outcome research should be broad enough to include these data, and outcome measures designed accordingly.

The issue of the cost-effectiveness of psychotherapy is a major one which has implications for any psychotherapeutic service delivery system. Howard *et al.* (1986) established that the relationship between the number of weekly psychotherapy sessions administered to clients and the percentage of clients showing measurable improvement was portrayed as a negatively accelerating curve. That is, while more clients improved the longer psychotherapy continued (that is, an accelerating function), the increase showed diminishing returns (namely, a negative function) with, for example, 53 per cent of clients meeting the criterion of measurable improvement after eight sessions but only 62 per cent after thirteen sessions. Indeed, many studies have reported the major impact of psychotherapy to occur within the initial ten sessions. Another way of phrasing this issue is in terms of 'How much psychotherapy is enough?' Operationalising change in terms of reliable and clinically significant change (see below), Kopta *et al.* (1992) have estimated that there is a 0.66 probability of a client improving after 20 sessions and rises to a 0.82 probability after 52 sessions (that is, one year). However, such estimates are functions of the measures employed and the criterion of improvement used.

In terms of evaluating psychotherapy outcomes, some general approaches have been described in an earlier section. In addition, a range of measures for use in psychotherapy is outlined elsewhere (Lambert *et al.* 1983). However, there are a range of readily available client self-report measures which can be easily acquired and implemented. Two complementary measures are the Symptom Checklist-90R (SCL-90R: Derogatis 1983), which is a 90–item measure tapping nine dimensions (such as depression, anxiety, somatisation and so on), and the Inventory of Interpersonal Problems (IIP: Barkham *et al.* in press; Horowitz *et al.* 1988), which comprises 127 items and taps a range of interpersonal dimensions (for example, assertiveness, intimacy and so forth). In terms of making comparisons, general agreement among researchers to adopt one core outcome battery would have distinct advantages for evaluating individual change as well as being able to make comparisons with clients in other practices or disciplines. However, although the notion of a core outcome battery has long existed in the literature (Waskow 1975a), there is currently no general agreement between professions about such a protocol.

In addition to considering change measures, there is also the issue of how best to manipulate data in order to reflect the change process. For example, how much change has to occur before a client can be said to have 'improved'? Recently, operational definitions of reliable and clinically significant change have been devised (Jacobson and Truax 1991) which provide a viable and meaningful criterion for determining change. In brief, these procedures establish 'how much' change is required to be reliable and 'at what level' the client needs to be functioning after psychotherapy in order for the change to be clinically significant (that is, is more likely to belong to the normal than to the dysfunctional population). What is important for the practitioner is that these procedures only require a pocket calculator and enable a database to be built up from a few clients which can be added to in order that any single client's progress can be set in the context of all clients seen within the practice. Ultimately, such data are both informative for the practitioner and can also be used as feedback for clients. In this way, evaluation becomes an important part of the therapeutic process rather than an adjunct. These features of cost-effectiveness, measures and the presentation of data are all central to current concerns with evaluating psychotherapy service delivery systems, and there is a growing body of literature in this area (such as Fonagy and Higgitt 1989; Parry 1992).

GENERAL GUIDELINES AND PITFALLS IN EVALUATING PSYCHOTHERAPY PROCESS AND OUTCOME

In this final section, we conclude with a number of practical hints which we believe will lead to better research or evaluation as well as more cost-efficient learning. As change is multifaceted, it is undesirable to rely on any single measure of change. To obtain an understanding of a particular phenomenon, it is generally best to employ more than one measure. For example, a phenomenon which is tapped only by a single measure will be extremely vulnerable to the specific 'noise', and unreliability carried by that one measure and findings may be an artefact of that one measure. Without the availability of a parallel measure, it is sometimes difficult to unravel this problem. Another issue concerns the frequency with which any phenomenon is tapped. A simple rule is to measure as often as possible. Two reasons underlie this rationale. First, how a particular measure performs can be better understood the more often it is used. Secondly, in line with current psychotherapy research, practitioner-scientists should be tapping the *process* of change. By implication, a measure used only once or twice (that is, pre- and post-psychotherapy) is unlikely to summarise adequately any process of change. A simple rule of mathematics is that only a linear relationship (namely, a straight line) can be deduced from two data points. Given that all practitioners know that change is not always linear, it is only when a minimum of three data points exist that a more accurate or clinically representative profile of the change process can be deduced.

Thirdly, we would recommend the adoption of multiple methodologies (that is, methodological pluralism). Psychotherapy research is unlikely to be sufficiently informed by practitioner-scientists selecting on principle one approach rather than another. Differing psychotherapeutic approaches are tools employed towards enabling clients to achieve improved well-being. The issue is being able to select a method or approach which is most appropriate to the phenomenon under investigation. And fourthly, we would encourage piloting of any procedures: implementing what may seem a very simple and straightforward evaluation procedure can throw up unforeseen obstacles. Often, the introduction of smaller components of a study in stages enables the evaluation of whichever aspect of the study is causing difficulties in implementation.

In designing any research or evaluation, it is best to be focused and arrive at findings which have a sense of clarity. Too many researchers spread themselves too thinly such that, while they take account of many possible moderating variables, they can say very little of substance which is clear and which has implications for other practitioners. In contrast, being able to state clearly a relationship between *two* variables does provide a scientific advance. The relationship between either of these two variables and a third variable can be investigated in a separate study. In designing and, in particular, reporting any study, however small-scale, it is important to remember a central component of science: replication. This is true whether the methodological approach is qualitative, quantitative, ideographic or descriptive. What is of interest is building upon single results and obtaining general theories of how psychotherapy works and under what conditions specific clients respond differentially. As argued elsewhere, this will not be obtained in any single study (Barkham and Shapiro 1992). However, to replicate the work of others, practitioner-scientists are required to record all characteristics of their sample and the procedures used.

ETHICAL ISSUES

When carrying out research, experience suggests that most clients appreciate the need for evaluation, both in terms of their own progress (similar to the medical profession taking readings of body temperature and blood pressure) and in order to enhance the quality of service for future clients. However, adherence to certain ethical procedures is required. General information about any evaluation should be passed to the client before starting psychotherapy. If data, be it questionnaire or audio-tapes, is to be used afterwards and worked on by other people, then the client's consent needs to be obtained. This is referred to as 'informed consent'.

To ensure that the client's rights are not infringed, agreement for the client to release material for research purposes can only be obtained *after* psychotherapy has finished, particularly in the case of audio-taped material. That is, only when the client knows what is on the audio-tapes can they make an informed decision whether or not to release them for research purposes. This procedure both empowers clients and saves clients guarding against speaking freely in the presence of a tape-recorder. Finally, any research which takes place in a public arena and which is beyond standard working practice should have ethical approval from the appropriate local body.

REFERENCES

Aveline, M. (1992) 'The use of audio and videotape recordings of therapy sessions in the supervision and practice of dynamic psychotherapy', *British Journal of Psychotherapy* 8: 347–58.
Barkham, M. (1990) 'Research in individual therapy', pp. 282–312 in W. Dryden (ed.) *Individual Therapy: A Handbook*, Milton Keynes: Open University Press.
—— (1992) 'Research on integrative and eclectic therapy', pp. 239–68 in W. Dryden (ed.) *Integrative and Eclectic Therapy: A Handbook*, Milton Keynes: Open University Press.
Barkham, M., Hardy, G. E. and Startup, M. (in press) 'The structure, validity and clinical relevance of the Inventory of Interpersonal Problems (IIP)', *British Journal of Medical Psychology*.
Barkham, M. and Shapiro, D. A. (1992) 'Response', pp. 86–96 in W. Dryden and C. Feltham (eds) *Psychotherapy and its Discontents*, Milton Keynes: Open University Press.
Barlow, D. H., Hayes, S. C. and Nelson, R. O. (1984) *The Scientist Practitioner: Research and Accountability in Clinical and Educational Settings*, New York: Pergamon.
Beutler, L. E. (1989) 'Differential treatment selection: the role of diagnosis in psychotherapy', *Psychotherapy* 26: 271–81.
Bohart, A. C. and Todd, J. (1988) *Foundations of Clinical and Counseling Psychology*, New York: Harper & Row.
Casement, P. (1991) Personal communication.
Clark, M. (1986) 'Personal therapy: a review of empirical research', *Professional Psychology: Research and Practice* 17: 541–3.

Corey, G. (1986) *Theory and Practice of Counselling and Psychotherapy*, Pacific Grove, CA: Brooks Cole.

Crits-Christoph, P., Cooper, A. and Luborsky, L. (1988) 'The accuracy of therapists' interpretations and the outcome of dynamic psychotherapy', *Journal of Consulting and Clinical Psychology* 56: 490–5.

Davis, J. D., Elliott, R., Davis, M. L., Binns, M., Francis, V. M., Kelman, J. E. and Schroder, T. A. (1987) 'Development of a taxonomy of therapist difficulties: initial report', *British Journal of Medical Psychology* 60: 109–19.

Derogatis, L. R. (1983) *The SCL-90R Administration, Scoring and Procedures Manual-II*, Towson, MD: Clinical Psychometric Research.

Dryden, W. (1985) *Therapists' Dilemmas*, London: Harper & Row.

—— (1991) *A Dialogue with John Norcross: Toward Integration*, Milton Keynes: Open University Press.

Elkin, I. E., Shea, M. T., Watkins, J. T., Imber, S. D., Sotsky, S. M., Collins, J. F., Glass, D. R., Pilkonis, P. A., Leber, W. R., Docherty, J. P., Fiester, S. J. and Parloff, M. B. (1989) 'NIMH Treatment of Depression Collaborative Research Program: general effectiveness of treatments', *Archives of General Psychiatry* 46: 971–82.

Elliott, R. (1983) ' "That in your hands . . .": a comprehensive process analysis of a significant event in psychotherapy', *Psychiatry* 46: 113–27.

—— (1986) 'Interpersonal process recall (IPR) as a psychotherapy process research method', pp. 503–27 in L. S. Greenberg and W. M. Pinsoff (eds) *The Psychotherapeutic Process: A Research Handbook*, New York: Guilford Press.

—— (1989) 'Comprehensive process analysis: understanding the change process in significant change events', pp. 165–84 in M. Packer and R. B. Addison (eds) *Entering the Circle: Hermeneutic Investigation in Psychology*, Albany, NY: SUNY Press.

Elliott, R., Hill, C. E., Stiles, W. B., Friedlander, M. L., Mahrer, A. R. and Margison, F. R. (1987) 'Primary therapist response modes: comparison of six rating systems', *Journal of Consulting and Clinical Psychology* 55: 218–23.

Elliott, R. and Shapiro, D. A. (1992) 'Client and therapist as analysts of significant events', pp. 163–86 in S. G. Toukmanian and D. L. Rennie (eds) *Psychotherapy Process Research: Paradigmatic and Narrative Approaches*, Newbury Park, CA: Sage.

Eysenck, H. J. (1952) 'The effects of psychotherapy: an evaluation', *Journal of Consulting Psychology* 16: 319–21.

—— (1966) *The Effects of Psychotherapy*, New York: International Sciences.

—— (1992) 'The outcome problem in psychotherapy', pp. 100–24 in W. Dryden and C. Feltham (eds) *Psychotherapy and its Discontents*, Milton Keynes: Open University Press.

Fiedler, F. E. (1950) 'A comparison of therapeutic relationships in psychoanalytic, non-directive and Adlerian therapy', *Journal of Consulting Psychology* 14: 121–53.

Fonagy, P. and Higgitt, A. (1989) 'Evaluating the performance of departments of psychotherapy', *Psychoanalytic Psychotherapy* 4: 121–53.

Garfield, S. L. (1986) 'Research on client variables', pp. 213–56 in S. L. Garfield and A. E. Bergin (eds) *Handbook of Psychotherapy and Behavior Change*, 3rd edn., New York: John Wiley.

Gaston, L. (1990) 'The concept of the alliance and its role in psychotherapy: theoretical and empirical considerations', *Psychotherapy* 27: 143–53.

—— (1991) 'Reliability and criterion-related validity of the California Psychotherapy Alliance Scales – patient version', *Psychological Assessment: A Journal of Consulting and Clinical Psychology* 3: 68–74.

Glass, G. and Kliegl, R. M. (1983) 'An apology for research integration in the study of psychotherapy', *Journal of Consulting and Clinical Psychology* 51: 28–41.

Goldfried, M. R., Greenberg, L. S. and Marmar, C. R. (1990) 'Individual psychotherapy: process and outcome', *Annual Review of Psychotherapy* 41: 659–88.

Greenberg, L. S. (1986) 'Research strategies', pp. 707–34 in L. S. Greenberg and W. M. Pinsof (eds) *The Psychotherapeutic Process: A Research Handbook*, New York: Guilford Press.

—— (1991) 'Research on the process of change', *Psychotherapy Research* 1: 3–16.

—— (1992) 'Task analysis: identifying components of intrapersonal conflict resolution', pp. 22–50 in S. G. Toukmanian and D. L. Rennie (eds) *Psychotherapy Process Research: Paradigmatic and Narrative Approaches*, Newbury Park, CA: Sage.

Greenberg, L. S. and Pinsof, W. M. (eds) (1986) *The Psychotherapeutic Process: A Research Handbook*, New York: Guilford Press.

Grunebaum, H. (1986) 'Harmful psychotherapy experiences', *American Journal of Psychotherapy* 40: 165–76.

Guy, D. G., Stark, M. J. and Polestra, P. L. (1988) 'Personal therapy for psychotherapists before and after entering professional practice', *Professional Psychology* 19: 474–6.

Harré, R. (1981) 'The positivist-empiricist approach and its alternatives', pp. 3–17 in P. Reason and J. Rowan (eds), *Human Enquiry: A Sourcebook of New Paradigm Research*, Chichester: John Wiley.

Heron, J. (1981) 'Philosophical basis for a new paradigm', pp. 19–36 in P. Reason and J. Rowan (eds) *Human Enquiry: A Sourcebook of New Paradigm Research*, Chichester: John Wiley.

Herron, W. G. (1988) 'The value of personal psychotherapy for psychotherapists', *Psychological Reports* 62: 175–84.

Hobson, R. F. (1985) *Forms of Feeling: The Heart of Psychotherapy*, London: Tavistock Publications.

Horowitz, L. M., Rosenberg, S. E., Baer, B. A., Ureno, G. and Villasenor, V. S. (1988) 'Inventory of Interpersonal Problems: psychometric properties and clinical applications', *Journal of Consulting and Clinical Psychology* 56: 885–92.

Horowitz, M. (1982) 'Strategic dilemmas and the socialization of psychotherapy researchers', *British Journal of Clinical Psychology* 21: 119–27.

Horvath, A. O. and Greenberg, L. S. (1989) 'The development and validation of the Working Alliance Inventory', *Journal of Counseling Psychology* 36: 223–33.

Howard, G. S. (1986) 'The scientist-practitioner in counseling psychology: toward a deeper integration of theory, research and practice', *The Counseling Psychologist* 14: 61–105.

Howard, K. I., Kopta, S. M., Krause, M. S. and Orlinsky, D. E. (1986) 'The dose-effect relationship in psychotherapy', *American Psychologist* 41: 159–64.

Howarth, I. (1988) 'Psychotherapy: who benefits?' *The Psychologist* 2: 150–2.

Ivey, A. E., Ivey, M. B. and Simek-Downing, L. (1987) *Counselling and Psychotherapy*, London: Prentice-Hall International.

Jacobson, N. S. and Truax, P. (1991) 'Clinical significance: a statistical approach to defining meaningful change in psychotherapy research', *Journal of Consulting and Clinical Psychology* 59: 12–19.

Jung, C. G. (1971) *Collected Works*, vol 6, *Psychological Types* (R. F. C. Hull, revised trans.), Princeton, NJ: Princeton University Press.

Kagan, N. (1980) 'Influencing human interaction: eighteen years with IRP', in A. K. Hess (ed.) *Psychotherapy Supervision: Theory, Research, Practice*, New York: John Wiley.

Kazdin, A. E. (1986) 'The evaluation of psychotherapy: research design and methodology', pp. 23–68 in S. L. Garfield and A. E. Bergin (eds) *Handbook of Psychotherapy and Behavior Change*, 3rd edn., New York: John Wiley.

Kelly, T. A. (1990) 'The role of values in psychotherapy: a critical review of process and outcome effects', *Clinical Psychology Review* 10: 171–86.

Kiesler, D. J. (1981) 'Process analysis: a necessary ingredient of psychotherapy outcome research', Paper presented at the Annual Conference of the Society for Psychotherapy Research, Aspen, CO, June.

Kline, P. (1992) 'Problems of methodology in studies of psychotherapy', pp. 64–86 in W. Dryden and C. Feltham (eds) *Psychotherapy and its Discontents*, Milton Keynes: Open University Press.

Kopta, S. M., Howard, K. I., Lowry, J. L. and Beutler, L. E. (1992) 'The psychotherapy dosage model and clinical significance: estimating how much is enough for psychological symptoms', Paper presented at the Annual Meeting of the Society for Psychotherapy Research, Berkeley, CA, June.

Kovel, J. (1976) *A Complete Guide to Therapy*, New York: Pantheon.

Lambert, M. J. (1986) 'Implications of psychotherapy outcome for eclectic psychotherapy', in J. C. Norcross (ed.) *Handbook of Eclectic Psychotherapy*, New York: Brunner/Mazel.

Lambert, M. J. and Asay, T. P. (1981) *Patient Characteristics and Psychotherapy Outcome*, New York: Pergamon Press.

Lambert, M. J., Christensen, E. R. and DeJulio, S. S. (1983) *The Assessment of Psychotherapy*, New York: John Wiley.

Lambert, M. J., Shapiro, D. A. and Bergin, A. E. (1986) 'The effectiveness of psychotherapy', pp. 157–211 in S. L. Garfield and A. E. Bergin (eds) *Handbook of Psychotherapy and Behavior Change*, 3rd edn., New York: John Wiley.

Liaboe, G. P., Guy, J. D., Wong, T. and Deahnert, J. R. (1989) 'The use of personal therapy by psychotherapists', *Psychotherapy in Private Practice* 7: 115–34.

Llewelyn, S. P. (1988) 'Psychological therapy as viewed by clients and therapists', *British Journal of Clinical Psychology* 27: 223–37.

Luborsky, L., Singer, B. and Luborsky, L. (1975) 'Comparative studies of psychotherapies: is it true that everybody has won and all must have prizes?' *Archives of General Psychiatry* 32: 995–1008.

McCullough, J. P. (1984) 'Single-case investigative research and its relevance for the nonoperant clinician', *Psychotherapy* 21: 382–8.

McLeod, J. (1990a) 'The client's experience of counselling and psychotherapy: a review of the research literature', pp. 1–19 in D. Mearns and W. Dryden (eds) *Experiences of Counselling in Action*, London: Sage.

—— (1990b) 'The practitioner's experience of counselling and psychotherapy: a review of the research literature', pp. 66–79 in D. Mearns and W. Dryden (eds) *Experiences of Counselling in Action*, London: Sage.

Malan, D. H. (1963) *A Study of Brief Psychotherapy*, London: Tavistock.

Maluccio, A. (1979) *Learning from Clients: Interpersonal Helping as Viewed by Clients and Social Workers*, New York: Free Press.

Meltzoff, J. and Kornreich, M. (1970) *Research in Psychotherapy*, New York: Atherton Press.

Mitroff, I. and Kilmann, R. H. (1978) *Methodological Approaches to Social Science: Integrating Divergent Concepts and Theories*, San Francisco: Jossey Bass.

Morrow-Bradley, C. and Elliott, R. (1986) 'Utilization of psychotherapy research by practicing psychotherapists', *American Psychologist* 41: 188–97.

Murphy, P. H., Cramer, D. and Lillie, F. J. (1984) 'The relationship between curative factors perceived by patients in psychotherapy and treatment outcome: an exploratory study', *British Journal of Medical Psychology* 57: 187–92.

Nietzel, M. T., Russell, R. L., Hemmings, K. A. and Gretter, M. L. (1987) 'Clinical significance of psychotherapy for unipolar depression: a meta-analytic approach to social comparison', *Journal of Consulting and Clinical Psychology* 55: 156–61.

Norcross, J. C. and Prochaska, J. O. (1986) 'Psychotherapist heal thyself – II: the self-initiated and therapy facilitated change of psychological distress', *Psychotherapy* 23: 345–56.

Norcross, J. C., Strausser-Kirtland, D. and Missar, C. D. (1988) 'The processes and outcomes of psychotherapists' personal treatment experiences', *Psychotherapy* 25: 36–43.

Oldfield, S. (1983) *The Counselling Relationship*, London: Routledge & Kegan Paul.

Orlinsky, D. E. (1989) 'Researchers' images of psychotherapy: their origins and influence on research', *Clinical Psychology Review* 9: 413–41.

Orlinsky, D. E. and Howard, K. I. (1977) 'The therapist's experience of psychotherapy', pp. 566–689 in A. Gurman and A. Razin (eds) *Effective Psychotherapy: A Handbook of Research*, Oxford, Pergamon.

—— (1986a) 'Process and outcome in psychotherapy', pp. 311–81 in S. L. Garfield and A. E. Bergin (eds) *Handbook of Psychotherapy and Behavior Change*, 3rd edn., New York: John Wiley.

—— (1986b) 'The psychological interior of psychotherapy: explorations with therapy session reports', pp. 477–501 in L. S. Greenberg and W. M. Pinsof (eds) *The Psychotherapeutic Process: A Research Handbook*, New York: Guilford Press.

—— (1987) 'A generic model of psychotherapy', *Journal of Integrative and Eclectic Psychotherapy* 6: 6–27.

Parloff, M. B. (1979) 'Can psychotherapy research guide the policymaker? A little knowledge may be dangerous', *American Psychologist* 34: 296–306.

Parry, G. (1992) 'Improving psychotherapy services: applications of research, audit and evaluation', *British Journal of Clinical Psychology* 31: 3–19.

Paul, G. L. (1967) 'Strategy of outcome research in psychotherapy', *Journal of Consulting Psychology* 31: 109–18.

Persons, J. B., Curtis, J. T. and Silberschatz, G. (1991) 'Psychodynamic and cognitive-behavioral formulations of a single case', *Psychotherapy* 28: 608–17.

Phillips, J. P. N. (1986) 'Shapiro personal questionnaire and generalized personal questionnaire techniques: a repeated measures individualized outcome measurement', pp. 557–89 in L. S. Greenberg and W. M. Pinsoff (eds) *The Psychotherapeutic Process: A Research Handbook*, New York: Guilford Press.

Prochaska, J. O. and DiClemente, C. C. (1986) 'The transtheoretical approach', pp. 163–200 in J. C. Norcross (ed.) *Handbook of Eclectic Psychotherapy*, New York: Guilford Press.

Rachman, S. and Wilson, G. (1980) *The Effects of Psychological Therapy*, New York: Wiley.

Reason, P. and Rowan, J. (1981) 'Foreword', pp. xi–xxiv in P. Reason and J. Rowan (eds) *Human Inquiry: A Sourcebook of New Paradigm Research*, Chichester: John Wiley.

Rennie, D. L. (1987) 'A model of the client's experience of psychotherapy', Paper presented at the Sixth Annual International Human Science Conference, Ottawa.

Robinson, L. A., Berman, J. S. and Neimeyer, R. A. (1990) 'Psychotherapy for the treatment of depression: a comprehensive review of controlled outcome research', *Psychological Bulletin* 108: 30–49.

Rogers, C. R. (1957) 'The necessary and sufficient conditions of therapeutic personality change', *Journal of Consulting Psychology* 21: 95–103.

Safran, J. D., Greenberg, L. S. and Rice, L. N. (1988) 'Integrating psychotherapy research and practice: modeling the change process', *Psychotherapy* 25: 1–17.

Shapiro, D. A., Barkham, M., Hardy, G. E., Rees, A., Reynolds, S. and Startup, M. J. (in press) 'Effects of treatment duration and severity of depression on the effectiveness of cognitive/behavioral and psychodynamic/interpersonal psychotherapy', *Journal of Consulting and Clinical Psychology*.

Shapiro, D. A. and Shapiro, D. (1982) 'Meta-analysis of comparative psychotherapy outcome studies: a replication and refinement', *Psychological Bulletin* 92: 581–604.

Silberschatz, G., Curtis, J. T. and Nathans, S. (1989) 'Using the patient's plan to assess progress in psychotherapy', *Psychotherapy* 26: 40–6.

Sloane, R. B., Staples, F. R., Cristol, A. H., Yorkston, N. J. and Whipple, K. (1975) *Psychotherapy versus Behavior Therapy*, Cambridge, MA: Harvard University Press.

Smith, M. L. and Glass, G. V. (1977) 'Meta-analysis of psychotherapy outcome studies', *American Psychologist* 32: 752–60.

Smith, M. L., Glass, G. V. and Miller, T. I. (1980) *The Benefits of Psychotherapy*, Baltimore, MD: Johns Hopkins University Press.

Southgate, J. and Randall, R. (1981) 'The troubled fish: barriers to dialogue', pp. 53–62 in P. Reason and J. Rowan (eds) *Human Inquiry: A Sourcebook of New Paradigm Research*, Chichester: John Wiley.

Stiles, W. B. (1980) 'Measurement of the impact of psychotherapy sessions', *Journal of Consulting and Clinical Psychology* 48: 176–85.

—— (1988) 'Psychotherapy process–outcome correlations may be misleading', *Psychotherapy* 25: 27–35.

Stiles, W. B., Elliott, R., Llewelyn, S. P., Firth-Cozens, J. A., Margison, F. R., Shapiro, D. A. and Hardy, G. (1990) 'Assimilation of problematic experiences by clients in psychotherapy', *Psychotherapy* 27: 411–420.

Stiles, W. B. and Shapiro, D. A. (1990) 'Abuse of the drug metaphor in psychotherapy process–outcome research', *Clinical Psychology Review* 9: 521–43.

Stiles, W. B., Shapiro, D. A. and Elliott, R. (1986) 'Are all psychotherapies equivalent?', *American Psychologist* 41: 165–80.

Stiles, W. B., Shapiro, D. A. and Firth-Cozens, J. A. (1988) 'Do sessions of different treatments have different impacts?', *Journal of Counseling Psychology* 35(4): 391–6.

Stiles, W. B. and Snow, J. (1984) 'Dimensions of psychotherapy session impact across sessions and across clients', *British Journal of Clinical Psychology* 23: 59–63.

Tarragona, M. and Orlinsky, D. E. (1988) 'During and beyond the therapeutic hour: an exploration of the relationship between patients' experiences of therapy in-sessions and between sessions', Paper presented at the Annual Meeting for the Society for Psychotherapy Research, Santa Fe, NM, June.

Waskow, I. E. (1975a) 'Selection of a core battery', pp. 245–69 in I. E. Waskow and M. B. Parloff (eds) *Psychotherapy Change Measures*, Rockville, MD: National Institute of Mental Health.

—— (1975b) 'Fantasied dialogue with a researcher', pp. 274–327 in I. E. Waskow and M. B. Parloff (eds) *Psychotherapy Change Measures*, Rockville, MD: National Institute of Mental Health.

Part II

Culture

Chapter 4

Psychotherapy and race

Pat Grant

'Race' is a term frequently used but not easily defined. Haralambos wrote that race is simply a group of people who see themselves, or are seen by others as a race (1983: 97). Black people do see themselves as a race and are seen by others as a race. Race plays a big part in group identity and it affects the belief systems of that group. Culture is also another factor influencing group identity and this is closely bound up with race. Marsella and Pedersen (1981) suggested that culture has to do with the passing on of a way of life from one generation to another – a way of life that becomes so ingrained within people that they become unaware of assumptions they make about themselves and others. As d'Ardenne and Mahtani (1989) suggested, it is very difficult to separate race from culture, and no attempt will be made to do so in this chapter. Fernando is correct in suggesting that 'In a multi-cultural society where racism is prevalent cultural issues are not easily differentiated from racial ones' (1988: 155).

Two races will be referred to in the chapter – black and white. Black is used in reference to all non-whites. 'Black had a highly pejorative connotation in England in and before the sixteenth century. White had a corresponding pure connotation' (Milner 1983: 7). Today there are still negative images attached to being black. The Moynihan (1965) report about black families in the United States, but which was also influential in Britain, painted a very negative picture of black people, seeing the black family as 'a tangle of pathology'. Generally the image of black people that is put across in society is quite poor, and does not in any way help to enhance the self-esteem of blacks. Fortunately that is now changing, and black people themselves are presenting a more positive view of black. Movements such as the Black Power movement have helped black people to see themselves as people of worth and beauty. There is, however, still a long way to go in getting society as a whole to see black in a more positive light.

The black race is not a homogeneous group (neither is the white race, of course). Black people come to Britain from different geographical regions, lifestyles, religious backgrounds, socio-economic status and so on.

There are, however, certain social and political realities attached to being black in British society. Black people stand out because of their colour. All of them to a greater or lesser extent are faced with the reality of combating discrimination on the basis of their colour, and they all develop ways of coping with racism. Throughout history, black people have found different ways of coping with racism – these strategies of coping have been passed on from generation to generation. A given individual may use a whole range of these strategies, some of these consciously and others unconsciously. One of the tasks of psychotherapy may be to help clients to become conscious of the strategies they use and to compare those strategies with other available options, in order that they might make a more active and conscious choice regarding the options they use.

This chapter will cover issues such as the black client finding a psychotherapist, expectations of psychotherapy and working effectively with the black client, particularly in cases where the psychotherapist is white.

FINDING A PSYCHOTHERAPIST

The choice of psychotherapist is governed by a number of factors, such as availability, cost, sex, race, psychotherapeutic orientation of the psychotherapist and so on. For many black clients, race may be a very important factor in their choice of a psychotherapist. Many black clients will actively choose black psychotherapists because they feel better understood by them, and are able to engage in greater self-disclosure with someone of their own race. Sue and Sue (1990) argue that, because of their past experience of racism and prejudice, black clients often find it difficult to trust a white psychotherapist, and so find self-disclosure difficult. They are wary of self-disclosure as it may lead to misunderstanding, hurt and vulnerability to racism. The author has had black clients who have actively sought out black psychotherapists because they did not want to discuss certain family issues with a white psychotherapist, whom they perceived might use the information to judge black people negatively.

The degree of importance that a black person might attach to having a black psychotherapist may say something about that person's view of themselves, and how they cope with living in a predominantly white society. There are those black people who cope with the 'white world' by acting like white people – that is, mimicking their mannerisms, speech patterns, way of life and so on. These people tend to see themselves as different from other black people, and as far as they are concerned, white is the way to be – it is 'correct'. These black people might actively choose a white psychotherapist because they believe white therapists are better than black ones.

There are also those black people who are very anti-white; they are angry with white people and they do not trust them. This group of black people would resist having a white therapist, and even if they appear to accept one they find ways to sabotage the therapy. They may also resist having a black psychotherapist, as they may see the black psychotherapist as 'selling out', adopting white middle-class values of counselling and psychotherapy, and giving up on their own people. Basically, they may see the black psychotherapist as a 'white man in black clothing'. There are those black people who are more interested in their own group, who, while not rejecting white people, see them as somewhat irrelevant. These black people might prefer a black psychotherapist. Finally, there are those black people who are more interested in the expertise of the psychotherapist, and the ability of the psychotherapist to share and accept their world views, rather than in the race of the psychotherapist (Jackson 1975; Sue and Sue 1990).

Marsella and Pedersen (1981) reported that a majority of the studies on the effects of race and treatment have concluded that black people responded more favourably to black therapists. This was backed up by Atkinson and Schein (1986), who indicated that certain similarities between psychotherapist and client may actually enhance therapy. They suggested that racial similarities between psychotherapist and client may indeed influence the client's willingness to return for therapy. In the light of the preceding information it would seem understandable that black clients would seek out a black psychotherapist. There are not many black therapists, however, and therefore many black clients are left with a choice of white psychotherapists.

In choosing a white psychotherapist there are certain factors to which black clients will pay particular attention. They will be concerned about the racial reaction of the psychotherapist. Marsella and Pedersen (1981) identified three types of racial reaction that the psychotherapist might exhibit – the illusion of colour-blindness, the 'great white father' syndrome, and the assumption that all black people's problems revolve around the issues of being black. Let us return to the issue of colour-blindness. Black clients do not want to be treated as just another white client, as this is only another denial of many of the factors unique to them. Psychotherapists who are colour-blind are not ready to work with black people, as they may still be resisting having to confront and deal with colour differences. While they are in that state, they cannot help the black clients to confront and develop ways of dealing with the reality of being a black person in this society. Often, psychotherapists who come across as colour-blind also have a fear of finding racism in themselves, and unless they face this, they will be unable to work effectively with black clients.

Some white psychotherapists take the view that they know exactly what the black client needs, and they understand the intimate working of the black person's mind. Their only wish is to do good to the black person – all the black client has to do is to put their trust in this 'great white father'.

This sort of response is offensive to many black people and they reject white psychotherapists who have this racial reaction. Similarly, they also reject psychotherapists who act as if all the problems of the black client revolve around their colour – they do not. Although it is true that black people are faced with the problem of combating discrimination on the basis of their colour, it is untrue to suggest or imply that all problems of black people are centred around their colour. It is good for white psychotherapists to have some understanding of black people as a group, but they should not stereotype them; they cannot afford to lose sight of blacks as individuals. Black clients will not truly engage in psychotherapy with psychotherapists who stereotype them.

Black clients, like white clients, are interested in finding psychotherapists who are experts. They prefer psychotherapists who are experts in a variety of theories and skills, because such a psychotherapist can choose the skills and theory appropriate for working with them, rather than clinging to a particular orientation which might not suit the client. Many black clients may not necessarily articulate this, but they will act it out by not returning for the therapy if the therapy is not meeting their needs. Black clients also prefer psychotherapists who have some knowledge and understanding of the socio-political forces affecting them.

So far there has been an implication that black clients are always active in the choice of their psychotherapist. Unfortunately this is not the case. Many black clients cannot afford to pay for psychotherapy and so have to take whatever psychotherapist they are offered by those doing the paying, such as social services, the NHS and so on. Often the people involved in allocating black clients to psychotherapists feel they are doing their black clients favours by referring them to black psychotherapists. A black psychotherapist might not necessarily be the best person to work with a black client, and indeed the black client might not want to work with a black psychotherapist. When referring a black client to a black psychotherapist, a good question to ask oneself is 'Why am I doing this?'

EXPECTATIONS

One's expectation of psychotherapy is influenced by one's view of the world and issues such as abnormality and health. Different racial groups have differing perceptions of health and normality. For example, a white middle-class psychotherapist with a British background may see the family relations of the nuclear family as normal, and view the black West Indian who was brought up by a family friend in a different home, a few streets away from the mother's home, as abnormal and an 'issue' for psychotherapy. What this psychotherapist fails to understand is the importance of the modified extended family which have ties that are just as important as blood ties. In fact, these people are chosen to be part of the family even though there are no blood ties. The other issue that the psychotherapist may fail to understand is that, even though streets may separate the home, in the family's minds it is like one home, with family members seeing one another just as often as if they were living in the same house.

Relationships with authority figures are often influenced by one's racial heritage. Psychotherapists are often seen as authority figures, and clients will expect to relate to them as they would to authority figures from their own culture. An example of this is the author inviting a middle-aged black client to address her by her first name and the client choosing to put 'Miss' before the first name as a sign of respect for the psychotherapist's position. According to Marsella *et al.* (1979), if a client comes from a background where they relate to authority in an autocratic way, then the tendency will be for them to do so in the psychotherapeutic setting. They also expect the psychotherapist to be active, instructive and assertive. It is the author's experience that some clients may even begin to doubt the credibility of the psychotherapist if expectations are not met. On the other hand, clients from a background of relating to authority figures in a democratic way will prefer a more equal relationship.

Many psychotherapists attach high status to goals such as self-exploration and personal growth. These goals may need to be examined when working with some racial groups.

Barbarin (1984) pointed out that, for lower-class black clients, goals such as these might be insufficient since the tendency for this group is to focus on external conditions rather than intrapsychic concerns. This is not surprising, as it is difficult to imagine how to concentrate on those issues when they may have immediate problems of survival such as housing, food, employment and other socio-economic issues. If the psychotherapists are expecting to pursue personal growth and self-exploration and the clients are expecting to find ways of meeting their needs as related to their external condition, then there will be a mismatch of expectations. This could lead to frustration and anxiety for both the client and the psychotherapist.

Sue (1981) indicated that many Puerto Ricans who came for therapy expected information, advice and direct suggestions. Asian Americans also sought advice and suggestions, and they preferred a structured, more practically orientated type of psychotherapy. The author's own experience of working with black clients of West Indian origin suggests that they too tend to prefer psychotherapy that is structured and practically orientated. Different racial groups experience the environment differently, and it is from their perception of the social/cultural environment that they draw their conclusions about how the world works and how they need to relate to it. As mentioned earlier, many black people experience racial prejudice or discrimination of one sort or another. This has led Jones to write, 'One of the tasks facing all Black Americans is the development of ways to cope with experiences of racial prejudice and discrimination' (1985: 364). Some might argue that this is a task facing black people in general. This may therefore be an issue that many black clients would expect to tackle in psychotherapy.

WORKING WITH THE BLACK CLIENT

To work with any client you first have to engage that client. Engagement begins with the psychotherapist's first contact with the client; it could take a few minutes or several sessions, or it might never happen. The initial contact that is made with the client is vital, whether this is by phone, letter or in person. A lot can be read into one's use of language or tone of voice. A client once told me that it was my voice which was the deciding factor in coming along to the session. Clients going for psychotherapy often feel vulnerable, and they need to feel the warmth of the psychotherapist if they are to open themselves up. The initial interview, which may also be the assessment interview or part of it, is also important; and the psychotherapist should remember that this is a two-way process. While the psychotherapist is assessing whether or not the client is someone he or she could work with, the client is making the same decision. If the psychotherapist fails to make this a meeting of persons and hides behind the role of psychotherapist, this could make the black client suspicious of the white psychotherapist.

Many black clients have little experience of psychotherapy, and so it is always helpful to discuss with them how the session will be structured, and how one will work with them. Failure to structure early may lead to clients not returning for psychotherapy. During the assessment interview it is necessary to find out what the concerns of the client are. Also useful is to explore 'the personal meanings that presenting concerns have for the client' (Nelson-Jones 1982: 281). For example, a black client had concerns about returning to his country. On exploration it emerged that the concern was related to the client's perceived failure – failure to live up to his village's expectation of him as a bright boy who had gone to England to become a doctor but who had not achieved this. Another kind of information that one would need to collect in the assessment interview is related to the client's personal and social history, as this will give some indication of their personal identity. Where the client is, in terms of their own black identity, may be significant for working with that client.

At the end of the assessment the psychotherapist has to make the decision whether to work with the client, or indeed whether he or she is the best person to work with that client. Psychotherapists may choose not to work with black clients because of their own personal biases or limitations in cross-racial psychotherapy. In cases such as these the psychotherapist may choose to make a referral to another psychotherapist;

maybe a black psychotherapist. This should not be seen as a failure on the part of the psychotherapist; it is best to refer rather than struggle to work with clients they are not yet ready to work with. Psychotherapists are human and they too can have a racist attitude, which may be conscious or unconscious. This attitude could come across as a feeling of superiority, or the psychotherapist viewing cultural differences involving lifestyle as negative and indicative of pathology (Sue and Sue 1990). A white psychotherapist who would never consider herself as someone who makes racist comments and who strives for racial harmony once said, 'Anyone who is decent would know that female circumcision is wrong.' The implication here was that the black group she was referring to was not decent. I suppose this is an indication of the biases we all carry around with us. Greene (1985) aptly stated that psychotherapists of all backgrounds must confront their own biases when dealing with any culturally diverse group. What is maladaptive in one situation maybe quite adaptive in another.

In working with black clients psychotherapists need to understand that there may be barriers to communication which arise from cultural differences, such as the psychotherapist's personal prejudices (mentioned earlier). There are also other problems such as lack of knowledge of the culture, which could result in the client and psychotherapist misunderstanding each other. As McGoldrick wrote, 'Often it is very difficult to understand the meaning of behaviour without knowing something of the value orientation of the group. The same behaviour may have a different meaning in families of a different background' (1982: 23). For example, in some black cultures it is disrespectful to make eye contact with one's elders or people in authority when they are speaking to one. The reverse is true in Britain, where one would be expected to make eye contact with the individual addressing one.

Language can be a problem in cross-racial psychotherapy. Black clients might use words and phrases not understandable to the psychotherapist. Sometimes they may even use words that are familiar to the psychotherapist but they do not use the words to mean the same thing as the psychotherapist would. For example, some black West Indians may use the term 'What's happening?' as a form of greeting. The psychotherapist might not see this as a greeting and begin to wonder what the client meant by 'What's happening?'. Vontress (1981) argued that differences in language pattern on the part of the psychotherapist and client can lead to rapport problems in the psychotherapeutic relationship. Although it is not always easy to pinpoint these rapport problems, one can always feel them. Lack of rapport between psychotherapist and client will often lead to premature termination of psychotherapy. One of the mistakes white psychotherapists sometimes make is to continue a dialogue with the black client when they are unable to understand. They often do this with the hope of catching on as the conversation progresses. Unfortunately, they often find out that the more they allow the client to talk without clarification, the more confused they become (Vontress 1981).

One of the important factors in the client–psychotherapist relationship is the power-authority dimension (which is discussed further in Chapter 22 of this book). This hierarchical dimension takes on an added significance when one of the participants in the relationship is a 'majority person' (in this case, the white psychotherapist) and the other a 'minority person' (in this case, the black client) primarily because it is a microcosm of the larger social context (Jewelle 1985). Many black clients find it difficult to disclose as they do not 'initially perceive Whites as persons of good will' (Vontress 1981: 97). Self-disclosure is dependent on trust, and this is in turn affected by the degree to which psychotherapists and clients perceive themselves as similar and acceptable to each other. A black client and a white psychotherapist are obviously dissimilar in appearance but there are a number of other ways in which the psychotherapist might seek to develop a trusting relationship in which the client feels accepted. This certainly is one of the tasks of psychotherapy.

Transference is important in any therapeutic relationship but it has a special slant in cross-racial psychotherapy, particularly when the psychotherapist is from the 'majority group' (Vontress 1981). It is therefore necessary for white psychotherapists working with black clients to have an awareness of their own and their client's feelings about blackness and whiteness and the possible effect of these on transference and counter-transference (Gurman and Razin 1977). For example, the client may transfer onto the psychotherapist negative feelings about a white teacher who treated him or her as stupid. Psychotherapists may also engage in their own counter-transference by becoming excessively sympathetic to the black client; so sympathetic that they set a lower standard for black clients than for white clients. Psychotherapists may also demonstrate a counter-transference reaction by overcompensating when they work with black clients. For example, out of fear of hurting the black client they suppress any negative feelings they might have and become all positive and over-accommodating.

An area that psychotherapists frequently neglect when working with black clients is the strengths of the black family. Black families often have strong family ties and family roles are quite flexible. They also tend to place high value on religion. For example, aunts or grandmother may take responsibility for child care. Here psychotherapists must not be too quick in making assumptions that this is a negative practice leading to rejection of the child. In fact, this might be a very positive experience for the child. Finding out about the family and who helps whom within the family is therefore a necessary part of working with the black client.

Finally, it is sometimes useful to examine issues to do with racial identity, as this might influence how you work with the client. For example, if the black client is at the conformity stage of black identity where they believe in the superiority of white ways and inferiority of black ways, they might find exploration of cultural identity difficult. Any psychotherapist working with a client at this stage will need to help the client sort out conflicts related to racial identity. Black clients at this stage are often eager to identify with the white psychotherapist, but this process could be used in a positive way as the white psychotherapist helps the clients work through their need to over-identify. It will also be important for the white psychotherapist to model positive attitudes toward blacks. Unlike the clients at the conformity stage, the clients at the resistance and immersion stage do not view white psychotherapists positively. White psychotherapists are often seen as belonging to the 'oppressors' and as such are often challenged by these clients. If challenged, it is important not to be defensive, as a non-defensive approach is best if one wants to help the clients to explore these racial feelings or beliefs. Sue and Sue (1990) give a number of ways in which a psychotherapist might work with clients at different stages of black identity.

SUMMARY

In this chapter the relationship between race and culture was examined and it was decided that a separation of the two concepts was difficult. While race was divided between black and white, the point was made that 'blacks' were not a homogeneous group. It was acknowledged that one thing all black clients had in common was having to combat discrimination at one level or another. The difficulty of finding black psychotherapists was highlighted; also some of the things black clients look for when they choose a white psychotherapist. The exceptions of black clients in relation to psychotherapy were explored, as well as how the white psychotherapist might work with a black client.

The chapter concentrated on white psychotherapists working with black clients, but there are, of course, cases of black psychotherapists working with white clients and black psychotherapists working with black clients. The concentration on the first is not a denial of the importance of the others but rather a statement of what is more common in Britain.

ACKNOWLEDGEMENT

The editors would like to acknowledge the life and work of the late Jafar Kareem in raising awareness of intercultural issues.

REFERENCES

Atkinson, D. R. and Schein, S. (1986) 'Similarity in counselling', *The Counselling Psychologist* 4: 319–54.

Barbarin, O. (1984) 'Racial themes in psychotherapy with blacks: effect of training on the attitudes of black and white psychiatrists', *American Journal of Social Psychology* 4: 13–20.

d'Ardenne, P. and Mahtani, A. (1989) *Transcultural Counselling in Action*, London: Sage.

Fernando, W. (1988) *Race and Culture in Psychiatry*, London: Croom Helm.

Greene, B. (1985) 'Consideration in the treatment of black patients by white therapists', *Psychotherapy* 22(2): 389–93.

Gurman, A. and Razin, A. (1977) *Effective Psychotherapy*, New York: Pergamon.

Haralambos, M. (ed.) (1983) *Sociology*, London: Causeway Press.

Hines, P. and Boyd-Franklyn, N. (1982) 'Black families', pp. 84–107 in M. McGoldrick, J. Pearce and J. Giordando (eds) *Ethnicity and Family Therapy*, New York: Guilford Press.

Jackson, B. (1975) 'Black identity development', *Journal of Educational Diversity* 2: 19–25.

Jewelle, T. G. (1985) 'Can we continue to be colour-blind and class bound?', *The Counselling Psychologist* 13(3): 426–35.

Jones, A. (1985) 'Psychological functioning in black Americans: a conceptual guide for use in psychotherapy', *Psychotherapy* 22(3): 363–9.

McGoldrick, M. (1982) 'Ethnicity and family therapy – an overview', pp. 84–107 in M. McGoldrick, J. Pearce and J. Giordano (eds) *Ethnicity and Family Therapy*, New York: Guilford Press.

Marsella, A. and Pedersen, P. (eds) (1981) *Cross Cultural Counselling and Psychotherapy*, New York: Pergamon Press.

Marsella, A., Tharp, R. and Ciborowski, T. (1979) *Perspective in Cross Cultural Psychology*, New York: Academic Press.

Milner, D. (1983) *Children and Race*, London: Ward Lock Educational.

Moynihan, D. (1965) *The Negro Family in the US: The Case for National Action*, Washington, DC: US Government Report.

Nelson-Jones, R. (1982) *The Theory and Practice of Counselling Psychology*, London: Holt, Rinehart & Winston.

Sue, D. W. (1981) 'Evaluating process variables in cross-cultural counselling and psychotherapy', pp. 181–4 in A. Marsella and P. Pedersen (eds) *Cross Cultural Counselling and Psychotherapy*, New York: Pergamon Press.

Sue, D. W. and Sue, D. (1990) *Counselling the Culturally Different*, New York: John Wiley.

Vontress, C. (1981) 'Racial and ethnic barriers in counselling', pp. 87–107 in P. Pedersen, J. Dragus, W. Lonner and J. Trimble (eds) *Counselling Across Cultures*, Honolulu: University of Hawaii Press.

SOME USEFUL ADDRESSES

Asian Family Counselling Service
2nd Floor Rooms
40 Equity Chambers
Piccadilly
Bradford
West Yorkshire BO1 3NN
Tel.: 0274 720486

Black and Asian Trainees Support Group
metanoia Psychotherapy Training Institute
13 North Common Road
Ealing
London W5 2QB
Tel.: 081 579 2505

Black and Ethnic Minority Health Development Team
MIND South-east Regional Office
24–32 Stephenson Way
London NW1 2HD
Tel.: 071 387 9070

Black HIV and AIDS Network (BHAN)
111 Devonport Road
London W12 8BP
Tel.: 081 749 2828

British Refugee Council
Bondway House
3–9 Bondway
London SW8 1SJ
Tel.: 071 582 6922

Chinese Information and Advice Centre
68 Shaftesbury Avenue
London W1
Tel.: 071 836 8291

NAFSIYAT Intercultural Therapy Centre
278 Seven Sisters Road
London N4 2HY
Tel.: 071 263 4130

Newham Alcohol Advisory Service
7 Sebart Road
Forest Gate
London E7 ONG
Tel.: 081 519 3354

RACE Race and Cultural Education in Counselling
c/o British Association for Counselling
1 Regent Place
Rugby CV21 2PJ
Tel.: 0788 550899

The BAC's Training Directory lists cross-cultural courses and also those which raise multicultural awareness. It also publishes a Counselling and Psychotherapy Resources Directory. *Details of these directories and other publications, from the BAC above.*

Transcultural Psychiatry Unit
Lynfield Mount Hospital
Heights Lane
Bradford BD9 6DP
Tel.: 0274 494194

Chapter 5

Psychotherapy and gender

Sheila Ernst and David Gowling

'Common sense' tells us that to know who I am is to know that I am a man or a woman, a boy or a girl. When a baby is born, the first question is 'What is it?' We know that does not mean is it a frog or a lobster, but 'Is it a boy or a girl?' When my third child was born the midwife said, 'It's a lovely boy. Oh . . . no.' She looked again: 'I mean a girl'. In those few seconds my mental image of my baby had to shift rapidly. The midwife was looking at the presence or absence of labia and a vagina or penis but for me, even in those brief moments, I had begun to think of my baby as a boy and in my head I had to reconstruct her as a girl. The journey towards establishing a gendered identity starts in those first few moments of life; that vivid moment of first realisation, 'It's a girl'; 'It's a boy'.

If gender is so much a part of who a person is, it is not surprising to find that when someone is in distress and seeking psychotherapeutic help, gender and gender-related complaints are often experienced as key issues.

For a man this might be expressed as: 'I don't feel like a man. I can neither live up to my own expectations of a man, nor other people's.' 'How can I be a father?' 'My girlfriends always complain that I am too remote and unaffectionate and in the end it ruins the relationship. I don't know how to be different. I think I'm just an ordinary bloke, but I can't be.' Even when the problem is not explicitly about masculinity it is often gender-related; difficulties at work, obsessive jealousy, fear of one's own violence, being preoccupied with pornography or feeling nagged or henpecked.

Women may come to psychotherapy because they feel disturbed about their femininity or because they fear that they cannot live up to their own or society's images of what a woman should be. Women may seek psychotherapy because in their struggle to survive and to resolve unbearable internal conflicts they find they are abusing themselves, for instance through anorexia, or because of the distress they suffer through being abused by others. Women also often need help in working out the conflicts that arise for them related to their reproductive cycle; pregnancy, childbirth, abortion or the menopause.

Often a woman will express her anxieties and fears about herself in terms of her capacity to develop satisfying, intimate relationships. Whereas with men, stereotypically, problems are to do with an experienced incapacity to be intimate and feelings of claustrophobia in a relationship, with women the difficulties may be expressed in terms of longings for closeness and intimacy which are never fulfilled. Popular books like Robin Norwood's *Women Who Love Too Much* (1986) reflect this aspect of women's experience, but unfortunately do not provide a sufficiently critical stance of social norms alongside the psychological account.

There follows an example of the kinds of difficulties which a couple may bring to psychotherapy. A young couple came to 'sort out their relationship'. She had been in individual psychotherapy for two years and had begun to acknowledge her dissatisfaction with her relationship.

Their phrases were poignant: 'I feel that I'm a chattel just like my mother. A child carer and a shopper.' 'But I'm a worker, always have been. I'm proud of that; my father brought me up to earn good money. You can't expect me to care for the children as well.' Her response is, 'I want more of you.' And his, 'You're too demanding. I don't have energy at the end of the day.' 'All I want is for you to share more.' 'You're always going on and on.'

The dynamic is familiar. The young woman wanting contact, intimacy and sensitivity while the young man is feeling threatened, tense and put-upon; one partner defining sharing as natural, the other experiencing the idea as inherently alien and unmasculine.

These subjective expressions of distress as being gender-related are backed up by statistics which suggest that seeking help with your mental health is something women are far more likely to do than men, whether this means going to the GP, using the psychiatric services or having psychotherapy (Barnes and Maple 1992: 11). In other words, there does seem to be a significant relationship between gender and emotional distress, although, we suggest, it is important for psychotherapists and their patients that we take a careful look at how this is understood. What have we learned about men and women's psychological formation and the way it is structured within society which can help us to understand why it is that far more women than men seek psychotherapy? Is it simply that women are more 'sick' or more troubled than men? Or is it that men simply refuse to go for help when they need it, and opt out? Is this something that could be affected by will-power or does it run deeper? How these questions are answered will affect the understanding of men and women's psychology which, in turn, determines the kind of psychotherapeutic understanding offered to our men and women patients.

CHOOSING A PSYCHOTHERAPIST: DO I WANT A MAN OR A WOMAN, AND WHY?

Men and women seeking help with their emotional difficulties may have many anxieties about how the psychotherapist tackles 'gender issues' even though they may not have formulated it in quite this way. A man may feel that he won't be able to talk freely about his feelings or that the psychotherapist will disapprove of his fantasies. He may also fear that dwelling on painful or distressing feelings in psychotherapy will incapacitate him; will turn him into a cissie. A heterosexual man may fear that his sexual habits with women will be criticised while a homosexual man may fear that a psychotherapist will want to 'cure him' of a disease rather than enable him to discuss freely the difficulties he is encountering in his sexual partnership. A woman may fear that her feelings about the conflicting demands of children and work will be pathologised and she will be deemed an 'unnatural mother', or that as a lesbian she will not be seen as womanly with womanly feelings.

THE PSYCHOTHERAPIST'S ANXIETIES

The psychotherapist may find himself or herself identifying with the young couple who were seeking help. Perhaps the psychotherapist has grown up in a similar environment, white and working-class where there was a firm, if unwritten, agreement, that men work and women stay at home. Lucy Goodwin expressed this vision succinctly: 'We see women as nourishment . . . embodied in the symbol of the ideal mother who is paraded before us in so many commercials, cooking, washing, caring, touching immaculate babies, loving and radiantly happy' (1990: 7).

Coming from this background the psychotherapist's early experience provided little challenge to this view. Few alternative dystonic values were ever presented. Growing men were asked to see women as sexual adventures or as potential wives and mothers but not as individuals separate from their roles. This strictly heterosexual value system influenced the psychotherapist's experience of themselves; how they formed an opinion of their self-worth and ultimately a sense of their existential place in society.

Inevitably, whatever background the psychotherapist comes from will affect how they see patients/clients, and they have a responsibility to understand fully the implications of these influences. We can then potentially meet the significant challenge of both the ego-syntonic restrictions described above and the ego-dystonic possibilities.

THE IDEAS BEHIND THE PRACTICE

We have looked at the thoughts and feelings of the client/patient and the psychotherapist as they approach working together. We will now look at the ideas which influence psychotherapeutic practice and theory on this topic, taking both a humanistic and psychoanalytical perspective.

Humanistic perspective on gender

From a humanistic perspective everyone, irrespective of gender, is born with as full a potentiality for self-actualising growth as they can have within the parameters of physical and mental health.

Berne, the founder of Transactional Analysis, named Physis as 'the growth force of nature, which makes organisms evolve into higher forms, embryos develop into adults, sick people get better and healthy people strive to attain their ideals . . . it may be a more basic force than libido itself' (1981: 369–70). Clarkson supports this view that Physis is 'nature, coming from the deepest biological roots of the human being and striving towards the greatest realisation of the good' (1992: 12).

Therefore, in considering gender as a very significant factor in life and psychotherapy, what are the influences, other than Physis, which we have to take into account?

Clarkson, in further quoting Berne, states that,

> the autonomous aspiration of individual human beings rises from the depths of the somatic Child (the oldest ego state) and transcends the limit-inducing downward pressures of the script which is shaped in the matrix of love and death in our earliest relationships.
>
> (1992: 12)

What is meant by the oldest child ego state and the limit-inducing downward pressures of the script?

Weiss said, 'Every ego state is the actually experienced reality of one's mental and bodily ego with the contents of the lived-through period. Some ego states are easily remembered, some are difficult to recall, some are strictly repressed!' (1950: 141). Specifically, our child ego state is archaic, from the past, and we can re-experience and relive fully those past experiences in the here-and-now, and the crucial emphasis here is that we are not just remembering, but reliving.

Applied to gender, the oldest child ego state is that moment in psychic and physical time when we are born, either as a boy or girl. In the fullest sense this oldest ego state is laid down at the moment of conception.

How does this concept relate to scripting theory? Our script is a life plan made in childhood, enforced by parents, justified by subsequent events and culminating in a chosen alternative: each child decides in childhood how they will live.

As the adults lean over the cot, the baby is clothed in many attributions such as big, bouncy, strong, beautiful, handsome, pretty, gentle, smiley and intelligent. These statements begin to attribute a socially acceptable identity to that newly arrived bundle of flesh and feelings. Although the grown-up cannot know if many of these attributions are true, they constitute the earliest projected wish from the influencing environment that the child grows in a certain way.

So in scripting theory the two essential influencing elements are the environment the child is born into and the sense he or she makes from a place of primitive understanding. From this he will lay down his personality and expectations of self relationships and life. So an accident of birth will determine my sex but, from that moment of birth, determining script influences on my gender identity are legion.* As above, determining descriptive language gives us an initial identity and as we grow the gender split becomes increasingly pronounced. 'He's just like his father/brother/ Uncle George/the Prime Minister.' 'She's going to be a beautiful girl, just like her aunt/Madonna/her mother.' Although the child may have some primitive aspirations to be a politician or a pop star, can she be allowed, and allow herself to be herself? This is a crucial question, because we can already experience the client being objectified, becoming a function of a prescribed set of gender-specific rules.

As a consequence, on many occasions in the therapy room individuals, having exposed and understood these prescriptions, begin to ask the question 'Who am I?' (as man/woman). There is often a profound sense of internal emptiness. A young, high-achieving man had 'all of a sudden' plunged into 'depression'. Over time he began to understand that he did not know who he was if he wasn't a worker. As he traced this further he realised that his father had been described by the family as a failure because he only held down seasonal or occasional work and he drank. His mother had often said to him, 'You won't be like your father, will you?' 'You're going to do all the things he never did!' and 'You're going to be Mummy's little success!'

Therefore our identity continues to be formed within the matrix of parental influence, class, money, cultural background, race, school and friendships. Take two of the above; the interrelation between gender and culture. How may these influences bear directly on the psychotherapy relationship?

For example: first, a young Jewish woman carrying the full weight of post-Holocaust survivor's trauma. Her identity as an autonomous woman is seriously impaired by her responsibilities to take into the next generation the episcript tragedy of her father's family (who were concentration camp victims). Her experience and life task was to find and take care of tragic, wounded men (her brother was not expected to care in this way).

Secondly, a young man from an aristocratic background, having authority

---

* It is important to note here the distinction between sex (physiological) and gender (socially formed).

vested in him by birth, class and status, not through personal qualities. He had presenting arrogance and belief in obedience to his word, and there was a tragic internal conflict between his wish to be his 'own man' and his profound sense of duty to the family tradition.

Thirdly, a middle-aged woman who read a book for the first time, and said she felt 'as if I fell to bits inside'. The book was *Women Who Love Too Much* (Norwood 1986). She had never seen her life portrayed so vividly and the consequent sense of profound personal loss precipitated a breakdown.

These are a few examples of the above scripting process, which, it is hoped, emphasise aspects of gender-splitting. They pose significant challenges to us as therapists which we discuss later in the chapter.

Psychoanalytic theory and gender

Gender has been a hotly debated subject within psychoanalytic theory. It is easy for us now to pick holes in Freud's theories from a modern feminist perspective, and indeed many feminists did do precisely that in the seventies; Freud was criticised for the sexism of his concept of 'penis envy', and his ideas of so-called normal sexual development culminating in genital sexuality which privileges the existing forms of heterosexual relationships and pathologises both alternative forms of heterosexuality and homo-sexuality. Yet gradually feminists, including myself (Sheila Ernst), found themselves returning to read Freud, for he was a great initiator of a new way of perceiving human beings. He himself compared the discovery of the unconscious to the discovery that the earth is not the centre of the universe, and that human beings are descended from animals rather than being the unique creation of God. He recognised that 'to prove to the ego that it is not master in its own house' but merely the recipient of 'scanty information' from the unconscious (Freud 1922: 241) would be a truly shocking notion which would in time transform people's understanding of human behaviour.

Recognising the immensity of this work, it is then fascinating to see what can be learned from the gaps and silences within his work; not only because of what it tells us about Freud, but more significantly because it can help us to understand subsequent psychoanalytic thinking and indicate the work that needs to be done to introduce a gendered or gender-aware psycho-analytic psychotherapy. For Freud was concerned with some of the most fundamental questions: What is gender? How and why do gender reactions have their current forms? Can these forms be changed and what would be the benefits of doing so? How are the relations of domination established, maintained and replicated? To what extent are such relations a necessary and unalterable aspect of human life? A re-reading of Freud reveals that he did not simply lay out a naïve theory which discriminated against women but rather that he was profoundly ambiguous in, I would argue, a good sense. He was prepared to allow himself to acknowledge that some of his theories were not consistent with others and that he could not simply pull them into shape. (I think that this can also be reassuring for prospective patients who fear that any psychoanalytic psychotherapy will 'tell' them what to think in a dominating way.) On the one hand, he maintained his belief that the natural state of the child is 'polymorphous perversity', which led him on to thinking that 'the exclusive sexual interest felt by men for women is also a problem that needs elucidating and is not a self-evident fact' (Freud 1962). On the other hand, he maintains his developmental model of sexuality which unfolds until the person reaches the 'normal' adult stage of genitally orientated, heterosexual sexual intercourse. Thus Freud opened up some questions which we might want any psychological theory to be addressing, but at the same time he did not question the division between men and women in his society but rather assumed them to be natural. It followed from this that he accepted the way in which to become a man was to define yourself as separated from the devalued world of mother and women.

Some of the subsequent development of psychoanalytic theory has laid a foundation for feminist theorists and practitioners to look at new ways of working which could challenge this conservative aspect of Freud's work.* This has important consequences for both men and women wanting help from psychotherapy. There were two crucial ways in which the British object relations school paved the way for contemporary thinking on gender. They began by questioning the centrality of the Oedipal conflict and suggested that the focus of the analyst's attention needed to go much further back into the child's earliest infancy. Klein's (1949) work as a child analyst provided controversial theories about the inner unconscious phantasy life of the child. Fairbairn (1952) and Winnicott (1960) took this work into a slightly different direction by stating much more clearly than Klein had done that the early psychic development of the child was a result of the interaction between the infant and the environment. Winnicott conceptualised this as the need for the mother and family to provide a 'holding' environment within which the child could develop; he saw the work of a psychoanalyst (and of others in the 'caring' professions) as being as much about providing a similar sort of 'holding' environment for the client/patient as it was about offering the 'correct' interpretations.

What was new and important about these psychoanalysts' work was that they were focusing on the importance of the environment and the early mother–infant relationship; what they were not doing was acknowledging fully what implications the different roles and power of men and women

---

* There has been a steady stream of psychoanalytic writing which has criticised Freud's views on women and gender, such as Jones (1927) and Horney (1967).

might have on boy and girl infants being reared by mothers; nor what this might mean from the mother's point of view. In the past fifteen years much work has been done on developing a theory and practice drawing on a psychoanalytic history but seeing how the social reality of gender relations is incorporated into the psychology of each individual man or woman. Inevitably, once social relations are seen as having such significance other differences between men and women have to be incorporated into the psychotherapy relationship (hence the fact that this book has a whole section entitled 'Structural Themes'). What feminism brings to psychoanalysis is the understanding that we can only grasp the different development of men and women if we understand that femininity and therefore mothering have been devalued in our society. We shall see how this affects the practice of psychotherapy with men and women.

Feminist psychoanalytic writers (drawing on the object relations tradition) recognise the importance of the mother–infant relationship, but they see it within the framework of a society in which mothers are responsible for mothering, may be idealised or denigrated and yet get little recognition or real status for the task they perform. Meanwhile they have little role in the external world, or where they do, this is either markedly inferior to men or they are expected to somehow maintain their family responsibilities without letting them interfere. (A good example of the latter is the MP Harriet Harman's complaint that the way that Parliament's sittings are organised makes it impossible for her to get home to see her children at tea-time. Clearly, Parliament does not relate to after-school child-care concerns, but it is interesting that no male MP seems to have made similar complaints.) Thus the early period of extreme dependency and all the often frightening and chaotic feelings and fantasies associated with this period are inextricably connected to the mother. For boys this means that to become a man means escaping from the dependency and intimacy that are associated with mother and identifying with father who is not seen as being part of mother's world. Thus masculinity becomes associated with independence and detachment, while femininity is associated with connection and dependency. The girl forms her identity through her awareness of the mother's role and position; she tries to get closer to mother by being like her or, sensitive to mother's deprivation, she feels that she has to care for mother.

Olivier (1990) gives some examples of the contrasting ways in which men and women typically relate to a psychotherapist. 'I don't know what I'm doing here. I haven't anything to tell you. There's nothing I feel like sharing with you,' and 'Got to keep quiet so as to keep a distance. I hate talking when we make love. I don't want to bring any feeling into it.' Here the man is expressing his fears of communicating with his psychotherapist, and this is connected to his attempt to prevent intimacy with his sexual partner by not talking when they make love.

'If I stop talking I'm afraid you will see that I don't amount to anything.'
'If I let the silence take over again, I won't be able to bridge the distance
between us. It frightens me.' In these two statements women are talking
about their low self-esteem and the need to be constantly reassured by
contact with the psychotherapist.

Within the relationship between patient and psychotherapist what
matters is that the roots of these two positions are understood. A
psychotherapist unaware of the gender issues may find themselves reacting
unconsciously in a way that reproduces these positions instead of analysing
them. The psychotherapist may unwittingly respond to the man's distancing
without recognising the fear that underlies it, or may feel distaste for the
woman's cloying demands rather than helping her to see how unrecognised
she feels.

Gender-awareness in practice

A session of a mixed psychotherapy group (a group analytic group) is in
progress. Alison is talking about how difficult she finds the weekends. She
explains that she doesn't know what to do with herself because everyone
else seems to have partners, husbands, wives or lovers to spend time with
and she feels she is always taking the initiative to ring up friends and try
to arrange to go out together. She thinks she always needs other people
more than they need her. This theme is taken up by Helga, who says that
having a partner doesn't really make any difference; she wants more from
her boyfriend than he seems to want from her. She finds herself starting
conversations, suggesting outings or inviting friends round and even, to
her surprise, having to initiate sex. Alison and Helga wonder what is wrong
with them; why do they always want so much; why do they always feel so
needy? The three men in the group listen attentively but do not say
anything, which suggests that they might identify with what is being said.
Mark seems particularly interested, and asks Alison and Helga some
searching questions about their previous relationships and then about their
family backgrounds. The woman psychotherapist is beginning to feel
uncomfortable. She doesn't like this image of poor needy Alison and Helga
and three solicitous and helpful men. While the conversation continues she
is examining her own reaction.

She thinks, 'What is it I don't like? Is it that I identify with Alison and
Helga and can't bear to acknowledge my/their neediness? Do I feel that,
as group conductor, I should be playing the good mother and helping them
to feel nurtured and cared for? Is what they are really talking about – my
lack of concern and attention; are they wanting to ask me for more
attention? Do I feel competitive with Mark, who is being the second
psychotherapist in the group?'

The psychotherapist is exploring some of the difficult feelings which she might be having because of her own personal reactions to the situation; in technical terms she is looking at the aspect of her counter-transference which may be to do with her own unresolved difficulties. She is particularly aware of the way in which a woman's neediness may be unacceptable to another woman because it puts her in touch with her own unmet needs. She is also aware that she may be ambivalent about her nurturing role; on the one hand, resenting it because she feels inadequately nurtured, but, on the other hand, threatened because this nurturing maternal role may be her way of defending herself against her own neediness.

She then feels ready to acknowledge to herself that some of her discomfort is to do with the painful way in which Alison and Helga are exposing themselves, but something else comes to mind. She feels that the attentiveness of Mark, Henry and Bill may be because they too feel many of the things which Helga and Alison are talking about but they cannot allow them to come to consciousness. Alison and Helga are working on their behalf to express the whole group's neediness. In gender terms, the women are expressing the emotions and making themselves vulnerable while the men are apparently concerned observers. The psychotherapist is now ready to make a comment or interpretation which will enable the three men to see how they are defending themselves against their own needy feelings and thus missing out on the opportunity to understand more about this aspect of themselves, while Alison and Helga are carrying the split-off parts of the men's vulnerability and in this way losing touch with their own capacity to begin to understand how and why it is that they have such difficulty in finding ways of getting some of their needs addressed.

Implications for users and psychotherapists, male and female, psychoanalytic and humanist

Patients and psychotherapists may be frustrated with traditional psycho-analytic theory which both offers a way of understanding the deepest roots of gender identity and at the same time can often to the modern reader appear to be sexist, patriarchal and pathologising of the experience of women and men, particularly if they are homosexual. As a psychoanalytic psychotherapist who has been very influenced by the 'second wave' of feminist thinking I (Sheila Ernst) have tried to give an account of how work has been done in the last twenty years, initially on women's psychology and more recently also about men too, which has revised and developed psychoanalytic thought and practice to encompass new thinking about gender and homosexuality. What this means in clinical practice is that there are a growing number of psychoanalytic psychotherapists who have begun to address these questions in their practice and have at least some awareness of the issues involved. For the patient who is concerned that within treatment their gender identity or sexual preferences will not be pathologised, as opposed to explored and analysed, it is important to search for a psychotherapist who is open to thinking in this way. (For the particularly problematic relationship of lesbians and gay men to psychoanalytic psychotherapy, see Chapter 8 on Psychotherapy and Sexual Orientation.)

For me (Dave Gowling), writing as a man from a humanist perspective, it is here as client and as psychotherapist that we are confronted by the interplay of gender-motivated forces. For instance, a male psychotherapist could be seen as Santa Claus, white knight, punisher, saviour, abuser or sought-after lover. We can see this as projection within the transferential relationship; that this is not necessarily me; this is an introjected and projected other, and we (the psychotherapists) have a responsibility to stay adult; empathic, confrontative, supportive, whatever is clinically appropriate in that time of our relationship. This does assume, however, that we have freed ourselves sufficiently from our counter-transferential influences. Can we assume that our emotional response is based on a 'correct interpretation' of our client's true intentions and meaning? Therefore, for instance, can the male psychotherapist see his client as distinct from his demanding or engulfing or marshmallow mother in the intensity of the moment-to-moment relationship?

If we store in our child ego state all experiences of our primary parenting, may the above intensity not press on a lesion (sore spot) in our child, such as a belief or decision that, say, we are not quite good enough to meet up to our parents' standards, their expectations of maleness? The effort to stay in 'integrated adult' in the intensity of that moment could be significantly costly to the quality of the ongoing relationship, and both psychotherapist and client's sense of self may be affected. The psychotherapist may trigger old felt incompetence and the client may experience that they have met another inept or incompetent male. So we are faced with ongoing, intense challenges to our sense of self, our sense of wholeness and intrapsychic integrity. This, I believe, makes essential a commitment to continue in personal therapy for our duration as a psychotherapist.

Can I as a man identify with issues of female sexual abuse, menstruation and sexual attraction, and stay non-threateningly, non-sexually involved without giving up on my essential maleness? I am challenged by the contrast between my archaic syntonic belief, about the 'place' women should have in society, and a wish to stay unbiased (or to use my bias constructively), a wish to see the wholeness of the person as they struggle to find their own unique path in psychotherapy and in life.

Furthermore, do we as men have an immutable problem, as Jung states:

> woman with her very dissimilar psychology is, and always has been a source of information about things for which a man has no eyes. She can be his inspiration, her intuitive capacity, often superior to man's,

can give him timely warning, and her feelings, always directed towards the personal, can show him ways which his own less personally accented feelings would never have discerned.

(Jung 1986)

This does seem to indicate an inherent problem which the male brings to psychotherapy: this separation, seemingly immutable, and only to be attained via a woman's intuitive capacity. Jung seems to speak of the very challenge and conflict manifested in the relationship of the young couple mentioned above.

Now I don't hold this as a truth, but perhaps in pursuit of this feminine 'source of information' Bly met his soft man: 'Men welcoming their own "feminine consciousness" and nurturing it'. He went on to say though, 'this is important, and yet I have the sense that there is something wrong. The male in the past twenty years has become more thoughtful, more gentle. But by this process he has not become more free. He's a nice boy who pleases not only his mother but also the young woman he is living with' (1990: 2).

Perhaps the challenge therefore is that as men we have to embrace what Bly calls 'the beast'. Embrace more fully those 'male values' of strength, anger, determination, hard work and comradeship, and integrate them with, not separate from, the seemingly feminine virtues of sensitivity, emotional awareness and expression of feelings. In this sense we could remove ourselves from fixed ego syntonic expectations and embrace them at the same time.

From the patient's viewpoint it is important to find psychotherapists and institutions which share an awareness of the importance of looking at the issue of gender. There are already organisations like the Women's Therapy Centre in London (see address below) which, as well as providing psychoanalytic psychotherapy, will help prospective patients to find a psychotherapist who concerns themselves with these issues. A patient seeking a psychotherapist can also feel entitled to ask his or her own questions, although we must recognise how difficult this can feel when one is in a state of distress.

It is important that the question of gender is continually raised in discussion amongst professionals and that pressure is put on training organisations to include and integrate a gendered way of thinking into their curriculum for trainees and for their members as part of their own postgraduate ongoing study. This is happening slowly, but requires constant attention because there is a tendency towards conservatism in this most deeply personal area; there is also a tendency towards an anti-feminist backlash (Faludi 1992). There is also a way in which psychotherapists, like other professionals, may find it more pressing to address other forms of discrimination, such as racial discrimination, believing them to have a stronger moral or political imperative. The competition within a hierarchy of discriminated groups is dangerous and, we would argue, unprofitable territory. I do not think that we can place gender above or below other forms of discrimination which need to be addressed, but rather would point out that gender is a fundamental part of any theory of personality development and therefore to discuss it in a new way could threaten existing theory and practice profoundly. This might be why it so easily slips out of consciousness.

SUMMARY

Another way of expressing this would be to say that addressing the issue of gender in psychoanalytic and humanistic psychotherapy means helping the patient to find the repressed masculine and feminine parts of themselves. To do this the psychotherapist must be aware of the ways in which social forces influence the girl's and the boy's psychological development. Psychotherapists themselves are also part of this society and will need to work on their own often unconscious adaptation to gender stereotypes; this needs to be as much a part of any psychotherapist's training as uncovering the other aspects of the life of the unconscious.

REFERENCES

Barnes, M. and Maple, N. (1992) *Women and Mental Health*, London: Venture.
Berne, E. (1981) *A Layman's Guide to Psychiatry and Psychoanalysis*, Harmondsworth: Penguin (first published 1947).
Bly, R. (1990) *Iron John*, London: Element.
Clarkson, P. (1992) 'Physis in Transactional Analysis', *ITA News* 33: 14–19; also published in *Transactional Analysis Journal* 22(4): 202–209.
Fairbairn, W. R. D. (1952) *Psycho-analytic Studies of the Personality*, London: Tavistock.
Faludi, S. (1992) *Backlash*, London: Chatto.
Freud, S. (1922) *Introductory Lectures in Psychoanalysis*, London: Allen & Unwin.
—— (1962) *Three Essays on the Theory of Sexuality*, New York: Basic Books.
Goodwin, L. (1990) *Moving Heaven and Earth*, London: Women's Press.
Horney, K. (1967) *Feminine Psychology*, New York: Norton.
Jones, E. (1927) *Papers on Psychoanalysis*, Boston: Beacon Press.
Jung, C. G. (1986) *Aspects of the Feminine*, London: Ark (first published 1982) (selection from *Collected Works* between 1954 and 1971).
Klein, M. (1949) *The Psychoanalysis of Children*, London: Hogarth Press.
Norwood, R. (1986) *Women Who Love Too Much*, London: Arrow.
Olivier, C. (1990) *Jocasta's Children*, London: Routledge.
Weiss, E. (1950) *Principles of Psychodynamics*, New York: Grune & Stratton.
Winnicott, D. W. (1960) *The Maturational Process and the Facilitating Environment*, London: Hogarth Press.

FURTHER READING

Chodorow, N. (1978) *Reproduction of Mothering: Psychoanalysis and the Sociology of Gender*, Berkeley, CA: University of California Press.

Eichenbaum, L. and Orbach, S. (1982) *Understanding Women*, Harmondsworth: Penguin.

Ernst, S. and Maguire, M. (eds) (1987) *Living with the Sphinx: Papers from the Women's Therapy Centre*, London: The Women's Press.

Estés, C. P. (1992) *Women Who Run with the Wolves: Contacting the Power of the Wild Woman*, London: Rider.

Jukes, A. (1993) *Why Men Hate Women*, London: Free Association Books.

O'Connor, N. and Ryan, J. (1993) *Wild Desires and Mistaken Identities*, London: Virago.

Pines, D. (1993) *A Woman's Unconscious Use of Her Body*, London: Virago.

Tannen, D. (1991) *You Just Don't Understand: Women and Men in Conversation*, London: Virago.

FURTHER INFORMATION

Albany Trust
Sunra Centre
26 Balham Hill
Clapham South
London SW12 9EB
Tel.: 081 675 6669

London Lighthouse
111–117 Lancaster Road
London W11 1QT
Tel.: 071 792 1200

Red Admiral Project
51a Philbeach Gardens
London SW5 9EV
Tel.: 071 835 1495

The Men's Therapy Centre
Tel.: 071 267 8713

The Women's Therapy Centre
6–9 Manor Gardens
London N7 6OA
Tel.: 071 263 6200

Chapter 6

Therapy with survivors of the Nazi Holocaust

Judith Hassan

I have chosen to write about my work with the survivors of the Nazi Holocaust, set in the voluntary sector of Jewish Care – formerly the Jewish Welfare Board (JWB) – because it is a subject I feel passionately about, both personally and professionally. Looking at it in the context of the agency is a new angle for me. It makes me reflect on the years of development in both my work and in myself within the agency and how the two have become intertwined. I write because I want to show the process I have been through in this special area of work; to spare others some of the pitfalls that have inevitably happened and also to pass on what I have learned.

Though the terminology I will use will be familiar to the therapeutically trained, the social work context of the agency as well as my training as a social worker will broaden the meaning of therapy. This may not only differentiate me from the more traditional therapist, but even alienate me in some circles. The world of the survivor is a unique one; not comparable, they would feel, to any other event in history. Obviously comparisons are made to other disasters and genocides, but the Nazi Holocaust remains on its own. Interestingly, I am writing this chapter on my own. Though various logistical reasons could explain why this happened, it is perhaps no coincidence that I have no co-author. Yet I have an important and urgent task, which is to make the work with survivors come alive, and engage other therapists whilst the need is still there. In ten years' time it may be too late.

This chapter is therefore not an academic exercise but a plea for those who can open themselves up to this work, both personally and professionally, to become involved. I have divided the chapter into three parts. The first part will concentrate on how, on the one hand, my training and theoretical framework gave me the foundation to work with elderly refugees from Nazi persecution using psychodynamic approaches. I will also look at how the organisational setting enabled this work to begin. I will examine how I became aware of the restrictions in what I could offer survivors from the concentration camps and those who had been in hiding, because I had become imprisoned by my professional boundaries as well as the organisational walls – I was at that stage mirroring the incarceration of the survivor in the camp.

Few survivors of the camps could or wished to penetrate the fortress. In the context of working therapeutically with Holocaust survivors, organisations take on a different perspective. In terms of the death camp experience the 'production of death became bureaucratised', wrote Kren (1989); death camps were literally death factories. With efficiency and care to meticulous detail, the genocide went on. Within this order, chaos ruled. The death camp was a mad world, a world turned upside down in which human dignity and humanity had no meaning. With this in mind, how could any organisation offer services to Holocaust survivors? Entering an office building and being greeted by a security guard could flash back to another place and another time.

In this first stage, I will concentrate on looking at contributing factors to this wasteland between the survivor and the professional. Factors such as the over-emphasis on pathology; survivors' feelings towards Anglo-Jewish organisations; the authority issues related to the helper and the resultant inequality and vulnerability of the relationship; the lack of understanding of the nature of extreme experience in making sense of the survivor and his world – these are but a few of the reasons why the organisation and professional framework kept death-camp survivors away.

The second stage of this chapter will look at how the organisation's fortifications were broken down by reaching out to survivors through an understanding of self-help support groups, social bonding, human reciprocity, power shifting from the therapist authority figure, the emergence of the coping, adapting survivor. The emphasis is on the meaningfulness of the therapy to the survivor – a question of being understood rather than diagnosed. New approaches then began to emerge such as the power of the testimony as a therapeutic tool and the relevance of ritual prayer and mourning. This stage was also mirroring the opening up of the camp gates, with the prisoners being set free. I have linked it to my experience of passing through the organisational doors to a world unknown. For me the 'prison' gates had opened up, but I did not know what I would find. As the survivors have reported, they faced a world that did not want to hear the atrocities they had been through. I, similarly at that stage, found many professionals unwilling or unable to hear and share the world of massive trauma I was uncovering forty years on.

The last stage of the chapter focuses on how a true sense of liberation is reached, contrasted with the disappointment of the 'setting-free' stage. The liberation is away from the psychopathology and victim role of the survivor to an image of strength and health. Through the empowerment of the survivor the possibility of meaning and healing can begin to happen. The development will be put in the context of the shift in setting to a new community-based location, as well as looking at my own professional metamorphosis.

The development of these stages can be seen metaphorically as a journey. It forms a link between the past, the present and the future. There is a beginning, a setting-out on the journey, a middle and an end or final part of the journey. The constant reflection between the camp experience, the 'therapy' and the setting and how these three component parts fit together will be focused on as an essential ingredient for this work to happen. It is in a sense my testimony, my story of a long and difficult journey which I have undertaken with survivors, but which ends with hope and optimism.

THE FIRST STAGE – THE BEGINNING OF A JOURNEY

The story began when I returned to the JWB, having been seconded to my social work training. This training had given me an excellent foundation in psychodynamic work which I hoped to put into practice. At that time I was in an area-based team in Swiss Cottage. The setting was a beautiful old house in an area in which a very high number of survivors/ refugees had settled. There was a day centre for the elderly beneath our offices, and so it was not unusual for elderly people to walk in and ask for help. This was mostly of a practical nature, because that was how the agency was perceived. However, I gradually began to notice patterns emerging related to unresolved issues that refugees were experiencing forty or fifty years on. There appeared to be a current loss such as the death of someone close, retirement, loss of health – all of which reactivated earlier losses which had not been worked through. Secondly, I knew from my work with the elderly that it is a natural process of ageing that short-term memories tend to grow weaker, whilst long-term memories become stronger, allowing events from the past to return to consciousness much more vividly.

Case study 1

An example from practice: Mrs H was a refugee in her eighties. Most of her family had perished in the war. She came to the JWB asking for a volunteer to help her to move. On first contact it seemed to me that her level of anxiety was excessive for the request she was making. This was conveyed to her, and we agreed to meet over a period of time to try and understand what had brought her to me at that moment. After all, she said she had managed for over eighty years. Before our meeting, however, she had a road accident and was admitted to hospital. I continued to see her there. Mrs H refused to be operated on for a fractured leg and, indeed, refused all treatment for infection. The staff in desperation called in a psychiatrist who diagnosed her as a paranoid schizophrenic, without taking into account her background. During her time in hospital, as she lay helpless and vulnerable, unable to move, she began to talk about her past, particularly her persecution under the Nazis. Her current helplessness seemed to reactivate similar feelings she had about being unable to save her mother, whom she left behind, from being killed.

She began to mourn for her mother, which she said she had never done before. Though she displayed considerable hostility with paranoid features towards the staff, she allowed me to continue to see her regularly. Our relationship was not without difficulty, and I felt I was always walking a fine line between colluding with her paranoid feelings, and becoming yet another persecuting 'Nazi' in her eyes by differentiating myself from her. However, I seemed to convey to her a sense that she was heard and understood, and some feeling of trust developed. I continued to see her weekly over one-and-a-half years. The move which had brought her to me initially turned out to be an eviction – a traumatic enough event at any time, but for her it was also a reminder of her enforced 'eviction' from Germany as a refugee. Mrs H was able to share with me her real fear of breaking down mentally and being admitted to psychiatric hospital. This did not happen, though she came very close to it. She made a successful move to new accommodation, thereby avoiding the trauma of eviction.

However, once the crisis was over, Mrs H's defences re-emerged. What she found so difficult to acknowledge was that through our relationship I had become significant to her. Once more in control of events, she defended herself against the feelings of vulnerability and helplessness, first by trying to use my sessions with her to do practical tasks which the local authority worker was already doing, and secondly by rejecting me altogether. Klein has noted that this 'fear of getting to love someone is not uncommon in survivors of the Holocaust' (1968: 73).

Understanding the reality base of her paranoia rather than labelling her as psychiatrically ill allowed us an opportunity to struggle with the fears and anxieties I had initially felt at our first meeting. Mrs H was a highly intelligent, articulate woman who internalised something from what transpired in our sessions. Despite a great deal of denial concerning the connections made between current and past trauma, we were able to work through some of the 'unfinished business' which had contributed to her vulnerability and sense of aloneness. Entering into Mrs H's world gave me a unique opportunity to learn how to relate to someone who, in another setting, would be labelled as paranoid, and consequently seen as having impaired ability to relate.

Mrs H had been touched by a 'mad' environment under the Nazis. She may have had some disturbance prior to this period, but there is no doubt that the reality of what she experienced affected her ability to trust. Despite her 'paranoia' she had amazing support from neighbours and friends as well as social services. There was a warmth that emanated from her, and it was these strengths on which I tended to build. I could so easily just have seen Mrs H as yet another victim of Nazi persecution, perhaps feeling that her state was unsurprising, considering what she had been through. Consequently, I might have tried to make reparation to her through practical provision and giving as much emotional comfort as possible. However, it was the struggle and fight which constituted our work together that I believe helped Mrs H to break out from the 'victim' category. It may have helped her to experience again a feeling of being in control of events so that her current trauma did not overwhelm her. Mrs H's other agenda was to tell her 'story' so that someone would know what really happened.

Interestingly, during the course of our meetings, Mrs H's son came from the United States to visit his mother for the first time in many years. He had written to her that he had wanted to know more about what happened to her and her family, and wanted to help her to write it down. The survivor who feels they can tell their story because they believe that it will be heard and thereby transmitted can sometimes unburden themselves dramatically. This may make great demands on the social worker, who often becomes the sole means for passing this on – it demands availability by the social worker to the survivor to an extent possibly not encountered with other clients.

The agency's specialisation of working with the elderly, plus my own psychodynamic training, encouraged me to undertake this work with the elderly refugees whom many would agree were beyond the age at which emotional growth or change was possible. My experience had shown me that chronological age was not the main factor in ability to grow emotionally. In addition, the flexibility to see her in hospital as well as at home allowed me to engage her in a therapeutic process so that she could subsequently live more comfortably with herself and die more peacefully. My increasing tendency to pick up on the underlying issues which brought these elderly refugees to the organisation allowed me to begin my involvement. It is very easy to miss the opportunities to confront these painful events from the past, especially as those who have been traumatised or persecuted do not easily verbalise them, as was seen in the hospital setting in which the client found herself. In addition, it may be the therapist who finds it difficult to face these painful areas. Survivors and therapists have become locked in to what has come to be known as a 'conspiracy of silence'. Consequently we must also focus on the therapists – on the counter-transference factors, as these too can imprison us in our defences in a similar way to the organisational walls which become impenetrable to the pain the survivor experiences.

I have often asked myself why I became involved in the work with survivors. Why did I start to see the patterns emerging in my work rather than another worker? Admittedly, at that time I did not even know what I was beginning to touch – my naïvety was in a sense a good thing. I felt that I could apply my psychodynamic training in any setting. I saw myself as a professionally qualified worker who just happened to be working in a Jewish organisation. As I entered the world of these persecuted refugees, so I started to look at my own Jewish identity. I began to think about issues of assimilation and how this has led to the persecution and in its extreme form to genocide. I began to appreciate how the organisation's separate identity in meeting the needs of the Jewish community *vis-à-vis* social/ health services seemed to fit with this theme of confronting my own separate Jewish identity.

I was also addressing this issue in my work with people who had been persecuted for being Jews, whether they adhered religiously or not. Just as their Jewishness could not be avoided, nor could mine. Now I knew why I had chosen to work in a Jewish setting – the work began to take on meaning for me on a level it had not done before. I also became more aware about my personal connection to the Holocaust, which had not been spoken about previously. My mother had come to England as a refugee from Nazi Germany in 1939, and my grandparents were interned in a camp in France. The memories of what happened to them returned to me vividly recently when I was preparing for our most recent conference in January 1992, called 'Creative Approaches to Working with Holocaust Survivors'. Looking at artwork from the camp at Gurs brought home to me in images the link between my work and my own family.

In the self-exploration which needed to be done for me to engage in this work, I had asked myself whether I was making reparation for the suffering my family had been through, but which I had been spared. Wishing to make reparation also brought with it the corollary that survivors who had been through such terrible happenings should be spared any more suffering. How then could I address the rage that was underlying the massive losses that the survivors had been through? In one sense the survivor would be treated as the victim who had suffered so much, and it would be anathema to confront the rage. Having worked this through, however, I was then able to use my personal experience as a bridge between myself and the survivor, and this ultimately led to my acceptance as a non-survivor. In turn this allowed the therapeutic work to take place.

Though my training has encouraged the boundary between the personal and the professional sides of myself, this had to be looked at again in terms of reaching out and encouraging survivors to look at their unfinished business from the past. This work depends on trust, but for people whose trust has been shattered, as many survivors had experienced, how does such a relationship come about? Krell, himself a survivor as well as a therapist, points out that 'in the psychotherapy with holocaust survivors/and or their children, the therapist may be sought out for precisely those reasons that make them feel that some degree of intimacy is possible' (1989a: 224). The adaptation process had started to happen in myself. Survivors in their incarceration or under persecution had to find new ways of coping with the extremely adverse environment they found themselves in. Similarly, if I worked in this world, I had to find new therapeutic ways of doing this.

In the world of the survivor, theory develops from contact with survivors – listening very closely to what they say helps them. However, much of the early work with Holocaust survivors tried to deal with the chaos they presented by trying to fit them into syndromes and theories. Steinberg wrote: 'The early investigations seem to struggle with understanding the survivor via pre-existing theories. Survivors were in a sense fit into the theories, but the fit, as critics have pointed out, was not quite right' (1989: 31). Much of the early work with survivors was based on compensation claims from Germany. Reparation claims looked for causal connections between current emotional difficulties and the experience in the Holocaust. The professionals were looking for 'damage' to justify the claim rather than looking for the survivors' ability to cope. Under these particular circumstances one can understand how the pathological aspects came to be accentuated. However, the model of survivor syndrome which was the medical model for understanding the survivor then transferred itself into different settings with which survivors came into contact; for example, treatment settings. Yet 'the limited power of this model to explain the behaviour of Holocaust survivors in treatment did not appear to inhibit its use' (Steinberg 1989: 27).

The implication of this has been that very little hope could be offered by psychoanalytic therapy for survivors, as their personalities were considered irreversibly damaged by their Holocaust experience. Certainly, survivors would agree that their experiences had scarred them, but in turn, survivor syndrome tended to incarcerate them further in the psychopathology with which they have been labelled. The setting again became of paramount importance in breaking away from this model of understanding survivors. The non-clinical setting of the JWB encouraged me to see the healthy, coping, adaptive side of the survivor. If we look again at the concentration camp setting we see, as Frankl (1987) has concluded, that it was the environment under persecution and in the camps which was abnormal; the survivor reaction to it was normal. We are talking about life in extremity, which cannot be understood within our normal framework.

When we do start to understand this dehumanised, degrading world of the camp, we can then re-examine such issues as the survivors' need to go over and over again what happened. Some therapists have interpreted this need as neurotic behaviour and an inability to complete the mourning process. Krystal (1984), for example, saw the survivor as locked into his anger, unable to accept his past. The answer, he writes, is that 'it must be accepted or we must keep waging an internal war against the ghosts of our past. This does not acknowledge the survivors' need to bear witness' (p. 113). As des Pres points out, psychiatric treatment is directed towards processes of 'adjustment, acceptance, forgetting' (1976: 39). However, these goals are at variance with the survivors' goal to remember so others will not forget. To assume that the need to bear witness is rooted in neurosis is to ignore entirely the nature of extreme experience. This view is supported by Davidson (1981), Baron (1977), Ornstein (1985) and many others. Baron concludes that bearing witness for the survivors is a duty, not a disease.

The pessimistic, pathological approach coloured much of the thinking on survivors at that time. With relatively little known about the long-term effect of massive trauma, the structure it offered was appealing. I was at the Survivor Syndrome Conference in London in 1980, attended by therapists from all over the world. It put survivors on the map as far as therapy was concerned. Interestingly, however, very few of the therapists remained involved in the work in Britain. This again may be linked to the overwhelming nature of the syndromes portrayed. The deskilling process experienced at the conference is something often felt in working with severely traumatised people, and there is a reluctance by many therapists to get involved. In a survey carried out at about that time concerning possible services needed by survivors, the results received were very negative. The questionnaire was sent to GPs in areas in which survivors were living. The response was either that we should not bring up the trauma again, or that anything we could offer would be too late.

Just as a survivor was trying to be fitted into a pre-existing framework, so my own work was not being understood. The excellent consultation I had been receiving for years at the Tavistock Centre could not help me deal with these issues that were emerging from the work. The JWB encouraged me to find an alternative consultant, which I did in Professor Shamai Davidson, who had many years' experience in this work. Without this intervention I might not have survived this stage of the work. The organisation's sensitivity and awareness of the need to invest in this support was crucial.

THE MIDDLE STAGE – OPENING THE ORGANISATIONAL DOORS

I began to realise that those who had been most traumatised in the concentration camps or in hiding rarely came forward to ask for help. One would have expected their emotional needs to be greater. This was a grave misunderstanding on my part. I have since learned through my contact with concentration camp survivors why they kept their distance from our professional organisation – anger towards our Jewish community for not having done enough to help them when they needed it after liberation; the indifference of Jews towards their suffering; their feelings towards authority and institutions; their fears of weakness and vulnerability which asking for help would imply. The office setting was therefore potentially an obstacle to reaching survivors of the death camps. The therapist as well as the organisation were seen as authority figures, which in terms of the camp experience could be equated with the Nazis. Vulnerability in the camps meant certain death, and hence the survivors tended to cope on their own. It should be stressed that most survivors coped extremely well without any professional support. They achieved well at work and raised families despite extreme difficulty. This was in some sense their victory over the Nazis.

The evidence of pathology and sickness among survivors which many professionals, as well as the media, wanted to emphasise, would have implied that Hitler had done the job extremely well. However, in reality this was not the case. The coping continued for many years and these years came to be known as the 'symptom-free interval'. The needs of the survivors changed as they grew older. However, it was difficult for the needs to find meaningful expression within the confines of the therapeutic office setting.

A turning point in my work with survivors came when a camp survivor (not a client) came to see me, having heard my name through an organisation in Israel that specialised in working with Holocaust survivors. The JWB had sent me to a conference in Israel to give a paper on my work, having recognised the importance of these links. This survivor asked me to help her set up a self-help group for some camp survivors whom she knew wanted to come together. They did not want therapy, but to help one another mutually. They would not need to explain why they were there. In this self-help group I was an honorary member (a non-survivor). Instead of the comfort of my usual professional role, I had to face role conflicts and paradoxes in enabling the group to get off the ground – being there as a catalyst but leaving space for the survivors to find their own way; hearing the hidden agendas but using the survivors to draw these out rather than interpreting them, acknowledging my own identity as a professional, but allowing the survivors to use my presence in a way acceptable to them – often in an informal social role.

To the survivor, the meaningfulness of the self-help group was in its mirroring of the camp experience. The non-clinical informal atmosphere of the group which met in premises of their own choice (non-institutional) was a far more acceptable environment for the therapeutic work to take place. The group created a sense of belonging, a sense of family and community which many survivors had been deprived of for a very long time. They celebrated the Jewish festivals together, they phoned one another outside of group meetings. In that sense of belonging and sharing they also fought with one another – as one survivor told me, 'This is the only place that we can bring our bestiality – in all other groups we have to behave'. Despite the hierarchies of suffering which developed, their experience was also in a sense normalised. From this experience of a self-help group, I learned about the power of a group as a therapeutic medium, particularly for camp survivors. Instead of trying to fit the survivor into the boundaries of my professional expertise, I began to develop my theoretical framework from the position that I saw working in practice.

I then turned to the literature and read that mutual aid constituted the key to survival in the camps. After overcoming the initial shock of being tossed into such debilitating circumstances, the prisoner gradually realised the struggle was a collective one (Baron 1977: 27). This mutual aid which had helped during the incarceration could then be translated into therapy in the self-help group. Des Pres refers to the teamwork aspect in the camp when talking about the importance of 'organising' – for example, sharing out clothes and food, or propping one another up during roll call to prevent being selected for death. 'In extremity life depends on solidarity for collective action is more effective than individual efforts' (Frankl 1987: 121). Through this understanding I was able to progress on from Krystal's (1984) account of the influence of the impact of massive psychic trauma with its emphasis on how the traumatic process relates to intrapsychic events, to a recognition of the importance of the interpersonal dimension – what Davidson calls 'social bonding' (1984: 556).

Such social support was not only important during the incarceration, but was also an important variable in preventing or modifying long-term effects of massive psychic trauma. It was in the interpersonal bonding that human dignity was in some way sustained and survivors continued with their struggle to live. It is recognition of this essential yet understated dynamic which gives credence to view Frankl's quotation from Nietzsche that 'he who has a why to live for can bear almost any how' (Allport 1987: iii). The social work context of this therapeutic work with survivors seems to fit comfortably with the shift from the individual surviving for himself, as proposed by Bettelheim (1986), to the wider context of the group, as proposed by des Pres (1976) and Davidson (1981). To see the survivor without a context is to misinterpret the experience.

In addition, it was in this agency context that the need for professionals to come together in groups as well as the survivors was realised. To be able to undertake this work takes courage as well as skill. The JWB recognised this through the consultancy arrangements they made for me with Sonny Herman, a therapist working with survivors in Holland. Together we run monthly groups for professionals working with survivors, where they can share their work in a supportive environment. Being a voluntary agency gives the space to address these difficult issues.

Prioritising this work and with the agency giving it its full backing has made my task infinitely easier than it would otherwise have been. Both in the groups and at the conferences we have organised on working with survivors, I have often heard counsellors/therapists declaring their sense of isolation in their organisations when they take on this work with Holocaust survivors. I spend considerable amounts of time visiting hospitals and other organisations, or receiving phone calls from professionals who have begun to work with survivors. The sense of not being alone with the trauma seems to bring relief, as well as the exchange of information on the services which have been developing.

Through the experience of the self-help groups the walls of the setting had become more elastic. My role of listener and facilitator overcame the authority issue and also the sense of vulnerability and dependency that the therapeutic relationship often brings. The importance of not knowing because I was not there (in the camp) was a humbling but essential part of my acceptance in the group. As Wiesel has written, 'Listen to survivors, listen to them very carefully. They have more to teach you than you them' (1982: i). There can be no assumptions, no sense of knowing. Listening and learning from survivors as witnesses of the unimaginable rebalances the relationship in such a way that therapy can then begin. With the survivor teaching us, we start to search with them for meaning in their survival, but the methods we use are varied. They are not patients or even clients but individuals whom we engage in a process which may lead to healing. They take us on a journey with them. Krell (1989b) has, for example, found the use of a map an excellent tool for encouraging the process of communication. Looking at the map conveys interest and involves both parties in a joint venture.

Some of these survivors from the self-help group were then able to come forward and ask for counselling. The office setting then became a safe place in which to conduct therapy. Just as they had become individualised to me, so had I to them. The myth of the 'pathetic victim' was fast disappearing and the strength of the survivor emerging. I became more aware of the variables which affected the coping – issues such as early childhood experiences; the age of the survivor on entering the camp; whether they remained with members of their family in the camp; what happened to them after liberation; whether they adhered to their religious beliefs. The myth of the professional was also broken down through personalising the experience and loosening the constrictions of my professional role. At the same time, when the location shifted to the office, there was no sense of undermining my professional status. The preparatory work of the self-help group enables the survivor's ego to be strengthened, so that, when the trauma is re-experienced, which it may be in the therapy, this is not so overwhelming. Ornstein emphasises the importance of the survivor being understood rather than diagnosed, and this seems to open up a possibility of survivors sharing some of their most painful memories. 'Feeling understood by the psychotherapist fosters the development of one of the self-object transferences. . . . Only when such a rehabilitation of the self has occurred can the process of mourning begin' (Ornstein 1985: 99).

Case study 2

A way of dealing with the process of mourning can be illustrated by reference to a particular survivor. This work contrasts a traditional psychodynamic approach with one which is more meaningful to the survivor. Mrs L came to the JWB at the point when her husband had died. She was seen at the office by a social worker, who assessed her need for bereavement counselling. The social worker was sympathetic of her need to mourn, but Mrs L could not make use of the counselling and so terminated. I met Mrs L six years later in the self-help group just described.

After I had got to know her in that setting, she asked if she could come and see me. She told me her command of English was not good, and she would like me to help her record what had happened to her before, during and after the Holocaust. She had never been able to tell her children what had really happened and she wanted them to know. We met regularly over several months. She would talk to me about her life before Auschwitz-Birkenau during the incarceration and what happened to her at liberation and later. Her imagery was vivid and we recorded vignettes about her experience.

The summer was very hot inside the overcrowded barracks – the air smelled fetid and rotten, the atmosphere was suffocating – it was a nightmare. I looked at these well-fed Germans who externally looked prime examples of the human race and yet inside were mere empty shells, devoid of those values which make them human. I looked at myself, whose outer shell was a pathetic specimen of life, yet inside I kept the values which my parents had given to me and which no one could take away. If I survived, I thought the world would be a better place because this would never be allowed to happen again.

(Survivor's testimony)

Mrs L would talk to me and I would record, writing it up after the session in the first person. She told me she found the process acceptable and helpful because she was also giving something to me – she was helping me to understand the incomprehensible. My recording seemed to demonstrate the success of her teaching. We shared the painfulness of what was recalled, and for the first time she felt heard.

One day I was ordered to search through some clothing and chanced to find a diamond hidden away in a shoulder pad. Yet I could so easily discard it – it had no usefulness to me – it could not get me what I needed – the food that would sustain me. The diamond had no value in that world. The beauty of the diamond only reflected me as I really was; dirty and full of lice.

(Survivor's testimony)

In that world beyond metaphor, this survivor's creativity and imagination are put to full use to convey her testimony.

Having completed our task, Mrs L arranged to go on an organised trip back to Auschwitz. She took her daughter with her. In this group of young people, she was the only survivor – this is how she described it:

As we passed through to Birkenau, the horror of the place struck me once more. I went up into the watchtower from which the Germans had looked down on me. The emptiness of the place struck me and the absolute silence. It appeared like a timeless place – time does not exist. I had expected the earth to be red with the blood of those murdered there, but only greyness could be seen – the greyness of ashes. It seemed so quiet and still. I tried to visualise again the seething bodies in that hell of forty years ago. I could see nothing, yet the smell of death still hangs in the air.

(Survivor's testimony)

We, as therapists, need to be looking at what helps the individual to survive and cope, both during the incarceration and after liberation. Our task is to help find meaning in their survival. Survivors cannot forget what happened, but we should try and help them find the means to have a present as well as a future. By helping them to record their testimony we help them to bear witness to what happened. With no graves to help in expressing the loss, the testimonies became the tombstones and the 'paper monuments' (Rosenbloom 1983).

In addition to the testimonies, the mourning process can also be helped through the survivors' participation in the ritual prayers for the dead. Many survivors have come to me and said that they felt so helpless in not being able to save their families, and some feel they should have died with them in the Holocaust. Many do not even know where their families were murdered. Finding out what really happened to them through the tracing service, saying kaddish (the mourners' prayer) for the family who died, setting up a memorial stone for those who died are all practical ways in which survivors can feel there is still something positive they can do, and that they have not survived in vain. I have been assisted in this spiritual task through the help of Rabbi Rodney Mariner, a rabbi whose congregation is largely made up of survivors. Rabbi Mariner chose to spend a three-month sabbatical with me in the team to learn about working with survivors. This link formed an essential part in a chain in developing approaches appropriate to survivors. He also conducted a memorial service for the child survivors whose families had perished, and this took place in our premises. The partnership between the spiritual and the therapeutic seems to happen naturally with the Jewish setting I work in. While I was writing this chapter, one of the survivors I had been seeing over some time said that she wanted me to know that she had started to believe in God, having previously wanted to take her own life. The ritualistic mourning had reconnected her to her spirituality which comforted her as she grew older.

THE FINAL STAGE – THE END OF THE JOURNEY

In January 1990 the work shifted out of the JWB office to a new location at a centre in Hendon called Shalvata. By this time my work with survivors had become well established, and hence the work came over with me. Though the work of Shalvata is for anyone over the age of 18 who is experiencing an emotional problem, the name also links with a centre in Israel that works with Holocaust survivors. Shamai Davidson had been director of that Centre but died some years ago. Shalvata is a memorial to his work.

The strength of Shalvata's work is firmly linked to what I have learned from survivors – the non-clinical approach; the Jewish dimension; the importance of groups; the balance of creative approaches with the therapeutic; finding the healthy, coping, adaptive side of those seeking help. Overall, the approach is to adapt the services we offer to the individual needs of those who come to us for help rather than asking them to fit into pre-existing frameworks. Our need to be creative is challenged constantly by survivors. The multidisciplinary nature of the team at Shalvata opened up opportunities to widen the scope of possible services.

For example, some survivors do not wish to return to the traumatic memories of their past, and yet nevertheless carry with them emotions that at times can be overwhelming. In my view, many survivors need their defences to cope. Some professionals have argued that those who do not wish to look at their past are resistant to help. It is my view that it is not the survivor who is resistant, so much as our inability to find the suitable channel or medium. A theatre workshop for survivors was started by the creative therapist at Shalvata. Again this idea was rooted firmly in the survivor experience, not conjured up from nowhere. We listened to what had helped survivors cope in the camps. When we talk to survivors we hear ample evidence of the use of creative imagination in helping to pass, minute by minute, the extent of their adversity. As one survivor told me, when she was hungry she imagined eating a slice of bread; another, who was so tired, imagined being asleep.

As an example from my work, I had been seeing a survivor weekly over a long period of time. Her divorce had been the trigger for bringing back the memories of what had happened to her when she was 'abandoned' at the age of five when her parents were taken away to the camp. She was left hidden in a cupboard and remained in hiding during the war suffering other tragedy during that time. The trauma returned in the present with such ferocity that she felt the only course open to her was to commit suicide – she felt she should have died with her family. She had also met me in a self-help group, and the trust which had developed allowed her to come and see me in my office. Gradually she came to feel that she could not reverse what had happened but she would have to find some way of making her life more bearable. She had told me how during her life she had enjoyed being the life and soul of the party and had a great sense of fun and laughter. She had now lost touch with this emotion, and would dearly love to find it again, but felt she had no right to enjoy herself.

I wondered whether, if she were able to take the part of someone else who did laugh, such as that role in a play, maybe she would reconnect with that emotion without experiencing any guilt. This survivor, who had thought suicide was the only option, now participates not only in the theatre workshop, but also the self-help group for child survivors (those who were children in the camps and in hiding during the Holocaust). She attends a weekly therapy group for child survivors run by a group analyst, as well as individual sessions with myself. Shalvata is the focal point for all those inputs. We as therapists meet together regularly and create in a sense the lost family. We acknowledge the 'missing years' for those child survivors – their childhood and the adolescence of which they were deprived. Our ability to come together as professionals has resulted in Shalvata being seen as their 'home' and not only a place for treatment. They tend to go around together, almost like an adolescent peer group or gang. They go on theatre outings, they meet socially in one another's homes – all factors which would traditionally not be acceptable in treatment situations. Again, in my view the only good therapy is the one that works, and the success of what we do is more dependent on our professional adaptability.

At this stage we are still breaking new ground, but it is our openness to look again at the traditional approaches which is crucial. The family model is one which is central in terms of the Jewish dimension of the work with Holocaust survivors. The client above commented in a recent meeting with me that her knowledge of my always being there for her at Shalvata reassured her at times when the absence and loss of her own mother could have overwhelmed her. I was her 'lifeline' as she called it, whether she was actually seeing me or not. Her ongoing need to do this is accepted by me, and perhaps more important than the in-depth work I could do with her.

The focus of much of the developments included in this chapter in working with survivors has to do with the concept of empowerment. Many saw survivors as pathetically going like sheep to the slaughter. Some ask, why did more people not resist? Some did, of course, but in the death camps, starvation ruled out the possibility of much physical force, apart from a lack of weapons. However, the survivors resolved that it should never happen again. Much of this positive energy was channelled into the creation of the state of Israel. Survivors are often passionate in their support of Israel. At the same time, however, their fears are growing rapidly concerning the rise of fascism again in Europe. The reunification of Germany and the Nazi war crimes trials bring back anxieties and remembrances of what they have been through in the Holocaust.

A sense of helplessness concerning these events could reactivate their fears of persecution and victimisation. How, then, do we offer alternative approaches which can liberate the survivor from their victim role to fight the rise of fascism? The remembrance of what happened can be translated positively into survivors becoming educators in schools. Survivors are the living witnesses: they are not out of history books, they were actually there. They can convey to children, for example, what it meant to be a child similar to them, but in very different circumstances. They can talk about the Holocaust through the eyes of a child. This can be digested and have meaning – a very different meaning from the media's portrayal of the survivor. The survivor who looks no different from you or me is a far more powerful messenger about the past, and can warn those they speak to about where fascism leads.

The survivor as teacher was also used by me at Jewish Care to train professionals in working with survivors. Six survivors spoke about what it meant to survive and how professionals could have helped but did not and how they now have a second opportunity. We worked with these six survivors for some weeks preparing them for the event. They feared they might break down as they recounted what had happened. In the event, it was the professionals who were in tears. The survivors were strengthened by the experience and have continued this role of teacher in various settings. 'Education as remembrance brought relief no sleeping pill or insightful analysis could match' (Krell 1989b: 222). There is still something the survivor can do, and make a contribution to the community they are living in. This political stance which the survivor can take fits into the notion of a voluntary agency's brief as a pressure group. We are concerned not just for the individual but in social change. The identification of the agency with this political role can be seen in their choice of speaker at the next annual public meeting; namely, Martin Gilbert. Fascism is brought into our consciousness and how we engage survivors in this task of speaking out is the therapy. It also unites the organisation with the survivor in a common cause, whereas before I had described the survivors' alienation from this Anglo-Jewish edifice.

Taking this notion of empowerment even further, Jewish Care and the Central British Fund for World Jewish Relief have created a new setting in which survivors will take responsibility for the development of the first Survivor Centre in the United Kingdom. This was opened in 1993 next door to Shalvata. It is a centre for survivors run by survivors. The co-ordinator's role as facilitator is to ensure that all the survivors who wish to can participate in the Centre. The focus of the Centre will be a café, and there will be a social programme which the survivors will help in organising. They will not be dependent recipients of services, but will be creating services which meet their needs. It is not a therapy centre in the same sense as Shalvata, and will have a separate entrance. The self-help groups which currently run both for the older survivors and the child survivors will transfer to the Centre, as well as the theatre workshop. The Spouses of Survivors Group, and the Second-Generation Group, will continue at Shalvata, as will the individual therapeutic work.

Recording the testimonies, the educational programme, advice on reparation claims, a library on Holocaust work and issues related to medical or legal matters as experienced by survivors will be on offer. Involvement of the second generation through participation in some of the activities may also have a therapeutic effect. This centre will in a sense re-create the lost community which survivors often perceive as the greatest loss they have experienced. As they grow older, so their need to be together in a 'home of their own' increases. With vastly diminished families, they need to support one another. Their collective voice is far louder and more significant than any individual effort and is thereby the most powerful tool towards empowerment and strength. The foundation for this ultimate goal had been laid during my years of struggle to find the most suitable approach with survivors. The Centre is both the end of a journey and a new beginning. When people are near to death their greatest fear is that they will not be remembered – that it will be as though they had never existed. This is even more so for the survivor who may have few people in whom they will live on. So the new Centre is there not only for them to enjoy but also to be able to let go of their lives – in the knowledge that their struggle will not have been in vain. For myself as well, the Centre represents the end of one piece of work but also unburdens me of the weight I have carried around in ensuring that the survivors' important message is heard and passed on. I am now free to go forward with them. The central role of the organisation in supporting me in my task, and the financial as well as emotional backing received for the projects I have undertaken need to be emphasised. The encouragement to innovate and to take risks in what some therapists may see as untraditional ways can perhaps only be done in the enlightened setting I have been working in.

CONCLUSION

Aspects of the organisation and setting have been crucial in the development of this work with Holocaust survivors: the Jewish dimension; the social work context; the non-statutory nature of the work; the role of the voluntary sector; the concept of a therapeutic community in a non-clinical environment. A personal conviction on my part towards the need to develop new ways of working with survivors seems to be an essential ingredient in transforming what could have been an intransigent setting into one which opened its doors outwards. It let me pass through to a world unknown which in turn had a profound influence on the organisation.

REFERENCES

Allport, G. W. (1987) 'Preface', pp. i–iv in V. E. Frankl, *Man's Search for Meaning: An Introduction to Logotherapy* (I. Lasch, trans.), London: Hodder & Stoughton.

Baron, L. (1977) 'Surviving the Holocaust', *Journal of Psychology and Judaism* 1(2): 27.

Bettelheim, B. (1986) *The Informed Heart*, Harmondsworth: Penguin (first published 1960).

Davidson, S. (1981) *On Relating to Traumatised Persecuted People*, Israel/Netherlands: Symposium on the Impact of Persecution II, 14–18 April, Dalfern, Amsterdam: Rijsvijk.

—— (1984) 'Human Reciprocity among Jewish Prisoners in the Nazi Concentration Camps', Proceedings of the 4th Yad Vashem International Conference, 1980, Jerusalem: Yad Vashem.

Frankl, V. E. (1987) *Man's Search for Meaning: An Introduction to Logotherapy* (I. Lasch, trans.,), London: Hodder & Stoughton.

Klein, H. (1968) 'On problems in the psychotherapeutic treatment of Israeli survivors of the Holocaust', in H. Krystal (ed.) *Massive Psychic Trauma*, New York: International Universities Press, p. 233.

Krell, R. (1989a) 'Alternative therapeutic approaches to holocaust survivors', in P. Marcus and A. Rosenberg (eds) *Healing their Wounds: Psychotherapy with Holocaust Survivors and their Families*, London and New York: Praeger.

—— (1989b) 'Psychotherapy with Holocaust survivors and their families', in P. Marcus and A. Rosenberg (eds) *Healing their Wounds: Psychotherapy with Holocaust Survivors and their Families*, London and New York: Praeger.

Kren, I. G. M. (1989) 'The Holocaust survivor and psychoanalysis', in P. Marcus and A. Rosenberg (eds) *Healing their Wounds: Psychotherapy with Holocaust Survivors and their Families*, London and New York: Praeger.

Krystal, H. (1968) *Massive Psychic Trauma*, New York: International Universities Press.

—— (1984) 'Integration and self healing in post traumatic states', pp. 113–34 in S. A. Luel and P. Marcus (eds) *Psychoanalytic Reflections on the Holocaust: Selected Essays*, New York: Ktav Publishing House.

Ornstein, A. (1985) 'Survival and recovery', p. 99–130 in D. Lewis and N. Averhahn (eds) *Psychoanalytic Inquiry 5*, Hillsdale, NJ: Analytic Press.

—— (1989) 'Treatment issues with survivors and their offspring: an interview with Anna Ornstein, Paul Marcus and Alan Rosenberg', pp. 16–106 in P. Marcus and

A. Rosenberg (eds) *Healing their Wounds: Psychotherapy with Holocaust Survivors and their Families*, London and New York: Praeger.

Pres, T. des (1976) *The Survivor – an Anatomy of Life in the Death Camps*, Oxford and New York: Oxford University Press.

Rosenberg, A. (1989) 'A joint interview', in P. Marcus and A. Rosenberg (eds) *Healing their Wounds: Psychotherapy with Holocaust Survivors and their Families*, London and New York: Praeger.

Rosenbloom, M. (1983) 'Implications of the Holocaust to social work', *Casework: The Journal of Contemporary Social Work* (April), Family Services Association of America.

Steinberg, A. (1989) 'Holocaust survivors and their children: a review of the clinical literature', pp. 27–31 in P. Marcus and A. Rosenberg (eds) *Healing their Wounds: Psychotherapy with Holocaust Survivors and their Families*, London and New York: Praeger.

Wiesel, E. (1982) 'The Holocaust Patient', Address to Cedars-Sinai Medical Staff, Los Angeles.

FURTHER INFORMATION ABOUT WORK WITH HOLOCAUST SURVIVORS

Jewish Care
221 Golders Green Road
London NW11
Tel.: 0181 458 3282

Shalvata
Parson Street
Hendon
London NW4
Tel.: 0181 203 9033

Chapter 7

Psychotherapy and sexual orientation

Paul Hitchings

Despite attempts to 'cure' homosexuality being reported in the scientific literature, even comparatively recently by methods such as psychosurgery on two gay men (Schmidt and Schorsch 1981) and by hypnotherapy on a young lesbian (Roden 1983), these are now exceptions and the last two decades have witnessed a shift in the attitudes of psychotherapists towards an affirmative view of homosexuality. In part, this shift reflects the failure of the medical model as a result of its simplicity (Gonsoriek 1977; 1985), the lack of success in attempts at 'cure' (Coleman 1978) and the questionable ethics involved (Symposium on Homosexuality and the Ethics of Behavioural Intervention 1977). This shift also reflects the modest changes in legislation, social attitudes and awareness over this time.

In moving away from a pathological model toward gay/lesbian affirmative models of psychotherapy a gap has been left that needs to be filled. This requires that practitioners share their clinical experience and develop and refine such alternative models. It is to these aims that this chapter intends to address itself.

The following discussion has, for the sake of clarity, made the over-simplified assumption of a discrete division between heterosexuality and homosexuality. The situation is clearly more complex. Kinsey *et al.* (1948) have suggested a seven-point scale to reflect that people could rate at any point of gradation between exclusive homosexual and heterosexual behaviour. In an effort to refine categories, Bell and Weinberg (1978) have suggested categories that reflect types of homosexual expression and lifestyle, and in a similar vein Coleman (1985) has suggested categories that reflect not only behaviour but also fantasy and emotional attachments. This measurement problem of course reflects the diversity of meaning that the term 'homosexual' can have for any particular individual. Consequently, the clinician and the reader need to bear in mind that we are always referring to individuals who are unique in their own sexuality, even if for the sake of clarity and simplicity we continue to refer to the abstraction of homosexuality.

THERAPIST ISSUES

Sexual orientation of the psychotherapist

Are lesbian/gay clients more likely to be helped by working with a psychotherapist of the same sex and orientation? The answer to this question is complex, and to a considerable extent depends on what the client hopes to gain from psychotherapy. There is very little direct research in this area; however, two studies (Beutler *et al.* 1978; Hart 1981) found that where there is mutual acceptance between client and psychotherapist of each other's sexual viewpoints, such acceptance is associated with facilitating global improvement within the client.

In summarising the effects of psychotherapist variables of sex and gender on outcomes, Beutler *et al.* (1986: 265) state that 'research is needed to explore the possibility that egalitarianism rather than sexual attitudes or gender roles themselves provoke change'. The above suggestion, which is in keeping with the author's experience, implies that the crucial variable is the ability of the psychotherapist to recognise fully and believe in the equal validity of a homosexual lifestyle and not so much the sexual orientation of the psychotherapist *per se*. This of course also applies to psychotherapists who have chosen a homosexual lifestyle since they are equally vulnerable to harbouring and communicating anti-homosexual prejudice.

There is a particular potential advantage for gay men and lesbian women in working with a heterosexual psychotherapist since it is less likely that particular prejudices, that perhaps could be fostered by the gay/lesbian subculture, would go unnoticed or be actively colluded with.

There are, however, arguments that a gay psychotherapist can provide a client with certain dimensions that a non-homophobic heterosexual psychotherapist would be unable to offer. Rochlin (1982) argues that three particular dimensions are of significance: first, the enhanced degree of empathy that can be communicated from having personally shared the experiences of growing up gay in a heterosexual culture; secondly, the provision of a role model for clients who are unlikely to have been exposed to any positive role models in their childhood or their adult life; thirdly, the personal knowledge and experience of gay culture and lifestyles, which allows the client to further their work without having to educate the psychotherapist along the way.

Therapist self-disclosure

Discussion in the preceding paragraphs might imply to the reader that the author believes that psychotherapists should automatically disclose to the client in a routine way their sexual orientation. Almost all schools of psychotherapy caution on the use of self-disclosure by the psychotherapist, from those that prohibit any information being proffered, to those which believe that appropriate self-disclosure is essential in maintaining the relationship as an authentic encounter. The question then becomes, when is it appropriate and when inappropriate for the psychotherapist in working with gay and lesbian clients to withhold information regarding their sexuality?

Malyon argues as follows: 'If the clinician is gay, it is often of therapeutic value to reveal this early in the treatment process in order to help assure the client that the details of his homosexual feelings will be understood and accepted by the therapist' (1985: 63–4).

In practice, where the psychotherapist is gay the client has often contacted them because they specifically want a gay psychotherapist and have gained this information from one of the various gay referral sources or via word of mouth within the gay community. Where the psychotherapist is not gay and the client clearly identifies as being gay, there is a value in the psychotherapist sharing explicitly with the client their value system with respect to a homosexual lifestyle.

Malyon follows his position on self-disclosure with a caution:

> There are instances where early therapist disclosure would be counter-therapeutic, particularly where the client has not yet come out and is deeply conflicted over his homo-erotic promptings. In this instance therapist disclosure might be too threatening to the client and result in a premature termination of treatment.
>
> (1985: 64)

Those clients who have not yet come out and might find such a psychotherapist disclosure too threatening are less likely to have been referred by such sources.

Homophobia in psychotherapists

In the same way that it has taken and continues to take considerable effort and self-awareness to recognise and eradicate sexism within ourselves, even for those who at a conscious level affirm anti-sexist values, so too does it take this effort with our own homophobia and heterosexism irrespective of an individual's sexual orientation.

When working with gay men or lesbians, irrespective of whether or not the psychotherapist is gay or lesbian themselves, a therapist needs to have explored their own sexuality and at least to some degree have transcended the sex-role stereotypes offered to us in our society. For gay or lesbian clinicians this probably means we have achieved the latter stages in the 'coming out' models which are discussed later in this chapter.

TREATMENT MODALITIES

In choosing between individual or group formats for psychotherapy, particularly where the presenting problem involves the acceptance and development of a gay/lesbian identity, there are considerable potential benefits to be gained from group psychotherapy, which are not as easily available in individual work. Working in a group provides a gay/lesbian client with an opportunity to be with others in an intimate but non-sexual way, and to own their homosexuality in a comparatively safe setting. The latter two points are worthy of amplification. Providing a comparatively safe place to own and explore their homosexuality can provide sufficient confidence for lesbian women and gay men to own their sexuality in other less safe groupings, such as with straight friends, colleagues and family. Additionally, a group that provides non-sexual intimacy is of particular value since frequently the main social groupings available to homosexual men and women are the sexualised meeting places of bars and clubs. Although such venues have an important place in the culture, they do not easily provide for a nurturing environment conducive to co-operation and intimacy. Such groups can be particularly effective in facilitating the homosexual client through the phases of the 'coming out' process.

Is a gay/lesbian client better placed in an all-gay or a mixed group? Yalom (1975), in advocating mixed groups, was among the first authors to describe the potential benefits to the homosexual client and the benefits that could accrue to the other heterosexual group members of being included in a mixed group. He defines success for the gay client when they no longer consider their homosexuality to be a particular problem and the benefits to the other members of being confronted with their own homophobia, which requires that they accept the homosexual part of themselves.

In contrast, Conlin and Smith (1985: 109) describe the psychotherapeutic value of homogeneous groups for gay and lesbian clients.

> The group provides community sanction and support for minority sexual orientation status as a valid lifestyle. Also, by reducing internal conflict over sexual orientation, it decreases maladaptive reactions, such as depressions, suicidal gestures, and dependence on alcohol and other drugs.

In determining which type of group is likely to be of most value to a gay person, Conlin and Smith (1985: 109) further conclude:

> We have found that mixed groups can be useful to the homosexual patient who is already functioning at a high level of self acceptance and adaptation as a gay person, and presents with problems unrelated to sexual orientation. . . . On the other hand when internalised homophobia is the major issue for the homosexual patient, all gay groups are better suited to facilitating homosexual adjustment.

My own clinical experience and that of numerous colleagues who run both types of group generally support Conlin and Smith's arguments. However, if the homosexual client is placed into a mixed group, then, as Yalom (1975) suggests, the psychotherapist needs to be alert to subtle attempts on the part of the group to convert the member to heterosexuality. With this provision, provided the client has sufficient ego strength to accept being different, there is no reason why a gay/lesbian client should not benefit from membership in a group of heterogeneous composition.

There are particular boundary issues that are worthy of mention at this point concerning the facilitating of all-gay groups. Because the gay/lesbian subculture even in a large city is essentially comparatively small, the psychotherapist does need to stress the importance of the group's maintaining confidentiality. Such an all-gay/lesbian group approximates to a group run in a rural area where the importance of confidentiality needs to be underlined due to the obvious increase in probability of known or unknown friendship/acquaintanceship connections between members. Another major boundary issue that needs to be made explicit by the group psychotherapist is that of clients not having sexual relationships with one another. The provision of this boundary allows the group to become and remain a safe place where the more significant intrapsychic issues can surface unclouded by the potential complications of sexual liaisons.

There are, of course, gay/lesbian clients whose ego boundaries are too fragile to benefit from group membership at all. A format of initial individual psychotherapy might be indicated as a preparation for group psychotherapy and later can be used concurrently with it.

Models of the coming out process

In my work with homosexual clients I have found it helpful to use a developmental model as a framework to inform my treatment planning. A developmental model is appropriate since adult identity development, a task that Erikson (1946) defines as belonging to adolescence, is unlikely to have been properly resolved, since this task includes the integration of sexuality including sexual orientation. This is likely to have been prevented since identity formation is an interactive process between the adolescent, their family and the wider society (Erikson 1946). Clearly, in Western societies the development of the homosexual person's identity is hindered by anti-homosexual norms and values which thwart the appropriate completion of developmental tasks at least from adolescence onwards and probably have had an impact on earlier experiences.

There are a number of such models in the literature (Cass 1979; Coleman 1985; Dank 1971; Henken and O'Dowd 1977; Lee 1977; Grace 1979) which all have broadly comparable tasks. For a brief account of these models, see Hanley-Hackenbruck (1989). The particular model I prefer to use is that of Coleman (1985), and in proposing this model he suggests that individuals who are homosexual need to negotiate certain stages in the formation of their identity development. However, the use of such a model does not assume that a person follows through each stage in a progressive, linear manner. A person may work at a number of stages concurrently and may need to recycle previous stages at particular points in their development.

The entire process of developing an identity has been referred to in the gay and lesbian community as 'coming out'. Cohen and Stein (1986), quoted by Hanley-Hackenbruck, define the term as follows:

> Coming out refers to a complicated developmental process which involves at a psychological level a person's awareness and acknowledgement of homosexual thoughts and feelings. For some persons, coming out ultimately leads to public identification as a gay man or lesbian.
>
> (1989: 21)

The five stages of Coleman's (1985) model are described below, together with some of the associated relevant psychotherapeutic considerations:

1 Pre-coming out

Of this stage Coleman states:

> Because individuals at the pre-coming out stage are not consciously aware of same sex feelings, they cannot describe what is wrong. They can only communicate their conflict through behavioural problems, psychosomatic illnesses, suicidal attempts, or various other symptoms. It is conceivable that some suicidal attempts by children and adolescents are due to this conflict.
>
> (1985: 33)

At this stage a person is aware that there is something different about themselves but cannot conceptualise this difference and/or admit this difference to themselves. This task is filled with confusion, and Cass (1979) refers to it as the stage of 'identity confusion'. This task is completed when an individual acknowledges to themselves their same-sex feelings.

Psychotherapeutic considerations

In the early part of this stage the client is not aware of homosexual impulses as being the conflict that underlies the presenting problem. This possibility is then a psychotherapeutic hypothesis. In both the early and latter part of this stage the client is likely to be experiencing a high degree of conflict. The significant psychotherapeutic task at this stage is to allow the client to explore their sexuality without any prejudice on the part of the psychotherapist as to which orientation they should further explore and develop. This will eventually allow the client to make a genuine choice, at a pace that is in keeping with their own readiness. Whilst the psychotherapist needs to guard against pushing the client in one direction or another the psychotherapist needs nevertheless to provide accurate information including correcting common misconceptions about homosexuality. This requires a fine balance of judgement on the part of the psychotherapist, since too frequent correction of misconceptions or, on the other hand, ignoring misconceptions, could be misinterpreted by the client as pushing towards one or other orientation. Of particular value at the latter part of this stage is suggested reading, such as Hart's (1984) text.

Coleman (1985) states that a healthy resolution to this stage is to face the existential crisis of being different.

2 Coming out

Coleman writes of this task,

> Once their same sex feelings have been identified and acknowledged, individuals face the next developmental task of the coming out stage: telling others. The function of this task is to begin self acceptance.
>
> (1985: 34)

At the beginning of this task it is important that the person chooses to tell people who are relatively 'safe', that is, those who almost certainly will be validating of their sexuality. The counsellor/psychotherapist is obviously within this category. When sufficient positive experiences have been accrued by the person, they are in a better position to tell people whose response is less predictable. On this point Coleman comments:

> This is a very critical point, for the confidants' reaction can have a powerful impact. If negative, it can confirm all the old negative impressions and can put a seal on a previous low self-concept. If positive, the reaction can start to counteract some of the old perceived negative feelings, permitting individuals to begin to accept their sexual feelings and increase their self esteem. The existential crisis begins to resolve in a positive direction.
>
> (1985: 34)

At this stage it is of particular value for the client to begin to develop a friendship circle that can offer support and guidance, since social isolation can be especially damaging. Many gay organisations run social groups either specifically for people engaged in the process of coming out or that would provide a supportive social environment.

In the latter stages of this task, telling significant people in their lives who are heterosexual is an important step, since homosexual people may still be perceived as of lower status. Particularly painful can be negative responses from family members, and the person might find it helpful to remind themselves how long the process has taken them and to appreciate the grieving process that their parents and other family members are likely to be involved in. 'It is important that they persevere with their parents and family through a grieving process. Parents will often grieve the loss of the image of their son or daughter as married and having children' (Coleman 1985: 35).

Psychotherapeutic considerations

Here the psychotherapist needs to praise new behaviour, from the initial statements the client makes that they are gay/lesbian, to finding information about homosexuality and to telling significant others. Sketchley (1989) notes the importance of helping the client distinguish between the first, possibly negative reactions of others and their later second reaction, which is more likely to be positive when they have had more time to respond.

The issue of telling significant others such as family members needs to be carefully dealt with by the psychotherapist. The client could possibly at this stage either approach the situation in a provocative manner or in an ill-thought-through way, motivated by euphoria at embracing their new-found self concept. The possibility of delaying this self-disclosure until the client is more psychologically ready needs to be explored.

3 Exploration

This period is the equivalent of the adolescent period of learning through exploring and experimenting with relationships. A particular cluster of issues is often of relevance at this stage. These are: development of interpersonal skills for meeting others, the development of skills of sexual competence, setting appropriate boundaries for self, recognising internalised self-oppression, awareness of the potential use of intoxicants to anaesthetise the pain and shore up a weak self concept. For gay men there is also the issue of the separation of self-esteem from sexual 'conquest'. Additionally, they must be aware of the danger of obtaining casual sex apparently for pleasure but in effect to reinforce a negative view of the self.

Cass (1979) describes this phase as the time when identity tolerance can lead to identity acceptance. This is a particularly intense phase of learning since the social rules and norms of gay culture need to be learned. In addition, this is a phase like adolescence but without the usual parental and economic constraints which would normally operate to provide safe boundaries for the person. Grace (1979) has suggested the concept of 'developmental lag' to describe the process.

Psychotherapeutic considerations

In relation to the cluster of issues discussed above there are a large number of potential psychotherapeutic tasks involved. Many of the tasks of the psychotherapist will be more clearly educative than at other periods in the coming out process. Frequently, the psychotherapist will need to teach certain social skills and/or encourage the client in order to overcome possible shyness and awkwardness. Additionally, the psychotherapist is well placed to help the client acquire the relevant information about health issues.

The possibility of the client being stuck at this stage needs to be borne in mind by the psychotherapist. In the author's experience clients often present for psychotherapy as a result of having been stuck at this stage for many years. This may well be indicative of internalised homophobia expressed in beliefs such as 'homosexual relationships will never last', which is then lived out as a self-fulfilling prophecy. The psychotherapist needs to be alert to subtle as well as more obvious manifestations of such belief systems.

Towards the end of this phase clients frequently need to experience and express their feelings of anger and sadness at not having had permission from their parents and the wider culture to live their sexuality properly. There is often a period of mourning for the decades of their life that cannot now be lived in a way that would have been healthy and satisfying.

4 First relationships

First relationships, irrespective of sexual orientation, are frequently over-romanticised and essentially function as learning grounds for relationship skill-building. However, for homosexual clients who are chronologically older than is usual for this task, first relationships can often take on an intensity and optimism that is unrelated to the reality of the two people involved. Also such relationships are often entered into before the previous tasks have been completed and consolidated. Frequently the individual attempts to use the relationship as a protection against dealing with a still delicate self concept. A further factor here is the lack of homosexual role models or cultural support offered. When such a relationship ends there is the possibility that it will not be used as a learning experience but that the ending is bitter or traumatic. Such a situation can lead to depression, recreational drug abuse and, particularly for gay men, the use of casual sex to feel guilty and reinforce negative beliefs about homosexuality. In this way, then, the individual may return to the previous developmental phase and become stuck in it.

Psychotherapeutic considerations

The psychotherapist needs to help the client think through the expectations made of the relationship and explore internalised homophobia which often is given expression in very subtle forms. When such a relationship ends the psychotherapist needs to encourage the client to appreciate what they have learned and to encourage the ending in as healthy a way as possible.

5 Integration

Cass (1979) refers to individuals at this stage as having moved from 'identity confusion' through 'identity comparison, tolerance, acceptance, and pride, to identity synthesis'.

Here, then, is the task of fully 'choosing' to be gay in an existential sense. Being gay at this stage becomes at one and the same time central to the individual's identity and paradoxically totally irrelevant. Against such a background the individual is then free to negotiate the tasks of the various stages of adult life that we all face irrespective of our sexual orientation.

During this stage, which is essentially an ongoing process of growth, the client is likely to be involved with choosing a lifestyle that fits with their own temperament and with the phase they are in, in their life journey. Frequently, clients will put some energy into the creation of 'families' of their own making and choice, which may or may not include their biological family. For some gay clients this may involve lifestyles that are not modelled on the heterosexual norms and might involve more than one ongoing committed relationship, none at all or an exploration of the variety of relationships that are possible.

Psychotherapeutic considerations

This is essentially the phase of existential psychotherapy when homosexual clients, who are less likely to be distracted by the prescribed meanings offered by the majority heterosexual culture, engage with the existential task of choosing a meaning for their lives. Typically this is an issue that comes to the fore in the forties and fifties, and can be all the more clearly highlighted as a result of living a life that does not conform to the usual traditions.

Discussion of stages

In outlining the above stages together with the associated psychotherapeutic considerations, the reader may well have questioned whether counselling/ psychotherapy is necessary to move through this process of coming out. Clearly the majority of homosexual people do negotiate these stages using the support of other homosexual friends as guides. What factors would seem to suggest that psychotherapeutic help should be sought? Hanley-Hackenbruck (1989) suggests five particular indicators:

1 The family environment was particularly rigid, especially if there was a religious emphasis.
2 The person experienced negative experiences relating to sex-role behaviour or body type.
3 Having experienced anti-homosexual prejudice.
4 There is serious underlying pathology.
5 Sexual abuse, especially same-sex, was experienced as a child or as an adolescent.

However, whilst such indicators are valuable to the clinician, it is also likely that an individual attempting to negotiate these stages does experience some stuck points in the process for which counselling/psychotherapeutic help would not be invaluable.

DIFFERENTIAL DIAGNOSES AND THE COMING OUT PROCESS

Each client negotiates the coming out process against their own particular psychological make-up. The complexity of the interaction between possible underlying pathology and that of the stress of the coming out process is one that every clinician needs to be aware of. This issue has been discussed succinctly by Gonsoriek, who states,

> There are a number of clinical conditions in which individuals at times manifest homosexual behaviour or concerns, and the client may therefore appear to be coming out or having a sexual identity crisis when, in reality, these behaviours or concerns are part of a serious pathology. On the other hand the coming out process in itself can produce in some individuals considerable psychiatric symptomatology reminiscent of serious underlying psychopathology; but, in fact, such pathology does not exist and the individual is having a particularly difficult time coming to terms with his or her sexuality. Finally, the coming out process may serve as a precipitating event for some individuals who do have severe underlying problems; that is, both may be present.
>
> (1985: 100)

In particular, here the clinician needs to be cautious in ascribing to the homosexual individual diagnoses of which paranoia is a prominent part. To have lived in a society with a strong anti-homosexual prejudice, to pass as straight and to have managed to make contact with other homosexuals often without the benefit of homosexual meeting places has required that the person develop a powerful sensitivity or heightened awareness. This at times may manifest in what appears to be paranoid thoughts and behaviour. In addition, given the real nature of prejudice that continues to exist, sometimes hiding behind liberal façades, some paranoia, if held in awareness, is healthy and adaptive.

THE IMPACT OF AIDS

Working with gay men, it is inevitable that the subject of AIDS will come up. If not worried about themselves, most gay men will have known other men who have died of AIDS or men who currently have AIDS or who are HIV positive. Eventually, fears and anxieties about AIDS are highly likely to emerge. The psychotherapist will often be asked to help the client decide whether or not to test for HIV. The question then arises as to whether the individual is better off not knowing his HIV status, or knowing and making life decisions accordingly. A frequent fear is that the client will not be able to cope if it turns out they are HIV positive. If there is a partner involved, this agonising decision becomes twice as difficult. Should they both test? What if one is HIV positive and the other HIV negative? Sometimes the decision to test is based on the premise that 'I'm so scared and worried now, that it could not be worse'.

Psychotherapists working with a large number of gay men are likely to have clients who are HIV positive or who have AIDS. The task for the psychotherapist and client is to work through the issues around illness and death, so that the client can get on with his life. Frequently, a client with HIV or AIDS will exhibit the stages of mourning set out by Kübler-Ross (1969). At first, there is often a massive denial. Then the client will go into the angry or bargaining phase. If the psychotherapist has been successful, eventually the client will move into the acceptance phase, although regression to earlier phases is frequently seen. In working with these issues, the work of the existential psychotherapists can be very helpful (Yalom 1975).

Together with the subject of AIDS goes the issue of safer sex. A psychotherapist working with gay men may be asked for specific information about safe sex practices, and should be well informed on the subject. The thorny question then arises about what to do in relation to a client who tells you that he is practising unsafe sex? The issue is similar to other kinds of destructive and self-destructive behaviour such as driving whilst intoxicated. During the period when psychotherapist and client are exploring the dynamics and aetiology of such other and self-destructive behaviour, it is often possible to use the power of the therapeutic alliance to contract with the client to cease this harmful behaviour. If the client refuses, the psychotherapist has the option of refusing to work with the individual.

Within this area it is obviously important that the psychotherapist validates the tragedy that this disease has brought, through bereavement work, and also is aware of the existential issues that are in terms of life stages prematurely brought to the fore. The psychotherapist needs also to validate the way in which the gay community has also transformed the experience of this tragedy to build a community based on genuine intimacy.

SUMMARY

Gay and lesbian clients deserve to work with psychotherapists who have resolved to as great extent as they can their own homophobia so that gay and lesbian affirmative models of psychotherapy can be most effectively utilised. The lives of homosexual clients, in having the courage to break with social norms and create healthy lifestyles and communities for themselves, offer us all the encouragement that oppressive social norms can be changed.

ACKNOWLEDGEMENTS

The author wishes to acknowledge the help of Nina Miller for suggestions and corrections, in the context of a lesbian perspective, to the initial drafts of this chapter.

REFERENCES

Bell, A. and Weinberg, M. (1978) *Homosexualities: A Study of Diversity Among Men and Women*, New York: Simon & Schuster.

Beutler, L. E., Crago, M. and Arizmendi, T. G. (1986) 'Research on therapist variables in psychotherapy', pp. 257–310 in S. L. Garfield and A. E. Bergin (eds) *Handbook of Psychotherapy and Behaviour Change*, New York: Wiley.

Beutler, L. E., Pollack, S. and Jobe, A. M. (1978) '"Acceptance" values and therapeutic change', *Journal of Consulting and Clinical Psychology* 46: 198–9.

Cass, V. C. (1979) 'Homosexual identity formation: a theoretical model', *Journal of Homosexuality* 4: 219–35.

Cohen, C. and Stein, T. (1986) 'Reconceptualising individual psychotherapy with gay men and lesbians', *Psychotherapy with Lesbians and Gay Men*, New York: Plenum.

Coleman, E. (1978) 'Towards a new treatment model of homosexuality: a review', *Journal of Homosexuality* 3(4): 345–59.

—— (1985) 'Developmental stages of the coming out process', pp. 31–43 in J. C. Gonsoriek (ed.) *A Guide to Psychotherapy with Gay and Lesbian Clients*, New York/London: Harrington Park (first published 1982).

Conlin, D. and Smith, J. (1985) 'Group psychotherapy for gay men', pp. 105–12 in J. C. Gonsoriek (ed.) *A Guide to Psychotherapy with Gay and Lesbian Clients*, New York/London: Harrington Park (first published 1982).

Dank, B. M. (1971) 'Coming out in the gay world', *Psychiatry* 34: 180–97.

Erikson, E. (1946) 'Ego development and historical change', *The Psychoanalytic Study of the Child* 2: 356–9.

Gonsoriek, J. C. (1977) 'Psychological adjustment and homosexuality', *JSAS Catalogue of Selected Documents in Psychology* 7(45): MS no. 1478.

—— (ed.) (1985) 'Introduction to mental health issues and homosexuality', pp. 18–22 in *A Guide to Psychotherapy with Gay and Lesbian Clients*, New York/London: Harrington Park (first published 1982).

Grace, J. (1979) 'Coming out alive', Paper presented at the Sixth Biennial Professional Symposium of the National Association of Social Workers, San Antonio, quoted by E. Coleman in J. C. Gonsoriek (ed.) (1985) *A Guide to*

Psychotherapy with Gay and Lesbian Clients, New York/London: Harrington Park (first published 1982).

Hanley-Hackenbruck, P. (1989) 'Psychotherapy and the "Coming out process"', *Journal of Gay and Lesbian Psychotherapy* 1: 1.

Hart, J. (1984) *So You Think You're Attracted to the Same Sex?* Harmondsworth: Penguin.

Hart, L. E. (1981) 'An investigation of male therapists' views of women on the process and outcome of therapy with women', *Dissertation Abstracts International* 42: 2529B.

Henken, J. D. and O'Dowd, W. T. (1977) 'Coming out as an aspect of identity formation', *Gai Saber*: 18–22.

Kinsey, A., Pomeroy, W. and Martin, C. (1948) *Sexual Behaviour in the Human Male*, Philadelphia: Saunders.

Kübler-Ross, E. (1969) *On Death and Dying*, New York: Macmillan.

Lee, J. D. (1977) 'Going public: a study in the sociology of homosexual liberation', *Journal of Homosexuality* 7(2/3): 59–70.

Malyon, A. K. (1985) 'Psychotherapeutic implications of internalised homophobia in gay men', pp. 59–69 in J. C. Gonsoriek (ed.) *A Guide to Psychotherapy with Gay and Lesbian Clients*, New York/London: Harrington Park (first published 1982).

Rochlin, M. (1982) 'Sexual orientation of the therapist and therapeutic effectiveness with gay clients', pp. 21–9 in J. C. Gonsoriek (ed.) *A Guide to Psychotherapy with Gay and Lesbian Clients*, New York: Hawarth Press.

Roden, R. G. (1983) 'Threatening homosexuality: a case study treated by hypnosis', *Medical Hypnoanalysis* 4: 166–9.

Schmidt, G. and Schorsch, E. (1981) 'Psychosurgery of sexually deviant patients', *Archives of Sexual Behaviour* 10: 301–21.

Sketchley, J. (1989) 'Counselling and sexual orientation', pp. 237–51 in W. Dryden, D. Charles-Edwards and R. Woolfe (eds) *Handbook of Counselling in Britain*, London: Tavistock/Routledge.

Symposium on Homosexuality and the Ethics of Behavioural Intervention (1977) *Journal of Homosexuality* 2(3): 195–259.

Yalom, I. D. (1975) *The Theory and Practice of Group Psychotherapy*, New York: Basic Books.

FURTHER READING

Kitzinger, C. (1987) *The Social Construction of Lesbianism*, London: Sage.

—— (1992) 'The regulation of lesbian identities: liberal humanism as an ideology of social control', pp. 82–98 in J. Shotter and K. J. Gergen (eds) *Texts of Identity*, London: Sage.

Part III

Modalities

Chapter 8

Individual adult psychotherapy

Christine Lister-Ford and Michael Pokorny

Although psychotherapy with individuals is commonly thought to have begun with Breuer and Freud (1893/1955) in Vienna around the turn of the century, and group psychotherapy with Moreno (1972), the problem of the meaning of life and human existence is as old as mankind itself. Forms of what we might now call psychotherapy have been in existence far longer than 100 years. Freud started with the analysis of hysteria, and with Breuer he gave meaning to the symptoms. At last the enigma of psychological symptoms had been solved by finding an interpretation of the hidden meaning to questions that had eluded thinkers for centuries. This was the great achievement from which the entire psychodynamic movement began, and which formed the basis of many of the psychotherapy methods that are in use today. Learning theory originated from different roots in the study of observed behaviour. As long ago as 1693 Locke was recommending a form of graduated exposure to the feared situation as a method of treatment. Interestingly, the development of all forms of psychotherapy is essentially a phenomenon of the twentieth century.

Even as the discovery of the known or unconscious mind was being made known to the world, Moreno (1965) was starting to work with children in the park, then later with prostitutes. Thus alongside the beginnings of individual adult psychotherapy, a start was being made on group psychotherapy with children and with other specific client groupings. Both these developments are now very widely practised from a variety of orientations. In this sense Moreno is also the ideological father (see Chapter 2) of all subsequent humanistic/existential approaches where group psychotherapy has always flourished alongside individual psychotherapy; including psychodrama, of which Moreno was the founder (1972).

We shall discuss the rationale and indications for individual psychotherapy as well as giving an idea of the range of psychotherapies that are available. A more detailed view of definitions and the nature and range of psychotherapy is available in Chapter 1 of this *Handbook*.

Why would an adult in our society choose to go for help to a psychotherapist? Socially and culturally, our society has evolved in such a way that we expect to go to a 'specialist' with our problems. When we are experiencing emotional difficulties, be they internal or in our interpersonal communications, or both, we can use the option of consulting someone who specialises in treating emotional problems. In the past this has been the role of the priest or the doctor, who offered reparative emotional relationships. Many people still consult their priest or their doctor as their specialist or first choice, as shown in the *Report of the Psychotherapy Working Party* (1989) of the South Tees District Health Authority. Today spiritual, medical and emotional help have evolved into separate specialisms, with the psychotherapist being trained as our modern-day emotional healer, offering a culturally congruent response to the emotional watersheds that daily life inevitably brings.

In general terms, a psychotherapist will help the client to face and work through emotional problems. Usually, this involves finding the past personal experiences that have contributed to present-day problems and re-experiencing these, to the point at which they become a phenomenological reality. At the point of impasse, where the old dilemmas and ways of solving them interfere with current needs by preventing an appropriate response to the here-and-now, the psychotherapist helps the client find new options for dealing with the old pain. Freed from the tyranny of his personal past, an individual is able to respond differently to present circumstances. Psychotherapeutic effectiveness depends upon the client having built a strong trusting relationship with the psychotherapist, such that the new choices uncovered during the psychotherapy can be accepted as more viable options than the old choices. Old relationship patterns which encouraged and supported these historical choices can be relinquished in favour of new ones discovered through the therapeutic relationship.

Individual psychotherapy offers the client the experience of an intense concentration by another human being on concerns of importance to him. He and he alone is the focus of interest and attention for at least fifty minutes every week. For most people this is an extremely rare, and therefore precious, opportunity. The need to be listened to with unswerving attention, for another actively and committedly to seek to enter into and understand life from 'my' perspective, to offer explanations and assist with the formulation of new choices, is something most of us crave at times of tension and difficulty in our lives. It is precisely to this that the psychotherapist commits herself.

With his psychotherapist as companion to the journey of self-discovery, the client, like the hero of yore, restructures both his internal psychological make-up and his relationship patterns to claim the holy grail of the full restoration of himself to himself.

TYPES OF ADULT INDIVIDUAL PSYCHOTHERAPY

It is extremely difficult to be specific about types of psychotherapy and remain brief. The United Kingdom Council for Psychotherapy has eight sections; each is meant to represent a different kind of psychotherapy, yet some clearly represent a client group, such as children or marriages. Others represent particular problems such as sexual problems, whilst the two largest sections contain quite a wide variety. So these sections will not serve as a working model for our purpose. If we turn to the *Handbook of Individual Psychotherapy* (Dryden 1990), we find eleven psychotherapies listed, although three of these are essentially psychodynamic in their foundation. Holmes and Lindley (1989) refer to the existence of over 300 types of psychotherapy. In this chapter we shall confine ourselves to a broad general classification (see also Chapter 2 of this book). The major schools we are able to identify are: psychodynamic, humanistic, integrative, behavioural, cognitive and experiential constructivist. Within these major schools there are great variations. Broadly speaking, the psychodynamic school is based on the idea of the dynamic unconscious, and there are very many derivatives of this school in existence. The best-known are those of Jung, Reich, Adler, Sullivan and Horney. The list could be very long. It is a moot point whether to include Klein with Freud or to list her work separately, as Dryden (1990) does. As well as individual adult work, this school has spread into child, group, organisational, marital and self-help modalities.

The basic root of the psychodynamic psychotherapies is the idea of psychic determinism, which is that all behaviour and thinking are influenced by our unconscious mind, which Breuer and Freud (1895/1955) originally called the 'Unbewusst' (literally translated as 'unknown'). That is not to say that the unconscious rules us, but that its influence will be greater in some ways than others. Fathoming out which is which is the essence of psychoanalytically based psychotherapy. This is done through the elucidation of the transference in the interaction between the psychotherapist and the client. By interpreting the underlying unconscious activity, the psychotherapist helps the client to understand and to feel the force of the way that the client's personal past is intruding into present-day reality. Any of the manifestations of the activities of the unconscious may be used in this process, from dreams to the common observation that actions speak louder than words. When Freud first came upon the fact of unconscious resistance he saw it as an obstacle to analysis. Soon, however, he became aware that the resistance was actually a feature of unconscious activity which repeats patterns of behaviour dressed up in modern clothing as a way of maintaining the repressions of the past. Thus Freud became aware that what the unconscious does is to produce in disguise what is hidden. So the elucidation of the new edition of the past became the central activity of the psychoanalyst. This is described as the analysis of the transference, meaning that the new edition appears as a version of the relationship to the psychoanalyst, and analysis of that new relationship uncovers the dynamic past in a meaningful way so that new reality-testing may take place. What may have been appropriate at an early age can be re-examined to see if it is still the best way of coping. Equally, emotions that could not be coped with when young may be reworked differently when the client is adult. Very often the reworking has to be done several times over because of the way that human beings use their existing defences as they progress through life. Any new situation will be dealt with by the defences that already exist. When these defences come under scrutiny, it is usual for some items to be taken over by other defences that already exist.

When in turn these defences are analysed, yet another way of dealing with all the items under their protection must be found. Far from being just a nuisance, the defence mechanisms serve an essential function, that of preventing the primary process of the unconscious from invading the conscious part of the mind. The unconscious parts of the mind work on what is called the pleasure principle. This means that gratification must be sought at once, that the passage of time is not appreciated, that opposites exist together without clashing and that a thing and its symbol are treated as the same. These features of the unconscious mean that repetition in the present can occur and that substitute gratifications can be just as satisfying as the original version. By contrast, the conscious mind works on the reality principle and has to manage conflict and ambivalence, and learn to wait for gratifications. The theory of the defence mechanisms is that they maintain the division of the mind into reality, or secondary process, on the one hand, and the pleasure principle or primary process on the other. When the defences break down the conscious mind is invaded by the fragmentary elements of the primary process which gives rise to phenomena that we regard as psychotic, such as delusions and hallucinations. The developing child utilises those defences that are available to it. As it grows and its defensive capacity expands, new experiences can be managed better and some old ones can be reworked with new techniques. Much of the upheaval of adolescence can be accounted for by the need to rework the past relationship to the parents in the light of the new situation of puberty. The Oedipus complex has to undergo a re-edition in the presence of physical sexual maturity, which was not the situation in the original version (Laufer and Laufer 1984). Thus, in the analysis of the personal history there has to be some repeat of this pattern of reworking, done retrospectively.

It is this need to re-edit several times that largely accounts for the long-windedness of psychoanalytic psychotherapy. Once the analysis of the transference became the central activity of the psychoanalyst, it was only a matter of time before analysts became aware that they also had unconscious reactions to the unconscious communications of their clients. Many of these reactions in the psychoanalyst become manifest through feelings that are derived from the unconscious response of the psychoanalyst. Learning to read their own unconscious responses became recognised as a reliable route to understanding the transference, and indeed eventually came to be seen as an excellent way to understand very obscure or very silent clients. Thus the capacity to understand became enlarged and gradually ceased to be dependent upon the client's being very articulate. Thus it has become possible to apply psychoanalytic understanding to an ever-increasing range of clients. Today it is commonplace for psycho-analytic psychotherapists to have clients who are deeply disturbed in all their relationships, who may have suffered severe deficit in their upbringing, leading to impairment of the capacity for relatedness in all directions. The actual severity of the pathology that is the usual psychoanalytic caseload has increased enormously over the years. As this process has gone on, less severe problems have been treated by shorter methods or group methods. This phenomenon of the shift in the content of the caseload is only a reflection of the shift that has also gone on in the severity of illness treated in hospital these days compared to thirty or forty years ago. It is the inevitable accompaniment to any increase in knowledge and skills.

Naturally, as knowledge of the transference and counter-transference increased, ways of shortening the period of treatment were sought. Psychotherapy based in psychoanalytic theory grew and in many senses reached its apogee in the use of knowledge of how the transference is formed to conduct short-term psychotherapy. If the theory is basically sound, then the deductions made from it should bring results. One can test psychodynamic theory by using it to predict the response to specific interpretations. However, it is also true that only some selected cases are suitable for brief psychotherapy, although the indications for this method are also widening.

An example of brief focal psychotherapy in practice is the story of the angry executive, which has been published in full (Pokorny 1984). An executive sought help because of frequent loss of temper to a serious degree, which was invading every area of his life. The diagnosis was displacement of affect with some reaction formation. His family had moved house twice early in his life and the rages had begun after the second move, and had worsened since that time whenever he had moved house. Thus the starting hypothesis was of loss at the first move which could not be coped with at the time and re-emerged at the second move as a symptom of displaced affect (in this case, rage). The question was: whom had he lost at the first move, why was nothing done about it at the time, and why had nothing been done till now? When the client reported that he had a recurrent nightmare starting after the second move of house in which he was trapped in a corner about to be crushed by a huge ball, the psychotherapist took the bull by the horns and interpreted the dream as representing his fear of being crushed by his feelings of grief and rage because he had lost someone important in the first house move. The response to this interpretation was dramatic, both in terms of the client's feelings and history. In a state of great emotional upheaval he began to pour out a story that he had 'forgotten' which not only explained a lot of his behaviour over the years, but also his present predicament. The outcome was that his relationships improved all round. His children and wife were no longer afraid of him and at work he coped more easily as well as more effectively. Finally, he moved house with his family with no hint of a recurrence in his symptoms.

One of the salient features of the treatment was the anger that the executive felt towards the psychotherapist during much of the treatment. He rationalised this as his distress that a stranger could so quickly understand and give expression to problems with which his own family had been unable to cope. However, it was in his anger with the psychotherapist that his displaced rage towards his parents first made its appearance. On several occasions the treatment almost broke down because of an unconscious pressure to re-enact the anger in the present, rather than understand its roots and origins.

The question of how such treatment works is of central importance. At first Freud thought that to repeat the experience by connecting the feelings with the fantasy brought about an abreaction which undid the repression. At that time the term 'repression' was used as a word for making something unconscious. Later, a variety of defence mechanisms were described, for instance by Anna Freud (1936/1966). Subsequently it was realised that simple abreaction was only reliable for very recent traumatic experiences and that the workings of the human mind are more complex. The discovery of the extent to which we are the author of our own misfortunes was enshrined in the theory of the repetition compulsion (S. Freud 1920/1961). This states that all human beings tend to stick with learned patterns of expectations and behaviour. It is in reality very difficult to get people to give up the habits of a lifetime, even when those habits are causing them frustration or harm. The determined clinging to old ways is another reason why psychoanalysis takes a long time and never has a perfect result. There is always something that a person will absolutely refuse to give up from their own personal past. It is also very hard to restructure the mind in the new ways that become available through an understanding of the past and its influence in the present. At least there is a comforting side to these difficulties. Many people seem to be afraid that psychoanalysis and its derivatives can unduly persuade people to change their beliefs. This is far from true. People may be fairly gullible over things that they wish to believe, but they are generally fairly obstinate about those things they regard or feel to be inconvenient to their outlook on life. To persuade someone into something that they would in any case be likely to favour is no achievement at all. To help someone see themselves in an entirely new light is very difficult indeed. The influence of the psychotherapist is thus very profound and very limited.

Humanistic and existential schools

Humanistic and existential schools have developed in many different ways from a rich variety of sources, including philosophy (Spinelli 1989). For an excellent account of existential counselling in practice, see van Deurzen-Smith 1988). Moreno (1965; 1972), initially working in Vienna and later in the United States, is widely recognised as one of the earliest, if not the first, exponent of the humanistic/existential school. Moreno gives 1921 as the date from which psychodrama may be considered a specific and discrete form of psychotherapy.

From his observations of and work with children and later with adults, Moreno came to recognise how enactment can provide a creative and spontaneous release of tension for an individual, known for the purposes of the enactment as the 'protagonist'. When this enactment is therapeutically directed by a competent psychotherapist, the protagonist can be helped to personal insights which facilitate the resolution of internal and interpersonal conflicts.

Enactment offers the client a satisfying vehicle for re-experiencing past moments that goes beyond merely recalling or recounting. The protagonist is able to relive moments from his own life, knowing them in their full emotional, physical and cognitive richness. The catharsis that comes from such phenomenological experience leads to release from old traumas and an increased openness to responding spontaneously and creatively to one's own living.

Philosophically, Moreno believed that enacting one's 'immortal primordial nature' (1946: 3) offers catharsis to a degree which releases the individual from the kind of self-constraint that is not merely necessary personal and social containment, but an unhelpful form of self-imprisonment. The therapeutic dialogue is opened up and enacted as part of the process of the psychotherapy, interpretation by the psychotherapist diminishes and the client creates new self-definitions.

Transactional Analysis

Transactional Analysis developed and grew from Berne's (1961/1980) interest in his patients' phenomenological experience of their personal past. Qualified as a psychiatrist, and having himself been in analysis with the ego psychologist Federn and later Erikson, Berne was well aware of the current trends in psychiatric and analytic thinking and practice. He integrated his knowledge in these areas with neurosurgeon Penfield's discoveries that during certain neurosurgical procedures people re-experience past situations with full emotional intensity. Berne created a tripartite system of the person, his ego state model (see Figure 8.1).

Emphasising that ego states are phenomenological realities and not

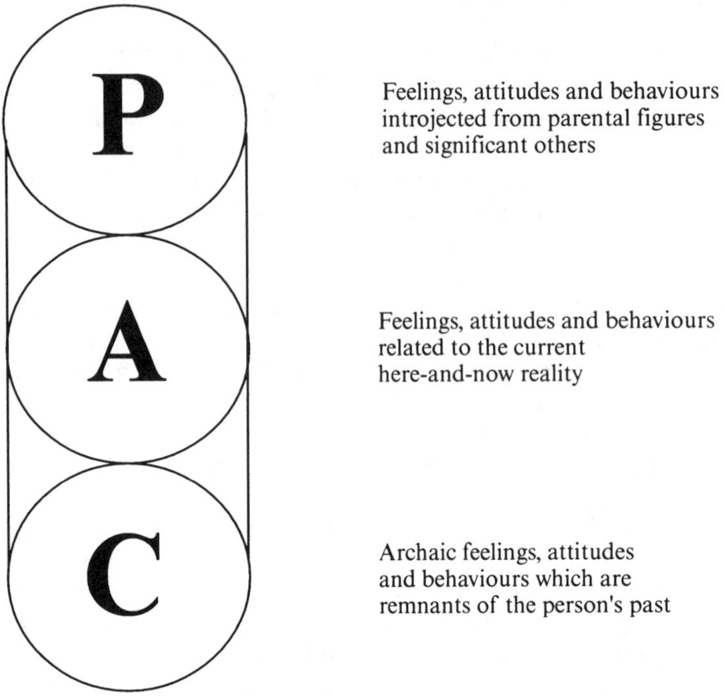

Feelings, attitudes and behaviours
introjected from parental figures
and significant others

Feelings, attitudes and behaviours
related to the current
here-and-now reality

Archaic feelings, attitudes
and behaviours which are
remnants of the person's past

Figure 8.1 Berne's original ego-state model (reproduced with permission from Berne 1964/1985)

merely abstract concepts, Berne writes: 'Parent, Adult and Child represent real people who now exist, or who once existed, who have legal names and civic identities' (1961/1980: 32).

Using the ego state model, a client can be helped phenomenologically to re-experience aspects of himself that are contributing to his immediate personal difficulties. By gaining insight into his inner world and the influences that are affecting and distorting his perceptions, relationships and behaviour, he is able to highlight sources of internal conflict. Once these conflicts are identified, a working-through process can commence.

One approach that can be useful in facilitating phenomenological awareness is the ego state dialogue. Three chairs are used, one to represent each ego state, and the client verbalises in a dialogue the internal conflicts which are contributing to his difficulties and the differing ego states within himself which generate these conflicts. The client moves between chairs as he speaks from each ego state. Normally, of course, he would contain this dialogue within his private world, but with the psychotherapist as guide he is able to externalise this, seeing and hearing himself in new ways.

Garth sought help for his lack of self-confidence which he saw as the source of his inability to achieve promotion successfully at work. It was clear from the way in which Garth spoke about himself that his difficulties arose from the harsh self-criticisms he made in his Parent ego state and the resulting despair and loss of self-esteem experienced in his Child ego state. Through a process of ego state dialogue Garth was able to experience the power of this internal dynamic. Protected and supported by the skill and care of his psychotherapist, he wept freely from his Child ego state, expressing his pent-up pain and despair. Garth was able to free himself from some of the effects of his internal tyranny. In the weeks that followed, he experienced a new sense of self-worth and, supported by further psychotherapeutic work, he eventually successfully secured the promotion he sought.

Philosophically, Berne stressed the importance of mutual respect between people which is expressed in his shorthand phrase, 'I'm OK – You're OK'. He translated this into practice in a number of ways. First, whatever occurs in the therapeutic relationship must be by explicit agreement between client and psychotherapist; contracting is, therefore, given high focus as a vital part of the psychotherapy. Contracts are open to review, renewal and change. Secondly, as a matter of professional practice, Berne taught that the only comments worth making about a client are those that the psychotherapist could make face to face to him. Anything else is immaterial. Thirdly, clients are encouraged to discover as much about the process and theoretical bases of the psychotherapy as is of interest to them. For example, those who wish may choose to attend a short introductory course in Transactional Analysis that offers opportunities for didactic and experiential understanding of the major aspects of the model.

Using the concept of Freud's repetition compulsion as his starting point, Berne emphasised the predictability of behaviour. This has become a major philosophical precept of Transactional Analysis. In practice this principle underpins the theory of psychological games which Berne defines in his book *Games People Play* as follows: 'A Game is an ongoing series of complementary ulterior transactions progressing to a well-defined, predictable outcome' (1964/1985: 44); in other words, engaging with others in predictable patterns of communicating whereby, without initially realising it, we either issue or respond to an unspoken message that is, nevertheless, fully apparent through voice tone, facial expression, physical posture or some other meta-communication. This leads to a familiar, unpleasant outcome, because we are involved in a psychological game. The long-term outcome of such patterns of transacting is to confirm and complete our script outcome; that is, to ensure that the life dramas, the scripts we have decided upon for ourselves, are played out to the last scene. The goal of TA psychotherapy is to help the client prevent these outcomes and recover his full capacity for spontaneity, intimacy and awareness.

The third major philosophical principle is that emotional problems can be resolved and changes made where the right approach and adequate knowledge are available. Berne writes of three major forces within the human psyche: Eros – the power of sexual drives; Mortido – the drive to self-harm; and Physis – the urge to transformation. The TA psychotherapist works with the client to help him harness his own Physis in the service of the metamorphosis. Physis has been defined by Clarkson as 'nature . . . coming from the deepest biological roots of the human being and striving towards its greatest realisation' (1992: 15).

Gestalt psychotherapy

Perls, the father of Gestalt psychotherapy, shared with Berne and Moreno a belief in the innate instinctual drive to health of the human being. He described this as organismic flow. He writes:

> The view here taken of the human organism is that it is *active*, not *passive*. For instance, inhibition of certain behaviors is not merely absence of these behaviors . . . [it is] an active holding in. If the inhibition is lifted, what was held in does not then passively emerge. Rather, the person actively, eagerly brings it forth.
>
> (in Perls *et al.* 1951/1989: 22)

Perls conceived of neurosis as a growth disorder. One's natural organismic flow is interrupted and the cycle of experience, which begins at the moment of sensing, is artificially arrested before it can reach completion or satisfaction. The natural drive to growth and satisfaction becomes stunted. Such interruptions lead to the unfinished business of an incomplete Gestalt (a German word with no exact English translation, meaning 'whole'). The individual holds and stores these incomplete fragments inside. The tension of holding what is incomplete is in direct opposition to the flow to healthy completion. This tension manifests through several dysfunctional ways of being which are known as interruptions to contact. Perls (in Perls *et al.* 1951/1989) makes reference to five interruptions; later Gestalt practitioners have added others. It is not our intention to discuss these in detail, but rather to give the reader a sense of Perls's understanding.

Desensitisation, numbing oneself to stimuli that are painful or evoke great fear, is a common method of interrupting contact with others and the environment. This interruption is found frequently in adults who as young children were subjected to persistent physical or sexual abuse. Clients report having used a variety of strategies to achieve desensitisation: 'By imagining myself sailing on a pink cloud I could pretend I was far away'; 'I would count backwards from one hundred, over and over until he had stopped'. As adults these individuals experienced difficulty in making full pleasurable contact during times of intimacy, usually desensitising instead, and were haunted by unexpressed pain and terror – their unfinished business. They needed to release this and make full resolution of their trauma before meaningful intimacy was possible in their current relationships.

Other interruptions include introjection – swallowing whole another's feelings or attitude – such as 'Never rest until your work is done'. Projection means imbuing the environment with a disowned aspect of the self. A client starts the session by saying to the psychotherapist, 'You look angry today', when in fact it is she who is experiencing unacknowledged anger towards the psychotherapist. Retroflection is the holding back of energy that is about to be expressed. A female client who had been brought up to hide her feelings was involved in a road accident in which another driver received serious injuries. Instead of expressing her horror she held it in, appearing calm and unmoved to rescue workers. Confluence is where there is neither a sense of boundary between two people, nor an awareness of their differences. Occasionally a client may request psychotherapy, and what emerges during the initial discussion is that the client is there because his partner has sent him. He has not paused to consider whether or not he has a need for psychotherapy.

When our organismic flow is interrupted, physical and emotional problems occur. The Gestalt psychotherapist helps the client to become aware of his interruptions and to restore his natural organismic rhythm.

Claire had returned to full-time education as a mature student. She was excited by the opportunities she saw opening before her. Within two weeks her excitement had turned to anxiety. Every time she entered the building where most of her lectures were held she felt nauseous. Her symptoms persisted and she began to experience panic attacks. She was concerned that she might not be able to enjoy her learning or fulfil her academic potential. Assisted by a friend, she referred herself to a Gestalt psychotherapist. What Claire discovered surprised her. Without her having been aware of it, Claire's senses had been restimulated by a combination of the smell of furniture polish used in the building and the high Victorian windows of the lecture hall. These were similar to those of the boarding school she had attended as a child of seven. Claire had loathed boarding school, feeling abandoned by her parents and homesick for familiar surroundings and routines. Here was her unfinished business, the unresolved grief and pain of her 'banishment'.

Claire's psychotherapist helped her fully to express these long-pent-up feelings. Through this Claire gained a new understanding of her past experiences at boarding school and her current difficulties at university. With her new awareness she was able to enter her university lecture hall free of the shadows of the past.

Philosophically, Gestalt is rooted in both existentialism and phenomenology. Influenced by thinkers like Buber (1937/1987) and Tillich (1973),

Perls placed great emphasis on 'response-ability', his belief in the ability of individuals actively to respond to themselves and their environment. Each of us must take responsibility for our own thoughts, feelings and behaviours, and thereby for our own existence. In the meeting between client and psychotherapist this is initially made explicit and continues to be assumed throughout the psychotherapy as the client is supported to discover and become fully aware of her subjective experience. Buber's influence is further discernible in Perls's model of the therapeutic relationship, which is based on Buber's 'I–Thou' relationship. The two partners to the therapeutic relationship are both present with the full range of their human resources, and the personhood of each is to be respected.

As a final point, it is interesting to note the importance of paradox in Gestalt psychotherapy. Based on the belief that people grow best by becoming more fully who they are already, striving to become the opposite of one's qualities is seen as unproductive and a barrier to growth. A client who wishes to become less timid is encouraged to express her timidity to its full in the therapeutic setting until she can go no further with it, at which point she is likely to be surprised to find herself having shifted her energy into a more outgoing mode.

Overall, the goals of the humanistic/existential psychotherapies can be summarised as assisting the client to learn to express himself at the boundaries of himself; at his heights, depths and breadth; to be fully himself, with all the richness that is implied. The diversity of methodologies within this school used in the service of these aims indicates the complexities and richness of the journeying. There are, of course, many other forms of humanistic psychotherapy which it has not been possible to include.

Integrative psychotherapy

Integrative psychotherapy is a new genre which is now widely accepted in the United States and is gaining a strong foothold in Britain. The integrative school uses those features that are common across the psychotherapies to create a meta-model of the therapeutic relationship. There are a number of these models, which are derived according to the philosophy and working practice of the integrative psychotherapist. Mahrer (1989: 2), using the work of Orlinsky and Howard (1987), identifies six basic components that constitute psychotherapy: a therapeutic contract; intervention strategies; a therapeutic bond; the nature of self-relatedness in client and psychotherapist; assessment of therapeutic realisation; and the interrelationships of these five components.

An integrative approach provides a way of understanding the therapeutic process and intervening with the client that extends beyond the bounds of any of the particular schools. Storr comments, 'research discloses the common factors which lead to a successful outcome in psychotherapy, which, to my mind, is largely independent of the school to which the psychotherapist belongs' (1979: viii). These themes are expanded by Norcross and Goldfried (1992), who offer an up-to-date view of the developments in integrative psychotherapy in their handbook. In Chapter 2, Clarkson's integrative model based on five kinds of therapeutic relationship is more fully discussed. This framework has been quite widely adopted and used in training and research in the group field and in integrative psychotherapy.

Behaviour therapy

Behaviour therapy is well described in detail in Dryden (1990) by Geraldine Sullivan, who goes into its background and historical roots. The actual term was first used by Skinner (1953). Behaviour therapy is based on applying learning theory to the treatment of psychological symptoms in a variety of ways. The main ingredient is the identification of methods of unlearning in which the client can work with the behaviour therapist to correct an unwanted pattern or symptom. There are fairly specific indications for this form of treatment: the problem should be defined in terms of observable behaviour, be current and predictable and have consistently identifiable triggers. Anxiety should be situational as opposed to free-floating, and clearly defined goals should be identified by client and psychotherapist. Lastly, client co-operation is essential. The most notable limitation is the degree of discomfort that the client must endure during the treatment in order to make worthwhile gains. As with all forms of psychotherapy, many clients do not have the will to undergo the required degree of difficulty.

Cognitive therapy

Cognitive therapy started with the observation that, whilst the behavioural school were concerned with external factors and the psychodynamic school with internal unconscious factors, nobody was paying any attention to the value and meaning of the thoughts that clients were aware of having and which they felt were central to their experience of life.

In 1955 Kelly put the emphasis on how people give meaning to their world, and the foundation stone of cognitive therapy was laid. Now there are about seventeen cognitive therapies, of which three are the most influential. These are the rational-emotive therapy of Ellis (1958), the cognitive-behaviour modification of Meichenbaum (1969) and the cognitive therapy of Beck *et al.* (1979). It is the latter, or a derivative, which is probably the most widely used form in Britain. In the cognitive model psychological disturbance is seen as one result of malfunction in the process of evaluating and interpreting the personal experience of the subject. Thus information is processed in a way that is biased, usually negatively biased, so that the experience of the world is distorted by the way the input is processed. This also tends to produce thinking which is more global, more absolute and more judgemental than normal. This primitive thinking leads to what are called 'logical errors', which characterise the thinking in emotional disturbance. Thus the basic assumptions that underlie cognitive therapy are that the person is an active agent who interacts with their own world through interpretations, inference and evaluation of stimuli. The results of these cognitive processes are conceptualised as accessible to consciousness in the form of thoughts and images. Thus each person has the potential to change what goes on in their mind. In other words, both emotions and behaviour are seen as being mediated by cognitive processes that are amenable to change. This is different from behavioural and psychoanalytic theory, the first paying little attention to the internal world, and the second regarding the internal world as all-important, but obscure, except to the professional guide.

So far, cognitive theory has remained focused on emotional disturbance and has not yet tried to offer a general theory of development that includes normal cognitive processes. The indications for cognitive therapy are expanding. So far it has been used in depression, generalised anxiety, panic disorders, eating disorders and hypochondriasis – a fairly large range of emotional problems. Selection is by clinical judgement, as the criteria have not yet been fully worked out. However, as with other forms of psychotherapy, motivation plays a key role in success. The client must be able to engage in the self-help programme, do the homework tasks and accept the underlying beliefs of the theoretical orientation. Clients with personality problems which are expressed as difficulties in relating will bring these difficulties into the therapeutic arena where they will interfere with the treatment. Work is currently being done on this problem area. The choice between individual or group cognitive therapy is under review. Generally, the more severe disturbances tend to be treated individually, but opinion is moving with experience, just as it seems to have moved in the choice between individual or group psychotherapy by the analytic method. Using more than one psychotherapist in a group setting can be helpful both as a training model for the psychotherapist and to help with difficult or stuck situations with clients. There is a developing tendency to use group therapy also as a follow-on from individual, to provide a type of laboratory setting in which to test the newly learned beliefs and behaviours. The method is limited in its application to those who can cope with its demands. People with severe mental disturbance are not suitable, particularly if they suffer from hallucinations or delusions. Severe obsessional behaviour can interfere too much with the homework programme. Depressives who prefer ideas of self-control do better than those who do not. Equally, where the symptoms are vague or generalised, such as global problems in relating, it can prove difficult to find a focus. An excellent account of cognitive therapy is given by Moorey (1990).

Personal construct therapy

Personal construct therapy is another derivative of the original work of Kelly (1955). It postulates that people construe the world according to what are known as personal constructs. If these constructs are rigid then that person will have difficulties in coping with everyday life. Those difficulties will appear in many different forms. One of the distinguishing features of personal construct theory is its emphatic rejection of the medical model. Thus it is in some contrast to the cognitive and behavioural schools, which are rooted in clinical psychology and appear to follow the medical model quite closely. The theoretical framework is expressed in the form of postulates, corollaries and other theoretical constructs. The fundamental postulate states that 'a person's processes are psychologically channelized by the ways in which he anticipates events' (1955). Three of the corollaries which elaborate this postulate are experience, choice and modulation.

The experience corollary states that 'a person's construction system varies as he successively construes the replication of events' (1955). This means that experience is only gained by having had to reconstrue a situation or some aspect of it, in a way that is different from previous constructions.

The choice corollary states that 'a person chooses for himself that alternative in a dichotomized construct through which he anticipates the greater possibility for extension and definition of his system' (1955).

The modulation corollary states that any variation within a construing system 'is limited by the permeability of the constructs within whose range of convenience the variants lie' (1955). New events, or new versions of events, are difficult to construe if many of the person's constructs are not open enough to receive them.

Change is conceptualised as cycles of movement which may, or may not, occur. The cycle of experience is about the process of reconstruing. The whole of psychotherapy is thus thought of in terms of human experience rather than in terms of treatment. Indeed, Kelly himself regarded the whole idea of treatment in relation to psychotherapy as misleading; a view that may well be shared by many psychotherapists of diverse schools.

The personal construct view of psychological problems is that the problem represents being stuck in a particular way of construing experience which keeps it always the same. As the person is seen as a form of motion, enabling the person to get on the move is in itself a goal of psychotherapy.

As everything is seen in terms of construing, there are no limitations of the client in terms of selection for personal construct therapy. The limiting factors are of time and place, and the personal limitations of any particular personal construct psychotherapist. Of course it is recognised that clients who already have the construct that it is possible to change, and that they themselves might change, will have a more favourable prognosis than those who have no such constructs. As in all forms of psychotherapy, the client must be able and willing to do his or her fair share of the hard work that is involved in psychological change. The most widely known tool is the Repertory Grid. There are, of course, many tools used in Personal Construct Therapy. For a clear account and references to the relevant literature, see Fay Fransella's chapter on the subject in Dryden (1990).

Neuro-Linguistic Programming

Neuro-Linguistic Programming began as an attempt to find out what were the factors in psychotherapy that made the difference to the client. It became a whole model of psychotherapy by the process of reframing. This means that any experience can be felt and seen as quite different if the context in which it occurs can be changed. The names that are particularly associated with Neuro-Linguistic Programming are Richard Bandler and John Grinder, and their book *Reframing* (1982) sets out their views very clearly. As a simple example, Bandler and Grinder (1982) describe a woman who spent all her time cleaning her house. The family were nagged remorselessly to take off their shoes, to enter by the back door and, in particular, not to walk on the living-room carpet as it showed dents from their footprints. Outside the house the family got on fine and there was no problem. The woman was asked to visualise her living-room carpet in its most pristine state – no footprints at all. She did so and felt happy. Then she was told that this image meant that none of her loved ones were in the home. She was entirely alone and, as long as the carpet remained perfect, not one of her family were at home with her. This made her unhappy. Then she was asked to imagine that the family had come home – she felt better – and finally that the footprints on the carpet meant that those she loved most in the world were with her. This kind of clinical example raises all the problems of small snapshots. Although in itself quite clear, it leaves us with the problem of what is being compared to what. The woman in this example is clearly not a true sufferer from obsessive compulsive neurosis, because if she were, she would not have been so happy and carefree outside the home. Whether that is a fair critique of the example is not clear, as there is no claim made to treat very severe pathology by Neuro-Linguistic Programming, as far as we know. It would be essential to study the whole matter much more thoroughly to arrive at a clearer understanding and to be able to envisage a set of indications and contra-indications for NLP. The systematisation of the techniques of reframing is currently the central concern for NLP.

It is perhaps a moot point whether personal construct therapy belongs to the cognitive therapies, as one of the variations that have arisen from the work of Kelly. Is it really any more than another version of the use of his work to provide a different framework for changing behaviour? The answer to this question is very complex, and no doubt it would be answered differently according to people's frames of reference. This raises the whole problem of the classification of the psychotherapies, which is not yet entirely satisfactory (see Chapter 1 of this *Handbook*). In this chapter we have followed the usual conventions as they exist today and, hopefully, they will be classified satisfactorily.

INDICATIONS FOR INDIVIDUAL PSYCHOTHERAPY

There are endless contradictions in the area of indications for different modalities of psychotherapy. It is helpful to remember that today's indications can easily become tomorrow's contra-indications.

Norcross and Goldfried suggest that individual psychotherapy is indicated in

> Problems of dyadic intimacy . . . require the development of a relationship with a therapist for some resolution to occur. Patients whose character or symptoms are based on firmly structured intrapsychic conflict, which causes repetitive life patterns that, more or less, transcend the particulars of the current interpersonal situation (e.g., family, job relationships). Adolescents or young people who are striving for autonomy. Symptoms or problems that are of such private and/or embarrassing nature that secrecy of individual treatments is required at least for the beginning phase.
>
> (1992: 466)

They continue by adding that relative contra-indications include patients who meet clear indications for family or marital treatment or patients who regress in individual therapeutic relationships.

This last caveat is something of a puzzle. It is difficult to imagine how problems of dyadic intimacy, their first indication, can be managed in individual psychotherapy without regression. Indeed, in the psychoanalytically based psychotherapies, regression is one of the major elements in the elucidation of the transference. It is possible that Norcross and Goldfried are thinking of uncontrolled regression, and not of regression that is confined to the psychotherapy sessions. Alternatively, what we are seeing is the difficulty inherent in any attempt to arrange a set of indications that are comprehensive enough to cover all forms of psychotherapy. For indications in the area of group psychotherapy, see Chapter 14 of this *Handbook*.

Dryden (1990) follows much the same pattern as Norcross and Goldfried, beginning with a quotation from Ellis, the founder of rational-emotive therapy, in which Ellis says that he usually lets the client pick the treatment modality. Dryden asked a number of psychotherapists to describe what they saw as the indications and advantages of individual psychotherapy as well as the contra-indications and disadvantages. The resulting list shows that the psychotherapists are generally in agreement:

Indications

Providing there is a situation of complete confidentiality it is suitable for clients to disclose 'secret' material. Thus greater openness is possible and the dyadic nature provides more opportunity for a close relationship between client and psychotherapist. It is indicated for more disturbed clients whose lives are chaotic and, where the development and resolution of a transference relationship is deemed curative, it is the treatment of choice. It can proceed at the clients pace, with the full attention of the psychotherapist and free from interruption from other clients. This is specially important for clients who are confused and who are struggling with value dilemmas, as well as those whose constructions of the world are loose and require tightening. It is indicated where the client's major problem is in relation to themselves or where others are not centrally implicated. It may be indicated for clients who wish to differentiate self from others or who have decided to leave a relationship and want to deal with the individual problems that this may involve. Individual sessions also allow the psychotherapist greater freedom to vary their own style of interaction free from concern about how this might affect other clients. In the dyad, a wider range of goals can be set than in other formats, and it is particularly appropriate where a major reconstruction of the self is called for. There are also a number of indications that are essentially negative, such as with clients who are deemed not likely to benefit from any other mode of treatment. The examples given are of clients who would monopolise a group or who would be too withdrawn to participate or are too vulnerable for group or family work. Other indications are extreme anxiety or depression.

Contra-indications for individual psychotherapy

To set against the criteria for individual psychotherapy, Dryden's psycho-therapists offer a list of criteria which they consider as contra-indications: clients who are likely to become too dependent and who are threatened by the intimacy of the close encounter of the dyad. As a group is less likely to be manipulated than an individual, manipulative clients or those diagnosed as 'borderline' are deemed to be better treated in a group. Individual psychotherapy may not be appropriate for those who use intellectualisation as a major defensive form, as well as for those who have a sexual problem that is maintained by their partner's response. Many of Dryden's psychotherapists are agreed that individual psychotherapy is contra-indicated when the client finds it too comfortable. This is based on the idea that change is facilitated by arousal. As a follow-on from this it is also suggested that it may be unhelpful to offer individual psychotherapy to clients who have had a lot of individual work in the past, except where the previous work has been ineffectively conducted.

Discussion of indications

In setting out fairly fully the indications for and against individual psychotherapy from two different textbooks, we hope to illustrate the difficulties in making general statements about which format to recommend in different circumstances. We did not want to give a picture of greater clarity than exists in reality. What we have to deal with is a situation where almost every indication and every contra-indication has a caveat that renders it fairly useless. The need for intimacy and structural change requires individual attention, but dependency can become a contra-indication even though it is an essential component of some psychotherapies. Secrecy is better dealt with in private, but manipulative clients should be offered a group format. Symptoms that are embarrassing or private are better not dealt with in a group, but if a partner is involved, group psychotherapy is indicated.

The problems of this attempt to create indications can be looked at as a secondary problem. The primary problem could be one of diagnosis, or classification (what is known in psychiatry by the Greek derivative, taxonomy). As we do not have a reliable means of identifying and classifying emotional problems, we cannot even begin to make sense of indications. Where we cannot categorise a condition, we are also not able to describe its history. In medicine this exercise is called the 'natural history of the disease', meaning that it is possible to describe the course of an illness if it is untreated. Only then can we say whether a treatment has been effective. Even then we have to be very careful that we do not confuse remission with cure. Quite a lot of work has been done, and is being done, in this area, but it is clear from what we have reported of psychotherapists' views on indications, as reported in the literature, that we still do not know enough about recognising and classifying emotional illnesses to have a comprehensive set of treatment criteria. Perhaps in this context it is more honest to let the client choose, as Ellis (1958) said he did, or to renounce the whole idea of illness and treatment in the context of psychotherapy. Either way does not actually solve anything, but it does provide a reframe that can illuminate the difficulties. Perhaps we should regard every form of psychotherapy as different from every other form. The problem here is that research suggests that no form of psychotherapy is demonstrably better than any other (Holmes and Lindley 1989). If we are to continue to use the term 'psychotherapy' in our title, we must find out more about how to recommend the most appropriate form of psychotherapy, or admit that it makes no difference which form is applied. This last option is probably not a realistic one for psychotherapists to adopt.

AVAILABILITY OF PSYCHOTHERAPY

As most of the psychotherapy in the United Kingdom takes place in the private sector, it is quite difficult to be clear about the availability. There is some provision in the NHS, mainly by psychiatrists and clinical psychologists. Some of the NHS Health Authorities have no, or only one or two, consultant psychotherapists, but although psychotherapy is provided by consultant psychiatrists and their teams it is 'invisible' because it is part of a general provision of services to a particular area. Departments of clinical psychology have offered a variety of psychotherapy services for many years; traditionally these have been mainly of the behavioural and cognitive schools, but by no means exclusively so. In addition, a number of other adjacent professionals have been pursuing psychotherapeutic activities within the NHS; most obviously, of course, in the Child Guidance Clinics within the interdisciplinary teams. Also social workers have at times and in different places become interested and active in providing psychotherapy either directly in relation to their social work activities, or instead of it. Occupational therapists have also developed some interest. For some years there has been a move to train suitably qualified nurses as psychotherapists, as part of their specialist psychiatric training, in the techniques of behaviour therapy, as well as in dynamic psychotherapy. In a recent article, Duggan et al. (1993) describe a clinical audit of behaviour therapy training of nurses from 1978 to 1991 at the Maudsley Hospital.

Reading through the list of the seventy organisations which are members of the United Kingdom Council for Psychotherapy, it is easy to see that the vast majority of psychotherapists are based in or near London. This is gradually changing as psychotherapists continue to spread. There are now groups of psychotherapists in several locations. Once the Register of psychotherapists is published it will be much easier to get an idea of the spread, and it will also be possible to buy, at a very reasonable fee, a list of psychotherapists in any named postal district. The Directory of Training of UKCP gives an overview of the availability of trainings in different locations. However, all of this does not catch those Health Service psychotherapists who are listed under their general professional title, nor does it indicate the whereabouts of those psychotherapists who do not belong to a professional organisation, or whose organisation does not belong to the UKCP. The only way that a comprehensive view of the availability of psychotherapy will be achieved, as well as the modality that is offered, will be the formation of a statutory register. Until then a certain amount of guesswork will be unavoidable.

CONFIDENTIALITY

This is a complex and thorny subject that applies to all forms and modalities of psychotherapy. In theory, confidentiality between client and psychotherapist is absolute. In reality, there are circumstances in which a court can demand that the psychotherapist, like the medical practitioner, must reveal the content of the psychotherapy sessions. This is very rare, and the only recorded instance of this was when a psychoanalyst was subpoenaed to appear in the High Court to give evidence about an alleged former patient. The psychoanalyst attended court and pleaded that it was essential to maintain confidentiality as an essential part of psychoanalysis. It was improbable that the material of sessions would provide the kind of objective evidence that the court was seeking, and that to divulge anything would amount to malpractice. The court accepted this plea. It was as though the practitioner had been treated like a priest with regard to the content of the confessional. The events were reported anonymously in *The Lancet* in 1965.

A new problem about confidentiality arose when the Access to Health Records Act (1990) came into force on 1 November 1991. This Act is an extension of the Data Protection Act and is part of the whole campaign for freedom of information. The first Act was to enable ordinary people to have a legal right of access to records held on a computer. Those rights have now been extended to handwritten records that had escaped the original legislation, so that the same rights now exist to any handwritten as well as computerised or typewritten records. There is an excellent summary in *Which?* magazine (1991).

Clients have the right to see their records from 1 November 1991 onwards if they make a written request. There is a time limit within which the records must be produced and there are some restrictions on who can make the request on behalf of minors. As there are no test cases so far, it is impossible to give definite advice. It is possible that if there are informal notes that do not carry the name of the client and are used only for supervision, that they might escape the Act, but it is not certain. The promoters of the Act take the view that if a client in any form of analytic treatment were to make a written request instead of trying the understand the meaning of the wish to see their notes, then the treatment would have already broken down and access to the records would not have a harmful effect on the psychotherapy (Frankel 1991). Included in the Act is the condition that technical terms must be explained. If the client asks for a change to the record, this must either be agreed to and carried out, or the wish of the client for a specific change must be noted in the record. Whether there will ever be a case that tests the Act remains to be seen. To whom does the Act apply? To professionals who hold records about health in the private sector as well as the NHS, except in Northern Ireland which will be covered by a separate law. Who is recognised as a professional? For practical purposes it boils down to registered professionals. That means psychotherapists will be included once they have a register. Whether this applies equally to a voluntary register as it will to a statutory register is not yet clear, but it is most likely that it will.

CONCLUSION

Psychotherapy for adults in the dyad is common to all schools of psycho-therapy and there is something of a confusion about when to refer to dyadic or group psychotherapy. This confusion spreads right across all the forms of psychotherapy. It could be that the problem of coherent indica-tions is secondary to a problem of definition and classification. Not enough is known about how much and what kind of psychotherapy is available in the United Kingdom, but that will change with the Register of Psycho-therapists launched on 20 May 1993. It is to be hoped that the need for psychotherapy will gain ground and that the provision of services right across the United Kingdom will soon begin to be a reality.

REFERENCES

Access to Health Records Act (1990) London: HMSO.
Anonymous (1965) 'Psychoanalyst subpoenaed', *The Lancet* 16 Oct.: 785–6.
Bandler, R. and Grinder, J. (1982) *Reframing: Neurolinguistic Programming and the Transformation of Meaning*, Moab, UT: Real People Press.
Beck, A. T., Rush, A. J., Shaw, B. E. and Emery, G. (1979) *The Cognitive Therapy of Depression*, New York: Guilford.
Berne, E. (1985) *Games People Play*, Harmondsworth: Penguin (first published 1964).
—— (1980) *Transactional Analysis in Psychotherapy: A Systematic Individual and Social Psychiatry*, London: Souvenir Press (first published 1961).
Breuer, J. and Freud, S. (1955) 'Studies on hysteria', in J. Strachey (ed.) *The Standard Edition of the Complete Psychological Works of Sigmund Freud*, vol. 2, London: Hogarth Press (first published 1895).
Buber, M. (1987) (R. Gregor Smith, trans.) *I and Thou*, Edinburgh: T. & T. Clark (first published 1937).
Clarkson, P. (1992) 'Physis in Transactional Analysis', *ITA News* 33: 14–19. Also published in *Transactional Analysis Journal* 22(4): 202–9.

Deurzen-Smith, E. van (1988) *Existential Counselling in Practice*, London: Sage.

Dryden, W. (ed.) (1990) *Individual Therapy: A Handbook*, Milton Keynes: Open University Press.

Duggan, C., Marks, I. and Richards, D. (1993) 'Health trends', *Journal of the Department of Health* 25(1): 25–30.

Ellis, A. (1958) 'Rational psychotherapy', *Journal of General Psychology* 59: 35–49.

Frankel, M. (1991) Personal communication.

Fransella, F. (1990) 'Personal construct therapy', pp. 127–48 in W. Dryden (ed.) *Individual Therapy: A Handbook*, Milton Keynes: Open University Press.

Freud, A. (1966) *The Ego and the Mechanisms of Defence* (rev. edn.) London: Hogarth and the Institute of Psycho-Analysis (first published 1936).

Freud, S. (1920/1961) *Beyond the Pleasure Principle*, London: Hogarth Press.

—— (1958) 'Remembering, repeating and working through', pp. 145–156 in A. Richards (ed.), J. Strachey (trans.), The Pelican Freud Library, vol. 12, Harmondsworth: Pelican (first published 1915–17).

Holmes, J. and Lindley, R. (1989) *The Values of Psychotherapy*, Oxford: Oxford University Press.

Kelly, G. (1955) *The Psychology of Personal Constructs*, vols 1 and 2, New York: Norton.

Laufer, M. and Laufer, M. E. (1984) *Adolescence and Developmental Breakdown*, New Haven and London: Yale University Press.

Locke, G. (1693) *Some Thoughts Concerning Education*, London: Ward Lock.

Mahrer, A. R. (1989) *The Integration of Psychotherapies: A Guide for Practicing Therapists*, Ottawa: Human Sciences Press.

Meichenbaum, D. H. (1969) 'The effects of instructions and reinforcement on thinking and language behavior of schizophrenics', *Behaviour Research and Therapy* 7: 101–14.

Moorey, S. (1990) 'Cognitive therapy', pp. 226–51 in W. Dryden (ed.) *Individual Therapy: A Handbook*, Milton Keynes: Open University Press.

Moreno, J. L. (1946) *Psychodrama*, vol. 1, New York: Beacon House.

—— (1965) 'Therapeutic vehicles and the concept of surplus reality', *Group Psychotherapy* 18(4): 213.

—— (1972) *Psychodrama*, New York: Boston House.

Norcross, J. C. and Goldfried, M. R. (eds) (1992) *Handbook of Psychotherapy Integration*, New York: Basic Books.

Orlinsky, D. E. and Howard, K. I. (1987) 'A generic model of psychotherapy', *Journal of Integrative and Eclectic Psychotherapy* 6: 6–27.

Perls, F. S., Heffenline, R. F. and Goodman, P. (1989) *Gestalt Therapy: Excitement and Growth in the Human Personality*, New York: Julian Press (first published 1951).

Pokorny, M. R. (1984) 'Brief psychotherapy and the validation of psychodynamic theories', *British Journal of Psychotherapy* 1(1): 68–76.

Skinner, B. F. (1953) *Science and Human Behavior*, New York: Macmillan.

South Tees District Health Authority (1989) *Report of the Psychotherapy Working Party*, South Tees District Health Authority (March).

Spinelli, W. (1989) *The Interpreted World: An Introduction to Phenomenological Psychology*, London: Sage.

Storr, A. (1979) *The Art of Psychotherapy*, London: Secker & Warburg.

Tillich, H. (1973) *From Time to Time*, New York: Stein & Day.

Which? (1991) 'Your right to know', *Which? Magazine* (Oct.), London: Consumers' Association.

A spectrum of psychological therapies for children

Peter Harper

> In childhood, with its rapid development of new modes of function, the therapeutic context of safety permits not only exploration and risks of change but also the emergence of more benign, healthy, adaptive modes at each developmental stage.
>
> (Pine 1985: 34)

This chapter presents an overview of several therapeutic schools, styles and structures used in therapeutic endeavours with children and young people. It highlights the universal and integrating factors of therapeutic frameworks from a meta-perspective. The setting and other contexts of working with children are discussed. Psychological literature is permeated with models of child development, and it is acknowledged that a knowledge of child development is useful in finalising treatment plans. However, developmental perspectives are not a focus in this review.

Common to therapeutic endeavours with children is the facilitation of particular forms of relationship in which the therapist will exhibit behaviours which consistently communicate acceptance, understanding and respect. Specific therapist behaviours will derive from the diagnostic acumen of the therapist, and the theoretical framework underpinning the therapy. However, influenced by a systemic awareness, many current therapeutic endeavours with children now place considerable importance on an assessment of the ecology of the child's life before intervention is planned. Accordingly, a broader range of interventions is made possible. Clarkson and Fish (1988) provided a categorisation of children's difficulties frequently encountered in therapy and summarised the advantages and disadvantages of individual, family and group work with children. In integrating children's difficulties in their model of overlapping subsystems, and in their promotion of an awareness of child, family and societal development and change, therapists working with children and young people are offered a robust model from which treatment choice, prioritisation and sequencing is made possible.

Although therapeutic endeavours with children have their origins in

Freudian analytic psychology, a wide spectrum of therapies from a variety of philosophical roots now prevails. The theoretical boundaries delineated for the purposes of this discussion may appear superficial, incomplete and even contradictory; however, they have been used in an attempt to summarise what is a broad and complex body of literature and knowledge.

THE PSYCHOANALYTIC SCHOOL

Although Freud himself did not work directly with children, his pioneering and classical analysis of 'Little Hans' (1909) exhibited that psychoanalytic concepts could be applied to work with the emotional disturbances of children. In this specific case, Freud directed his work through the father. The therapeutic goal was the reliving, during the therapeutic hour, of the affect associated with repressed experiences. In this process the ego was restored to control, co-ordinate and integrate the impulses which were previously repressed by neurotic defences. For adults in analysis the technique of free association was used to bring these repressed experiences to consciousness. However, the method was not practicable in the case of children undergoing analysis, and changes in technique were necessary.

From observations of children's play, Hug-Hellmuth (1921) noted the expressive quality of play and its potential, when used with verbal comments, to establish effective therapeutic alliances with children. Anna Freud (1946) noted the natural resistance of children to the use of free association, and modified the classical psychoanalytic technique to include the use of play. She used play too as a way of producing a positive emotional attachment to the analyst, and thereby to facilitate the analysis.

Klein (1932) maintained that her efforts extended the psychoanalytic understanding of the individual to early childhood, and thereby to deeper levels of the unconscious. Klein treated her first patient, Fritz, in his home in 1919, and noted the manner in which he used his toys symbolically to represent his experiences, fantasies and anxieties. 'Klein assumed that the child's play activities, including his accompanying verbalisations, were quite as motivationally determined as the free associations of the adult. Hence they could be interpreted to the child, in lieu of interpretations based on adult-style free associations' (Dorfman 1955: 236). In the Kleinian frame, the child is considered able to distinguish between play and reality, and to have the capacity to re-create real world objects and situations in play. Thus it is possible for the child to experiment with mastering life's predicaments using play. Adhering to two core tenets of psychoanalysis (namely, that psychoanalysis is based upon insight and exploration of the unconscious, and that insight is gained by an analysis of the transference relationship), Klein used the play of children as a *via regia* to the unconscious in the same manner that dreams were used by the adult analysts. She commented that 'we soon find that the child brings as many associations to separate elements of its play as do adults to the separate elements of their dreams. These separate play elements are indications to the trained observer; and as it plays, the child talks as well, and says all sorts of things which have the value of genuine associations' (1932: 30).

Klein's child play analyses were largely child-directed, with the analyst providing non-judgemental interpretations which were intended neither to encourage nor suggest courses of action to the child. The child is allowed to experience their fantasies as they occur, and to present them in whatever way they choose: using toys, drawing or dramatisation. The psychotherapist gives clear, succinct psychoanalytic interpretations geared to the child's level of understanding. The past is thereby uncovered, and the ego is strengthened to be better able to cope with the demands of the id and the super-ego.

PSYCHOANALYTIC VARIANTS

Child psychoanalysis in its pure form (in which children were seen in analysis several times a week) was unable to meet the increased public and clinical demand that treatment of childhood psychological disorders be made available to all children presenting with problems. Gradually, psychodynamic psychotherapies and techniques, as variants of child psychoanalysis, began to emerge. Horney, Fromm, Sullivan, Fromm-Reichmann and others began to practise more goal-directed treatments, incorporating into their theories a psychoanalytic understanding of pathology and its development.

For these theorists the primary focus of the child's psychotherapy is the strengthening of ego defences and the amelioration of specific symptoms or problem areas. The child is allowed to exercise free choice in play, and a positive transference relationship is encouraged. The containment offered by the transferential relationship enhances the ventilation of conflicts and the overcoming of resistance. Interpretations are used, but these are delivered with caution, at less depth and less systematically than is the case in classical psychoanalysis. The attainment of insight is seen to be a precursor of therapeutic change with constructive action being in place by the termination of therapy.

Concurrent with individual therapy for the child, the parents may be engaged in psychotherapy. Close attention is paid to contextual/environmental issues and their active modification.

Expressive or release psychotherapy

Building on the early psychoanalytic concepts of catharsis and abreaction, Levy (1939) carefully structured and directed his play therapy with children to facilitate the reliving of previously traumatic experiences which the history suggests may have contributed to the child's disturbance. Levy's 'release therapy' does not focus on the development of a transference relationship and he made no attempt to point out the feelings implicit in the child's play, or to promote changes in behaviour. Instead the child's own imaginative play was considered to be the medium by which anxiety was released. The therapeutic purpose then is the expression of blocked emotion in the security of the relationship with the therapist in the working through of traumatic experiences.

Clearly, this is a therapeutic method which is sufficiently flexible to accommodate a wide range of specific situations in which the child may have experienced trauma. The purpose is to provide the child with the opportunity to express emotional material without having it interpreted and without having to verbalise the nature of the specific trauma and the child's associated emotions. The method demands careful diagnosis of the specific trauma and is contra-indicated in situations in which serious parental pathology exists.

Relationship child therapy

Rankian (1945) theory, elaborated by Taft (1933) and Allen (1942), highlighted the curative potential intrinsic in the healing dynamic of the therapist–child relationship, and it viewed the analytic effort to recover the past as superfluous. Rogers (1957) later encapsulated the essence of the 'Rankian therapeutic relationship' in his work 'The necessary and sufficient conditions for therapeutic personality change'. The therapist–child relationship, with its focus on the present, does not dwell on the patient's earlier trauma and emotion. Relationship therapy is concerned with emotional problems as they exist in the present and the provision of a friendly and supportive relationship with an accepting adult, and a therapeutic environment in which the child's inherent capacity for growth and self-help can develop and flourish. This notion is conceptually similar to that of 'Physis' (Berne 1971; Clarkson 1992).

The core purpose of the therapeutic hour was to provide the child with the opportunity to define themselves in relation to the therapist, to differentiate and re-evaluate their conceptualisation of themselves in the therapeutic process. The therapy hour was seen to belong truly to the child, who was guaranteed acceptance and was given the freedom to feel, say and do whatever they chose, within clearly defined limits of time, and rules against damage to the property, the self and the therapist. In using therapeutic reassurance, active encouragement and the clarification of reality as primary therapeutic techniques, the use of interpretation was relegated to a role of lesser importance. The need for the patient to retrace developmental steps and to relive earlier relationships was therefore minimised. The therapeutic focus was on healing, and the restoration of the child's capacity for growth and self-help resulted in a considerable reduction in the time-span of therapy.

Non-directive or client-centred therapy

Client-centred play therapy has not extended or made use of the psycho-analytic premise that it is necessary for the patient to relive earlier emotional relationships and to retrace any developmental lines within the therapeutic hour. Instead, Rogers (1951), Axline (1947), Moustakas (1953) and others incorporated the notion of the Rankian (1945) theory that it is the therapeutic relationship that is curative in its own right. The previous history of the child's emotional problems is unimportant. The manifestation of the problem in the moment, and a focus on present feelings was considered the most important focus for therapy. With its fundamental postulate that play is the child's natural medium of expression, play therapy offers the child the opportunity to 'play out' their feelings, problems and difficulties, and thereby to develop an image of self rather than to 'reality' as others see it.

The child's free expression of themselves is facilitated by communicating three basic therapist attitudes: faith, acceptance and respect. It is in the context of these attitudes that 'children may achieve feelings of security, adequacy and worthiness through emotional insight' (Moustakas 1953: 2). It is by the constant recognition and clarification of the emotions in the non-directive play therapy relationship that the child's insight into the feelings that motivate behaviour and self-definition can emerge.

With its roots in Rankian relationship theory, the central philosophy of client-centred play therapy holds that the individual has the potential for growth and the capacity for self-direction. A primary therapeutic objective is to provide the child with the maximum opportunity to express their feelings so that these can be recognised and clarified, and that the child is eventually enabled to identify their own feelings and thereby to become master of them. The child

> needs good growing ground to develop a well balanced structure – the individual needs the permissiveness to be himself by himself, as well as by others . . . the right to be an individual entitled to the dignity that is the birthright of every human being, in order to achieve a direct satisfaction of this growth impulse.
>
> (Axline 1947: 10)

Diagnosis is not an endeavour undertaken by the non-directive play therapist. Meeting children where they are does not necessitate knowledge of symptomatic behaviour. Equally, with its focus on the present, the techniques of interpretation and probing have no place in the therapeutic hour. The individual will select the issues most relevant to them and their lives when they are ready to do so. Instead, recognition and clarification of the expressed emotional attitudes using reflection constitutes the essence of the therapist's activity.

Play therapy is a unique experience for any child. The relationship offered has wider boundaries than the child is ever likely to have experienced. In the play-room children are given the opportunity to be completely themselves. Emotions across the spectrum from anger and hate through to love and affection can be expressed in the confidence of complete acceptance. 'The therapeutic relationship does not set up standards or social values for them – it honours every impulse, need or projection as it is expressed' (Moustakas 1953: 19). Play therapy challenges the child to 'be', to take responsibility for themselves, to make their own decisions and ultimately to be masters of their own emotional destiny.

The Lowenfeld method

A therapeutic method which gave credence to both individual biography and socio-historical processes, and one which was strongly influential in establishing child psychology as a separate endeavour, was that developed by Margaret Lowenfeld (1935) and her founding of the Institute of Child Psychology in 1928. Lowenfeld believed that disturbances in children emerged not only from emotional conflicts but also from the conceptualising and experience of the infant or young child in their development of an understanding of the world in which they live. Thus it was that Lowenfeld developed her ideas on the importance of the 'non-verbal thinking' of children. She contested the analytic supposition that the meaning of children's play, and therefore the interpretations given in the course of analysis, could be derived from adults. Instead, as a result of her observational studies, she based her psychotherapeutic method on the conclusion that play was not only a mechanism for the release of tension, but also a medium through which children could access their feelings and fantasies, and 'think' about the world. She postulated that children 'cluster' inner experiences in making sense of their worlds, and considered this process to be primary in the development of personality. Where such conceptualisations were incorrect and disturbing, the mental work the child undertakes is aberrant and emotionally painful.

Lowenfeld's psychotherapeutic method was facilitated through the careful design and selection of play materials which, when presented by various projective methods, allowed the child to externalise thoughts and feelings and to clarify and come to an understanding of the experiences which were causing conflict. Play and action gave therapeutic access to the child's 'natural idiom', and in work with the child 'connections were observed and the attention of children was drawn to them, but comparatively few interpretations were offered' (Trail and Rowles 1964: 21). Lowenfeld was predominantly 'non-interventionist' in style, and by making constant reference to observational studies she guarded against getting her client material to fit a theoretical perspective.

Psychodrama

This systematised method of role playing is essentially a group therapy method in which enactment rather than play or verbalisation is the primary means by which a patient explores and achieves varying degrees of resolution in problem situations.

Psychodrama as a therapeutic method was initiated and developed by Moreno (1972). Classically, the method is now applied in a wide variety of settings which range from mental health facilities through the military to education resources and even professional training. However, psychodrama has its roots in Moreno's informal work with children's play in the parks of Vienna, during his years as a student. Moreno established himself as a story- or tale-teller, and noticed how the children who gathered around him spontaneously acted out themes from their histories or from their fantasies. He observed that these children were able to express their feelings powerfully through role play, and noticed that the children's improvisations followed an observable process in which hostility diminished in favour of a blossoming of creativity.

These early observations formed the basis of Moreno's (1974) spontaneity-creativity theory and influenced the development of his therapy located philosophically in existentialism and based on an action method. In favouring active expression over repression, Moreno's ideas are in stark contrast to Freud's prohibition against the acting out of neurotic defences. Moreno moved on from his work with children to develop meetings with prostitutes, and further developed the ideas which formed the beginnings of group work as a psychotherapeutic method. Like many therapies, psychodrama offers the individual an opportunity for catharsis and relief, insight and self-understanding, making modifications of behaviour possible.

Unlike the Freudian preoccupations with the past and the client-centred focus on the present, 'Psychodrama is concerned with an individual's personal life, past, present or future; his interpersonal relationships, his feelings, his fears, his concerns, and his fantasies, and even his delusions and hallucinations' (Rabson-Hare 1975: 3).

Group therapy

Group therapy for children had its origins in the 1930s work of Slavson (1943), who facilitated activity groups for pre-pubertal children with behaviour problems. Although derived from psychoanalytic theory, Slavson's groups were non-interpretative and experiential. A desire for group acceptance was seen to serve the same function in the group as transference serves in individual therapy. The expression of conflicting feelings while sustaining a relationship with a permissive therapist was seen as the therapeutic means by which egocentricity could be eradicated.

Slavson was one of the first to stress the role of the conductor and the importance of the relationship as the foundation of therapy. From Slavson's early work a variety of group therapies utilising play as a therapeutic medium were developed in the psychoanalytic school. Later developments in the analytic tradition, based on the natural inclination of children and adolescents to form peer relationships, were to include Bion's (1984) analysis of the group, and Foulkes's (1948) introduction of talk to facilitate analysis through and by the group.

In Axline's (1947) original formulation of non-directive, client-centred play therapy she placed little emphasis on group therapy. Her acceptance of group therapy as an adjunct for the child in individual therapy was limited, and only in the case of children who were poorly socially adjusted did she acknowledge the merits of group therapy.

However, Ginott (1961) dealt more fully with therapy in a group context. In accordance with Slavson's formulation, Ginott considered the group setting to provide a corrective emotional experience. Through the group and the therapeutic relationship children are provided with an opportunity to experience a sense of belonging and understanding, to experience support, and to have opportunities for vicarious catharsis. In group therapy the child is forced to re-evaluate behaviour in terms of peer relationships. The group provides a more tangible setting in which the child can discover and experiment with different styles of relating to peers by externalising aspects of themselves onto other members and onto the group therapist. Finally, in the case of younger children, separation from mother was considered less problematic when other children were around.

Group analytic drama

Willis (1988) developed group analytic drama, a therapeutic method, used in the treatment of disturbed adolescents, in which the principles of group analysis in the Foulkes (1948; Foulkes and Anthony 1965) tradition is applied, and use is made of a dramatic method which lies between classical psychodrama and sociodrama.

The interaction in group analytic drama with adolescents is entirely verbal. This is based on the notion that adolescents use activity as a defence against change. The conductor assumes a low profile in the group analytic drama session, and the therapist facilitates the group members becoming therapists in their own right.

Action groups in therapy with adolescents

Loftus (1988) documented his use of action group methods in his work with adolescents presenting with a wide range of emotional and behavioural problems. Social skills groups are based on the assumption that social behaviour is learned and should therefore be facilitated and taught by structured methods. By contrast, action groups, with their origins in the Gestalt philosophy, focus primarily on emotions, and maintain that young people have both the responsibility for themselves and the resources and skills to deal with their problems.

The therapeutic task in action group therapy is to put young people in touch with their own resources by encouraging them to experience their feelings. Based on the Reichian assumption that feelings are held in the body, the group members are encouraged to experience their feelings by physically moving themselves. Action groups occur within a therapeutic environment in which clear boundaries and limits exist, and the leadership function is made overt. The locus of decision-making is a key therapeutic issue, with the decision to attend being located as a parental function. Decisions to make the personal changes which are necessary to facilitate a decision for discharge from the group rests squarely with the young person. The pace of action groups is fast, and the major focus is on facilitating the experience of feelings. Interpretations are not made, but an atmosphere of intimacy and closeness is facilitated and enhanced by the shared experience and feedback which occurs during the course of the group.

COMMONALITIES IN THE SPECTRUM OF THERAPIES WITH CHILDREN AND YOUNG PEOPLE

The therapeutic relationship

A common theme running through all therapies is the delineation, with various degrees of importance, of the role of the therapist and the nature of the therapeutic relationship. The therapeutic relationship is the primary tool of the therapist's 'trade'. Research indicates that therapist qualities (rather than the gender, age or physical appearance of the therapist), and the nature of the relationship developed in the course of therapy will have a powerful impact on the efficacy of therapy (Norcross 1986).

In the psychoanalytic tradition, the analyst classically assumed a role of emotional distance in order to promote the transference relationship, the primary vehicle of the analysis. In her work with children Anna Freud (1965) made reference to the role of the analyst in the child's pursuit of a new relationship. Such a relationship was seen to not only have a corrective emotional capacity, but was also considered to be the springboard from which deeper interpretations were made.

Rogers (1957) listed the ingredients of empathy, genuineness and unconditional positive regard as therapist prerequisites for bringing about therapeutic change. The therapeutic relationship is one characterised by faith, acceptance and respect. Commitment to the Transactional Analysis concept of 'Physis', a creative force aspiring to growth and perfection (Berne 1971) is an act of faith and a belief in the potential of the individual. A 'consumer response' to such a demonstration of faith is reflected in the following statement: 'You were the first person who believed in me – who didn't think I was all bad' (Moustakas 1953: 3). Stability and consistency in the therapeutic relationship are also important in facilitating change. Unconditional acceptance too is an important therapeutic ingredient in the journey to mental health. Clarkson (1990) illustrated five different kinds of psychotherapeutic relationship potentially available to the therapist (see Chapter 2 of this *Handbook*). These distinct treatment modalities are useful as an integrating meta-perspective on the essence of all therapeutic endeavours, therapy with children and adolescents being no exception. As a very minimum a 'working alliance' between therapist and client has to be forged. In the case of children and adolescents, this contractual agreement to embark on a course of therapy frequently involves a 'three-cornered' commitment to the therapeutic endeavour. The literal dependence of children on their caretakers is an important consideration in treatment planning, and regarding 'customership' as being located in those persons who separately or jointly have the authority, the need and the means is an important consideration in therapy with children and young people.

The therapist

The therapist's role is a demanding one. The therapist must continually be sensitive to, aware of and alert to the child, their issues, actions, verbalisations and therapeutic needs. In spite of the child or young person being the chief architect of their own therapy, it is incumbent on the therapist to facilitate the provision of an environment in which the child is permitted free expression, in the context of protection from a therapist prepared to exercise potency in the therapeutic endeavour. An examination by therapists of their therapeutic role and the skills and personal qualities which they bring to bear in the therapeutic relationship should be undertaken, both in the context of regular case review and of supervision. Training analyses have long been a prerequisite for those working in an analytic frame, and increasingly an emphasis is being placed on the importance of therapists' knowledge of their 'inner maps', and the nurturing and replenishing potential of personal psychotherapy. This is particularly pertinent in work with children and young people, which has the potential to reverberate powerfully with unresolved issues in the therapist's own life.

The child or young person

The child or young person entering therapy is, in most cases, in serious personal trouble. The distress of the child may be exhibited in the behavioural or emotional symptoms precipitating referral, and a careful dynamic diagnosis of the problems and the systems in which they are located is required. Therapy is not, however, reserved for those in 'serious personal trouble'. It has been used successfully with children with physical handicap (Cruickshank and Cowan 1948), for children suffering situational disturbances, and the categories delineated by Clarkson and Fish (1988).

The session

The therapy hour belongs to the child and to the child alone. It is the prerogative of the child or young person to determine the pace and direction of their therapy. However, it is the role of the therapist to ensure that the psychologically pertinent issues are addressed in a client-relevant manner.

The wider context

Consent to treatment and the way in which therapeutic content will be communicated to parents and others (teachers or care-workers where relevant) should be clarified in the process of negotiating the therapy contract. Respecting the ethic of confidentiality, whilst also taking account of the implications of the Children Act (1989) and the Access to Health Records Act (1990), often raises difficult issues for the therapist. Unless these issues are clarified during the initial contractual negotiations, they may interfere with the therapeutic process. In practice, many therapists negotiate permission to communicate the themes and general issues arising from the therapy rather than communicating exact therapeutic content. Issues involving the disclosure of child abuse always override the ethic of confidentiality.

Some therapists insist that if a child is accepted into treatment, one or both parents should also enter therapy. It is acknowledged that there are occasions on which children are presented as a 'foil' for difficulties in an associated system (Clarkson and Fish 1988). However, some propound that unless the core and background issues are addressed, anti-therapeutic forces are likely to overwhelm the child and negate any change achieved in therapy. Others question this notion, believing that having undergone personal change, the child will change in relation to the environment in which they live and, in so doing, acquire a stimulus value of their own, drawing changed perceptions and reactions. Generally, an awareness of the implications of the interaction between the child and the various systems which are relevant will require consideration when deciding on treatment direction and goals.

The treatment setting

Psychological therapies with children and young people are undertaken in a variety of settings. These may range from specially equipped consulting rooms to sparsely furnished offices. Wherever therapy is undertaken it is important that time, space and boundaries are safeguarded. Attention to the detail of safety is an important consideration in finalising the setting in which children and young people are seen.

The therapist must be sure that the issues highlighted in the diagnostic formulation will be appropriately addressed during the course of therapy. Clearly this necessitates therapist knowledge of the developmental relevance of the materials provided, and an ability to respond in ways which take account of both the cognitive capacity of the child and their level of developmental maturity.

CONCLUSION

Therapeutic endeavours with children and young people are wide and varied, requiring specialist training and expertise. Further scientific research into the efficacy of the psychological therapies with this target population is required before their undisputed validity is established. None the less, the anecdotal evidence of large numbers of children and young people who have undertaken a therapeutic journey continues to bear testimony to the creative capacity of these endeavours.

Early concepts developed in therapy continue to influence the field, though latterly increasing service demands have led to their modification, revision and replacement with new theory and enhanced therapeutic techniques and styles.

REFERENCES

Access to Health Records Act (1990) London: HMSO.
Allen, F. H. (1942) *Psychotherapy with Children*, New York: W. W. Norton.
Axline, V. M. (1947) *Play Therapy*, New York: Ballantine Books.
—— (1950) 'Play therapy experiences as described by child participants', *Journal of Consulting Psychology* 14: 53–63.
—— (1964) *Dibs: In Search of Self*, London: Gollancz.
Berne, E. (1971) *A Layman's Guide to Psychiatry and Psychoanalysis*, Harmondsworth: Penguin.
Bion, W. R. (1984) *Elements of Psychoanalysis*, London: Karnac.
Children Act (1989) London: HMSO.
Clarkson, P. (1990) 'A multiplicity of psychotherapeutic relationships', *British Journal of Psychotherapy* 7: 148–63.

—— (1992) 'Physis in transactional analysis', *Transactional Analysis Journal* 22(4): 202–09.

Clarkson, P. and Fish, S. (1988) 'Systemic assessment and treatment considerations in TA child psychotherapy', *Transactional Analysis Journal* 18(2): 123–32.

Cruickshank, W. M. and Cowan, E. L. (1948) 'Group therapy with physically handicapped children', *Journal of Educational Research* 39(4): 193–215.

Dorfman, E. (1955) 'Personality outcomes of client centred therapy', *Psychological Monographs, General and Applied* 72(3): 1–22.

Foulkes, S. H. (1948) *Introduction to Group-Analytic Psychotherapy: Studies in the Social Integration of Individuals and Groups*, London: Maresfield Reprints.

Foulkes, S. H. and Anthony, E. J. (1965) *Group Psychotherapy: The Psychoanalytic Approach*, Harmondsworth: Penguin Books.

Freud, A. (1946) *The Psychoanalytic Treatment of Children*, New York: International Universities Press.

—— (1965) *Normality and Pathology in Childhood*, New York: International Universities Press.

Freud, S. (1909) 'Analysis of a phobia in a five-year-old boy' ('Little Hans'), *Standard Edition*, vol. 10, London: Hogarth Press.

Ginott, H. G. (1961) *Group Psychotherapy with Children*, New York: McGraw-Hill.

Hug-Hellmuth, H. (1921) 'Zur Technik der Kinderanalyse', *Internationale Zeitschrift der Psychoanalyse* 7: 179–97.

Klein, M. (1932) *The Psychoanalysis of Children*, London: Hogarth Press.

—— (1975) *Envy and Gratitude and Other Works*, London: Hogarth Press.

Klein, M., Heimann, P. and Money-Kyrle, R. E. (1955) *New Directions in Psychoanalysis*, London: Tavistock.

Levy, D. (1939) 'Release therapy', *American Journal of Orthopsychiatry* 9: 731–6.

Loftus, M. L. (1988) 'Moving to change: action groups in an out-patient setting', *Journal of Adolescence* 11: 217–29

Lowenfeld, M. (1935) *Play in Childhood*, London: Gollancz.

Moreno, J. L. (1972) *Psychodrama*, New York: Boston House.

—— (1974) 'The creativity theory of personality: spontaneity, creativity and human potentialities,' pp. 73–84 in I. A. Greenberg (ed.) *Psychodrama: Theory and Therapy*, vol. 33, London: Condor/Souvenir Press.

Moustakas, C. (1953) *Children in Play Therapy*, New York: Ballantine.

—— (1967) *Creativity and Conformity*, New York: Van Nostrand.

Norcross, J. C. (ed.) (1986) *Handbook of Eclectic Psychotherapy*, New York: Brunner/Mazel.

Pine, F. (1985) *Developmental Theory and Clinical Process*, London: Yale University Press.

Rabson-Hare, J. (1975) Psychodrama, Unpublished paper.

Rank, O. (1945) *Will Therapy and Truth and Reality*, New York: Knopf.

Rogers, C. R. (1951) *Client Centred Therapy*, Boston: Houghton Mifflin.

—— (1957) 'The necessary and sufficient conditions of therapeutic personality change', *Journal of Consulting Psychology* 21(2): 95–103.

Slavson, S. R. (1943) *An Introduction to Group Therapy*, New York: International Universities Press.

Taft, J. (1933) *The Dynamics of Therapy in a Controlled Relationship*, New York: Macmillan.

Trail, P. M. and Rowles, F. H. (1964) 'Nonverbal "thinking" in child psychotherapy', in M. Lowenfeld, P. M. Trail and F. H. Rowles (eds) *The Nonverbal 'Thinking' of Children and its Place in Psychotherapy*, London: Institute of Child Psychology.

Willis, S. (1988) 'Group analytic drama: a therapy for disturbed adolescents', *Group Analysis* 21: 153–68.

FURTHER INFORMATION

Association of Play Therapists
11 Hanover Street
Brighton
East Sussex BN2 2ST
Tel.: 0273 691166

The Institute for Arts and Therapy in Education
70 Cranwich Road
London N16 5JD
Tel.: 081 809 5866

Analytical psychotherapy with children

Miranda Passey

This chapter describes the work of child psychotherapists. It discusses what sorts of disorders can be treated by child psychotherapy, the settings in which child psychotherapists work, and the historical development and theoretical framework which underlie the work. There is a brief description of the training undertaken and some clinical examples to give a flavour of the child psychotherapist's approach. The wide range of consultative and supportive work offered to other professionals working with children is described.

A great variety of standpoints coexist within the general framework of present-day child psychotherapy. These are unified, however, by a fundamental belief that 'the immediate causes of psychological stress arise from internal conflict' (Reeves 1981: 271), whatever theoretical description may be given as the source of this conflict.

CHILDREN IN NEED

Children are especially vulnerable to disturbance; their emotional immaturity makes it difficult for them to discriminate between fantasy and reality. Events in childhood or within their families can either strengthen their capacity for healthy development or lead to self-destructive behaviour and a damaged capacity to make healthy relationships.

Up to 10 per cent of British children and young people (1.2 million) have some psychiatric or psychological problem which handicaps them for a year or more, and this percentage rises to 25 per cent in inner city areas. Of this 1.2 million at least 2 per cent (240,000) need psychiatric help.

There is increasing evidence that early effective intervention can be important in preventing adult mental ill health (Department of Health 1992). While many forms of intervention are available (family therapy, casework and so on), a high proportion (30 per cent) of those children referred to child psychotherapists (Beedell and Payne 1988) have failed to respond satisfactorily to other forms of treatment. Even when external changes have taken place, some children and young people are still unable to gain relief from their emotional disturbance because it is very deeply rooted.

THE CHILD PSYCHOTHERAPIST'S ORIENTATION

The chief concern of the child psychotherapist is the child's inner world. That is the subjective picture of people and things we all carry around within us, sometimes without being aware of it, and which may or may not sufficiently correspond to outward reality. The child psychotherapist attempts to help the patient understand his or her own situation and, in particular, any unconscious factors which may be contributing to the current difficulties. The aim is to help the patient come to terms with their past experience, their response to it, and their own present personality characteristics. This is achieved through the relationship the patient makes with their child psychotherapist, onto whom they transfer the attitudes and feelings that determine their relationships outside the psychotherapy. The psychotherapist endeavours to identify these attitudes and feelings and to put them to the child in such a way that they can see and feel them and, in the experience of them, make changes in the way they behave. Such changes do not imply that the child is enabled to put up with ill-treatment or abuse. Indeed, the child may become angry for the first time about what has happened or is happening, or become able to perceive correctly a situation of cruelty or abuse, however painful this may be.

External events may prove incomprehensible to children and be mis-interpreted in terms of existing fears or worries. Divorce, family break-down, the death of a parent or sibling are all experiences which may feed the child's picture of a baffling or hostile world where mistrust and hatred thrive.

WHO CAN BE TREATED?

Child psychotherapists treat children with a wide variety of difficulties and disorders. These range from symptoms arising from family breakdown, bereavement, child abuse, difficulties related to mental and physical handi-cap, developmental failure, behavioural problems, bed-wetting, soiling, eating or sleeping difficulties, school refusal, to severe conditions such as autism and anorexia.

In addressing the child's difficulties, child psychotherapists work closely with others to enable other aspects of the problem to be understood. This might involve arranging for help for the child's parents, for foster parents or others caring for the child, or addressing the needs of the family as a whole.

WHERE ARE CHILDREN SEEN?

Child psychotherapists work in a range of Health Service establishments, usually as part of inter-disciplinary teams, which may include child psychiatrists, clinical psychologists, family therapists, educational psychologists, social workers and others. These teams may be in Child and Family Treatment Centres (Child Guidance Clinics), Departments of Child and Family Psychiatry or Psychological Medicine, in hospitals, in special schools, in consultation centres for young people and in student health centres. Some also work in private practice.

WHO REFERS?

Referrals can come from GPs, teachers, social workers, paediatricians, from parents directly and from adolescents in their own right. These self-referrals often have the best outcome.

HISTORICAL DEVELOPMENT

A variety of developmental perspectives underpin theories and methods of psychotherapy with children; all are rooted in Freud's theories. Although the different trainings have particular orientations, in practice individual child psychotherapists tend to find a broad measure of agreement in their common aim of understanding children's communications and working together to bring to light the unconscious aspects of experience.

I propose to give a brief description of the development of two child psychotherapy perspectives, to indicate both how these methods of working sprang from adult analytic work and how they differ from them, so as to be able to reach children directly. Early child psychoanalysis contributed vitally to our understanding of children's emotional lives and to present-day practice.

Little Hans

Though Freud never treated a child directly himself, in the case of Little Hans (1909) he had the opportunity to study in depth a phobia in a five-year-old boy, through the boy's father. In common with other 'close adherents' of Freud, Hans's father had already been sending Freud observation of the child's sexual development before the onset of symptoms, and these enriched Freud's understanding of the way in which the difficulties developed. Freud enabled Hans's father to treat his son, by encouraging him to confide his fantasies, act out his hostility and describe his dreams. Together, Freud and Hans's father found a way of understanding this material and of talking to little Hans about it. Freud stresses that the father's position of trust and intimacy with his son is a crucial factor in making the treatment possible. As a result of this work of understanding and bringing to light the meaning of Hans's fears and anxieties, Hans seemed to have recovered from his symptoms. The treatment Freud supervised was essentially 'reconstructive' (Meltzer 1978); that is, aimed at an understanding of the pathology looking backwards at the internal meaning of significant events in the child's life.

The Oedipus complex

His work with adults, coupled with his researches into the sexual develop-ment of children, led Freud to the discovery of the crucial stage of emotional development known as the Oedipus complex. In simple terms, this is a normal stage of development when the young child desires the parent of the opposite sex, in rivalry with his father or mother, but at the same time loves and fears the retaliation of his rival in love. Freud emphasised how crucial it was for this conflict between desire, love and fear to be negotiated and resolved. If all proceeded well, the child's 'ego', the organising, reality-based part of the personality, would have mastered the instinctual 'I want it now' desires of the 'id'. The child would give up his immediate desire for his mother or father and postpone the satisfaction of his genital longings for the prospect of future rewards: 'When I'm grown up, I'll marry someone just like Daddy!' The healthy negotiation of this stage, he believed, would lay the foundation for future growth and personality development.

The infantile neurosis

Freud coined the term 'the infantile neurosis' to describe the conflicts engendered by the Oedipus complex. He believed that an unresolved infantile neurosis would be forgotten and repressed, but would form the basis for a reappearance in adult life of neurotic symptoms (Meltzer 1978).

In her pioneering work with children, which began in 1927, Freud's daughter Anna challenged critics' assumptions that the 'infantile neurosis', if it existed at all, was just a stage of development, and not to be interfered with. She took the view that disturbance in children which she could identify as stemming from unsuccessfully negotiating the Oedipus complex constituted neuroses in the proper sense – a source of intrapsychic conflict. At the start of her work, she saw the child analyst's primary task as that of helping to resolve the conflicts which arose directly as a result of the child's Oedipal longings (A. Freud 1986). In formulating the nature of the child's difficulties, Anna Freud and her followers would attempt to determine the stage of development which the child had reached (which she conceived of in terms of the oral, anal and genital stages) and to describe the earlier levels where the child might have retreated or become stuck because of the conflicts which this stage aroused.

Adapting the technique

In order to make psychotherapy with children effective, Anna Freud believed children would need a preparatory phase of analysis in order to build a trusting and positive relationship with the psychotherapist (this was later abandoned). She did not, at first, see the transference as equally important to child analysis because she believed it was precluded by the child's primary involvement with their parents, and felt the negative transference would be actively unhelpful, preventing the child from co-operating with treatment. Anna Freud also saw the child psychotherapist as having an implicitly educational role towards the child; for example, inherently influencing the child's attitudes or their conscience. These early views have been developed and altered in the light of experience, as have those of Melanie Klein.

Melanie Klein

For Melanie Klein, the child developed a sense of self as part of their earliest relationship with their mother, first experienced in the feeding situation. The taking in of food, comfort and good experiences were seen alongside the expulsion of urine and faeces, and of painful or fearful feelings. The baby could begin to organise a sense of themselves as a result of being responded to both physically and emotionally in a way which gave their experiences meaning, based on the mother's attempts to understand their different states of mind, and think about them.

The paranoid-schizoid position

As Klein described it, at the onset of life, the baby splits its good and bad feelings and experiences, as they cannot be tolerated or contained together by the immature ego. The good feelings maintain the baby's sense of being part of a mother who is wholly good. The bad, aggressive or destructive feelings which arise out of hunger or frustration are got rid of, projected, and are therefore experienced initially by the infant not as belonging to them but as coming from outside, thereby giving rise to terrifying per-secutory experiences. For example, night terrors, anxieties about separa-tion and difficulties about eating may all indicate feelings of persecution coming from projected hostile feelings. Her observations led Klein to describe this early 'position' (predominant mode of mental functioning) as the paranoid-schizoid position. As she conceived them, these positions overlap and are not superseded, as they continue to characterise our basic attitudes towards ourselves and others throughout life.

The depressive position

Gradually, the baby realises that the good mother who comforts and feeds them is the same mother whom they hate when angry and frustrated. This realisation brings feelings of guilt and concern at the aggression and phantasied attacks that they carried out on those they love. The struggle to maintain concern for others' welfare over predominant self-interest continues throughout life. The integration of these opposing feelings leads to a strengthening of the personality.

Theory to practice

Melanie Klein differed from Anna Freud in undertaking analytic therapy with extremely young children, as young as two years old. As she believed that anxiety, guilt and conflict were all present in the young child, and could be coherently expressed, they should be able to be addressed and described directly. This, she believed, would be a relief to the child.

Anna Freud believed that unconscious impulses and phantasies were at first unorganised and unavailable as raw data for conscious thought. Consequently she suggested that these impulses could only be reached by means of analysing the 'resistances' or defence mechanisms the child had erected against knowing about its feelings, thus allowing for the subsequent emergence of the unconscious content.

Play as communication

It was Klein's genius to see that play, as a way of communicating for a child, could replace adults' free association to words; also that the development of a direct and expressive way of talking was required, that could have meaning to the child, and would include using the child's own special words for such things as bodily functions and parts of the body (1932a and b).

> We soon find that the child brings as many associations to separate elements of play as adults do to the separate elements of their dreams. These separate play elements are indications to the trained observer, and as it plays the child talks as well and says all sorts of things that have the value of genuine associations.
>
> (Klein 1932a: 8)

Here is a vivid illustration of Klein's direct and expressive communication with a child. She describes her first session with Peter, aged three years and nine months:

At the beginning of his first session, Peter took the toy carriage and cars and put them first one behind the other and then side by side, and alternated this arrangement several times. In between he took two horse-drawn carriages and bumped one into another so that the horses' feet knocked together and said, 'I've got a new little brother called Fritz.' I asked him what the carriages were doing. He answered, 'That's not nice' and stopped bumping them together at once, but started again quite soon. Then he knocked the toy horses together in the same way. Upon which I said, 'Look here, the horses are two people bumping together.' At first he said, 'No, that's not nice', but then 'Yes, that's two people bumping together'. The material develops from here as Mrs Klein links his statement about Fritz's birth with his curiosity about how Fritz came, which he thinks is because of two people bumping together: 'You thought to yourself that Daddy and Mummy bumped their thingummies together and that is how your little brother Fritz came.' Peter's play continues to describe his phantasies of his parents' intercourse, and what it led to.

(Klein 1932a: 17)

As this passage indicates, Klein carefully gathers evidence before she suggests to Peter that the two carriages bumping together represent Mummy and Daddy. Child psychotherapists do not jump to conclusions, but carefully gather clues to help them understand the child's communications.

Developments and modifications

Klein's direct experience and observations opened up the study of some of the more primitive states of mind. This enlarged the scope and range of both adult and child psychotherapists' work to allow for the treatment of psychotic and 'borderline' children (Tustin 1969) as well as neurotic ones, although with some important modifications of technique. Tustin (1990, 1993) has been a pioneer in this field. Alvarez's (1992) book *Live Company: Psycho-analytic Psychotherapy with Autistic, Borderline, Deprived and Abused Children* is a brilliant example of the development and achievements of this sort of work.

Differences between child analysis and child psychotherapy

As work developed, psychoanalytic child psychotherapy became distinguished from child analysis. The main differences were that, while child analysis aimed at the transformation of the personality, child psychotherapy focused on the removal of symptoms.

Practical developments

The impact of the Second World War led to fundamental developments in the understanding of the meaning of separation and bereavement for children. The films made by James and Joyce Robertson (1972) showing the effects of separation from parents are still compelling today. They showed the crucial difference that might be made by the provision of good substitute care for a child faced with a separation, and the disastrous effect of such separation in a context where there was a constant change of caretaker for the child. Bowlby's research (1951, 1969) brought into vital focus the importance of a continuous, loving relationship between mother and baby; although this was later misused to suggest that mothers should never leave their children. Linked in with this work, it became possible to see how much the whole emotional context of the family could contribute to a child's difficulties. The establishment of multidisciplinary teams in Child Guidance Clinics which became more widespread after the war allowed for the concurrent treatment or support of a child's parents.

TRAINING IN CHILD PSYCHOTHERAPY

In 1928, Margaret Lowenfeld, one of the pioneers in child psychotherapy, established a children's centre in London where play was observed and studied. In 1933 she set up a training here for a small number of child psychotherapists. In 1935 her department became the Institute of Child Psychology, and this training continued until the close of the ICP in 1978 (Lowenfeld 1935).

The Anna Freud training dates from 1948, and the Tavistock (Kleinian) training from 1948, when it was set up to address the need for an analytical training for non-medical personnel practising psychotherapy in clinics.

The application of Jungian ideas to child psychotherapy arose from the work of Dr Michael Fordham at the London Child Guidance Clinic before the war (Astor 1988). Fordham's writings (1957, 1977, 1985) explain the development of his ideas about the treatment of children. A Jungian training was established in 1973.

The British Association of Psychotherapy child training course was started in the early eighties in association with a body well established in training adult psychotherapists. This training represents the 'middle' or 'independent' school of thought whose theoretical position embraces some of both Anna Freudian and Kleinian viewpoints, and whose stance is perhaps most fully represented by the work of Winnicott (1981).

Child psychotherapy in the United Kingdom has been organised since 1949 under the Association of Child Psychotherapists, which has members from four recognised training schools and two new provisionally recognised training schools. These are listed on page 191. The trainings are recognised by the Department of Health. The ACP is also the designated authority for the European Community.

Prerequisites for training

The basic prerequisites for training are an honours degree and professional experience in a relevant field such as education, social work, medicine and psychology. Following this, the training lasts a minimum of four years. The trainee undergoes a personal psychoanalysis, preferably five times weekly.

Pre-clinical training

The training falls into two parts, pre-clinical and clinical. During the pre-clinical years, along with the study of psychoanalytic theory and developmental research, the trainee will probably be involved in work in some other related field of work with children. During this time the trainee will undertake detailed observations of infants and young children and their families. In practice, each trainee follows an infant for the first two years of its life, and a young child for a year – making weekly visits for an hour at a time and writing up observations in depth. Each student's observations are then discussed in seminars. The work in these baby observation seminars can have a profound impact on the trainees, and deepens their conviction about the power of unconscious processes and the rich meanings inherent in non-verbal communication. This work develops in the trainee the capacity to observe and think about initially confusing or incomprehensible states of being encountered in the infant. The observations also provide a model for understanding the process of emotional growth and development in depth. As well as studying the unique impact of each child's personality on its family and environment, the observer is also introduced to the powerful experience of the counter-transference, as they discover that their own feelings are a useful source of information about what they are observing. This work has been described in *Closely Observed Infants* (Miller *et al.* 1989), and wider interest in infant observation is spreading due to the work done by child psychotherapists.

Work discussion

Trainees also bring their current work for discussion in work experience seminars. Here students are introduced to the application of psychoanalytic ideas to the different kinds of work with children they may be undertaking; for example, work in children's homes, individual casework with children in care, or work in a day nursery.

Trainees are able to explore different aspects of communication with children, and can study the meaning of behaviour and interaction, and the significant impact that working with particular children has on the worker, which can become a vital ingredient in understanding the communications of the child.

Clinical training

The second part of the training involves intensive (three times weekly) psychotherapeutic work with three children of different ages and developmental stages – a young child, a latency child and an adolescent. Trainees also see a number of non-intensive cases weekly. They also gain experience of working with parents and families, of doing assessments for psychotherapy and in offering brief counselling to adolescents and young people. All clinical work is carried out under the supervision of a senior child psychotherapist. When the training requirements have been satisfactorily carried out, the candidate is eligible for membership of the Association of Child Psychotherapists.

WHAT CHILD PSYCHOTHERAPISTS ACTUALLY DO

Setting up treatment

Child psychotherapists see children once weekly; or more frequently, where appropriate to the child's needs and to clinical resources. A child psychotherapist will usually carry out an assessment of perhaps three sessions. This is in order to gain some first-hand picture of the child and their difficulties and, by giving the child a direct experience of what psychotherapy is like, to give them a flavour of what is involved and to establish whether they can make use of this form of treatment.

The child psychotherapist first meets with the parents to hear their description of symptoms and events, to gather a valuable early history of the child, and of course to give them a chance to meet the person who will be treating their child. In this meeting the psychotherapist will also be able to explain the boundaries of treatment, and address the anxieties and doubts the parents may have.

In this meeting the child psychotherapist also explains that the content of the child's sessions are generally confidential, which will allow the child to explore painful or hostile feelings without the fear that these will be disclosed to their parents, whom they also love and on whom they depend.

Parental support

With our increasing awareness of the power of the family system to affect its members and sometimes to work against the improvement of an individual member, in the treatment of children consideration of the needs of the child's parents and the rest of the family is vital. Where possible, another worker will offer the parents or family regular appointments to help them with their own difficulties.

The setting

The child psychotherapist aims to provide a consistent and reliable setting for the child. This comprises the same, simply furnished room, available at the same regular time, for the same length of time; and the regular presence of the psychotherapist without interruptions and without avoidable alteration to the regular pattern of sessions. Holiday breaks are carefully prepared for and much advance notice is given.

The room should have simple furniture, if possible, access to water, and should be safe for the child to explore. It should not contain intimate or personal items belonging to the psychotherapist or drawings or materials belonging to other children, which would affect the nature of the child's transference. The aim of this consistency is to create conditions of reliability and predictability, which will allow the child to communicate and explore ideas in a context where they can feel reasonably sure that they will be contained both physically and emotionally.

These boundaries can, of course, also constitute frustrations which the child resents and seeks to destroy, thus also giving useful indication of the child's response to other boundaries or restrictions in the outside world.

The materials

Depending on the child's age, the child psychotherapist provides simple play materials for each child's exclusive use, contained within a separate box or drawer, which can be locked away or otherwise kept safe for the child between sessions. These materials are designed to facilitate expressive play, and as far as possible are simple and neutral. It is the understanding of the communication made by the play rather than simply the opportunity for free play which is therapeutically important. The materials might include small figures and animals, wild and domestic, fences, paper, crayons, scissors, glue, Sellotape, Plasticine, string, some small cars or trucks and bricks or building materials. For adolescents who find talking difficult, the provision of paper and crayons can provide a means of beginning communication.

Of course, some children cannot 'play' in any organised way, and the child psychotherapist's task is then to work with the states of mind, often of terror or confusion, which the child conveys (Hoxter 1988) in order to develop the capacity for symbolisation.

The technique

While adults use the capacity for words to express and communicate thoughts and feelings to others, children need to do this by playing. The young child may communicate by creating a three-dimensional play situation into which they can put themselves, or at least toys representing themselves or aspects of themselves. In this way, the child can describe or enact unbearable emotions or painful situations.

> Easing the impact of the child's anxieties by reassurance, guiding his instinctual drives along educational or creative lines, stimulating him with our own ideas, attempting to civilise his hostile impulses by control or by presenting him with our own values, and providing safe outlets for 'letting off steam' – all these aims can be undertaken by adults in sensitive rapprochement with a child. But these have no part in the Kleinian Child Psychotherapy technique, which aims to open the doors to the unconscious and scrutinize what can seem unacceptable or even unthinkable.
>
> (Hoxter 1988: 209)

Working from what the child says and does, and from the way the child is in the room, the psychotherapist attempts to understand the child's state of mind. This may be gathered from small, apparently insignificant details, or from powerful feelings stirred up in the child psychotherapist in relation to what is happening (or not happening) in the session.

The child psychotherapist has first to make sure that these feelings do not come from their own life and relationships. Of course, their own analysis is intended to enable them to separate the two. Given this, the feelings a child is able to evoke in their child psychotherapist can be an intense form of communication of otherwise unreachable states of mind in the child (Brenman-Pick 1988).

The child psychotherapist has to be receptive, to allow for the impact of the child's communications, both verbal and non-verbal. It can be very difficult to maintain this receptivity, perhaps under a barrage of violent speech or destructive behaviour in the room or of attempts to drown out the child psychotherapist's interpretations. An open state of mind relies most profoundly of all on the psychotherapist's self-knowledge, gained through their own analysis. This awareness allows for receptivity to their patients' more painful or unacceptable communications about parts of themselves.

Interpretations

Interpretations have to be based on the living evidence unfolding in the experience of each session. The timing of the interpretation is important, as what the psychotherapist says will have the most impact if it is most emotionally immediate for the child. There may be many aspects of the child's behaviour worthy of note, but what is actually said must correspond to the here-and-now of the session to enable the child to feel understood and to illuminate the meaning of their actions as they are engaged in them.

I want to give an example of a session with a ten-year-old boy, 'Eric'. I am not aiming to describe his treatment in any depth but to give a flavour of the work and the way in which he communicated his feelings before a holiday break, the second in the treatment. What a child makes of holidays or breaks in treatment is one very useful way of seeing how the child perceives themselves in relation to others. Do they feel rejected, or do they fear that they have damaged the psychotherapist, making them unable to continue?

Eric is in once-weekly treatment. He was referred for aggression at school, poor relationships at home and at school, failure to learn despite high intelligence, and a challenging of all authority. For large parts of his early life his mother was clinically depressed. He seems to have reacted to this by becoming 'impossible to manage', having tantrums which frightened and overwhelmed his mother, and spending much of his time pretending he was 'Superman'. His parents' relationship is a deeply dissatisfied one, with father feeling equally powerless to help Eric or to help his wife. There is a 'much easier' younger sister.

In Eric's sessions there is much evidence of his contempt which wrecks things for him, including an opportunity to use the helpful aspects of his parents, and often the potential usefulness of my interpretations. He finds it very hard to acknowledge any loving feelings, distancing them in himself – for example, by making a Valentine's Day card as a trick for another boy at school to give to someone he knew the boy liked, but without the boy's knowledge.

In this last session before a holiday break, Eric had been ill during the preceding week. He came into the room listlessly and sat slumped in his chair. He flashed open his jacket to reveal a glimpse of the T-shirt of his favourite football team, and muttered something, but wouldn't repeat it. I said something about his T-shirt and his giving me a glimpse of it and yet not letting me hear what he had said. Again, I could not hear his muttered words. I said that I couldn't hear him properly, and that I wondered if he was showing me something about a feeling of slipping out of touch with me because of the holiday, perhaps he was testing me out to see if I was really watching, listening or interested? In his cryptic, baffling communications perhaps he was both tantalising me and wondering if it was worth the effort in the last session before a break, as perhaps he felt *I* was tantalising *him* with my holiday absence.

Eric responded to this by moving from his chair to a chair at the table where his box is. He then spent some time carefully constructing a paper 'fortune teller', using a ruler I had got for him to make accurate measurements of paper. He abandoned his first one in distress, as he had made one black mark on it in a place clearly not intended. To him the 'mistake' seemed irreparable. I linked his upset at the one black mark's spoiling the fortune teller to his worries about damaging me, perhaps making me weary or depressed or needing a holiday, and how he had to abandon it completely as if it felt too awful.

In his second attempt (although he had made several in previous sessions), he couldn't seem to remember how to make the pockets into which the child inserts his fingers to make the fortune teller open like a mouth. I watched his struggles, finding myself thinking how closed up the paper construction seemed, how impossible to imagine how one could fold it so as to make the pockets. I felt he was showing me his sense that I was closed off to him in the holiday, there would be no way in. He responded by asking me if I had seen a *Streetfighter* film. When I asked him to tell me about it, he commented that I didn't watch much television, and I suggested that he was wondering what I did do when I wasn't there with him, and what I would be doing over the holiday. Was there anything we could share (a 'way in' to me)? He then began to construct the pockets and write the 'fortunes'. These were 'You will meet a tall dark man' (he is small and blond), and 'A dog will bite your trousers'. He said they were meant to be 'secret' but also asked for more ideas as he couldn't think of any. I suggested that 'fortunes' indicated his thoughts and mixed feelings about what would be happening for both of us in the holidays. Part of him wanted to hurt me or bite me for going away, part of him hoped for good things for me, part of him was very curious about who else there was in my life, the 'tall dark man' who might take his place or absorb my interest. These thoughts seemed to amuse and interest him without his having to be contemptuous of them, and I felt he was able to face the holiday in a more positive frame of mind.

The development I can see in him will, I hope, lead to his being able to form better relationships with his family and at school, and prevent him from discouraging their best efforts on his behalf.

Interpretations may have several functions. They may begin a sorting out of powerful, frightening or confusing feelings the child has depicted – naming the confusion and making it available for thought. They may describe in simple terms the way in which the child seems to be experiencing the psychotherapist. When a psychotherapist can gather impressions together, they may make an interpretation which can link the here-and-now way in which the relationship between psychotherapist and patient is proceeding to significant experiences in the child's past which may be colouring what is seen to be happening now. Understanding the impact of past experience which can come alive in this way through repeated interpretations in different but related situations can enable the child to become more aware of the difference between the past and reality, to think about the fantasies which may have distorted his perception of reality, and to come to terms with both.

Much of the time, unfolding themes or the meaning of a particular piece of play may need to be held in mind by the psychotherapist for some time, until the most appropriate moment comes to put them together for the child. Often the psychotherapist may not know what is 'going on' and may have to bear states of confusion or fear with and on a child's behalf until some understanding can be gained and expressed. This process also provides a model for the processing of emotional experience for the child, of 'containing' it (Bion 1962), which may in time become part of the child's own mental capacities to contain and understand.

THE AIMS OF PSYCHOTHERAPY

By means of an attentive presence, the psychotherapist aims to provide an 'internal mental space' for the patient in which he and his communications can be thought about. Her interpretations make links between his behaviour, feelings and anxieties, and also describe the nature of the here-and-now relationship he is making with her. Gradually, if all goes well, the child will integrate an understanding, thinking capacity for themselves. Their ability to sort out and come to terms with different, previously unthinkable aspects of their personality and experience will in turn diminish their fears of external persecutors and strengthen their sense of self. The child becomes capable of a greater capacity for concern for others, and as their internal world changes, they are enabled to make more positive relationships in the outside world. To illustrate some of these issues, I want to describe the effect of psychotherapy on Kay.

Difficulties related to mourning

Kay was referred to me by her GP at the age of five. Her own mother had died of leukaemia on Christmas Eve when Kay was three-and-a-half. She had seemed unaffected by the death (according to her father), and he thought she was too young to have made much of it. Within a year the father remarried, and it was her developing relationship with this new stepmother, who really made enormous efforts to reach Kay, that made her feel sufficiently safe for her difficulties to emerge. She was clingy and had bouts of uncontrollable weeping. She seemed cut off at school and was terrified of rain, of baths, showers and any running water, and seemed to become frozen with fear especially when going to the lavatory.

In our early sessions (I saw her three times a week), Kay showed me by her frightened looks and her miserable attempts to alter drawings to cover up anything I had referred to, how persecuting she felt my presence to be. Gradually this began to shift and she began to look at me for reassurance as she drew something frightening, as if beginning to trust that there might be something helpful about my attempts to understand. She drew frightening things. Bodies in coffin-shaped boats surrounded by fire, scenes with a dangerous witch in them who, she said, wanted to kill her and cook her for her husband's dinner, children being spirited away by this same witch with no chance of escape. Gradually we could understand that she felt me to be a potentially persecuting witch, and that this was connected to fears that her dead mother would come back to attack and murder her with 'black rain', as she called it.

Kay feared that her mother had died because Kay had damaged her in some way, or at least failed to keep her alive. Perhaps she also confused in her mind her normal, infantile demands, seeing these as being too much for her mother. She drew a picture of a lady having a shower and, as I watched, drew in the 'black rain'. She and I together worked out that this hail was like the 'pooh' she didn't feel mother had been able to manage. Mother's loss had in fact occurred at Kay's developmental stage of being preoccupied with toilet training. This material threw some light on her fear of water, which she felt became contaminated with wee and pooh, and her fear of her real waste products when she went to the toilet, as if they were potentially extremely dangerous and unmanageable. The fantasy was at times inseparable from reality.

Gradually Kay became able to play with the farm and wild animals, using drawing less. At first the scenes she created showed the animals all muddled up and uncertainly protected by a male caretaker who was often asleep or absent, leaving the animals in great danger. It seemed that this caretaker vividly represented the father who she felt had 'allowed' mother to die. However, she was gradually able to allow for the possibility of something more hopeful. The part of a session I describe shows how vividly she responded to my interpretation. This was a Monday session following a weekend break.

Kay arranged the animals in a long procession with the families all muddled up, saying, 'It doesn't matter because they're all friends'. She said they were all going somewhere because of the man; he always wanted them to do things or go out to places when they didn't want to, and they didn't like it. I suggested that perhaps she was seeing me as the 'man' who made her come for her session when she didn't want to, especially with a weekend to get through, and that this made her not want to come again, at least with a part of herself.

She responded to this by getting out some fences. She said there were people in the house who put food out for the animals because they knew they were coming, and the animals had thought there was nothing there but houses and people asleep in them.

It seems that, in response to my interpretation, she is able to modify her expectation that there will be nothing there for her when she comes and that I will be like the people asleep, unthinking and unprepared. She then feels that I can 'feed' her and think about her needs.

Gradually her sense of persecution lessened. In her play she was able to protect the vulnerable animals and allow important food supplies to be shared out fairly between the animals. It seemed that this indicated her feeling that there could be 'enough' for her in the sessions, and that there could be enough for others, the beginning of a capacity for concern. As she began to tackle an awareness of the power of her destructive rage and her fear that it was dangerous to take the good things she might be offered, she explained to me (indicating the crocodile), 'When he's hungry, he's not nice, he'll eat anyone, even his best friend'. Gradually this crocodile part of herself became more manageable. She began to experience a delight in 'putting things right', which I think indicated a renewed hope that the fantasied damage and destruction which she felt had been confirmed in her inner world by the real death of her mother could be repaired, and her inner world began to be restored.

Work with adolescents

Work with adolescents poses particular challenges and may make extra demands on the psychotherapist's capacity to sustain a therapeutic role (also see Chapter 10 of this *Handbook* regarding adolescents). Adolescents are often in turmoil, with conflicting states of mind, as they struggle to establish their sexual and personal identity. They often seem to need to set themselves up in opposition to parents and figures in authority, and this can colour the transference relationship to the psychotherapist.

Adolescents are particularly prone to acting out their intense emotions rather than being able to think about them, and this can lead to threats of suicide and sexual experimentation which brings the risk of unwanted pregnancy and disease. In the adolescent's conflict between identification with their parents and separation from them, and their anxieties about entering the wider world, they may bring very highly charged material to sessions, or attend spasmodically or not at all, leaving the psychotherapist worried.

Issues relating to the adolescent patient's uncertainties about being able to manage all the different tasks of adulthood can also produce wishes to retreat and regress. Intense and unresolved feelings belonging to infancy can be re-evoked. This work can also provoke correspondingly intense anxieties in the psychotherapist about their capacity to contain the adolescent patient. The fears stirred up by such work are also an indication of what a frightening process adolescence can be. Because of these difficulties, it may be especially hard to sustain long-term treatment with adolescents. Although this work involves a different focus, sometimes brief work can address a particular moment of crisis with good results, because repressed experiences and unconscious fears may be more available for understanding and working through (Wittenberg 1988).

How long does treatment last?

The length of a child's treatment will often depend on external circumstances and available supports for psychotherapy, as well as on ideal therapeutic goals. Although, of course, there are wide individual variations, in a study of child psychotherapists' working practices (Beedell and Payne 1988) it was found that 59 per cent of individual psychotherapy treatments were closed within eighteen months, and 76 per cent within two years. The preliminary study (Beedell and Payne 1988) suggested that there is a satisfactory outcome in 74 per cent of cases.

Short-term psychotherapy

This might range from three to ten sessions.

> Sometimes very short-term psychotherapy can be a great help. This holds true when the child is aware of the problem, the difficulty is actually near conscious level, and there is good co-operation. If a child or adolescent is seen at a time of crisis when he very much wishes to focus and work on his problem, it may be that long-term psychotherapy is unnecessary.
>
> (Lush 1988: 84)

This kind of work has been described by Wittenberg (1988).

DEVELOPING FIELDS OF WORK

Child psychotherapists have made pioneering developments in working with mentally handicapped children (Sinason 1992) and with children with severe emotional deprivation (Boston and Szur 1983). In addition to the work already described, child psychotherapists work with severely ill and dying children and their families (Judd 1989), in departments of oncology, paediatric endocrinology and orthopaedics, and in a regional burns unit. Recent extensions of fields of work include those with refugee children, children who have been the victims of torture or religious persecution, and children who have been involved in natural disasters. There is also a growing field of work with parents and infants in which child psychotherapists apply the knowledge gained from intensive work to address the difficulties that parents may experience with infants, for example with feeding and sleeping. Such difficulties can often be resolved in a few sessions and interventions of this kind may well forestall problems, which, unaddressed, might lead to more serious ongoing symptoms. An example of this is the Under-Fives Counselling Service with Infant–Parent Couples at the Tavistock Clinic, where parents and infants may be seen for up to five sessions at short notice.

Another means of extending fields of work is through teaching or supervisory and consultative work with other professional groups or institutions. For example, a child psychotherapist working alongside nurses and paediatricians in a neonatal intensive care unit can support the staff and parents in thinking about the experiences of very ill babies, often in incubators (Earnshaw 1981; Bender and Swan-Parente 1983). This work enables staff to suggest alterations in nursing or management practices which have direct benefit for the babies, or help parents feel they can make more contact with babies from whom they may feel both actually and emotionally cut off, and to whom they may also feel useless.

Professionals who use child psychotherapists in a consultative capacity may include residential care workers, social workers, health visitors, day nursery staff, neonatal intensive care nurses, midwives and teachers in special schools. Such work may also be carried out with GPs, paediatricians, occupational therapists and play therapists.

People working with disturbed children in a variety of settings often find it helpful to be able to describe the impact that these children have on them, and to explore the ways in which the child's behaviour affects their capacity to respond in a consistently helpful way.

Publications

Another significant aspect of far-reaching work being carried out by child psychotherapists is in writing for parents and others about children's normal development and their special difficulties. An example of this is the series of books *Understanding Your Baby* by Lisa Miller (1992) and *Your One-Year-Old* by Deborah Steiner (1991). Another book with broad application is *Through the Night: Helping Parents and Sleepless Infants* by Dilys Daws (1989), which tackles the enormously widespread problems of sleeping difficulties in children.

Research

Psychotherapy with children is still developing, and research into its methods and outcome is being undertaken – for example, the current (1993) Anna Freud Centre project, examining nearly 800 completed psychoanalytic treatment cases. This project aims to examine variables predictive of outcome and to generate hypotheses and measures to be used in a prospective study of treatment processes and outcomes. It also aims to identify particular groups for further study of their treatment, such as children with specific learning difficulties or with physical handicaps. Other projects aim to examine individual psychotherapy with sexually abused children.

Research has been done into the evaluation of psychotherapy with particular groups of children; for example, those fostered and adopted (Lush, Boston and Grainger 1991). Other fields of research with mentally handicapped children (Sinason 1992) are being developed. As another example, the study by Beedell and Payne (1988) retrospectively rated outcome in terminated cases, and there are further projects in progress.

SUMMARY

In this chapter, I have tried to describe the historical and theoretical development of psychotherapy with children, the training and orientation of child psychotherapists, and have given some examples showing how psychotherapy with children is carried out. I have discussed some of the wider applications of the work of child psychotherapists, which reaches parents and children through publications and brief work, and explained how consultation can contribute to the thinking of other professionals working with children in many settings. Finally, I have mentioned recent developments in the research and evaluation of practice and methodology.

APPENDIX

Child psychotherapy training:

The Tavistock Clinic
120 Belsize Lane
London NW3 5BA
Orientation: Kleinian and Post-Kleinian
Status: NHS

The Anna Freud Centre for Psycho-Analytical Study and Treatment of Children
21 Maresfield Gardens
London NW3 5SH
Orientation: Freudian and Contemporary Freudian
Status: Registered charity

Society of Analytical Psychology
1 Daleham Gardens
London NW3 5BV
Orientation: Jungian
Status: Private

British Association of Psychotherapists
37 Mapesbury Road
London NW2 4HJ
Orientation: Independent
Status: Registered charity

Scottish Institute of Human Relations
56 Albany Street
Edinburgh EH1 3QR
Orientation: Psychoanalytic, but non-specific
Status: Registered charity

Birmingham Trust for Psychoanalytic Psychotherapy
96 Park Hill
Moseley
Birmingham B13 8DS
Orientation: Kleinian and Post-Kleinian
Status: Registered Charity

REFERENCES

Alvarez, A. (1992) *Live Company: Psycho-analytic Psychotherapy with Autistic, Borderline, Deprived and Abused Children*, London: Routledge.
Astor, J. (1988) 'A conversation with Dr Michael Fordham', *Journal of Child Psychotherapy* 14(1): 3–11.
Beedell, C. and Payne, S. (1988) 'Making the case for child psychotherapy: a survey of the membership and activity of the Association of Child Psychotherapists', commissioned by the ACP, Unpublished manuscript.
Bender, H. and Swan-Parente, A. (1983) 'Psychological and psychotherapeutic support of staff and parents in an intensive care baby unit', in J. A. Davis, M. P. M. Richards and M. R. C. Robinson (eds) *Parent–Baby Attachment in Premature Infants*, London: Croom Helm, pp. 165–76.
Bion, W. R. (1962) *Learning from Experience*, London: Heinemann.
Boston, M. and Szur, R. (1983) *Psychotherapy with Severely Deprived Children*, London: Routledge.
Bowlby, J. (1951) *Maternal Care and Mental Health*, Geneva: World Health Organization.
—— (1969) *Attachment*, London: Hogarth Press.
Brenman-Pick, I. (1988) 'Working through in the counter-transference', pp. 34–47 in *Melanie Klein Today*, vol. 2, London: Tavistock/Routledge.
Daws, D. (1989) *Through the Night: Helping Parents and Sleepless Infants*, London: Free Association Books.
Department of Health (1992) *The Health of the Nation* (Green Paper), London: HMSO.
Earnshaw, A. (1981) 'Action consultancy', *Journal of Child Psychotherapy* 7(2): 149–51.
Fordham, M. (1957) *New Developments in Analytical Psychology*, London: Routledge & Kegan Paul.

—— (1977) 'Maturation of a child within a family', *Journal of Analytic Psychology* 22(2): 57–77.

—— (1985) 'Explorations into the self', *Library of Analytic Psychology*, vol. 7, London: London Academic Press.

Freud, A. (1986) *The Ego and the Mechanisms of Defence* (C. Baines, trans.), London: Hogarth Press (first published 1936).

Freud, S. (1909) 'Analysis of a phobia in a five-year-old boy' ('Little Hans'), pp. 167–305 in J. Strachey (ed.) (A. Strachey and J. Strachey, trans.), *The Standard Edition of the Complete Works of Sigmund Freud, vol. 8: Case Histories I*, London: Hogarth Press.

Hoxter, S. (1988) 'Play and communication', pp. 202–31 in M. Boston and D. Daws (eds) *The Child Psychotherapist*, London: Karnac.

Judd, D. (1989) *Give Sorrow Words: Working with a Dying Child*, London: Free Association Books.

Klein, M. (1932a) *The Psychoanalysis of Children*, London: Hogarth Press.

—— (1932b) *The Technique of Early Analysis*, vol. 2, London: Hogarth Press.

Lowenfeld, M. L. (1935) *Play in Childhood*, London: Gollancz.

Lush, D. (1988) 'The child guidance clinic', pp. 63–85 in M. Boston and D. Daws (eds) *The Child Psychotherapist*, London: Karnac.

Lush, D., Boston, M. and Grainger, E. (1991) 'Evaluation of psychoanalytic psychotherapy with children: therapist assessments and predictions', *Journal of Psychoanalytical Psychotherapy* 5(3): 191–234.

Meltzer, D. (1978) 'The case history of Little Hans', p. 52 in *The Kleinian Development*, part 1, London: Clunie Press.

Miller, L. (1992) *Understanding Your Baby*, London: Rosendale Press.

Miller, L., Rustin, M., Rustin, M. and Shuttleworth, J. (1989) *Closely Observed Infants*, London: Duckworth.

Reeves, A. C. (1981) 'Freud and child psychotherapy', pp. 251–71 in D. Daws and M. Boston (eds) *The Child Psychotherapist*, London: Wildwood House.

Robertson, J. and Robertson, J. (1972) 'Young children in brief separation: a fresh look', in A. J. Solnit, P. D. Neubauer, S. Abrams and A. S. Dowling (eds) *The Psycho-analytic Study of the Child*, vol. 26, London and New Haven: Yale University Press.

Sinason, V. (1992) *Mental Handicap and the Human Condition: New Approaches from the Tavistock*, London: Free Association Books.

Steiner, D. (1991) *Your One-Year-Old*, London: Rosendale Press.

Tustin, F. (1969) 'Autistic processes', *Journal of Child Psychotherapy* 2(3).

—— (1990) *The Protective Shell in Children and Adults*, London: Karnac.

—— (1993) *Autistic States in Children* (rev. edn), London: Routledge.

Winnicott, D. W. (1981) *The Child, the Family and the Outside World*, Harmondsworth: Penguin (first published 1964).

Wittenberg, I. (1988) 'Counselling young people', pp. 136–59 in M. Boston and D. Daws (eds) *The Child Psychotherapist*, London: Karnac.

RECENT PUBLICATIONS BY CHILD PSYCHOTHERAPISTS

Alvarez, A. (1992) *Live Company: Psycho-analytic Psychotherapy with Autistic, Borderline, Deprived and Abused Children*, London: Routledge.

Boston, M. and Daws, D. (eds) (1988) *The Child Psychotherapist*, London: Karnac.

Daws, D. (1989) *Through the Night: Helping Parents and Sleepless Infants*, London: Free Association Books.

Fonagy, P., Moran, G. and Higgett, A. (1989) 'Psychological factors in the self-management of insulin dependent diabetes mellitus in children and adolescents', in J. Wardle and S. Pearce (eds) *The Practice of Behavioural Medicine*, Oxford: Oxford University Press.

Judd, D. (1989) *Give Sorrow Words: Working with a Dying Child*, London: Free Association Books.

Miller, L., Rustin, M., Rustin, M. and Shuttleworth, J. (1989) *Closely Observed Infants*, London: Duckworth.

Sinason, V. (1992) *Mental Handicap and the Human Condition: New Approaches from the Tavistock*, London: Free Association Books.

Szur, R. and Miller, S. (eds) (1991) *Extending Horizons: Psychoanalytic Psychotherapy with Children, Adolescents and Families*, London: Karnac.

FURTHER INFORMATION

**The Association of Child
Psychotherapists**
Burgh House
New End Square
London NW3

The Child Psychotherapy Trust
21 Maresfield Gardens
London NW3 5SH

Chapter 10

Adolescent psychotherapy

Robert Jezzard

It is not difficult to find young people during the adolescent phase of development who seem to 'need' psychotherapy or counselling. The need is usually defined by a concerned adult, but the young person may have different views! Perhaps less frequently a young person may themselves declare a wish for help but find that the relevant adults, whether they be parents, other carers or professionals, are either unsupportive or even actively against the idea. Therefore, the mutually agreed decision between all concerned that psychotherapy is 'a good idea' cannot be assumed, however obvious the 'need' appears to be.

There are a number of prerequisites that need to be satisfied before psychotherapy with young people can start. Once it has been established and agreed that psychotherapy is both desirable and acceptable then it can begin. But it is then that the psychotherapist's real difficulties may start! There are further hurdles to be crossed before the useful components of theory and technique can be utilised. Some understanding of the adolescent's way of dealing with the world is required, but of even greater importance is a capacity on the psychotherapist's part to be resilient, flexible without being unprofessional, and, at the most basic level, being able to 'survive' in a therapeutic context with the young person without being totally humiliated and de-skilled. The 'rules' of therapy are not well understood by many young people, and they do not readily take for granted that those put forward by even the most benevolent of psychotherapists are necessary or appropriate.

WORKING WITH TROUBLED ADOLESCENTS

Anyone who has attempted to understand what is troubling a distressed but inarticulate adolescent will be able to describe the feelings of helplessness that can arise. To offer advice and an understanding ear and to have them summarily rejected or ignored leaves the 'helpful' adult bemused, humiliated and frequently angry. Many of us can still hear the phrase 'You just don't fucking understand!' ringing in our ears. The desire on adults' part may then be to just let them get on with it. However, it must be remembered that it is often the failure on the part of adults that has contributed to the development of the problem in the first place. In these circumstances, the psychotherapist may feel that he is having to bear the total burden of guilt of all those adults who have somehow failed to meet the hopes and expectations of the young person. It is easy to feel angry on behalf of your client, even to the point of giving voice to views about the shortcomings of their parent(s). This may lead to an extraordinary display of loyalty by the young person to even the most apparently abusive of adults. It is rare to come across a parent who has not tried to do their best to bring up their child. They may have been misguided or brought their own unresolved issues into their child's life, but none the less they will have wanted to be a good parent. At present, more than ever, parents are exhorted to take greater responsibility for the behaviour of their children, but we all know that is easier said than done. It is incumbent upon the professionals to retain some humility in their dealings with the parents or carers. In the face of turbulent or painful emotions, the task is one of 'survival', for parent and psychotherapist alike. There may be few tangible rewards for the effort or indications that either has got anywhere near 'getting it right'.

Theoretical models of adolescent development and therapy rarely offer much in the way of practical advice about how to cope with a first inter-view, let alone continue a constructive long-term professional relationship with a young person. Whether it be trying to elicit psychotic phenomen-ology from a bemused or frustrated teenager thought to be suffering from schizophrenia or whether it be trying to understand why an overdose has been taken by a young person who hides her face and remains mute, some practical tips are required to help the adult remain in contact with the young person with some confidence. Psychodynamic theories, however well understood, may seem totally irrelevant if the client is hostile or unco-operative; practical ways of working have to be found. A firm, secure anchor with a rope that offers some flexibility and leeway is required for a teenager who is being tossed around in a sea of turbulent emotions. Too rigid or restricting a hold may pull the young person under. Too insecure and changeable a base may allow the young person to drift too far away or drown.

PREREQUISITES FOR PSYCHOTHERAPY

An understanding of developmental issues and a knowledge of the law are first required. Adolescence is often described as a time of identity acquisition (Erikson 1968). A secure identity is not an ideal that is acquired exclusively in adolescence, but during a process that occurs throughout life, and which happens to present crucial tasks in adolescence. It is the time when 'given' values from family and school are re-evaluated. It is the time when alternative beliefs are more obviously on offer, and these must be explored in the struggle to individuate from parents. It is a time of considerable change. Not only is it a time of physical and sexual development or a time in which social relationships are explored, but also a time in which there are cognitive changes. The capacity to reason, to think ahead and gain a perspective of the future, and to make connections between present and past events may develop during this period; but for each young person the process is slightly different and the stage of development may not match the chronological age. This must be borne in mind during the psychotherapy sessions; an immature seventeen-year-old may require a more structured method of working, while a more mature fourteen-year-old may be able to tolerate a more open-ended, reflective approach.

Legislation, as far as it is relevant to children, has changed a great deal over the last few years. The Children Act now encompasses most of that which is relevant for a therapist to know. However, there are areas which are still being clarified, such as consent to treatment *vis-à-vis* the rights of children as opposed to the rights of parents to give or withhold consent. There is not the scope in this chapter to address these issues, but it needs to be said that it is incumbent upon all therapists to have sufficient understanding of the legal framework in which they have to operate.

Who is requesting the help? If it is the client, they may have unrealistic expectations of what therapy can mean. They may not want to be there at all, perhaps from a profound ambivalence about authority figures, and therefore not maintain contact. If it is the parents, they may be asking the psychotherapist to change the young person, but their views on what needs changing may be very different from the young person's or the psychotherapist's. If it is private work, the parent(s) may be paying, therefore the contract is with them rather than with the young person. For example, if the young person's attitude is a product of how the family functions, it may be necessary to negotiate with the family about what is and what is not possible, and what part they may play.

The mere existence of a 'need' for help is an insufficient guide to the appropriateness for therapy. In assessing a young person for psychotherapy the therapist must have a clear understanding of the origins of a young person's problems, the extent of the need and the time-scale required. It is not uncommon for the wish to 'rescue' a person from their plight to lead to unrealistic hopes being encouraged. There is also a danger of the psychotherapist becoming a surrogate parent, if the child is living in an awful world. No matter what the time period, the therapy will usually end before the child in this situation is ready. The form of the therapy must be taken into account; for example, whether individual, group or family therapy would be the more appropriate.

Not all adolescents are in a position comfortably to explore new values and ideas. If they have grown up in an environment riddled with inconsistency and lack of clarity, this task is made especially difficult for them. Exploratory behaviour in toddlers occurs safely when there is a secure base from which to operate. Similarly, in adolescence exploration of ideas and beliefs can only really occur if childhood experience has offered some clarity about the child's place in the world. They cannot face painful feelings without a support system. If the adolescent is in 'limbo' (e.g. awaiting placement with a foster family) psychotherapy cannot take place. Equally it can be extraordinarily difficult for re-evaluation of beliefs and values to occur when the adults 'hold on' tightly and restrict the process of exploration and discovery too rigidly. The impending loss for them of their child may be unbearably painful. These restrictions may be associated with parental rigidity or unwitting over-protection, and nearly always imply some lack of understanding about the developmental needs of the young person. The therapist needs to check which adults are prepared to support the intervention. The psychotherapist's views may differ from those of parents and teachers. If there is the possibility of work being undermined by an unsupportive adult, then an additional worker may be required to work with them.

FIRST STEPS

So how do we cope with these young people? How do we ensure that they do take advantage of helpful adults? How do we listen to them and understand them? In what context do we see them – alone, with their family, or in groups? Whatever the context, whatever the theoretical model, and whatever the problem, the first aim is to ensure that no interview with a young person makes it less likely in the future that a young person will go for help or talk to an adult. A short meeting which elicits little information but which makes the young person feel that there is some prospect of being understood *may* be more helpful than a long interview with a laborious dissection of problems. The latter type of interview will feel persecutory at worst, and irrelevant at best, and may put them off seeking help for ever. If a 'need' of a fourteen-year-old cannot be met when first noted, we must ensure that we do not compound the problem by making this young person less amenable to help at a later stage.

To achieve these minimal aims a young person's view must be respected, even if an alternative adult view is presented. For example: 'I appreciate that you feel the only way to make teachers hear is to shout at them and that at present this is what you may have to do, but it is possible that this makes the problem worse and may make them less likely to listen than before. Maybe we need to look for another way of helping them to understand you.'

In addition, there is the issue of trust and the effect of past experiences. An adolescent who has been let down, perhaps by the abuse of power in the context of child abuse, who has been denied a good experience of parenting, perhaps by an alcoholic parent or who has suffered many losses, may just not feel able to trust even the most well-intentioned adult. It is no wonder that young people in this position are uncommunicative, surly and avoiding. Rekindling trust can take a long time and the process may have many genuine ups and downs.

A further issue to tackle early are the rules of the basic psychotherapy session itself. Don't be afraid of explaining the strange ways of the professional world, because it is probably new to them. After working for a while with teenagers it can seem by contrast that adults are surprisingly compliant about the basics of the session: that it starts at, say, 10 a.m. and ends at 10.50, that if they arrive late the session is shortened, that they give notice of not attending, and that it is their role to 'do the telling' about their particular difficulties. Adolescents can find this structure extremely difficult, so it may be necessary to be flexible, to negotiate a fairly formal way of seeing the young person, and to give explanations if necessary.

What information goes where, and to whom? Negotiating issues around confidentiality is a big issue in working with adolescents. For example, in working with under-sixteens a contract may need to be negotiated allowing contact with or work with parents. Under-sixteens may disclose experience of sexual or general abuse. If the contract is 100 per cent confidential, the psychotherapist may feel unable to take appropriate action to protect the child. If the contract is to work with another agency then it is less likely to be 100 per cent confidential. A typical example of this issue is the fourteen-year-old who says he feels like committing suicide: if you have told him, 'Our session is just between us and these four walls', then he states he is suicidal with 'Don't tell Mum and Dad, I want to kill myself', you are left with the dilemma of whether to go to the parents or the social services.

Finally, the various expectations that the therapist may have of the young person or vice versa can sometimes be helpfully written down in the form of a contract. If there are rules – for instance, about lateness or cancelled sessions – they must be specified. Too often young people are assumed to appreciate what is required of them or how they are meant to behave. The flexibility that may be built into such negotiations will depend upon many factors and, above all, must bear some relation to the capacity of the young person to abide by them.

SOME PRACTICAL PROBLEMS

Whether it is your first interview with a young person or your fiftieth, you can still find yourself beset with a practical communication problem which makes the task of being 'helpful' very difficult indeed. Often you will want to be finding out information, establishing trust, negotiating a problem, giving a view, reinforcing parental authority and understanding the young person all at the same time. You may find the young person walking out after ten minutes or difficult to persuade to leave after ninety minutes. It matters very little whether your task is 'in depth' psychotherapy, persuading them to take unpleasant medication, taking a medical history or advising them about their smoking habit – you still have to feel comfortable in their presence for them to feel comfortable in yours. You still have to respect them even if they give the impression of not respecting you, and you have to find a way of coping with the barriers to easy and open communication; that is, *if you wish to have a positive influence and be helpful.* Be prepared to feel incompetent and humiliated sometimes, and be prepared to learn from others about ways of communicating and listening effectively. Above all, learn from your own experiences, both positive and negative.

The young person may not want to tell you anything at all – why should they? – especially if they did not want to see you in the first place. If you manage to negotiate this first issue, it may become clear that the young person does not trust adults, for very good reasons; whether consciously or unconsciously. They may be frightened, anxious and depressed; such overwhelming feelings make it hard for many adults to talk easily, let alone teenagers.

The young person may feel they will be rejected, disliked or disbelieved if they tell you what is wrong. It may be concretely expressed, in terms of 'If you really knew, you'd never want to see me again'. Underlying this may be fear, conflicts of loyalty or belief systems, or a fragile self-esteem. The young person may feel that they will appear stupid or silly if they put their feelings and problems into words. Equally, they may just simply want to please you and collude with the psychotherapist's hope that things are getting better. These very basic doubts in the young person's mind can also contribute to the feelings of persecution that are engendered by even the most benevolent and well-intentioned question.

Denial that a problem exists presents a very real challenge – for example, 'There's nothing wrong' or 'The teachers are lying' – and this makes it very hard to solve. Equally the projection of the problem onto others, such as 'Teachers pick on me' or 'My brother keeps destroying my clothes', may deflect the psychotherapist from the task. There may some truth in their views about the problem, but equally they may be reluctant to own their part of it. If they only see themselves as 'victims' it is hard to get them to address the part they play in the process. Another version of denial to be aware of is the protest of recovery; for example, 'It's all right now! It won't happen again! I'm going back to school on Monday!' It is so easy to accept such statements against your better judgement, as it is always a relief to think a problem has been solved. However, always check the real likelihood from past experience and history.

The young person may also understate the problem, acknowledging the problem but in such a casual and/or dismissive fashion that it is hard to pursue. It is easy to collude with the expressed view that the problem is insignificant. Psychotherapists wish to believe what they hear, need to respect a young person's perception, but may be fooled in the process. A thirteen-year-old charged with the attempted rape of an adult woman commented, 'I only touched her bum.' This understatement rendered it very difficult for the psychotherapist to address the serious nature of the problem. At times it will be necessary to seek confirmation from others – school, parents, perhaps – if you are going to address the problem at all. This always requires negotiation if trust is to be preserved and does not necessarily mean that you are going to break confidentiality. To deny yourself necessary knowledge about a child's behaviour or experiences may mean you simply collude with that child's unrealistic hopes and views of the world around them.

Some young people adopt a pseudo-sophisticated manner, such as the twelve-year-old who could not play with his peers and refused to go to school, who told me, 'The child inside me has been kidnapped'. Much of his conversation and most of the explanations for his difficulties were intellectually challenging, fascinating to listen to and fertile ground for endless intriguing discussion. It is easy to be hoodwinked by apparently sophisticated discussions which, if looked at more closely, are masterpieces of illogicality, 'second-hand', or simply mechanisms to avoid painful realities.

Some young persons are very adept at avoiding serious discussions by their witty repartee. It can be very seductive and it is easy to join in if it is mutually advantageous not to deal with painful issues – especially when you are busy. Equally the 'butter-wouldn't-melt-in-my-mouth' look of angelic innocence can produce a similar response, for it misses the point and can mask despair.

Racist or sexist remarks which offend can make it very difficult to work with a young person. They nevertheless have to be dealt with in a way which does not deny the young person's right to receive help. A typical retort was 'Women should do all the housework' as a response from a male who refused to help with the washing-up at home. It can be quite difficult to address such assertively held views which are contrary to what you or others believe.

Occasionally a young person will refuse to see you. Once a fourteen-year-old travelled across London by bus and arrived for his appointment on time to tell me that he did not want to see me. After a period of much verbal abuse, running away and then returning, he eventually burst into tears and told me that he had been beaten by his father that day. Be ready to consider that the surface statement may mask real distress and over-whelming need. Equally, a request to see you less often *may* be a test of your interest in them and capacity to take them seriously and to care about them.

One of the most incapacitating modes of communication is silence. A fifteen-year-old girl attended regularly, sat down with her hair hanging in front of her face, head down, biting her nails, and if she said anything it was in an inaudible whisper. At times she would curl up into a tight, silent ball. It can leave you feeling truly helpless, hopeless and incompetent. In fact, this girl rang the clinic years later, now able to talk; and during the discussion, I asked her why she had been so quiet then. She said: 'I had so much to say I just didn't know where to begin.' This leads naturally to the next point: take care with silence, as it is often, but not always, threatening. Be sensitive to this. However, be careful not to fill up silence with conversation if it is your discomfort that you are dealing with rather than the young person's.

Another practical problem sometimes arises when verbal expression is impoverished and in its place come frequent shrugs, frequent replies such as 'I dunno!', 'I don't care', ''Cos it's boring' or 'I can't remember'. The capacity to express a viewpoint or to engage in debate requires ease with the use of language. The child brought up in a family with limited verbal stimulation or a family where feelings are rarely expressed finds themselves handicapped in adolescence when struggling to account for themselves or make themselves heard. The young person's shorthand for painful emo-tions can so easily not be interpreted by the psychotherapist. Taking these phrases at face value may prevent any understanding from taking place. These responses frequently stop the discussion by simply blocking it, or diverting attention away from important areas, and a way around them needs to be found. For example, 'bored' is a word that can be used to sum up almost any negative emotion, such as angry, depressed, worried, muddled and so forth. Equally, 'I don't care' almost never means what it says. I have never yet come across a young person who does not care. Finally, 'Dunno' or 'Can't remember' may simply mean they can't face telling you.

It may simply not be possible for an adolescent to name the feelings they are experiencing, for they are often diffuse and mixed emotions which are not easily differentiated; or the feelings may simply be new to the young person. This is one reason why the young person may not feel confident about, or even know, the best word for their experiences. 'I've got the hump' may be their best phrase for 'depressed', and this slang expression may mask the true despair which the psychotherapist is none the less expected to understand. To some extent, this problem may be one of cognition, so assessment of the stage of development of the young person is always an essential part of the process.

A very common problem encountered in day-to-day practice is the secret trap, such as: 'My step-father is sexually abusing me, but I don't want you to tell anyone'. The attempt to establish confidence, confidentiality and trust can lead you into the trap of not being able to take necessary action to protect a young person who is seriously at risk. Never promise what you can't deliver.

Some young people make disrespectful comments, such as 'You're a goat!' I have been called many things in my time, from the above to the misuse of my name, from 'Dr Jedi' to Bob to Sir, and it is not a matter which I waste time over. It is also easy to be totally thrown by very personal questions coming out of the blue: 'Have you ever been to dirty movies?' Often these are more genuine and innocent than they appear. They challenge your boundaries very effectively, however!

Hostile remarks such as 'Stop being so nosy' or 'You don't bloody well understand' or even a physical threat, particularly if said in a venomous tone, can render the interviewer powerless and defensive. At times they may make you angry and/or frightened – not exactly the most fertile ground for a sensitive and understanding discussion.

The 'yawn' or the sudden trip to the loo are things to look out for. Take note of when these imposed breaks in interviews take place, for you may well find that you are approaching the important issue. It may be a time to respect the young person's need to stop there, or the opposite. Maybe they simply need extra time to think. Sometimes it can be a difficult judgement to make.

SOME USEFUL PRINCIPLES

Behaviour tends to be the main communicative modality rather than words, but its interpretation is frequently misunderstood by adults. A search for meaning becomes replaced by insensitive management. Unexpected difficult behaviour usually has a 'meaning'. You may not need to interpret it directly, but the young person needs to know that you've picked up the meaning or, at the very least, that it *has meaning* even if at the time you do not understand what it is all about. This does not stop the adult from responding to the behaviour if this is required, but a search for meaning may make the management of the behaviour fairer and more consistent. For example, an attack on another child by a teenager brandishing a billiard cue may have to be managed without words in order to prevent harm. The behaviour must be stopped and contained before any attempt at understanding is achieved. This does not even preclude the use of appropriate sanctions. However, whether the young person wishes to talk about the event afterwards or not, the adult should share their bemusement as to why it happened and what was trying to be communicated. No compromise should be adopted over defining the acceptability or otherwise of such extreme behaviour, but this does not preclude understanding. A brisk, firm, authoritative response to control a situation will ultimately be more acceptable if the young person perceives the benevolent intent of the adult and the adult's interest in the background to the event. If the behaviour has no meaning, then no harm has been done; but if the behaviour is indeed meaningful and is a maladaptive communication, then much may have been lost by failing to address it.

In order to build a good relationship you need to treat the views of young people with respect. You do not have to agree with a young person to have respect for their right to hold their own opinion. They are unlikely to listen to you or reflect on their views if they feel you have not listened to them, heard what they are saying and respected their right to have a view different from your own. Make a clear distinction between hearing them and offering them your own alternative viewpoint. The latter cannot be imposed upon a young person but it can be offered to them to consider. At times they may take your opinion very seriously and value it *but* nevertheless appear to reject it; they absorb it privately and the last thing they may want to admit is that they have valued you. Self-respect and pride can very often be eroded by the clever guy imposing his own viewpoint.

Always assume the young person's interest in being helped. Many young people will make considerable efforts to give the impression that they think that you are useless and are not valued. If they have come to see you, that may say much more than the attitude presented to you. Many mistakes are made by too readily accepting the surface statements and demeanour.

In working with young people, it is important to avoid fruitless battles; and to try not to win. There are some issues which it is right to be firm about, and those require no discussion, as this often leads to deadlock or futile battles which you are likely to lose. On the other hand, many 'disagreements' are fairly minor, and it may be important to allow teenagers some sense of autonomy and independence by judiciously conceding to their view. If you are 'right', your view may then ultimately be more readily accepted.

Don't be put off if discussion seems superficial and irrelevant. Many issues are worked out 'in the metaphor' and may never require explicit clarification. The need for clarification is often the professional's need rather than that of the young person. For example, the psychotherapist may feel at times that the discussion is about trivialities, e.g. about last weekend's camping trip, but often a surprising amount of 'private' work is being done within the adolescent's mind at the same time, or after the session, which may or may not ever be acknowledged or expressed.

If possible balance the discussion, as a totally 'heavy' discussion may become unbearable. Do not avoid painful issues that can be discussed if they need to be discussed. But periods of more neutral inquiry or even light-hearted discussion may make the addressing of difficult material more bearable.

It is important to be adult. The young person won't necessarily thank you for your teenage reminiscences. They may need you to be adult and different. A frequent cry in adolescence is 'I am different', expressed through clothes, tastes, rebellion: all sorts of means. If you reply, 'Yes, I am the same', a barrier is immediately built and the young person's identity development is thwarted. Your job as an adult psychotherapist is not to join in with younger people or to 'share' their experience with, say, a reminiscence of the music of your day – although the obvious irony is that they *do* need to be understood – but to remain adult, and above all to be tolerant. Understanding can grow through the very fact of being different. 'The best thing to do is to behave in a manner befitting one's age. If you are sixteen or under try not to go bald' (Woody Allen).

You need to find a common language, which does not mean talking to them like a teenager. However, there may be words and phrases which they find comfortable in using that have more meaning to them than your own. A manifestly severely depressed young person may prefer to talk about being 'fed up' rather than depressed. Do not talk down to them and do not try and use phoney or age-inappropriate language, but 'tune in' to their key words and use them judiciously if it helps you to communicate more effectively. Develop a language common and useful to you both.

When 'stuck', asking a teenager for their three wishes can sometimes be very revealing. It can also be useful to have activity bridges. These are a shared activity which may facilitate a useful discussion. How often in residential settings have 'breakthroughs' occurred while doing the washing-up? Clearly, the activity has to be appropriate to the context.

Feedback is often better than interpretation. This is not a universal rule, but, for many, an interpretation can feel persecutory, or like an imposition of your views. Don't assume anything until you can be sure that they have heard you at face value; remember that they are giving their construction, their view. There is a tremendous temptation for adults to impose their sophisticated understanding and beliefs about 'meaning' before listening and acknowledging the communication first. For example, a psychothera-pist working with an individual in a group said, 'What you're really trying to tell me is you're angry with your father' and received the angry retort, 'Stop fucking twisting everything I say!' The psychotherapist had not negotiated early with the adolescent, or respected him, but turned his statement into the therapist's own idea, own language. Later in the group session, the psychotherapist understood enough to say, 'Do you mind if I twist it around . . . ?' and got a grunt of half-acknowledgement. Later the young person said, 'I suppose you want to twist that around?' – but at least offering an opportunity for this 'twisting' or interpretation to happen. Unless the process of interpretation is both 'negotiated' and also presented with benevolence and humility (as opposed to arrogant dogmatism!), personal feedback is preferable. 'What you have just said makes me feel very sad for you' may be better than 'You are depressed about the loss of your mother'. The idea about the issue – sadness, depression – is offered in a way which respects the young person's right not to acknowledge that you are correct. It also clarifies the mood of the interaction and it does not impose an idea or a word upon the young person which does not feel right for them.

Views and comments offered as choices, for the adolescent to reject or disregard if they wish, may lead to greater use being made of helpful and clarifying remarks from the interviewer. If an adolescent is having trouble labelling an emotional state, then 'multiple choices' of feeling states offered on a series of cards can be of help; see if one card carries a better word. Don't allow the stuckness with words, for feelings block further discussion. It may be helpful to offer the choices verbally in terms of 'What I'd feel/think if I were in your shoes'. Maybe describe the choices as being like a tray of hors d'oeuvres for you to take what you like the look of best.

For the sensitive young person, eye contact also may be threatening at points in an interview. Sometimes even averting your gaze may make a young person feel less vulnerable. However, it may be useful to regain eye contact when making an important positive point, particularly if it relates to your attempt to confirm that you have heard and are sensitive to their view or their problem.

Do not leave a young person exposed, vulnerable and traumatised at the end of an interview. Some attempt to check out how they are feeling and efforts to rebuild necessary defences before they leave may be essential.

CONCLUSION

We are often unaware of when we are being at our most helpful. You will be disappointed if you expect acknowledgement or thanks; but there may be some quite unexpected and indirect thanks if you look hard. Remember, adults may often feel irritated by not hearing 'Sorry' or 'Thank you', but it gets said by teenagers in other ways.

It is important to be flexible and not restrict therapeutic opportunities by sticking rigidly to the rules of therapy; *but* don't give up those rules which have evidently some value. The main job of the adult is to survive and 'stick with it' in the face of adolescent murder, to paraphrase Winnicott (1958), but not to become punitive or impatient in response to attack or passivity. Remain tolerant and a way will be found to provide that securing anchor.

REFERENCES

Erikson, E. H. (1968) *Identity, Youth and Crisis*, New York: Norton.
Winnicott, D. W. (1958) *Collected Papers*, London: Tavistock.

FURTHER READING

Bazalgette, J. (1971) *Freedom, Authority and the Young Adult*, London: Pitman.
Klein, J. (1987) *Our Need for Others and Its Roots in Infancy*, London: Tavistock Publications.
Rutter, M. and Hersov, L. (eds) (1985) *Child and Adolescent Psychiatry: Modern Approaches*, Oxford: Blackwell.
Steinberg, D. (1983) *The Clinical Psychiatry of Adolescence: Clinical Work from a Social and Developmental Perspective*, New York: Wiley.
—— (ed.) (1986) *The Adolescent Unit: Work and Teamwork in Adolescent Psychiatry*, New York: Wiley.
York, P., York, D. and Wachtel, T. (1982) *Toughlove*, New York: Bantam/Doubleday.

Chapter 11

Short-term psychotherapy

Gillian Butler and James Low

That there is no simple correlation between therapeutic results and the length and intensity of treatment has been recognised, tacitly or explicitly by most experienced psychoanalysts and is an old source of dissatisfaction among them. Among psychoanalysts there arise two types of reaction to this dissatisfaction. One was constructive like Ferenczi's relentless experimenting with technique in an effort to isolate the factors responsible for therapeutic results. The other was a self-deceptive defence in the form of an almost superstitious belief that quick therapeutic results cannot be genuine, that they are either those transitory results due to suggestion or an escape into 'pseudo-healthy' patients who prefer to give up their symptoms rather than obtain real insight into their difficulties.

(Alexander, in Alexander and French 1946: v)

Alexander's words are as true today as they were in 1946. This chapter is concerned with psychotherapy that is intentionally carried out over a short period of time. Many psychotherapies that might become long-term are cut short due to crises, the non-establishment or collapse of the psycho-therapeutic alliance, staff changes and so forth. Although NHS psycho-therapy departments tend to allocate resources in favour of patients receiving long-term therapy, there is little evidence to suggest that most continue treatment beyond six months. Howard *et al.* (1987) provide clinical evidence from the United States that suggests that this may be a common experience.

However, there are many forms of psychotherapy that are intentionally short-term. Such psychotherapy is done with individuals, couples, families, groups and organisations. Many different theoretical perspectives are made use of, including behavioural, cognitive-behavioural, cognitive-analytic, analytic, systemic and solution-focused. Sledge *et al.* (1990) made a distinction between time-limited psychotherapy, brief therapy and long-term psychotherapy. They see time-limited psychotherapy as one where the psychotherapist offers a pre-arranged, non-negotiable number of sessions and the client agrees to this at the beginning of psychotherapy, whereas brief psychotherapy lasts for three to four months but with no pre-fixed ending date. The end occurs when the particular topic that has been the focus of psychotherapy is satisfactorily addressed. In their research they found that the drop-out rate for time-limited psychotherapy was half that for each of the other types of psychotherapy. It would seem that when patients know how long the psychotherapy will last they are able to feel more in control, and are able to work in a focused way towards the goal set. Their conscious understanding of the contract may limit the explora-tion and help to reduce fears of engulfment and/or abandonment (see Ryle 1990).

DIFFERENT MODELS OF SHORT-TERM PSYCHOTHERAPY

The various models of short-term psychotherapy are united in the desire to provide an effective psychotherapy in as short a time as possible, and they share a belief in the possibility of significant change occurring in months rather than years. But they have very different ways of concep-tualising the problem and the processes of change. In a short chapter like this we cannot spell out all the significant differences. What we will do is present some general features of short-term psychotherapy, look at suitability and contra-indications and the process of assessment with examples from a range of short-term psychotherapists. We will then provide an account of two psychotherapies, one cognitive-analytic and the other cognitive-behavioural, to give a sense of the issues as they arise in practice.

We are using the term 'short-term psychotherapy' to indicate a therapy of up to twenty sessions, each lasting an hour, spaced at weekly intervals. Malan (1976) refers to cases of brief analytic psychotherapy ranging from four to fifty sessions. Mahrer (1989) described two-hour sessions, Ryle (1990) sixteen- or eight-session therapies, and many other permutations have been written about.

The approaches to short-term psychotherapy can be usefully classed into four 'families': dynamic or analytic, cognitive-behavioural, systemic and integrative. Existing literature seems to show little interest in short-term psychotherapy amongst humanistic practitioners. This may be due to the fact that most of the developments have occurred in public service institutions where cost-effectiveness and reduction of waiting lists have always been pressing concerns. The history of analytic brief psychotherapy is well documented, for example by Malan (1976), and Flegenheimer (1982) has provided useful summaries of the theories and techniques of the main approaches. Crits-Christoph and Barber (1991) describe recent advances highlighting the important role given to research, both process and outcome, in the development of specific applications of short-term dynamic psychotherapy. Ashurst (1991) provides a very clear, brief and comprehensive introduction to the key issues in dynamic brief psychotherapy.

Cognitive psychotherapy was developed as a short-term method of treatment, and included both cognitive and behavioural techniques.* So cognitive behaviour therapy (CBT) is based on a theoretical model of emotional disorder which explains how the relationships between thoughts and feelings can provoke and maintain distress. Theoretically, long-term improvement can be achieved in a short time by working to identify, examine and test out different ways of thinking. Precise techniques were first developed for working with depressed patients (Beck 1976; Beck *et al.* 1979), and have been elaborated for work with many other emotional disorders (for example, Beck *et al.* 1985; Hawton *et al.* 1989; Scott *et al.* 1989). A large body of research now documents the clinical effectiveness of short-term cognitive behaviour therapy and continues to contribute to the development and elaboration of the theoretical model. In contrast to more dynamic psychotherapies, longer-term treatments are being developed after the short-term ones have become established (for example, Beck *et al.*, 1990; Young 1990), and new theoretical developments continue to broaden the potential scope of this approach (for instance, Safran and Segal 1991).

From the beginning family psychotherapy, informed by a systems theory, operated with a sharp awareness of the importance of short-term interventions. When the prime concern of psychotherapists is to promote change in the system, their own position *vis-à-vis* the system should not be one that promotes stabilising dependence. Out of this basic notion a wide range of interventions have developed and with them a permission for the psychotherapist to be active and creative. This finds its most radical development in solution-focused psychotherapy where the focus of attention is consistently on difference, on what is new. The psychotherapy affects a shift in interest in the client away from problems and their convolutions and origins towards any and every event that is different. The psychotherapy has no contracted time limit but tends to be short-term (Shazer 1991).

The integrative approach to psychotherapy has opened up new ways of combining effective features of different models in order to optimise sustainable change within short-term psychotherapy. Norcross (1986), Marteau (1986) and Ryle (1990) each offer a skeletal structure which can

---

* The terms 'cognitive therapy' and 'cognitive behaviour therapy' are confusing as they have often been used interchangeably. It is fair to say that the main types of cognitive therapy make use of some behavioural strategies. These strategies play a crucial part in the treatment, as they involve carrying out 'behavioural experiments' which help to determine whether certain ways of thinking are unrealistic or unhelpful. The term 'cognitive behaviour therapy' (CBT) will be used in this chapter to make clear the distinction from cognitive analytic therapy.

be fleshed out with different emphases and techniques according to the precise needs of the individual client. Indeed, short-term models often have a predetermined feel about them, an 'off-the-peg' quality which requires a skilful adaptation by the psychotherapist so that the psychotherapy is tailored to suit the client rather than vice versa.

GENERAL FEATURES

Although there are many models of brief psychotherapy, certain general features can be identified. These are both a consequence of the brief focus and significant determining factors in its efficacy.

First, the psychotherapist is active, taking on a variety of functions including teaching, modelling, encouraging and structuring the work. This activity is designed to stimulate and support a matching activity in the patient. If it promotes dependence, something has gone wrong. The psychotherapist needs to be explicit about what is on offer at the beginning of psychotherapy so that the patient can make an informed choice. The psychotherapist needs to believe in the value of short-term work since their confidence, empathy and availability are key factors.

Secondly, the psychotherapeutic alliance is a central feature. In most forms of brief psychotherapy the alliance is strengthened by the conscious agreement to focus on an explicit problem that has been identified together. Psychotherapist and patient find themselves working together with a shared goal but different tasks. This shared belief in the possibility of solving the problem promotes negotiation and the creative channelling of difference into the further development of self-confidence and self-esteem.

Thirdly, the patient's motivation is affirmed, responded to and developed. The desire for change must be linked to the implementation of strategies that will make change a reality. These strategies may be implemented through communication or by means of tasks that shift cognition, affect or behaviour. This may include interpretation within the psychotherapeutic relationship, behaviour monitoring, set homework and so on.

Fourthly, the focus is on supporting patients in their ordinary lives. Whatever is learned during the session needs to be generalised through application in the wider social environment. Particular ways of understanding are linked to patterns and procedures in such a way as to lead the patient towards a resolution of the present difficulties.

Fifthly, the containment and structure provided by the temporal focal issue and active development of the psychotherapeutic alliance provide a context within which patients can try out new ways of thinking, feeling and behaving. Negative expectations of the patient are explored or interpreted and also confronted through reality-based feedback – for instance, about efforts and achievements in psychotherapy. The clearer the focus, the easier it is for patients to evaluate their own progress and to use the support of the psychotherapist to avoid self-sabotage or the tendency to discount their own success.

Obviously, a great deal more could be said about these points, and of course many of the factors mentioned are shared with long-term psychotherapy. Weakland *et al.*, writing of their focused problem resolution model of brief psychotherapy, make a point that short-term psychotherapists of many persuasions would agree with that.

> Our fundamental premise is that regardless of their basic origins and aetiology – if, indeed, these can ever be reliably determined – the kind of problems people bring to psychotherapists persist only if they are maintained by ongoing current behaviour of the patient and others with whom he interacts. Correspondingly, if such problem-maintaining behaviour is appropriately changed or eliminated, the problem will be resolved or vanish, regardless of its nature, origin or duration.
>
> (1974: 144–5)

Different models will give different accounts of the ongoing current behaviour that maintains problems. In short-term psychotherapy the relevant behaviours have to be readily identifiable and easily recognised by the patient.

SELECTION OF PATIENTS

The short-term psychotherapies that have an analytic approach often include selection criteria that are difficult to assess accurately or objectively. These tend to become qualities that psychotherapists learn to identify intuitively through the distillation of experience rather than being able to tick off on a checklist. This is one of the reasons why some writers believe that short-term psychotherapy is best performed by very experienced psychotherapists (Marteau 1986).

Lists of selection criteria have been provided by many writers (for example, Ashurst 1991; Malan 1976, 1979; Crits-Christoph and Barber 1991). Crits-Christoph and Barber (1991) have very usefully compared the selection criteria and disqualifiers of a range of short-term dynamic psychotherapies. Although there are wide variations, typical exclusion criteria are addictions, psychosis, severe personality disorders and suicidal acting out. In contrast, Ryle (1990, 1992) has described the successful use of cognitive-analytic psychotherapy with very disturbed borderline patients. In all cases the basic concern must be whether a short-term psychotherapy is likely to make the patient worse – a judgement that is necessarily based on accumulated wisdom and experience in the absence of an accepted body of relevant research and information.

Nielsen and Barth (1991) suggest that the patient's ability to define a circumscribed chief complaint is indicative of ego strength, reality testing, tolerance of frustration, and capacity for delaying gratification. Thus the ability of the patient to identify a focal problem in the first few sessions is an indication of their having the resources to make effective use of this psychotherapy. Of course, the patient's capacity to participate in this way is influenced by the psychotherapist's ability to respond in a flexible way in order to promote dialogue and the development of a psychotherapeutic alliance.

When psychotherapy is short-term it is important for patients to be able to engage quickly in treatment, and to make a commitment to it. The degree to which they can do this, and opt positively for the treatment offered, has therefore to be weighed up during assessment. Some patients may select themselves, or their behaviour may provide important clues. Those who can ask questions about what is on offer, and think about what they want to get out of it, may be better able to set achievable goals, less likely to be troubled by disruptive avoidance or fantasy, and more likely to develop realistic expectations about psychotherapy.

We now offer two examples of short-term psychotherapy which illustrate some of the points made above.

COGNITIVE-ANALYTIC THERAPY (CAT) WITH A BORDERLINE PATIENT

Ryle (1990) provides a clear account of the theory, structure and practice of this model. The intention here is to give an account of a case highlighting the particular concerns of a time-limited psychotherapy approach.

Mary was thirty-eight when she was referred for CAT from a sexual problems clinic where she had presented with vaginismus. Mary has had several psychiatric admissions over the last fifteen years stemming from suicide attempts, alcohol and drug problems, anxiety and depression. She met all eight of the DSM-111-R criteria for Borderline Personality Disorder. Angry and withdrawn at the beginning of psychotherapy, she treated every comment by the psychotherapist as an invasive attack and replied with disparaging remarks regarding the quality and efficacy of the psychotherapy. Once this pattern was identified the psychotherapist outlined the structure of the psychotherapy, going over what would be required of psychotherapist and patient, repeating the details until anxiety diminished and the work could begin.

Mary's mother had died shortly after her birth and she was taken care of by an aunt and uncle whom she took to be her real parents. When she was five they told her that her mother was dead and that her 'uncle' was in fact her father. She went with him to Australia for several years and then back with him to England to be passed from one set of unwilling relatives to another. Her father was drunk and violent and she often felt unsafe in his company. He was also sexually provocative with her, and she is haunted by the thought that he may have done more than she can remember.

By her late teens she was taking a lot of amphetamines and living in a chaotic manner. Her life since then had been marked by violent relationships, severe alcohol abuse and an absence of supportive relationships. Her father had died six years previously by falling into the River Thames. She was never sure if it was a drunken accident, suicide or murder, and was terrified that her own life might end in a similar way.

There were obvious specific problems that could have become the focus for the sixteen-week psychotherapy that was on offer, but through the discussion of the first two meetings, Mary came up with an existential question: 'How can I be in life when death, abandonment and confusion are so woven into my story?'

The open-endedness of this question could easily lead to wide-ranging exploration that might have become a way of avoiding distressing issues. However, the psychotherapist felt that the structure of the psychotherapy was precise enough to provide momentum and direction to the inquiry. As she said several times, 'If I know how to live, how to be alive, if I know that in myself, then I will be able to control myself. But I don't exist.' Having been deprived of so much, it seemed very important that she be allowed to stay with her question. Developmentally, the absence of consistent and reliable parenting and especially the confusion of identity of key figures in her early years had led to all her object relations being permeated by uncertainty and suspicion. She was convinced that her birth had caused her mother's death and so she was a monster whom no one could bear to be close to. 'I deserve nothing.'

This uncertainty and suspicious hostility was very evident in the transference, with each attack being followed by apologies and remorse. At the end of the first session, Mary had been given a psychotherapy file to fill in. This file gives brief descriptions of common procedures, and the patient is invited to identify the ones that they recognise some involvement with – see Ryle (1990) for a detailed description. This self-identification of the procedures facilitates the elaboration of more precisely customised procedural descriptions since it bypasses the resistance that interpretation can evoke. By the fourth session two procedures were identified as maintaining her problematic being in the world.

1 *The dilemma*: either I keep feelings bottled up, strive to be perfect and feel angry and depressed, or I let things out, risk not being perfect, hurting others, being rejected, making a mess, feeling guilty, angry and dissatisfied.
2 *The trap*: feeling depressed and uncertain about myself, I try to please others and do what they want. I have no time to meet my own needs

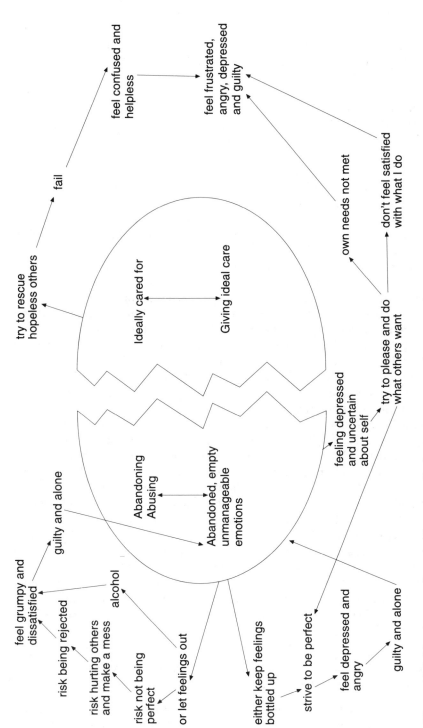

Figure 11.1 Mary's procedures in diagrammatic form

and so I feel frustrated and angry. I then get drunk, out of control, and feel guilty, depressed and confused, back where I started.

For Mary these procedures were a revelation, especially when presented in diagrammatic form (see Figure 11.1).

The split core of the diagram highlights the gap across which Mary flipped in her mood swings. The arrows indicate the way in which the procedures arise from a core state, either as a direct expression of it or as an attempt to gain distance from it. The procedural movement always returns to the core, illustrating the way the system is self-perpetuating.

Mary's intelligence, which she had never really utilised, blossomed, and she was able to make connection after connection, each week bringing new accounts of how she had recognised herself being pulled into a familiar response and being able to try something new. It was as if the diagram, apart from its cognitive heuristic value, was acting as a symbolic representation of the containing maternal mirroring that she was expecting through her relationship with the psychotherapist. The fact that the diagram was acting in some way as a Winnicottian transitional object helped to lessen regressive dependence on the psychotherapist and to encourage a movement towards seeking more reliable objects in her social life. The tasks of observing her behaviour in the light of the identified procedure and reporting back to the psychotherapist optimised the nurturing potential of setting and attaining achievable goals under the supportive and watchful eye of the psychotherapist.

Half-way through the psychotherapy Mary got a job in the canteen of the psychiatric section of another hospital. She was able to use this situation to explore her own belief that she was mad. 'They're trapped, they're mad – I'm just crazy and I'm getting better.' As her sense of herself and her identity in the world of others developed she was able to make sharper distinctions of both her own internal states and the qualities displayed by others.

As the end of the psychotherapy approached she said she felt she would be able to cope now because she was on her own side, not divided against herself. 'It is as if all of me is pointing in the same direction and I'm moving along in my own life finding out more and more about who I am.'

At three-months follow-up she reported promotion at work, minimal alcohol consumption with no episodes of drunkenness, and had taken a week's holiday for the first time in her life. Her score on the SCL94 dropped from a pre-therapy 101 to 55 at follow-up.

COGNITIVE BEHAVIOUR THERAPY (CBT) FOR MIXED AFFECTIVE DISORDER IN A DEPENDENT PERSONALITY

Karen was twenty-six when she was referred by her general practitioner for help with long-standing, intractable depression and anxiety, and she was described as 'rather a dependent personality'. At this time both her anxiety and depression were moderate to severe (Beck Depression Inventory score = 36: Beck *et al.* 1961; Beck Anxiety Inventory score = 28: Beck *et al.* 1988). She had taken an impulsive overdose two months previously after a row with her mother and had been given two courses of anti-depressants and one of counselling in the last four years without obvious benefit. She worked as a clerical assistant for the local council, and her fiancé, Robert, was a telephone engineer.

At assessment Karen was tearful and appeared flustered. She described high levels of tension, panic attacks two or three times a month, moodiness and irritability when at home in the flat she and Robert shared, feeling overwhelmed by difficulties and unable to control her feelings. She failed to go to work because of high levels of anxiety at least twice a month, frequently telephoned her mother asking to be brought home from work because she felt panicky, met Robert for support every lunch hour, and regularly demanded time and reassurance from her boss.

She was easily able to explain what she wanted from psychotherapy: to feel less anxious and panicky, especially before leaving for work every morning, and to feel less miserable and fed up, which was more of a problem in the evenings and at weekends. She also made it clear that she hoped the psychotherapist 'would make her better' – an expectation that was discussed during the first meeting when explaining the rationale for CBT. This made the point that psychotherapy requires joint, collaborative work, that patients are expected to carry out assignments between psycho-therapy sessions, and that these assignments are designed as tests of different ways of thinking and behaving. Karen was willing to play an active part in treatment provided she was clearly directed. But she was frightened by the thought that 'others can make suggestions but ultimately I've got to do it myself'. For her first homework assignment Karen read a booklet describing CBT for anxiety.

Sessions 1–3

Information about the development and background to Karen's difficulties was collected over this time but will be described later, as the main work of this stage focused on her numerous worries and present symptoms. A number of 'vicious circles', or maintaining factors, were unravelled and illustrated using diagrams. One of these concerned anxiety: for example, worrying about work tasks → feeling tense and tearful → inability to concentrate → more worry about work. Another concerned her need for support from others: for example, when she felt anxious, worried or miserable → she thought 'I can't handle this' → then sought someone (Robert, her mother, her boss) on whom to 'unload' → felt better → and concluded 'I was right. I can't handle things alone.' Various behavioural strategies were introduced to start testing the idea that she was helplessly trapped in these vicious circles: relaxation and breathing exercises, graded task-setting to build up her independent work skills, and problem-solving to use before going to others for help. Karen learned these methods assiduously, and gradually came to terms with the idea of 'self-help'. But progress was slow and she continued to bring numerous different, and in her view, urgent problems to each session. These included anxieties about her performance at work, avoiding social engagements, the possibility that PMT could account for her symptoms and her irritability and lack of sexual interest in Robert.

Session 4

When Karen introduced yet another urgent problem for discussion the psychotherapist asked her to think about what was happening in psycho-therapy, and about the effects of this ever-changing focus. She said that it reflected exactly the way she felt: overwhelmed, confused and never sure what the next problem might be. This provided the opportunity to focus together on formulating the information she had so far brought to psychotherapy, looking for patterns and themes, and working out how they might fit together. At the end of this session she concluded, 'It's not that everything is a worry. It's that one problem spreads, and that's not being confident.' This conclusion, or hypothesis, provided the basis for the formulation which guided the rest of the work.

Two comments are pertinent at this stage. First, much weight is placed in this form of short-term psychotherapy on helping patients draw their own conclusions and formulate thoughts and beliefs in their own words. The aim is to engage them in sharing the work of psychotherapy at an affective as well as at a cognitive level. Secondly, it is possible that Karen's insistence, in psychotherapy also, that other people fix her problems for her, made it hard to come to such a conclusion and difficult to focus on issues other than the urgent ones she brought to each session until this pattern became obvious in psychotherapy also.

The development of Karen's problem

Karen's father left home when she was four. She was a shy child and had been bullied at school. One of her mother's boyfriends was physically violent towards both Karen and her mother, and they fled from him together, moving from house to house for three to four years. When Karen was seventeen and had just started work, they were living with an aunt. She was asked to leave the aunt's house as it was overcrowded, and did so briefly, but insisted on returning when she missed her mother. They moved into temporary accommodation with her mother's new friend John, and stayed there until Karen and Robert found their own flat about two years ago. Putting all the information together as simply as possible produced the following formulation:

Early experience
Father left home (age four)
Bullied at school (age eleven to twelve)
Violence at home: both witnessed and received
'There was nowhere that was home'

Dysfunctional assumptions: i.e., underlying, initially unrecognised beliefs such as
'I need people to look after me'
'I am not safe on my own'
'I can never be confident'
'I am not as good as others are'

Critical incidents: i.e., events that trigger the assumptions, such as
Making mistakes, especially at work
Disagreements, in particular with those in close relationships
Living away from mother, and dislike of her mother's new friend John
Threats to stability of all kinds

These activated the assumptions, for example:
'They will think I'm no good, and I'll lose my job'
'They will leave me, and I won't be able to cope alone'
'Mum doesn't need me now she's got John'
'I'm all alone in the world'

Present symptoms, for example:
Feelings: mostly anxiety, but also sadness, frustration, anger, resentment, feeling helpless and hopeless
Physical symptoms: tension, panic, headaches, agitation, apprehension
Behaviours: avoiding social contact, writing endless lists of things to do but procrastinating, disrupted sleep, 'making muddles'
Thoughts: 'I can't cope', 'There's nothing I can do', 'I need to talk to someone', and so on
Vicious circles (e.g. of anxiety and reassurance-seeking) keep the problem going in the present, reinforce the assumptions and make it hard to build confidence

Subsequent sessions

Karen said that the formulation, which had been sketched out using both diagrams and written material, enabled her to fit the problems together and make sense of what was happening in the present. Two main strategies were helpful to her subsequently. First, when she felt anxious she asked herself: 'How does this fit with not being confident?' Working this out made her feel less at the mercy of a host of unpredictable problems and better able to think what to do next. Secondly, she carried out a typical CBT homework assignment, the purpose of which was to help her think again about how confidence develops. This involved asking others how they became confident. Her findings led her, with some help, to the following main conclusions: many people who appear confident are not so underneath; you can be confident about some things but not others; confidence can be learned – it comes with practice.

In order to test out whether these conclusions applied in her own case she carried out a number of behavioural assignments, and made better use of the strategies introduced in the first sessions (problem-solving, and so on). By the end of treatment (sixteen weeks) she had joined an evening class (entitled 'Speaking with Confidence'), ate lunch without Robert on work days, and made fewer 'unreasonable' demands on her mother, Robert and her boss. She was much less depressed (BDI = 14) and somewhat less anxious (BAI = 18). During the next six months she had a couple of 'booster' sessions, and at follow-up had maintained these gains, attended work daily, had made more friends at work and now understood that her mother 'needed John as well as, and not instead of, me'. She had at one stage broken off her engagement to Robert, but returned to him a few weeks later having decided that the relationship was valuable to her, and not just rooted in her former dependence.

CONCLUDING COMMENTS

The two case examples given here outline approaches that are clearly structured and systematic, and we would suggest that the early development of a focus for the work, and a theory-backed treatment plan, help both patient and psychotherapist to optimise the potential of their brief encounter. Where the nature of the institution or the structure of the model determine the number of sessions available, the psychotherapist is freed from having to consider the duration boundary. Where that is not the case, more questions about the task of psychotherapy are often raised, and this is an area of some complexity (Frank 1961). The patient may well arrive with a difficulty that has recently been troubling, the 'presenting problem', which the psychotherapist sees as being an aspect or symptom of some longer or deeper malaise. And so a difference of desire makes itself apparent. The patient wants care while the psychotherapist seeks to promote exploration, change and development. But the route to the relief of suffering and the promotion of satisfaction and well-being may be either long or short. So perhaps it is the clinician's duty to ensure that the client is helped on a journey determined by each client's precise situation and not by the psychotherapist's curiosity or the dictates of a theoretical model.

As we have tried to illustrate in the case examples provided above, an awareness of, and competence in, the skills of short-term psychotherapy can help to keep psychotherapist and patient on course. When the course runs smoothly any conflict between focusing on presenting problems and on a 'deeper malaise' may disappear.

These two cases were obviously selected to illustrate how similar but strikingly different types of short-term psychotherapy were successfully used to help with relatively long-standing difficulties. We are well aware that psychotherapy does not always proceed smoothly but, instead of concentrating on the problems and difficulties of working in this way, and on ways of overcoming them, we have chosen instead to illustrate how complexity and the long-standing nature of difficulties need not impede progress.

It is tempting in this context to speculate a bit more about the processes that help to facilitate change, especially with two such different kinds of psychotherapy in mind. The following ideas are put forward purely in that spirit. As yet not enough is known either about process or outcome for anyone to be certain about exactly which methods and strategies used with which problems are most likely to be most beneficial.

First, the ability to specify limited goals in each case focused the work, especially at the start of psychotherapy. Discussion of goals may also have helped define appropriate expectations for psychotherapy, and to build trust between patient and psychotherapist. At the same time, this focused work enabled the psychotherapists to develop hypotheses about how to formulate the cases in terms of the theoretical frameworks they were using. Significantly, the first patient decided to focus not on her symptoms or presenting problem but on the meaning of her life. Her profound existential inquiry was then opened out and sharpened by the structure provided by cognitive-analytic therapy. The second patient initially wished to focus on symptoms and presenting problems. When doing so within the framework of cognitive-behaviour therapy she came to recognise recurring patterns and used the method to broaden and generalise the field of inquiry.

Next, the process of coming to a shared understanding, not only of the problem in the present but of the problem placed in a wider historical and developmental context, played a central part in both psychotherapies. In neither case was this achieved immediately, and in both cases it was achieved only after the psychotherapists had had the opportunity to observe the patients' different ways of engaging, and of having difficulty in engaging, in psychotherapy. Once arrived at, coincidentally by the fourth session in both cases, the formulations encompassed more issues than were raised by the specific goals. They incorporated 'critical' information about each patient's developmental history and ideas about the factors supposedly maintaining the distress. The formulation may thus have served many functions, but three of these seem to be particularly useful: explanation, understanding of the past and about why patterns repeat themselves, and specification of how to deal with these in ways relevant to specific problems arising in daily life. Using Persons' (1989) terminology, the formulation helped in both cases to relate overt difficulties to underlying mechanisms.

Sharing the formulation in an open, explicit way seemed to help the patients to define and then recognise these patterns, so as later to become free of their constraints. It is assumed that these patterns have generality; that is, they are exemplified in many different ways in the patients' lives. If the formulation offered makes sense then it can help the patient make the move from the particular to the general. A particular incident of behaviour can be seen as an instance of the general pattern, so that whatever has been learned on one occasion can more easily be generalised to other contexts and occasions. Thus, starting from a limited goal, and working with specific difficulties as they emerge in the here-and-now, provides the context for developing a good working hypothesis, or formulation. Recognising this – presuming it is accurate, of course – then enables people to become free of previous restrictions and repetitions, increases their options for adaptation, and frees up more adaptive processes of change and development. The approach of CAT, by incorporating an understanding of transference and counter-transference, makes use of what happens between patient and psychotherapist to deepen and intensify the living experience of the reality of the self-managing and reciprocal role procedures identified in the reformulation.

An important aspect of the relationship that facilitates this kind of work is that it is built up on the (often undeclared) assumption that patients have resources that they are able, or can become able, to use to their advantage. Growing independence is thus a sign of the successful use of short-term psychotherapy, and dependence will inevitably inhibit progress.

This speculation about some of the processes that may facilitate change in short-term psychotherapy assumes that there are specific reasons why psychotherapy is effective when it works, and why it is not effective when it fails. This is an important assumption underlying the different approaches to short-term psychotherapy, and one that motivates continued search and research. However, the speculation also illustrates how difficult it is to be certain about which of the aspects of short-term psychotherapy account for its effectiveness. Given the present state of our knowledge, it could therefore be tempting to conclude that there is nothing to choose between one form of short-term psychotherapy and another. In practice, the choice of method is indeed made by psychotherapists on the basis of their particular training, theoretical orientation and working context, and by patients on bases that we are not at all clear about and which are probably determined as much by chance factors and local availability as by rational matching of patient to treatment. It is important, if this somewhat unsatisfactory state of affairs is to change, that psychotherapists continue to communicate and to speculate about their methods. There are two developments which will help to support short-term psychotherapy: patients need to be supported in making informed choices about the kind of psychotherapy they enter into; and psychotherapists would benefit from an emphasis on flexibility and responsiveness in their training rather than on induction into the pseudo-safety of a system.

As short-term psychotherapy is likely to continue to develop fast, the demands on psychotherapists today are large. Perhaps their main tasks, in addition to clinical practice, should include constant appraisal of new ideas in their own as well as in related fields, and a willingness openly to examine their own practice. The more we know about one another's ways of working the more likely it is that we shall in the end be better able to select the right approach for the right person.

REFERENCES

Alexander, F. and French, T. (1946) *Psychoanalytic Therapy*, New York: Ronald Press.

Ashurst, P. (1991) 'Brief psychotherapy', pp. 187–212 in J. Homes (ed.) *Textbook of Psychotherapy in Psychiatric Practice*, London: Churchill Livingstone.

Beck, A. T. (1976) *Cognitive Therapy and the Emotional Disorders*, New York: International Universities Press.

Beck, A. T., Brown, G., Epstein, N. and Steer, R. A. (1988) 'An inventory for measuring clinical anxiety: psychometric properties', *Journal of Consulting and Clinical Psychology* 56: 893–7.

Beck, A. T., Emery, G. and Greenberg, R. (1985) *Anxiety Disorder and Phobias: A Cognitive Perspective*, New York: Guilford Press.

Beck, A. T., Freeman, A. and associates (1990) *Cognitive Therapy of Personality Disorders*, New York: Guilford Press.

Beck, A. T., Rush, A. J., Shaw, B. I. and Emery, G. (1979) *Cognitive Therapy of Depression*, New York: Guilford Press.

Beck, A. T., Ward, C., Mendelson, M., Mock, J. and Erbaugh, J. (1961) 'An inventory for measuring depression', *Archives of General Psychiatry* 4: 561–71.

Crits-Christoph, P. and Barber, J. (eds) (1991) *Handbook of Short-term Dynamic Therapies*, New York: Basic Books.

Flegenheimer, W. V. (1982) *Techniques of Brief Psychotherapy*, New York: Aronson.

Frank, J. D. (1961) *Persuasion and Healing*, Baltimore, MD: Johns Hopkins University Press.

Hawton, K., Salkovskis, P., Kirk, J. and Clark, D. (1989) *Cognitive Behaviour Therapy for Psychiatric Problems: A Practical Guide*, Oxford: Oxford University Press.

Howard, G. S., Nance, D. W. and Myers, P. (1987) *Adaptive Counselling and Therapy*, San Francisco: Jossey Bass.

Mahrer, A. R. (1989) *Experiential Psychotherapy: Basic Practices*, Ottawa: Ottawa University Press.

Malan, D. H. (1976) *The Frontier of Brief Psychotherapy*, New York: Plenum.

—— (1979) *Individual Psychotherapy and the Science of Psychodynamics*, London: Butterworths.

Marteau, L. (1986) *Existential Short Term Therapy*, London: The Dympna Centre.

Nielsen, G. and Barth, K. (1991) 'Short-term anxiety provoking psychotherapy', pp. 45–79 in P. Crits-Christoph and J. Barber (eds) *Handbook of Short-term Dynamic Therapies*, New York: Basic Books.

Norcross, J. C. (ed.) (1986) *Handbook of Eclectic Psychotherapy*, New York: Brunner/Mazel.

Persons, J. B. (1989) *Cognitive Therapy in Practice: A Case Formulation Approach*, New York: W. W. Norton.

Ryle, A. (1990) *Cognitive-Analytic Therapy: Active Participation in Change*, Chichester: Wiley.

—— (1992) 'Critique of a Kleinian case of presentation', *British Journal of Medical Psychology* 65: 309–17.

Safran, J. D. and Segal, Z. V. (1991) *Interpersonal Processes in Cognitive Therapy*, New York: Basic Books.

Scott, J., Williams, J. M. G. and Beck, A. T. (1989) *Cognitive Therapy in Clinical Practice: An Illustrative Casebook*, London: Routledge.

Shazer, S. de (1991) *Putting Difference to Work*, New York: W. W. Norton.

Sledge, W. H., Moras, K., Hartley, D. and Levine, M. A. (1990) 'Effects of time-limited psychotherapy on patient drop-out rates', *American Journal of Psychiatry* 147(10): 1342–7.

Weakland, J. H., Fisch, R., Watzlawick, P. and Bodin, A. (1974) 'Brief therapy: focused problem resolution', *Family Process* 13: 141–68.

Young, J. E. (1990) *Cognitive Therapy for Personality Disorders: A Schema-focused Approach*, Sarasota, FL: Professional Resource Exchange.

Chapter 12

Marital psychotherapy

Tom Leary and Gillian Walton

Marital therapy in the United Kingdom as a separate discipline came to birth pragmatically to address the concerns which arose in the earlier twentieth century about perceived changes in marriage and family life. There was an increase in divorce. Families were easier to limit in size, and the changing social status of women, which began in the nineteenth century with the Married Women's Property Act and continued in the twentieth century with female emancipation (not fully implemented until 1928), had a growing effect on the national consciousness.

Naturally, it is never possible to be simplistic about cause and effect, but the phenomenon of the idea of 'companionate marriage' written about as early as 1909 began to gain ground and take root as the century progressed, and we would suggest that this had an important effect on the way marriages were treated therapeutically. Marie Stopes and some of the earlier radical feminist writers were concerned about the male/female power issues. The pioneers in the field of marital work in the 1930s had a concern about the place of birth control and personal choice in marriage. Relationships other than marital relationships were barely addressed. Even as late as 1952 the Marriage Guidance Council was writing officially that its work in the field of family planning and sexuality was to be explored only within a marital relationship.

Nevertheless, in the late 1940s the Family Discussion Bureau, which was closely connected to the psychoanalytic work of the Tavistock Clinic, was beginning to formulate some of the thinking which came to underpin the work of marital counselling and psychotherapy in the United Kingdom. Notable amongst this writing was Dicks's famous book, *Marital Tensions* (1967), which took some of the thinking further and introduced the concept of the marital relationship being a place where people could, within a safe container, explore some of the unconscious issues which preoccupied them. Perhaps the nursery rhyme 'Jack Sprat' provides a simple illustration of this basic theory of projection within marriage. Jack Sprat ate only 'lean'. Mrs Sprat ate only 'fat'. Together they were content, each doing something of value for the other. Only when tastes changed would there be any difficulty, and at this stage possibly some help might be acquired.

The work of Jung was also seminal, especially to the work of the early Marriage Guidance Council workers, since it was he who first described marriage as a 'psychological relationship' and wrote of marriage as a container within which individuation could happen (1931/1981: 195). He also pointed out the impact of the unconscious lives of parents on their children, a belief which has continued to inform family and marital workers. Important too was the work of John Bowlby (1969), whose study of attachment and loss and whose belief in the possibility of repair during the course of subsequent attachment experiences inspired workers in the field with faith in the value of work in this area.

From the psychoanalytic field came the belief in and exploration of the relationship between the worker and the client as a way of understanding better the relationship between the couple. Some of the technical basis for this has come from the field of object relations with its description of projection and projective identification.

There are now many agencies working in the field of marital counselling. Although there will be variations in their orientation, from the psycho-analytical on the one hand to the pure behavioural on the other, they will have a common belief in the value of committed couple relationships both inside and outside marriage. London Marriage Guidance, for example, saw an almost equal number of married and unmarried people in 1992. For the purposes of this chapter we shall be describing a mainly psycho-dynamic approach, by which we mean that attention is paid to both the unconscious and conscious processes in the relationship and in the work, and to the way in which this is experienced through the transference and counter-transference and reflection processes. In work with couples we take the view that it is preferable to interpret the transference sparingly, concentrating rather on the dynamics of the relationship between the couple themselves.

The first task for the worker is to engage the couple to work in the psychotherapy. Couples present for psychotherapy in a variety of ways. There is often ambivalence about asking for help either on the part of one or both partners. Sometimes there is an immediate crisis such as an affair or a bereavement. At other times the search for psychotherapy is a secret and an approach is made by only one partner, the other partner not being informed. The way in which the approach is made is important and gives valuable information about the clients' feelings about psychotherapy and their feelings about themselves. An example of this would be a young couple both engaged in the caring professions who came to a first appointment saying that their problem was not grave and that they were happy to go on a waiting list. It transpired on further exploration that the problem was in fact quite urgent and pressing. That the clients found it difficult to ask for their needs to be met immediately was indicative of their difficulty in their lives in general to express their feelings and therefore to get their needs met. Another young couple came with the wife saying rather humorously, 'I've dragged him along'. Had the worker not addressed the husband's feelings of ambivalence about being present, then the work would have been jeopardised from the start. It is a cardinal rule that any ambivalence should be addressed openly and fully at the beginning of the work in order for both partners to be engaged. At this time more women than men present initially for couple therapy, but it is becoming increasingly acceptable for men to make the first move.

A mixture of warmth, firmness and confidence is required from the psychotherapist at this stage, since bringing a relationship to psychotherapy is a courageous and potentially risky thing to do, for it can expose clients more than when a partner's views are reported at second hand. It is rather like allowing another person into the most intimate part of one's life.

Psychotherapists come to the initial session with some information concerning the clients before they are met, and, as with any therapeutic encounter, the fantasies are checked out against the reality so that the psychotherapy begins with this very first contact. Attention is given to which of the parties made the approach, and why. The process of making the arrangements for the first meeting is taken seriously, and significance is given to whether the couple come together or singly at the beginning. Most marital psychotherapists have some sort of structured intake model, the aim of which is to explore whether the clients are willing to make a therapeutic alliance with the psychotherapists. Even if a partner comes alone to the first session the psychotherapist will always be keeping the other partner in mind. It can often be useful to think of intake in three stages. The first of these is the presenting problem; the second, the history of the relationship linked with a brief history of the two partners; and the third the establishing of a contract which is mutually acceptable to the client and to the worker. Equal time and attention would be given to all these three stages.

The exploration of the presenting problems relates to the question of why the couple have come now. At this stage the psychotherapist will try to find specific examples of the problem; for example, if there is a communication problem, the psychotherapist would encourage the clients to give actual and specific instances. At this stage no interpretations will be given but attention will be paid to the details of what the clients say, how they say it and how they relate with each other as they are saying it in order to get some understanding of the interaction between the clients and to discover what hurts enough for them to ask for help. The psychotherapists will be looking for the place where the pain and dysfunction are to be found. They will be trying to get some understanding of how the clients heard about marital therapy and of why they have chosen the particular agency they have at the particular time they have. When exploring the history of the relationship attention will be given to how the couple first met and what initially attracted them to each other. It will be useful and important at this stage to have some detail about the courtship and about the form of marriage ceremony chosen if it is a married couple. Couples usually have quite a clear view of when things first began to go wrong and for whom, and they would usually at this stage be encouraged to talk about the good times and the bad times, about any specific life events that they had to face such as bereavements, and the place of children in the relationship.

The physical relationship of the couple is a very important area. This clearly needs to be handled sensitively, but it is essential that it is addressed since it is so very often an indicator of the other areas of communication between the couple and of the life experience they bring to the relationship. When brief personal histories are taken, the couple will be asked to outline details of the family of origin and their place within it and, metaphorically speaking, to introduce the psychotherapist to their parents. At this stage it is useful to know about previous close relationships and whether there is any previous history of therapeutic help or any medical or psychiatric treatment which would be of significance in the work. In order to offer the clients something of value at this introductory point, the psychotherapist would gather the session together in a form which the clients might find meaningful. This would require an analysis of the convergence of knowledge – that is, the clients' impact on the worker and the worker's impact on the clients, in the light of the presenting problem. At this stage, it may be possible to suggest a time-span within which the work might take place, but this might also equally often be left open-ended for the time being. The way in which the financial arrangements are negotiated is also of great significance, and can offer insight into how the couple value each other and their relationship, and potentially the therapeutic endeavour.

The majority of marital work is carried out in a triangular situation; that is, one psychotherapist with two clients. Both clients and psychotherapists can experience this as a challenging and sometimes problematic configuration since it often reflects and re-creates some of the clients' original dilemmas; for example, if there has been a difficulty about adequate resources, then being in a situation where both parties have to share the same hour and the same psychotherapist can revive some of the pain and panic of an earlier time. There is then the opportunity to explore and rework some of the issues involved. An example would be Peter and Joan, each of whom had for different reasons felt uncertain of their value in their lives when younger. Peter's younger siblings were born soon after him and he was then sent abroad to preparatory school, whereas Joan was one of a large family in which the mother's emotional life took up much of the available energy. Whilst young and travelling the world Peter and Joan coped quite well, but marriage and the arrival of children were unexpectedly very difficult for them. They were once again having to share the available resources with others and deeply resented this, using different coping mechanisms. In psychotherapy they found using the same therapeutic space difficult also, and for perfectly good, conscious reasons for a while took to coming separately. It was as a result of allowing this to happen and being influenced by it that the central issue of whether there was enough of the worker to go round could be raised and the couple work could begin with both parties in the room at the same time.

The triangular configuration is of course of enormous significance to everybody. Classical psychoanalytic theory stresses that the original Oedipal experience stays with human beings throughout life. It is therefore important that a couple worker who works alone is very conscious of his or her own attitude to this, since arguably what is experienced by the worker is to be in the omnipotent position of being able to see another marriage from the inside and to share its secrets, rather than to have the experience of the parental relationship of being on the outside. The threat presented to marriages from third parties is often what brings couples to psychotherapy. If the therapeutic session also involves three people, then, although it inevitably mirrors the problem, it can also be used creatively to work with it. Simon and Sarah came to seek help because Simon had been expressing doubts about their ten-year-old relationship which had begun when they were at university. It very soon emerged that this doubt had been triggered off by a recent affair and, on more exploration, that there had almost always been a third party present in the relationship both in reality and certainly in their fantasy since each carried inside them an image of a damaging and intrusive parent, fathers in both cases. In neither case was the mother experienced as either powerful or protective. In the therapeutic relationship with the female psychotherapist the couple explored a different experience of being in a three-person relationship, one which eventually allowed them to be the couple and the psychotherapist the outsider.

Inevitably, one psychotherapist must be either male or female, and this can impose limitations since it is more difficult for some things such as gender issues to be addressed so effectively. Nevertheless, it is by no means ruled out, but it does demand that the psychotherapist is able to draw on both his or her masculine and feminine qualities. The gender of the psychotherapist can indeed be an important factor in constellating important themes in the work. For George and Ruth, a powerful, shared inner object was a parental couple where the father was controlling and dominating and where value was measured by external markers of success, usually examination results. Both George and Ruth were high achievers and successful professional people. However, now that they had small children Ruth was increasingly torn between her career and her maternal instincts and wish to be intimate with her children; George, although a tender father and outwardly supportive of his wife's wishes, was nevertheless torn between sharing with her this change of direction and holding on to the well-known means of valuing her. The female worker for some time was also aware of being measured and evaluated, and indeed the couple would often give feedback on the failures and successes of the previous session. It was only after some time of holding and containing this couple that it was possible to demonstrate the value of the more feminine qualities, and both George and Ruth were able to speak longingly of their mothers and to be less hard on the psychotherapist and each other. Jung's (1981) concept of a psychotherapeutic relationship as a crucible within which things can be explored and in time perhaps re-arrange themselves in a more creative form is as applicable to couples therapy as it is to one-to-one psychotherapy. In both cases the psychotherapist approaches the work open to experience what the clients bring, and open to working with them on the search for their own values and meaning.

REFERENCES

Bowlby, J. (1969) *Attachment and Loss: I – Attachment*, London: Hogarth Press.
Dicks, H. V. (1967) *Marital Tensions: Clinical Studies Towards a Psychological Theory of Interaction*, London: Routledge & Kegan Paul.
Jung, C. G. (1981) 'Marriage as a psychological relationship', pp. 187–201 in H. Read, M. Fordham, and G. Adler (eds) R. F. C. Hull (trans.) *The Development of Personality: The Collected Works*, vol. 17, London: Routledge & Kegan Paul (first published 1931).

Further information

London Marriage Guidance Council
76a New Cavendish Street
Harley Street
London W1M 7RG
Tel.: 071 580 1087

Westminster Pastoral Foundation
23 Kensington Square
London W8 5HN
Tel.: 071 376 2404

Some couples courses are run by:
metanoia Psychotherapy Training Institute
13 North Common Road
Ealing
London W5 2QB
Tel.: 081 579 2505

Chapter 13

Family therapy

Gill Gorell Barnes and Alan Cooklin

THE NATURE OF PSYCHOLOGICAL CHANGES

The nature of psychological change has always been controversial, both within groups of psychologists, sociologists and anthropologists, and between them. Disputes have often been framed in terms of causality – what causes psychological development and its defects? An alternative framework, which will be the focus of this chapter, is to consider where psychological change occurs. Is psychological development to be described, for example, in terms of changes in a young person's observable behaviour, or in terms of the unconscious processes or 'dramas' imputed to be associated with these behaviours? Alternatively, is development to be viewed as a family event in which all generations participate and all actually change, or is it to be seen as a socio-cultural event in which the changes differ markedly depending on the cultural context?

Individual psychotherapies, whether based on a model of learning theory or on psychodynamic understanding, have one thing in common. They view the patient from the standpoint that he or she is an integrated, discrete organism. Family and other 'systems' therapies view the patient as one component in a system or 'organism' (for example, the family) which can manifest malfunction through the behaviour of that component – the patient. That is the major difference.

WHAT IS FAMILY THERAPY?

Family therapy refers, on the one hand, to a 'treatment' – an activity whereby a therapist sits down for one or more sessions with various members of a family to help them change something – and, on the other hand, to a framework for conceptualisation, a way of understanding and thinking about human behaviour which may then be used in a variety of ways. This thinking can then be applied to the family or to other contexts in which human beings live in proximity and may develop intimate relationships.

THE PRINCIPLES

Two important components of the thinking are as follows. First, people are not islands, and their behaviour can only be understood in the context in which it occurs. This is an interpersonal description, which sees behaviour as principally responsive to the context of a person's relationships. This differs from most psychodynamic views in which the individual's 'internal world' is seen as the principal organiser of behaviour. In the latter framework this term 'internal' is frequently used as a synonym for 'psychic' or 'mental', on the assumption that psychic processes are located in an inner space (Rycroft 1968). Thus, 'internal reality' and 'internal conflict' are defined in contrast to the external equivalents, or actual 'external' relationships in which people are currently engaged.

Thus, while the internal world may be seen as a relatively 'closed shop', viewed principally through dreams, associations and play, or manifested by one's behaviour in aspects of relations, in this chapter the individual's internal world is also seen as accessible through the day-to-day interactions with others. These interactions themselves, and the meaning individuals attribute to them, are dependent on the context in which they occur. The meanings are co-constructed within the belief systems of the family over time, or may have been previously attributed to such interactions in former contexts of a similar kind. Such contexts might include families of origin, former marriages or cohabitations, or family interactions from a first family, highlighted for potential action replay in the context of a step family or foster family. The mental representation of sets of relationships and their 'carry-forward' into other contexts is an important contribution to family systems thinking from the field of child development research (Sroufe and Fleeson 1988).

The second major component of family systems thinking therefore is that people in close emotional proximity readily set up stable patterns of interaction. These patterns are made up from a whole series of sequences; repetitive short events involving two or more people. The sum of all these possible sequences can be called the family pattern. This is illustrated later under 'Family patterns and the "family dance"'.

This way of thinking assumes that the actions of all participants in a sequence – the players in a drama – affect one another and, inasmuch as each is reacting to the behaviour of others, the sequence becomes self-regulatory, within boundaries of time, place and role. This in turn assumes that there are no protagonists or victims but that both enter into an interaction and complement one another's behaviour. For this to happen, however, each participant must be bound by the ground rules of the group, and to some extent share similar sets of beliefs and habit responses. This concept has been problematic at times, particularly if one weaker member in a family is seen to be abused by the power – sexual, physical or economic – of another. In any interaction people may not be equal in the degree to which they choose to be bound by a particular set of beliefs. Each person's degree of choice may be dependent on their relative power related to age. Whereas each adult participant to some extent chooses to continue to participate in the drama, the cost of trying to give up that participation may be dramatically different for different family members. The child cannot leave home, and this is frequently also true of the abused wife.

If the family presents a problem, either through an individual's symptom or behaviour, or through showing a set of 'problem' relationships, it is assumed in a family system framework that the problem is in some way connected with the wider organisation of the family. It is not necessarily the case that the family 'causes' the problem, but rather that the problem, as it develops, becomes part of the life and context of the family, and over time may become part of what is familiar and comforting. A practitioner who does 'family therapy' will, therefore, be concerned with the relevant wider family organisation and how this relates to the problem, rather than with any one individual in isolation.

PATTERN AS A CONCEPT IN FAMILY STUDIES

From a research perspective, the idea of systemic properties in family pattern has been built up over the last fifteen years. The interactions between two people, the way aspects of this interaction continue to affect individuals when they are apart and the way the qualities of that interaction are affected by the introduction of a third person have been studied in a variety of family situations. Whereas some studies have focused on behaviour, others have looked at less tangible aspects of mutual influence such as changes in perception and expressed emotion. A summary of these studies can be found in Gorell Barnes (1985, 1993). How much the individual's freedom is actually curtailed by family pattern can of course only remain at the level of hypothesis (both in relation to constraints on the freedom of a client as well as constraints on any therapist who works with that client).

Family therapists address 'pattern' at different levels; some work primarily at the level of observable behaviour, and generally assume the principle that change in behaviour will be followed by changes in beliefs. Others address patterns of belief on the principle that unless beliefs change, what is permitted in the way of behavioural change will remain constrained. Some of these differences in approach will described below.

SYSTEMIC PATTERNING AND INDIVIDUAL FUNCTIONING

The common core of the systemic approach to family life is the belief that family members, engaged in the task of rearing dependent and developing beings, are necessarily interconnected. They both contribute to the formation of patterns between them and are organised in their individual behaviour by their ongoing participation in patterns of mutual influence. Over time, patterns may retain the capacity for change and adaptation or, in situations of threat or fear, may become rigidified and unamenable to adaptive change. The idea of rigidity will be discussed further below.

THE THERAPY

A practitioner who does 'family therapy' will, therefore, be concerned with the total family organisation and how this relates to the problem, rather than to any one individual. In order to do this the practitioner may use various methods, may work through individuals, but keeping their sights on the whole organism of the family. They may work with parts of the family, with the whole nuclear family or with the nuclear and extended family of three generations or more, or even include other members of the community (especially where the family is an ethnic minority in the host culture). The therapy may last for one, two or many sessions of one or more hours. The most common is for the therapist to work for a fairly small number of sessions, averaging about ten.

DISTINCTIONS FROM OTHER THERAPIES

The differences in practice and underlying model of thinking between family (or 'natural group') therapy, group ('stranger group') therapy and individual psychodynamic therapies are summarised in Table 13.1. This summarises differences in the goals of change, the locus of change (that is, between family members rather than between patient and therapist in the first instance), and the process of change, including the role of the therapist in this process.

To summarise, the family systems perspective assumes that

1 people are intimately connected, and those connections can be as valid a way to both understand and promote change in behaviour as can any individual responses;
2 people living in close proximity set up patterns of interaction made up from relatively stable sequences of interaction;
3 therefore the patterns that therapists engage with must, to some degree, and at the same time, act as cause and effect of the problem that they are presented with;
4 problems within patterns in families are related to incongruous adaptation to some environmental influence or change.

Family therapy then addresses itself to changes in patterns of relationships: to those which are lived and witnessed on a daily basis; and to those

Table 13.1 Comparison between family group therapy, 'stranger' group therapy and individual therapy

Individual therapy	'Stranger' group therapy	Natural (family) group therapy
The patient/therapist relationship exists only as a context for psychotherapy.	The group exists only as a context for psychotherapy.	The family has a life of its own, with a history and an anticipated future.
Psychotherapy occurs in the context of the intensity of relationship between therapist and patient.	Psychotherapy occurs in the context of the intensity of relationships between the therapist and group members, and between group members.	Psychotherapy occurs in context of a change in relationship pattern in the context of the current intense family relationships.
Thus the therapist is central.	Thus at different times the therapist or some part of the group may be central.	Thus the therapist is principally an agent of change rather than a central actor.
The therapist *allows* the intensity of affect from the patient to him/her to develop (although the setting may provoke it).	The therapist facilitates the 'integration' or 'gelling' of the group in the service of psychotherapy.	The therapist is more likely to be concerned to develop the differentiation of the group.
Therapist and patient maintain a non-social relationship (to varying degrees, depending on the model).	The members are discouraged from meeting between sessions.	The members remain in an intense relationship between sessions.
The therapist does not try to develop a structure in the therapeutic relationship, and interpretations may be used to highlight inappropriate structural patterns sought by the patient. In child psychotherapy the therapist *may* be forced to be a parental adult.	There is no permanent structural organisation of the group. That which evolves is transient and often seen by the therapist as a re-creation of past or 'inner' families of the members. The members are usually of similar age, as may be the psychotherapist. The psychotherapist aims to be 'meta' to the group.	The family has an inherent and necessary hierarchical organisation, relating to the different ages, developmental positions and responsibilities of the members. As the therapist is an adult, this will affect how he or she is used by the family. The therapist aims to *think* from a meta-position, but may *act* in a partisan manner.
Change occurs through understanding the meaning of an old pattern in a new context. This change has then to be generalised to other contexts. The pattern in the original context may or *may not* change.	Change occurs through understanding of the meaning of an old pattern in a new context. This change has then to be generalised to other contexts. The pattern in the original context may or *may not* change.	Change occurs through changing the pattern in an 'old' context, so that the context itself is changed.

Source: reproduced with permission from Cooklin (1990).

which are carried in people's minds. These can usefully be conceptualised as 'mental representations of sets of relationships' (Main 1991), a development of the idea of 'inner working models' of relationship, originally postulated by Bowlby (see Byng-Hall 1991).

RESISTANCE, HOMEOSTASIS, RIGIDITY AND INCONGRUENT ADAPTATION

A key concept in individual psychodynamic therapies is that of resistance. This assumes that change, particularly in terms of the acquisition of new insights, is avoided or 'resisted' in the service of preserving some aspect or fantasy of the self. In the family systems literature there is no equivalent to this notion, although two concepts are to some degrees analogous. These are the concepts of homeostasis and rigidity. The former (Jackson 1957) assumed that interactions in the family tended towards the maintenance of a steady state, rather as the biological organism uses feedback of biochemical processes to maintain a sufficiently steady internal environment. Such an idea would be in conflict with the changes inherent in growth and development and would therefore postulate possible sources of conflict at such developmental transitions as adolescence. Many writers have pointed out the potential flaws in such a concept; particularly that change is happening all the time in family life and not only at critical transitions. Furthermore, the concept assumes an almost pernicious holding-back against change. A wider sensitivity to issues of power, particularly in relation to gender, race and poverty, suggests a less 'obstructive' framework for such processes (see 'Incongruent adaptation' below).

A concept related to homeostasis was that of 'rigidity' of family pattern, meaning that roles (who dominates, who submits, who leads and who is led) and responses are rigidly organised, and that roles and responses do not adapt to changes in context. For example, if a particular adult is accustomed to making decisions about issues in which they have competence, in a 'rigid' system that person would be unlikely to defer to someone with greater competence in a context in which they may have no expertise.

The concept of rigidity has been similarly criticised as giving no recognition to the possible underlying forces that may have played a part in the failure of a family to adapt to a new context, whether this be of place – in cases of migration; of lifestyle – in response to economic changes or illness; or resulting from the changes inherent in development.

Thus, throughout all families, there is a constant tension between these contradictory forces for change and stability. Many problems can be understood in terms of the failure to resolve this conflict in the family, or, put another way, in terms of the adaptation becoming incongruent to the current focus of development in the family, although it may have been quite congruent to an earlier set of circumstances. Within this chapter this will be referred to as 'incongruent adaptation'.

The term 'incongruent adaptation' has been chosen in order to stress

1 that many problems are based on genuine attempts at adaptation to a problem or new situation, rather than on any inherent 'resistance' or pathology;
2 that the form of adaptation to a problem may have fitted well with some early situation, or some different context – but is ineffective in, or aggravates, this situation.
3 that the use of earlier and inappropriate (or incongruous) ways of adapting to a problem is often provoked or intensified in situations of fear or threat. These could include severe illness, various forms of persecution (such as ethnic or racial persecution) or disasters.

MODELS OF FAMILY THERAPY

No attempt will be made here to describe the many different models of psychotherapy used within the field over the last thirty years. These may be followed up through texts referenced at the end of this chapter. Key approaches have included strategic work, structural work, psychodynamic approaches, multigenerational approaches, the study of family myths and scripts, the 'Milan' approach, and a number of approaches which have been included under the heading of 'constructivism' (Jones 1993).

All the models include at least the premise that the connections between people are as valid a way in which both to understand and promote change in the behaviour of those individuals as any individual responses. In general, in all approaches the therapist is less concerned with pathology and with dysfunction, and more concerned with the promotion of both latent and actual strengths in the family; with encouraging the discovery of latent and new repertoires of behaviour, whilst in some way blocking those which promote dysfunction.

Gurman *et al.* have further defined family therapy as

any psychotherapeutic endeavour that explicitly focuses on altering the interactions between or among family members, and seeks to improve the functioning of the family as a unit, or its subsystems and/or the functioning of individual members of the family. This is the goal regardless of whether or not an individual is identified as the patient.

(1986: 565)

Three main groups of models have had a major influence on work in Britain and Europe. These are the structural approach, strategic approaches, and the Milan (and 'Post-Milan') approaches.

In structural work the therapist attempts to achieve small changes in sequence and pattern as they occur in a session. Such small changes are themselves unlikely to be lasting, unless they are repeated with sufficient intensity and frequency that they become part of a new folklore in the family. In these situations, a small shift in current behaviour becomes the focal point for the initiation of a new set of perspectives between family members about one another. Thus there can be some mutual revision of the perceptions of one another, and ultimately of their views of such relationships.

Structural family therapy addresses itself to the developmental context of the problem, the family itself; and works directly with the interactions as they occur, whereas a group of psychotherapies known collectively as 'strategic' look at the problem in a variety of social contexts. Therapists address themselves to the meaning attributed to the symptom, in the context in which it had a lived existence. Practitioners differ in their view as to whether the symptom is primarily a failed solution to another problem; or whether it carried an important meaning in relation to some other aspect of the successful functioning of the family. Strategic therapists tend to divide into those concerned with problems as a manifestation of failed solutions, and those interested almost exclusively in the 'exceptional' solutions which 'worked', and which are then amplified as the focus of psychotherapy.

Therapists who follow the solution-focused brief therapy model take as their premise the essential resilience of people which becomes depleted at times of critical life transitions, or stressful life events. At such times options for solving problems may diminish, and small problems may assume greater significance. As energy becomes increasingly directed into trying to solve a particular problem, so the attempted failed solution becomes the problem. Time in psychotherapy is therefore spent looking at the solutions that family members have used and particularly those that have 'worked' – that is, are exceptional – however rarely. It is assumed that people will have attempted more than one solution and that some of these may have had a glimmer of success. The exception to the rule of failure is therefore sought and amplified. Since people usually apply what seem to them to be common-sense solutions, uncommon solutions may be proposed, thus interrupting the usual pattern of behaviour.

A second group of strategic therapists understand the symptom primarily as part of the mechanism by which particular families regulate themselves. To lose the symptom would be to face a change in the overall organisation of the family, and a change in the beliefs by which the family regulate their collective identity. Many families would seek change for one member without wishing for change in their own living patterns. Working this way, therefore, the therapist links the symptom to the system in a number of ways, expressing curiosity and interest in the part it played in wider family life, and the maintenance of the stability and coherence of the system as it became organised over time. The goal of working this way is to create a perceptual redefinition of the problem and its 'lived existence'. However, the meanings attached to the problem may have been developed through a number of differing time-spans (Cooklin 1982). Sometimes they have come from one generation only, and sometimes they have been handed down over a number of generations without re-examination as to their usefulness.

In recent years this way of working has been developed alongside ideas of 're-authoring', or 'restorying', and narrative. The impact of the more openly politicised voices of women, of groups of different cultures, of victims of racism and of survivors of abuse, as well as work with victims of political oppression and torture, has increased awareness of the distinction between the 'dominant' and 'marginalised' discourse in different societies. It has also highlighted the way in which people only have access to part of their own history through the impact of larger systemic forces such as gender, race, class, economic status and age.

The Milan approach, developed in many settings within Britain, extended strategic thinking to address the complex mesh of meaning systems that families develop around problems; both of everyday life, and inherited from former generations. Campbell *et al.* have lucidly distinguished the value of this approach in the following way:

> We would apply this approach to any family in which the alternative solution to the problem has over time become entwined with the family's meaning system so that the alternative solutions are constrained by belief and relationships at one remove from the problem behaviour. . . . We assume that some feedback will create conflict about people's beliefs and relationships. When this happens an individual becomes preoccupied with the context of the message and the relationship to the giver of the message and the content of the message is lost. The result of this loss is that the conflict is incorporated into the family's meaning system.
>
> (1991: 325–62)

FAMILY SYSTEMS AND SOCIAL CHANGE

As family life and its structures have themselves changed in the United Kingdom, the integration of a systems perspective that pays attention to wider systems affecting family life has become more urgent. Early family therapy theory and training was largely based on the theory of the family as a stable, two-parent system. With one-third of first marriages and nearly two-thirds of subsequent marriages ending in divorce, stability can no longer be assumed. In addition, awareness of the many other disruptions and transitions experienced by families through economic pressures, such as unemployment and migration, challenged a theory based on ideas of a regulated society functionally organised at different levels with similarities of patterns between the different levels. Within Britain, attention was additionally paid to families formed by fostering and late adoption, and to the multiple serial transitions experienced by many children as a result of changes in marriage, cohabitation and separation experiences.

The diversity of race and culture within British society has led to wider recognition of many functional structures for bringing up children that differ greatly from the former norms of a family theory based on Western ethnocentric life-cycle traditions. Awareness of their own ignorance among family therapists has therefore led to the development of a more constructivist or exploratory approach in clinical settings, alongside a sensitivity to the need to understand the strengths inherent in cultural patterning that may be radically different from the therapist's own. These require changes within family therapy theory, as with other psychotherapy theory, at the levels of individual development, family and kinship structures, assumptions about health and normality within widely differing cultures, and new understandings of religion and spiritual meaning systems and their impact on culture and custom. In addition, assumptions based on the idea of stability of family life and the internal coherence of systems patterned over time, which developed in the 1950s and 1960s, have to be reconsidered in the light of the transitions and disruptions experienced by many families seen in clinical settings in the 1990s.

The degree to which social issues and psychotherapy connect within the domain of the family therapist varies widely within the field, but within a feminist perspective these are seen as part of the essential process of change. The discussion of the personal in the political, and the recognition of both client and female therapist as subject to the same socio-political forces within a patriarchal society, lead to a more open and even-handed discussion of the problem in context (Jones 1989). Women's thinking about the commonality of structured oppression within society has been amplified by the development of black commentaries on transracial and transcultural psychotherapy. The need for white professionals to develop a structural pluralist view of society, to recognise and acknowledge that there are many perspectives of equal validity, rather than one predominant homogeneous view with others marginalised or discounted, has amplified the awareness of family therapists that the way in which they think about the task of psychotherapy plays a part in a number of wider political debates.

FAMILY PATTERNS AND THE 'FAMILY DANCE': PATTERN IN ACTION

Imagine an event where you are sitting at dinner with some members of your family – say, your parents if they are alive, or perhaps your children.

Maybe there are others: grandparents, siblings, aunts, uncles or cousins. Imagine that a small and common or familiar conflict develops. Perhaps it starts with the question of who is to visit whom at the weekend, or some comment on your dress or diet. If you can imagine such a scene, you may be able to predict more or less accurately who would say what, roughly in what order, and the sort of tone in which each would speak. You may be able to go further. You may be able to predict to what degree of tension or passion the conflict will develop and two or three ways in which it will 'end'. What you will have remembered is an interactional sequence and one which is likely to be repeated with a similar shape and similar attitudes taken by the various members, despite the fact that the subject of conflict might differ markedly. We put the 'end' in inverted commas because, of course, it is not really the end. It is only the punctuation of a sequence which, together with other sequences, makes up the interactional pattern of the family. This sequence could 'end' with a senior member of the household perhaps looking stern, raising his voice, perhaps shouting, banging the table, perhaps threatening violence or perhaps carrying out violence. The amount of feeling and the level of conflict tolerated in different families will be idiosyncratic to that family. However, the ending of a sequence with one member taking a strong and challenging position is one pattern which will occur in many families in a predominantly patriarchal culture. In cultures with a different orientation to gender and power this may be different.

There are many alternative punctuations (or ways of 'slicing up' a circular event into an apparently 'linear' causal series of events) to such a sequence. It could end with somebody becoming upset, bursting into tears, leaving the room or the house, or with another member placating and 'calming things down'. It could end with a diversion: someone making a joke, an external intrusion such as the telephone or perhaps a child becoming excited or misbehaving. Diversion by a child is a common ending to such a sequence of conflict in many families. In some families, however, the child's overreaction to increasing tension is in somatic form. If the child has a predisposition to asthma, for example, the child is likely to have an asthma attack at times of high tension, particularly if this concerns the parents. Such an attack will often then divert attention from the conflict in the family, as members of the family co-operate to assist the afflicted member (Minuchin *et al.* 1978). At this point, the problem of considering causality can be seen. It could be said that the tension in the family precipitates the asthmatic attacks; alternatively, it could be said that the asthmatic attacks control tension in the family. The important point is that these patterns do not occur because somebody 'makes' them happen. Rather, they are a function of the organisation of relationships which has become set up in the family. We could postulate unconscious motives for each member which propagate such patterns, but an important aspect of these patterns is their provision of some stability to the family. Inasmuch as maintaining stability is often experienced by the members as a way of protecting the family and those in it, therefore one function of such behaviour is to achieve a degree of mutual protectiveness.

THEORIES OF ORGANISATION AND INTERACTION IN FAMILIES

Two related sets of ideas have provided frameworks for considering the family as a system rather than just a set of individuals. These are general systems theory and cybernetics (Ashby 1956; Von Bertalanffy 1950; Hoffman 1981).

General systems theory

General systems theory is not a theory of causality, but a theory of organisation. It is a way of categorising systems throughout nature both living and inanimate. It considers the family as a living system and considers its capacity to adapt in terms of the following:

1 The boundary around the family and around the subsystems in the family. This relates to the degree to which family members maintain a close unity within the family, or engage actively with the outside world. This, in turn, controls the input and output of information to and from the family. Information includes people. Thus a family with a very imperme-able boundary will be likely to adapt poorly to the arrival of new members – babies, grandparents, boyfriends or girlfriends – and will be intolerant of members moving out (such as around the time of adolescence).
2 The theory also considers the differentiation of the subsystems within the family and the degree to which the boundary around these is clear. For example, the marital relationship is a separate subsystem from, say, the parental subsystem. In a family in which the members say 'We always do everything together', the differentiation of the parents having a separate relationship may be poorly recognised. This, in turn, may militate against the development of any other set of separate relationships.

In addition to the degree to which the family is differentiated into subsystems, it will also form part of other subsystems to varying degrees. For example, the family may be part of an extended family network and the different members may be part of other suprasystems within the community, such as work, school, and/or social groups.

Cybernetics

Cybernetics is a set of principles adapted from electronic control systems. The thermostat in a central heating system is the simplest example.

Cybernetic principles are used to consider ways in which the family has developed habits that tend to neutralise or stabilise any change. In an example of Susan, an anorexic girl of seventeen, the father became depressed after she was admitted to hospital, began to eat and to make relationships with boys in the same unit. Strains in the marriage appeared and her mother developed a number of hypochondriacal symptoms. Susan's younger brother, Ben, began to steal. Susan eventually became so worried about them all that she discharged herself from hospital, soon after which she resumed her fasting behaviour. The others then improved.

Thus, the behaviour of the members of the family could be seen as responding to a change (the young girl leaving home), whilst the effect of their behaviour was ultimately to maintain stability, albeit an inappropriate stability and at a high cost. It was from observations such as these that the term 'family homeostasis' was coined (Jackson 1957).

DEVELOPMENT AS MULTI-PERSON EVENT

Most child development literature considers the development of thoughts, traits or attachments as 'inside' the child (Kessen 1979), and most studies provide more information about *what* happens in large samples than about *how* it happens. As Radke-Yarrow *et al.* (1989) point out, the research data of developmental psychology do not seem to be capturing what appears obvious to the naïve observer of society: namely, the degree to which children and their environments are connected.

If we take adolescence as an example, it is not only an individual, but also a family stage of development. 'Adolescent' parents are different from the parents of young children. They are likely to be reciprocally ambiguous in their responses, may even be preoccupied with questions about separation and individuation for themselves, may have disturbing sexual fantasies precipitated by the young person's emergent sexuality or sexual behaviour, and so on.

EXAMPLE

An example of the way in which individual development and behaviour can be seen as functionally related to or 'fitting' the wider organisation of relationships in the family is given below.

Joanna, her husband Billy and baby Jemima had been referred to us during Jemima's first year of life. When Jemima was five months old Joanna's grandmother, who had been the 'good grandmother' in her family, died. She had acted as a support to Joanna when her own mother had become severely incapacitated, after suffering brain damage in a car accident. This had left Joanna as the eldest responsible female in her family of origin, in which she had been responsible for the upbringing of her three siblings. The grandmother's death recreated for Joanna a pattern in which she felt left alone to take care of others, and also posed a new challenge about how she was to do this. Was she to do it in the style of her family of origin which had made many unusual adaptations to give the handicapped mother the 'illusion' that she was still in charge, or was she to adapt to a carefully cultivated norm of health and well-being that her husband's family consciously paraded? She became acutely depressed, started drinking heavily and experienced three admissions to psychiatric hospitals, subsequently discharging herself and refusing to take medication. She and her husband both came to see us with baby Jemima throughout most of the first two years of Jemima's life. Joanna retained a hostile view of the whole process of these 'conversations'. These often consisted of her long monologues about her precarious attempts to maintain a daily structure by driving around London with her dog and her baby in a small car, and dropping in unexpectedly on friends who became less sympathetic as the time went by. She described her home as a 'trap', talked obsessively of 'being inside a concrete box' and 'a tiny dirty window' through which she would peer at a hostile world from which she felt excluded. She would often respond to any attempt at contact by the therapists or by her husband by repeating *ad nauseam*, 'I only see four walls'. None the less Jemima continued to thrive, the house was kept at a reasonable standard, and Joanna remained outside the hospital. Joanna clearly enjoyed aspects of the therapeutic conversation, in which much teasing and humour would go on, introducing a number of other frames through which her dilemmas might be considered. However, her continued obsessive preoccupation with 'the four walls' suggested to us that the choices she saw herself facing needed to be contextualised in a wider family arena for her to believe that her position could ever change.

We called together both sets of grandparents and all the living siblings. One brother had hanged himself the previous year, and the reasons for his suicide remained obscure. However, it was clear that in Joanna's mind his death was associated with staying within the domain of his parents' family home, a farm in a remote part of England. Joanna herself used to visit this farm, where her father and mother still lived, nearly every weekend. She also expressed a longing to be free of the compulsion to visit. The rationale we gave to the family for this 'clan' gathering was that together we would explore the way in which people carry into marriage the traditions, cultures and influences of the families they come from, and the way in which these cultures may form part of the difficulties any couple are having. As the whole family were very concerned about the well-being of the joint grandchild, as well as the couple, all four grandparents and the adult siblings on both sides of the family attended.

The definition of the couple as part of the wider family system was well received by Joanna's father, who had been described to us previously as highly eccentric. Throughout the meeting he remained highly self-referential, continuing an uninterrupted stream of talk which seemed at first unrelated to the concurrent family discussion. However, he also interjected messages that suggested he had a better understanding of his daughter's dilemma than anyone else. Observing that he and his wife also had problems, and that while the focus might be on the young couple today, it might more appropriately be on the senior generation tomorrow, he commented, 'Joanna has had to evolve by herself over the last twenty-five years since her mother's accident.' He described how he saw himself and his wife as actors, playing the part of normality. He constructed this for the two of them, with himself acting as his wife's memory (the young adults confirmed that her memory was lost). He contrasted the positive qualities of the grandmother Joanna had lost (his own mother) with the more eccentric and formally disturbed qualities of his wife's family: 'Everyone used to go to psychiatrists in Jane's family.' He represented a world in which all figures who were 'parental' were perceived by society as psychiatrically disturbed and in need of treatment. This presented a marked contrast to Billy's parents. They busied themselves with trying to pin down the many ways in which Joanna's 'mad' behaviour was an annoyance to the rest of the family, and ways in which this might be changed, making many practical suggestions about what would constitute good child care for Jemima.

During the course of the conversation Joanna revealed that she thought she would never make the transition from being a Brown, her family of origin which she visited each weekend, to being a Drewitt, the family name of her husband. This became a metaphor for the two different worlds of experience she was contending with, the world of her brain-damaged mother and illogical, eccentric father; a domain within which her elder brother had recently killed himself, and a world of healthy child development which she saw herself as having lost following the loss of an active participant 'mother' in her own childhood. This world was now represented by the Drewitt family, as her husband's sisters had many healthy, bright small children, and Joanna did not always feel that her own child was welcome there. To join the 'normal' world was experienced by her as an active betrayal of the world of her childhood and the current world of her family of origin. To be 'normal' was taboo. Confronted by the power of her father's rambling and random stream of interruptions, her husband challenged her more directly with the dilemma.

'Your father's world is more real to you than my world.' She denied it, but went on to show how compelling the reality of the world of her family of origin was for her: 'Every weekend when I visit, I feel I am going back into a Brown world. I have this hammering in my head to become a Brown again.' Her husband engaged her in an intense conversation about his family's readiness to have her 'enter' their family, although he was unaware of all the connotations of disloyalty outlined above. In the middle of this her father began to talk at the same time in a compelling, low-key voice on the other side of her. Gradually her head turned as her attention was drawn back to her father, who was saying without any logical sequence 'I don't worship any family . . . Jo and Billy have got to find their own way somehow . . . they got married in the Western Isles . . . where do you want to be on Friday, Saturday and Sunday?' At the point where her head turned, both therapists, her husband and her father engaged in a lively and direct critique of the very brief and intensely highly packed sequence that had just taken place. The taboo against discussing the interconnection of Joanna's behaviour with that of her father, the Brown world; and the pain of transition from her father's domain of logic (in which as the keeper of his wife's memory he held the power for two parents) to that of a more everyday reality, was vigorously debated. Her father, accepting both his power and the necessity of its overthrow, cheerfully said, 'I'm older you see . . . some weeks I accomplish nothing, other weeks I write to Washington, I write to Moscow.' His inability to achieve much in the 'everyday' world and Joanna's competence in surviving in it were highlighted.

The dangers of parenthood in this family were discussed in the context of Joanna's mother's injury. Many constuctions could be made from this dense text, but those which overtly showed themselves as freeing Joanna began with the open highlighting of the power of her father's voice in a context where other voices, her husband's and her own, could be heard in a new way by the whole family. This allowed the beginning of new constructions of how she herself could be a parent; differences both of generation and gender. These could develop because her husband, far from 'holding' her memory during her 'mad' episodes, as her father had done for her mother had always held out for them having their own validity, although their meaning was not yet revealed. Joanna and Billy needed much further support as their family grew in size, but the intervals between our meetings became longer and longer as they gained in confidence.

WHAT WERE THE FUNCTIONS OF THERAPY FOR THIS FAMILY WITH THESE PROBLEMS?

This case illustrated the vonvening of the family to face the highly complex forces (many of which could be defined as unconscious) mutually acting on the different members of the two sets of families, and which were destructively manifested in the form of Joanna's restricted life and perspective, as well as in the risks to her children. The therapists worked at three main levels:

1 challenging Joanna and Billy to accept the control of their own definitions of good and bad, close and distant, and so on;

2 Thus encouraging Joanna and Billy to view Joanna's complaints as relevant if falling in the framework of a need for new definitions of how a family should be;
3 challenging the absolute definitions of 'truth' expounded by Billy's family, while connecting to, and redefining the apparently 'crazy' world of Joanna's family.

CONCLUSION

In this chapter we have aimed to illustrate both the different and complemtary frames of thinking implicit in the family systems framework in relation to individual psychodynamic thinking. We have been at pains to stress the framework of thinking as a useful field within which other forms of thinking can easily be connected, rather than prescribing a 'therapy' as a 'cure-all'. We hope the reader will find ways to use the ideas in his or her day-to-day work, whatever the orientation.

REFERENCES

Ashby, W. R. (1956)*Introduction to Cybernetics*, New York: Wiley.

Byung-Hall, J. (1991) 'The application of attachment theory to understanding and treatment in family therapy', pp. 199-215 in C.M. Parkes, J. Stevenson-Hinde and P. Marris (eds) *Attachment Across the life Cycle,* London: Routledge.

Campbell, D., Draper, R. and Crutchly, E. (1991) 'The Milan systematic approach to family therapy', pp. 325–62 in A. S. Gurman and D. P. Kniskern (eds) *Handbook of Family Therapy*, vol. 2, New York: Brunner/Mazel.

Cooklin, A. (1987) 'Change in here and now systems vs. systems overture', pp. 37– 74 in A. Bentovim, G. Gorell Barnes and A. Cooklin (eds) *Family Therapy: Complementary Frameworks of Theory and Practice,* London: Academic Press.

——(1990) 'Therapy, the family and others', pp. 73–90 in H. Maxwell (ed.) *Psychotherapy: An Ouline for Trainee Psychiatrists, Medical Students and Practitioners*, London: Whurr.

Gorell Barnes, G. (1985) 'Systems theory and family therapy', pp. 216–32 in M. Rutter and L. Hersov (eds.) *Modern Child Psychiatry*, vol. 2, Oxford: Blackwell.

——(1993) 'Family therapy', pp. 944–65 in M. Rutter, L. Hersov and E. Taylor (eds), *Modern Child Psychiatry*, vol. 3, London: Blackwell.

Gurman, A. S., Kniskern, D. P. and Pinsof, W. M. (1986) 'Research on the process and outcome of marital and family therapy', in S. L. Garfield and A. E. Bergin (eds) *Handbook of Psychotherapy and Behaviour Change: An Emperical Analysis*, 3rd edn, New York: John Wiley.

Hoffman, L. (1981) *Foundations of Family Therapy*, New York: Basic Books.

Jackson, D. D. (1957) 'The question of family homestasis', *psychiatric Quarterly Supplement* 31: 79–80.

Jones, E. (1989) 'Feminism and family therapy: can mixed marriages work?', pp. 63–81 in R. J. Perelberg and A. C. Miller (eds) *Gender and Power in Families*, London and New York: Routledge.

——(1993) *Family Systems Therapy: Developments in the Milan Systematic Therapies*, Chichester: John Wiley.

Kessen, W. (1979) 'The American child and other cultural inventions', *American Psychologist* 34: 815–20.

Main, M. (1991) 'Metacognitive knowledge, metacognitive monitoring and single (coherent) vs multiple (incoherent) models of attachment: findings and directions for future research', in C. M. Parkes, J. Stevenson Hinde and P. Marris (eds) *Attachment across the Life Cycle*, London: Routledge.

Minuchin, S., Rosman, B. and Baker, L. (1978) *Psychosomatic Families*, Cambridge, Mass.: Harvard University Press.

Radke-Yarrow, M., Richards, J. and Wilson, W. E. (1989) 'Child development in a network of relationships', pp. 48–63 in R. A. Hinde and J. Stevenson-Hinde (eds) *Relationships within Families: Mutual Influence*, Oxford: Oxford Scientific Publications.

Rycroft, C. (1968) *A Critical Dictionary of Psychoanalysis*, Harmondsworth: Penguin.

Sroufe, L. A. and Fleeson, J. (1988) 'The coherence of family relationships', in R. A. Hinde and J. Stevenson-Hinde (eds) *Relationships within Families: Mutual Influence*, Oxford: Oxford Scientific Publications.

Von Bertalanffy, L. (1950) 'The theory of open systems in physics and biology', *Science* 3: 25–9.

INFORMATION ON TRAINING

The Institute of Family Therapy
43 New Cavendish Street
London W1M 7RD
Tel.: 071 935 1651

or

The Association for Family Therapy
5 Heol Seddon
Cardiff
Wales

A learning video/computer pack, 'Family Therapy Basics', is available from

Marlborough Family Service
38 Marlborough Place
London NW8 OPJ
Tel.: 071 624 8605

Chapter 14

Group psychotherapy

Oded Manor

Group psychotherapy usually refers to situations in which between seven and twelve people meet together with one or two specially trained psychotherapists for between one and three hours, usually once or twice a week. Sometimes the number of these meetings is agreed in advance – for example, six sessions at the minimum – but a year's duration is more common. The membership of the group may be closed or open. So-called slow open groups may continue for many years. Yet, even when membership is open – that is, new members can join whenever a vacancy is available – usually there is a core membership of people who have participated long enough to sustain the therapeutic momentum while others find their way in what is, after all, a rather unusual group situation.

Most groups meet in the same middle-sized room, where they sit in a circle so that each person can see all the others. Usually the culture is rather informal. However, in the more strict psychoanalytic groups surnames are still used, particularly in relation to the psychotherapist. Equally, the more psychoanalytically orientated the psychotherapist, the more she or he is likely to say nothing at the beginning of the session. Instead, the group members themselves are expected to say whatever comes into their minds so that free association emerges. Other psychotherapists may begin in this way or they may begin by expressing their own feelings first. Some would add to these also a theme, or a query which is on their minds. Still a third style may involve giving members a topic or even suggesting and conducting an exercise related to interpersonal relationships. Whatever the therapeutic style, full and reasonably even participation of all the members is usually considered desirable.

I would suggest that group psychotherapy is utilising experiences which are unique to group situations in offering individuals psychotherapeutic help in their personal, interpersonal and social relationships. Broad as it is, this definition marks out group psychotherapy from other uses of small groups as a way of helping people. For example, the term 'psychotherapeutic' is there to suggest that whatever else is experienced, in group psychotherapy attention is deliberately focused on processes which may be out of awareness. This is not necessarily the case in behavioural group therapy, in group counselling and in social group work.

Another difference is the focus on 'individuals'. Group psychotherapy is there first and foremost for each of its individual members. The major experiences of group psychotherapy have to be helpful to its individual members; not necessarily to the group as a whole, nor to other people involved with those individuals. This emphasis on the needs of the individual members marks out group psychotherapy as different from small-group training for managers, the T-group approach, and from social action groups.

The emphasis on relationship is included in the definition in order to acknowledge that in group psychotherapy practical help is usually not provided to members directly. Whereas some group psychotherapists encourage members to explore what they themselves can do to obtain or earn money, to secure their accommodation, or to receive legal protection, others do not do even that. Seldom would a group psychotherapist act directly for or on behalf of any of the members. This type of involvement is more typical of group counsellors and social group workers.

Before pointing to the reasons for all this and to some of the advantages of group psychotherapy, I would like to emphasise strongly that this method is only one among others, and will not always be effective.

WHEN GROUP PSYCHOTHERAPY MAY NOT BE SUITABLE

Individual situations

It is my experience that group psychotherapy is not likely to be suitable for a minority of one. People who present conditions that are likely to be recognised by other group members as totally different from those presented by the rest of the group, and cannot be changed, seem to suffer in group psychotherapy rather than benefit from it. Examples could include particularly low intelligence, psychotic difficulties in a person joining a group where everybody else presents neurotic ones, marked hearing and vision impairment, or vastly different characteristics such as age or race. However, some remarkable exceptions exist – for example, one person with very short-term memory has benefited a group and from a group in unexpected ways.

Total confidentiality is another constraint. If the person is struggling with issues that require total professional confidentiality, that person may feel too anxious to participate in a group even when the members commit themselves to such a level of confidentiality (Norcross and Goldfried 1992). For example, a bisexual married man holding a secret relationship with a man while raising his family may find a group of heterosexually involved adults not only too different, but also too threatening to his family constellation.

Disabling past experiences can also be counter-indications. Some people were so badly bullied at school that they would not entertain joining any other group for the rest of their lives. Others were so badly and continuously scapegoated that they became paralysed in group situations and no group psychotherapist can change that. Such people may well begin psychotherapy with one individual psychotherapist.

Couple situations

Not all couples should be offered group psychotherapy either. For example, couples who are struggling with immediate issues in their sexual relationship may need the detailed attention of a psychotherapist, and the privacy of couples therapy for themselves.

Family situations

When a family is concerned, some situations call for family therapy instead of group psychotherapy. It is clearly recognised now that children can influence the dynamics of their own families over and above their parents' influence (Boer and Dunn 1992). When difficulties are presented in which children are involved, and the parents show sufficient concern accompanied with the potential to change the situation, group psychotherapy may miss the point. Only family therapy can address the immediate relationships between parents and children and among the siblings themselves.

GENERAL ADVANTAGES

Detailed research findings can be found in Garfield and Bergin (1986). For this brief chapter, six general features can be mentioned in relation to all types of group psychotherapy.

1 *Strength in numbers*: If the group becomes supportive of its members, each is then appreciated by quite a number of others. The mere expression of approval, appreciation and encouragement while a group member is remembering painful past experiences or trying to change certain behaviours seems a great help to many.
2 *The anonymity of the crowd*: Almost the reverse of strength in numbers, the group also offers members escape from attention. As some talk, others can temporarily withdraw their attention. It is noteworthy that some people find the continuous attention offered in individual psychotherapy too demanding. Group psychotherapy offers them a safe haven where they can participate in their own time. Other people tend to enter such intense conflicts, particularly with authority figures, that no individual psychotherapist can contain them for long enough to effect change.

Such people can diffuse their anger by letting others take over for a while, and still benefit.

3 *The advantage of being weak*: Group situations offer their members a distinct power balance. Since each individual is to some extent unique, no two people are totally alike. Therefore, at a certain level each member is pitched against the whole group and is unable to change the group culture alone. Groups do generate the experience of helplessness as much as they raise self-esteem. When people feel helpless they easily feel as if they were children, and with those child-like experiences can come the warm acceptance of being held unconditionally, as a child is held by an accepting parent. Being so 'contained' seems to provide strong emotional encouragement to members.

4 *Going back to go forward*: Feeling helpless in the group has another consequence. As each member realises their weakness in relation to the whole group, each feels like a child. With these child-like feelings aroused, memories of earlier years surface rather easily and quite spontaneously. Such surfacing is called 'regression' and seems helpful in re-evaluating earlier experiences and altering patterns of feelings, behaviour and thoughts in the present. By being forced to go back to their childhood, members are offered the opportunity to go forward into a different adulthood.

5 *The group as a psychosocial microcosm*: If the group is properly constituted, the members have enough in common so they identify with one another while, at the same time, they also differ sufficiently to receive a wide range of responses to their feelings, thoughts and behaviour. Such diversity within commonality creates ambiguity in relationships, and ambiguity leads people to make guesses. When people begin to guess how to behave they fall back on their habits; they re-enact central patterns of their other relationships. It is assumed that these patterns – dominating others, clowning, reasoning, and so on – sustain the problems for which people come for help. At some point or another during the development of the group, each member is likely to reconstruct their prevailing pattern. So the group becomes an intense miniature of the members' relationships in the outside world. When such re-enactment occurs, each member's pattern is amenable to exploration, to change and to generalisation outside of the group.

6 *Free experimentation*: The group is usually composed of members of equal formal status, joining the group on the same basis. Therefore, during the group's development each has potentially the chance of entering many different roles: assertive, receptive, humorous, supportive and so on. Because the members are not bound to one another in any way outside the group, each can experiment with new behaviour without immediate consequences in their daily life. This freedom to experiment without consequences seems to enable the testing out of

feelings, thoughts and behaviours that have been out of bounds for the members before they have joined the group.

SPECIFIC FACTORS

Yalom (1970) was probably the first to distil the more specifically unique therapeutic experiences. Yalom identified ten 'curative factors' of group psychotherapy:

1 Imparting information
2 Instillation of hope
3 Universality
4 Altruism
5 The corrective recapitulation of the primary family group
6 Development of socialising techniques
7 Imitative behaviour
8 Interpersonal learning
9 Group cohesiveness
10 Catharsis.

Rather than merely summarising Yalom's discussion, I would like to reflect on the possible relevance of these curative factors to three major ways of offering group psychotherapy. In doing so, I shall not attempt to review all the existing approaches to group psychotherapy (for examples, see Long 1988; MacKenzie 1992; Dryden and Aveline 1988). Clearly, such a variety cannot be conveyed within one chapter. Instead, I shall highlight examples that illustrate what I, as a systems-orientated practitioner, believe to be the crucial differences. As noted by Roberts (1982) among others, these differences are among:

psychotherapy	OF	the group
psychotherapy	IN	the group
psychotherapy	THROUGH	the group.

For a useful comparative evaluation of therapeutic factors, also see Bloch (1988: 297).

Psychotherapy OF the group

Although it is rare by now, some group psychotherapists address only the group as a whole. They do not refer to individual members, nor to pairs or sub-groups. Instead, their interventions usually begin with 'the group is . . . ', and follow with what the psychotherapist feels group members want from her or him. For example, the group psychotherapist may say: 'The group is trying to force its will on me.'

This was the main contribution of Bion (1961), who began work in the late 1940s. For Bion, the major therapeutic achievement was the rational clarification of relationships, particularly relationships with authority figures. He focused on authority figures since, so he thought, they always stood for early relationships with parental figures.

Bion believed in enhancing people's ability to pursue their goals rationally. Other modes which developed in the group were seen by Bion as defences against the rational one, which he called 'work'. When the group was not able to work, it regressed to what Bion called 'basic assumption', and he identified three of these: pairing, dependency and flight–fight. The psychotherapist is concerned mainly with maintaining her or his position as a 'projection screen'; sustaining an impersonal presence to which group members can attribute feelings, thoughts and behaviour they find intolerable in themselves. This rather impersonal presence of the psychotherapist seems to lead members to focus on their experiences of the psychotherapist.

It must be said that not everybody at the Tavistock Institute in London shared Bion's purity. For example, Ezriel (1950, 1956) developed a different model. Like Bion, Ezriel too maintained a relatively impersonal, analytic stance and always began with an interpretation of the group as a whole. Yet, he would then go on to articulate how each individual member contributed to the pattern presented by the whole group. These individual contributions he saw as three types.

Ezriel saw group psychotherapy as a process through which the 'required relationships', which led to problems and symptoms, were given up. Giving up these disabling relationships was possible only once certain 'calamitous relationships' were experienced as not leading to the expected disaster. Only then can the 'avoided relationships' develop. Having pointed out the situation as a whole, Ezriel would then spell out the fears; that is, the calamitous relationships each individual harboured so that each could venture certain avoided relationships. By doing so, Ezriel involved group members with one another more than Bion did. Very specific anxieties, such as favouritism, loyalty to both parents or sexual attraction to one of the parents, could probably be explored in such groups.

Psychotherapy OF the group was further extended into peer relations by Whitaker and Lieberman (1964). As Yalom (1970: 141) points out, their approach had parallels with that of Ezriel. Ezriel's 'required relation-ships' could probably be seen as equivalent to Whitaker and Lieberman's 'group solution': the manifest behaviour pattern which group members adopted.

Ezriel's 'avoided relationships' seem to serve a function similar to Whitaker and Lieberman's 'disturbing motive': behaviours that group members found too disturbing to attempt. This motive was seen as too disturbing because of a fear which Whitaker and Lieberman called the 'reactive motive': for example, a negative reaction from the psychotherapist or other group members which was too risky to contemplate. The reactive motive seems rather similar to Ezriel's 'calamitous relationship'.

Similar to Ezriel, the dynamics among the solution, the disturbing motive and the reactive motive were seen as largely unconscious. The interpretation of these dynamics always revolved around a 'focal conflict': some tension between a wish (the disturbing motive) and the fear of pursuing it (the reactive motive). The focal conflict always referred to the here-and-now situation of that particular group.

However (and this is where Whitaker and Lieberman differed from Ezriel), the focal conflict was not always between the psychotherapist and the group members. Such conflict could also arise among the members themselves. This active response to peer relationships and their possible conflicts seems to have led Whitaker and Lieberman towards a wider range of responses to their groups. Although they did offer interpretations of the group as a whole, they also showed members alternatives to their restrictive solutions by modelling them, and so would express their own feelings, ask direct questions, and at times respond also to an individual rather than the whole group.

This wider version of psychotherapy OF the group seems to allude to the recapitulation of the primary family group (Yalom's factor no. 5). It can contribute towards developing socialisation techniques (Yalom's factor no. 6) in relation to impersonal authority figures, and to group cohesiveness (Yalom's factor no. 9). The combination of having to cope with the impersonal authority of the therapist and the increased cohesion often gives rise to altruism among the members (Yalom's factor no. 4).

Psychotherapy IN the group

From a systems point of view the opposite of psychotherapy OF the group is probably psychotherapy IN the group. In psychotherapy OF the group, the psychotherapist always begins with their view of the group as a whole: what pattern of behaviour is evident in the session which is different from the various contributions made by individual members of that group. Psychotherapy IN the group begins from the other end: the pattern each member shows as a unique individual in relation to the group as a whole. So, in these methods the group psychotherapist is likely to begin by asking each member, 'What do you want now?' It should be said that, like the former, pure psychotherapy IN the group is rare by now. Its original forms could probably be found in the pioneering work of Moreno's psychodrama (1972), in Rogers' encounter (1957), Perls' Gestalt therapy (Perls et al. 1951), and Berne's Transactional Analysis (1977). Modern practitioners of these approaches have considerably developed and/or modified these founders' theories and practices.

Transactional Analysis as developed by Eric Berne (1961/1980), being more of an integrative model than the other three, includes their central emphases on the one hand, while extending their range and ability to the interpersonal level on the other. Transactional Analysis made its unique contribution in studying the transactions between individual group members. The method offered a way of working with these to extrapolate, understand and resolve the group members' intrapsychic conflicts, outdated decisions and harmful or ineffective life scripts. TA's unique contribution is in relating past or borrowed ego states to present ways of relating to other people. Ego states are conceived to be the basic phenomenological structure of the human personality: 'An ego state may be described phenomenologically as a coherent system of feelings, and operationally as a set of coherent behaviour patterns, or pragmatically as a system of feelings which motivates a related set of behaviour patterns' (Berne 1977: 123).

Most methods of psychotherapy IN the group include the detailed enactment of earlier relationships. Therefore, Yalom's factor no. 5, the corrective recapitulation of the primary family group, is powerfully activated. Because of their active mobilisation of bodily processes, Gestalt therapy and psychodrama share an emphasis on deep release of feelings. The members intensify the expression of their feelings through bodily gestures, through direct beating of soft objects, and through acting various parts of themselves. So, it is likely that Yalom's factor no. 10, catharsis, is extremely deep in such groups. Also, in such methods the members rally round each individual as sources of support. At one point or another, each member has the opportunity of being physically held by others as well as supportively holding them. Each person experiences the ability to give and receive unconditionally and very directly. Therefore, Yalom's factor no. 4, altruism, becomes very important. The intense mutual support that comes from such physical closeness seems to generate Yalom's factor no. 9, group cohesion, to an unusual degree. At times such groups can become the most important association for their members. Coupled with the experiences of altruism and group cohesion is Yalom's factor no. 2, instillation of hope. These methods are anchored in humanistic psychology which rests on the assumption of self-actualisation rather than cure. The emphasis on self-actualisation implies an unlimited belief in the potential of each individual person to evolve further and reach a richer life. So instillation of hope can be most powerfully evoked. There is another aspect to these body methods. The psychotherapist works in detail with each individual on their very idiosyncratic patterns of physical, emotional and cognitive behaviours and on the relationships among these three levels. So, after a while, each member develops very intimate knowledge of these processes and should be able to prevent the establishment of disabling ones without any help from the psychotherapist. Yalom's factor no. 1, imparting information, is not only central but is extended to become a form of psycho-education in intimacy.

Psychotherapy THROUGH the group

Psychotherapy OF the group can be seen to begin from the top: the group as a whole. If so, then psychotherapy IN the group begins from the bottom: each individual. In this sense, psychotherapy THROUGH the group focuses on the middle: the relationships among group members and the ways in which they try to involve the psychotherapist in them. Again, the psychotherapist OF the group is likely to begin with the phrase 'The group is . . . '. The psychotherapist IN the group would begin by asking each member, 'What do you want now?' However, the group analyst is likely to wait until a member speaks and then ask, 'What do other members feel?' A great deal is turned back to the group, and only when group members are clearly stuck in their attempts to resolve issues on their own does the group therapist become involved in suggesting group phenomena that stand in the way.

Foulkes's (1948, 1964) group analysis began not long after Bion proposed his model, but took a markedly different direction. Foulkes's attention was focused on what he called 'the matrix': the intricate web of relationship, fantasies and fears that group members were developing towards one another. The individuality of each group member was seen as emerging within this overall context of the matrix. Therefore, the members' relationships with him seemed to Foulkes of secondary importance. Due to their orientation towards peer relationships, group analysts have not restricted their view of the causes of difficulties to early family influences alone. Most group analysts consider early experiences in play groups and at school important too. Furthermore, many group analysts are usually socially minded; they may express their own feelings during the session, and they may encourage members to explore practical solutions to their problems.

However, as noted by Roberts, 'Foulkes did not leave us with a clear and coherent presentation of the underlying theories . . . from which group analysis was developed . . . . Each concept is developed differently with each appearance' (1982: 112). Quite a number of group analysts are very aware of this, and would privately express the view that very little would be lost if group analytic ideas were couched in systems terms. Indeed, Roberts himself discusses the relationship between the parts and the whole and the paradox involved in ways which raises the question why the connection had not been made explicit long ago.

In fact, in the United States psychotherapy THROUGH the group seems to have progressed mainly by drawing upon general systems theory. By now, one can find psychotherapists who have come from an object relations perspective (Ashbach and Schermer 1987), a Jungian approach (Boyd 1991), psychodrama (Williams 1989), or Transactional Analysis (Peck 1981), all expanding their perceptions by resorting to various aspects of the systems approach. The most thorough work was probably done by the 'Task Force' led by James Durkin (1981). The advantages of the systems approach to group psychotherapy are almost obvious. This approach enables us to relate the parts (the members) to the whole (the group). It also accounts for step-by-step changes as much as it focuses on transformation. Systems group psychotherapists do not invent their own theory. Some link it with a vast body of knowledge developed in other disciplines (Manor 1992). Others see their theory as an over-arching model providing a framework within which different approaches can be coherently integrated (Clarkson 1990; Clarkson and Lapworth 1992).

Insight is emphasised by them as much as it was by psychotherapists OF the group. Disequilibrium and the deep release of feelings are intensified as much as was done by psychotherapists IN the group. Interaction among group members is as important to systems therapists as it was for group analysts working THROUGH the group. In addition, no group member is seen as isolated from their present network, be it marital partner, children, friends, colleagues or other affiliates. Seen as part of the member's system, all are included when change is considered. Change itself is understood in rather wide terms: from intrapsychic transformation, through interpersonal clarification, to step-by-step modification of behaviour.

Sluzki (1983) encapsulated the systems approach in his seminal paper 'Process, structure and world views: towards an integrated view of systemic models in family therapy'. This integration can be achieved by concentrating on those influences that constitute feedback. James Durkin explains that feedback arises when 'part of the output . . . is returned as input' (1981: 343). Group psychotherapists who concentrate on the processes express this somewhat more simply. They usually say that the group psychotherapist should use mainly that which the group gives her.

Feedback can be offered in various ways. Simple to understand is the communication of empathy: the facilitator captures the essence of the contents expressed by the members in relation to the most emotionally charged utterances. By focusing only on this segment, the practitioner responds to part of the group's output. She then rephrases it and communicates it back to the group as an empathic input. Repeating the process of offering a certain input gives rise to a structure. Let us see how a structure emerges.

Emerging structures

For example, let us take a situation where one member, John, dominates the interactions. The group psychotherapist can say, 'John is raising an important issue. I wonder what other members feel about this.' In such a situation, the psychotherapist has effected a certain judgement. She acted on the assumption that equal participation by group members is more desirable than being dominated by one of them. A desired level, that of equal participation, was in the psychotherapist's mind, and she was trying to steer the group towards it. This level is called 'homeostasis'. In that situation the behaviour of the dominating member disrupted and deviated from the homeostasis. The psychotherapist's intervention used part of the output ('John is raising an important issue'), and then returned it to the group as input, but that input 'negated' John's domination; it focused on 'what the other members feel'. Such 'negative feedback' counteracts the impact of the deviation and restores the homeostasis by steering the system back to a desired level of activity. If the group continues to allow John to dominate its interactions and rely on the psychotherapist to offer such negative feedback when they want to speak too, a pattern will be established. This pattern will set up a structure whereby the psychotherapist will act as a buffer between John and the group members. Although not necessarily desirable, such a structure provides the group with continuity. Other, more enabling structures can be enhanced in the same way: that is, by resorting to negative feedback. Enabling such structures requires a good understanding of the process.

Facilitating processes

Through the process of negative feedback, other step-by-step, linear changes can be introduced. Offering tasks during the session as well as homework tasks, not unlike those offered in cognitive-behavioural group psychotherapy (Alladin 1988), is a good example. These highly planned programmes aim at specific levels of interaction, and can therefore be seen as another form of negative feedback. Within the systems approach all these planned step-by-step changes are called 'first order changes'. I prefer the more humanistically meaningful expression 'incremental changes'. Incremental changes are often part of learning new interpersonal skills, and so give rise to a great deal of interpersonal and social learning (Yalom's factors nos. 8 and 6) and to imitative behaviour (Yalom's factor no. 7).

Incremental changes facilitate the often-needed continuity of patterns in relationships. We do need the continuity involved in turning up on time, in learning to say 'hello' as well as 'goodbye', or in taking care to sustain eye contact while talking with certain people. Continuity of patterns is very helpful for living. Yet, when patterns of behaviour are repeated so rigidly that they reinforce too closed a structure, they do not enable people to cope with unexpected exceptions, such as the need to change a subject or just to be in silence in the group. In such situations instability is positively needed. Imagine John, in our example, continuing to dominate the group for four or five sessions. What will happen then? Quite likely, at some point someone will shout 'For God's sake, John, stop this!' When that member protests, John's initial deviation will be temporarily intensified: someone else will assume power in the group too. The pattern comprised of John's domination, the members' passivity, and the psychotherapist as a buffer, will be destabilised. From then on, it will not be possible to predict the results; these will depend on the reactions of other members, of the psychotherapist, and John. In some instances the protest may turn out to be merely another deviation which the group will suppress again. If so, the group will soon revert to the same buffering pattern, perhaps with someone else dominating it instead of John. In systemic terms, negative feedback may be affected to return the group to its uneven pattern. In more fortunate circumstances, other members will join in, saying that they too had had enough of John's 'Sermon on the mount'. In such a case, the deviation produced by the protesting member will be further amplified. If allowed to run its course, the protest is likely to enable the group to revise its way of working together. The members are likely to question the value of allowing one of them to dominate – while trusting their psychotherapist to rescue them from the consequences. Instead, a more participative pattern may then be developed.

Instability can also be facilitated deliberately through the persistent intensification of a deviation from a too-stable structure. Helen Durkin was probably one of the first group analysts to describe how 'seemingly accidental and very fleeting emotions, thoughts and actions' were given 'conscious expression' (1981: 188). Further along these lines, the use of growth games, as initially developed by Schutz (1966), and the 'hot seat technique' used in Gestalt psychotherapy (Perls *et al.* 1951) can also be incorporated as offering such forms of feedback. Such an intensification is called 'positive feedback'. Whenever a deviation from the homeostasis is persistently intensified and the system is not directed towards a specific level of activity in advance, positive feedback is applied. Such feedback often leads to a great deal of upheaval as roles, rules and norms are fundamentally revised. The course of change cannot be planned in advance in these circumstances, exactly because it leads to some transformation of previous structures. Transformation often involves catharsis (Yalom factor no. 10). Such a deep release is often of feelings related to earlier relationships, particularly with parents and other earlier carers. The result is often the re-evaluation of the meaning of previous relationships, and the rules of future ones. So the corrective recapitulation of the primary family group (Yalom's factor no. 5) is very much part of this. This ability of psychotherapy to lead to transformation of relationships tends to charge it with hope (addressing Yalom's factor no. 2, instillation of hope) quite dramatically.

As can be seen, the processes lead to both incremental changes as advocated by behavioural psychotherapists, as well as transformational change, pursued by humanistic and existential psychotherapists. Indeed, the systems approach goes even further. This is where the 'world views' mentioned above come to bear on practice.

Reflecting a world view

Let us go back to John's behaviour in our example. The psychotherapist could have responded in other ways to John's domination. For example, the psychotherapist could have expressed how the situation affected her: contributing self-disclosure. This would be characteristic of the psychotherapist IN the group. Alternatively, she could have described the pattern of domination and submission between John and the members. She could also have suggested an unconscious dynamic underlying that pattern. Both would have suited psychotherapists OF the group. The systems approach does not exclude any of the others. Instead, this approach broadens the spectrum of responses by referring to our ability to reflect upon our own experiences and communicate their meaning to others. This ability to offer connections among various messages is called 'meta-communication' (Simon *et al.* 1985: 223).

Yet we do not simply communicate. Whenever we offer a connection we affect human judgement about the relevance of certain elements and, by implication, the irrelevance of others. In our example, the psychotherapist referred to the dominance–submission pattern. This was her choice. She could have talked about other experiences which were no doubt available to her, but she chose to focus on the theme of power in the group. Systems thinkers have been intensely interested in unearthing the moral bases of such choices. They call it 'punctuation': the ways in which each participant 'subjectively perceives different patterns of cause and effect' (Simon *et al.* 1985: 284). When Wilden explored the processes involved in punctuation, he showed that they always evolved out of certain moral values, which were often suppressed (1980: 50–6). These moral values can be related to what Sluzki called 'world views'. The uniqueness of the systems approach is in its insistence that each practitioner must make explicit the world views underlying their work. For example, I hold humanistic world views. These direct us to punctuate experiences in groups which promote such human values as pluralism, genuineness and mutuality in relationships. The freedom of the psychotherapist is considerable within the systems approach, but the burden of responsibility is quite heavy. No ready-made ideological recipes are offered. Instead, every time each practitioner is with clients they are expected to articulate the world views guiding their practice.

Through such comments, as well as those offered by the group members, the universality (Yalom's factor no. 3) of problems as well as possible solutions can be highlighted. Both psychotherapist and members impart a great deal of information (Yalom's factor no. 1), and group cohesiveness (Yalom's factor no. 9) is likely to increase.

Two beneficial aspects are particular to the systems approach. Both relate to Yalom's factor no. 8: interpersonal learning. One is the group as a 'rehearsal stage'. Sufficient evidence exists by now (Goldstein and Kanfer 1979) to accept that changes achieved during the session do not necessarily transfer to situations outside it. Special procedures have to be developed to ensure that group members actually translate their group psychotherapy experiences to real life. Therefore it is vital that the group psychotherapist offers exercises to each member during the session, rehearsing with him or her how to cope with specific external situations differently now. The systems approach would lead to such work being done by virtue of its understanding of structural inequalities in every society, such as between women and men or black and white people in Britain. Structural inequalities mean that members have actively to alter the power balance outside the group. Also, each group splits itself from the world to some extent: 'we' are different from 'them'. In view of this universal tendency for closure, group members then have to explain the change to people outside the group. Awareness of closure leads to 'linking'. The systems approach suggests that, whether consciously or not, everything which happens to one part of the system is likely to affect all the other parts. Therefore, everything that happens to a group member in psychotherapy is likely to affect their relationship in all the subsystems to which that member is committed: first and foremost those involving intimacy, such as parent or child, or any partnership between adults (marriage, cohabitation or an open relationship). The systems approach would see the member as a person-in-relationships, and would strive to involve those outside the group as each plays their part in the member's relationships.

SUMMARY

Even a single chapter already conveys the richness and diversity offered by group psychotherapy, and many approaches are not included here for lack of space. The discussion was confined to highlighting three major pointers to the differences among the approaches: psychotherapy OF the group, psychotherapy IN the group, and psychotherapy THROUGH the group. Each includes quite a number of different styles, yet some of Yalom's curative factors seem to be particularly relevant to one of them more than others.

It was suggested that, by alluding to recapitulation of primary family relationships, psychotherapy OF the group is likely to give particular prominence to coping with authority figures, and so contribute to socialisation techniques related to this level. The emphasis on the group as a whole seems to lead to increased group cohesiveness, and the combination often encourages members to help one another; that is, altruism.

Psychotherapy IN the group also promotes group cohesion and altruism. In addition, it is particularly conducive to enhancing deep catharsis, and to enabling the corrective recapitulation of the primary family group. The emphasis on self-actualisation embedded in deep cartharsis often contributes to a great deal of optimism, that is, to the instillation of hope. This strand is also an effective forum for imparting information, particularly about intimate relationships.

Psychotherapy THROUGH the group, especially when drawing on the systems approach, can address all the former curative factors, and then go further to enable a great deal of interpersonal and social learning as well.

Much more research is needed to validate these observations. If supported, this line of thinking might help us see the wood for the trees. It may suggest that the systems approach has the potential to integrate many of the others, and so link group psychotherapy more clearly to other forms of therapeutic help, notably those concerned with the family, but also couples and individual psychotherapy.

REFERENCES

Alladin, W. (1988) 'Cognitive-behavioural group therapy', pp. 115–39 in M. Aveline and W. Dryden (eds) *Group Therapy in Britain*, Milton Keynes: Open University Press.

Ashbach, C. and Schermer, V. L. (1987) *Object Relations, the Self, and the Group: A Conceptual Paradigm*, London: Routledge & Kegan Paul.

Berne, E. (1977) *Intuition and Ego States*, San Francisco: Harper & Row.

—— (1980) *Transactional Analysis in Psychotherapy: A Systematic Individual and Social Psychiatry*, London: Souvenir Press (first published 1961).

Bion, W. (1961) *Experience in Groups and Other Papers*, London: Tavistock.

Bloch, S. (1988) 'Research in group psychotherapy', pp. 283–316 in W. Dryden and M. Aveline (eds) *Group Therapy in Britain*, Milton Keynes: Open University Press.

Boer, F. and Dunn, J. (eds) (1992) *Children's Sibling Relationships: Developmental and Clinical Issues*, Hillsdale, NJ: Lawrence Erlbaum Associates.

Boyd, R. D. (1991) *Personal Transformation in Small Groups: A Jungian Perspective*, London: Tavistock/Routledge.

Clarkson, P. (1990) 'A multiplicity of psychotherapeutic relationships', *British Journal of Psychotherapy* 7(2): 148–63.

Clarkson, P. and Lapworth, P. (1992) 'Systemic integrative psychotherapy', pp. 41–83 in W. Dryden (ed.) *Integrative and Eclectic Therapy: A Handbook*, Milton Keynes: Open University Press.

Dryden, W. and Aveline, M. (eds) (1988) *Group Therapy in Britain*, Milton Keynes: Open University Press.

Durkin, H. E. (1981) 'The technical implication of general systems theory for group psychotherapy', pp. 172–98 in J. E. Durkin (ed.) *Living Groups: Group Psychotherapy and General Systems Theory*, New York: Brunner/Mazel.

Durkin, J. E. (ed.) (1981) *Living Groups: Group Psychotherapy and General Systems Theory*, New York: Brunner/Mazel.

Ezriel, H. (1950) 'A psycho-analytic approach to group treatment', *British Journal of Medical Psychology* 23: 59–74.

—— (1956) 'The first session in psychoanalytic group treatment', *Nederlands Tydskrift voor Geneeskunde* 111: 711–16.

Foulkes, S. H. (1948) *Introduction to Group-Analytic Psychotherapy*, London: Heinemann Medical Books.

—— (1964) *Therapeutic Group Analysis*, London: Allen & Unwin.

Garfield, S. and Bergin, A. E. (eds) (1986) *Handbook of Psychotherapy and Behaviour Change* (3rd edn), New York: Wiley.

Goldstein, A. P. and Kanfer, F. H. (eds) (1979) *Maximising Treatment Gains: Transfer Enhancement in Psychotherapy*, London: Academic Press.

Long, S. (ed.) (1988) *Six Group Therapies*, New York: Plenum Press.

MacKenzie, K. R. (ed.) (1992) *Classics in Group Psychotherapy*, London and New York: Guilford Press.

Manor, O. (1992) 'Transactional analysis, object relations, and the systems approach: finding the counterparts', *Transactional Analysis Journal* 22(1): 4–15.

Moreno, J. L. (1972) *Psychodrama*, New York: Boston House.

Norcross, J. C. and Goldfried, M. R. (1992) *Handbook of Psychotherapy Integration*, New York: Basic Books.

Peck, H. (1981) 'Some applications of transactional analysis in groups to general systems theory', pp. 158–71 in J. E. Durkin (ed.), *Living Groups: Group Psychotherapy and General Systems Theory*, New York: Brunner/Mazel.

Perls, F. S., Hefferline, R. F. and Goodman, P. (1951) *Gestalt Therapy: Excitement and Growth in the Human Personality*, New York: Julian Press.

Roberts, J. P. (1982) 'Foulkes' concept of the matrix', *Group Analysis* 15(2): 111–26.

Rogers, C. R. (1957) 'The necessary and sufficient conditions of therapeutic personality change', *Journal of Consulting Psychology* 21(2): 95–103.

Schutz, W. (1966) *The Interpersonal Underworld*, Palo Alto, CA: Science and Behavior Books.

Simon, C. B., Stieling, H. and Wynne, L. C. (1985) *The Language of Family Therapy*, New York: Process Press.

Sluzki, C. E. (1983) 'Process, structure and world views: towards an integrated view of systemic models in family therapy', *Family Process* 22(4): 469–576.

Whitaker, D. S. and Lieberman, M. (1964) *Psychotherapy through the Group Process*, New York: Atherton Press.

Wilden, A. (1980) *System and Structure* (2nd edn), London: Tavistock Publications.

Williams, D. (1989) *The Passionate Technique*, London: Tavistock/Routledge.

Yalom, I. D. (1970) *The Theory and Practice of Group Psychotherapy*, New York: Basic Books.

Part IV

Settings

Chapter 15

Psychotherapy in and with organisations

Peter Hawkins and Eric Miller

Freud said the whole business of therapy was to bring a person to love and to work. It seems to me we have forgotten half of what he said. Work. We have been talking of what goes wrong with love for eighty years. But what about what goes wrong with work, where has that been discussed?

(Hillman 1983)

Most people entering psychotherapy training already have another professional identity – as social workers, teachers, psychologists and so on. Many, when they have finished their training, develop a part-time practice as psychotherapists while continuing with their previous occupations, more often than not as full- or part-time employees of organisations. The training may in some cases lead to changes in the context of their jobs and will invariably have some influence on their working practices and relationships; but they carry on wearing their original professional hats.

The alternative is to start explicitly from one's professional identity as a psychotherapist and to apply in wider settings the skills and insights gained from working with individual patients. This is happening increasingly. Some training institutions are beginning to include consultancy to groups (as distinct from group psychotherapy) as an element in the final year of training. In doing so they are enlarging the professional definition of 'psychotherapist'.

This chapter is aimed mainly at this second category – psychotherapists who are thinking of using their training and experience to take up roles as counsellors, trainers or consultants in organisational settings, or who are already doing some work of this kind and want to reflect on the roles they have now or might want to take up in the future. However, it may be also relevant to the first category – the 'employees' – by offering them different perspectives from which to look back on their own situations. Some of the ideas in the chapter may also be useful to therapists in private practice who have only second-hand, consulting-room knowledge of organisations. A growing proportion of individuals seeking psychotherapy come not for treatment of an 'illness' but to enhance their lives and self-understanding. Many are successfully working in organisations. Indeed, they may have been referred on to psychotherapy by their work-based counsellor, or management consultant. The psychotherapist working with such patients/clients needs to be attentive to the constant interplay of the psychodynamics of the individual and those of the organisation. This is sometimes like working with a relationship difficulty, such as a marital problem, where only one side of the relationship is present. The psychotherapist has to be able to distinguish when patients are projecting their own disturbance onto the organisations they work for, and when they are carrying some of the distress and disturbance that is a symptom of the organisational dynamics. Organisations play a significant part in most people's lives, starting with childhood experience in schools. Adults may spend more time in and relating to their work organisation than to any single individual, and often their self-image and self-esteem are greatly determined by the setting in which they work, and the amount of work satisfaction and positive feedback they receive. All psychotherapists therefore need to understand the complex interplay between individuals, the groups they belong to and the organisations of which they are a part.

In this chapter we suggest that psychotherapy in and with organisations has to keep a constant balance in understanding the interrelatedness of three key factors; *task*, *process* and *environment*. These can be seen as a triangle with each element affecting both the others (see Figure 15.1). We give a series of typical examples, progressively more complex; first involving work with the individual and proceeding through the levels of group, inter-group and the organisation as a whole. Working with individual

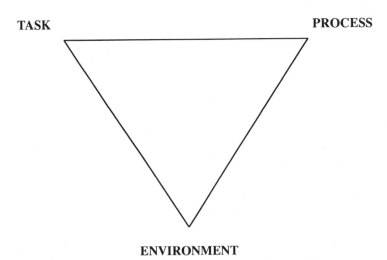

Figure 15.1   Task, process and environment

members of an organisation, the task of the psychotherapist is to help them to achieve a healthy alignment between self, work and the environment of the work organisation. Likewise, when we come on to look at the level of team development, the task of the team consultant is to help the team find a healthy alignment between their group process, their collective task and the organisational context, including customers and stakeholders who create the environment in which that team exists. The same triangle and task can also be taken one level higher, when the consultant works with the alignment of task, process and environment for the whole organisational system. Each successive level, in our view, involves more complex issues and consequently more training, and at some point in this progression the identity of 'psychotherapist' has to be discarded – or, rather, subsumed in a broader identity, such as 'organisational consultant'.

First, however, we need to say something about what psychotherapists bring to an organisation and to offer some perspectives on the nature of organisations themselves: a simple but perhaps useful framework.

WHAT PSYCHOTHERAPISTS BRING

Two great assets that a psychotherapist brings to the organisation are as follows:

1 A capacity to work at the *transaction* between patient and psychotherapist; using the transference and counter-transference as data for understanding the dynamics of the patient. Consultants drawn from other disciplines tend to see their clients as 'out there' and deny themselves the insights that could be yielded by looking at their subjective experience.
2 Related to this is an alertness to unconscious processes.

Not unconnected with these is the readiness and capacity to listen and to wait. Listening to the music as well as to the words is clearly also important; but simply to be able to listen non-judgementally and refrain from premature interpretation is an asset missing in many consultants and most managers.

The main liability is a predisposition to see problems in terms of individual pathology and interpersonal difficulties. With rare exceptions, such as combinations of individual and family therapy, the psychotherapist is accustomed to working with problems as residing in individual patients. Work, family and partner relationships are contextual. When one shifts to the organisational setting it is useful to turn this on its head and to approach the situation as if the organisation itself were the client/patient. One might then take as a working hypothesis that the apparent pathology of the individual is a symptom of organisational illness. If the organisational problem is identified and tackled, the individual's symptoms will evaporate.

That represents, in slightly exaggerated form, the shift in perspective that is appropriate. Much the same applies to so-called 'personality clashes'. These presenting problems all too frequently turn out to spring from ambiguity and confusion in definition of roles. If one colludes in accepting that the problem lies in the individual or in interpersonal relations, then the pathogenic factors in the organisation will go on producing more and more casualties.

Another potential liability is the actual label of 'psychotherapist'. This mobilises fantasies and projections even before one arrives. One of the co-authors, not a psychotherapist, has run into similar fantasies about his associations with 'Tavistock'. Arriving by car at a Lancashire factory, he was greeted with the not entirely jocular question: 'Do you carry your couch in the boot?' Although the image of psychotherapy is shifting, stereotypes remain, such as: 'They must think we're nutcases'; 'They can read our minds'. It will be prudent to be aware of such likely transferences and to avoid compounding them by also introducing our own jargon. We need to learn and respect the language of the organisation.

THE NATURE OF ORGANISATIONS

Most psychotherapists have the experience of being an employee in an organisation. Valuable though this is, it has its disadvantages. First, there may be a tendency to extrapolate from these experiences and to assume similarities – and indeed differences – that may not be valid. Secondly, one may be tempted, without recognising it, to identify with those members of the client organisation – perhaps front-line workers or middle managers – whose position and dilemmas resonate most closely with one's own past experience. If recognised, this can be informative; unrecognised, it will mean getting caught in projections that are a threat to one's professionalism.

Learning the language of the organisation includes gaining an under-standing of its technology, of its relations with its environment, and of the kinds of responsibilities attached to various functions and roles. Psycho-therapists coming from health and social service institutions, as many do, may well feel lost at first when they enter, for example, an industrial company. They have to devote some serious effort to discovering how it works and who does what. Acknowledging one's ignorance and asking questions does more for one's credibility than operating from ill-informed assumptions. If you acknowledge the competence of others in areas where you are ignorant, they may be readier to accept that you have professional competence that they lack.

Beyond this acquisition of practical knowledge about the specific organisation, the incoming psychotherapist needs conceptual frameworks or models that offer a perspective on the functioning of organisations as wholes – analogous to the models of individual functioning that one has learned during training. There is no shortage of these: Gareth Morgan (1986) has devoted a substantial book to the subject, while writers such as Pugh and Hickson (1989) and Handy (1976) offer accessible introductions.

Some of these models or metaphors are less helpful than others in contributing to our understanding. Unhelpful, for example, is the traditional mechanistic metaphor – a managerialist perspective – in which the organisation is a machine and good management seen in terms of a well-designed engine: 'oiling the wheels', 'changing gears' and driving the machine. We confine ourselves here to offering four perspectives which we find illuminating and of practical use.

1 *Organisation as a socio-technical system* Originating at the Tavistock Institute in the 1950s, this framework sprang from a pioneering study in coal-mines (Trist and Bamforth 1951) and was further developed by Trist himself, Rice, Emery and others (e.g., Rice 1958, 1963; Trist *et al.* 1963; Emery and Trist 1969). It views the organisation as an interplay between a system of technical activities necessary for task performance and a social system of relationships which meet the psychological and social needs of the work-force. Technology does not determine organisation: there are choices; and some forms of organisation are more effective than others in optimising the functioning of these systems.

2 *Organisation as an open system* A systemic perspective alerts us to the interconnectedness of the parts of an organisation to one another and to the whole: a change in one part will have repercussions in others. The notion of the organisation as an open system (also developed at the Tavistock Institute: cf. Rice 1963; Miller and Rice 1967) draws on the analogy with the biological organism. It depends for its existence and survival on a process of interchange with its environment. A manufacturing company imports raw materials, converts them into widgets, sells them, and uses the proceeds to buy more raw materials, maintain the system and pay a dividend to shareholders. In an educational institution, the intakes are students, the outputs are graduates (and drop-outs), and through its perceived success in doing this it generates more inputs and the resources to 'process' them. These import-conversion-export processes are the *primary tasks* of these institutions – the task they must perform in order to survive; but they will also be engaged in ancillary input-output processes related to supplies, personnel and so on. The organisation as organism seeks to maintain a 'quasi-stationary equilibrium' through making internal and external changes to match shifts in its environment. There is also another type of interchange with the environment. Organisations are shaped by external perceptions, expectations

and projections; for example, societal projections onto health systems, the police, prisons, social work and so on – and they themselves project onto their environment. Similar processes pervade the interaction of subsystems: for these, the organisation as a whole is a significant feature of their environments.

Another aspect of looking at organisations as organisms is the recognition that organisations have their own stages of human growth and development (Lessom 1990; Lievegoed 1991). As with working with individuals, it is important to see the problems of the organisation in the context of its 'life history' and the 'life transition' it is currently facing.

3 *The political dimension* An organisation is a political system, engaged in negotiating and allocating power between groups and individuals. Maintenance of this system depends much less on the actual exercise of coercive power – the manager firing a subordinate, the union going on strike – than on the shared belief that it *may* be used. The experience of the authoritarian regimes in the communist bloc is relevant. For forty years or so they had seemed invulnerable. The year 1989 showed that in maintenance of the order the secret police were much less significant than people's collusive assumptions. When they discovered that these assumptions could be questioned, the regimes collapsed like houses of cards. The key point is that shared assumptions about the distribution of power are a significant factor in holding an organisation together. Psychotherapists working in organisations, in whatever role, need to be alert to the power structure for another reason: whether they want to or not, they become part of it: simply by relating to this person or group and not to that one they will be perceived as exercising power and therefore will be exercising it. They therefore need to be aware of the consequences of the alignments they make.

4 *Organisational culture* The culture perspective (Peters and Waterman 1982; Schein 1985; McLean and Marshall 1989) likens work organisations to tribal cultures, with their own rituals, codes of behaviour and belief systems, which derive from the ecological context in which the tribe lives and evolves over time in relation to the changing environment. The definitions of organisational culture are extremely varied: how things are done around here (Ouchi and Johnson 1978), values and expectations which organisation members come to share (van Maanen and Schein 1979), and the collection of traditions, values, policies, beliefs and attitudes that constitute a pervasive context for everything we do and think in an organisation (McLean and Marshall 1989).

As the variety illustrates, this approach does not provide an exact science but a rich multiple-level perspective for viewing and influencing organisations. Bath Associates (1989) have created an integrative model that views organisational culture as residing at four distinct but linked levels:

Artefacts – the rituals, symbols/logos, mission statements of the organisation, buildings, organisational structure.

Behaviour – the unwritten rules which constrain how people behave, what is and what is not talked about and how people relate to one another.

Mind sets – the spectacles through which members of the organisational culture view themselves, the environment with which they interact and problems that arise.

Emotional ground – the collective feelings that underlie and influence the other three levels of culture; the emotional mood and feeling within the business.

It is important to recognise that only the top level of the culture is fully visible and conscious. The behavioural norms may operate without people being aware of the conventions they are acting within. The mind sets may be subconscious, for we see not the spectacles that we see through. The emotional ground may be fully unconscious. When you first join an organisation there are many things that you notice about the culture, that three or four months later you stop noticing because you have been socialised and enculturated. You have begun to wear the collective spectacles that occlude the cultural norms that are taken for granted. As the Chinese proverb says, the last one to know about the sea is the fish.

Unconscious processes within groups and organisations contribute to and are shaped by the organisational culture. There have been many seminal studies on the unconscious dynamics of the emotional ground of organisations (Bion 1961; Jaques 1953; Menzies 1959; Merry and Brown 1987; Miller 1993). Jaques (1953) believed that the defence against psychotic anxiety was one of the primary cohesive elements binding individuals into institutionalised human associations. Menzies (1959) showed in her seminal paper on social systems as a defence against anxiety, that many of the cultural norms of nursing could be seen as designed to keep the nurses from becoming too involved with the patients, so as to avoid, for example, the anxiety that attends emotional attachment to those who are seriously ill. The culture also has a norm that the emotional ground of distress about the patients is not discussed and the system then has a deep cultural split between the feelings and the institutionalised behaviour. Thus an organisation designed for performance of a task is both used for, and to some extent subverted by, the defensive functions that it serves for its members. Although these phenomena are most prominent in hospitals and other service institutions, where staff are working with sick and dependent patients or clients, they are part of all human organisations; and indeed Jaques (1953) illustrated his paper with a case study from industry.

That, as we have said, is by no means an exhaustive set of perspectives. What they have in common is that they focus attention on the organisation as a whole – its structures, political processes, culture and unconscious dynamics. This, we argue, is the appropriate focus for psychotherapists taking up roles in relation to organisations. Their work will be informed by their therapeutic training and experience, but that is background: as a rule of thumb, if you find yourself looking at people through your psychotherapist's spectacles, you are out of role.

We go on now to consider the range of more common roles.

The individual level

More and more organisations are setting up employee assistance programmes. These come in various forms. Some are generalised counselling and welfare services, which may be contracted from outside or provided internally. Clients bring a wide range of problems – for example, housing, debt, alcoholism, divorce, bereavement – not all of which psychotherapists will be equipped to deal with: divorce may raise legal and financial as well as emotional issues; for bereavement counselling some specialised training is desirable. Much the same applies to post-trauma counselling, now routinely provided by, for example, most police forces and by British Rail. Some organisations provide stress counselling services and some out-placement counselling for redundant personnel and assistance for people approaching retirement. These, again, call for a mix of practical and therapeutic help.

What an organisation 'buys' when it hires someone is a set of skills, mental or manual (factory-floor workers, in some companies, are still called 'hands'). It is, perhaps rightly, not interested in the whole person, except when something goes wrong that interferes with the work. That is regarded as best dealt with off the job, by someone else. Now, it may well be that the 'something wrong' presents itself in another part of the individual's life-space – the marital problem or the bereavement. But, as psychotherapists well know, people's internal worlds are not so neatly compartmentalised (or, if they are, that is indeed pathological). For many years, pursuing this holistic way of thinking, some industrial medical officers have paid attention to individual illness as a symptom of organisational illness, and seen their job as promoting the health of the enterprise (Bridger *et al.* 1964). Some departments or units may generate more than their share of illnesses, absences, turnover and so on. (One industrial medical officer even used expense claims as an indicator: inflated expense claims in one section would be a sign of low morale.) Attention can then be given to the pathogenic parts of the organisation. However, note that these in turn may be a manifestation of a malaise in the system as a whole: organisations are adept at localising and concentrating their pathology into 'problem departments' and casualty roles.

This by no means implies that, say, the stress counsellor should march into the chief executive's office to protest. What is most appropriate is for the organisation providing the employee assistance programme to give feedback to the host organisation on the spread of problems emerging and what part the organisational dynamics may be contributing to the emerging personal issues. In order to preserve confidentiality, this feedback needs to be based on data that are not attributable or recognisable to the individuals on whom it is based. But even if the psychotherapist takes no action at all, merely the recognition that organisational malfunctioning is a contributory factor will make it possible to reframe the individual's problem – and perhaps prevent the client from becoming a patient.

Another type of activity in which such issues can be addressed more directly is what we call here 'role consultancy'. Here the client is typically a person having difficulty in the organisational setting (for example, a marketing manager who is seen as too abrasive; a health service manager who feels trapped between conflicting demands; a medical consultant who keeps getting scapegoated; or a manager introducing a major change and looking for help in predicting and coping with the consequences). The client may be self-referring or referred and paid for by the employing organisation. In the latter case, the issue of 'Who is the client?' is pertinent: accountability and confidentiality have to be explicitly negotiated. The focus is on the person/role boundary; the task is to help the client to clarify the issues. The role consultant can be mainly a sounding board but usually needs to do more than that – and provide a form of non-managerial consultancy supervision (Hawkins and Shohet 1989) which explores the complex interplay of the dynamics of the individual and the work setting. Sometimes the client may seem to be the victim of an impossible organisational situation; sometimes the problem seems to lie in the individual's psychopathology. Both factors will be present, in varying proportions. Clients can be helped to consider what actions they might take to influence the organisational factors and how far they are unconsciously colluding. The boundary is difficult to manage, though the consultant's experience of the difficulty offers valuable data. If the consultant is convinced that psychotherapy would be useful, this should be referred to someone else, enabling work on the role to continue.

The group level

A mental health day centre is looking for someone to run a weekly staff support group. A small voluntary welfare agency is asking for a facilitator for monthly meetings. A board of directors of a commercial company want help in being a more effective team. Requests of this kind are becoming increasingly common, and often they are directed to psychotherapists. Sometimes the proposed contract is for a limited period, while the group is managing a transition; sometimes they are open-ended: the time and the budget are built in as an inherent part of the weekly work.

The groups are usually by no means clear about what it is they are asking for: one sign of this is the fluid terminology in which 'consultant', 'facilitator', 'supervisor', or even 'leader', become interchangeable. Regrettably, psychotherapists who accept such assignments may be equally imprecise about what they are undertaking. A vague request for 'staff support' is met by an equally vague quasi-therapy group.

We argue for a much more professional response in which a number of questions have to be asked and dealt with, for example:

- What is the work-task of this group?
- What is its relatedness to the task of the wider organisation?
- What is the problem that the group seeks to address in these sessions?
- Are weekly meetings the most appropriate format for working on this problem? (For a psychotherapist with a fixed weekly time-schedule it may be very convenient to slot a group into a vacant Tuesday afternoon, but is the convenient solution actually the most appropriate to the client's needs?)
- What is the task of the meetings? What is the output to be achieved?
- What is the task of the consultant in relation to this? What kind of role is appropriate?
- If the contract is to be open-ended, what arrangements are to be built in for review? This allows both parties to consider whether the method of working matches the original intentions and either party to terminate the contract.

The answers to such questions tend to be taken for granted in individual psychotherapy – perhaps too much so: arguments about that belong elsewhere. Here we want simply to emphasise that in professional work with groups they cannot be taken for granted: they have to be discussed, negotiated and periodically re-examined (see chapter 9 of Hawkins and Shohet 1989).

Very often such a group is working with severely damaged and deprived people. This disturbance is imported into staff; staff in turn export disturbance into clients. Care and treatment suffer. Thus an appropriate task for the consultant may be to collaborate with the group in examining the specifics of this import/export process; the desired output of a session would then be a set of staff restored to effective working roles and relationships, in which they can again distinguish what belongs to them and what to the clients. If what belongs to them includes, say, differences over approaches to treatment, then these have to be identified and explored. The consultant's role is both to provide some containment and to intervene in ways that will further the task of the group. Containment alone is insufficient. Too often we have seen so-called 'sensitivity groups' which are spittoons or worse: staff merely evacuate their negative feelings and return to roles and relationships that are at best unchanged and may even be exacerbated by unbridled exchanges of abuse. In the late sixties and early seventies there was a popular trend to introduce sensitivity groups into many work settings. The research evidence shows that this had very mixed results. Some managers clearly benefited, some became worse and the benefits for the organisation as a whole were very dubious (Cooper 1972; Mangham 1975).

There are other traps for the unwary psychotherapist embarking on work with groups. One, already mentioned, is to become preoccupied with the psychopathology of an individual. Groups are adept at projecting disturbance or distress onto the most suited recipient. To treat this individual as 'the problem' is counter-productive: if that person is extruded, another potential casualty will readily be found. 'The problem' belongs to the group and has to be addressed as such.

Another trap is where the group projects its difficulties onto the wider organisation – for example, a children's home in a local authority social services department. The group may well see itself as the victim of uncaring management and there may well be an element of reality in this. The trap is identification with the oppressed: the consultant who colludes with this projection is inhibiting the group from using its own capacities to tackle those problems that actually do belong to it. The group then becomes the impotent victim; and the effect on the people in its care is, to say the least, unlikely to be beneficial.

Another group-level activity that a psychotherapist may become drawn into is 'team-building'. Outside expertise is sought because perhaps they are 'not pulling together' or there are 'interpersonal rivalries'. The client team may be a working group at any level; or an organisation may embark on a team-building exercise for, say, all levels of management (the latter is best seen as a version of organisational consultancy: see below). Writers on organisation development offer a number of useful exercises and approaches (Hastings *et al.* 1986; Woodcock 1979). However, they do not always mention the pitfalls. Identification with the oppressed is one of them: it is not difficult to mobilise cohesion against top management as a common enemy: the mobilisation of what Bion (1961) called 'basic assumption fight/flight'. Another pitfall is that warm, positive interpersonal relations are not necessarily a recipe for effectiveness. Some task-related conflict is necessary and constructive: for example, if the production director and the marketing director are in each other's pockets, both functions are likely to be less effective than they could be. Hence the intervention should not be simply people-centred: the shared work-task is also a critical element.

The inter-group level

In a large university social science department two research units are at loggerheads with each other. Each is highly critical of the other's approach, not only privately but also publicly in conferences. They are often competing for grants from the same funding bodies. One or two less senior members from each unit are so disturbed by the situation that they ask a psychotherapist for help.

Two large companies have been merged. Their cultures are very different. A regional sales manager from one company has been put in charge of a merged department and finds that so much energy is being expended on in-fighting that sales are way below target. He wants a professional to help bring the two factions together.

Requests for intervention at the inter-group level almost invariably involve conflictual situations like this. How can one respond? There is no one system for resolving such conflicts, but we can point to some pitfalls and to possible building-blocks.

The first and obvious pitfall for a psychotherapist is to attribute the problem to powerful and possibly pathological leaders. Pathological they may be, but as we suggested when we looked at organisations as political systems, they are held in position with the collusion of the followers, who, if one leader is removed, may well produce another with similar characteristics. So it is more prudent to focus on the pathology of the relationship. Here the psychotherapist is well placed to identify projective processes – the tendency to split off and project onto the other group aspects of one's own group that are to be disowned. But, as in work with individuals, if those projections are structured into defence mechanisms, there remains the problem of getting one's interpretations heard and used. Parties to a conflict are volatile: ambivalent about any resolution – perversely, each needs the other – they are quick to find excuses to withdraw. So there is the issue of containment to be considered; and to convey security it may be useful to work with a colleague.

There remain some difficult choices about methods of working. In the university example, how far does the conflict belong to these two units and what is being projected onto them by the wider organisation? Should other departmental representatives be drawn into the process? Then there are questions of how to structure meetings: with the parties separately; joint meetings with all protagonists; meetings of representatives? This last approach could well be a good starting point in the university case, but it could also misfire if members of the small negotiating group committed to conciliation become split off from their constituents, who then carry more of the fight.

The literature on conflict resolution is substantial and some of it is useful. Marital therapy offers one paradigm: nearly thirty years ago Burton (1967) began to apply a version of marital casework to settlement of international disputes. Game theory and Transactional Analysis also have their place (see Hawkins and Shohet 1989: chapter 10). A psychotherapist may sometimes need reminding that conflicts of interests are not entirely fantasy. Then there are various practical techniques, such as role reversal, which can be used in the course of a conciliation process. (In the case of the merged sales department, this revealed that each side was both envious and contemptuous of different aspects of the other's culture.) Although a combination of psychotherapeutic experience, political nous and luck may sometimes work, it will be prudent to familiarise oneself with some of these other ideas and approaches, and/or start by attaching oneself to a practitioner with more experience in these arenas.

The organisational level

At the still more complex level of consultancy to organisations – at least to those organisations that are larger than face-to-face groups and that are internally differentiated by function – some training or apprenticeship is required. Psychotherapeutic skills are nevertheless very relevant. We have noted a growing trend, not only for psychotherapists to train in the world of organisational consulting, but also for some organisational consultants from other disciplines to embark on psychotherapy training. This is leading to useful dialogue and cross-fertilisation.

Requests for consultancy at this level come in many guises. A chief executive is tired of mutual back-biting and recrimination among her heads of departments. The board of a holding company is dissatisfied with the performance of one of its subsidiaries. A production director is worried about a non-committed work-force: quality is declining and the scrap-rate is going up. There is a corresponding array of possible responses that may be made by a traditional management consultant. In the first example, it may be that definition of responsibilities is fuzzy and that the problem could be alleviated by a structural change – re-drawing the boundaries between the subsystems. In the second, one needs to discover how far the deficiency lies in the subsidiary and how far in problems of power and authority in the relationship with headquarters. The third example may point to re-examination and possibly re-design of the socio-technical system to produce a form of work organisation that is both more effective and more satisfying to the workers. In problems such as these, therefore, the perspectives outlined earlier may all be relevant and then the organisational consultant may have some practical ideas to contribute. What they have in common is that they involve management of change, particularly change in culture – a factor often neglected by management consultants using mechanistic models but central to the task of the organisational consultant.

For the organisational consultant involved in change, therefore, all four of the perspectives outlined earlier are useful, but supplementing them is the fifth perspective of the organisation as a learning organism. This sees learning as the most central task of all organisations. The approach has been developed by Argyris and Schon (1978); Senge (1990); Pedler *et al.*

(1991); Hawkins (in press). It builds on the earlier work by Revans (1972) who coincidentally, like Trist and his Tavistock colleagues, also worked for the British Coal Board in the late 1940s. Revans argued that an organisation must learn at an equal or a greater rate than that of the environmental changes around it or the organism will die. Since that time environmental changes have grown exponentially and the need for organisations to learn at a faster speed has thus also dramatically increased.

Organisational learning is clearly dependent on the continuous learning of all its members, and in particular those in senior and influential positions. However, the organisation's learning cannot be reduced to the sum of the learning of those within it, for:

> The learning organisation approach has explored ways of creating continuous learning for individuals within organisations, and how this is built into effective team learning and development. Then, how learning, feedback and communication between teams and departments is fostered and how this in turn is harvested into organisational learning. At the same time as there is this upward spiral of learning within the organisation, the system has to be helped to learn in relation to its environment, with the fostering of dialogical learning between the organisation and its key customers and stakeholders.
>
> (Hawkins, in press)

What each of these approaches does is to link the complexities of the task with a psychological understanding of individuals, groups, inter-groups and whole systems. The consultant in such traditions can be seen as functioning as a corporate psychotherapist, or what an earlier Tavistock writer termed as a 'sociotherapist' (Sofer 1961), who helps the organisation to carry out its task better by attending to the collective dynamics of the whole system, including those that are unconscious to the system itself.

If we return to our triangular model, we can see how the model can be expanded to include the hidden and unconscious elements of the organisational world, at both the team and whole organisation levels (see Figures 15.2 and 15.3). Only by reconnecting the behaviour to the emotional ground in which it has grown can the culture become conscious and the organisation learn new ways of managing its internal and external tensions.

The consultant does not focus just on the task, or just on the process, or just on the external environment, but on the relationship between these three key elements. Also the consultant needs to be more an educational facilitator than an expert surgeon, for it is important that in learning more about the relationship between the three elements of task, process and environment at one particular time the organisation also 'learns how to learn', and increases its own ability continuously to attend to the interfaces and relationships that are key to its successful development (see Figure 15.4). Humanistic psychotherapy and co-operative research methodology have provided useful and wide-ranging techniques for working with

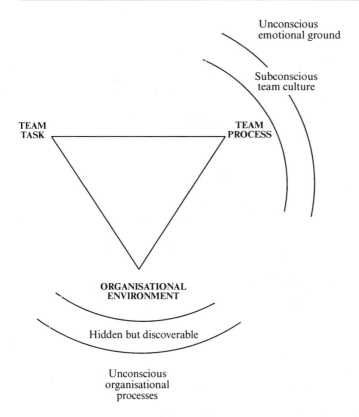

Figure 15.2 Team task, team process and organisational environment

organisations to help them get some distance on their own culture and gain fresh insight into their unwritten rules and mind sets (Bath Associates 1989; Reason 1988; Hawkins and Shohet 1989; McLean and Marshall 1989). This provides the organisation with an expanded awareness from which to make choices about future direction.

Gestalt psychotherapy has also made a major contribution to understanding the emotional learning blocks within organisations as well as approaches to help organisations overcome their stuckness (Merry and Brown 1987; Critchley and Casey 1989).

THE CONSULTING PROCESS

Psychotherapy has also informed the world of organisational consulting on how to manage the complexities of supporting a system through the processes of change.

The consultant may go through similar stages to the individual psychotherapist: building a relationship, helping the organisation tell its story;

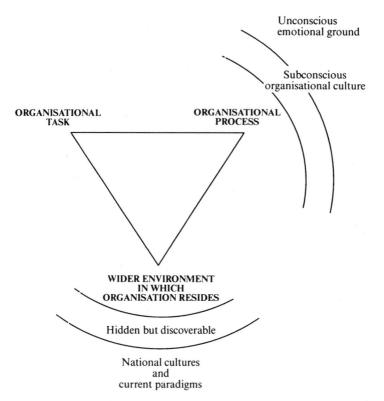

Figure 15.3 Organisational task, organisational process and the wider environment

initial formulation of the dynamics within the system; helping the client focus on the key areas of difficulty; creating new forms of dialogue within the client system; helping the client system to reframe its problems, seeing them in a new perspective; supporting experimentation with new forms of behaviour and learning from these; supporting the consolidation of new ways of being; and finally reflecting on the change process and managing the separation from the consultant and the internalisation of the consultant's contribution.

Consultants have traditionally paid less attention to their own process than have psychotherapists. For some this has been costly and the consultant team have ended up paralleling the dynamics of the client organisation rather than recognising that they can use themselves as instruments for registering those dynamics. Psychotherapy has some useful concepts and approaches for helping consultants to understand their involvement with the host organisation. These include projective splitting; supervision

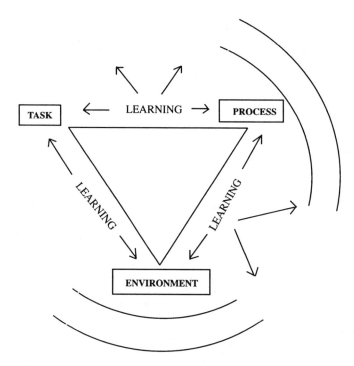

Figure 15.4 Task, process, environment and the learning organisation

processes for the consultant(s); the use of psychodrama re-enactment (Hawkins 1988) and parallel process (Hawkins and Shohet 1989).

CONCLUSION

To sum up, psychotherapists can take up valuable and effective roles in organisations as counsellors, trainers and consultants at various levels. To do this they have to be prepared for some unlearning and some new learning. They have to be alert to a number of dangerous temptations: pathologising individuals or systems; reducing collective processes to individual dynamics; inability to understand the technical, commercial or operational realities of the organisation; inability to switch levels appropriately and understand the interconnections between the individual, the team, the inter-departmental, the organisational and the environmental; and over-focusing on process while under-focusing on task. In order to be effective they need to acquire a 'good enough' knowledge of the task and technologies of the client system that impact upon the people they are working with, and also to find a language through which they can communicate. Depending on their orientation – psychodynamic, humanistic and systemic – they will bring with them some variations in perspectives, metaphors and language, but, in our view, once they take up their roles in the organisational setting the differences will be much less significant than the commonalities – in particular, attention to unconscious dynamics.

REFERENCES

Argyris, C. and Schon, D. (1978) *Organisational Learning*, Reading, MA: Jossey Bass.

Bath Associates (1989) *Organisational Culture Manual*, Bath: Bath Associates.

Bion, W. R. (1961) *Experiences in Groups*, London: Tavistock Publications.

Bridger, H., Miller, E. J. and O'Dwyer, J. J. (1964) *The Doctor and Sister in Industry: A Study of Change*, London: Macmillan (Journals) Ltd; reprinted from *Occupational Health* (1963) 15.

Burton, J. W. (1967) 'The analysis of conflict by casework', *Year Book of World Affairs*, XXI, London: Stevens.

Carlisle, J. A. and Parker, R. C. (1989) *Beyond Negotiation*, Chichester: Wiley.

Cooper, C. L. (1972) 'An attempt to assess the psychologically disturbing effect of "T" group training', *British Journal of Social and Clinical Psychology*, pp. 342–5.

Critchley, B. and Casey, D. (1989) 'Organisations get stuck too', *Leadership and Organisation Development Journal* 10(4): 3–12.

Emery, F. E. and Trist, E. L. (1969) *Systems Thinking*, Harmondsworth: Penguin.

Handy, C. (1976) *Understanding Organisations*, Harmondsworth: Penguin.

Hastings, C., Bixby, P. and Chaudhry-Lawton, R. (1986) *The Superteam Solution*, Aldershot: Gower.

Hawkins, P. (1988) 'A phenomenological psychodrama workshop', pp. 60–78 in P. Reason (ed.) *Human Inquiry in Action*, London: Sage.

—— (in press) *The Heart of the Learning Organisation*, London: Sage.

Hawkins, P. and Shohet, R. (1989) *Supervision in the Helping Professions*, Milton Keynes: Open University Press.

Hillman, J. (1983) *Interviews*, New York: Harper & Row.

Jaques, E. (1953) 'On the dynamics of social structure', *Human Relations* 6: 3–24.

Lessom, R. (1990) *Development Management*, Oxford: Blackwell.

Lievegoed, B. (1991) *Managing the Developing Organisation*, Oxford: Blackwell.

McLean, A. and Marshall, J. (1989) *Cultures at Work: How to Identify and Understand Them*, Luton: Local Government Training Board.

Mangham, I. (1975) *Some Assumptions, Objectives, Methods and Results of Team Development Activities*, CSOCD Working Paper, University of Bath.

Menzies, I. E. P. (1959) *The Functioning of Social Systems as a Defence Against Anxiety*, London: Tavistock Institute of Human Relations.

Merry, V. and Brown, G. I. (1987) *The Behaviour of the Neurotic Organisation*, Cleveland, OH: Gestalt Institute of Cleveland Press.

Miller, E. J. (1993) *From Dependency to Autonomy: Studies in Organization and Change*, London: Free Association Books.

Miller, E. J. and Rice, A. K. (1967) *Systems of Organisation: Task and Sentient Systems and their Boundary Control*, London: Tavistock Publications.

Morgan, G. (1986) *Images of Organisation*, Beverly Hills, CA: Sage.

Ouchi, W. G. and Johnson, J. B. (1978) 'Types of organisation control and their relationship to emotional well-being', *Administrative Science Quarterly* 23: 292–317.

Pedler, M., Burgoyne, J. and Boydell, T. (1991) *The Learning Company*, Maidenhead, Berks: McGraw-Hill.

Peters, T. and Waterman, R. (1982) *In Search of Excellence*, New York: Harper & Row.

Pugh, D. S. and Hickson, D. J. (1989) *Writers on Organisations* (4th edn), Harmondsworth: Penguin.

Reason, P. (1988) *Human Inquiry in Action*, London: Sage.

Revans, R. (1972) *The Origins and Growth of Action Learning*, Bromley, Kent: Chartwell Bratt.

Rice, A. K. (1958) *Productivity and Social Organisation: The Ahmedabad Experiment*, London: Tavistock Publications.

—— (1963) *The Enterprise and its Environment*, London: Tavistock Publications.

Schein, E. M. (1985) *Organisational Culture and Leadership*, San Francisco: Jossey Bass.

Senge, P. (1990) *The Fifth Discipline: The Art and Practice of the Learning Organisation*, New York: Doubleday.

Sofer, C. (1961) *The Organisation from Within: A Comparative Study of Social Institutions Based on a Sociotherapeutic Approach*, London: Tavistock Publications.

Trist, E. L. and Bamforth, K. W. (1951) 'Some social and psychological consequences of the longwall method of coal-getting', *Human Relations* 4: 3–38.

Trist, E. L., Higgin, G. W., Murray, H. and Pollock, A. B. (1963) *Organisational Choice: Capabilities of Groups at the Coal Face under Changing Technologies*, London: Tavistock Publications.

van Maanen, J. and Schein, E. M. (1979) 'Towards a theory of organisational socialisation', in B. M. Straw and L. L. Cummings (eds) *Research in Organisational Behaviour*, vol. 1, Greenwich, CT: JAI Press.

Woodcock, M. (1979) *Team Development Manual*, Aldershot: Gower.

FURTHER READING

Clarkson, P. (1990) 'The scope of "stress" counselling in organisations', *Employee Counselling Today* 2(4): 3–6.

Clarkson, P. and Shaw, P. (1992) 'Human relationships at work – the place of counselling skills and consulting skills and services in organisations', *MEAD, the Journal of the Association of Management Education and Development* 23(1): 18–29.

USEFUL ORGANISATIONS AND TRAINING COURSES

Bath Consultancy Group
(formerly Bath Associates)
Consulting Service for
Organisations and Managers
24 Gay Street
Bath
Avon BA1 2PD
Tel.: 01225 333737
Fax: 01225 333738

The Tavistock Institute
Advanced Organisational
Consultation Programme
Tavistock Centre
Belsize Lane
London NW3 5BA
Tel.: 0171 435 7111

PHYSIS
12 North Common Road
Ealing
London W5 2QB
Tel. and fax: 0181 567 0388

Chapter 16

Psychotherapies within the NHS

Adele Kosviner

A BIRD'S EYE VIEW

The psychotherapies, by their very nature, evolve and change. The National Health Service, too, is evolving and changing, as are the professions within it. Psychotherapeutic services within the NHS are therefore hard to capture as a given static picture at any one moment. Looking at things positively, there have been considerable improvements in the quality of provision of the psychotherapies in the NHS over recent years, and these continue: services aim to offer a broader range of psychotherapies and so be responsive and flexible to individual needs; collaboration between providers of the psychotherapies is improving, so more efficient and effective use can be made of all resources in the field; and standards for training and accreditation are being made more explicit, which is leading to improved standards of care. On the more negative side, service provision is still inadequate and patchy; even where it exists, it is hard to find one's way to the service one may need and there is room for further improvement in collaboration between those providing the services.

Casting an eye to the future we may envisage, in response to market forces, perhaps a greater efficiency and quality of service, or perhaps a greater fragmentation of services and emphasis on advertising our wares, rather than providing them. Improved monitoring and audit of psychotherapy services should ensure that only the best survive. We shall, I think, have to fight hard to ensure that it is the best in the psychotherapies that survives, not the best in the packaging, or the cheapest.

WHAT WE DO AND WHAT WE SAY WE DO

The professions providing the psychotherapies in the NHS can no longer rest on their laurels. Apart from the very important developments in the psychotherapies in the independent sector, the whole climate towards the professions in the NHS is increasingly one of 'demonstrate what you do', and of decreasing interest in what we merely say we do. This emphasis on actual skills and competencies rather than professional training alone is spearheaded by the Department of Employment's National Council of Vocational Qualifications (NCVQ), and is likely to be attractive to NHS Trusts and Directly Managed Units, which need to be increasingly vigilant on questions of cost-effectiveness, especially in the short term. We need to be able to demonstrate, through the effectiveness of our work, the importance of the breadth and depth of understanding that comes from years of professional training. It will no longer be taken for granted.

One of the aspects of 'what we say we do' is entangled in the very use of the word 'psychotherapy'. Within the history of the NHS the word has been used as much to demarcate territory as to describe services. Used ambiguously, it has sometimes confused the issue of whether the psycho-therapeutic services being referred to are primarily psychoanalytic or are those covering the full range of psychotherapies. It has also led to confusion when services in psychotherapies in the NHS have been assumed to be coterminous with the relatively few posts specifically *labelled* 'psychotherapy' (as with some medical posts), rather than referring to the full range of psychotherapy services, both generalist and specialist, that are available within the NHS.

THE STATUS QUO

That broad psychotherapy services do exist within the NHS is not under question. It is their quality, coherence, cohesion and accessibility that has been the main concern of those involved in their practice. Different professions and, within them, different professionals, differ in the propor-tion of time and expertise they contribute to the provision of formal psychological therapies, in the type and range of psychotherapy they offer, and in the breadth and level of specialist training in different therapeutic approaches that they have received. Specialised psychological therapies are provided mainly by clinical psychologists and medical psychotherapists; with nurse specialists, social workers, occupational therapists and related professions (such as drama, music and art therapists) playing an increasing role. However, in many areas, services in formal psychotherapies are often uncoordinated, unevenly distributed, and poorly integrated with other psychiatric and psychological services. Some are inadequately resourced to meet even minimal public demand. Further, they are often fragmented and subject to inter-professional tensions, themselves fed by anxieties about professional roles and by anxieties that conceptual differences between psychological therapies may contaminate rather than enrich a psychotherapy service. The current changes and uncertainties in the NHS are perhaps exacerbating these tensions, but they should also provide some pressure to resolve them. The present situation is not conducive to good patient care, is incomprehensible to most referrers and will undoubtedly become an anathema to purchasers.

For this reason a Joint Statement addressing these issues has recently been prepared by the British Psychological Society (BPS) and the Royal College of Psychiatrists (1993), the two professional bodies whose members at present constitute the major source of expertise in the psychotherapies within the NHS. This statement is concerned with issues of good practice and principles underlying working arrangements within NHS psychological therapy services. It stresses that the range of psychotherapies offered should be broad and balanced, with the contribution of each approach integrated within a co-ordinated service. It suggests that co-operation between professional groups providing psychological therapies at general and specialist levels is in the best interests of service users. It emphasises the need for high standards to be ensured through specialist assessment, treatment and training resources, having at least one specialist in each of the major psychotherapies provided, and for such resources to be co-ordinated by those with a broad appreciation and understanding of all aspects of services in the psychotherapies, not just one model of psychotherapy.

We are not yet there. This chapter will now cast an eye at history before going on to look at existing needs and services, and finally look again to the future. It will ask why we need psychological therapy services in the NHS; explore existing provision and how to gain access to it; and in doing so consider some features of particular relevance to NHS provision of the psychotherapies, such as the need to prioritise demand, the need for comprehensive assessment and therapy services, implications for training and supervision of staff, and evaluation of services provided (including the effectiveness and efficiency of the psychotherapies available). In the course of this it will identify areas that, one hopes, will be the targets for improvement and development.

THE HISTORY OF THE PSYCHOTHERAPIES IN THE NHS

Psychiatry and psychotherapy

In the mid-1970s psychotherapy became a separate medical speciality within psychiatry. An original intent behind the appointment of consultant psychotherapists was to enable medical staff to think about the role of psychological factors in their treatment of and their interaction with their patients. Guidelines for staffing levels were published in 1975, with a long-term goal set at 250 whole-time equivalent (WTE) consultant psychotherapists in England and Wales, an equivalent of 1 WTE for a population of 200,000. In 1984 there were 84 consultant posts established, in 1990 there were 127 (of which thirteen were vacant). Almost half of these posts are part time and the majority of them (61) are in the London area (Royal College of Psychiatrists 1991a).

The Royal College began to establish requirements for training in the psychotherapies for General Professional training (as a general psychiatrist), for training in General Psychiatry with a Special Interest in Psychotherapy, and for specialist training in Psychotherapy (leading to eligibility for consultant psychotherapist posts). Included in the latter were accredited Senior Registrar 'in-service' training schemes, as well as accommodation for those who had received their specialist psychotherapy training in private training institutions, independent of the NHS. In-service training approaches tended to develop away from established centres of psychotherapy training, which themselves were mainly in London. Standards of training between in-service training and external centres were different, resulting in some unevenness. There was an initial preponderance of psychoanalytic interest amongst medical consultant psychotherapists but this is now being redressed, with greater numbers becoming interested in other therapeutic orientations, including cognitive and behavioural approaches. In addition the General Psychiatry section of the Royal College of Psychiatrists is becoming more interested in the integration of psychological therapies in general psychiatric practice, rather than leaving its provision and development to the separate specialty alone.

Psychology and psychotherapy

The professional Division of Clinical Psychology was established by the BPS in 1968. At that time the psychotherapeutic orientation within the Division was largely behavioural, but with vigorous, if smaller, enclaves in psychoanalytic and humanistic approaches. Over the years this has balanced out so that the core curriculum for Clinical Psychology training now covers all major psychotherapeutic approaches (Kosviner 1992).

Post-qualification further training in the psychotherapies began to be recognised by the BPS in the late 1970s. The Department of Health Manpower Advisory Group commissioned an independent review in 1989 (Management Advisory Services to the NHS 1989) which concluded that the ability to combine or change psychological approaches as appropriate, while remaining rigorous in their application, was what distinguished clinical psychologists from other practitioners of formal psychological therapies. There are now approximately 2,500 Clinical Psychologists in the United Kingdom, most of whom consider their primary responsibility to include the provision of psychological therapies. Others have specialised in specific approaches such as neuropsychology, or are working in a more educational capacity with both clients and their carers. Career structures within Clinical Psychology have now developed to include continuing professional development in specialist areas (including the psychotherapies) after professional qualification, and permit progression to the higher consultant grades within the profession on the basis of clinical expertise as well as managerial responsibilities. This is encouraging more clinical psychologists to embark on further specialist trainings in the psychotherapies. The Society has now established the necessary internal structures to enable it to address the task of formally demarcating criteria for training and accreditation of its members within the psychotherapies at general and specialist levels.

Other NHS professions

The Royal College of Nursing revised its basic mental health course for psychiatric nurses in 1982, introducing a significant emphasis on 'counselling' and on acquiring some psychological therapy skills. The establishment of posts for clinical nurse specialists within mental health is likely to increase interest amongst nurses in gaining further expertise in counselling or the psychotherapies. Occupational therapy within mental health services has for some time fostered the development of skills in some of the psychotherapies, especially perhaps the therapies based on creative activity (art, music, drama) as well as skills-based approaches; for example, anxiety management, social skills and problem-solving.

Independent psychotherapists

A few posts have been established in the NHS in response to service demand, for psychotherapists – usually of a psychoanalytic orientation – for whom a career path in the psychotherapies is not possible within their core NHS profession, or who indeed have no such 'core profession' prior to their training in a particular psychotherapeutic model.

WHY WE NEED THE PSYCHOTHERAPIES WITHIN THE NHS

A high proportion of GP consultations and referrals for specialist hospital treatments, from headaches to heart attacks, involve psychological factors. The over-prescription of psychotropic medication such as the benzodiazepines has lead to public and professional awareness of the need to provide psychological treatments as an alternative or adjunct to medication, both for the conditions which have led people to seek help in the first place, and for those who have become dependent on such medication to cope with their original problems. It is increasingly recognised, too, that psychological therapies are the treatment of choice for a wide range of psychological and psychiatric presentations, including severe personality difficulties, acute and chronic neuroses, and adjustment to the aftermath of life crises, traumatic events and disasters. There is increasing demand for psychological treatments in the prevention as well as the amelioration of major psychiatric and physical illnesses, substance misuse, and other major habit disorders such as anorexia and bulimia, sexual deviations and some criminal behaviour.

INFINITE DEMAND, FINITE RESOURCES

No National Health Service can ever meet all the demands placed upon it, and providing psychotherapies is obviously no exception. Choices have to be made at every level, from those involving individual patients to those involving government strategies. There is a need for guiding principles to inform these choices, and currently there is some concern that market forces should not be the only ones. The goal of offering the highest quality service to the greatest number who need it most should clearly guide us, but matters are not so simple. Who decides who is most in need? Increasing awareness of the need for cost-efficiency may lead to the NHS becoming a specialist service of last resort for those who are unable to obtain help elsewhere, or because they cannot afford it. It is possible that NHS resources will become more focused either on the more seriously disturbed, or on those groups which demonstrably respond well to psychological interventions, and which thereby raise any given NHS Trust's reputation for making a contribution to the 'Health of the Nation' (Department of Health 1992), not just its ill health.

MAKING BEST USE OF ALL RESOURCES

Just as medicine is not only practised at consultant level within the NHS, so formal psychological therapies are carried out both by specialists in particular orientations and by professionals with less training and experience, under their supervision, in order to make fullest use of existing resources. This has implications for standards in supervision and training within the National Health Service (BPS 1990; Royal College of Psychiatrists 1990, 1991b).

SHORT-TERM AND GROUP APPROACHES

Services in the psychotherapies are under pressure to focus increasingly on shorter-, rather than longer-term treatment approaches, and on group rather than individual work, whenever appropriate, in order to treat greater numbers of people more efficiently. This undoubtedly makes sense where such approaches can be shown to be effective, and some research is encouraging in this field. The Joint Statement from the BPS and the Royal College of Psychiatrists (1993), while recognising the need to maximise efficiency and effectiveness, has also stressed the need to ensure that an appropriate range and choice of treatments are available. It is as cost-inefficient, they have argued, to give short-term treatments which are not effective as it is to provide long-term treatments where short-term treatments would be just as effective. The choice of treatment is a matter of clinical judgement, which should none the less be influenced by issues of cost-effectiveness. This has implications for the essential skills in differential assessment for the psychotherapies, required in National Health Service provision (Fonagy and Higgitt 1989, 1992; Menzies *et al.* 1993).

WHO RECEIVES HELP?

Services in the psychotherapies within the NHS have either to prioritise the more seriously 'dis-eased' or to use resources only where they are maximally effective. These demands on the service are sometimes contradictory, since many practitioners wish to help to alleviate the distress of those with more severe or chronic psychiatric or psychological conditions, where results may not be achieved quickly nor be easy to register clearly on any gauge of 'success'. Those in need of psychological therapies presenting to the NHS are not the 'worried well', nor do they usually represent the 'YAVIS' end of the spectrum (young, attractive, verbal, intelligent and successful). In a recent patient population audit in West Berkshire, for example, 45 per cent were aged forty and over, 20 per cent had never worked, only 8 per cent had higher education or professional status and 35 per cent had had psychiatric hospital admissions in the past two years. In addition, 25 per cent acknowledged sexual abuse, 35 per cent physical abuse (often both as children and adults) and 15 per cent had at least one conviction (Jane Knowles, personal communication 1994).

THE RANGE OF PSYCHOTHERAPEUTIC SERVICES AVAILABLE WITHIN THE NHS

Any one district or unit may possess anything between a comprehensive, well-organised provision to very little in the way of range or quality of services. At best there will be the possibility of a full and comprehensive consultation followed by the treatment of choice from well-trained and experienced professionals. At worst a patient will at least be guided to the best locally available help. Most services, whether those provided by clinical psychology or medical psychotherapy services (or both in a co-ordinated endeavour), will offer both individual and group work, some short-term, some longer-term. The range of therapeutic approaches available (for example, analytic, cognitive-behavioural, humanistic, systemic) will vary considerably, depending on local resources. Some larger clinical psychology services offer them all. With limited resources available to them, many services offer 'eclectic' psychotherapy. This term covers a multitude of meanings, from a well-informed flexibility of approach according to the needs of the individual presenting, to a 'mish-mash' based on very little understanding of anything. Some services offer psychotherapies practised by clinicians with considerable training and experience; others rely heavily on staff with very little or even no previous experience of psychotherapy – for example, doctors being trained in psychiatry – under the supervision of those with greater training and experience. Sometimes this supervision is full and frequent, but at other times it may amount to little more than infrequent consultation, with any one practitioner presenting their case for supervision in a group setting perhaps once in six weeks. There is clearly room for improvement and standardisation in the provision of supervision just as in the psychotherapies themselves.

ASSESSMENT

The assessment received in the initial consultation is of key importance to psychotherapy services within the NHS. It should be informed by an understanding of the range of different psychological therapies and their applicability to different types of difficulties and in different settings – whether in individual, group, couple or family therapies. Ideally, the assessment process should be informed by a broad understanding of human development and of the range of psychological approaches which can help in any particular case; it should be dispassionate and not biased towards any particular therapeutic orientation; it should be flexible and tailored to individual needs, and helpful in empowering people to make informed choices about which psychotherapeutic approach may best suit them. It should also be able, where necessary, to adjust psychological treatments to the individual rather than the other way round. The consultation service should further be able to offer a base for continuing flexibility during treatment if, for example, psychotherapy aims change as a result of increased understanding or changing priorities, perceptions or external circumstances.

TYPES OF PSYCHOTHERAPY PROVIDED WITHIN THE NHS

Services should aim to provide a full range of the main psychotherapies. Some of them do, and in an accessible, co-ordinated way that allows the flexibility mentioned above. Other districts or regions may have the full range, but they may be offered in differently managed units in a way which makes access to them quite a problem for patients and referrers alike. However, expertise does exist within the NHS (albeit not uniformly) in all major psychological therapies which are substantiated by sound psychological theories and/or empirical research findings. These include:

- Psychoanalytic psychotherapies which involve re-experiencing, exploring and changing feelings, assumptions and basic difficulties (especially in personal relationships) in the context of a developing relationship with a psychotherapist.
- Cognitive and behavioural psychotherapies which involve problem-solving approaches based on an analysis of how a person's experiences – and their interpretations of them – relate to how they feel and behave at any one time, and to bring about change through systematic 'real life' exercises.
- Systemic psychotherapies which are usually used in family therapy but may also be helpful in working with groups of people in a work place or other context, and also shed light on individual problems. Indeed it is sometimes the case that problems which an individual perceives as their own may best be understood as a problem within a group or organisation in which the person experiences the difficulties. In such cases it may be that, after full assessment, consultation to the group or organisation rather than the individual may be appropriate.
- Humanistic or existential psychotherapies which may use a range of approaches, including various aspects of the relationship with the psychotherapist, to help a person achieve their therapeutic goals.
- Counselling approaches which help individuals help themselves, in the context of a supportive relationship.

In some cases it may be appropriate to adopt an integrative approach where different psychotherapies may be combined, according to individual needs, so long as this is done in a way that is informed by the principles underlying these different approaches so that incompatible procedures are not mixed to brew an inherently contradictory or meaninglessly eclectic cocktail. Approaches such as cognitive-analytic therapy and some combinations of systemic with behavioural or analytic approaches are instances where therapeutic approaches may be tailored to service demands or individual needs. There has to be space within the NHS psychotherapies for innovation and development, but it is important, in my view, for its practitioners to be well grounded in the orientations they practise before combining or shortening them.

Different approaches suit different people and even different problems in the same person. They can almost all be offered on a short- or longer-term basis, in a variety of settings. These settings include individual psychotherapy with a psychotherapist; group therapy, where a number of people meet together regularly with one or two psychotherapists; couple therapy where couples meet together with one or two psychotherapists to work on their relationship difficulties (which may include sexual difficulties); and family therapy, where the whole family will meet with one or two psychotherapists. Most of these psychotherapies are offered on an 'out-patient' basis. In very severe or intransigent cases, residential or day-care psychological therapy may be recommended.

ASSESSMENT REVISITED

In short, clarifying problems and goals for NHS psychotherapy is only the start. There is then the need to determine which type of therapy (cognitive-behavioural, psychodynamic, systemic and so on), in what setting (individual, group and so forth), its frequency and its duration. Judgements must then be made about the implications of differing degrees of emotional and time commitments, and judgements too about available resources both within the NHS and within the voluntary or independent sectors, or within social services. Thorough assessment at this stage also has implications for monitoring demands on the service and how to prioritise resources, present and future.

This task of assessment is clearly broader than that available to any-one who is familiar, however deeply, with only one psychotherapeutic approach. The BPS/Royal College of Psychiatry Statement (1993) has recommended that there should be collaboration between providers of psychological therapy services, which would allow integration of assess-ment procedures, such that all referrals could be initially screened by a small team of those members of the service with a substantial under-standing of the range of different psychological therapies available, and the respect of their colleagues in all professions. The Statement suggests that the screening team will be an important source of information and advice to other services and agencies, especially potential referrers, and will be in a good position also to identify gaps in the treatment provision and to audit aspects of the service. Such a system, following the spirit of the Patients' Charter, should be able to facilitate informed patient choice.

ORGANISATION OF PSYCHOTHERAPY SERVICES IN THE NHS

While all NHS clinical staff in mental health services use psychological skills with their patients, the two professions presently providing the bulk of formal psychotherapies are clinical psychology and medical psycho-therapy. Both may also offer supervision and consultation to other NHS professionals carrying out formal psychotherapy. Some formal psycho-therapy is also sometimes carried out independently of either of these two departments, by, for example, nurses or occupational therapists, with varying amounts of formal training or supervision.

Both medically organised and clinical psychology psychotherapy services (whether or not they are co-ordinated) take direct referrals from outside agencies as well as from within psychiatric and hospital services. They usually have waiting lists, either for assessment and/or for treatment. They may or may not use pre-interview assessment aids such as self-completion questionnaires.

HOW TO GAIN ACCESS TO NHS PSYCHOTHERAPEUTIC SERVICES

The usual way for a referral to be made is through a GP directly to either the consultant clinical psychologist (in adult or child services, as appropriate) or to the consultant psychotherapist (for adult services) or to child psychotherapy services (psychoanalytic only) where these exist. Different departments may have different specialities or may overlap in the service they provide. It is to be hoped that local GPs are familiar with the resources available within their local mental health services, although one cannot blame them if they sometimes become confused about which department is offering what, at what level of therapist competence. The sooner services can integrate themselves without threats to professional or psychotherapeutic identity, autonomy or status, and without any one claiming precedence over the other, the better. Easier said than done, but the present situation, as emphasised by the Joint Statement, is clearly not in the best interests of service users. Clarifying and acknowledging differences in types and levels of competencies should go some way towards minimising wasteful internecine tensions.

TRAINING IN THE PSYCHOTHERAPIES AMONGST NHS PROFESSIONALS

It might be helpful at this point to summarise the training of psychiatrists and clinical psychologists within the psychotherapies.

Psychotherapy training within the medical profession is at a general level (within training as a general psychiatrist) and at a specialist level (for training as a consultant psychotherapist) (Royal College of Psychiatrists 1990, 1991b; General Medical Council 1987). Training criteria in the psychotherapies within psychiatry are divided into that deemed appropriate for any general psychiatrist, and that required for specialist practice as a consultant psychotherapist.

Junior psychiatrists will have completed their basic medical education and have full registration as doctors, but they will not generally have received any training or experience in the psychotherapies prior to starting to practise as psychiatrists. Rather, they acquire it in the course of their 'in-service training' over a period of at least two years as psychiatrists in training.

Senior registrars in psychiatry (who will have had a minimum of two to three years of general professional training as psychiatrists) will therefore have had a minimum of eight to nine years' professional training, a minimum of two of which will have included training in the psychotherapies.

Consultant psychotherapists have had, in addition to the minimum of two to three years' training within their general professional training as a psychiatrist, a further four years' (minimum) training in a chosen psychotherapy. Consultant psychotherapists will have had a minimum of twelve years' professional training, including a minimum of six years' training in the psychotherapies.

Psychotherapy training within clinical psychology is similarly at different levels. It requires first a degree in Psychology followed by a master's or doctoral degree in Clinical Psychology (minimum three years, full-time), the core curriculum of which covers all major models in the psychotherapies (Kosviner 1992; BPS 1990).

Junior clinical psychologists (formally called 'basic grade') will therefore have had a minimum of three years' general training in the psychotherapies before starting practice as chartered psychologists in the NHS. They are expected to consolidate this by a further two years' 'continuing professional development' which, for those working in general adult or child services, includes specialist supervised practice in the psychological therapies. They are expected to continue to receive supervision in specialist psychotherapies thereafter.

Senior clinical psychologists (that is, those who have had a minimum two years' general professional experience after qualifying as chartered clinical psychologists) will therefore be required to have had a minimum of eight years' professional training, a minimum of five of which will be concerned with the psychotherapies. At this stage some may consider going on to specialist training, which takes a further minimum three to four years, depending on the psychotherapeutic orientation, and qualifies them as fully independent practitioners within a specified model of psychotherapy.

Specialist clinical psychologists in a specified psychotherapy will have had a minimum of twelve years of professional training, including a minimum of eight to nine years of psychotherapy training (Kosviner 1993).

Both professions consider 'breadth' as important as 'depth' in training in the psychotherapies. This enables those appropriately qualified to fulfil consulting roles in assessing the most suitable form of psychotherapy in any individual case. The Working Party on the Psychotherapies set up by the Joint Consultative Committee between the Royal College of Psychiatrists and the BPS will in all likelihood be addressing criteria for competence in this field in the near future.

SUPERVISION

As much NHS psychotherapy is practised at basic and intermediate as well as specialist levels, the issue of adequate standards in supervision is of paramount importance. At the present time there are guidelines within the main professions serving this field, but greater shared standards can only be a good thing. There are still inadequate numbers of either profession trained to specialist level, which is where specific expertise in particular psychotherapies (which may be held by some independent psychothera-pists as well as by existing NHS professionals) should, where it is lacking, be brought into services to ensure the quality of services provided.

AUDIT, EVALUATION AND RESEARCH

The unmonitored practice of psychotherapy within the NHS is no longer acceptable. There is a need to provide more and better services within available resources, and this cannot be achieved without systematic audits of services. Measures of service relevance, equity, accessibility, acceptability, effectiveness and efficiency can be built into the process of delivering services in the psychotherapies (Parry 1992). These may include measures of psychotherapeutic outcome and process, provided that the measures used are sensitive to the variables being assessed (Fonagy and Higgitt 1989). There is a slightly dangerous tendency within the current tensions in the NHS to embrace a mock 'glasnost' about all its services, in which rapid (and sometimes meaningless) assessments have replaced thoughtful reflections about the service. The Society for Psychotherapy Research is a helpful organisation for those wishing to become more familiar with research issues in this complex field.

WHOSE CRYSTAL BALL?

We all probably have different ideas about what we think will happen to the psychotherapies within the NHS. It is reasonable to assume, in the short term at least, that there will be little increase in resources available for the psychological therapies. That means we will need to make the best possible use of all existing resources – both generalist and specialist – and so create maximum availability for the service. This, in turn, will demand improved co-ordination and organisation in any one area in order to achieve as comprehensive, effective and efficient a service as possible. We will also need enough specialists in all major psychotherapy orientations available to ensure adequate levels of supervision and quality of service. In the same way, in-service training in the psychotherapies should be encouraged and developed, with special attention paid to developing appropriate shared standards and training by specialists. The need for comprehensive assessment to be carried out by those with knowledge of all the options in the psychological therapies will be necessary to ensure the maximum effectiveness of any psychotherapy service. Consultation in the psychotherapies to medical disciplines and health-care professionals will enable these services to appreciate the psychological dimensions of physical health and illness. Finally, we need to stay grounded in an empiricism sensitive to the complexities of the service which we provide, and adequately monitor and research our services (Department of Health 1992). We need to protect the service from becoming a victim of a paradox of factuality, where what is recorded becomes more important than the actuality of what we do, and where we may lose our bearings, or, worse, our integrity, in the winds of the marketplace or political fashion.

REFERENCES

British Psychological Society (1990) *Policy Statement: Psychological Therapy Services: The Need for Organisational Change*, Leicester: BPS Publications.

British Psychological Society/Royal College of Psychiatrists (1993) *Joint Statement: Psychological Therapies for Adults in the National Health Service*.

Department of Health (1992) *Health of the Nation*, London: HMSO.

Fonagy, P. and Higgitt, A. (1989) 'Evaluating the performance of departments of psychotherapy', *Psychoanalytic Psychotherapy* 4(2): 121–53.

—— (1992) 'Psychotherapy in borderline and narcissistic personality disorders', *British Journal of Psychiatry* 161: 23–43.

General Medical Council (1987) Education Committee, *Recommendations on the Training of Specialists* (Oct.), London: GMC.

Kosviner, A. (1992) 'The psychotherapies in the curriculum of clinical psychologists', pp. 84–8 in G. Powell, R. Young and S. Frosh (eds) *Curriculum in Clinical Psychology*, Leicester: BPS (Division of Clinical Psychology) Publications.

—— (1993) *Smatterings, Standards and Snobbism in Psychotherapy and Psychology*, Psychotherapy Section Inaugural Address, BPS.

Management Advisory Services to the National Health Service (1989) *Review of Clinical Psychology Services* (Oct.), London: HMSO.

Menzies, D., Dolan, B. M. and Norton, K. (1993) 'Are short term savings worth long term costs? Funding treatment for personality disorders', *Psychiatric Bulletin* 17(9): 517–19.

Parry, G. (1992) 'Improving psychotherapy services: applications of research, audit and evaluation', *British Journal of Clinical Psychology* 31: 3–19.

Royal College of Psychiatrists (1990) *Handbook of the Joint Committee on Higher Psychiatric Training*, London: RCP.

—— (1991a) 'The future of psychotherapy services', *Psychiatric Bulletin* 15: 174–9.

—— (1991b) *Statement on Approval of Training Schemes for General Professional Training for the MRCPsych* (April), London: RCP.

Chapter 17

Psychotherapy and social services

Kenneth Kirk Smith and Jonathan Smith

Social services departments in Great Britain cost the taxpayer £5,591 million in 1991, approximately £100 for every man, woman and child. At £2 a person a week, you may be surprised it is so little. Social workers are responsible for providing a range of services (including counselling) to children and families, disabled people, the elderly, and people who are mentally ill. Social workers deal directly and indirectly with human growth and development, dependency, transference and counter-transference, and unconscious processes in individuals and organisations; yet the relationship between social work and psychotherapy is an uncomfortable one. The reasons for this, and some of the implications, will be considered in this chapter.

THE RISE AND FALL OF PSYCHODYNAMIC SOCIAL WORK

The first set of reasons is to be found in social work's own history. Social work is not a new profession. Its origins were observable in the 1870s, and it has an interesting history of which it can be justly proud. Though social conditions influence how people live and behave, individuals are unique and deal with adversity in different ways; and so both psychology and sociology are needed to understand behaviour, even if at times it is hard to hold them together in the same frame. Social work recognises this, and also the importance of the family as the social institution that creates individuals and prepares them for independent existence in the community. It has established an identity as a profession committed to helping people in need, by working with individuals, families, groups or communities.

Social work was greatly advanced in the 1950s by psychoanalytic ideas, which it took in from Dr John Bowlby and the Tavistock Clinic, from Donald Winnicott at the London School of Economics, and from the American social work profession. These ideas provided social work with the psychology that it had been looking for. The publication of Bowlby's *Forty-four Juvenile Thieves* (1946), for example, helped people to see that, in many cases, delinquents were deprived people in need of help. This psychology, which saw difficult behaviour as a way of dealing with deprivation, or as defences for the personality against anxiety and loss, provided a method that improved the practice of work with individuals, traditionally called 'case-work'.

With the addition of psychodynamic psychology, case-work became a powerful way of helping people, which was rather seductive to some members of the profession. It certainly contributed to the effectiveness of social work. In the 1950s and 1960s, social work had not caught the attention of the public, as it later would. It was an activity known only to a few; but this group, which included members of the local authority Children's Committees, judges and lawyers who knew of the work of the Probation Service, and doctors aware of the contribution made by mental welfare officers to the mentally ill, was influential. People who were aware of social work approved and some even idealised what they saw.

Psychodynamic psychology led to the 'generic principle'. Social work increasingly became aware of the common human needs underlying a variety of defensive and disruptive behaviours, and began to find the division of the profession into agencies specialising in certain kinds of client problem to be a constraint. The 1969 Children and Young Persons Act, which went a long way towards blurring the distinction between delinquent and deprived children, was an example of the application of this principle.

In pursuit of a generic approach, social workers decided to form themselves into a single professional body, the British Association of Social Workers. To achieve this, they voluntarily surrendered the smaller and highly effective organisations which supported the practice of child care and of psychiatric social work, published excellent journals, and organised well-attended annual teaching conferences. Unfortunately, BASW, the large new organisation, took some time to learn to manage itself, and for some years was not an organisation that could represent the profession and support its members. Even today, fewer people attend its Annual General Meeting than attended that of the Child Care Officers Association in 1968. This left social workers in an exposed situation when, after legislation implementing the Seebohm Report (Seebohm 1968), they found themselves working in enormous local authority departments, responsible for services to a wide range of client groups.

The Seebohm Report gave power, responsibility and independence to social work. It recommended that there should be one large social service department in each local authority, directed by a social worker, thereby confirming the high standing in which social workers were regarded at the time, and giving its assent to the generic principle.

Social workers who lived through this re-organisation will remember the chaos it brought. At a time when they were disorganised, without adequate management skills to survive in such large departments, or the practice skills to co-operate to provide a generic service, they were totally overwhelmed by legislation. The 1969 Children and Young Persons Act, an exciting and liberal piece of legislation, transferred to people who had been child-care workers the responsibility for juvenile offenders who had been the responsibility of the Probation Service. This imposed a responsibility to offer corrective relationships to young offenders onto workers who had a welfare ideology, and no experience of the creative use of authority. The skills that the Probation Service had been developing, of using a relationship sanctioned by an order to help young people in trouble, were lost. The first indication of things to come for social work was a barrage of complaints from magistrates, the police and the public, taken up in the press, that social workers had no answer to delinquency. This was followed by the Chronically Sick and Disabled Persons Act (1972), which was full of creative ideas for workers to improve the lot of disabled people, but with no offers to provide the money to do so.

Social work has found ways of coping with the constraints and opportunities of a social services setting. It has evolved new partnerships, new management and new practices, and now does work in response to community demands which would not have been possible in the 1960s. But it has never regained the confidence, the cohesion and the public approval which it once enjoyed. One aspect of this is that there is no agreed language to describe its practice. Some of the influences that led to this have been described, but there is one more significant influence to consider.

The introduction of psychodynamic psychology to social work helped it to advance, but it polarised opinion in the profession, as it has done in medicine and in society generally. As Butrym pointed out (1976), it professionalised one aspect of social work – that is, individual case-work – and it took some time for other aspects of social work practice to catch up. Group work was rediscovered in the 1960s, family therapy in the 1970s, and finally community work, mentioned in the Seebohm Report, took a higher profile after the Barclay Report (1980). Before this, however, individual case-work on psychodynamic lines had become such an interesting and powerful method that some people saw it as the whole of social work. In her classic paper, Irvine (1956) showed that psychodynamic case-work had a proper place in the repertoire of responses of social work. But other people were less accepting. Baroness Wootton (1959) attacked psychodynamic methods. Mayer and Timms (1970) questioned the relevance of case-work for working people. Radical social workers said that too much psychology detracted from the social, structural contribution to poverty and failure. A debate was in progress about the identity and practice of social work.

Unfortunately, partly due to the organisational changes going on, this debate was never finished. One result is that social work is ambivalent about, or even resistant to, psychodynamic work. Some people anticipated what was about to happen, and established a pressure group (GAPS, or the Group for the Advancement of Psychotherapy and Psychodynamics in Social Work), but it has never had more than 400 members. Another rather tragic example of the failure to resolve the contradictions inherent in providing social services is that the generic debate has never been properly dealt with, so that social services departments are even now reorganising themselves backwards and forwards from 'specialist' (based on special client groups) to 'patch' (taking all comers from a neighbourhood).

Finally, the recognition of child abuse, and later sexual abuse, in the community has created a situation which has changed social work. Since Maria Colwell, the first case to come to public notice (Department of Social Services 1974), social workers have found themselves, with the police, in the front line of services to protect children from physical and sexual abuse in their families. When this fails there is, quite properly, outrage and a demand for the allocation of responsibility, and this operates as one of the major anxieties for workers in social services departments.

To conclude this part of the argument, it is submitted that psychodynamic psychology empowered social work, and contributed to the progress that led to the creation of social services departments. Social workers evolved a form of psychotherapy which they called 'case-work' which was instrumental in helping individuals and families. At the same time, in search of the 'generic principle', social work transformed the institutions that maintained its professional identity. As a result, under the pressure of organisational change, the debate about the place of psychodynamic work was never concluded, and the profession has lost some of the practice skills and the position that it had established.

This has been a painful loss. In some ways social work has moved on, and now tackles more difficult things than it could have attempted in the 1960s, and some of the practice from that time has been shown to need improvement (Reid and Shine 1969). But in other ways it has lost cohesion and confidence, and the ability to work with people in need. It is a profession dominated by the needs of clients and employers, without a core that allows it to make its own contribution to events. Reflecting on this, and how it has happened, one can see that in the 1970s there was some idealisation and a little hubris: but there also seems to have been a kind of self-destructiveness, a determination not to form a strong professional identity, but to identify with the deprived and the outcast, in a way that contributed to its inability to speak to them.

SOCIAL SERVICES – IS ANY PSYCHOTHERAPY PRACTISED?

Social services departments are large and complex bureaucracies, with responsibilities under legislation to a range of client groups, employing a variety of professional people with different kinds and levels of training.

The range of different kinds of helping activities is considerable, and social work is only a part of the activity. Staff include foster-parents, residential and day-care workers, occupational therapists and administrators. The tasks vary from the mundane to matters of life and death, some of the work is long-term, and some of a crisis nature. Social workers are meeting the results of deprivation, delinquency, mental illness, handicap of all kinds and marital disharmony. Stress is considerable. Social work training is usually for two years, which the profession does not regard as adequate. In these circumstances, is it meaningful to talk of psychotherapy, or anything like it, in social services departments?

Our answer (this may be controversial) is a qualified 'yes'. Some social workers share with psychotherapists the belief based on experience that if dependency needs are recognised and understood, the client's growth process can continue. Understanding the client in the here-and-now of a relationship can help this to take place. This cannot be learned from a textbook, but needs to be experienced in relation to the worker's own need to be cared for and accepted. One of the most potent experiences in training to help other people is an experience of having been a patient oneself. Not everyone will want to work this way, but for those who do it is a vocation, in the sense that workers will continue to work like this whether they are sanctioned by their agency or profession, or not. Some social work training courses still prepare students to work in this way. In other cases, social workers subsidise their training by taking courses at their own expense, sometimes in psychotherapy or counselling.

Even where the demands of the agency inhibit thoughtful relationship work, workers find ways to do this by subverting the system. The study of mental health practice by Fisher et al. (1984) showed that social workers manage to keep a part of their case-load where they can do long-term work, while offering a crisis service to the majority of people for whom they are responsible.

DIFFERENCES OF SETTING

Now we can turn to the question of the differences that the setting makes to psychodynamic work in a social services agency.

The first difference is that sometimes social workers in social services departments intervene with the environment directly. This enables them to help people by providing foster-care, by financial and other kinds of help, and by engaging in community development programmes. However, it means that there are times when the social worker can no longer operate as a counsellor or psychotherapist to help a client to come to terms with and respond to difficulties in the environment, as the worker has become a part of the environment, and thus a part of the problem to be overcome. It is extremely difficult for clients to seek psychotherapeutic help from a worker who has been instrumental in removing their children. It is not easy to work with a client who needs psychological help or counselling and who also wants or needs money, unless there is a clear understanding, accepted by the client, of the circumstances, if any, in which the agency can offer financial help.

A second major difference is that usually in psychotherapy there is a contract between the worker and client, whereas, in social services departments, payment is by a third party. This could be seen as A doing something with B while C pays. This means that social workers are able to help people who need it, but could not or would not afford to pay for it. However, the price of this is a built-in confusion, as it is not always clear who C is, what he expects to happen, and even whether this is possible. At various times, C can be represented by an officer of the local authority, or by elected members, or officers or elected members of the national government, or indeed by the electorate itself. Where psychotherapy is provided in the National Health Service, it is at least fairly clear that it is psychotherapy that is being paid for. One of the disadvantages of the changes in social work described above is that it lost control of its own identity, which is now determined by a diverse variety of organisations, including employing authorities, so that what is called social work may be rather different in, say, Islington and Hackney.

A consequence of providing a free service is that it may both meet a need and uncover (or even appear to create) a demand. Some health professionals, for example, think that if people who attempt to commit suicide are given too much help with their problems, this will increase the number of attempted suicides. Without some sort of control, there is a risk that social work is either strangled by the demands arising from its own effectiveness or, alternatively, that the service may become inefficient, inappropriately defensive, and not subject to financial control. Recent legislation has made a radical attempt to clarify this. Under the NHS and Community Care Act (1991), the law separates providers or services from purchasers, devolves responsibility to a level as near the client as practical, and envisages a pluralist economy, strengthening the voluntary sector. The intention is to bring a realistic appreciation of the costs of treatments to the notice of those prescribing them, and to allow 'market forces' to exercise some control. Ultimately this may help, though there are theoretical and practical problems to deal with. In the short term, it is reducing the time available to workers in social services departments to help people themselves, and there is a real danger that it will erode even further their ability to carry out interventions that constitute clinical work.

A third major difference is that social services meet and work with people for whom psychotherapy would not be possible or helpful. Some clients want advice, information or services, and manage well enough once they have these. Others are too ill to cope with the kind of help that can be offered in regular appointments, even if they are frequent. They may need day care or support to manage at home, or even residential care or compulsory admission to hospital. Other people find ways of dealing with their problems, such as delinquency, which maintain the omnipotent defensive belief that they are all right, and it is the world that is out of step: they can only be helped with some kind of structure, court process or containing order.

DIFFERENCES OF THEORY

Now we can turn to some of the differences of theory between social work and psychotherapy, with particular reference to work with children.

Social workers are daily confronted with the realities of child abuse, deprivation and neglect in all its many and varied forms. The social worker may focus appropriately upon the parents' social situation, their here-and-now environment, and look for the factors that frequently (though not always) correlate with the problem of abuse; that is, poverty, homelessness, poor housing, racism, deprivation and inequality. These connections are valuable in helping the social worker to understand what may have precipitated the crisis.

Aware that parents are themselves desperately in need of help with their psychological as well as their social needs, social workers have at times looked hopefully to psychoanalysis and psychotherapy for maps and models to guide them in their task. It is these disciplines that have concerned themselves specifically with the subjective experience of the individual, with the feelings and emotional conflicts that reside in the psyche. Aware of the beleaguered social worker struggling to meet the demands of the desperate families on her case-load, it is to the relationship between psychotherapy and social work that we now turn.

Psychotherapy and social work are concerned with a large overlapping area of human experience, and yet their perspectives seem to be worlds apart. Communication between the two disciplines is befogged by the use of very different language and concepts. Instead of a creative cross-fertilisation of ideas they have diverged, as each has charted its own largely separate course.

There are many reasons for this. One is that professionals tend to move from social work towards psychotherapy. Social workers who go on to become psychotherapists, learning and growing on the way, with considerable expenditure of time, money and effort, must be forgiven for assuming that the end is superior to the beginning. This assumption may be reinforced if it cloaks the fact that they cease to work with the people and situations that are the most demanding, chaotic, needy and possibly least hopeful. Although psychotherapy and social work are different, and social workers are on average less trained, the task of social work is as difficult as psychotherapy, as demanding and as valuable.

The relationship between reality and fantasy, as conceived by psychotherapists, has also contributed to the divergence between the two disciplines. Whereas social work is daily confronted by the all-too-obviously painful realities of children's lives, psychotherapy and psychoanalysis have often seemed to focus attention more upon the fantasy life and imagination of the individuals who come in search of relief from their suffering.

There have been periods, however, when a cross-fertilisation of ideas between the two disciplines has taken place. Winnicott (1965), while making a significant contribution to the object relations school of psychoanalysis, shifted the focus of analysis onto the real nature of the infant–mother relationship and the traumatic effect of failures by the environment to meet the needs of the child. At the same time, Bowlby's (1969) pioneering research focused on the effects on the child of real events of separation and abandonment. (By its very nature, attachment theory focuses on the child's relationships with the primary carer.)

More recently, attachment theory researchers have begun to focus their attention on the effect of abuse on the child's attachment relationships with parents, and how the damage to the attachment relationship results in the abuse being transmitted generationally. It is unfortunate that attachment theory has had a limited reception in social work. Marris (1982) points out that it has been misunderstood as a sociological theory about family structure, rather than as a psychological theory about child development in the context of the relationship with the primary carers. It has not always found favour, for ideological reasons, with those who hold strong views either for or against the traditional family structure, and this has reduced the extent to which it has been accepted.

Alice Miller's (1985) focus upon the psychotherapist's function as advocate for the inner child, with an unequivocal focus on the realities of childhood trauma and abuse, has also made a significant contribution to bridging the gulf between social work and psychotherapy.

In the United States, Selma Fraiberg's work (1980) has raised important issues about the nature of psychotherapy with socially and economically deprived and disadvantaged groups. She raises questions about the need to change and modify the techniques of psychotherapy if clients from these groups are to be successfully engaged in psychotherapy, and to be helped in the process.

During the initial encounters with a client from such a background, the type of client who will frequently appear at the doors of a social services department, it is likely that motivation to seek psychotherapeutic assistance will be low. The psychotherapist will need to be prepared for such clients to be very difficult to engage in psychotherapy. Often a client will have experienced the involvement of statutory agencies in the family for several generations. Social workers may have intervened and removed children into care, or the client or members of their family may have been compulsorily admitted to hospital under a section of the Mental Health Act. Such a client may therefore be very wary of, or indeed hostile to, any offer of psychotherapy, and fearful that this may be yet one more intrusive and interfering intervention in their life. Furthermore there is unlikely to be much support in such a person's cultural background for the notion that psychotherapy, and the exploring of one's feelings, can be of help in life. Current external environment pressures may seem all too clearly to be overwhelming. This may sound very familiar to social workers; significantly, a psychotherapist working in a social services department will need to employ techniques and skills borrowed from social work if clients are to be successfully engaged in psychotherapy.

First, the psychotherapist will need to assume a large amount of responsibility in the process of creating and maintaining an attachment relationship with the client (Reiner and Kaufman 1959). In the initial stages of the psychotherapy, there may be repeated missed appointments and cancellations, as the client expresses uncertainty, ambivalence and hostility about the notion of engaging in psychotherapy. The psychotherapist will therefore need some understanding and acceptance of the very tenuous nature of the attachment relationship, and may need to be prepared to wait patiently for the client who fails to turn up for appointments, for several weeks, before a successful therapeutic alliance is established. It needs to be recognised that this is an important part of the work, otherwise such clients are likely to fail to engage in the psychotherapy.

Part of this process of engaging the client in psychotherapy also centres on the issue of the client's uncertainty of how far they can trust the psychotherapist. This will emerge in psychotherapy generally, whatever the setting. However, where the encounter between client and psychotherapist takes place in the particular social context described above, working through the issue of trust, recognising the effect which the social context has upon the client's doubts about how far they can trust the psychotherapist becomes a crucial issue, especially in the initial period of psychotherapy. These issues are best addressed by the psychotherapist at the first suitable opportunity.

Fraiberg gives a most graphic and telling account of the simple and straightforward, and yet highly unconventional, way in which she worked with this issue of trust, and the negative transference that had to be worked through, before one highly anxious and abusing mother was able to make use of the psychotherapeutic support that was being offered to her.

Her past was filled with broken and disappointing relationships, meaning that a formidable negative transference had to be dealt with immediately. My acknowledgement of Beth's (the mother's) fury, disappointment and distrust enabled her to visit me twice a week. She made constant demands on me. She changed the meeting times. I agreed. She asked for Trudy's (her baby's) hospital records. I got them. She wanted to scold the hospital administrator, I summoned him.

(1980: 223)

This example is quoted because it illustrates so clearly the kind of modification of technique and flexibility of approach that may be needed of the psychotherapist working in a social services department. It also illustrates how working therapeutically in such a context may involve combining psychotherapy with social work functions. The psychotherapist, as well as providing in-depth assistance with the client's subjective experience, with the way in which past traumatic experiences may be re-enacted in the present, also provides practical material assistance which may be in the form of financial assistance, help with food or clothing, or negotiation with other agencies such as hospitals, doctors, children's hospitals or the income maintenance services. The psychotherapist may also provide a non-didactic and supportive form of guidance in child development for those young mothers whose basic knowledge of the needs and developmental stages of babies and infants is inadequate. The provision of these forms of assistance contributes significantly to the therapeutic relationship, assisting in the formation of a therapeutic alliance, and reducing a highly self-protective negative transference. It communicates to the client in a symbolic way that the psychotherapist is there to help her find her own pathway out of her nightmare, rather than to interfere, intrude and betray her, as others are likely to have done.

The choice of location and settings may also involve the psychotherapist in adopting unconventional approaches. There are many clients whose motivation to seek therapeutic assistance is so low that they are unlikely to become engaged in psychotherapy unless the psychotherapist is prepared, initially at least, to visit them in their own homes, to conduct the psychotherapy sessions in the living room, the kitchen or the children's playroom. The psychotherapist will need to address the issue of boundaries and maintain the privacy necessary for the therapeutic work, but creative flexibility can mean that even intrusive visits by others can be worked with therapeutically. Where mothers with young children are concerned, reaching a psychotherapist's office can create practical problems and be a real disincentive to engaging in psychotherapy. This affords additional impetus for the psychotherapist to be flexible, and to find ways of conducting psychotherapy with babies or young children present, using the interactions between parent and child as potential material for exploring the parent's past childhood experience. Where seeing a client in her own home may create serious difficulties around the boundaries of a therapeutic relationship, then finding alternative locations near the client's home, such as a private room in a community centre or a church hall, can be considered. Such a setting would need to convey symbolically the psychotherapist's separateness from institutions that undertake statutory child-care and mental health responsibilities, which the client may perceive as intrusive and interfering.

IS PSYCHOTHERAPY POSSIBLE IN A SOCIAL SERVICES DEPARTMENT?

We have begun to touch upon an important issue: namely, whether it is possible to combine the therapeutic role with other social work functions, particularly the statutory ones; or whether it is necessary to create a separate agency and structure offering psychotherapy and other therapeutic forms of assistance, an agency that is clearly and distinctly separate from the social services department.

Events in social services in recent years have increased the likelihood of the development of an insurmountable negative transference in some of its clients. The greater awareness of the incidence of abuse, particularly sexual abuse, coupled with a number of critical inquiries into situations where children have been killed by a parent whilst being supervised by a social worker, have resulted in a concentration of resources upon the investigation and assessment of child abuse, and upon the child protection aspect of the service. The contribution of preventive or long-term supportive case-work to the field of social services has diminished appreciably, so that increasingly social services have become identified with the highly interventionist aspects of the work on child protection cases. A psychotherapist who is a social worker, or is clearly a member of a social services department, will begin by being identified as a part of this interventionist child protection service.

For psychotherapists to create the safety of the therapeutic space, they will need to be sure that the contents of the session remain completely confidential. Psychotherapists need to develop their own guidelines for breaching the confidentiality of the therapeutic space when, for example, a child's life is judged to be seriously at risk, or when there is a subpoena to give evidence in court. These guidelines are likely to be different from the procedures and policies created for social workers as part of their role in child protection, where the emphasis is of necessity more upon the sharing of information with other agencies. A single agency could not contain such differing guidelines in relation to confidentiality with any ease.

Another advantage of separating the two roles and functions can be stated as follows. There are many clients whose sense of self has been so fragmented and shattered by their experience of childhood abuse and trauma that, when they begin psychotherapy, they could not be contained in a relationship with a psychotherapist who was also clearly a member of an agency which receives children into care, or compulsorily admits people into mental hospital. The anxiety, fear and distrust of the psychotherapist would create such a formidable negative transference that the psychotherapist would be unlikely to reduce it sufficiently to engage the client in a working therapeutic alliance.

The disadvantage of separating the roles of child protection and the provision of therapeutic support into separate agencies is that collaboration between workers carrying child protection responsibility and the worker undertaking the therapeutic task remains essential. Working from separate agencies is likely to increase significantly the difficulties of facilitating a high level of collaboration between workers, and to create a barrier to the necessary continuing cross-fertilisation of ideas between social workers engaged in child protection and psychotherapists engaged in preventive work. Such a barrier would increase misunderstanding and miscommunication between workers. This is likely to occur when both workers are faced with the same client expressing very intense deeply distressed feelings (Mattinson and Sinclair 1979). Linked to this, such a separation of roles could easily increase the possibility of clients splitting into a good and a bad worker, a good and a bad agency, with all the problems of inter-agency conflict that could result if this was not dealt with successfully.

CONCLUSION

Surveying the history of social work and the relationship between social work and psychotherapy, we reached a point where a synthesis of conflicting ideas in the social work profession was much needed. For a number of reasons, the moment was lost, and social work was overwhelmed by political, social and economic forces which have sapped its vitality and strength. The need for a synthesis of ideas remains as urgent as ever, and particularly there is a need for an agreed working psychology which will contribute to the practice and language of social work, in understanding and describing work with the elderly, the handicapped, mentally ill people, and most of all, in work with children and their families.

In the field of child abuse, this is of the utmost importance. There is a need to understand and work with both the victims and the perpetrators of abuse to children, but to do this means having to manage such upsetting and conflicting emotions that it would not be surprising to see the profession and its practitioners in flight. There is a danger that 'child-protection' will dominate the concerns of employers and professionals alike, and that this will be justified in terms of scarce resources or market forces. However, social work has been creative when its practitioners established relationships with those at the margins of society who needed help, and saw them as human beings with the need for understanding, help and time. The origins of abuse are to be found in the objective social world, and subjectively in the inner world of experience. The relationship between the latter and the real events of childhood trauma need to be more fully explored and understood. This is a task of the utmost urgency, and it needs the co-operation of those who work with adults who have been abused, and of those working with the family situations where abuse is currently being perpetrated. It is in the interests of social work and its clients for there to be a strong profession of psychotherapy, with clear boundaries and high standards, and for the two professions to relate to each other with respect and understanding.

REFERENCES

Barclay, P. M. (1980) *Social Workers: Their Role and Tasks*, London: NCVO/ Bedford Square Press.

Bowlby, J. (1946) *Forty-four Juvenile Thieves: Their Characters and Home-life*, London: Baillière Tindall & Cox.

—— (1969) *Attachment and Loss: 1, Attachment*, London: Hogarth Press.

Butrym, Z. T. (1976) *The Nature of Social Work*, London: Macmillan.

Department of Social Services (1974) *Report of the Committee of Enquiry into the Care and Supervision Provided in Relation to Maria Colwell*, London: HMSO.

Fisher, M., Newton, C. and Sainsbury, E. (1984) *Mental Health Social Work Observed*, London: Allen & Unwin.

Fraiberg, S. (1980) *Clinical Studies in Infant Mental Health*, London: Routledge.

Irvine, E. E. (1956) 'Transference and reality in the casework relationship', *British Journal of Psychiatric Social Work* 3(4): 1–10.

Marris, P. (1982) 'Attachment and society', pp. 185–201 in C. M. Parkes, J. Stevenson-Hinde and P. Marris (eds) *The Place of Attachment in Human Behaviour*, London and New York: Routledge.

Mayer, J. E. and Timms, N. (1970) *The Client Speaks*, London: Routledge & Kegan Paul.

Mattinson, J. and Sinclair, I. (1979) *Mate and Stalemate*, Oxford: Blackwell.

Miller, A. (1985) *Thou Shalt Not Be Aware*, London: Pluto Press.

Reid, W. J. and Shine, A. W. (1969) *Brief and Extended Casework*, New York: Columbia University Press.

Reiner, B. S. and Kaufman, I. (1959) *Character Disorder in Parents of Delinquents*, New York: Family Service Association of America.

Seebohm, F. (1968) *Report on the Committee on Local Authority and Allied Personal Social Services*, Cmnd 3703, London: HMSO.

Winnicott, D. (1965) *The Maturational Process and the Facilitating Environment*, London: Hogarth.

Wootton, B. (1959) *Social Science and Social Pathology*, London: Allen & Unwin.

FURTHER READING

Balint, M. (1968) *The Basic Fault*, London: Tavistock Publications.

Bowlby, J. (1988) *A Secure Base*, London: Routledge.

Delozier, P. P. (1982) 'Attachment theory and child abuse', pp. 95–117 in C. M. Parkes, J. Stevenson-Hinde and P. Marris (eds) *The Place of Attachment in Human Behaviour*, London and New York: Routledge.

Yelloly, M. A. (1980) *Social Work Theory and Psychoanalysis*, New York: Van Nostrand Reinhold.

Chapter 18

Psychotherapeutic communities
The contemporary practice

David Millard and Haya Oakley

Psychotherapy is influenced by the setting in which it occurs. Nowhere among the settings considered in this section of the *Handbook* is this more true than of therapeutic communities, a defining feature of which is the deliberate attempt to use the characteristics of a residential or day-care organisation in a therapeutic way. They constitute:

> a place in which people can discover that they live IN a community. Indeed they are a constant meditation on the different ways in which this 'IN' exists – from the fact that one cannot live purely in one's 'head', to the way in which themes and issues that apply through the house are not ultimately located IN anyone.
>
> (Freidman, in Cooper *et al.* 1989: 73)

'Therapeutic community' refers to a model – or family of models – which may be applied to the organisation of residential or day-care settings. These may be either within the Health Service – namely, in-patient units, wards or 'day hospitals' more or less directed by doctors – or in hostels or 'day centres' providing predominantly non-medical accommodation and staff. In this chapter we have both in mind, but principally the non-medical settings. This reflects the current trend, in Britain as elsewhere, away from treatment in psychiatric hospitals and towards care in the wider community provided either through national or local government or by private or voluntary organisations.

HISTORICAL BACKGROUND

The term 'therapeutic community' was introduced by Main in 1946 to denote one aspect of the changes then beginning to take place in psychiatric hospitals in Great Britain. The kernel of this wide-ranging process was, perhaps, a movement from an essentially authoritarian towards a more collaborative style of staff behaviour and consequently from institutionalising and repressive residential regimes towards a more liberal, humane and participative kind of culture.

Subsequently, the partial but more general application of ideas associated with the therapeutic community became described as the 'therapeutic community approach' (Clark 1965). This influence persists, often unacknowledged, in psychiatric units employing occasional ward meetings and the like. It is to be distinguished from the therapeutic community proper, the model originally associated chiefly with the pioneering work of Maxwell Jones (1968) at the Henderson Hospital in south London. Characteristically, such communities have regular, usually daily, community meetings, one of whose functions is to examine significant events in the daily life of the community – the 'other twenty-three hours' of the residential work literature – together with an accompanying staff group and an array of other group activities: psychotherapy, work groups, creative therapies and so forth. The processes of living within the community are understood to be in themselves potentially therapeutic.

As we describe below, this places a good deal of the therapeutic influence and responsibility with the users of the service ('members', 'residents', 'patients' and so on) and constitutes, to use the title of Rapoport's (1960) classical monograph on the Henderson Hospital, the *Community as Doctor*. Jones's earlier work had been with military personnel under treatment during the Second World War for psychosomatic disorders ('effort syndrome'). Initially, he had lectured to groups of about eighty men on the dynamics of this condition, but soon discovered that they preferred to talk with one another and that the outcomes of this approach were better! This, incidentally, is an early and significant illustration of the therapeutic community principle that staff through modifying their own behaviour can change the culture even when that culture includes a good deal of active participation by the patients.

Therapeutic communities have, however, developed both within and outside the hospitals. One group exists in 'progressive' education, originally represented by the work of pioneers such as A. S. Neil, Lyward and David Wills (for contemporary examples, see Table 18.1). These had in common an emphasis on self-government, even within communities of disturbed young people. Another derives from the residential care of alcohol and drug abusers and is associated with American institutions such as Synanon and Phoenix House (Ziegenfuss 1983). These, often known as Concept Houses, have a more directive culture and frequently employ as staff members people who were themselves previously substance abusers.

Yet another derives from so-called 'alternative' psychiatry. In 1962 Dr David Cooper set up an experimental unit (Villa 21) in Shenley Hospital; he believed that breaking down the hierarchic barriers between patients and staff would enhance the understanding and treatment of the patients. This was the movement later extended and developed by the Philadelphia Association, chaired at the time by R. D. Laing, which started by setting up households where the emphasis was on ordinary living

Table 18.1 Examples of therapeutic communities classified by type of provider

Local authority social services departments

Mental health day centres;
e.g., Kensington and Chelsea (Blake *et al.* 1984); Leeds
Mental health hostels; e.g., Wandsworth; Buckinghamshire

Criminal justice system

Probation hostels; e.g., Norris 1979)
Probation day centres (Cook 1988)
Grendon Underwood Prison (Gunn *et al.* 1978)

Voluntary sector

Education and therapy; e.g., New Barns School; Peper Harow (Rose 1982);
  Thornby Hall (Worthington 1989); Cotswold Community (Whitwell 1989)
Hostels, households, etc. (mentally ill); e.g., Richmond Fellowship (Jansen
  1980); Philadelphia Association; Arbours (Berke 1982)
Residential homes (handicapped children and adults); e.g., Camphill Village
  Trust (Baron and Haldane 1992)
Crisis centres
  Will admit a person in an acute condition; e.g., Arbours Association
  Will accommodate severe crisis within their normal brief;
  e.g., Philadelphia Association; Shealin Trust

National Health Service

District-level in-patients units (may accept some day patients)
Adults (general); e.g., Oxford (Pullen 1986); Leicester, West Berkshire
Substance abusers; e.g., Alpha House; Ley Community (Donnellan and Toon
  1986)
Adolescents (Boakes 1985)
Regional or super-regional units; e.g., Henderson Hospital (Whiteley 1970b)

– hospitality rather than hospitalisation – and where people who had lost their way would be able to wander safely and freely until they could find their way. For nearly thirty years these ideas have evolved with experience, and currently there are a number of such communities in London and other parts of the country.

THE THERAPEUTIC COMMUNITY IN CONTEMPORARY BRITISH MENTAL HEALTH PRACTICE

It is not possible to enumerate accurately contemporary psychotherapeutic communities; in the present political climate, institutions tend to open and close, the function and model of practice of those remaining may change, and institutions may vary in the extent to which they would describe themselves or be recognised by others as therapeutic communities. A fairly comprehensive *Directory* is obtainable from the Association of

Therapeutic Communities. Accounts have been published of several institutions which currently operate with some version of the model (see Reference and Notes at the conclusion of this chapter), and examples of such institutions may be classified as in Table 18.1.

A distinct feature of the British tradition in the field is the part played by the voluntary sector (see also Chapter 19 of this *Handbook*). Psychotherapeutic communities are set up by charities using government funding; for example, housing associations and local authority grants, and private means. Within the voluntary sector two approaches may be distinguished. One, as exemplified by the Richmond Fellowship, uses the treatment modality of 'community as doctor' and centres on providing a care regime aiming to care for or rehabilitate residents. The emphasis is usually to get people better so that they can rejoin society as working, valuable members. In the other type, therapeutic communities are mostly referred to as 'households' and run by organisations like the Philadelphia Association, Arbours and the Shealin Trust in Scotland; 'these communities started from a recognition of the need for places of sanctuary, asylum, refuge or dwelling felt by some people who find themselves in extreme mental distress' (Cooper *et al.* 1989: 21).

THEORY AND PRACTICE

We shall first give some introductory theory and comments on indications and contra-indications; then offer a short and perhaps rather idealised account of therapeutic community practice. The third section offers a more detailed theoretical justification for this practice, a note on effectiveness, and finally suggestions to the reader for discovering more about this type of work.

Theory I: some preliminary concepts

Institutions offering residential or day care for whatever purposes should do so in the light of explicit theories of institutional functioning (Millard 1972). This term denotes the kind of narrative which describes as precisely as possible how a particular regime actually produces the changes which it exists to bring about. Our starting point is a value assumption that such 'group care', as residential and day care may collectively be termed, is indeed to do with *change* in members, including, obviously, the minimising of deterioration where this is inevitable, and the enhancement of the quality of life, rather than *warehousing*. Theories of institutional functioning must therefore include theories about personal change. It is only on the basis of this kind of understanding that: (1) staff can be helped to see how they can best act, (2) the work of a place, including matters such as the indications for admission, can be clarified for referring agencies and others, and (3) research and the evaluation of outcomes can be conducted.

Where group care is not guided by the clear application of a theoretical model, the risk is that the problems brought by residents create such levels of anxiety in the staff that features arise in the regime, 'institutional defences' (Menzies 1960), which are often damaging both to residents and staff, and prevent the work being done most effectively. Paradoxical as it might seem, it is the professionalisation of the staff which allows the client members of a residential institution to contribute most to their own well-being. This chapter is therefore written from the perspective of the staff member.

Psychiatry is well used to the existence of a number of 'models of madness'; that is, theoretical systems for considering the fundamental nature of mental disorder. Thus, behind the use of the particular family of theories of institutional functioning underlying therapeutic community models are important theoretical notions of the nature of mental disorder. A number of models of group care are available; some are based on learning theory as applied in behaviour therapy ('token economies' and the like), others on pedagogical or pastoral theories (Arthur 1985), still others, including therapeutic community theory, on the basis that human behaviour, whether deviant or normal, is influenced by the *meanings* which people attach to their own activity and that of others. We shall return below to the significance of this viewpoint.

The variety of forms of therapeutic community practice which occur in community care settings place us firmly in the territory of Clark's (1965) *therapeutic community approach*. The differing circumstances in which community care is practised, the range of characteristics of those using such services and the constraints imposed by the parent service-delivery agencies upon individual therapeutic communities all contribute to variety within the arrangements they make. Does this then mean, as some critics have suggested, that the whole concept runs away into the sands and that we cease to be able to identify anything specific as belonging to the therapeutic community? We believe not. Manning (1989) uses the idea of a *common core* of practices. Having carefully surveyed the evolving definitions of the therapeutic community and, acknowledging the existence of some confusion among both proponents and critics of the idea, he writes:

> We can conclude from the review that, first, therapeutic communities are distinct from other therapeutic practices in terms of theoretical aims, organisational structure and process, and self identity. Second, there are three broad originating streams of therapeutic work which are beginning to converge towards one general type, most clearly related to the democratic community.* Third, that there is nevertheless, and

* Manning is here referring to what might be called the 'Maxwell Jones type' of therapeutic community.

not surprisingly, variation around this common core in terms of therapeutic ideology, client type and the purity with which the therapeutic
community principles are put into practice.

(Manning 1989: 47)

We can therefore accept as falling within the scope of this chapter the
application of a range of psychotherapeutic community ideas to a range of
client groups; we return below to consider the balance between common
and specific features.

Indications and contra-indications

People may be referred to a therapeutic community by their doctor or
psychotherapist, or may refer themselves. The reasons for coming vary.
Sometimes their current living conditions cannot sustain the degree of
stress. Sometimes it is in order to try and prevent hospitalisation. At other
times a person will wish to spend some time in a therapeutic community
as a buffer between a period in hospital and ordinary living. In many
communities residents are admitted or accepted for membership because
their specific problem might be shared by present residents (for example,
drug addiction). Some communities have a limit on length of stay; others
are open-ended. Some regard participation in all the community's activities
as a condition of acceptance; others leave this open to negotiation. Some
therapeutic communities would wish that the whole of the treatment
during the stay would be carried out within the community; others permit
or encourage ongoing individual psychotherapy outside the community
activities.

In general, it may be said that clients are potentially suitable if

1 their problems (whether primarily behavioural or psychological) *include
   or are significantly caused by psychological events* – this yields a wide
   spectrum, including most varieties of mental disorder, problems in social
   relationships and many behavioural problems, criminal or otherwise;
2 such psychological events are crucially to do with the *meaningfulness* of
   human experience and behaviour.

This is of course the case since therapeutic community practice aims
precisely to operate on the meanings which people attribute to their
experience and behaviour. It does so by providing a setting in which people
are allowed in a relatively non-directed environment to 'experience' and
'behave'; then by subjecting these matters to examination, comment and
interpretation, and encouraging experimentation with appropriate new
behaviours and subsequent reinforcement by both fellow users and staff
(Millard 1989). Communities vary in the extent to which their understanding of meaningfulness is confined to the conscious level, in which case these

practices might be described largely by cognitive psychology (secondary process), or also take as essential unconscious or primary processes. Behind this statement is the obvious point that the important thing about mental disorders is that they reduce the patients' social competence.

Psychotherapeutic communities, working with psychoanalytic principles, would shift the emphasis from patterns of behaviour and reinforcement to an attempt to reach and resolve unconscious conflict via a process of psychoanalytic interpretation of what goes on between the members of the community and between them and the psychotherapist. This, as noted earlier, may take place alongside individual psychotherapy and would usually work on the understanding that the community is the patient, and that this would in turn benefit the individual members. The free development of the community is the condition of the free development of each.

The clinical categories within which such persons might fall include the more severely disabled adult neurotics; people with most varieties of personality disorder, including alcohol and drug abusers not actively taking such substances during the admission; and people with chronic disability following major psychosis, whether or not they require maintenance medication. Chronic schizophrenics, of course, form a substantial majority of those in need of long-term care. Note that this insistence on psychological meaningfulness does not exclude an organic component in the aetiology in any case.* Another clinical category is children and adolescents displaying the range of psychiatric problems which are, of course, only partly comparable to those of adulthood.

Within this large reservoir of potential users of community mental health services, two other points may be made.

1 Obviously, since this is predominantly a group technique, the clinical problem should be of a type and severity which on the ordinary criteria would require management in a group setting: most of those whose problems can be managed individually in out-patient or case-work settings are excluded. Naturally, different institutions employing the therapeutic community model will admit patients having a particular *profile* of clinical and social characteristics (Blake *et al.*, 1984).

2 Patients who need short-term, acute treatment are generally not suitable. Or to put the same point in a different way, units which are set up specifically for short-term treatment probably cannot make much use of therapeutic community models of working. This is because it is necessary

* Presumably, psychological function in all of us is related to the activity of whatever brain we have. We must get along as best we may in solving the everyday problems of psychosocial adjustment, whether our brain function happens to be capable of producing Nobel Prize-winning research or to be modified by whatever physiological change it is that leads to, say, schizophrenia.

for patients to be in the unit sufficiently long to be able to understand its culture and to make that culture work in a way that meets their own needs. Clinical experience suggests that this takes a minimum of three weeks' stay, but many of the users we have in mind actually require much longer. In one study of the residents in mental health hostels who for the most part were reasonably able, two-thirds needed to stay for more than a year; 80 per cent of this sample were in whole time open employment (Hewett *et al.* 1975).

An unusual exception to this generalisation are the Crisis Centres run by the Arbours Association and therapeutic communities run by the Philadelphia Association and the Shealin Trust who are prepared to take in from time to time an acutely disordered, short-term resident.

Therapeutic community practice

Therapeutic communities require a defined space: a hospital ward, a hostel or day-centre accommodation, for instance, but the characteristics of such premises are not specialised. What is needed is essentially a 'domestic' type of building: outside hospitals, something like a large flat or house, or (for a day centre) a public hall which provides rooms for large and small group meetings, cooking and communal eating, and perhaps some accommodation for creative therapies, together, of course, with sleeping and toilet arrangements if the setting is residential. It is best if the space does not have to be shared with other users. The costs of accommodation can often be relatively modest. The users of the community should be able to make a substantial contribution to their own support and the daily care of the building.

The features of therapeutic community practice may be summarised in three defining principles:

(a) therapeutic communities have a characteristic kind of social structure;
(b) therapeutic communities have a characteristic timetable for daily or weekly living;
(c) therapeutic communities have a characteristic set of expectations of the behaviour of their members – both staff and users.

In what follows we shall refer to each of these in turn.

Systems theory defines its subject in terms of *elements* and their *connections*. Figure 18.1 shows diagrammatically the principal elements in the therapeutic community model: various groups, the 'in-between' or background space/time and boundaries. These exemplify the first of the defining principles.

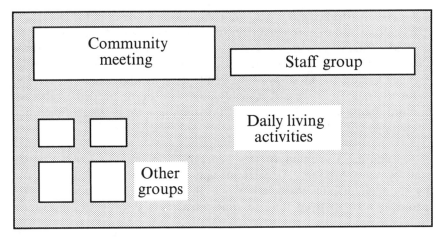

Figure 18.1 The principal elements in the therapeutic community model

(a) Community meeting

This is possibly the single most characteristic feature. Generally, such meetings are considered to have essentially two types of function (Gilman *et al.* 1987): the patient/staff administration meeting and large group psychotherapy. Other authorities distinguish a third category dealing with inter-group (or systems) analysis. These functions may be the subject matter of separate meetings, in which case important issues of boundary maintenance arise, or they may be combined. Importantly, community meetings constitute the main forum for 'feedback'; that is, they are the place where events elsewhere are reported, discussed and used for learning. As far as possible the community is self-governing, 'democratic' (to use Manning's term), both staff and users having an important measure of responsibility. Some communities operate on the principle of 'one person, one vote'; others will modify this to a variable extent.

It is impossible to differentiate entirely between the ordinary daily living, the running of the place and the psychotherapeutic input. The following illustration of a meeting in a community household may illustrate that point.

S was a young woman who had spent most of her adult life in and out of mental hospitals and various residential care settings, having been diagnosed as schizophrenic. At that time she had been living in a community for a while, convinced that all the other residents and psychotherapists were 'aliens' whilst she was the only human being. She did not formally take part in community activities, spent a great deal of time in her room, appeared periodically during meal times to take some food upstairs with her and has never sat through a whole community meeting. On the particular night a business meeting of residents and psychotherapists was discussing amongst other things some spare cash and how it would be used to redecorate the house. S was particularly agitated, and came in and out of the meeting room accusing people of being aliens, and slamming doors. The meeting decided that each resident could paint their own room the colour of their choice but that the communal space should be painted in a colour agreed upon by democratic voting procedure. Just as the vote was about to be taken someone said, 'Wait a minute, go and get S.' Someone called out and S came to the room and duly cast her vote for the colour of her choice. This was not experienced by any of the residents or the psychotherapists as a particularly unusual or dramatic event, nor would it have necessarily been listed amongst the psychotherapeutic assets of the community. However, it had a deep psychotherapeutic effect on everyone involved and in particular on S, who conceded for a brief moment that everybody else was a member of the human race that she herself could join.

A single community may also be part of a wider network sharing similar psychotherapeutic cultural elements. Cross-community activities will also affect the community's life.

(b) Staff groups

Conventionally, every community meeting is immediately followed by a staff meeting ('after-group') but staff groups often occur also at other times. From the beginnings of the therapeutic community movement it was found that the opening of communication networks and flattening of staff hierarchies created high levels of anxiety, especially among staff trained in conventional nursing or medical settings. In fact, it is virtually an axiom of residential and day care that good staff communication reduces anxiety, raises morale and improves outcomes (Revans 1976).

Although it is widely known that any psychotherapeutic team does not have to be in complete agreement and total harmony to be effective, unresolved tensions in the team will bring out the worst in the community and could even lead to occasions of serious acting out. For example: R was acutely disturbed for many months, draining the community's emotional and physical resources. The two house psychotherapists differed in their opinion as to R's future in the community, and so one of them agreed that R should stay if the other was very keen to keep him. This ambivalence was played out throughout the household, culminating in the residents 'not noticing' one day that R had wandered off in a state of confusion, only to be picked up by a totally unambivalent policeman and hospitalised.

This is a rare and extreme example, but it illustrates the need for any psychotherapeutic team to work together to understand the agreements, disagreements, competitiveness, rivalry and the multitude of anxieties and pressures generated from being involved in such a demanding and delicate field of work. Furthermore, it is known that covert staff disagreement is liable to result in high levels of disturbed behaviour among users (Stanton and Schwartz 1954).

(c) Other groups

Groups have been shown to be a defining feature of therapeutic communities (Crocket *et al.* 1978; Hinshelwood 1964/1987). They may be roughly classified as follows:

(i) *Verbal psychotherapy*: Group analytic ideas (Foulkes 1964) have been widely influential. Some communities will place little emphasis on individual work with members, and the small therapy group is then the most intimate and intensive site for psychotherapy.

Perhaps the most notable difference between such groups within a community and those elsewhere is the impossibility – indeed, the undesirability – in this situation of maintaining anything like a 'rule of abstinence'. Not only is there inevitably a good deal of passage of information into and out of the group and of social contact between members other than during group meetings, but often *feedback*, an account of the proceedings within a small group given to the community meeting, may be established as a community norm. A larger circle of confidentiality is therefore called for than is characteristic of ordinary group psychotherapy, and this probably induces systematic differences in the material typically communicated.

(ii) *Creative therapies*: Art therapy and drama therapy, psychodrama and related psychotherapies are widespread (McMahon and Chapman 1987); music therapy occurs in some places; movement, dance and the use of puppets have been reported; doubtless, other modalities are possible. In expert hands, these may enable the exploration of emotionally laden material to take place among members for whom exclusively verbal methods are too threatening.

'A good illustration is the story of Peter who was too fragile to participate in any verbal activity and whose first form of expression and contribution to the community life was the ability to participate in yoga classes' (Oakley, in Cooper *et al.* 1989: 150).

(iii) *Work groups*: Work groups which may be routine, as in shopping for and preparing community meals, and 'special occasion', to plan an outing or a party, occur widely. For these and various other types of group it is common to arrange that members, rather than staff, should take leadership roles such as convenor, reporter-back, etc. This is *sociotherapy*, the precise connotation of which is the deliberate psychotherapeutic use of the occupancy of particular roles in a social structure. It is to be sharply distinguished from *social therapy*, which may refer to no more than participation in recreational activities. The examination in small and large groups of the individual's performance in such roles forms a vital feature of most communities.

(iv) *Others*: Because of the contemporary awareness of the social tensions surrounding gender, *women's groups* (Collis 1987) and *men's groups* are frequently found in therapeutic communities. Special groups to participate in the *selection of members for admission*, or induction groups for *joiners* or preparation groups for *leavers* (Parker 1989) are not uncommon. A specific problem often arises for members where developments within the individual come into conflict with homeo-static mechanisms in her or his family, thereby tending to resist and subvert such changes; in some places, this has led to the development of *families groups*. In addition, depending on the particular client group, there may be a place for special focus groups, such as for alcohol abusers.

(d) 'In between' time

This is represented by the grey background in Figure 18.1. Here we note the significance of the structured timetable in therapeutic community practice: this is the second *defining principle* (above). The importance of this has long been recognised, such as Jones's (1968) concept of the 'living-learning' community. Recent research has pointed to it with renewed interest. In studies asking members to identify where psychotherapeutic-ally significant happenings take place, 40 per cent identify this space/time. Van der Linden (1988), in discussing this matter, relates it to Winnicott's (1971) emphasis on the importance of play. It is also consistent with the generalisation that

> It is central to the theory of operation of therapeutic communities that no action-based programme is successful unless the gains (however small) made by patients are brought to some form of conscious recogni-tion and verbal expression, and no verbal approach is complete unless the gains are tested and reinforced in action.
>
> (Blake *et al.* 1984: 54)

Robin Cooper (1989) tells the moving story of Richard, who was too disturbed to join the normal activities and who could not be left behind when the whole community went away for their summer holiday. Richard had been living almost as a recluse within the community as he claimed he needed complete peace to think his thoughts. On that occasion,

> he comes along bundled into the back of the Volkswagen van with his shitty mattress and stinking blankets. The cottage in fact is no more than a large converted barn, so now there is absolutely no chance of Richard getting any quiet at all. One very solitary member of the house has already pitched her tent in the nearby field, and, even on the

marshes flits between field and barn. But now there is another tent in the field – in the opposite corner of the field – and here Richard spends his days screaming at the sheep because now they are interfering with his thinking.

(Cooper *et al.* 1989: 54)

(e) Boundaries

The importance of 'background time' points to the need to define boundaries, represented by the heavy lines in Figure 18.1, including that around the community within which members need to remain to some extent. The question of boundaries is central to the life of most communities, if we allow the crude assumption that most residents are there because of some degree of inability to articulate themselves in the world. For some the task may essentially be to define their own psychic and social boundaries. We can then appreciate the importance of the acute sensibility required and attention paid to issues as mundane as: Who has which room? Can they lock it? Can you go into someone else's room? Who can visit and who says so? Who represents the law and who carries the authority?

The way in which boundaries will be defined will affect relationships both among the staff and between staff and members of the community. The extent to which detailed definitions of do's and don'ts are established, the written and unwritten rules, will also have an effect on the nature and the style of the psychotherapy which will take place in a particular therapeutic community, as well of course as the question of who defines the boundaries and who draws up the rule-book.

> it was very significant that Peter chose to touch me as he did at the community household, in his room rather than mine, a private yet public place, a playground that was personal and neutral, where we were alone, yet surrounded by others whose presence was benign, where there were no tight rules about going into people's rooms or about touching them. I did not have to look over my shoulder in case a member of the nursing staff 'caught me' in the patients' dormitory. Therefore what happened remained uncluttered, a gesture of trust and closeness, an expression of genuine tenderness and love, made possible by the milieu.

(Oakley 1989: 158)

And another example:

> A group of teenagers who spent most of their lives in care were used to receiving a packet of biscuits on a Friday, which they would lock away in their room. When they moved to a household with two resident workers, they took to raiding the kitchen cupboards at night only to discover it was their communal food they were eating and that there

would be none there provided magically by a nameless 'big brother' administrator. They promptly demanded to join the workers on the weekly trip to the supermarket, so that they could choose the biscuits and make sure they lasted until the next trip. Youngsters from the neighbourhood were attracted to the house ('without parents'). At first they were welcomed by the residents, who rejoiced in the seemingly permanent party, only to realise their home was being abused and then decided to draw a firm boundary around it.

(Oakley, written for this chapter)

FURTHER CONSIDERATIONS

Theory II: why do we do things this way?

(a) Rule-governed behaviour

Although therapeutic communities have sometimes been stigmatised as wild and lawless places, they typically have a quite clear structure and set of social expectations. Users of the service are not required to conform to the highly structured behaviour often required of patients in institutional settings, though there may be rules about participation in meetings and so forth. Much scope is left for them to 'find their own feet' – that is, their behaviour within the therapeutic community must draw on their own resources, however inadequate these might be. This is the *third* of our *defining principles*.

How, then, does it actually work?

In Philadelphia Association households people go to sleep when they wish. They get out of bed under their own steam and in their own time. When they are moved to, they shop, cook, eat, clean, stay in their rooms, watch television. . . . All this takes place in every household in the land. . . . What, if indeed anything, is therapeutic about this?

(Freidman, in Cooper *et al*. 1989: 56)

No doubt, a number of mechanisms might be identified operating at various social and psychological levels of analysis. As in all psychotherapies, the essentials must be to do with some psychological change in the user which can, so to speak, be exported from the psychotherapy. These psychological events may be thought of as having to do with the *rules* which link an individual to their social context. The central idea here is that how we act is *not* precisely in accordance with learned and fixed patterns of behaviour but rather in accordance with a stock of general principles which form (or generate) our action in particular social situations and which are therefore called *generative rules*. People are more socially competent precisely because they have generative rules which adapt them well to the demands of specific situations, but people whose stock of generative rules is somehow inadequate are those whom we recognise as disabled by one or another of the mental disorders (Millard 1981). Life in psychotherapeutic community care is therefore designed to encourage the kind of internal changes which enhance the individual's competence in social behaviour. Thus the link between a particular model of mental disorder and a particular theory of institutional functioning becomes clear.

(b) Psychotherapy and sociotherapy

The model depends crucially on a *combination of interventions* into the clients' psychological world ('psychotherapy') with those into their social world ('sociotherapy'). Edelson regards these not as alternatives, with beliefs and aims in treatment antagonistic to one another, but rather as: 'inextricably *interrelated* enterprises in any attempt to understand and influence or change persons, but enterprises *differentiated* by having different systems of intervention and analysis' (1970: 175).

Nevertheless, the technical literature generally, and perhaps inevitably, takes one orientation or the other as its starting point. On the psychotherapy side, there are two important aspects: individual and group. Since these are the subject of other chapters in this volume, we identify here only some specific emphases.

(i) Psychotherapy

Naturally, in psychotherapeutic communities opportunities often arise spontaneously, or are contrived, for staff to sit with users as individuals or groups for formal therapeutic activities; exactly as they are found in individual case-work or in group-work settings. But among *individual* psychotherapies we note that residential and day-care settings offer uniquely the possibility of 'on the hoof' or *peripatetic therapy* (Millard 1992). This is indeed a major and insufficiently recognised skill of group-care practice. It is one in which work with individual users may be fragmented into quite short interventions, but where these accumulate in a coherent fashion over hours, days, months or even years. The technique of 'holding' such a thread is demanding. And the demand is often compounded by the need to hold several such threads simultaneously for different users, and to manage the complex ways in which they may be plaited together in the ever-shifting daily interactions of the unit.

Concerning group-work, a clear distinction must be drawn between group psychotherapy and therapeutic community practice, however much the latter may draw upon the insights and the techniques of the former. Users and staff inevitably share in the common social life. Thus, discussions primarily concerned with psychotherapy within the therapeutic community make necessary, and not incidental, reference to matters of social structure. Correspondingly, social phenomena are seen as having an essential psychological importance.

An example is worked out by Hinshelwood (1979) in the paper 'The community as analyst'. His thesis starts from the proposition that the group can offer individuals such participation in a collective defence system that they may be protected from their emotional distress and overlook it. Alternatively, by offering some form of psychotherapeutic insight and confrontation with their distress and defences against it, members can be helped to mature. Such confrontation employs the notion of transference; thus far we are in the domain of group psychotherapy. However, in a community there are not one or two psychotherapists to participate in a transference relationship but a *staff group* which is defined over against the patient group by all manner of social events in the community life. The boundary thus created between staff and patients may be used defensively to protect against anxiety or may be part of the healthy, effective structure which enables the daily life of the community to proceed in an orderly fashion. On an analogy with the analysis of transference, Hinshelwood suggests that the discussion of problems around this boundary is a crucial task for the community, and a primary tool for this purpose is the community meeting which 'exists to release and control this anxiety, not to alleviate it' (1979: 109).

(ii) Sociotherapy

Similarly, the bringing together of social events and the combined efforts of staff and residents to understand their significance, and to grow in social competence through this understanding, occur in those who take sociotherapy as their starting point.

For example: Whiteley (Whiteley *et al.* 1973) uses the term 'sociotherapy' in describing the well-known work of the Henderson Hospital. Here there exists an array of explicit social roles and tasks. Patients have the opportunity of testing themselves, in many of these supported and exhorted by a continuous stream of comments from other community members. But it will, of course, be what is learned and internalised from that experience which individuals will take away as a permanent acquisition when they leave.

Secondly, the Concept Houses, mentioned previously, employ a very rigid formal hierarchical social structure to which members are required to commit themselves completely, severing their ties, at least initially, with the outside world. Residents progress up and down (!) the hierarchy as they are able to conform to the community's morality. This is enforced by intensive group surveillance and the existence of a fearsome array of sanctions. Such communities are generally staffed by those who have themselves recovered from the problems, alcoholism or addiction, with which they deal. They usually have more conventionally qualified staff in an external, consultative role. Here also, a psychotherapeutic element is clearly present. Wilson writes:

> This rigid structure of the community seems to have the effect of enforcing the distribution of 'internal objects' along particular channels – transference is highly focused in staff, who come to represent health and the possibility of giving up addiction. Hostile and destructive inputs are acknowledged . . . initial regression is encouraged . . . [people] may complain that they are being infantilised or depersonalised . . . those who remain for long periods of time in such programmes, however, often experience a strong internal change.
>
> (1979: 98)

(c) Theory of institutional functioning: Rapoport's principles

In *Community as Doctor*, Rapoport (1960) established a framework of four principles: *permissiveness, communalism, democratisation* and *reality confrontation*, which have become widely accepted. Characteristically, users newly admitted to a therapeutic community will receive much less guidance about how they are expected to conduct themselves than they would if entering an institution of another type. This is the notion of *permissiveness*:

> the Unit's belief that it should function with all its members tolerating from one another a wide degree of behaviour which might be distressing or seem deviant according to 'ordinary' norms. Ideally, this should allow both for individuals to expose behavioural difficulties, and others to react freely so that the bases for both sides of social relationship patterns may be examined.
>
> (Rapoport 1960: 58)

The individual tends rapidly to replicate within the institution the problems experienced outside, and which are probably among the indications for admission. The extent to which the member's behaviour is constrained by the situation is modified; it does not allow, for example, the individual to fall into the stereotyped activities of the patient role. Their behaviour will be formed by whatever rules they can draw upon for guidance in only partly familiar situations.

In addition, the ideology provides that much of what goes on is regarded as public property – the user's 'symptoms' – which are likely to include both subjective (mental) discomforts as well as distorted (unsocial) patterns of behaviour, are not a private affair, to be shared only with some species of professional psychotherapist. This is the idea of *communalism*: 'the Unit's belief that its functioning should be characterised by tight-knit, inter-communicative and intimate sets of relationships. Sharing of ameni-ties, informality (e.g. use of first names) and open communication are prescribed' (Rapoport 1960: 58).

This is an example of a therapeutic community rule. It is ethically justifiable, since all members are in the same situation; it makes an open reality of matters which are usually kept covert in other settings; and it is an essential precondition of *democratisation*: 'each member of the community should share equally in the exercise of power in decision making about community affairs – both psychotherapeutic and administra-tive . . . conventional hospital status hierarchies should be "flattened" to produce a more egalitarian form of participation' (Rapoport 1960: 55).

Further therapeutic community rules are implied here. Democratisation involves a conscious abrogation by otherwise powerful staff members of decision-making prerogatives in the interest of members' experimentation with revised social performances.

Thus far, nothing in this exposition points to an explicitly psychothera-peutic function nor to any notion of personal change. For these elements we need to add *reality-confrontation*: 'Patients should be continuously presented with interpretations of their behaviour as it is seen by most others' (Rapoport 1960: 63).

This is essentially the mechanism through which the meanings which individuals attach to their own experience and behaviour, and those of others, are challenged and modified. It is such modifications, translated into an improved level of social competence, which comprise the essential gain to participants in a therapeutic community regime.

Some further problems

It is not possible to make this section comprehensive, but some typical issues are noted which readers may pursue through the References list.

(a) Issues for staff

Our approach to theories of institutional functioning suggests that the characteristics of the regime should derive from the specific needs of the user group. There exist, of course, other interests which may conflict with this: public prejudice, the manager's desire to ration resources, the self-interests, legitimate or otherwise, of staff members, and the like. Some therapeutic communities will have nurses or house parents who will carry out the care function as well as doctors, social workers and other professionals who may or may not participate in the daily routine and in community meetings. Other therapeutic communities may largely be run on a daily basis by the residents, with a warden to carry out the administrative functions and a team of visiting psychotherapists. However, the task of planning the regime and, broadly, of maintaining the culture once established belongs ultimately with the staff. Therapeutic community practice will delegate such matters to users to the maximum possible extent; and thereby arises a continuing tension within which the work is done.

Typically, therapeutic communities make arrangements through some form of staff supervision or consultation to maintain the effectiveness of the staff group. These matters are widely discussed in the published literature (for example, Millard 1992).

(b) Issues for users

Whereas for some individuals being in the company of other people who share similar problems and needs can be a source of instant relief, others may initially find the close-knit atmosphere of the therapeutic community, and its push towards sharing, a little oppressive. Some may wish for greater privacy and need to form 'special' intimate relationships with a member of staff in lieu of integrating with the group as a whole. Issues of confidentiality and split loyalties to outside carers and family may also arise.

The published literature includes several accounts of experience in therapeutic communities written by users (see Mahony 1979; Hudson 1990).

(c) Issues for the community

The organisational problems of running a psychotherapeutic community are manifold and, in general, beyond the scope of this chapter. One example must suffice.

A problem familiar to practitioners of any residential care is that what constitutes a true description of events at one time may not be true at another, yet the published descriptions of communities almost necessarily have a static quality about them. Savalle and Wagenborg (1980) have given a clear description of *oscillations* with the de Spiegelberg therapeutic community in Holland. The characteristics of the periods of less effective functioning are described as: expressions of dissatisfaction and lack of confidence, with grumbling, threats to leave or aggressive outbursts; strongly increasing demands for individual treatment; increasing polarisation between staff and patients; inadequate use of treatment facilities with much irrelevant talking and absenteeism; decrease among patients of interest in one another and in care for their physical surroundings; increasing use of alcohol or tranquillisers; development of 'night-life' with many occurrences of which staff and fellow-patients are only partly aware. This author considers some of the determinants, both from within and outside, of such periods of 'low tide' in the life of a community and describes in some detail the methods available to staff for the fruitful management of such crisis periods.

Effectiveness

The therapeutic community movement in the last twenty years has been well aware of need for evaluative research, but the field combines some of the classical difficulties of psychotherapy research with that in residential or day care (Clark and Cornish 1972). Early attempts at empirical evaluation would include Whiteley (1970a) on the Henderson Hospital and Clark on the management of chronic psychotic patients in Fulbourn (Clark and Myers 1970). But methodology in the behavioural sciences has developed, and two recent examples illustrate a more sophisticated approach:

1 Dutch researchers, working with a model which is well towards the psychotherapeutic end of the therapeutic community spectrum, have used the technique of large samples and conducted a study, the NVL project (Koster and Wagenborg 1988) on a cohort of 1,340 patients admitted to eight institutions over a three-year period and assessed at intake, discharge and at one, three and five years of follow-up. The results are complex but, for instance, a global 'well-being' score rose significantly from 36.8 (s.d. 7.6) at intake to scores around 45.0 at discharge and slightly rising at follow-up.
2 Manning assessed Richmond Fellowship houses in Australia and used path-analytic statistics to demonstrate that in this instance the observed outcomes (significant improvements in cognitive and emotional functioning, general behaviour, interpersonal behaviour and performance at work) could not have been due to a combination of spontaneous improvement with a sophisticated selection of 'suitable' patients but must have been contributed to by their experience in the therapeutic community.

The broad thrust of the evidence suggests that properly conducted therapeutic community regimes are capable of producing measurably effective outcomes in a number of client groups where this question has been examined, but for further discussion of this question the reader must be referred to the technical literature.

Where to go for further information

(i) *General information* The Association of Therapeutic Communities operates both individual and group membership, the latter to permit junior and less well-paid members of therapeutic community staff to attend conferences, and so on. This organisation is a good general source of information and publishes a *Directory of Communities* in the United Kingdom. The ATC is at 14 Charterhouse Square, London EC1M 6AX.

(ii) *Training* The Royal College of Nursing and Association of Therapeutic Communities have operated since 1986 a one-year day-release course, leading to the Certificate in Therapeutic Community Practice of the two organisations. The course meets once weekly from 2 to 8 p.m. at the Royal College of Nursing. Each session includes a formal lecture, a student-centred 'workshop' period, experience in small groups conducted by members of the Institute of Group Analysis and periodic large groups. In addition, there are two residential long weekends, operated on therapeutic community lines. The course is modular and students are able to accumulate credits towards a diploma and ultimately the BSc in Health Studies of the University of Manchester.

Among the voluntary organisations, Philadelphia and Arbours Associations run their own training programmes and there are occasional short courses based elsewhere.

(iii) *Books* The following are useful introductory texts:

Barnes, M. and Berke, J. (1972) *Two Accounts of a Journey Through Madness*, Harmondsworth: Penguin.
Cooper, R., Freidman, J., Gans, S., Heaton, J. M., Oakley, C., Oakley, H. and Zeal, P. (1989) *Thresholds Between Philosophy and Psychoanalysis*, London: Free Association Books.
Hinshelwood, R. D. (1987) *What Happens in Groups: Psychoanalysis, the Individual and the Community*, London: Free Association Books.
Kennard, D. with Roberts, J. (1983) *An Introduction to Therapeutic Communities*, London: Routledge.

In addition, the quarterly journal *Therapeutic Communities* is essential reading for serious practitioners in this field. The list of References and Notes that follows also offers an introduction to the extensive literature now available.

REFERENCES

Arthur, A. R. (1985) 'A psychotherapeutic community for religious and clergy', *International Journal of Therapeutic Communities* 6: 103–8.
Baron, S. D. and Haldane, J. D. (1992) *Community, Normality and Difference: Meeting Special Needs*, Aberdeen: University of Aberdeen Press.
Berke, J. H. (1982) 'The Arbours Centre', *International Journal of Therapeutic Communities* 3: 248–61. (See also Berke, J. H. (1990) 'Editorial: reflections of Arbours', *International Journal of Therapeutic Communities* 11: 191–5, which introduces a 'Special Issue on the Arbours Association: Twenty Years On'.)
Blake, R., Millard, D. W. and Roberts, J. P. (1984) 'Therapeutic community principles in an integrated local authority community mental health service', *International Journal of Therapeutic Communities* 4: 243–74.
Boakes, J. (1985) 'Different, or the same? Theory and practice in adolescent psychiatric units', *International Journal of Therapeutic Communities* 6: 231–8.

(See also Roosen, C. (1985) 'The psychotherapeutic community – a residential treatment for adolescents', *International Journal of Therapeutic Communities* 6: 205–18, papers among others comprising a Special Issue of this journal on work with adolescents.)

Brigland, M. (1971) *Pioneer Work with Maladjusted Children*, Birkenhead: Willmer Bros.

Clark, D. H. (1965) 'The therapeutic community concept: practice and future', *British Journal of Psychiatry* 111: 947–54.

Clark, D. H. and Myers, K. (1970) 'Themes in a therapeutic community', *British Journal of Psychiatry* 116: 534.

Clark, R. V. G. and Cornish, D. B. (1972) *The Controlled Trial in Institutional Research*, London: HMSO.

Collis, M. (1987) 'Women's groups in the therapeutic community: the Henderson experience', *International Journal of Therapeutic Communities* 8: 175–84.

Cook, R. D. (1988) 'A non-residential therapeutic community used as an alternative to custody', *International Journal of Therapeutic Communities* 9: 55–64.

Cooper, R., Freidman, J., Gans, S., Heaton, J. M., Oakley, C., Oakley, H. and Zeal, P. (1989) *Thresholds between Philosophy and Psychoanalysis*, London: Free Association Books.

Crocket, R. S., Kirk, J., Manning, N. and Millard, D. W. (1978) 'Community time structure', *ATC Bulletin* 25: 12–17.*

Donnellan, B. and Toon, P. (1986) 'The use of "Therapeutic techniques" in the Concept House model of therapeutic community for drug abusers: for whose benefit – staff or resident?' *International Journal of Therapeutic Communities* 7: 183–9.

Edelson, M. (1970) *Psychotherapy and Sociotherapy*, Chicago: University of Chicago Press.

Foulkes, S. H. (1964) *Therapeutic Group Analysis*, London: George Allen & Unwin.

Gilman, H. E., Russakoff, L. M. and Kibel, H. (1987) 'A bipartite model for community meetings: the separation of tasks', *International Journal of Therapeutic Communities* 8: 131–4.

Gunn, J., Robertson, G., Dell, S. and Way, C. (1978) *Psychiatric Aspects of Imprisonment*, London: Academic Press.

Hewett, S., Ryan, P. and Wing, J. K. (1975) 'Living without the mental hospital', *Journal of Social Policy* 4: 391–404.

Hinshelwood, R. D. (1979) 'The community as analyst', pp. 103–12 in R. D. Hinshelwood and N. Manning (eds) *Therapeutic Communities; Reflection and Progress*, London: Routledge & Kegan Paul.

—— (1987) *What Happens in Groups: Psychoanalysis, the Individual and the Community*, London: Free Association Books; first published 1964.

Hudson, P. (1990) 'We never promised you a rose garden', *International Journal of Therapeutic Communities* 11: 289–97.

* In this study of one week in 1977, among the 18 communities surveyed the distribution of groups was:

For all staff/some patients	1 to 88
For some staff/some patients	3 to 88
For patients only	1 to 15

The more group meetings, and the more time spent in groups, the more like a therapeutic community did the respondents consider themselves to be. ($r = 0.61$ (number of groups); $r = 0.64$ (time spent in groups).)

Jansen, E. (ed.) (1980) *The Therapeutic Community Outside the Hospital*, London: Croom Helm.

Jones, M. (1968) *Social Psychiatry in Practice: The Idea of a Therapeutic Community*, Harmondsworth: Penguin.

Koster, A. M. and Wagenborg, J. E. A. (1988) 'The follow-up project on therapeutic communities: a collection of measures for change', *International Journal of Therapeutic Communities* 9: 163–76. (See also the group of related papers on the NVL project in the same Special Issue of this journal.)

McMahon, B. and Chapman, S. (1987) 'Psychodrama and the therapeutic community', *International Journal of Therapeutic Communities* 8: 63–6.

Mahony, N. (1979) 'My stay and change at the Henderson therapeutic community', pp. 76–87 in R. D. Hinshelwood and N. Manning (eds) *Therapeutic Communities: Reflection and Progress*, London: Routledge & Kegan Paul.

Main, T. (1946) 'The hospital as a therapeutic institution', *Bulletin of the Menninger Clinic* 10: 66. (Reprinted in Barnes, E. (ed.) (1968) *Psychosocial Nursing: Studies from the Cassell Hospital*, London: Tavistock.)

Manning, N. (1989) *The Therapeutic Community Movement: Charisma and Routinization*, London: Routledge & Kegan Paul.

Menzies, I. (1960) 'A case study in the functioning of social systems as a defence against anxiety', *Human Relations* 13: 95–121.

Millard, D. W. (1972) 'Generic Concepts and Specialised Institutions', Lecture given at a conference on Professional Boundaries and Residential Social Work, London, 20 May 1972.

—— (1981) 'Generative rules and the therapeutic community', *British Journal of Medical Psychology* 54: 157–65.

—— (1989) 'Editorial: When is it not a therapeutic community?', *International Journal of Therapeutic Communities* 10: 192–4.

—— (1992) 'Educated intuition', *International Journal of Therapeutic Communities* 13: 83–106.

Miller, E. J. and Gwynne, G. V. (1972) *A Life Apart*, London: Tavistock Publications.

Norris, M. (1979) 'Offenders in residential communities: measuring and understanding change', *Howard Journal* 8: 29.

Oakley, H. (1989) 'Touching and being touched (the negotiated boundaries and the "extended" consulting room)', pp. 146–66 in R. Cooper, J. Freidman, S. Gans, J. M. Heaton, C. Oakley, H. Oakley and P. Zeal, *Thresholds between Philosophy and Psychoanalysis*, London: Free Association Books.

Parker, M. (1989) 'Managing separation: the Henderson Hospital leavers group', *International Journal of Therapeutic Communities* 10: 5–16.

Pullen, G. P. (1986) 'The Eric Burden community', *International Journal of Therapeutic Communities* 7: 191–200.

Rapoport, R. N. (1960) *Community as Doctor: New Perspectives on a Therapeutic Community*, London: Tavistock Publications.

Revans, R. W. (1976) *Action Learning in Hospitals*, London: McGraw-Hill.

Rose, M. (1982) 'The potential for fantasy and the role of charismatic leadership in a therapeutic community', *International Journal of Therapeutic Communities* 3: 79–87.

Savalle, H. J. and Wagenborg, H. (1980) 'Oscillations in a therapeutic community', *International Journal of Therapeutic Communities* 1: 137–46.

Siegler, M. and Osmund, H. (1974) *Models of Madness: Models of Medicine*, New York: Macmillan.

Stanton, A. H. and Schwartz, M. S. (1954) *The Mental Hospital: A Study of*

Institutional Participation in Psychiatric Illness and Treatment, New York: Basic Books.

Van der Linden, P. (1988) 'How does the large group change the individual?', *International Journal of Therapeutic Communities* 9: 31–40.

Whiteley, J. S. (1970a) 'The response of psychopaths to a therapeutic community', *British Journal of Psychiatry* 116: 534.

—— (1970b) 'The Henderson Hospital', *International Journal of Therapeutic Communities* 1: 38–58. (See also Norton, K. (1982) 'A culture of enquiry: its prevention or loss', *International Journal of Therapeutic Communities* 13: 3–26.)

Whiteley, J. S., Briggs, D. and Turner, M. (1973) *Dealing with Deviants*, London: Hogarth.

Whitwell, J. (1989) 'The Cotswold community: a healing culture', *International Journal of Therapeutic Communities* 10(4): 53–62.

Wilson, S. (1979) 'Ways of seeing the therapeutic community', pp. 93–102 in R. D. Hinshelwood and N. Manning (eds) *Therapeutic Communities: Reflections and Progress*, London: Routledge & Kegan Paul.

Winnicott, D. W. (1971) *Playing and Reality*, New York: Basic Books.

Worthington, A. J. (1989) 'The establishment of a new therapeutic community: Thornby Hall', *International Journal of Therapeutic Communities* 10(3): 165–73.

Ziegenfuss, J. T. (1983) 'The therapeutic community and addictions: a bibliography', *International Journal of Therapeutic Communities* 4: 307.

Chapter 19

Psychotherapy in the voluntary and independent sector

Sara Llewellin

The potential usefulness of psychotherapy to the voluntary sector is made evident if we look briefly at the sector's functions, history and philosophies. Equally, the obstacles to developing the interface between the two are firmly located in the sector's financing, management and, in some instances, political history.

WHAT IS THE VOLUNTARY SECTOR?

Also known as the charitable, and now part of what is known as the independent sector, the voluntary sector is made up of projects, organisations and groups running a wide variety of services. The key distinguishing feature is managerial independence from the statutory or commercial sectors, even where the statutory sector provides funding. Voluntary sector agencies are so named because the legally responsible managing body (usually the management committee or board of trustees) is entirely voluntary. This has its origins in philanthropic charity work and is still supported by the requirements of charity law. Many voluntary sector agencies have paid staff, whilst others operate entirely by the use of volunteers.

There are many thousands of voluntary sector organisations in the United Kingdom. They cover a broad spectrum of community-based and human service-based activities and needs. Some work very closely with statutory agencies, whilst some work in clear opposition to them. They range from small volunteer outfits to housing associations employing more than 1,000 staff members. The focus of their work may be agitational or practical or both. They may provide services, for example, to

- the general public (e.g., community centres, advice centres, law centres, arts or recreational groups), or
- ongoing specific client groups (e.g., play groups, pensioners' lunch clubs, after-school clubs, people with physical or mental special needs of a long-term nature), or

- groups of people in crisis (e.g., homeless people, those living with HIV/ AIDS or other life-threatening illnesses, women experiencing domestic violence or rape, people with substance dependencies), or
- groups of people fighting discrimination (e.g., black and ethnic minority people, refugees, lesbians and gay men, women).

It can be seen from this diversity that the sector has no homogeneity or common focus, which is in large part advantageous but which also leads to difficulties of documentation and strategic development. The disparate nature of the sector is a reflection of its history, an understanding of which is crucial when considering its relationship to psychotherapy.

PHILOSOPHICAL UNDERPINNINGS

The contemporary voluntary sector has its genesis in more than one philosophical base. The National Council for Voluntary Organisations (NCVO) was established in 1919 as the representative body for the voluntary sector, which was at that time (before the welfare state) operating from a base of charitable philanthropy. 'Voluntary work' was often religiously motivated or church-based and largely the domain of the middle classes 'doing good'. Still in existence, the NCVO is now in the forefront of contemporary strategic development and integration of philosophy and political ideology.

The emergence of the social and political movements of the 1960s and 1970s led to great changes in this philosophical base. Influences such as the modern women's movement, the development of black and other minority politics and more public money in the form of statutory grant aid (primarily through local authorities) led to enormous changes. The principles of autonomy, collectivism, self-determination, user participation and community-led initiatives came into the ascendancy. Concepts such as oppression, power, access and empowerment came to replace those of misfortune, assistance and succour to the poor. Above all came the integration of the demands of the grass-roots activists for equality of opportunity.

The voluntary sector mushroomed, and, during the late 1970s and eighties, especially in the inner cities and urban areas, the philosophy outlined above was prevalent. Many of these principles now form the bedrock on which practice is built.

However, we now operate under a new and different set of constraints, fraught with contradiction. As the 1990s unfold, we see the development of the contract culture where, ironically, the voluntary sector is being seen by the statutory sector as part of the private sector, now renamed jointly as the 'independent' sector. Anti-professionalism and collectivism have largely been replaced by new emphases on performance, hierarchy, cost-effective management, monitoring, evaluation, public accountability and public relations.

Agencies are now entering into negotiations for contracts with local authorities for the provision of services in line with community care legislation. Hard-pressed authorities have been squeezing and shaving grant budgets over the past five years. As the current recession has deepened, the need and demand for services has escalated. These two taken together have necessitated a return to fund-raising as an alternative, or addition, to grant aid – with all the attendant compromising which that of necessity entails. All these factors are current influences informing the internal battles of inherent contradictions.

COMPATIBILITY WITH THE HUMANISTIC TRADITION

The close resemblance between the philosophies of the humanistic therapies and those outlined above will be seen quite clearly by those familiar with either. Key parallel issues which concerned the early humanists were accessibility, autonomy, mutual consent, demystifying medical procedures, and giving people structures which they could understand and through the use of which they could effect personal change. The psychiatric and psycho-analytical traditions seemed incompatible with much of the radical thinking of the period, steeped as they were in medical mystique and hidebound by inreasingly challenged frames of reference. The humanistic psychotherapies, on the other hand, offered readily accessible models of human interaction and pathology which proved able to accommodate – and indeed promote – key concepts of rights, dignity, autonomy and self-actualisation.

The psychotherapist as an 'expert facilitator' rather than just an 'expert' placed more emphasis on process than was present in psychiatry, and more emphasis on current here-and-now functioning than was evidenced by psychoanalysis, although certainly both those traditions have undoubtedly also been influenced by developments in social and political critiques. Examples of these are Community Psychiatric Nursing (CPNs) working at the interface between psychiatry and the community, feminist psycho-analysis integrating an understanding of patriarchal structures and the social construction of femininity. Centrally important to this development is the work of Juliet Mitchell (1974, 1984), reconciling modern feminism with the legacy of the structuralist movement which integrated an under-standing of sociopolitical structures with the psychoanalytical traditions. (For further material on this, see Reading list B below.)

PHILOSOPHICAL TENSIONS

It can be seen then that there is very real historical commonality between psychotherapy and the voluntary sector. There have also been, however, philosophical tensions which proved a block to wide-scale development of the use of psychotherapy within significant parts of the sector for a number of years.

Some of these tensions had their origin in the political resistance to anything which could potentially pathologise – or appear to pathologise – the oppression or marginalisation of certain groups of people. For example, during the decade 1975–85 it was widely held in the Women's Aid Federation, which runs refuges for women leaving violent men, that any suggestion of counselling or psychotherapy carried with it the implication that violent men were not being held responsible for their actions, and women were being blamed yet again for male violence. This must be seen in the context of an emerging politic still struggling against a cultural belief system which, indeed, does 'blame' women for much of the violence they experience. However, the notion of counselling, at least, as a tool which can empower women rather than pathologise their experience has certainly been adopted now by many. At the time of writing, Camden Women's Aid refuge are advertising a post as 'Woman Counselling Worker', qualified, who 'will be providing a counselling service for CWA therefore an understanding of the complex issues surrounding domestic violence, and appreciation of the trauma associated with such violence in terms of its impact on women and children, is essential' (*Guardian*, 1993b).

There have also been philosophical tensions around the issues of money, access to knowledge, qualifications, 'professionalism' and power dynamics. The very strong anti-professional trend which dominated parts of the voluntary sector during the seventies and eighties, whilst usefully promoting access and self-determination, often had the concomitant effect of devaluing real and useful skills along with paper tigers . . . or chucking out the baby with the bathwater.

It has taken time and integrative creativity for some of the very real contradictions between need and process to begin to be resolved. Using new models and ways of working, various agencies and groups have managed to promote services which both acknowledge the concrete social realities which lie behind the historical resistance, while also skilfully tackling the needs of real people in situations of real psychological stress. These services would largely fall into the category of counselling.

COUNSELLING

Counselling services, as opposed to psychotherapy, have proliferated in the sector over the past decade and are now thoroughly well established as a legitimate and desirable part of overall provision.

The new Advice and Counselling Lead Body set up to develop national standards and incorporate them in NVQs estimates that there are 50,000 people engaged in these activities assisted by some 500,000 volunteers. A further 2 million people have the delivery of advice, guidance and counselling as an essential part of their job.

(Advice, Guidance and Counselling Lead Body 1992)

The success of many of these initiatives lies in their pro-activity in relation to the politics and philosophies of the sector. Counselling models have been determined which have creatively and sensitively addressed the thorny issues of sexual, racial, cultural and gender identity, for example, and which respond to a variety of different presenting needs. Areas covered include:

1 issue-based crisis counselling, such as bereavement, redundancy, debt, rape;
2 counselling services run by and for specific minority groups, thereby sympathetically partnering clients with counsellors whom they are predisposed to trust, and who may be less likely to hold incompatible frames of reference, such as PACE counselling service for lesbians and gay men, incest survivors' groups run by survivors;
3 general counselling services; often community-based and usually short-term – in practice therefore this often means crisis counselling, such as services based in community centres, or serving a catchment area and having a general brief;
4 issue-based counselling specifically picking up where a statutory service has left off, such as HIV/AIDS counselling services accepting referrals from on-the-spot counsellors at antibody testing centres; and
5 counselling, and in this instance often also psychotherapy, as part of a residential recovery programme designed to equip people for good-quality independent living, such as hostels for people becoming sober.

WHY COUNSELLING AND NOT PSYCHOTHERAPY?

Largely because of appropriateness, but also because of financial, organisational and operational constraints, counselling is usually the more appropriate response to crises or difficulties which may be attended to discretely, rather than requiring an examination of belief systems, behaviour and their genesis in childhood. A good illustration of this would be bereavement counselling.

In an exploration of bereavement counselling in the voluntary sector, Charlotte Sills says:

it is [my] belief that a 'normal bereavement' may not need psycho-therapy. There is a national network of skilled and experienced agencies offering support and counselling for the bereaved, which provide a more appropriate response than psychotherapy. The use of psychotherapy at a time of normal bereavement is, at best, misusing the therapist's skills and at worst appearing to pathologise and thus interfere with a normal process.

There are recognised patterns of loss that a bereaved person tends to follow. The individual experience will of course be unique. However, there will be a process starting with disbelief and acute distress and progressing over time to adjustment, and eventual acceptance. During this time a variety of emotions will be felt and expressed – for example anger, fear, despair, relief. The degree of difficulty a bereaved person experiences in 'believing in' the loss and its significance will depend on the degree of impact on his or her assumptive world. The amount of grief expressed will depend on the greatness of the loss, as well as the personality of the person and how he or she generally functions in the world. This process inevitably leads to periods of pain, disorientation or depression. However, if the process takes its normal course, the person will not need the services of a psychotherapist. What is needed is the support of someone who will help the person give time, space and recognizance to his reactions and feelings, and be a witness to the process. He can then help him re-establish the coping functions that have perhaps been temporarily overwhelmed or unsettled by the loss. In many cases, this support is provided by family and friends, but often the help of a Bereavement Service can be invaluable. Usually these services offer a trained bereavement counsellor. This may be on a short-term basis, perhaps during the early, difficult times, to help the person develop a support network for himself. Equally, counselling may take place over several months, during which time, in weekly sessions a person has a life-line to hold onto while he explores his feelings. He can then begin to build a new life, which may have to include a new sense of personal meaning – for instance the person who has always thought of himself as part of a couple and now needs to discover an identity as an individual.

Local bereavement services are organised by many organisations including Cruse, Mind, Age Concern and Local Authorities. There are also specific organisations for Gay Bereavement, Jewish Bereavement and many others. All will offer some sort of counselling. Some also offer groups for bereaved people ranging from structured, closed short-term groups led by a facilitator, informal social meetings to self-help groups.

(Sills 1992)

It should also be noted that the label 'counselling' is more acceptable to many people than anything which starts with 'psycho-', conjuring up as it can images of madness, illness, dysfunction and disorder. Whilst not entirely without a stigma factor, counselling has become far more integrated into popular culture either than it was, or than psychotherapy still is

(Clarkson and Carroll 1993). Even *London's Burning*, a television drama series about a London fire station (ITV 1992), promotes its usefulness in the modern fire service!

At the same time many people working as voluntary sector counsellors are also psychotherapists and maintain that in some circumstances the distinctions are decidedly blurred. When researching counselling in the field of HIV/AIDS in London, Andrew Henderson found the following:

> In London there are two AIDS hospices in the voluntary sector, the London Lighthouse and the Mildmay. Both employ specialist counselling teams and run a range of support groups, some of which are led by therapists. Individual counselling is mostly undertaken on the basis of time-limited contracts of a few weeks or months. However, the Lighthouse has a policy of offering some longer-term therapy. The distinction between counselling and psychotherapy is raised by AIDS in a particular form. Apart from the usual discussion amongst practitioners as to the length, intensity and depth of the work, those affected by HIV seem to fight shy of what they suspect to be the pathological implication of the psychotherapy label.
>
> This point is confirmed by other counselling/therapy services which employ some qualified psychotherapists. The Red Admiral Project is one such specialist AIDS contract-counselling service. The Terrence Higgins Trust and the Landmark Centre both offer short-term counselling. All these agencies focus on crisis counselling, while emphasising that the distinction between counselling and therapy is often hard to hold.
>
> This is especially true of the needs of partners, families and friends. Facing the life-threatening condition of a loved one will often bring to mind a previous death; the prejudice and stigma of AIDS may uncover related reactions, say, to an abortion and problems of inner rejection can emerge. An AIDS diagnosis for a child or a sibling may open up the need for family therapy.
>
> Most AIDS agencies recognise that in such instances HIV disease has been the occasion for wider therapeutic issues to emerge and will seek to refer on for generalist psychotherapy. Some agencies have their own list of private practitioners: others will use sympathetic independent and voluntary agencies. In London the Westminster Pastoral Foundation and metanoia have established links with AIDS agencies.
>
> (Henderson 1992)

He also gives a thumbnail outline of the specifics of the context in which this work has developed. In doing so he clearly illustrates both the resistance to being pathologised and the interplay between the political and the therapeutic in developing appropriate services.

The AIDS voluntary sector has developed with great speed since HIV disease emerged in the UK in the early 1980s. Perhaps because of the high level of public alarm in the face of the epidemic there seems to have been early agreement between statutory authorities and service users that community services would be most acceptably developed by the voluntary and self-help sectors. The Department of Health makes AIDS-specific grants to health and social services authorities; these authorities in turn commission a range of community services, including counselling, from voluntary organisations. So in London alone, where probably about half the UK incidence of HIV infection occurs, there are some 300 voluntary organisations and community groups. The next most significant centre of HIV disease in the UK is Edinburgh.

While current public concern in the UK tends to focus on the growing threat from HIV to the heterosexual population, the majority of those diagnosed with full AIDS continues to come from two other groups – gay men and intravenous drug users and their sexual partners. Because of the long period of latency in the body before HIV infection results in AIDS, this pattern is likely to continue for some time. The consequences for therapy and counselling support services are that the usual range of issues arising when young people face an incurable and life-threatening disease are inextricably bound up with the impact of social prejudice towards two marginalised groups.

Young people facing a life-threatening disease in a death-denying society also commonly have to contend with negative and hostile attitudes around drug use, homosexuality, sexual transmission of disease and irrational fears of contagion. The support and counselling services have focused on the crisis of an HIV/AIDS diagnosis for individuals, but from the start there has been recognition of the underlying issues outlined above, not only for those living with HIV, but also for their partners, friends and carers.

STD and specialist HIV clinics will normally undertake pre-HIV test and post-HIV test counselling, but will usually refer more long-term counselling and therapy needs to outside agencies. The same pattern is common in hospital in-patient units; crisis counselling is undertaken, but as hospital stays are typically short, longer-term support is sought from community agencies.

A further dimension of support services drawn upon by the specialist agencies are those set up to meet the needs of groups generally covered by 'equal opportunities' policies. Agencies for women, lesbian and gay people, black groups, addiction services and many others are developing AIDS awareness in their services, and particularly in the counselling dimension. For some people living with HIV, AIDS is not the most pressing issue in their lives and therapy if indicated may best be mediated through whatever organisation offers the individual most safety.

(Henderson 1992)

It would seem, then, that there is some psychotherapy taking place where the overt remit is a counselling one. There are also some voluntary sector agencies which incorporate some psychotherapeutic work in their brief, although this is still much more unusual. To give an example, Leeds Women's Counselling and Therapy Service advertised in January 1993 for a 'qualified analytical psychotherapist . . . [to head] the staff team of three psychotherapists and four counsellors . . . to provide a therapeutic service BY women FOR women in Leeds' (*Guardian* 1993a).

FINANCIAL CONSTRAINTS AND OPERATING MODELS

There can really be no doubt that (especially) one-to-one work over any sustained period of time is both expensive and often difficult to evaluate in concrete output terms, especially to the lay person. Voluntary sector funding is as precarious as it is varied. The holders of the public purse usually want tangible evidence, often in crude numerical terms, of services being provided, at what cost, to whom and with what outcome.

The context of financial insecurity in which most of the voluntary sector operates can militate against taking on long-term commitments. Funding is often on a yearly, renewable basis and this may deter the introduction of work which can require a long time.

Money is also an issue with respect to service users. Many who would seek the services of counselling or psychotherapy agencies do so because of their inability to pay in the private sector. The sector itself is largely resistant to the idea of charging commercial rates to individuals and, in many cases, to that of charging at all.

Inevitably, then, among the popular working models which keep costs down are those which involve the use of volunteers, often trainees. Hard money is then only required for administrative posts and volunteer supervision. The following is an extract from an interview with a counselling co-ordinator for a project whose counsellors are volunteers:

My role is for 15 hours per week as counselling co-ordinator for a voluntary mental health organisation. These 15 hours include administrative time. I manage a team of 10 counsellors. I do the assessment interviews of clients and then the referrals, matching them up with counsellors. I oversee/supervise the whole process. There are three groups of three counsellors, and I offer one person one-to-one supervision on a fortnightly basis. Five are training at metanoia. Of the other five, four are on courses such as Kingston Polytechnic, Windsor College and Hounslow.

On the team there are also a project co-ordinator for 28 hours per week who oversees the whole project, and a full-time Administrative Manager who works 28 hours per week.

The difference between the voluntary sector and the NHS is the high level of liaison with the many other professionals in the field in other organisations. For example, there are referrals from psychiatrists in the community, from probation officers (counselling is part of the probation requirement), and doctors. In the independent sector this level of liaison would be similar but in the voluntary sector it means that my colleagues are volunteering their time.

Our policy is that counsellors see a maximum of three and a minimum of two clients per week, with supervision in accordance with the BAC Code of Ethics which means one supervision to four hours of client contact. We ask for a minimum of two years' commitment to the Project, with three months' notice of leaving. There is a management committee, with one volunteer counsellor who represents the counselling team who is on the management committee.

We do not accept any volunteer without one year of counselling skills training of ongoing counselling skills to diploma level. Supervision is offered here but personal therapy is not a prerequisite. Supervision helps to clear up what is a therapy and what is a supervision issue.

(Moore 1992)

Other, less well-funded organisations which use volunteer practitioners pay for their external supervision. For trainees this can be an advantageous arrangement, involving them in no financial transactions at all while providing them with the clients and working environment they need in order to become qualified. This would seem to be a model equally well suited to psychotherapy trainees, although both for ethical and practical reasons the length of time committed may need to be longer and contractually more firm.

Some of the problems encountered by this model are: maintaining a slow turnover of the volunteers, quality control, and matching experience to presenting needs. The interviewee above elaborates:

We notice an increasing number of people coming for counselling who have psychiatric problems. I need to liaise with the psychiatric hospitals, but they like to keep their distance. We are inviting them to be more supportive and to liaise more closely. The volunteer counsellors are scared by the psychiatric cases who are close to suicide and very damaged. The clients have not learnt to take care of themselves psychologically and may be seen as high-risk.

(Moore 1992)

PSYCHOTHERAPY AS AN ORGANISATIONAL TOOL

Consultancy work within the voluntary sector has been a key growth area of the past five years and more. Organisational and personnel training, group or individual non-managerial supervision, crisis intervention, assertiveness training, facilitation of events, performance reviews and interpersonal skills training are some of the more common examples of consultancy bought by agencies with training and supervision budgets. The work can be one-off or ongoing.

Psychotherapeutic group skills are clearly among those most useful in this kind of work, especially since often the subtext to what is required is an external person to 'sort it all out' or mediate between people who are not communicating well. A skilled psychotherapist will be able to resist such invitations and effectively facilitate groups to take responsibility for performing these functions for themselves, even though the brief is not a psychotherapeutic one.

Some such consultancy work can be a useful addition to a private clinical caseload, requiring a different application of the same skills but in a setting, and with a contract, of a very different nature.

As a purchaser rather than a provider, I would emphasise the importance of contractual clarity as central to a useful outcome. It is also vital for working in this sector to have a good grounding in equal opportunity politics in order to facilitate people or groups to understand and resolve their own conflicts in a safe and contained way. It will be hard for a consultant to gain trust in this setting if they are not familiar with the history and development of equality critiques (see Reading list E below).

Similarly, a more positive outcome is likely if the facilitator is able to convert 'therapy language and style' into language and style in keeping with the working culture of the agency. 'How might you sabotage yourself' might draw a cynical snigger in some places when 'How might you fuck up?' will be immediately and powerfully understood (Lacey 1992).

So, because of the nature, scope and variety of work undertaken by the voluntary sector, it can be seen that there is a great potential for new collaborative initiatives between the sector and the psychotherapeutic world. Much is already happening. The key elements to be addressed for further successful development are funding packages, on the one hand, and a better popular definition (or public profile) of psychotherapy as a non-judgemental and empowering tool for the individual, on the other.

REFERENCES

Advice, Guidance and Counselling Lead Body (1992) Feasibility Study undertaken for the Department of Employment and produced February, pp. 22–6, London: AGCLB.

Clarkson, P. and Carroll, M. (1993) 'Counselling, psychotherapy, psychology and applied psychology: the same and different', in P. Clarkson, *On Psychotherapy*, London: Whurr (1993).

Guardian (1993a) Classified advertisements, 20 Jan., London and Manchester.

—— (1993b) Classified advertisements, 21 Jan., London and Manchester.

Henderson, A. (1992) Personal communication.
Lacey, F. (1992) Personal communication.
Mitchell, J. (1974) *Psychoanalysis and Feminism*, London: Allan Lane.
—— (1984) *Women: The Longest Revolution: Essays in Feminism, Literature and Psychoanalysis*, London: Virago.
Moore, J. (1992) Personal communication.
Sills, C. (1992) Personal communication.

FURTHER READING

List A: the origins of humanism and anti-psychiatry

Berne, E. (1968) *Games People Play*, Harmondsworth: Penguin (first published 1964).
—— (1969) *A Layman's Guide to Psychiatry and Psychoanalysis*, London: André Deutsch.
—— (1975) *What Do You Say After You Say Hello? The Psychology of Human Destiny*, London: Corgi (first published 1972).
Laing, R. D. (1969) *The Politics of the Family and Other Essays*, New York: Pantheon.
Maslow, A. H. (1962) *Towards a Psychology of Being*, Princeton, NJ: Van Nostrand.
Middleton, F. and Lloyd, S. (1992) *Charities – the New Law: The Charities Act, 1992*, Bristol: Jordons.
Perls, F. S. (1969) *In and Out the Garbage Pail*, New York: Bantam.
Perls, F. S., Hefferline, R. F. and Goodman, P. (1951) *Gestalt Therapy: Excitement and Growth in the Human Personality*, New York: Julian Press.
Rogers, C. R. (1980) *A Way of Being*, Boston: Houghton Mifflin.
—— (1980) *On Becoming a Person: A Therapist's View of Psychotherapy*, Boston: Houghton Mifflin (first published 1961).

List B: the history of the interface between psychoanalysis and sociopolitical thinking up to modern-day feminism

Althusser, L. (1964) 'Freud et Lacan', *La Nouvelle Critique* 162, 163, Paris: Larousse.
Ehrenreich, B. and English, D. (1979) *For Her Own Good: 150 Years of Experts' Advice to Women*, London: Pluto.
Eichenbaum, L. and Orbach, S. (1982) *Outside In, Inside Out: Women's Psychology – a Feminist Psychoanalytical Approach*, Harmondsworth: Penguin.
Foucault, M. (1967) *Madness and Civilisation: A History of Insanity in the Age of Reason*, London: Tavistock Publications (first published 1961).
Lacan, J. (1977) 'The Significance of the Phallus', pp. 281–91 in *Ecrits: A Selection* (A. Sheridan, trans.), New York: W. W. Norton (first published 1966).
Marcuse, H. (1969) *Eros and Civilisation*, London: Sphere (first published 1955).
Metcalf, A. and Humphries, M. (eds) (1985) *The Sexuality of Men*, London: Pluto.
Mitchell, J. (1974) *Psychoanalysis and Feminism*, London: Allan Lane.
—— (1984) *Women: The Longest Revolution: Essays in Feminism, Literature and Psychoanalysis*, London: Virago.
Showalter, E. (1987) *The Female Malady: Women, Madness and English Culture 1830–1980*, London: Virago.

List C: sociology resisting pathologising male violence/female victimisation

Dobash, R. E. and Dobash, R. P. (1979) *Violence against Wives: A Case against the Patriarchy*, New York: Free Press.
Dobash, R. E. and Dobash, R. P. (1992) *Women, Violence and Social Policy*, London: Routledge.

List D: contemporary useful texts for practitioners

Fernando, W. (1988) *Race and Culture in Psychiatry*, New York: Croom Helm.
Littlewood, R. and Lipsedge, M. (1982) *Aliens and Alienists: Ethnic Minorities and Psychiatry*, Harmondsworth: Penguin.
d'Ardenne, P. and Mahtani, A. (1989) *Transcultural Counselling in Action*, London: Sage.
Chaplin, J. (1988) *Feminist Counselling in Action*, London: Sage.

List E: 'starter kit' for understanding equality critiques

Barnes, C. (1991) *Disabled People in Britain and Discrimination*, London: Hurst (in association with the British Council of Organisations of Disabled People).
Cant, B. and Hemmings, S. (1988) *Radical Records: Thirty Years of Lesbian and Gay History*, London: Routledge.
Fryer, P. (1984) *Staying Power: The History of Black People in Britain*, London: Pluto Press.
Gay Left Collective Publications (eds) (1980) *Homosexuality: Power and Politics*, London: Allison & Busby.
Information Ireland (eds) (1985) *Nothing but the Same Old Story: The Roots of Anti-Irish Racism*, London: Information Ireland.
Moraga, C. (1981) *This Bridge Called My Back: Writings by Radical Women of Color*, New York: Persephone.
Rodney, W. (1972) *How Europe Underdeveloped Africa*, London: Bogle l'Ouverture Publications.

List F: bereavement

Bowlby, J. (1980) *Attachment and Loss: Loss, Sadness and Depression*, New York: Basic Books.
Murray-Parkes, C. (1986) *Bereavement: Studies of Grief in Adult Life* (2nd edn), London: Tavistock Methuen (hardback), and Pelican (paperback).
Murray-Parkes, C., Stevenson-Hinde, J. and Marris, P. (eds) (1991) *Attachment across the Life Cycle*, London: Routledge.
Pincus, L. (1974) *Death in the Family*, New York: Pantheon.
Worden, J. W. (1983) *Grief Counselling and Grief Therapy*, London: Tavistock (first published 1982).

ADDRESSES

National Association of Bereavement Services
68 Chalton Street
London NW1 1JR
Tel.: 071 247 0617

Feltham Open Door Project
The De Brome Building
77 Boundaries Road
Feltham TW13 5DT
Tel.: 081 844 0309

Chapter 20

Psychotherapy in private practice

Alexandra Fanning and Michael Pokorny, with additional material by Helena Hargaden

It is quite remarkable that, although in many respects psychotherapy is the same wherever it is practised, in other ways it is quite different in private practice from both the public Health Service and the voluntary sector. We shall focus primarily on these differences as they run right through the therapeutic process, from the beginning to termination. Whereas it is commonplace for there to be a definite end-point in an institutional setting, especially when the staff member moves to another job, in private practice our experience has been that the practitioner remains personally available to the former client in perpetuity. Even clients who return to their country of origin, or migrate, may expect to drop in when they visit the city of the psychotherapist. We imagine that, if we were to migrate, some of our former clients would visit us in our new location. Whether such visits are professional consultations or more in the nature of a social call will depend on the nature of the agreement at the time.

Most of the training of psychotherapists as well as most of the practice of psychotherapy takes place in the private sector. The increasing numbers of academic courses tend not to offer the clinical component that is so essential to becoming an independent practitioner. It is to be hoped that efforts now starting to bring together the private trainings and the university courses will be successful to the benefit of all the training enterprises. Training in psychotherapy has developed by groups of psychotherapists joining together to set up a clinic or a training course. The two endeavours always go together because of the need to provide clients for the trainees and to provide practitioners for the clinic clients, very often in the form of supervised trainees, who work for very low fees. In this way psychotherapy can be offered to those who could not afford to pay an economic fee. Thus a variety of training courses have sprung up, mostly in London, but now spreading all over the United Kingdom. These courses and their attendant clinics have all been staffed on a voluntary basis by practising psychotherapists, almost like the days when medicine was a private enterprise and it was usual for doctors to spend some of their time working in public hospitals run by charitable bodies. A very large segment of voluntary and low-fee psychotherapy activity has grown up inside the private sector and supports voluntary activity by private practitioners. Some of this has worked its way into the voluntary sector, where local authorities have funded specialist clinics run by psychotherapists at very low fees. Thus an important component of private practice is work in this voluntary and low-fee area.

All the committee work of actually managing the psychotherapy organisation's training and treatment is currently unpaid and usually takes place in the evening, or at weekends. It is very important to keep this feature of private practice in mind when considering all the other issues. Many people seem to believe that private practice normally excludes this area of voluntary work, which can nowadays seem so old-fashioned. We doubt whether there are many, or any, whole-time private psychotherapists who do not undertake a significant amount of voluntary professional work. It would be very interesting to conduct a survey to try to find out just how much unpaid and low-paid work is being done from private practice.

In addition to this, all the work involved in the organisation of psychotherapy as a profession is also done on a voluntary basis. Thus, psychotherapists who have to attend daytime meetings for any aspect of professional organisation, whether this is for their own organisation or for the United Kingdom Council for Psychotherapy, must juggle their commitments to their clients and at times forgo some fees.

Currently anyone with little or no training can set up in private practice in Britain. In the absence of any regulation, it is not possible to control the activities of unscrupulous practitioners. It is hoped that this will change with the introduction of the National Register of Psychotherapists, launched on 20 May 1993 by the United Kingdom Council for Psychotherapy. With regulations agreed amongst the seventy member organisations, UKCP will be able to monitor the ethical and professional conduct of its registered psychotherapists. It will also be possible to check the orientation and affiliations of any registered psychotherapist by looking them up in the register. For the first time a public document exists giving access to the range and kinds of psychotherapy available to the public.

Turning to the private practice component, we will discuss the special features of this by comparing private practice with institutional practice, whether that is in the voluntary or National Health sector. One of the main distinguishing features of private practice is its independence from medical, welfare and penal systems. With no established structures, there is neither a line manager nor organisational ethos. Private practitioners are essentially answerable to themselves, and any structures that exist must be self-created.

Thus we can start with the observation that access to the psychotherapist is much more direct and immediate in private practice than in a clinic setting. Clients can be referred direct to the psychotherapist of choice, or indeed can approach a psychotherapist themselves on the recommendation of a friend or relative. As reputable practitioners rarely advertise, that is not a usual route into psychotherapy. The advantage of direct access is that the client consults the chosen practitioner in person, and this is generally much faster than through a clinic. The most obvious disadvantage is that there is almost no way of checking the credentials of the psychotherapist. It is much easier to behave in an unethical manner in the privacy of a private consulting room, and it is much easier to practise with little or no training in a private consulting room. Whereas in a clinic the work is shared to some extent with a team, in private practice the psychotherapist works alone. There is no one to keep an eye on the health and welfare of the private practitioner. The National Register of the United Kingdom Council for Psychotherapy will make some improvement, but until there is a statutory register it may be impossible to control the activities of unscrupulous practitioners.

Psychotherapists will vary according to the type of training they have had. What follows is therefore a generalised account or outline of the common factors in private practice. It is not intended to be a definitive outline.

At the first consultation the limitation of single-handed practice means that there is a very clear limit to what can be offered to the client. One person can only offer their own capacity. It is very important that the needs of the client and not those of the psychotherapist are kept in mind at this stage. It can be hard to send a client to another practitioner or another kind of psychotherapy when one needs more work oneself.

In a clinic setting there is usually someone to answer the telephone and make an appointment. In private practice it is usually the psychotherapist who performs these tasks; some clients are very surprised by the directness of the access, and may find it rather disconcerting.

As well as ease of access, private practice offers a personal and more intimate setting than a clinic. Indeed, as many practitioners work at home, the personal aspect of the setting is very obvious. This may be experienced by the client either as cosy and warm, or as too personal and threatening. It can be felt to be intimidating to enter the home of the psychotherapist, especially if the client needs to be critical and demanding. Much more information about the psychotherapist is readily available than would be the case in a more formal setting of a hospital or clinic. The different perceptions of the available evidence are often more striking. It is a mistake to expect every client to see the same things or make the same deduction from what they see. The simplest example is that your taste in furnishings and wallpaper will, in the course of one day, be seen as wonderful and awful, with many shades in between. It is important to remember that what you are hearing is the counterpart to the phenomenon of the institutional transference. Whether you work with the transference or not, there will always be some degree of expectation of the institution in which you work, and whatever the client feels about the treatment will, to some extent, reflect their state of mind in relation to those institutional expectations. In the absence of an actual institution, those expectations will be attached to the premises and the person of the psychotherapist, in addition to the usual transference phenomena. This means that you have the advantage of carrying a greater burden of responsibility.

In addition, there is more of a problem of separating work from home life when both happen in the same premises. We think that psychotherapists who work at home develop routines to make this separation. In clinic or office practice the difference is made routinely by the journey between home and work, however short that journey may be. However, being in single-handed practice means that the clients invade the home life to some extent. The practitioner will have to decide about availability for telephone calls and for extra sessions. This takes skill in juggling personal needs for quality time with the knowledge that it might be appropriate and useful for some clients to have the opportunity for telephone contact and extra appointments. For others it might be important that the psychotherapist not be available outside the agreed session times. These boundaries have to be worked out by each practitioner; there is no automatic answer to the boundary problem. It is usual for some clients to telephone in the evenings and at the weekends – for example, to cancel or change appointments – sometimes leaving messages with various family members. This phenomenon is very unusual when working from an institutional setting. There are interesting variations in the capacity of the family to answer the phone appropriately and take clear messages, without giving away extra gratuitous information.

One of the important features of the additional responsibility of working alone is the provision of the holding function that an institution or clinic provides. In a sole private practice there is no automatic third party to give support or back-up in times of crisis, nor to provide cover when the psychotherapist is either ill or on holiday. Whereas it is quite usual to ask another private practitioner to be available for emergencies during holiday breaks or illness, it is very difficult actually to perform this function, because the emergency visit will be to new and unfamiliar surroundings just when the client is least able to cope with such strangeness. At least in a clinic, the place where the emergency consultation takes place is the same, even if the actual office used is different. The private practitioner can feel very alone when faced with an emergency, such as an attempted suicide, a sudden death or other crisis. This is all the more reason to pay attention in advance to the creation of a back-up system and a support network. A shared private practice often combines the best features of single-handed work with clinical or supportive back-up.

In the private setting the contract is at a much more personal level and continuity is as assured as it ever can be in reality. Even in private practice there is no guarantee of immortality. It is easy to see that the private practitioner must exert a sufficient degree of self-discipline in order to run an effective practice where both the clients and the psychotherapist will be looked after appropriately. It is important not to overwork nor to work unsocial hours, nor to agree to an arrangement that does not suit you, because of the needs that a client may have. Flexibility must have its limits as well as being informed by the needs of the practitioner. The isolation can be alleviated both by seeking the advice of colleagues, often known as supervision, as well as by the voluntary activities of helping in the training of others. Working in an organisation also improves the network available and helps to develop the practice.

The issue of personal safety is highlighted in private practice where the practitioner is often the only person on the premises with the client. It is therefore essential to be alert to the possibility of violence, and have some understanding of how to contain it. Often the first contact is by telephone, and from this brief contact the psychotherapist must make a decision on whether to offer the client an assessment session, or not. As well as relying on the personal 'sense' of whether this client is safe or not, it is possible to identify the referral source and check on the nature of the problem before agreeing to see the client. If there is any doubt, it is the responsibility of the psychotherapist to arrange that there is some back-up available, preferably by ensuring not only that someone else is on the premises, but also that they are aware of the possible risk.

Another element of the isolation of private practice lies in the question of contact with the client outside the psychotherapy sessions, and contact with relatives or friends of the client. There is no simple advice that will cover all these aspects.

In general, it is easier not to see or speak to friends or relatives of the client, even if the client gives permission. This is true for individual, marital or group therapy, which includes family therapy. The client group, of whatever size, should have sole right of access. However, that is not possible if you are treating a child or adolescent who is dependent on the parents, whether the parents are paying the fees or not. Equally, if you are the only psychotherapist in the town where you practise, you will have to see everybody, and cope with the problems that causes. If you practise a form of psychotherapy that requires the involvement of the spouse or partner or parent of the client, we would regard them as belonging to the client group. It may be difficult to resist the intrusion of other family members into the psychotherapy, but it is important for the psychotherapist to maintain the boundaries of the therapeutic enterprise at all times. Help from a colleague may be very welcome before responding to a request for an interview or telephone conversation. You are entitled to delay a decision by saying that you wish to think about a request. At least you will appear to be serious and thoughtful, even if the answer is disappointing.

Similarly, it is important to manage the boundaries of the treatment with regard to the possible intrusion of clients into the time of another client. Staying on after the session is over, arriving early and ringing the door-bell repeatedly, going to the lavatory after the session and spending ages so that the next session will be due to start with the previous client still in the house – all of these are ways of intruding. Any practising psychotherapist will be able to expand on this list. Of all the possible intrusions, one of the most important aspects for the client and the psychotherapist is the guarantee of safety from interruption across the external boundary. There is no simple answer to how to cope with these threats to the integrity of the space that you try to provide for your clients.

The private psychotherapist is thus responsible for all aspects of the setting and the treatment of the client. In return, the client pays the fees directly to the psychotherapist. Thus from setting up the consulting space to arranging money management, private practice covers an entire range of human work-related activities. Private psychotherapy practice is a one-person business, with all that that entails.

The first task in entering practice is to decide where you will practise and how you will arrange your consulting space. Remember that you hope to spend a lot of time in your consulting room and should therefore make sure that you are comfortable. As a simple matter of courtesy, a similar level of comfort should be provided for your clients. People vary enormously in the degree of personal or impersonal decoration that they think is appropriate to a psychotherapist's room. We think that we fall somewhere in the middle, having rooms that are far from clinical or institutional, but not containing personal memorabilia. The real problem is that the same artefacts can carry very different messages for different people. A shelf of books on fairy stories and books written in Hebrew may suggest wisdom and caring, or equally may give rise to feelings of alienation.

Having selected your consulting room and its furnishings, the question of how the clients will get in and out of the premises must be thought about. The most usual method seems to be the remotely activated door buzzer. The client presses a bell push which sounds a buzzer that is audible in the consulting room, and the psychotherapist presses a button which activates a buzzer on the door lock and allows the door to be pushed open. We think that this method is very intrusive to the client already in the consulting room. The alternative is, however, also difficult. If one answers the door-bell for each client, the clients have to arrange to ring the door-bell only at the appropriate time, as the door will not be answered during the session of another client. A different method that is more appropriate to office practice as opposed to domestic practice is to have a digital lock that the clients can operate for themselves. The client can enter and go to the waiting room in good time for the appointment. However, it may well be felt as threatening to have clients entering one's home unaccompanied.

The next question is how to start to have clients. Usually this begins during the training with the supervised clients that are an obligatory part of the training. The teachers and supervisors are generally only too glad to have another psychotherapist to whom they can refer clients once training has been completed. Although advertising to the public is considered unethical, advertising to one's professional colleagues is not. The simplest form is to circulate a notice that from a particular date one will be practising at a certain address. The inference is clear enough. Having started, it is very important to look after your sources of referral as well as your clients. Just as it matters to respond quickly to the client's request for help by making contact and fixing a date and time for a first interview, it is also important to let the referrer know what is happening – that you will see the client, that you have seen the client and what will happen next. It is helpful to inform the referrer at intervals, however briefly, about progress or lack of it. It is essential to give a brief report when the client's psychotherapy is over – first, to let the original referrer know what has become of their referral; secondly, to convey the fact that you now have a space in your timetable for another client.

However, if the client is a direct referral, some form of diagnostic or assessment interview will be needed. Whatever it is called, it will involve an assessment of the client's stage of psychological development, the severity and acuteness of the crisis and the actual or potential risk to the client or to others. If the decision is to offer psychotherapy, several criteria will have been satisfied; that a particular form of psychotherapy is the most appropriate treatment, that the client is capable of supporting it emotionally and financially, and that the practitioner will be able to carry through the psychotherapy for as long as required. The question of the inclination of the psychotherapist to work with a particular client, aside from the question of competence, raises complex difficulties. Not wanting to work with a particular client could be seen as unprofessional on the grounds that we should offer our skills equally to all who seek our help. On the other hand, to take on all comers, provided that they are suitable for our kind of psychotherapy, could be a form of omnipotent denial, a wish to be able to do anything and everything.

Continuing professional development is becoming a fashionable part of our vocabulary, partly in relation to the move to create a formal profession of psychotherapy. Under another guise it is something that most of us in private practice have been doing since we entered practice. It involves a number of activities which are designed to increase our knowledge and skills, both directly in helping our clients, and in adjacent areas of expertise. The training of a psychotherapist is never complete simply because it is only during the practitioner's day that new problems, or new versions of old problems, can emerge. It is at that point that the psychotherapist needs help with thinking about the problem. It is not possible to help anyone with a problem that they do not yet have. Unfortunately, it has become the habit amongst psychotherapists to call this process of seeking to enlarge one's range and depth of understanding by the rather inappropriate term 'supervision'. This term is easily misunderstood as belonging to student days, and is often queried by tax inspectors. In other professions it is recognised that any practitioner needs to seek the opinion of another practitioner about some cases – not necessarily difficult cases, nor must the help be sought from a more senior practitioner. Two heads are better than one. Seeking an opinion is normal in almost all walks of life. As all psychotherapists in private practice are being consulted, and therefore work as consultants, it is quite usual to consult another consultant for an opinion. As our clients are in long-term treatment with us, our seeking of another opinion has also to be relatively long-term. A one-off consultation has its usefulness and its limitations. In addition, it is vital to attend clinical and theoretical meetings in order to keep up with the thinking of one's professional colleagues, as well as to meet and chat with one's fellow professionals. It is good for the practitioner to be seen to be active so as to help referrers to keep a range of psychotherapists in mind during the consultation process.

Ending the psychotherapy of a client is as varied as human nature, and much has been written about it. Some clients end suddenly and without warning, some suddenly with some sort of warning. Most come to the natural end of the useful work and leave in an agreed way. When you know that you will have a vacancy at a certain date, you can let your usual referral sources know. It is important not to start a new client within six weeks of a holiday break, as it normally takes six weeks to settle in to a new place and a new routine. This is as true of job changing as of psychotherapy. You may want to arrange to see the client again after a set period or after some months. You are free to make any ethical arrangements that you think are needed for the welfare of the client. Follow-up is a good idea. It is, however, also important not to intrude into the life of the client once the psychotherapy is over. Some follow-up occurs by former clients writing or telephoning, or seeking an occasional session. Often such contact resolves into the sending of Christmas cards for a few years, or a letter during the early part of the New Year. We always respond to these contacts partly because of common courtesy and partly because we are glad to have news of former clients. But we keep our response to a brief and fairly formal level. The other sort of follow-up happens when one becomes involved with the training of psychotherapists and has the responsibility for the training psychotherapy. The former client becomes a colleague and the relationship changes. This can make it hard for the former client to seek further help if it should be needed. As the mind of the psychotherapist is the main tool of their trade, some further servicing may well be a good idea. As far as we know, a second personal psychotherapy is common amongst analytically trained psychotherapists, usually with a different psychotherapist from the training psychotherapist.

The vulnerability of the client is the key to a discussion of ethical practice. People seek psychotherapy because they are in psychological distress. Rogers (1951) describes the desire for psychotherapy as the wish to make the most and the best of life, instead of the least and the worst. Two extracts from Lapworth illustrate the goal of autonomy and the degree of vulnerability that precedes autonomy.

> I knew it was a process, or I knew it ought to be a process – something that I did for me with you, *not what you did to me*. And it seemed to be a process of working myself out, explaining myself to myself and sorting myself out. . . . I just knew I had to do something but I wasn't quite sure what. . . .
>
> There were a number of things about me and my situation that I wanted to sort out. I was very stuck. I was very unhappy. I was extremely frightened of everything – of the world, of other people, of change and I knew I couldn't go on being that way and so I wanted to do something to change those things.
>
> (1989: 3)

It is clear from these two extracts that the client exposes fears and vulnerability in a way that the psychotherapist does not. This power imbalance in the relationship is reflected through the process of transference and involves cultural, class, racial, economic and sexual elements; in short, all the ingredients that go towards making power relationships within the community of the world in which we all live. Professionally trained psychotherapists will subscribe to a code of ethics which will have as its focus the need to protect the client from any abuse, be this financial, moral or sexual. Accountability for this protection rests with the psychotherapist. These concerns are as relevant for the private practitioner as they are for the practitioner working in an institution of any kind. A structure conferring authority and guidance on the profession would be most welcome. It is hoped that this will be achieved by the Register of the UKCP.

A feature common to all types of psychotherapy practice, and indeed to all walks of life, is the pervasive intrusiveness of gossip. During the working day we all hear gossip about our fellow professionals. It can at times be too easy to believe what we are hearing as though it is anything other than gossip. Whereas good advice should always be passed on, gossip should be discarded as a sadistic attack on the entire profession. In order to facilitate this a courteous attitude should be maintained towards one another at all times. We are all struggling with the same problems, and may be making similar mistakes.

As private practice is a small business, it is essential to write about the money management aspect. Unhappily, that can only too easily be seen as mercenary. However, it is a nettle that must be grasped. It is striking that it receives very little attention at all either in the literature or in the training of psychotherapists. In spite of the fact that private practitioners earn their living from fees paid by clients, it seems to be thought wrong to be too interested in money and how to manage it.

There is a whole range of considerations that are applicable to all business enterprises and are not specific to psychotherapy in private practice. The practitioner will need to be aware of the pitfalls and opportunities of annual financial audit, tax returns, allowing for overheads and for renovations and repairs. The importance of keeping adequate records need not be stressed. It is also very important to be aware of being adequately insured against foreseeable misfortunes. Advice in these areas is easy to obtain if one is aware of the need to examine present and future monetary arrangements.

How much to charge for your work? There are two ways of approaching this question. What is the usual fee that your contemporaries charge (that is, the going rate)? It can be difficult to ascertain with any accuracy. We think that at present fees for psychoanalytic psychotherapy range from about £20 to about £50 per session. There are, of course, wide variations beyond these figures. Some low-cost schemes are much cheaper and some practitioners are much more expensive.

It is usually quite hard to find out how much your contemporaries are charging and there is no really established going rate. So we all have to struggle with the fact that the fee is a difficult matter for both the psychotherapist and the client. In a positive state of feeling a client may easily agree to a fee that turns out to be too high and has to be adjusted. In a negative state of mind a client may get the fee agreed at a level that turns out to be lower than usual and lower than could actually be afforded. That is difficult to adjust, and maybe even more difficult is the need to raise the fees during the course of a long psychotherapy. Without a set price there is always room for the psychotherapist to feel guilty about charging fees that, although realistic, can amount to quite a lot of money for the client. Equally, there is room for the client to feel guilty if the psychotherapist charges a fee that is obviously not enough. We have even heard of clients insisting on paying more when they felt that the psycho-therapist was under-charging. We know that money arouses very strong feelings in all of us. To set a fair price without the indignity of detailed means testing can be tricky. As the psychotherapist is both the beneficiary and the judge of fairness, there is plenty of room for discomfort. In addition, the client will often have some level of conflict between diverting finite resources to psychotherapy and protecting the needs of a family. This can also activate guilt in the psychotherapist, who may agree to a fee that is lower rather than higher, and may even be too mindful of the needs of the family of the client at the expense of the needs of the family of the psychotherapist.

All of these factors are going to have an influence on the psychotherapy, which will become clear in the transference-based psychotherapies. To feel able to take up the transference meanings of money and fees with the client can be a delicate but necessary matter. The relationship between the client and the psychotherapist can be intense and very personal. The client is dependent on the psychotherapist, who may come to represent parental figures. The introduction into the psychotherapeutic relationship of the unwelcome reality of the dependency of the psychotherapist on the fees paid by the client can be very intrusive for both parties. We think that this may induce some psychotherapists to avoid raising their fees after some time, and then to ignore the fact that the failure to re-assess fees after an interval can lead to a situation where the client is not able to discuss finances at all. Thus an important part of the transference may become hidden in an awkwardness about the reality of money and fees. Often clients are relieved if the fee is discussed from time to time. Equally often, a client may feel affronted that the size of the fee has been brought back into the sessions, even when a long time has elapsed since starting. All of these issues are much more pointed during periods of high inflation, when the real value of the fee can be eroded at an alarming rate if the psychotherapist does not take some appropriate action.

It is difficult yet essential to keep in view that what we are providing is an intense kind of emotional contact, within a setting where fees are charged. It can be felt to be a brutal reminder of the professional and fiscal nature of a very demanding and intimate experience to discuss the meaning of money or to touch upon the size of the fee in relation to the current session. We must always remember that psychotherapy is demanding of both the practitioner and the client. Thus a balance has to be achieved between the need to charge fees to earn a living, the need to provide a service that is therapeutic and the need not to let the outside world interfere too much in the psychotherapeutic enterprise. It has often been said that clients have to pay in order to benefit from psychotherapy. We have serious doubts about that. If it were true, no one would be helped by NHS, voluntary or reduced-fee psychotherapy. We know that is not true. It is possible that the idea of the client having to pay to benefit arose as a way of trying to cope with the guilt in the psychotherapist about having to charge fees of clients who are often in desperate need. If so, then it would illustrate some of the points that we have been trying to grapple with in relation to charging fees.

After many years of interesting practice, you can look forward to retirement with pleasurable anticipation, provided that you have planned carefully for it. Meantime, it is vital to plan for the unlikely event of sudden or early death which would leave your clients stranded. The usual measure is to have an agreement with a colleague who will have access to your records, see your clients and help them to come to terms with the death. The closer the colleague is, the more difficult will be the task. There is one very good article by Traynor and Clarkson (1992), but otherwise there seems to be very little written on this topic.

In conclusion, we would like to emphasise that private practice has been, and still is, an exciting challenge and a very worthwhile endeavour. The difficulties that we have outlined of being in sole charge of everything are compensated by the enormous relief of not having to accommodate colleagues or sit on endless committees. Private practitioners really can run their own working life according to their own wishes and needs. Of course, the service provided has to be excellent, but that is part of the fun of private practice. We can recommend private practice without reservation.

ACKNOWLEDGEMENTS

We are grateful for the advice that we have had from Dr R. D. Hinshelwood and Professor W. Dryden in writing this chapter.

REFERENCES

Lapworth, P. (1989) 'A customer's perspective', *ITA News* 24: 3–9.
Rogers, C. R. (1951) *Client-centred Therapy*, London: Constable.
Traynor, B. and Clarkson, P. (1992) 'What happens if a psychotherapist dies? The role of the psychotherapeutic executor', *Counselling* 3(1): 23–4, and *ITA News* (1992) 33: 20–1.

FURTHER READING

British Association for Counselling (1992) 'Code of ethics and practice for counsellors'/'Counselling skills'/'Trainers'/'Supervision of counsellors' (4 leaflets), Leicester: BAC.
International Transactional Analysis Association Training Standards Committee (1991) 'ITAA Statement of Ethics', Appendix 28, pp. 115–16 of *Training and Certification Manual for the Training and Certification Council of Transactional Analysts, Inc.*, San Francisco: ITAA.
Journal of the British Association for Counselling, 3(1).
—— 2(3).
metanoia Psychotherapy Training Institute (1990) *Code of Ethics and Professional Practice*, London: metanoia.
Turpin, M. (1991) 'Professional status', *ITA News* 30: 7.

Part V

Issues

Chapter 21

Psychotherapy and learning disability

Janet Bungener and Brendan McCormack

This chapter is primarily addressed to the psychotherapist contemplating individual work; however, some of what we say will also be relevant in the group setting. The chapter is in three main parts: context, treatment and themes. We begin with context, as this client group has a particular context, historically, culturally and within the family, out of which they have grown. Knowing something about this context can be of help clinically. We then move on to treatment. This section is to give general advice to the prospective psychotherapist and to consider communication with learning-disabled patients. In the third and final section we pick out particular themes and concepts that we have found useful and that commonly arise.

CONTEXT

The concept of learning disability

'Sticks and stones will break my bones, but names will never hurt me': this has never been less true than in relation to the names or words in the language used over the years to describe disability. No sooner has a new name been invented than it too becomes pejorative and there is pressure to change it (Sinason 1992). This naming gives a location to the disability, and giving it a location implies ownership on the one hand and disowner-ship on the other. Disability is more safely located in someone else rather than in oneself. There have been medical, psychiatric, psychological, social, educational and legal attempts at such definitions which have changed over the years. The obsession with definitions and classifications has served more to cloud understanding of the meaning of disability, and it is in this spirit that we would like to quote a pioneer in the field, Maud Mannoni, a French psychoanalyst, who said: 'But what in fact is feeble-mindedness? . . . Quite deliberately I have chosen not to know' (1973: 15). Disability is something which can only exist in relation to something else, or someone else, and therefore it is not only a problem for one person or another, but also a problem of discourse. In other words, the location of disability could be said to be between people rather than in people (McCormack 1991a).

Historical and cultural background

Looking back at the history of psychoanalysis and psychotherapy, it seems hard not to come to the conclusion that people with learning disability have never been considered easily for therapeutic treatment. In fact it could be said that, apart from the few pioneers, this patient group has been actively avoided and considered unsuitable for treatment. There have been other groups in the past who have been similarly considered unsuitable for treatment, such as the severely deprived and the borderline. These groups are now part of the general caseloads, as techniques have developed to meet their particular needs, in line with theoretical advances in the under-standing of early psychological development. The debate about treatment for people with learning disability has been around for almost as long as psychoanalysis itself. Yet, this group has still not been incorporated into the general psychotherapy caseload.

Social attitudes towards people with a mental disability must have had an impact on the way this group was considered in relation to psycho-therapy. The Eugenics Movement, which was a preoccupation in Northern Europe and America in the early part of this century, was arguing very strongly in favour of segregation of the mentally deficient. The Eugenicists' main fear was that the intelligence of the race would deteriorate if the mentally deficient were allowed to reproduce (Jones 1972). After the 1913 Mental Deficiency Act in England and Wales, colonies were developed where children and adults with learning disabilities were sent to live out the rest of their days. Similar colonies were built in most Northern European countries. They were later called hospitals, and aligned with the mental hospitals, or asylums for the insane. In Nazi Germany, the mentally deficient, along with Jews, gypsies, homosexuals and the mentally ill, were sent to the gas chamber. If society in general accepted that segregation was necessary, and that nothing more could be done about mental deficiency, it should not be surprising that psychotherapists, as part of that society, should feel somewhat similarly. However, there may be other reasons too. The unconscious fear of sexuality in relation to disability could lead psychotherapists to avoid this group of patients by rationalising that they are incapable of responding to treatment (Sinason 1988).

Psychodynamics of disability

We know that psychological trauma can cause actual specific learning difficulties in children, such as sexual abuse affecting reading. This is apart from general emotional disturbance, which may affect a child's ability to concentrate and perform at school. Some psychoanalytic theory can give us insights, or help us to consider, how learning disability might come about, and subsequently be maintained. Klein (1931) has suggested that the mother's body should be felt to be well and unharmed if the infant is to develop a desire for knowledge.

Bion (1962a) describes how the development of normal thinking may be disturbed to such an extent that in the place of normal thinking, projective identification occurs as an 'evacuating' process. This interferes with the ability to learn by experience.

Sinason (1986) has described how thinking can be attacked as a defence against the memory of trauma. Janet will be describing how the psychotherapist's thinking can be attacked and Brendan will describe thinking being attacked in psychotherapy as a defence against being thought about; (see 'Sustaining gain' (page 375) and 'Counter-transference' (page 379)).

The individual and the family

Social, cultural and religious beliefs all contribute to our desires and fears about procreation. The fantasies that people have about conceiving and producing children can have a significant impact on their subsequent relationship with the child, and how they view themselves. When presented with a damaged, handicapped or disabled child, the fantasy of the idealised child is shattered. The fantasy of the woman as the producer of perfect children, and the man's potency, is also shattered. Instead, they are replaced by images or beliefs that the disability has resulted from a curse, a sin of the forefathers or 'bad sex' that produced something damaged (Sinason 1988). This can result in much guilt and blaming. Thus, rather than being associated with a sense of hope for the future, the arrival of the child can be associated with the sense of a catastrophe, about which nothing can be done.

Bicknell (1983), in her classic paper 'The psychopathology of handicap' has emphasised the impact of the arrival of a handicapped child upon the family, and the subsequent problems which can arise as a result of a failure to resolve this crisis. She emphasises the importance of loss in disability, the loss which is experienced by both the individual, and by the family, not only at the time of birth, but at all subsequent developmental stages. This loss can also be re-experienced at critical periods in the family's life cycle. Primarily, the sense of loss is about the loss of intelligence, as well as the symbolic loss of the idealised intelligent child of the parent's fantasies. Bicknell describes the common reaction to the birth of the handicapped child as being similar to that of grief, or the bereavement process. Failure to resolve the grief surrounding these losses can result in a variety of problems, such as early rejection, seeking alternative diagnoses, chronic grief and late rejection. Critical periods for families occur not only around the time of birth or diagnosis of the disability, but also later on, as the child reaches, or does not reach, developmental milestones. In addition, the grief can re-surface when other siblings who are not disabled achieve developmental milestones such as going to school, going to university, getting married. A common crisis period for a family is when their child with a disability reaches young adulthood, or the age when young adults usually leave home.

Ageing parents are reminded of the fact that they have a dependent child, who, despite being a young adult, needs some degree of supervision and care for which they feel responsible, but feel increasingly less able to provide. The parents have difficulty letting go of the child when they can see, more than anybody, the vulnerability and other problems which their child has to face. On the other hand, the child, now an adult, may be feeling frustrated at being kept as a child and not allowed the independence of non-disabled peers.

The intense mother-and-baby relationship, which is normal in the neonatal and infant period, can persist for years when a child is disabled. This can continue right into adulthood, preventing normal separation and individuation. This situation can result in a cutting-off, or excluding, of the father (Thompson 1986). It is not uncommon in clinical practice to come across a family where the father has either left at an early stage in the family's life cycle, or absents himself in some other way, by working night shifts, for instance, or working long hours during the day. We are often quick to blame the father for opting out, but further exploration sometimes reveals that the father often feels left out and frustrated, and has difficulty finding a way into the intense mother-and-child relationship. This, of course, can match cultural expectations of male and female roles, the father typically saying: 'I leave all the decisions up to her, I just provide for them.' In one such family, the father had saved £1 million for his disabled son to inherit, and meanwhile the mother was saying that father was never around and she needed more support. These problems are compounded by the way the expression of affection is made difficult for men in this culture.

Disability, death and sexuality

'The mother–child relationship in such cases [disability], will always have an aftertaste of death about it: of death denied, of death disguised, usually as sublime love, sometimes of pathological indifference, and occasionally, as conscious rejection; but the idea of murder is there even if the mother is not always conscious of it' (Mannoni 1973: 4). The result of the death wish, or the unconscious desire of the parents that the disabled child had not been born, or had died early, leaves some disabled people with a very strong sense of being an outsider, of not belonging. At worst, they may feel that they should not exist. However, if we see the death wish as a prominent issue in development, then so too is the wish for life. The wish for life must be enormous in some who have survived against all the odds.

One aspect of life for people with a disability is the extent to which they have to form, and then break, relationships with significant others. In some cases this can stretch right back to infancy, particularly for people who were in care as children. A considerable number of doctors, social workers, residential social workers, physiotherapists, occupational therapists, key-workers of various sorts and various centres may have become involved for varying lengths of time. This can make the adult with a disability wary of forming yet another significant relationship, or so-called significant relationship on offer in the form of psychotherapy.

The links between disability, death, sexuality and independence have been described by Hollins and Evered (1990). Sexuality has been a major taboo area for disabled people and the emergence of secondary sexual characteristics in adolescence, and the desire for sexual relationships in later adolescence and young adulthood, can result in considerable conflict within the family, and also within the individual.

It should be noted that a history of sexual abuse is commonly encountered in people with a learning disability who are referred for psychotherapy (McCormack 1991b). It is also increasingly recognised that the problem is widespread amongst people with learning disabilities. Children with disabilities are over-represented in groups of children who have been sexually abused. Perhaps a combination of factors contribute to this: the self-image of being damaged as a result of 'bad sex'; dependency and vulnerability exciting hostility in the abuser; poor knowledge about sex and sexuality due to lack of education; poor self-esteem, poor communication skills and a lack of an ability to protect oneself.

TREATMENT

Communication and language

Learning-disabled people have rarely been considered for psychotherapeutic treatment and, though this is changing, some common concerns still arise about undertaking such work. An immediate concern many people have is about understanding and being understood when there is a recognisable difference in IQ and verbal ability between patient and psychotherapist.

On encountering her first learning-disabled patient, a psychotherapist was faced in the early sessions with a leaden silence. She strained to think at all. There was a sense of pressure building up. She had a thought, a gaping hole, then a thought again. 'How are she and I to connect? Can I make sense to her? Can she make sense to me? How capable is she? Is there anything there? Is my treatment going to transform her? Are we going to feel very different from each other? Are we worlds apart? Oh God, is there just going to be this dumb emptiness?' Of course that was not all there was, and the meaning in the silence and concern was slowly understood by the psychotherapist and the patient. In revealing to the psychotherapist her most handicapped self, the patient showed her anxiety that she was going to be a disappointment and an unwanted burden to the psychotherapist. Although this psychotherapist has since discovered that she and the patient can understand each other, the issue about language and understanding commonly arises both prior to and at the onset of treatment.

Communication happens on more than one level. We know this from everyday experience when we look at the expression on a person's face, or listen to the tone of their voice, or even to the quality of someone's silence to discern their mood, or meaning, or state of mind. Developmental psychologists such as Stern, Bruner, Brazelton and Trevarthen have researched and described communication processes that we use unawares by studying in minute detail the patterns of interaction between infants and children and their carers (Stern 1974; Bruner 1968; Brazelton *et al.* 1974; Trevarthen and Hubley 1978). Although these forms of social experience first arise in the very early periods of our lives, they remain intact within us and between us throughout life with the potential for development. We are most aware of what goes on in the verbal domain, but we continue to relate in other domains. As psychotherapists, we can become more aware and attuned to those other domains through supervision, training, personal psychotherapy and the findings of developmental psychologists.

These different levels and forms of communication, as described by the psychologists, dovetail with the concept of 'emotional intelligence', where a person can be emotionally aware and knowledgeable despite major deficits in cognitive intelligence (Sinason 1992: 74). An encouraging common finding regarding language is that expressive abilities often increase and become more coherent in psychotherapy as the patient has an ongoing experience of the psychotherapist trying to make sense of their communications, be they verbal or non-verbal.

Another important contribution that the developmental psychologists can offer to us in this work is the growing body of understanding about the interpersonal nature of the growth of a person's mind and sense of self. Again these findings are emerging from detailed mother–infant studies and represent a move away from a simple one-person psychology to a two-person psychology which can be of relevance to the two-person situation of psychotherapy. For example, when faced with the fragility and inertness of Shona, a severely developmentally delayed four-year-old with autistic features, Janet found herself responding as a mother would to an infant a few weeks old. With the idea that Shona needed help in sustaining a sense of purpose and a sense of herself as continuous, Janet began to describe very little things Shona did in an ongoing way, speaking as perhaps Shona would have spoken herself, had she the capacity to do so.

Shona came in, sat down and looked up at Janet, smiling with an open look. Janet did the speaking. 'Hello, Mrs Bungener. Nice to see you.' Shona went to the locker and picked something out. 'I've got Plasticine.' She handed Janet some: 'Here, Mrs Bungener, I want you to have some too.' Then every tiny thing she managed to do, Janet described. 'I'm squeezing it. I can press it. Put it down, now. What can I do with it? I can put my finger in it, my nail in it, I can make a mark.'

This type of describing is like the process of 'amplifying', identified by Brazelton as a function that mothers perform for the early infant:

> Most mothers, in sum, are unwilling to deal with neonatal behaviours as though they are meaningless or unintentional. Instead, they endow the smallest movements with highly personal meaning and react to them effectively. They insist on joining and enlarging on even the least possible interactive behaviours, through imitation. And they perform as if highly significant interaction has taken place when there has been no action at all.
>
> (Brazelton *et al*. 1974: 68)

It is also like acting as the child's self-awareness, like an auxiliary ego or like a mother processing the infant's experience through alpha-function as described by the psychoanalyst Bion (1962a, 1962b). At this stage, what was important was for Shona to know that she was actually moving herself and another object and that she was capable of shaping and making an impression on the Plasticine. Ultimately, after many repetitions of similar experiences, she will be abstracting from these experiences a belief that she can shape and make an impression on life and others, including Janet.

The concern about language and intelligence is also a concern about difference. Whenever a group in society is identified as being different, it generates a concern about whether there can be a shared reality. Historically and currently, differences between people have often led to wars, injustice and exclusion. When we first meet someone, we use different types of identification as part of the process of trying to find links. One of the most immediate types of identification we use is adhesive identification; we relate to the surface qualities of a person in a two-dimensional way (Bick 1968; Bungener 1992). If the surface is very different from the surface we are used to – for example, sound of the voice, colour of the skin, shape of the body – the links or coherence we are looking for feel less within reach. We cannot avoid this level of identifying, we all make use of it and build our stereotypes from it. We also cannot avoid being faced with difference when we meet a mentally handicapped person.

Therapeutically, we can be aware of and address the issue of difference and the two-dimensional reactions we and others have to it. We can also make use of identificatory processes of a three-dimensional nature to assist in the search for the individual and not the stereotype. Later we shall describe how mentally handicapped persons themselves can make defensive use of stereotyping.

Suitability

As there are very few psychotherapists working or specialising in this field, there is, as yet, a lack of research about suitability. The best way to address this question is not so much in relation to the prospective client or patient, but in relation to the psychotherapist and what the psychotherapist can bear.

Sinason (1986, 1988, 1992) has shown that patients with severe or profound disabilities can be seen, and make use of psychoanalytic psychotherapy. It is important to remember that the process of psychotherapy is not just about speaking. Apart from this, we recommend that therapists exercise the usual caution where psychosis may be present, or where there may be risk of violence or suicide.

Technique

The best technique is the one with which the psychotherapist, through their training, feels most comfortable. As the psychotherapist gets to know the patient better, it may be that a particular emphasis or adaptation to the basic technique would be helpful. We indicate – see 'Communication and language' (page 369) and 'Counter-transference' (page 379) – where we have found some adaptation helpful such as the emphasis on the counter-transference with non-verbal patients and also, if comfortable for both psychotherapist and adult patient, providing them with materials or toys. Children of course would naturally be provided with such materials: we refer the reader to the chapters on psychotherapy with children for further details.

Boundaries

Many people with learning disabilities have grown up in an atmosphere of poor boundary keeping, where personal privacy is at a minimum. This means that the privacy normally associated with psychotherapy may be difficult to appreciate, both for client and psychotherapist. There is often pressure from carers on the normal confidentiality one would expect. This can stem from carer anxiety and a need to know.

The role of the carer in treatment

The dependency associated with disability means that many are dependent on carers to make practical arrangements for psychotherapy. This dependency affords an opportunity for carers to interfere, consciously or unconsciously, in the process. It is not uncommon, particularly in the early days, for carers to make alternative arrangements, such as a day trip for the client, so that they are unable to attend the psychotherapy. Many people working in learning disability services are working in highly stressful situations on low salaries. It should not be surprising that the luxury of individual psychotherapy should be envied. It is often helpful to acknowledge this, and to suggest ways that they might address their own needs.

It may be helpful to meet carers occasionally in order to deal with possible boundary problems, sabotage or envy. Such meetings should be carefully thought through, and discussed with the patient. Confidentiality need not be breached in such meetings, but they may be helpful in protecting the psychotherapeutic space, and in promoting understanding.

Timing

The question may be asked: how will someone with a poor appreciation of time be able to understand the regular nature of the psychotherapy, and the time of the session itself? Virtually all of us working in this field have found that a sense of time improves with ongoing psychotherapy. Sometimes it is useful to give a card to the patient, with boxes representing each planned session, and these can be shaded in, or ticked off, as the psychotherapy unfolds. This may also help in planning for termination or ending. Termination in the psychotherapy is likely to re-activate issues of abandonment, the struggle for existence and despair. Termination should be well planned to allow for working through some of these issues. Therapeutic despair, which may result from a sense of stuckness or an inability to think, may make the psychotherapist consider terminating the psychotherapy early. If this despair is encountered in the assessment stage, and not understood, it may result in psychotherapy not being offered in the first place.

Supervision

Psychotherapy is not generally available in learning disability services, and very few generic psychotherapy services are willing to take on such cases. This means that adequate supervision can be hard to come by. We would like to re-emphasise its importance and warn against taking on psychotherapy without adequate supervision. We would recommend that, in the first instance, those interested should approach local generic psychotherapy services.

THEMES

The concept of secondary handicap

One of the most important concepts of psychotherapeutic work with the learning disabled is that of secondary handicap. The handicap the psychotherapist meets is not necessarily a fixed, immovable mass. Although there may well be some primary organic damage that cannot be changed, there is the potential to move in and out of stupid states of mind caused by secondary handicapping processes. Although such fluidity in disability makes for uncertainty, it also allows scope for therapeutic change.

A secondary handicap may come after the original handicap as an exaggeration and extension of it. It may come as a newly created handicap, perhaps brought into existence as a defence against trauma and abuse. Often the secondary handicap pervades the personality to such an extent that initially, and perhaps for a long time, there is little possibility of identifying the patient's real potential. In our experience, one of the most interesting and challenging aspects of psychotherapeutic work in this field is the exploration with the patient of secondary handicapping processes. What can then be allowed to emerge is a more intelligent patient. A learning-disabled woman, for instance, managed to stay wheelchair-bound for ten years before revealing that she could walk. Undermining one's abilities or handicapping oneself is, of course, not the sole province of the disabled: our capacity to use our intelligence can vary enormously even without the burden of a disability. Days in which we perform at our best are rare for most of us, and we often do things that we regard as being stupid or forgetful.

We have found Sinason's distinction between three types of secondary handicap very useful (1992). The first is called 'mild secondary handicap', where a person with an already existing handicap exaggerates that handicap to make themselves as inoffensive and easygoing as possible. Its most distinctive feature is the handicapped smile: 'some handicapped people behave like smiling pets for fear of offending those they are dependent on' (1992: 21). It can form the so-called friendly, happy demeanour of handicapped people; their uniform, disguising underlying sadness and insecurity. In conjunction with the handicapped smile, jokey, cheery atmospheres are often created by others around handicapped people in an unconscious attempt to defend against the feelings such handicaps arouse.

The second is called 'opportunist handicap' because severe psychological disturbance in the personality takes the opportunity to use the handicap as an outlet and a home: 'The handicap can become a magnet for every emotional difficulty and disturbance the individual has. In this difficult constellation we regularly find envy of normality, hatred for parental sexuality that created them and refusal to mourn or acknowledge the loss of the healthy self' (Sinason and Stokes, 1992: 56).

An example given is where a handicapped young man waiting at a bus stop would consistently only stick out a finger to indicate his wish for the bus. As a result of course, the bus driver drove past, unable to see such a small indication. The young man could therefore continue to blame the bus driver and the world for failing to acknowledge him and meet his requests. What he was unwilling to face was his own contribution to his unmet needs and psychological immobility.

The third handicapping process is where handicap is used as a defence against the memory and knowledge of trauma and abuse. Many cases have now been treated where 'going stupid' and cutting off one's thinking are a direct result of, or greatly exacerbated by, trauma and abuse that have gone on unrecognised. With the recovery of the knowledge and memory of the sexually intrusive or violent experiences comes the retrieval of intelligence. A vivid clinical description of such a recovery is in Sinason's narrative of her treatment of eight-year-old Ali (1992: 136–77).

Sustaining gain

Ali, like many others who have suffered environmental deprivation or abuse in an extensive way, may find it very difficult to sustain the recovered intelligence in the world outside of psychotherapy if the weight of the disability, an inadequate environment and continued effects of trauma overburden an already depleted ego. When some patients come to acknowledge that they are more capable than people realise, they may also painfully feel that, outside of psychotherapy, both internal and external pressures will inevitably push them backwards into their blunted, but familiar, ways of being.

In addition to carrying their own concerns about their ability, the fears of others about stupidity and failure are often heavily projected into learning-disabled people. A competitive society like ours that places considerable value upon intelligence can use an identifiable intellectually disabled group as a repository for unwanted aspects of itself. Disability and ability in this sense are relational and fluid. The vested interest in locating all the inability in one group happens by a process of stereotyping and projection rather than struggling to own and understand the disabilities and abilities within each of us. When the projections are ongoing through-out life, the experience of damage, slowness and stuckness can take a strong hold over the personality.

The re-activating of thought processes that takes place in psychotherapy can be extremely painful. Mark was a thirty-five-year-old patient with a 'mild' learning disability. Five months on in the treatment, after a long silence in the session, he reported that his speech had been 'going funny' at work, by which he meant that he had been talking fast again and people had been finding it difficult to understand him. This had come up already in the sessions and had been discussed as one of the reasons he was regarded as handicapped or stupid. He said he had been getting feelings of anger. He was just trying to get back to his old self. The psychotherapist said it seemed as if Mark had had these kind of difficulties all his life, and he said yes, his parents never listened to him and his brother and sister never listened to him, and then he said: 'If somebody sits and listens it opens the claw in my head. It's one side of the claw says everybody is going to believe you, otherwise not at all. It's like a claw and each time I come here it goes in deeper.'

The psychotherapist felt at first as though he were being attacked for not listening to Mark. We can see, however, that the real pain was in being listened to, which is also to be thought about. Over the two years of this therapeutic relationship, much of what they thought about was indeed very painful. Thinking and memory can lead to a knowledge of trauma that is unbearable. In some cases it may not be possible to continue with the psychotherapy and the patient stops coming.

For patients fortunate enough to have good family, community or vocational support, sustaining the gains is more possible. One mother of a learning-disabled young woman noticed a subtle but important change between herself and her daughter during the daughter's third year of psychotherapy. When the daughter had returned from an outing one evening, the mother suddenly realised that she had not known exactly where her daughter had been. She was shocked, because for as long as she could remember she had acted as an auxiliary brain for her daughter, holding all information about her life, based on the belief and experience that her daughter was incapable of doing so herself. This mother had not known where her daughter was going because her daughter now knew that she had a mind of her own which could hold information, and a mother who could bear and support such separation and growth.

Fluctuations in capacity also occur within the treatment itself. In many session, patients will show an in-and-out or back-and-forth movement, in terms of being in touch with their intelligence. The job of the psychotherapist is then to work at the interface between emotional and cognitive development: the psychotherapist explores the feelings that are around as well as what happens to intelligence in the face of those feelings. It may be difficult, however, for the psychotherapist to recognise and work with the defensive loss of intelligence and to sustain a belief in more intelligence being there. At points when the patient has succumbed to 'going stupid', the psychotherapist can likewise experience in their counter-transference a thickness in their own brain and a belief that very little intelligence exists in the patient. (This experience of damage and stuckness will be discussed in more detail in the section on counter-transference.) In psychotherapeutic work, we have found that in the face of mental stuckness the psychotherapist has first of all to take into themselves the catastrophic feeling of stupidity, which means bearing a total thickness in their own brain. They need to stay with this appalling experience for some moments until they realise that it is a feeling they are dealing with rather than a fact. They then know that they have material they are equipped to work with: the treatable rather than the untreatable. It is a process of containing and transforming catastrophic feelings as described by Bion (1962a: 93–119).

Transference

There are particular, commonly occurring types of transference that arise in the work with the learning-disabled, but they are expressed in ways that are highly individual. Today transference is generally understood as being 'everything that the patient brings into the relationship. What he brings in can best be gauged by our focusing our attention on what is going on within the relationship, how he is using the analyst, alongside and beyond what he is saying' (Joseph 1988: 62).

Mannoni (1973) has described a particular type of relationship that is easily set into motion with the learning-disabled. The patient can see the psychotherapist as somebody they must try to fit in with. Through a fear of being rejected for a perceived lack in ability, the learning-disabled person seldom opposes other people and tries if they can to mould themselves to the desires of others. What can result is a neutralised patient, and a dependent relationship where everything is kept nice even though the cost is the loss of self-determination. It can feel far safer to fit in when what you represent to others is unwanted difference and damage.

Another aspect of this transference of dependency onto the psycho-therapist is not only the handing over of all self-determination, but also of the act of thinking itself. In one particular session where a patient called Dana is asked for her ideas, Dana is silent and eventually tells the psychotherapist that she has no idea, and giving the impression of complete emptiness, gazes up into the eyes of the psychotherapist, quite content. The psychotherapist comments on how Dana is looking to her for an idea. Again Dana agrees. She is passively handing over to the psychotherapist all the ability in a parasitic way and is quite prepared to inhabit the psychotherapist's mind. In situations like this there is a tremendous pull to take the easy way out; to be educative and supply the answer. Instead, the psychotherapist says to Dana that Dana finds it hard to believe that if she just looked in her own mind she might find an idea. There is a pause and Dana comes forth with her own idea. When the psychotherapist can believe in the patient's capacity to think, the patient can have some belief in herself and her ability returns. This dependency in the relationship can be a major dynamic in the maintenance of stupidity in the learning-disabled.

Envy can also often appear in the transference, though in a rather disguised form. The patient may unconsciously hand over their ability, but at the same time they can feel envious of the psychotherapist's capacities and will find ways of attacking those capacities, particularly in the form of rather 'silly' types of question. The patient described above, who was characteristically passive, at the same time began almost every session for over two years with the question, 'Aren't you speaking?', well aware of the tone of stupidity and ridicule in her voice. It was always said as the psychotherapist had just sat down, allowing no time for thoughts to develop and thus was simultaneously attacking and mocking of the psychotherapist's capacity to think and speak. It was not the patient who was to be the stupid, silent baby who could not converse with ease and intelligence, but the psychotherapist.

Lack of independence in their lives may lead learning-disabled patients to transfer into the therapeutic relationship their paranoid feelings about confidentiality. Although initially they may appear very accepting of arrangements, their actual feelings may be quite different. They may bring into the relationship an expectation of their privacy and views being disregarded.

A further regularly occurring feature that learning-disabled people bring into their relationship with a psychotherapist is the expectation of abandonment or being unwanted. This is linked with the transference of dependency already described. Before and after holidays, cancellations, absences due to illness, in fact at any breaks in the treatment, fears about abandonment are generally to be found in some form. Because handicap and disability are basically unwanted in our competitive society, those born with a disability are aware that they often represent a burden or something which has gone wrong. They are also aware that, had it been possible to detect the defect *in utero*, it is unlikely that they would have been born. With the increasing sophistication of scanning procedures and genetic research, detection of even minor abnormality is becoming possible and abortion an option that is taken for granted. Around breaks in the relationship with the learning-disabled patient, the expectation that arises is that the psychotherapist must have become tired of the burdensome patient, unable to stand them any longer. On returning from a summer holiday break, a psychotherapist found herself thinking of the treatment and relationship as monotonous and dull; very little was expressed and there seemed to be no new ideas around. After several sessions like this, the psychotherapist had a feeling that seemed unacceptable and surprising:

she did not feel pleased to be seeing her patient again. It was possible to understand the sense of boredom and displeasure in the treatment, as the patient bringing into the relationship the expectation that the psychotherapist prior to the holiday was glad to see her disabled patient go and was not pleased at seeing her back again. Once this transference was understood and recognised between the patient and psychotherapist, more alive and interested feelings and material followed.

For patients who have been abused, their experience of breaks in the treatment can have an added distressing element. Around separations, it is common for these patients to transfer the experience of abuse onto the relationship. The psychotherapist will often hear of abusive incidents in the present as well as the past, prior to or following a holiday or absence. Being left reminds the patient of the lack of protection they felt at the time of the abuse, and this can become synonymous with being abused. It is very painful to be seen as abusive and abandoning at the time of separations, but it is clinically very useful.

Counter-transference

Simply put, counter-transference could be said to be the psychotherapist's emotional response to the patient. As a concept, it has undergone considerable change since Freud. The feelings aroused in the psychotherapist used to be thought of as an impediment to the work and only indicative of the psychotherapist's psychopathology or blind spots. Today, the counter-transference is considered to be an important indicator of the patient's state of mind. It involves a process of self-analysis and struggle, where psychotherapists try to work through and discern what their thoughts and feelings are telling them about the internal world of the patient (see Brenman-Pick 1988: 34–47).

Making use of the counter-transference can be particularly important with patients whose verbal capacities are limited or non-existent, or where they fluctuate. In fact, it is one of the main therapeutic tools which makes psychotherapy possible with the non-speaking, profoundly handicapped person. The other tools are the use of materials such as toys, drawing and modelling aids, and being alert to non-verbal communications such as facial expressions, body movements, breathing, state of alertness and so on. Janet has already described working with Shona, a severely delayed young child and, for a moving and detailed description of a treatment of a profoundly handicapped, non-speaking patient, see Sinason's description of her work with Maureen (1992: 221–55).

Sinason (1992) writes of the need to work far more intensively with counter-transference feelings with non-verbal patients but also of the need to monitor carefully the patient's responses to interpretations or comments based upon counter-transference impressions. She warns, 'Sometimes, a patient can provide a nod which might be compliant rather than a sign of real agreement' (p. 251). When unsure of her impressions, she phrases her comments to take account of this uncertainty and to give the patients a sense of their right to assess for themselves whether her perception feels correct or not. It is also re-emphasised that to use one's emotional responses to patients with increasing depth and effectiveness requires supervision, personal analysis and training.

One of the most common counter-transference feelings is the experience of drowsiness or an inability to stay alert and thinking. At these times, it is helpful in the first instance simply to try to register the fact that drowsiness or heaviness is the feeling that one is experiencing because the effect of such a counter-transference is that thinking, even of the most rudimentary kind like recognising a feeling, becomes very difficult to activate. Registering the feeling is the beginning of digesting and processing the feeling in order to identify which aspects have arisen from the state of mind of the patient and why. With one moderately handicapped patient with IQ 51, a state of thickness and heaviness that arose in the psychotherapist was an important indicator that something unbearable was being experienced by the patient leading to an attack on the patient's and the psychotherapist's capacity to think. In this particular session, the patient had learned that the psychotherapist was having to cancel the next week's session. Initially the patient was able to allow herself to be in touch with the shock of the cancellation. She was able to let a difficult question develop – why was the psychotherapist not seeing her? – and she acknowledged a negative feeling that she was fed up about it. But when the psychotherapist tried to allow the negative feeling some development by saying, 'Fed up and angry with me', the patient responded flatly with 'I don't mind'. The psychotherapist then inquired, 'Now you say you don't mind?' The patient, with her eyes deadened, replied, 'Never mind.' The psychotherapist queried, 'But first you did feel fed up with me?' The patient replied, 'No I didn't, I don't mind.'

This patient had rid herself of her mind. She attacked and obliterated her intelligence in the face of a painful situation: she feared that the psychotherapist did not want to see her. However, that was not the way the psychotherapist experienced it. The psychotherapist felt as if her brain had gone into a state of seizure, it was thick and numb, and her thought was: the patient is handicapped. She knew that, from listening to what had been said, it was possible to recognise defensiveness and denial, but so powerful was the obliteration of this patient's mind that the psychotherapist believed herself to be in the presence of permanent, untreatable damage. The psychotherapist's anxiety was that if she stopped to think about it, she would get stuck in a shapeless, thick, timeless substance – a quagmire. Her urge was to forget it, to leave it behind, to keep moving. The psychotherapist struggled to stay with the feeling and process it and finally managed to resist the urge to give up and escape. The psychotherapist said, 'I think you have got rid now of that part of your mind that knew you were angry.' She made a rubbing-out movement to demonstrate. The patient, looking alert, replied, 'Like a rubber with a mistake.' With the registering and processing of the mind-numbing counter-transference, the psychotherapist retrieved her capacity to think and enabled the patient to do likewise.

The second commonly occurring counter-transference is most often found in a trio of feelings. Contempt, guilt and pity all come together to create an important set of feelings which can be difficult to detect. This arises from the situation of difference between the psychotherapist and patient, apparent as well as real: to have a nice new hairstyle, an attractive jumper, legs to walk with, to be a wife or husband, mother or father, to have a job, to be travelling independently – any attribute that the psycho-therapist appears to have or have more of than the patient – can produce feelings of guilt. This guilt can be greatly exacerbated by an underlying feeling of contempt that exists unrecognised. The psychoanalyst Neville Symington writes of being confronted in the Tavistock Mental Handicap Workshop by the shocking knowledge of previously unrecognised con-tempt that he and other colleagues felt towards learning-disabled people (1992). On a conscious level they had only been aware of their sympathy and goodwill towards this group, but when they began to examine the detail of their practice, it emerged that in many small procedures, contempt towards the learning-disabled was lurking unawares. For example, they would accompany such a patient to the room and not do so with 'normal' patients. When they tested out whether this was based on a real perception of need or patronising care, they discovered that all their patients could make it to the room in the normal fashion; that is, by themselves. Other colleagues were brave enough to bring forth other examples such as not bothering to dress as carefully or to be as punctual for learning-disabled patients, on the unexamined assumption that they would not notice or would not mind. A further attitude which conceals this contempt is revealed in making all sorts of allowances for learning-disabled people that we would not do for 'normal' clients, letting them off being accountable or responsible for their behaviour.

Guilt is paralysing and unproductive and results in no change, no development. Symington's thesis is that the handicapped person them-selves tries to induce this cycle of contempt and guilt in the psycho-therapist, aided by the psychotherapist's intolerance of their own areas of disability. Omnipotently, the client believes themselves to be unwanted, and sets about to prove this to be the case; omnipotently, the psycho-therapist believes that the only handicap in the room is in the client; both views seek to maintain the status quo. What is being defended against on both sides is developmental change, as it entails the working through of considerable psychic pain for the client, the retrieval and integration of disabled aspects in the psychotherapist, and a stepping into the unknown for both. Symington writes, 'We do not desire development in the person we feel sorry for, or pity' (1992: 137). He considered the recognition of contempt in the counter-transference to be a vital step in breaking out of these stagnant cycles.

CONCLUSIONS

We have shown in this chapter that it is quite possible for the generic psychotherapist to take on patients with a learning disability. It is also now a statutory requirement, under the Children Act (1989), that children with a disability must have access to all services available to children in general, which includes psychotherapy. The more generic psychotherapists assess and treat the learning-disabled, the greater the pool of knowledge will become in relation to technical and theoretical issues, as well as in our understanding of the meaning of disability. There is room also for the specialists, such as those associated with the Mental Handicap Workshop at the Tavistock Clinic, as this concentration of work and sharing of experience is helpful in advancing theory, and promoting and supporting research.

REFERENCES

Bick, E. (1968) 'The experience of the skin in early object relations', *International Journal of Psychoanalysis* 49: 484.

Bicknell, J. (1983) 'The psychopathology of handicap', *British Journal of Medicine* 56: 167–78.

Bion, W. R. (1962a) 'A theory of thinking', pp. 110–19 in W. R. Bion (1967) *Second Thoughts*, London: Maresfield.

—— (1962b) *Learning from Experience*, London: Heinemann.

Brenman-Pick, I. (1988) 'Working through in the counter-transference', pp. 34–47 in E. Bott-Spillius (ed.) *Melanie Klein Today*, vol. 2, *Mainly Practice*, London: Routledge.

Brazelton, T. B., Kolowski, B. and Main, M. (1974) 'The early mother infant interaction', pp. 49–77 in M. Lewis and L. A. Rosenblum (eds) *The Effect of the Infant on its Caregivers*, London: Wiley Interscience.

Bruner, J. S. (1968) *Processes of Cognitive Growth: Infancy*, Worcester, MA: Clark University Press.

Bungener, H. (1992) 'From link to skin', Paper given at Ninth Tavistock Model Conference, Larmor-Plage, France (Aug.).

Children Act (1989) London: HMSO.

Hollins, S. and Evered, C. (1990) 'Group processes and content: the challenge of mental handicap', *Group Analysis* 23(1): 56–67.

Jones, K. (1972) 'A history of the mental health service', Routledge & Kegan Paul: London.

Joseph, B. (1988) 'Transference: the total situation', pp. 61–72 in E. Bott-Spillius (ed.) *Melanie Klein Today*, vol. 2, *Mainly Practice*, London: Routledge.

Klein, M. (1931) 'A contribution to the psychogenesis of intellectual inhibition', pp. 219–33 in M. Klein (1975) *Love, Guilt and Reparation*, London: Hogarth.

McCormack, B. (1991a) 'Thinking discourse and the denial of history: psychodynamic aspects of mental handicap', *Irish Journal of Psychological Medicine* 8: 59–64.

—— (1991b) 'Sexual abuse and learning disabilities', *British Medical Journal* 303: 143–4.

Mannoni, M. (1973) *The Retarded Child and the Mother*, London: Tavistock.

Sinason, V. (1986) 'Secondary mental handicap and its relation to trauma', *Psychoanalytic Psychotherapy* 2(2): 131–54.

—— (1988) 'Richard III, Hephaestus and Echo: sexuality and mental/multiple handicap', *Journal of Child Psychotherapy* 14(2): 93–105.

—— (1992) *Mental Handicap and the Human Condition*, London: Free Association Books.

Sinason, V. and Stokes, J. (1992) 'Secondary mental handicap as a defence', pp. 46–58 in A. Waitman and S. Conboy-Hill (eds) *Psychotherapy and Mental Handicap*, London: Sage.

Stern, D. (1974) 'Mother and infant at play: the dyadic interaction involving facial, vocal and gaze behaviours', pp. 187–214 in M. Lewis and L. A. Rosenblum (eds) *The Effect of the Infant on its Caregiver*, New York: Wiley.

Symington, N. (1992) 'Counter-transference with mentally handicapped clients', pp. 132–8 in A. Waitman and S. Conboy-Hill (eds) *Psychotherapy and Mental Handicap*, London: Sage.

Thompson, S. (1986) Dissertation for Diploma in Family Therapy, Institute of Family Therapy, London.

Trevarthen, C. and Hubley, P. (1978) 'Secondary intersubjectivity: confidence, confiding and acts of meaning in the first year', pp. 183–229 in A. Lock (ed.) *Action, Gesture and Symbol: The Emergence of Language*, London: Academic Press.

Waitman, A. and Conboy-Hill, S. (1992) *Psychotherapy and Mental Handicap*, London: Sage.

Chapter 22

The personal and the political
Power, authority and influence in psychotherapy

Louise Embleton Tudor and Keith Tudor

THE POLITICAL AND THE PERSONAL

We write this chapter at a time in which political and psychological contexts are characterised, on a global scale, by conflict and change. Old orders are giving way as old and new conflicts emerge, often with bloody and tragic consequences. Many peoples, particularly in Eastern Europe, are dealing with rapidly changing and emerging societies that are as yet unable to establish new order, to operate and to grasp the reality of unemployment, poverty, consumerism (and other free-market commodities, such as pornography). The increase in violence and the false gods of nationalism and racism may be some reflection and acting out of the intrapsychic pain people experience in their extrapsychic new worlds. The apparent passion for destructiveness can be understood politically and sociologically in terms of alienation, anomie and divisiveness; and psychologically in terms of splitting. Such theories describe experiences which are inextricably bound up with both political and personal struggles in the world. At the same time as societies, communities, organisations, groups, families and individuals appear to be concerned with division and subdivision and smaller and smaller identifications, there are also a number of moves to negotiate how people come together in different forms of economic, political and psychological union. Alongside the horror and terror of war and conflict, there is also great excitement and potential in the changes we have witnessed in the world in recent years – perhaps exemplified in the actuality and the metaphor of the tearing down of the Berlin Wall.

This fear (terror, horror) and excitement (joy, potentiality) both characterises the diversity of response to crisis, chaos and change and represents different traditions within psychotherapy. The psychoanalytic and psychodynamic traditions tend to emphasise the destructive capacity of human beings and inevitable conflict within and between them, whereas the humanistic tend to focus more on human beings' capacity for self-actualisation, their social nature and commonality. These tensions have been significant in our own development (separately and together) as individuals and in our psychotherapeutic practice, as it has been in our respective political experience and work. Three themes have brought these issues together.

The first is represented by the 1970s slogan – 'The personal is the political' – which summarised the notion that the personal realm was the subject of (and subject to) political analysis. Influenced particularly by Marxism, feminism, both Gramsci (1971) and Althusser (1969, 1976), and books such as *Psychoanalysis and Feminism* (Mitchell 1975), *Capitalism, the Family and Personal Life* (Zaretsky 1976) and *Beyond the Fragments* (Rowbotham *et al.* 1980), we sought in different ways (and in different organisations) to advance 'the personal', through 'the political' through campaigning, being 'active' in trade unions, consciousness-raising groups and local community work. The second theme relates to the difficulty of this enterprise in the face of the rise of the political right and the Thatcher hegemony in the 1980s, and the subsequent shift of the British Labour Party to the political centre-ground. This, with the marginalisation of Marxism as a political theory and practice, particularly in Eastern Europe, and in Britain of the radical socialist tradition, together with the current political and psychological culture of the individual, means that it is difficult to adopt and pursue critical ideas as political ones. At the same time many people who were involved in politics in the 1970s and eighties turned away from confronting society to confronting themselves through the medium of various therapies, psychological or otherwise – although some, notably Holland (1979, 1985, 1990), Banton *et al.* (1985), and Hoggett and Lousada (1985), formulate and maintain some integration of *psycho*therapy practice with political commitment. The third theme, and one which currently exercises us, is the evolution of such integration in two spheres: how to maintain political perspectives and activity, particularly in our psychotherapeutic practice and the organisation(s) of psychotherapy; *and* how to influence the political world to take account of individual biography and personal distress: an integration of psyche with concerns about society.

It is significant that we begin this by contextualising our concerns about issues of power: political power, personal power and, in seeking integration of the personal and the political, the expression of power in the psychotherapeutic relationship. The issue of power in psychotherapy is, in our view, not sufficiently considered in the literature or in research, training, supervision or practice. The *abuse* of power by psychotherapists has, in recent years, been importantly highlighted by Masson (1989), Rutter (1990) and Miller (1990). However, not much has been written either on definitions of power or the positive *use* of power – what we refer to as *authority* – in psychotherapy and the impact, or *influence* this has on clients. In this chapter we explore issues of power, authority and influence in psychotherapy, outlining a framework for analysis, practice and action.

The subjective–objective dimension

SUBJECTIVE _____ OBJECTIVE

The subjectivist approach to power   The objectivist approach to power

Assumptions about
Voluntarism   human nature   Determinism

Power and power relations are   *Power and power relations are*
representative of human nature,   *determined by people's*
which is autonomous and free-willed   *situation/environment*

Section I   *Human nature and child development*
                   Discussion – change in psychotherapy

Nominalism   Ontology   Realism
                           (assumptions about
                         the essence of phenomena)

Power is a concept/label   *Power is definable and exists*
which structures my reality   *independently as a concept*
                                                     and structure

Section II   *Unconscious and conscious processes*
                    Discussion – choice in psychotherapy

Anti-positivism   Epistemology   Positivism
                           (assumptions about
                          the grounds of knowledge)

I am a participant-observer in my   *Power can be studied objectively*
own power and my study of it   *through analysis of its constituent elements*

Section III   *Transference and counter-transference*
                     Discussion – therapeutic touch

                          Assumptions about
                             methodology
Ideographic   Nomothetic

We can only know about power   *The use and abuse of power can*
subjectively, personally through   *only be researched through*
biographies, journalistic accounts   *systematic protocol and technique, e.g. by*
and the process of research   *testing hypotheses and data analysis*

Section IV   *Psychotherapy and the notion of difference*
                    Discussion – the role of the psychotherapist

---

Figure 22.1 The subjective–objective dimension

We identify four central aspects of psychotherapeutic theory which we introduce and develop in relation to four discussions with implications for practice. The sections and discussions are framed by a conceptual schema, based on Burrell and Morgan's (1979) analysis of a subjective–objective dimension to theories and assumptions about the nature of social science (see Figure 22.1). These four aspects form the four sections in our discussion of the use of power, authority and influence in psychotherapeutic practice and its relation to the personal and the political, namely: different theories of human nature and child development; the relative emphasis on unconscious and conscious processes in psychotherapy; transference and counter-transference and the presence of the psychotherapist; and the notion of difference. The discussions developed within each section are, respectively: change in psychotherapy; choice in psychotherapy; the use of touch in psychotherapy; and the political role of the psychotherapist in psychotherapeutic practice.

I. HUMAN NATURE AND CHILD DEVELOPMENT

One of the fundamental ideological differences between, on the one hand, psychoanalytic and psychodynamic and, on the other, humanistic and existentialist approaches rests on their respective assumptions about human nature. Within the humanistic/existential tradition philosophical assumptions rest on the wholeness of human beings, their social nature and potential for autonomy and, crucially, the subjectivist nature of knowledge. Maslow, the founder of 'third force' psychology, identifies two main emphases of existential psychology: 'a radical stress on the concept of identity . . . [and] great stress on starting from experiential knowledge' (1968: 9). At the subjective end of Burrell and Morgan's (1979) subjective–objective dimension these assumptions are represented and reflected by humanistic views about self-concept (Rogers 1951) and self-actualisation (Maslow 1968); an existentialist emphasis on being and existence (existence comes before essence); and phenomenological streams of consciousness in which the subjective is the source of all objectivity. Psychoanalytic and psychodynamic critiques of such perspectives highlight such subjectivism, unfounded and unwarranted optimism and idealised bonhomie. Political critiques are more damning: 'the rejection of theory which seeks insight into objectivity in favour of subjective feelings reconstitutes a suspect Cartesian tradition in the reverse: I feel therefore I am' (Jacoby 1977: 104).

Extreme subjectivity denies the extent of power and conflict in the external world and the powerful intensity and frightening aspects of the internal, unconscious world of the client. The psychoanalytic/psychodynamic perspective is that human nature and child development are based on conflict. The importance of the centrality of conflict in any psychological theory, it is argued, is the link with power (and control) and the consequent implications for the theoretical and practical stance of the psychotherapist. The passion for destructiveness, for instance, can then be understood psychologically in terms of repetition-compulsion, being led by the unconscious and understood only in the transference and particularly the negative transference (see below). Such understanding may also provide insight into conflict and destruction at a political level.

More recent and more sophisticated humanistic and integrative approaches acknowledge both constructive and destructive forces: the aspirational Physis (the force of nature) quality of human nature as well as the Freudian drives, libido (the sexual instinct) and mortido (the death instinct) (Berne 1969/1981; Clarkson 1992).

It follows – from different beliefs about human nature – that there are differences about how people grow and develop from that 'first nature'. Psychoanalytic and psychodynamic approaches to child development are founded on the belief that we are born with some notion of survival, comprising *both* the capacity for love and nurturing and nourishing relationships *and* the capacity for annihilation; that is, the destruction of that love, either from without or from within, an example of which is the baby who simultaneously loves and attacks the mother's nipple. Indeed, it is argued that one thing which distinguishes psychoanalytic/psycho-dynamic theory from more humanistic approaches is its willingness to describe these important drives and early experiences. As personality is built up then, essentially in a pre-thinking phase, it is the quality of our actual experience and the environment which will determine the personality and character structure which emerges. The most deeply problematic aspects of people's personalities are the repression of very murderous notions and debates which actually threaten the self, either by virtue of the child's wish to assault those people considered to be threatening or by a belief that the outside world is actually hostile. Personal and social change takes place only if the murderous aspects of the human psyche are understood and brought into some sort of relation with the positive aspects. Power, therefore, is predicated upon inevitable and necessary conflict and is something about which we are all highly ambivalent – with consequent implications for the psychotherapeutic relationship (further developed below).

The implication of more humanistic approaches to child (and adult) development is that the child develops a sense of their own power(s), as well as an appreciation of the limits of those powers. This is particularly in relation to others, traditionally through the resolution of developmental processes, stages or tasks – for example, Erikson (1965, 1968) (who, from a psychoanalytic background, introduces a social element to his psychosocial description of growth and crisis in the life-cycle) and, more recently, Stern (1985), who develops a more interpersonal, process description of development. These views are predicated on a notion of power which emphasises the autonomy and negotiability of power relationships.

What both the psychoanalytic/psychodynamic and humanistic/existential traditions agree upon is that childhood is an experience of a power relationship. Nowhere is this argued more eloquently – and the destructive consequences elaborated – than in the work of the former psychoanalyst and now writer and advocate for children, Alice Miller (1985, 1987a, 1987b). The parent–child relationship is by its nature a relationship of power, authority and influence; indeed, a child cannot flourish without its parents having and using these appropriately. When power is simply equated with oppression, however, and oppression is associated with all power relationships, this leads to psychological and ideological tautology and confusion – to the extent that Masson (1989), for instance, argues against all forms of psychotherapy (except self-help therapy) on the basis of the power (structure) inherent in psychotherapy and the psychotherapeutic relationship which he regards as necessarily abusive, commenting that imbalance in power rarely leads to compassionate behaviour. The answer to this debate on power – between determinism and voluntarism – lies not in such defeatism (as Masson's); or in ignoring the existence of power; or in (the mistaken) thinking that we can share it (the logic of co-counselling), do away with it (Rogers 1957/90c), or give it away (which informs much of the discussion about empowerment in the field of mental health). Although power relationships may be inadequate, invasive and even abusive (Masson 1989; Rutter 1990), our perspective is that they are not *per se* deforming. There is, however, in some psychotherapeutic circles, a deep ambivalence about power, about owning knowledge, having skills and definable roles that distinguish one person from another – a concept of difference which we expand later. At the same time there is an ideological context to this rejection or denial of power. Certain ideas about power have prominence at certain, particular times – which brings us back to 'the political' and the extent to which the dominant culture, class, race and gender determine our thinking and beliefs as against the degree of autonomy we have and can develop for ourselves and in relation to one another.

Discussion – change in psychotherapy

People come to psychotherapy wanting a change in their lives and, indeed, can be viewed (assessed, diagnosed and so on) by the psychotherapist in relation to their stated aims or wishes for change. Often the initial stage of the psychotherapy comprises a process of mutual definition of the issues or problems and the aims of the client regarding their solution. During this process, the psychotherapist may (or, almost inevitably, will to some extent) initially be (re-)defining 'the problem/s' according to their own theoretical orientation and framework, even using concepts which have no meaning to the client or to which the client might object. Knowledge is power and the framing of knowledge has a powerful impact on practice: the psychotherapist has, by virtue of his authority and ability to conceptualise, greater knowledge in this respect than the client; and herein lies the potential both for abuse *and* for the enabling of healthy change and autonomy. The key practice issue in this respect is to what extent our own assumptions as psychotherapists about human nature (determinist or voluntarist) influence our beliefs, notions and practice about our clients' ability to change. In terms of our conceptual schema (Figure 22.1), determinist approaches to psychotherapy will rely more on diagnosis, classification and treatment, whilst voluntarist approaches (and to power relations in general) will emphasise mutual and ongoing assessment: 'if we could empathically experience all the sensory and visceral sensations of the individual, could experience his [*sic*] whole phenomenal field . . . we should have the perfect basis for understanding the meaningfulness of his behaviour and for predicting his future behavior' (Rogers 1951: 494–5).

Working alongside – and at times against – such power, authority and influence expressed consciously or unconsciously by the psychotherapist, we need to consider the influence of social factors on aspects of and prospects for change in psychotherapy.

Despite the encouragement and development of individual autonomy (voluntarism), there are situations and times when social disadvantage will be a (determining) factor on a client's capacity and/or options for change. To claim otherwise is at best naïve and at worst persecutory. In practice, we can consider the conceptual schema (Figure 22.1) and reflect its range: as a client denies their ability to change we can confront such denial and discounting (for example, Schiff *et al.* 1975); if they claim undue or grandiose free choice in given situations we can balance this with an appreciation of what is in some way determined.

II. UNCONSCIOUS AND CONSCIOUS PROCESSES

Freud was the first of the nineteenth-century writers who were aware of the existence of the unconscious to delineate its particular characteristics and later to distinguish three aspects of the unconscious: from the recollection of an event which was not in mind but which is easily accessed by a trigger (the preconscious); to a level where access is difficult but may or may not be accomplished after weeks, months or even years of application; to 'a mental province rather than a quality of what is mental' (Freud 1923/1973: 104), hidden from the ego. The contents of the second layer of the unconscious were generally held to relate to matters of personal experience and history which were too traumatic or threatening for the individual to remember. Jung (1954/1959) calls this the personal unconscious and added the notion of the collective unconscious, the contents of which, irrespective of historical moment, racial or ethnic group, gender, class or age, relate to (arche)typical reactions to universal human circumstances. Subsequent writers have not significantly disagreed with these definitions although they may differ in the importance they attach to these systems and phenomena in their clinical work.

A crucial question in the psychotherapeutic relationship arises in relation to the unconscious and the use of power, authority and/or influence by the psychotherapist. Whose consciousness prevails? For it is only through consciousness that the unconscious can be understood, and it is in the nature of the unconscious that its contents are obscure to the conscious. It is questionable, for instance, whether at the beginning of any psychotherapy the client is in a position to know what is being agreed in relation to the function of the psychotherapist. Whilst neither psychotherapist nor client can know what material will emerge or how, the psychotherapist at least knows about his or her own assumptions and techniques and, even at the assessment stage, can make some hypotheses about some aspects of the psychotherapy. However the client is presenting and however empathic the psychotherapist, different theoretical constructs will inevitably occur to the psychotherapist as the interaction proceeds. The psychotherapist is necessarily involved in a conscious process. However, in terms of understanding the impact of the essence of such phenomena – for example, the psychotherapist's conscious conceptual processing (let alone the psychotherapist's unconscious material) – the important question is: to what extent is the client influenced (unconsciously) by the internal processes of the psychotherapist? The answer depends partly on what we believe about power. If we believe that power is definable and exists independently as a concept and a structure (realism), then we will believe that the psychotherapist's conscious and unconscious processes will influence the client; if, on the other hand, we believe that power is a concept which we use in different ways to structure our reality (nominalism), we will believe that the psychotherapist's power, authority and influence will be questioned and mediated by the client's own sense and grasp of issues of power throughout their psychotherapy. Lukes (1974) stresses the importance of the power to define: the statement 'power is not a property, but a relation' is a nominalist definition of power which wrests it from 'objectivist' realism; and Schiff *et al.* stress the priority and necessity of understanding the patient's frame of reference, suggesting that 'the whole question, "What is really real?" is necessarily an ongoing consideration' (1975: 54). Either way (subjectivist or objectivist), there are implications for psychotherapeutic practice.

Discussion – choice in psychotherapy

This (ontological) discussion about the essence of things – which might be subtitled 'Whose reality is it anyway?' – is important in ascertaining how power is defined and how choices are made in the psychotherapeutic relationship. From choosing a psychotherapist; to the first point of contact; finding out how the psychotherapist works; what sort of person they are; even what information the client wants; through to the choices the client has within the psychotherapeutic relationship (not forgetting the occasions and situations in which there is even less or no choice in the process): all these, commonly unconscious choices and decisions, are based on assumptions about the essence of phenomena. To one client who wanted to 'get on with' her psychotherapy in the initial session the psychotherapist pointed out that she was taking a lot 'on trust' with the result that the client highlighted various (implicit) assumptions she had, particularly about the professional authority of the psychotherapist. Again, we can draw on Burrell and Morgan's (1979) conceptual schema to clarify and work with such issues as they arise in practice. Two common positions are found: in one (as in the example above), the client abdicates their reality to the psychotherapist's, often unconsciously; in the other, the client rigidly adheres to their own reality, even in the face of an objectivist 'reality'. One client's relationship with their group psychotherapist was shaken when he heard his psychotherapist define himself as black; he had hitherto and unconsciously 'seen' his psychotherapist as white and subsequently had to (re-)examine his assumptions, his relationships and his racism. Such discussion about what is 'real' (realism) and what is a concept or a label (nominalism), such defining and reclaiming is often an important stage in psychotherapy: 'it is the uniqueness of the individual that is apparent in the ancient idea of naming' (Jacobs 1985: 23). Jacobs understands naming in itself as an alternative to – and, as such, a reclaiming of the essence of – labelling.

For the psychotherapist's part, if we are aware of these largely unconscious processes and assumptions and common positions, we can respond to how our power may be viewed, being sensitive both to defining another person's reality and, equally, to rigidly defended realities. This discussion has practical implications, for instance, for diagnosis and treatment planning in psychotherapy. Rogers (1951) discusses the problems of diagnosis in terms of encouraging dependency and a reliance on an external locus of evaluation (realism). Clarkson (1992) summarises 'the case against diagnosis', referring to the dangers of alienation, reductionism and 'false certainties'. Whilst it would be a denial of our power and authority as psychotherapists to deny our experience in assessment and treatment, we need to be aware of and be explicit both about our views of human nature and about the essence of phenomena in order to be clear about our clients. One psychotherapist, in working with a client who was concerned about the process of her psychotherapy, agreed initially to answer the client's questions about his conceptualisations – thereby opening up the process as well as the content of the psychotherapy – and modelling a power-sharing which the client had not previously experienced. This also had the effect of establishing trust which, as it transpired, was a core, developmental issue for the client – reflecting the practical and conceptual link between issues of human nature and of ontology.

III. TRANSFERENCE AND COUNTER-TRANSFERENCE

For psychoanalytic and psychodynamic psychotherapists the constant examination of the transference relationship is crucial both as an expression of the client's self and as a vehicle for the negative defences central to the pathology of the client. It is thus only a transferential relationship which can stand the issue of whether the client destroyed the parent. People do not conceptually understand their internal world, it is argued, simply through thinking about it; rather, if the patient is to do so in a sustained way, they do so through an emotional experience also; namely, the vehicle of the transference. It is a criticism of more humanistic/existential approaches that they do not have this way into the destructive and negative organisation of the client's internal world.

There are implications for the person and conduct of the psychotherapist who believes in the therapeutic usefulness of the transference. The psychotherapist who adheres rigidly to a technique without paying attention to the clues from the client about exactly what was enraging, frightening or demeaning in the original responses to their anger or negativity runs the risk of compounding the original trauma; the maintenance of a 'blank screen' is one obvious example of this. It is not enough for the client to understand that their hostility against their psychotherapist derives from earlier experiences; they also need the experience of a different response in the present. At some time or other probably all psychotherapists are tempted to act as if clients only need a good experience in the present to obliterate the effects of deprivation or abuse in the past and therefore to focus on reparative interventions rather than those which facilitate the client to connect with feelings towards the psychotherapist which both might find difficult. As Casement points out: 'the analytic "good object" is not someone better than the original object: it is someone who survives being treated as a "bad object"' (1990: 87).

Whatever the orientation of the psychotherapist, they are most likely to provide a genuinely therapeutic experience for the client when they demonstrate to the client total respect for that person as an individual, a continuing interest in the relationship between themselves and the client and a commitment to examine their own defensiveness in the face of criticism from the client. This responsiveness to the individuality of the client necessitates a degree of spontaneity, flexibility, open-mindedness and creativity incompatible with over-strict adherence to any technique, whether psychoanalytic, psychodynamic or humanistic. The contributions of experienced practitioners in Dryden (1992) are examples of serious and critical self-reflection on practice, often questioning the grounds of knowledge of such practice. Such epistemological assumptions – about the grounds of knowledge – are crucial and especially so in relation to discussions about power; the challenge to Freud's seduction theory and the belief in the subjective experience and reality of the abused child represents a subjectivist (anti-positivist) knowledge based on the participation of the client in recalling and reclaiming their own experience (for example, Kelly 1988; Kelly and Radford 1990/1991) in relation to sexual abuse and violence). Abuse – and its denial or disguise, maybe as love or affection – represents a denial of the very grounds of such self-knowledge in a perverted form of (adult) 'objectivist' (positivist) knowledge.

The willingness to own and examine their own negativity and other feelings toward the client (counter-transference) will enable the psychotherapist to withstand criticism and hostility from the client without defending, retaliating or collapsing. For example, one psychotherapist was misheard by a client who then reacted to what he understood the psychotherapist to have said with sharp criticism, intending to hurt her. She was hurt. Liking the client and wanting to be liked, the psychotherapist quickly readied herself to correct the client's misunderstanding; she was also angry and formulated a retaliatory reply. Fortunately, the psychotherapist, recognising this counter-transferential invitation, was instead able to offer the client an opportunity both to acknowledge how deeply and how frequently he wanted to wound her and see her hurt, and to examine his willingness to 'hear' her make what would have been a persecutory remark. Thus, an understanding of counter-transference and continuing awareness of its impact on the psychotherapist is essential for the psychotherapist to maintain contact with the potential for the use and abuse of his power.

There is a variety of approaches within humanistic/existential psychotherapies to the concept and use of transference and counter-transference. Rogers represents one view against the use of transference:

> 'The client-centred therapist's reaction to transference is the same as to any other attitude of the client: he endeavours to understand and accept' . . . . acceptance leads to recognition by the client that these feelings are within her, they are not in the therapist.
>
> (1951: 203)

This follows from Rogers' theory of personality and behaviour (1951) and theory of psychotherapy and personality change (1959/1990a, 1977/1990b). Many humanistic psychotherapists will, following this, discourage or 'cut through' the transference rather than encouraging or working in it. From a transactional perspective Berne was concerned to explore the underlying dynamics of transference transactions (Berne 1966); more recently Novellino (1984) and Moiso (1985) suggest ways of working *with* rather than *in* the transference. Clarkson (1991) offers an in-depth analysis of both psychotherapist and client transference and counter-transference. Such attempts to integrate an understanding of transference and counter-transference are not simply cognitive exercises: the symbolic meaning of the client's transference will often be realised or expressed emotionally or in behavioural terms. Schiff *et al.* illustrate their approach to transference, linking this to their understanding of power: 'Major exchanges of power occur in therapeutic relationships. Patients often wish to invest therapists with authority and responsibility . . . our policy is to accept the patients' investment of power [transference] to the extent we believe it possible to utilise that power for their welfare' (1975: 102).

Discussion – therapeutic touch

In discussing the use of touch in psychotherapy we distinguish between touch on greeting or parting; touch which the client asks for or the psychotherapist gives in an isolated incident; and touch which is part of the treatment, such as in biodynamic massage or other post-Reichian psychotherapies which focus on the body as the repository of tension and dis-ease, resulting from unexpressed or unacknowledged feelings about past traumas. The second case is less ambiguous, especially if, at or near the beginning of psychotherapy, there is discussion and agreement about the use and purpose of therapeutic touch. Nevertheless, there are implications for the power relationship if, for example, the client is undressed and prone on a massage table. For this reason biodynamic psychotherapists do not work in the transference. Southwell (1990) argues that the work is focused on the energy within the client's body and not on the relationship between psychotherapist and client. It can be argued that the degree of intimacy in the physical relationship between the biodynamic psychotherapist and their client is such that it could not tolerate the additional intimacy of the transferential relationship: the client would have no place if the psychotherapist did not 'touch' – and the psychotherapist no way of not touching. It can be further argued that, without a place in which there is no 'touch', the client cannot fully experience the touch that is.

With some separation along these lines, whoever or whatever is evoked in psychotherapy can be explored. The technique of separation between the physical (touch) and the transferential raises the question of whether the psychotherapist acknowledges counter-transference. In an attempt to answer this, many psychotherapists using body-orientated techniques do not touch, but maintain close contact with their clients through the nature of their presence and their verbal interventions or, in accordance with their observations of the transferential processes at work, exercise considerable judgement in their use of touch. There is some evidence that Rogers, for instance, towards the end of his life, began to regard 'presence' as another 'condition' for therapeutic change (Rogers 1986; Thorne 1992). (Although Tudor and Worrall, in press, take issue with the notion of presence being viewed as a condition.) Such psychotherapists, like their psychoanalytic/ psychodynamic colleagues, may 'touch' their clients deeply with the appropriateness and usefulness of their verbal and non-verbal interventions.

A further aspect of the use of touch is the reparative need on the part of the client for being held or touched appropriately by the psychotherapist/ parent figure; to withhold this, it could be argued, only compounds the original lack or trauma and may be a lack on the part of the psychotherapist. Traditionally, psychoanalytic and psychodynamic psychotherapists perceive such reparation (or reparenting) as an avoidance of the client experiencing the original pain and as undermining of the client's ability to deal with it, although Woodmansey (1988) argues for the use of touch in treatment: as communication and as 'primary experience', suggesting contra-indications such as clients' sexual difficulties, and pointing out the need for professional responsibility. Humanistic psychotherapists have, on the whole, tended to be more open to considering touch and to touching clients, although recent research into and publicity about the abuse of such power relationships (for example, Rutter 1990) have, properly, highlighted the need for a coherent theoretical stance and consequent appropriate practice; good professional practice and ethics and, therefore, psychotherapeutic discretion; and regular supervision.

IV. PSYCHOTHERAPY AND NOTION OF DIFFERENCE

As psychotherapists the authors both come from a socialist tradition and share a belief that, as active agents in our lives and therapeutic practices, we have a view of politics which we try to relate to our understanding of our clients. As socialists we come from traditions which have an analysis of society which is essentially conflictual; traditions which, at the same time, value *inter*dependence. Yet we live in a Western society in which the value of independence (through market forces) is paramount and 'the nanny state' and *dependent* relationships are attacked. Simons (1992) points out the partiality of such attacks – as if necessary and appropriate dependence is inherently damaging. What draws these strands together is the notion of difference. The negotiation of difference, in psychotherapy, allows for some idea about ambivalence – often missing in critical politics. There *is* a structural and emotional difference between the patient and the psychotherapist, just as between many other structural differences – of class, race and gender. The difference in different psychotherapies is just how *difference* is negotiated. (Stereo)typically in the psychoanalytical tradition it is emphasised and highlighted, whereas within the humanistic tradition it is emphasised less and even ignored. In elaborating the notion of difference, we identify three areas in which psychotherapy and politics interact: psychotherapy *and* politics, politics *in* psychotherapy and the politics *of* psychotherapy.

Psychotherapy and politics

> Politics, in present-day psychological and social usage, has to do with *power and control* . . . with the *locus of decision-making power*: who makes the decisions which, consciously or unconsciously, regulate or control the thoughts, feelings, or behaviour of others or oneself.
>
> (Rogers 1957/1990c: 377)

In practising both politics and psychotherapy, one solution to such issues of power and control is to separate the two as Kopp does: 'the roots of most of women's problems are political and social. The solution to such political problems must be revolutionary rather than psychotherapeutic' (1974: 33). Certainly, such separation avoids any danger of 'psychologising' a client's politics or political involvement. However, in practice, to split off an aspect of one's life is an untenable position or – as the gay men and lesbians who entered the psychoanalytic establishment at a time when homosexuality was more widely considered pathological experienced – was and is, at the very least, a difficult road to travel.

Politics in psychotherapy

The alternative to such separation (or splitting) is the exploration and/or resolution of political issues, aspirations and ideals in and through the process of psychotherapy. This puts a client's politics on the agenda in psychological terms and therefore offers a more whole (holistic) approach to the client. In the authors' experience this is where it is possible and, indeed, necessary to explore the function and meaning of politics; power relations; the notion and experience of difference; the client's own sense of power; their relation to authority; and capacity to be influenced and to influence others. Only through such expansion and exploration is it possible to achieve a true integration – or, in Piagetian terms, a mature assimilation, rather than an immature accommodation – of the political world.

The politics of psychotherapy

As distinct from politics *in* psychotherapy, the politics *of* psychotherapy specifically puts the politics of *the psychotherapist* on the agenda and, more generally, focuses on psychotherapy from a political perspective. This first point immediately poses personal, political and ideological challenges to the psychotherapist – how much of ourselves and our views are we willing to reveal in the service of our client? How do they learn about power in the psychotherapeutic relationship? How do we negotiate our differences, whether personal, political or structural? For example, when asked in an initial interview by a lesbian client about the nature of her own sexuality and her theoretical, psychological view of the origin of lesbianism, one psychotherapist was willing to answer directly and before embarking on any exploration of the impact of her answers (or of other possible answers) on the client. By doing so, the psychotherapist intended to convey that, as a psychotherapist, she did not exist independently or isolated from social relations; and that she understood their impact on the client and that this impact would also be experienced in the psychotherapeutic relationship and process.

On the more general point, it was Reich who first developed a politics of psychotherapy both in his theoretical attempt to link his ideas about the body with what he saw as liberated societies and in practice through the establishment of his Sexual Hygiene Clinics for Workers and Employees in Germany during the 1930s: 'at this time Reich still visualised himself as a Marxist psycho-analyst, and as such he still hoped to find some measure of support for the mental hygiene work he was engaged on, in both Marxist and psycho-analytic circles' (Boadella 1985: 72). Reich was to be disappointed in and rejected by both circles. In our own personal, political and psychotherapeutic journeys we have also found it difficult to 'marry' these two worlds: within our political world and organisations to acknowledge the impact of and on the psyche; and for politics to be on the agenda within our psychological worlds.

Discussion – the role of the psychotherapist

It follows from these distinctions and brief discussions that, depending on the psychotherapist's strategy in relation to their psychotherapeutic work and politics (whether *and*, *in* or *of*), their practice and methodology will vary and differ – on Burrell and Morgan's (1979) and our analysis – from the ideographic (or symbolising) to the nomothetic (or legislative). Thus, the psychotherapist who emphasises systematic protocol and technique, typically, through diagnosis and treatment planning represents a nomothetic approach to social science and the methodology and practice of psychotherapy. A psychotherapist, on the other hand, whose method is more subjective, 'getting close to one's subject and exploring its detailed background and life history' (Burrell and Morgan 1979: 6), using, for instance, active listening, empathy (Rogers 1961) or metaphor (Kopp 1974), has an ideographic methodology. This dimension provides an understanding of debates about methodology; for instance, in psychotherapy research.

The psychotherapist's role will also vary according to their views and assumptions about the nature of society – this is another (vertical) dimension in Burrell and Morgan's (1979) work (and worthy of further consideration and development in this field). A proponent of the status quo will, however unconsciously, tend to support ways in which their client expresses their sense of social integration, of cohesion and of social order. Whereas, as an advocate of radical change, the psychotherapist/guru, 'arising in a revolutionary context . . . sets himself [*sic*] against both the traditional authority of patriarchal domination and the bureaucratic legalistic defining of power. Unintimidated by cultural expectations . . . overturning the usual ways of understanding the meaning of life' (Kopp 1974: 8).

Our own perspective is that the separation of politics and psychotherapy is a false one; and that one of our tasks and roles as psychotherapists/ activists living in a political world is to help clients understand, interpret, mediate and act on their extrapsychic as well as their intrapsychic world, to paraphrase Maslow (1968): 'intra-psychic success is not enough; we must also include extra-psychic change'. Unhappiness is informed by conflict, including conflict within power relationships: working class and ruling class, women and men, black and white, the unemployed and elderly and the productive world, children and the adult world. An ignorance or naïve understanding of such conflicts only fuels the criticism of the individualising focus and depoliticising effect of psychotherapy. A false understanding leads to attempts to substitute happiness for unhappiness, in a way in which both false humanism and commodity fetishism elevate pleasure as an end in itself, thereby minimising genuine suffering and alienation. Such naïve and unrealistic views are, in psychoanalytic terms, symbiotic organisations of and defences against the world. Just as a part of the psychotherapist's task is to confront apolitical resolutions of such crises, idealised happiness can be as destructive as rage: real health, psychologically and politically, allows for both to be expressed constructively and creatively.

Banton *et al.*, in their discussion of radical therapeutic practice, highlight the need to separate the positive and negative functions of power relations: 'radical practice must involve the subversion of discourse in a manner which maximises the positive possibilities for change' (1985: 135). They go on to argue that the (psycho)therapist's acceptance of power facilitates the opening up of experiences and connections, whilst their refusal of power leaves the client better able to integrate the connections between psychological stress and social reality and to 'maintain them independently of the therapist' (p. 139). As psychotherapists we therefore need to be able to distinguish between positive and negative power relations and to use our authority in confronting and connecting with our clients appropriately.

CONCLUSION

Lord Acton observed that 'power tends to corrupt, and absolute power corrupts absolutely' and, rather like the empirical research scientist who hung a horseshoe over the door of his laboratory as a sign of doubt and humility, perhaps Lord Acton's quotation would be well displayed or at least borne in mind in psychotherapists' consulting rooms. In this chapter, we have distinguished between the ab-use of power and the appropriate use of power – or *authority* – on the part of the psychotherapist; and have discussed the influence psychotherapy and the psychotherapist may have on the client, particularly at an unconscious level. We have suggested a conceptual framework for identifying four sets of assumptions about power and for working with issues of power, authority and influence in psychotherapy, precisely so that neither psychotherapists nor clients are corrupted by the power which necessarily and properly lies in the psycho-therapeutic relationship – advocating rather that such issues are made explicit and resolved with clients and, with Banton *et al.* (1985), that this is ultimately a subversive activity, psychologically and/or politically.

In concluding, we distinguish two fallacies, the identification of which may clarify future thinking and practice in these areas: one is the fallacy of empowerment and the other, of the authoritarian nature of power – what might be referred to, respectively, as 'giving over power' and 'having power over'. Just as one cannot truly be sent for psychotherapy, one cannot truly (passively) *be* empowered; we can actively learn about power, 'own' our own power and take power: this is genuine and positive psychotherapeutic potency or authority – 'power to' and 'power for'. In response to the second fallacy – and one which also proposes a way of modelling potency ('passing on', rather than 'giving over') – Steiner objects to the concept of power being universally linked to the control of and over others and concludes poignantly that 'the greatest antidote to the authoritarian use of power . . . is for people to develop individual power in its multidimensional forms and to dedicate themselves to passing on power to as many others as can be found in a lifetime' (1987: 104).

ACKNOWLEDGEMENT

Thanks and acknowledgement to Julian Lousada for his contribution to earlier drafts of this chapter.

REFERENCES

Althusser, L. (1969) *For Marx*, London: Allen Lane.
—— (1976) *Essays in Self-Criticism*, London: New Left Books.
Banton, R., Clifford, P., Frosh, S., Lousada, J. and Rosenthal, J. (1985) *The Politics of Mental Health*, Basingstoke: Macmillan.
Berne, E. (1966) *Principles of Group Treatment*, New York: Grove Press.
—— (1981) *A Layman's Guide to Psychiatry and Psychoanalysis*, Harmondsworth: Penguin (first published 1969).
Boadella, D. (1985) *Wilhelm Reich*, London: Arcana.

Burrell, G. and Morgan, G. (1979) *Sociological Paradigms and Organisational Analysis*, London: Heinemann.

Casement, P. (1990) *Further Learning from the Patient*, London: Routledge.

Clarkson, P. (1991) 'Through the looking glass: explorations in transference and counter-transference', *Transactional Analysis Journal* 21: 99–107.

—— (1992) *Transactional Analysis Psychotherapy: An Integrated Approach*, London: Routledge.

Dryden, W. (1992) *Hard-earned Lessons from Counselling in Action*, London: Sage.

Erikson, E. (1965) *Childhood and Society*, Harmondsworth: Penguin (first published 1951).

—— (1968) *Identity, Youth and Crisis*, New York: W. W. Norton.

Erskine, R. G. (1975) 'The ABCs of effective psychotherapy', *Transactional Analysis Journal* 5: 163–4.

Freud, S. (1973) 'The dissection of the psychical personality', pp. 88–112 in J. Strachey (ed. and trans.), *New Introductory Lectures on Psychoanalysis, The Pelican Freud Library*, Harmondsworth: Penguin (first published 1923).

Gramsci, A. (1971) *Selections from the Prison Notebooks*, Q. Hoare and G. Nowell-Smith (eds) London: Lawrence & Wishart.

Hoggett, P. and Lousada, J. (1985) 'Therapeutic interventions in working class communities', *Free Associations* 1: 125–52.

Holland, S. (1979) 'The development of an action and counselling service in a deprived urban area', pp. 95–106 in M. Meacher (ed.) *New Methods of Mental Health Care*, London: Pergamon.

—— (1985) 'Loss, rage and oppression: neighbourhood psychotherapy with working class, black and national minority women', Paper presented at the Pam Smith Memorial Lecture, June, Polytechnic of North London.

—— (1990) 'Psychotherapy, oppression and social action: gender, race and class in black women's depression', pp. 256–69 in R. Perelberg and A. Miller (eds) *Gender and Power in Families*, London: Routledge.

Jacobs, M. (1985) *The Presenting Past*, Milton Keynes: Open University Press.

Jacoby, R. (1977) *Social Amnesia*, Hassocks: Harvester.

Jung, C. G. (1959) 'Archetypes of the collective unconscious', pp. 3–41 in H. Read, M. Fordham, G. Adler and W. McGuire (eds) *The Archetypes and the Collective Unconscious: The Collected Works*, vol. 9, part 1, London: Routledge & Kegan Paul (first published 1954).

Kelly, L. (1988) 'What's in a name? Defining child sexual abuse', *Feminist Review* 28: 65–73.

Kelly, L. and Radford, J. (1990/1991) ' "Nothing really happened": the invalidation of women's experience of sexual violence', *Critical Social Policy* 30: 39–53.

Kopp, S. (1974) *If You Meet the Buddha on the Road, Kill Him!* London: Sheldon.

Lukes, S. (1974) *Power: A Radical View*, London: Macmillan.

Maslow, A. H. (1968) *Towards a Psychology of Being*, New York: Van Nostrand.

Masson, J. M. (1989) *Against Therapy*, London: Collins.

Miller, A. (1985) *Thou Shalt Not Be Aware: Society's Betrayal of the Child* (H. and H. Hannum, trans.), London: Pluto.

—— (1987a) *For Your Own Good*, London: Virago.

—— (1987b) *The Drama of Being a Child* (R. Ward, trans.), London: Virago.

—— (1990) *The Untouched Key* (H. and H. Hannum, trans.), London: Virago.

Mitchell, J. (1975) *Psychoanalysis and Feminism*, Harmondsworth: Penguin.

Moiso, C. (1985) 'Ego states and transference', *Transactional Analysis Journal* 15(3); 194–201.

Novellino, M. (1984) 'Self-analysis of countertransference in integrative Trans-actional Analysis', *Transactional Analysis Journal* 14(1): 63–7.

Rogers, C. R. (1951) *Client-centred Therapy*, London: Constable.

—— (1961) *On Becoming a Person*, London: Constable.

—— (1986) 'A client-centred/person-centred approach to therapy', pp. 197–208 in I. L. Kutash and A. Wolf (eds) *Psychotherapists' Casebook*, San Francisco, CA: Jossey-Bass.

—— (1990a) 'A theory of therapy, personality and interpersonal relationships, as developed in the client-centred framework', pp. 236–57 in H. Kirschenbaum and V. L. Henderson (eds) *The Carl Rogers Reader*, London: Constable (first published 1959).

—— (1990b) 'The necessary and sufficient conditions of therapeutic personality change', pp. 219–35 in H. Kirschenbaum and V. L. Henderson (eds) *The Carl Rogers Reader*, London: Constable (first published 1977).

—— (1990c) 'The politics of the helping professions', pp. 376–95 in H. Kirschenbaum and V. L. Henderson (eds) *The Carl Rogers Reader*, London: Constable (first published 1957).

Rowbotham, S., Segal, L. and Wainwright, H. (1980) *Beyond the Fragments*, London: Merlin.

Rutter, P. (1990) *Sex in the Forbidden Zone*, London: Unwin.

Schiff, J., Schiff, A. W., Mellor, K., Schiff, E., Schiff, S., Richman, D., Fishman, J., Wolz, D., Fishman, C. and Momb, D. (1975) *Cathexis Reader*, New York: Harper & Row.

Simons, H. (1992) 'There is no such thing as a free market', *Living Marxism* (June) 12–15.

Southwell, C. (1990) 'Touch and the psychotherapeutic relationship', Paper presented at the Conference of the Institute of Chiron Psychotherapy Centre, July, London.

Steiner, C. (1987) 'The seven sources of power: an alternative to authority', *Transactional Analysis Journal* 17: 102–4.

Stern, D. N. (1985) *The Interpersonal World of the Infant*, New York: Basic Books.

Thorne, B. (1992) *Carl Rogers*, London: Sage.

Tudor, K. and Worrall, M. (in press) 'Congruence reconsidered', *British Journal of Guidance and Counselling*.

Woodmansey, A. C. (1988) 'Are psychotherapists out of touch?', *British Journal of Psychotherapy* 5(1): 57–65.

Zaretsky, E. (1976) *Capitalism, the Family and Personal Life*, London: Pluto.

FURTHER READING

Clarkson, P. (1987) 'The bystander role', *Transactional Analysis Journal* 17(3): 82–7.

—— (1993) 'Bystander games', *Transactional Analysis Journal* 23(3): 158–72.

Hutcheon, L. (1989) *The Politics of Postmodernism*, London: Routledge.

Samuels, A. (1993) *The Political Psyche*, London: Routledge.

Chapter 23

Psychotherapeutic work with adult survivors of sexual abuse in childhood

Arnon Bentovim and Marianne Tranter

As professionals have become aware of the direct traumatic impact of child sexual abuse, there has also been a growing realisation of the potentially devastating long-term effects of such abuse on the adult life and functioning of victims of abuse, both male and female. It is thus not a question of whether sexual abuse may be traumatic, but to what extent and what are the factors which mitigate or potentiate such effects.

Until recently there has been a major process of denial of the phenomenon of sexual abuse in childhood. Herman (1981) outlined what she described as three historical 'discoveries' of the prevalence of sexual abuse in our society.

The first discovery of the awareness of the occurrence of sexual abuse as a traumatic experience is attributed to Freud's early psychoanalytic work when female patients revealed childhood sexual experiences with adult men in their families. Freud, using the notion of seduction theory, suggested that such experiences were causal of hysterical symptoms in adult life. He later identified such perpetrators as perhaps more likely to be other children, caretakers or distant relatives, not fathers, and he later repudiated seduction as a theory; instead he claimed that his patients' frequent reports of sexual abuse were incestuous fantasies rather than actual childhood events. Masson (1989) and others have traced the way in which such a view organised perceptions of psychotherapists for many years.

The second discovery of the prevalence of child sexual abuse was in the 1940s, when incest was 'discovered' by social scientists conducting large-scale survey studies of sexual practices, including the Kinsey study (Kinsey *et al.* 1953). Between 20 and 30 per cent of women reported having had a sexual experience as a child with a male, 1 per cent reporting sexual experience with a father or step-father. One researcher (Landis 1956) reported that 30 per cent of male participants in a survey reported childhood sexual experiences with an adult, again most typically male. Despite this description of the prevalence, the reality of the phenomenon continued to be denied by both the researchers and the public.

The third discovery of incest occurred during the 1970s, credited to the feminist movement and child abuse concern professionals who brought problems of childhood sexual abuse, together with other taboo issues, such as battering of women and rape, into public awareness. Undoing the historical legacy of denial is one of the major tasks for psychotherapists who are attempting to help victims become survivors, improve their mental health, their capacities to relate sexually, and to break the dangerous intergenerational cycle whereby abusive activities become re-enacted in the next generation.

RELEVANT EMPIRICAL RESEARCH

A variety of different approaches have now established the prevalence of childhood sexual abuse in both women and men. Finkelhor's (1979) classic study with college students revealed an incidence of 19 per cent of girls and 9 per cent of boys who had had a significantly stressful sexual experience in childhood. The review by Peters (1986) of prevalence studies in North America reported figures ranging from 6–62 per cent for female samples, and 3–31 per cent for male samples. The differences are often due to the way that sexual abuse was operationally defined, the types of activities, the characteristics of the sample studied and variations in research methodology.

Certain populations of patients have a higher rate of abuse, such as those with general psychiatric problems, anorexia/bulimia, self-mutilating behaviour, borderline and dissociative states and, particularly in those individuals, male and female, perpetrating abuse. Consistently 95 per cent of abusers are male (Bentovim *et al*. 1988), but there is a sub-group of women who themselves abuse (Finkelhor and Russell 1984; Tranter, 1992). Such women abuse alone or jointly with partners, creating a polyincestuous abusive context. There is a markedly high incidence of both sexual abuse and other forms of traumatic experiences in such individuals.

Children of all ages are abused in a ratio of about four girls to one boy. However, younger boys are relatively more at risk than younger girls, and boys are more at risk of extrafamilial abuse than girls. The oldest girl in a family is more at risk, as are children who have disabilities which render them more powerless and less able to communicate.

There is now a growing literature which is examining the longer-term effects of abuse, clinical and empirical (Haugard and Repucci 1988). Clinical descriptions include sexual dysfunction, depression, suicidality and guilt, isolation and disturbed interpersonal relationships, post-traumatic stress symptomatology, substance abuse, and other self-destructive behaviour and somatic complaints. Controlled studies demonstrate more marital and family conflicts, physical and sexual problems, adolescent turbulence, less sexual activity, greater amounts of sexual anxiety, sexual dysfunction, younger age of onset of problem drinking, more depression, lower self-esteem, less assertiveness: the (1989) study of Mullen *et al.* demonstrated a convincing link between abusive traumatic events in childhood and subsequent affective and phobic disorders in the adult life of women. Indeed, they put forward the view that the higher incidence of such disorders in adult women compared to men may be accounted for by abusive events in the childhood and adult life of women, compared to men. Watkins and Bentovim (1992) have brought together the literature describing the longer-term effects of abuse on men, and differences in abusive effects upon men and women.

TRAUMA ORGANISED SYSTEMS – A CONCEPTUAL MODEL TO UNDERSTAND THE PSYCHOPATHOLOGY AND LONGER-TERM EFFECTS OF ABUSE*

One way of understanding the longer-term effects of sexual abuse is to see it as a traumatic event which 'organises' subsequent emotional life and relationships. The notion of an organised system was introduced by Anderson *et al.* (1986). This is defined as a social action system which involves those engaged in communication about a particular problem. The language and way in which problems are communicated about creates the problem. In the sexual abuse field, a process of talking about the problem – such as Freud's first discovery – was replaced by silence. It is only following the phase of the third phase of discovery that the issue has fully been confronted and is now the subject of major communication and exploration. Sexual abuse is a traumatic event, and the way in which traumatic events are processed, and communicated about, is the heart of the problem. The way they are handled organises individual, interpersonal and professional relationships; the way they are represented or deleted from communication comes to determine the resulting system.

The notion of trauma suggests events of such intensity or violence that there is a breach in the defensive organisation of the organism. Helplessness overwhelms the individual; mastery, control and defence fail; there is a sense of unprotected disintegration, and acute mental pain. Helplessness and powerlessness thus become the central emotional experience. Sexual abuse represents often repeated overwhelming events, and represents a failure to respond to the core of the child's being.

There has to be a response to repeated trauma, and Bentovim and Kinston (1991) described a number of responses: the development of a self-sufficient shell; a compliant, clinging identification with the victim stance; or alternatively an angry identification with the abuser.

Flashbacks of the original event or avoidance of any contact which

---

* Bentovim and Davenport 1992; Bentovim 1992

reminds of the event can persist for many years. Feelings of guilt, soiling and disgust are common, fear maintains secrecy, disbelief and a sense of self-blame. Traumatic responses can be maintained in a frozen state for many years, and overwhelming feelings are deleted and the whole process obliterated leaving a 'hole' in the mind – a disaster to be avoided. This can orientate self-perception, relationships and personality development.

Finkelhor and Browne (1985) described the way in which such trauma-genic dynamics organise and create a style of perception and personality for the child who has been abused. Powerlessness is associated with the invasion of the body, absence of protection and repeated feelings of fear and helplessness. Stigmatisation is linked to the contempt, secrecy, blame and denigration so often associated with abuse. Betrayal through the manipulation of trust, violation of care and a lack of protection within the family unit, and traumatic sexualisation occurs through inappropriate responses being rewarded and an identification with victim or aggressor role activities often associated with gender effects.

Goldner *et al.* (1990) attempted to link psychodynamic social learning, sociopolitical and systemic notions to understand the development of abusive patterns of relating. The development of self and gender occurs during the same developmental phase. Abuse during childhood in addition gives rise to a conflict-laden layering of internalised self-representations that become the child and adult.

Gender is seen as a key concept in the development of self (see Chapter 5 of this *Handbook*). Boys construct themselves from a childhood negative – not being the mother, the primary caretaker. Gender structure in boys is thus threatened, and experiences such as separation conjure up echoes of the maternal bond. Women are seen as existing as reminders of what has to be given up. Girls, by comparison, see themselves as part of mother's psychological space; they identify, become empathic and claim their own voice by being the power behind the throne, the object of desire, or subject as object.

Marital violence is seen as an illusory way for males to seek personal power and psychic autonomy, to sustain the denial of dependence and dis-integration. Women have to submit to this reality, silencing their own voice and become organised into a cycle of violence, forgiveness and redemption.

For men who have experienced sexual abuse in childhood, the image of a child evokes their own experiences of powerlessness, sexual arousal and betrayal. An illusory way of seeking power and competence is to divest the self of traumatic experiences by projecting these onto a child. The child is perceived as the source of sexual interest, and the impulse to be sexual is felt to be beyond control, and addictive. A sexual orientation towards the child can take over the sexual life. Such an orientation can emerge during adolescence, and organise adult sexual patterns of relating. Alternatively, there may be a profound avoidance of sexuality since sexuality conjures up the same sense of powerlessness, and perhaps a profound fear of homosexuality in terms of a conviction that something special made the abuser choose them. The confusion of identity is even more profound for boys if the abuser is a woman in terms of who was the initiator, who the victim and who the victimiser.

Not all men who abuse have themselves been sexually abused, but there are frequent accounts of emotionally or physically abusive experiences in men who later abuse sexually. It may well be that the discovery of sexuality in adolescence provides an illusory way of creating emotional closeness out of a sense of profound emptiness and powerlessness.

There is a raised risk of homosexual activity as response to abuse in childhood for men. Eroticisation of abusive experiences may be a response which reduces the sense of powerlessness, stigmatisation and betrayal which organises thinking and feelings.

In girls who have been abused, through their identification with mother's role, they develop a conviction of being the cause of their own abuse. They are blamed for their sexual attractiveness by the perpetrator and they blame themselves. This leads to a feeling of stigmatisation, betrayal and/ or powerlessness, leading to self-destructive action, anorexia/bulimia, self-mutilation and profound deficits of self-esteem, depressive mood and the danger of taking victim roles.

It is striking that the majority of women who abuse have been abused sexually themselves, but only a small proportion of women who have had abusive experiences do perpetrate abuse themselves. There is a clinical impression that women who do abuse have often been inducted into active roles, with siblings in a polyincestuous family contact. Again, as in boys, there may be an eroticisation of abuse experienced with perverse role development which encapsulates the abusive experience and maintains it in an addictive fashion.

The interlocking choice of partners is often striking. Mothers of children who have been abused by their partners describe a high level of sexual and physical abuse themselves, and both mothers and abusive fathers describe childhoods with few happy memories. Whether this is because men with an abusive orientation instinctively sense which potential partners with children can be organised into a compliant mode, or whether this is on a mutual unconscious basis, is not clear.

However, studies on families where abuse has occurred (Madonna *et al.* 1991) reveal that such families are characterised by high levels of marital dysfunction, parents focused on their own needs rather than their children's, being emotionally unavailable to their children; and children expected to comply with adult needs.

What becomes clear is that sexual abuse occurs in highly dysfunctional contexts, and that as a result the thinking, feeling and actions of children who are subjected to rejection, physical, emotional and sexual abuse render them vulnerable to future victim or perpetrator behaviour. There are likely to be profound effects on their functioning, self-esteem, sexual functioning, and their ability to become partners or to parent. The meaning attributed to the self is profoundly affected, and therapeutic work with such individuals has to take a broad-based view.

THE THERAPEUTIC PROCESS IN WORKING WITH THE LONGER-TERM EFFECTS OF CHILD SEXUAL ABUSE

Working with the longer-term effects of child sexual abuse into adult life implies the following:

1 The original 'frozen' effects of sexual abuse have to be processed on both an emotional and cognitive level. The core sexually abusive experience needs to be fully disclosed and shared, and a variety of therapeutic approaches are often needed to accomplish this task.
2 The effects of such experiences on the development of the individual has to be tracked, on the sort of man or woman they have become, the degree in which particular roles as partners and/or parents occur; adult functioning in the sexual field, in the relationship field, relationships with men, with women; the development of the self in terms of capacities needs to be addressed; and assessment of unrealised potential.
3 There is no one therapeutic modality which will achieve all these goals, nor therapeutic style. Just as working with sexual abuse in childhood demands individual, family and group work, with a variety of approaches – psychodynamic, behavioural, psycho-educational (Bentovim *et al.* 1988) – so work with those adults who have been abused in childhood requires a variety of therapeutic contexts and therapeutic modalities.

Draucker (1992) describes the following stages:

1 disclosing the experience of child sexual abuse;
2 focusing on the abuse experience itself;
3 addressing the context of the sexual abuse;
4 focusing on current desired life changes;
5 resolving issues of abuse.

These represent helpful stages of therapeutic work.

Disclosing an experience of child sexual abuse

Although currently an increasing number of survivors of abuse are explicitly seeking therapeutic help – for example, following accounts in the media – many cases still present in a hidden way. Both individuals seeking therapeutic help for the distressing effects of their abuse, and those who may be less aware of the connection between current symptomatology and previous experiences, may be testing the capacity of the psychotherapist to be able to hear, understand and respond in an appropriate way to such experiences. The psychotherapist's capacity to hear and know about the possibility of abuse is a major factor in the discovery of abusive experiences. Many individuals previously reported the disbelief of their psychotherapists, and the perpetuation of blame for their own abuse through the interpretation of incestuous wishes. This reinforces the attribution of guilt and responsibility for the adult's sexual interest towards them as children.

A therapeutic context of silence and waiting for disclosure may itself re-create an abusive context and reinforce the silence which accompanied abuse. Many survivors of abuse describe the silence and the secrecy of their abuse, the father who comes in the night, the silence that is taken as consent. A therapeutic silence may trigger the sense of helplessness, powerlessness and even the flashbacks of the memories of abuse that characterise the longer-term effects. Not surprisingly, the patient or client then leaves feeling retraumatised by the psychotherapist.

Children who have been abused report a positive response to a therapeutic stance which joins with them, leads rather than follows, gives them a structure of questions and activities rather than leaving uncomfortable silences. This reflects the qualities of non-possessive warmth and accurate empathy which characterise good therapeutic work (Monck *et al.* 1993). The issue is to find a therapeutic approach which meets the needs of known traumatised individuals, and also encourages the disclosure of those who may have been traumatised. It is not surprising in this particular field that group work, self-help groups and survivor groups have had an important developmental role since they conquer the sense of aloneness, isolation and conviction of responsibility for their own abuse.

Disclosing sexual abuse

Such are the multiple effects of abuse in men and women that a screening approach is necessary for the many different presentations. Direct, blunt questions such as 'Were you a victim of incest or sexual abuse?' are not helpful. It is far more useful to ask questions such as: 'Many more people with complaints similar to yours are telling us about distressing or uncomfortable experiences in their childhood – experiences which they often found themselves thinking about, and being cross that the thoughts about it remain. Have you had such experiences? As a child, for instance, were you touched in a way that felt uncomfortable, embarrassing, even frightening? As a child did anybody ever ask you to do something sexual that you did not like? Were you hurt in a sexual way? If something like that had happened would it be worse if it was somebody close in the family or someone more distant? What would be the effect of revealing something of this nature at the time or now?'

If there is a denial but if the psychotherapist feels that there are strong possibilities of abuse, it may be helpful in recalling the effects of abuse to ask about and explore such possibilities, but without the force and conviction which can inappropriately 'lead' the patient. Ellenson (1990) suggested that the following should be explored as being possibly connected with abuse:

1 nightmares of recurring catastrophe; nightmares or dreams which describe harm to the self or children, death or violent scenes;
2 intrusive obsessions – for example, to hurt one's child, to feel one's child is endangered;
3 dissociative sensations, feeling that one is a child, or one's self is experienced as a stranger, feelings of being 'spaced out';
4 persistent fears of being alone, or in physically compromising situations;
5 a variety of perceptual disturbances such as illusions of an evil entity being present; auditory phenomena being called out to; intrusion of sounds;
6 visual or tactile hallucinations, movement of objects in the peripheral vision, feelings of being touched or thrown down.

These are all reminiscent of abusive experiences which have been partially 'deleted' from consciousness – the return of the repressed.

Disclosing abuse for men is particularly difficult because of the powerful fears of homosexuality associated with their being chosen as a sexual object, in many cases by men. Associated with this is a fear of not fulfilling a masculine image, or the reverse effect, identification with the aggressor, and adopting a 'hyper'-male invulnerable stance and the development of an abusive orientation. Being treated as a thing can result in a compliant response, an angry, battling, manipulative response, or an invulnerable stonewall response reminiscent of some descriptions of borderline personality.

Struve (1990) pointed to the following issues in the abuse of males. It is necessary to think of the possibility of abuse when the following patterns are noted:

1 Dynamics of shame, based on the perceived failure to protect oneself, or the desire to achieve revenge. This can have a very real and dangerous effect; e.g., a boy of twelve who had been abused by a man who had befriended him. Some three years later such was the intensity of his feeling of shame and desire for revenge that he killed the man in a way which had obviously been planned over a period of time. A major sense of rage and angry outbursts may be associated with such experiences of abuse.
2 Major difficulties occurring with male identity, including avoiding behaviour, which may be associated with body sensations of head or body parts shrinking. The avoidance of behaviour which may be perceived as feminine, including emotional intimacy, may also be noted.

3 Difficulties with sexual identity due to fears of being perceived as passive, or associated with sexual arousal triggered by a member of the same sex.

4 Denial of feelings, a sense of unreality and invulnerability, minimisation of the effects of any contact which is reported. There is frequently a report of less traumatisation by men who have been abused by women, perhaps related to the notion that sex with an older woman is a 'macho' privilege. Associated with such a sense of invulnerability may be very poor social functioning.

Therapeutic responses to disclosure

It is essential for the psychotherapist to respond in an appropriate way when a disclosure is made. The disclosure should not be responded to as a surprise; emotional support should be given, and links made between such experiences when revealed and current disturbances in an appropriately tested way. The opportunity should be taken to point out how such childhood responses and feelings can persist in a more or less repressed way. Also an explanation needs to be given that talking and remembering is painful, and that there may well be a period of regression following the initial relief at having shared a long-standing painful matter. Tolerating memories and returning reminiscences whilst matters are talked through will require a good deal of strength and support, but is the route to real forgetting.

Without real forgetting it can be asserted that memories will recur unexpectedly; they will be triggered by somebody who looks like, or reminds the patient of, places, people and events. Thus a world of fear is created rather than one which can be controlled. Remembering, working through and 'forgetting', or at least placing in a known area of mastery, with some of the major painful affect removed, is the aim of therapeutic work. Understanding the confusions and avoidances often associated with current relationships, sexual dysfunction, parenting and partner difficulties can make a tremendous difference. It can be pointed out that the aim is 'to develop a coherent narrative of one's life, rather than one broken up with major areas of pain, distress and deletion, literally to fill the holes in the mind' (Bentovim and Kinston 1991: 284).

Such explanations form a part of the initial therapeutic contract in that it spells out the task. Until there is further exploration of the extent of abuse it is difficult to estimate the intensity of therapeutic work that would be required. There should be a contract of regular work; the individual should be living in a safe context in terms of the availability of social support outside the therapeutic context. Significant others in their lives should know that support is necessary, and enough of the reason to understand the process. There are major advantages in family meetings – for example, with siblings, supportive parents, partners and children – so that there can be proper explanations given for what is happening, and if necessary joint meetings to explore issues which are focused on the links between past and present.

Specific tasks in therapeutic work

Reviewing experiences

It is essential early in the therapeutic process that a detailed description of abusive experiences is shared. This means reviewing the duration and frequency of abuse, identity of the offender(s), the form of abuse and method used to carry out abuse – use of physical force, methods to achieve and maintain silence. Types of sexual activity need to be explored, and it is important to ask about all sexual activities which are possible with children in a way which implies that the psychotherapist is aware that children are involved in all forms of sexual activity. The psychotherapist may well need to explore such matters gently but confidently, so that the patient does not have a projected fear that the psychotherapist cannot hear or bear to think of such possibilities. The ages of child and offender need to be explored.

Contextual matters also need to be explored, which include the role of other family members in the abuse, or their response to attempts at disclosure. If disclosure did occur, what happened, how did other members of the family respond? Who was protective, comforting, blaming? Did the offender take responsibility? What happened then? Were there other important family matters in context? How did the patient make sense of what was happening, both the abuse and responses to it?

It is helpful to have such information in a factual way and to be clear that this information will form the basis of the exploration of associated feelings and beliefs which developed and which persist. Getting such information in a non-emotional way is important, and the notion of 'assumptive interviewing' is helpful in such an exploration.

Assumptive interviewing implies that the interviewer has a detailed knowledge about abusive activities, so that if the patient talks about a digital touch in the vaginal area it may be appropriate to ask not only, 'Did he touch you with any other part, such as his penis?', but 'How long was it before he started to use his penis?'

Investigative interviewing techniques need to be more cautious; for example, when interviewing children the questions would be, 'Did he touch you with any other part of his body?' rather than making assumptions about a penile touch. But to trigger memories the possibility of the fact has to be raised; also all possibilities need to be explored – oral, anal, genital – all possible abusers need also to be explored, and any use of threats, bribery, force and so on.

Exploration of feelings

It is almost inevitable that in the exploration of what actually happened, feelings will undoubtedly be aroused and such explorations can themselves be therapeutic. The essential task in exploration of feelings is to process the event emotionally in a similar way to the processing of traumatic events involved in post-traumatic phenomena. This implies the retelling of events in an emotionally supportive context to separate the event from the overwhelming accompanying defects.

Sharing feelings has a cathartic effect and can also begin to help process matters cognitively. This implies the re-editing of the distortions involved in abuse through retelling. An adult conversation automatically re-edits experiences and beliefs which emerge from childhood. Internalised conversations and beliefs about such events and about the self may have persisted for many years (White 1989). White and his colleagues introduced techniques to externalise such conversations, rather than to maintain internalised dialogues and narratives. They point out that techniques such as the following may be helpful in co-constructing a new reality and understanding:

1 Were there days you did not feel that way about what happened to you? What did you do, or what did somebody else do, that managed to make you feel differently? What could you do now that could have the same effect, and find an 'exception'?
2 Are there days when you feel more powerful than the abuse experiences, when you know that you are in control of it rather than it being in control of you? What do you do on those days that seems to make a difference?
3 If a miracle happened and all these memories and distressing events were no longer to be in control of your life, how would you know that it was the case? What would be the signs?
4 When patients report feeling less anxious, more of a survivor, they may be asked, 'When did you first realise, perhaps even years ago, you had it in you to recover, even though you felt so overwhelmed by such events for many years?'

This approach to constructing a new reality has an important application to many areas of developing survival rather than victim roles.

The advantages of doing such work in a group context may be considerable. Such groups may need to be single-sex, with individuals sharing similar experiences. They need to be theme-centred, or task-structured so that a clear brief can be developed in terms of encouraging participants to be open about experiences, to share, support and confront when necessary, and to look at specific issues in a variety of ways.

There is a major drive towards self-help survivor groups, which may indeed be extremely valuable. But it may be more difficult for such non-led groups to confront issues such as the attachment to abusers, sexual responses and wishes to resolve and forgive. Such groups can maintain a sense of anger, outrage and revenge which may give solidarity to other members of the group, but may be destructive to the individual who wishes to move on.

Dealing with traumagenic effects

Recalling experiences and discussing the details, and the feelings associated with abusive experience, will re-evoke the feelings themselves. The traumagenic effects of sexualisation, powerlessness, betrayal and stigmatisation will reveal themselves in self-description of relationship, reflected within transference/counter-transference responses with the psychotherapist, in the interactional patterns revealed between partners, and within the current and extended family revealed in family meetings.

The advantage of group contexts to share and confront traumagenic dynamic effects is very considerable. Finding a similarity of responses, and seeing reflections and mirroring, can help define them as 'not only me' responses and can begin to trigger 'new' conversations and narratives of the self as powerful, confident, normally sexual and a survivor, not a victim. Responses within the one-to-one therapeutic setting can elicit profound reflections of traumagenic effects. Indeed, there is a danger of a psychotic transference formation. The advantage of a face-to-face approach in dealing with these feelings is considerable in terms of being able to modulate and help containment rather than an escalating runaway effect.

Cole and Barney (1987) described two phases of the 'stress response cycle', and the way intense emotional responses can be regulated, to cope with severe emotional responses. These are as follows:

1 *Denial phase*: this is characterised by amnesia, repression, minimisation, withdrawal.
2 *Intrusive phase*: this is one of intense affect, perceptual experiences, hallucinations, nightmares associated with tremors, sweating, re-experiencing.

There is a therapeutic need to maintain a balance using what Cole and Barney described as the 'window' between the two states to make the situation manageable. Group work can help break through the denial phase, but may reinforce the intrusive phase. There is a need to develop coping techniques, and to structure sessions to maintain an appropriate degree of containment.

A progressive toleration of the memories of experiences and their associated affects is a key in the therapeutic process itself and the move towards survival. It is important that patients should know what to expect, and should be helped to feel in control to be able to take matters at their own pace, yet to be encouraged to move forward. Crisis services may need to be in place, linking with family and extended support networks during this phase.

The management of traumatic symptomatology

General aspects

The importance of describing and locating traumatic responses such as flashbacks is to help not to suppress them, but to recapture the original experience so that there can be a working through. This is essential in the coming to terms with the victimisation experience. However, techniques may need to be developed to help maintain control. These include the following:

(a) *Control techniques*: e.g., grounding techniques. This can consist of planting the feet firmly on the floor, grasping the chair, focusing on breathing, perhaps by breathing out and letting anxiety out by counting to three. Developing an internal conversation which asserts that one is in the present not the past.

(b) *Self-hypnotic techniques*: associated with this may be the teaching of self-hypnotic/relaxation techniques. The 'ten steps down' induction process, associated with sitting in a comfortable seat with control levers to take control of the situation, can be a helpful way of gaining control. Other possibilities are the notion of finding a warm, comfortable space to assist in coping, which has been found particularly useful when there is an urge to self-mutilate.

(c) *Cognitive techniques* restructure flashbacks and nightmares by, for instance, changing the ending, bringing in a protector in imagination.

(d) *Role-play psychodramatic techniques and/or re-editing techniques*: such techniques may be used in groups, families or individual contexts. They are intended to re-edit the context in which the traumatic symptoms originated by literally bringing in the abusing parent in imagination, role-play, the Gestalt empty chair, through letters, art forms, simulated conversations, or the use of non-verbal sculpting.

These are all means of re-editing, changing realities, creating a different belief or reality structure.

In dealing with emotional responses and/or traumatic effects, it is essential to maintain both a 'symptomatic' and 'systemic' approach. Although traumatic events have an organising effect on relationships, undoubtedly current relationships also reorganise and reshape experiences and responses. Making major changes for the individual in symptom control, re-editing or restructuring can be very valuable, but it is also important to bear in mind the way in which current relationships may have been shaped, choices of partners made, or even responses induced in the other, which can all have a reinforcing and maintaining affect on symptomatic patterns.

It is important to maintain a systemic view at all times which considers the living context and relationships of the patient, and the effects of change: improvements, worsening, competence and incompetence. Work with partners may well be indicated. Such responses include the way in which the psychotherapist is made to feel, or find themselves reflecting some of the processes. The importance of supervision and training aspects of this work cannot be stressed too greatly.

Specific traumatic symptomatology

Self-destructive behaviour

Mutilation, overdosing and substance abuse are all ways of 'avoiding' painful affects and memories by creating perhaps other sources of pain or escape. It is essential to be able to use symptomatic approaches to take control, but also to be aware of long-standing patterns of response in significant others. Similar methods need to be used to deal with self-destructive behaviour as with any other symptom as described above; for example, control techniques, cognitive, hypnotic, role-plays, re-editing, and working with the individual and significant others.

Aggression against others

Distress is an affect which can be described with ease by women, but far less easily by men. Anger is a far more difficult emotion to help women express initially, whereas for men this may have already been institutionalised as an interactional mode. Bruckner and Johnson (1987) described within male survivor groups the problem that, after disclosure, men made plans for retribution, physical assault and validation of anger. It is essential to confront and help individuals be aware of the very major danger to themselves of such assaults.

The role of retaliation as a post-traumatic effect is now being increasingly well recognised. Powerful emotional responses emerging as anger need to be managed, facilitating the development of the verbal expression of anger and the constructive use of assertion.

Substance abuse

Substance abuse, as already indicated, is an aspect of self-destructiveness based in poor self-esteem. To admit powerlessness in the face of alcohol and substance abuse may be a major problem, since it confirms the original sense of powerlessness associated with abuse. To help patients admit that they are powerless in the face of alcohol may be the first step towards taking control of the abuse itself. Alcoholics Anonymous can provide a major support for such problems, but individuals need to be aware that they will be asked to tell their stories and helped to decide how much and what is appropriate to say in the context of the AA groups. The use of detoxification as a part of the treatment will also be essential.

General self-care

A key role in the long-term effects of abuse is around the focus of self-care. There may be a drive towards obsessive, perfectionistic approaches; alternatively, the disguise of any attractiveness, whether in women or men. Women wear clothes that cover themselves up, making themselves deliberately unattractive. Group members can give positive feedback in a variety of ways, and help with self-esteem, gradual acceptance of the body and an increasing sense of attractiveness and sexuality.

Body image problems are associated with anorexia/bulimia (Oppenheimer et al. 1985), and may represent a form of avoidance, of oral reminders of abuse. Anorexic responses mean that one area of life, the body, is controlled; but feelings of the body, being the 'cause' of the abuser's interest, remain.

The link between eating disorders, the emotional aspects of borderline states as described in DSM III and early traumatic experiences is now being convincingly demonstrated.

COGNITIVE PROCESSING OF SEXUALLY ABUSIVE EXPERIENCES

The traumagenic dynamic effects which have been outlined in children and young people have a major organising effect on the young person and future adult's view of themselves. There is a maintenance of the child's views and beliefs concerning the events – such as they were to blame, they are bad, dirty, responsible for the adult's interest in them, or that any sexual responses on their part confirm their sense of responsibility.

Children generally, in fact, have fairly clear views at the time of the abuse that the abuse is not their responsibility. It may well be that secrecy or failure to process experiences can gradually result in an increasing sense of responsibility for their own abuse. Abuse may represent affection or attention. They may feel that this is a form of sacrifice of their own lives to benefit their families. A small proportion of children (5–15 per cent) feel that the abuse was a positive aspect of their lives, a normal part of family life. There may be positive feelings about the abuse earlier on, but with later development in adult life the individual may feel to be in a different role to contemporaries. A young girl of twelve felt that her father's abuse of her was a major source of affection. Later she felt outraged at the degree of his betrayal when she discovered herself to be very different from her peers. She had sexual needs they did not, she became pregnant and angry with herself. Fundamental beliefs about self and the meaning of events require a good deal of processing and reframing.

Changing fundamental beliefs: reframing abusive experiences

There are a variety of corrective questioning techniques which can be valuable in cognitively processing abusive experiences and leading to a more functional set of beliefs. Circular questioning, future questioning, questioning expecting a variety of responses can achieve these goals. A young person of fifteen felt that her parents would not have continued abusing her seriously if they had realised that it was wrong. She felt that if they had known they would have stopped. She was asked: if she had read her story in a newspaper, then hypothetically what would she say – would she say the young person was responsible? Feel angry with the parents? Introducing other realities helped her re-edit her own self. A more formal approach to achieve this goal is cognitive restructuring (Jehu 1988).

Cognitive restructuring

Jehu's approach consists of the following:

1 Giving an understanding of the way that events and experiences can result in a variety of unhelpful beliefs.
2 Identifying the beliefs that automatically accompany cues and feelings. This may require a variety of approaches, relaxation, imagery to re-experience, description of flashbacks. All these trigger beliefs; e.g., about being responsible for the adult's sexual interest in them; that there will never be a possibility of feeling sexually towards a peer; that being abused creates a sense of dirt, worthlessness, inevitable damage. Out of such responses it is possible to outline beliefs and distortions.
3 Exploring alternatives. Using a variety of resources such as videos, written information, assertions, information from other group members, the patient is encouraged to explore alternative beliefs, to build up a different view of themselves, and to experiment with their new beliefs.

Structured group approaches

A similar approach has been developed in what has been described as a psycho-educational group approach, although there is often a combination of dynamic group therapeutic approaches together with a more cognitive psycho-educational approach. There are a variety of models used in such groups, but the majority follow a more or less structured theme in terms of topics to be discussed and ways of working. They may use experiential techniques, maybe watching videos, role play, Gestalt techniques, empty chairs, writing letters to abusers, re-enacting and re-editing experiences; exploring topics such as mothers' attitudes, the abuser's attitudes, sibling attitudes, exploring issues of self-protection and difficulties of being able to protect; issues of relationships with same and opposite sex; sex education, sexual anxieties, the care of children, heterosexual and homosexual issues.

Such issues may, of course, come up spontaneously, but it may well be helpful to have a series of themes and different ways of exploring them.

THE THERAPIST ROLE AND RESPONSES

Using a clearly structured approach with a sense of purpose, an approach which understands the processes and follows through themes in a logical fashion can maintain the task of emotional and cognitive processing. The use of male and female co-therapy teams in working with families and groups may help both to enact and deal with re-experiencing within the patient–psychotherapist relationship by offering a model of a consistent male and female partnership.

At the same time, whatever approach is used – group context, individual or family work of a structured nature, a non-directive approach relying on the development of transference/counter-transference – the original traumatic experience may well be re-created and re-experienced. Patients who have been abused are often exquisitely sensitive to the therapeutic atmosphere. Feelings of rejection or abuse may be re-experienced, responses from the psychotherapist may be interpreted as enactments of abusive relationships. The sex of the psychotherapist can bring forth stereotypes of maleness and femaleness depending on how the self and other have been structured through early experience. Breaks, interruptions, time issues, all confirm feelings of powerlessness and betrayal, and the appropriate interpretations may have mutative effects.

Psychotherapists often require consultation to deal with the identification with the patient's sense of despair, damage, feelings of being soiled, sexual responses and confusion that may be experienced by the psychotherapist. Whatever may be traumatising to the patient can also awaken and put psychotherapists in touch with their own traumatic experiences. Such reflections can both help in terms of an understanding of a patient's experience, and can also have its own devastating effect. The bringing forth of responses and fantasies of a disturbing nature for psychotherapists is also a by-product of dealing with adult survivors. Transference responses which can move from neurotic to psychotic need careful monitoring.

Family work benefits greatly from having live supervision or a reflective team, but the need for openness between the observing team and the family is an essential part to avoid feelings of being traumatised through a fear of voyeurism and excitement; for example, the use by Anderson *et al.* (1986) of the reflective team.

It is also possible for psychotherapists who work extensively in this field to feel burnt-out and overwhelmed, and unable to respond to patients' distress, or to minimise and disregard feelings and experiences. When this occurs psychotherapists need the support of a team, and the opportunity for a variety of work to counter the pervasive effects of traumatic experiences and effects and supervision.

Filling the hole in the mind which is created in the face of overwhelming stress by remembering, reminiscing and working through is a highly stressful experience for both patient and psychotherapist, and needs to be held and contained towards resolution.

Dealing with the context of abuse

It is essential that connections are made between previous experiences, the way in which they have been processed and the way in which this affects current life. This is part of the process of exploring the context of the abuse rather than personal response to it.

Exploring past contexts

There are a variety of ways of exploring the original family contexts which may have played an important role in the creation of traumagenic dynamic effects. Such exploration plays an important part in the resolution of persisting feeling states. This includes explorations through geneograms with the individual and/or the convening of meetings with original family members. An example is the case described by Bentovim and Davenport (1992) of a woman abused in childhood who had a meeting with her male siblings who, it turned out, had also been abused, although less seriously, then had subsequent meetings with her mother and finally with the abuser.

Bentovim *et al.* (1988) described a sequence of treatment stages in working with the family. This commences with working on the relationship with the mother. She is often felt to have played a key role in terms of the feeling of betrayal, not listening or hearing. Work with siblings is also important in terms of the resolution of emotional cut-offs.

Work with the abuser is very much to do with final resolution of abusive experiences. This may require specific work with the abuser to assess whether there is any possibility of such a meeting. The question has to be asked: can the abuser take responsibility for his abusive action and make a real apology to the individual who has been abused?

Meetings without preparation can be counter-productive, in the sense that fresh rejection and denial can occur. Old alliances and blaming of the adult who has been abused in childhood can renew a sense of helplessness and powerlessness. It is often necessary to do some extensive individual and family work with family members to co-construct a more satisfactory resolution.

The alternative is to use a variety of techniques within a peer group or with the psychotherapist to look at previous relationships; for example, using sculpting, non-verbal techniques, using the empty chair, letters, role plays, and creating a different belief system in terms of views of self and experiences.

Current issues

Self-esteem

Self-esteem is one of the major personal issues which survivors have to deal with. Dealing with guilt and shame, the process of listening, sharing experiences, change of attributions and beliefs regarding the abuse, all play an important role in building self-esteem. A variety of different interventions are often necessary, ranging from cognitive restructuring in terms of deeply held negative views of self as worthless, blameworthy or soiled. The routine use of positive statements to one another in groups can be a helpful reinforcer in terms of building on small changes that have been made; the seeking for exceptions and exploring how this came about in order to co-construct and reconstruct different realities of the self; for example, days when the individuals felt good about themselves.

Interpersonal functioning

There are some basic major issues of interpersonal functioning which need to be considered, which include the development of trust, maintaining appropriate boundaries between self and other, maintaining an appropriate affective contact with others, and dealing with important issues such as parenting and partnering, particularly sexuality and sexual relationships.

Such issues need to be dealt with in a variety of different contexts. Trust arises through the therapeutic process itself in terms of the consistency and appropriate response of individual psychotherapists, or within group and family contexts. Work needs to be done with the individual and significant others in his or her life, whether these be partners or family members, where appropriate. It is likely that the traumagenic effects will translate into structural family interactional patterns. Even if the individual has dealt with some of the personal traumatic issues, this may be insufficient to change the interpersonal structural responses once they have been initiated. Thus marital psychotherapy and more extensive family therapy is often necessary to deal with these issues.

Sexuality and sexual functioning in women

There can frequently be an extensive abusive effect on the capacity to function sexually. There are major differences between a sexual relationship which was not sought, and one which is freely entered. Sexual contact of any nature can trigger off experiences of powerlessness or flashbacks of inappropriate experiences, and lead to major avoidance. Women need to deal with a number of stereotypes which exist in any case in society; for example, women's roles to 'please men', to be submissive, are all reinforced by abusive experiences and traumagenic dynamic effects of abuse. Such beliefs need to be changed in a variety of ways, whether this be in group contexts, individual or couples therapy.

There may need to be a classic Masters and Johnson's programme, followed by couples therapy, to help a woman regain a sense of sexual freedom and control, and to begin to change the context. It is important to ensure that those individuals who have developed a homosexual orientation are helped to reinforce their choice of partner, but at the same time to ensure that appropriate attention is paid to the re-enactment of victim/perpetrator roles within the relationship.

One of the most difficult issues for women to deal with is the fact that a sexual response can be brought forward in the sexually abusive context and may have a major effect on sexual orientation for women; for example, choice of partner, sexual response patterns and experiences. This may well be one of the most difficult issues to discuss within group contexts because it would imply acceptance and even a compliant response to abuse. Psychotherapists, whether in group contexts or individually, need to be able to show an understanding and almost an assumption that such responses are possible, and to expect sexuality to be shaped by an abusive experience.

Although the adoption of a sexually abusive role for women is a less frequent response than for men, it has now been recognised that it does occur and must be acknowledged. Work with such women needs to follow a similar sequence to work with men; for instance, identifying the cycle of abuse, what triggers an abusive impulse, the nature of abusive actions, what follows abusive action, masturbatory reinforcement, and the connection to abusive experiences.

Adult experiences may also be processed through an internal 'conversation' which leads to the development of perverse sexuality and the eroticisation of abusive context. A woman in her thirties described a split way of relating to her husband, the father of her children, who was non-sexual and caring and looked after her and her children, and her exciting lover, who was not at all parental but with whom there was an intensity of relating, considerable excitement and arousal accompanied by sadistic fantasies of a beating nature. She was a woman who had been abused more by the intense interest and voyeuristic behaviour of her step-father, and later physical contact. She was able to 'resolve' her split following an extensive piece of therapeutic work by finding a partner who 'brought together' the two men into one. She had also been able to write to her brother, to 'construct' a narrative which made sense of her experiences.

Male sexuality and sexual functioning

The sexual responses of males to victimisation is, in many ways, similar to the responses of female survivors, such as the feelings of avoidance, the danger of intense eroticisation of experiences. Flashbacks and memories of abuse may be transformed through masturbation to sexually active arousal patterns and may trigger the sexualisation of other children. Powerlessness is a particular danger for men, and power is regained by abusing others in a retaliatory fashion. There may be the reverse – total avoidance or a passive, victimised response.

The fact of being abused generally by somebody of the same sex brings in the issues of conflict with the general societal view that males are not victims. The link with later homosexual patterns and major problems of sexual identity are also evident. A form of abuse which is perhaps not so explicit is the cross-dressing of boys by mothers who both pour themselves into their child and have an intense wish for a female child. This is a common pattern (for example, Green and Money 1961; Stoller 1968) in transvestism and possibly transsexualism, with far more profound issues of identity.

The danger for men of developing a violently aggressive sexual pattern, an abuser pattern towards other children or a rapist's profile is a very real risk depending on the particular context in which the boy has grown up (Watkins and Bentovim 1992). For men, as with both sexes, dealing with sexual problems requires an exploration of orientation; understanding the details of sexual avoidance and sexual dysfunction; exploring the details of impotence, ejaculation failures, non-responsiveness or hyper-responsiveness; a detailed examination of behavioural patterns, sexual preference, use of pornography, masturbatory patterns, and an examination of both the victim cycle in terms of the response within sexual encounter, and abusive cycles if they have been initiated.

The importance of partner work where sexual dysfunction has become part of a couple's problem is important for both men and women, and it is necessary to look at various contexts to work in, such as groups for men who have been abused and have begun an offending pattern. Most practitioners feel that it is preferable to commence by working on offender patterns, before dealing with issues of empathy for victims and victim experiences. A variety of cognitive behavioural programmes, group work approaches, have been devised to 'process' and construct more functional sexual patterns.

Forgiveness and resolution

It can be helpful to work with the extended and current family in group contexts so that those who have abused take responsibility either directly or by proxy through re-enactment, role play or psychodramatic techniques. In any therapeutic process the act of forgiveness and understanding something of what led to abuse is an essential component of resolution. It is impossible to do so at an early stage in therapeutic work, and abusers who ask their victims to 'forgive them' may compound an abusive situation.

Also what can be helpful is for an abuser to say 'sorry' for any act on their part. We have found it helpful with abusers who have 'forgotten', repressed or deleted their own abusive actions, to say that they had forgotten what happened, but they are sorry for any act which they did commit. This sometimes enables situations to move on and for the possibility of the establishment of a new situation. A failure to resolve or begin to understand and forgive can have an entirely negative effect on recovery from abuse. Long-standing grievances can have a 'corrosive' effect on the self and relatedness. To be healthy and feel undamaged implies that the abuse was not so bad; it is better to be angry and feed grievances. The use of a variety of group and family contexts to 'enact' the abuser's guilt, 'grieving' the loss or absence of a caring parent, may all assist resolution.

Research on the outcome of therapeutic work with survivors of abuse is very much in its infancy. We know very little about the long-term effects of specifically organised treatment programmes since they have come into being so very recently. It is essential that we do a variety of different outcome research to know what components are the most helpful, and with whom (see Chapter 3 of this *Handbook*). It would be helpful to know who can be best helped through group work, individual work, a psychodynamic approach, a cognitive-behavioural approach, self-help groups, leader-led groups, the use of enactment, role play and psychodramatic techniques.

One suspects that carrying out such research would be extremely difficult because almost inevitably each group of practitioners who have developed and practised a particular approach to psychotherapeutic work will inevitably use what they are familiar and comfortable with.

It would be valuable if the different elements of a therapeutic programme could be looked at critically, and that there could be some agreement to be pragmatic in terms of what actually works and is helpful.

The impact on mental health of early sexual abuse is considerable, and deserves the attention now being given to the topic.

CASE STUDY: JANE

Jane, a teacher aged forty-five, referred herself to Marianne Tranter on the recommendation of a friend who had consulted her in the past.

At the first meeting Jane sketched out her current difficulties: she was cohabiting with Giles, a musician aged forty-eight with whom she had a relationship of two years' standing. Although Jane felt basically happy with Giles, she experienced some anxiety/aversive responses during lovemaking which had led her increasingly to avoid sexual contact and situations which might lead to sex, such as ordinary affectionate contact. This was creating a significant strain on the relationship, and Jane was increasingly fearful of losing Giles whom she described as 'very attractive (to women) and highly-sexed'.

Jane, mindful of this, therefore tried to overcome her apprehension of sexual contact, feeling she owed Giles a 'sexual outlet' or else he might seek one elsewhere. However, in accommodating Giles in this way she was at the same time feeling considerable resentment towards him and was also doubting herself as woman, feeling very much a failure.

In subsequent weekly sessions the following information emerged. Jane's parents had separated when Jane was three and her sister Deborah was five. Their mother, Mary, subsequently met and married Stephen, who joined the household when the girls were seven and nine and became their step-father. Within a year it became customary for the girls to have a Sunday morning 'cuddle' in the parents' bed – an experience which was remembered as 'horrid' by Jane. She began to remember with more clarity what happened: her step-father would have one girl sit next to him whilst the other sat next to mother. When it was Jane's turn, he would stroke her thighs and vaginal area and digitally penetrate her. Because of his forceful personality, although Jane tried to avoid this contact and wriggle away, he would pull her back and glare at her, making her feel terrified to say anything. She had to appear as though nothing was wrong; she was very puzzled as to whether or not her mother knew and had never felt able to tell her. She was very aware as a child of her mother's dependence on Stephen; the marriage was sometimes violent and Stephen drank excessively on occasion but her mother always appeared to make allowances for him.

Jane wondered whether her sister suffered in the same way when she was next to step-father – but she gave no clue and Jane felt unable to ask her.

Eventually, when Jane was thirteen, her mother and step-father separated. Her mother had several other partners and always enjoyed going out, even though she and her daughters were living in virtual poverty and Jane could remember having to hide from bailiffs and debt collectors.

Jane left home as a young adult and, after having one or two boyfriends, married at twenty-three. Her husband (a doctor) was very demanding sexually, and Jane assumed that she should comply with his demands because that was expected of her. She was unable to express some of her negative feelings about their sexual relationship. Her husband became very impatient with her and rather intolerant, and undermined her. She developed a depressive state, the relationship deteriorated and eventually they separated, with her husband forming a new relationship with one of Jane's friends. Jane had various other fairly short-term relationships, interspersed with periods of living on her own. She had good, close contact with a circle of women friends, although in some ways found herself seeking in them some of the closeness she felt she lacked with her mother and sister (who both emigrated fifteen years before to America).

She had had a very difficult and ambivalent relationship with her mother whom she felt had betrayed her. She could acknowledge angry feelings towards her for having 'allowed' her abuse by her stepfather, and never having stuck up for her (Jane) or herself. She could remember the fuss her mother would make of him and other male partners and her fear of being alone.

She felt her mother had over-accommodated the men in her life for fear of losing them, and could see some similarity here in her relationship with Giles. Jane felt she had had to tolerate her step-father's abuse of her for fear of rocking the boat, provoking a family row, and risking marital breakdown between her mother and step-father. Similarly she had felt she had to tolerate her husband's sexual demands and avoid causing an argument. She felt too embarrassed/intimidated/unsure of herself to confront him with how she felt, remained silent and became depressed. With Giles she had a fear that a similar pattern was repeating itself, and this had precipitated her decision to seek psychotherapy.

Continuing therapeutic work

Over the following weeks and months Jane was encouraged to explore further her memories and feelings about the abusive experiences. She felt guilty and 'dirty', and as though she were defiled by her step-father. She became contemptuous of herself (and others); she had an aversion to her own body, not liking to touch her own private parts, let alone have her lover do so. Once lovemaking progressed beyond foreplay, however, she could enjoy intercourse. The psychotherapist suggested Jane explore her own body more and engage in some masturbatory activities where touching of her genitalia could be associated with pleasure in an anxiety-free context.

Jane was also encouraged to discuss her aversion to foreplay with Giles and let him know what other erogenous zones could be touched without causing anxiety. She found that oral genital contact was more pleasurable and less anxiety-provoking than digital penetration.

She was also encouraged to take the lead sometimes in lovemaking so that she felt in control rather than passive/anxious as before, and to help construct contexts in which she could feel relaxed and anticipate sexual contact without becoming anxious. Giles was perfectly amenable to Jane's requests and alternative suggestions for their lovemaking, and responded positively to Jane's attempts to communicate more openly about their sexual relationship. The fact that he wanted sex more often than she did still posed a certain dilemma for Jane. Should she 'give in' and accommodate him, or should she let him know she 'wasn't in the mood', and so risk losing him (a constant fear) like her mother's fear of losing Stephen and others? Jane felt both indignant at being so contained, but apprehensive of 'rocking the boat' and fearing conflict and/or rejection.

Her self-esteem was quite precarious, and she had difficulty, despite her obvious intelligence and ability, in being assertive; she often 'put up' with people and situations for 'an easy life', although would sometimes be furious with herself for doing so. She blamed herself for 'putting up' with her abuse and not telling her mother, although she came to understand some of the constraints which had prevented her from doing so. When, after a year in psychotherapy, she finally found the courage to ask her sister if Stephen had ever done anything to her, she was mortified to discover that he had, and that her silence and self-sacrifice had not managed to protect Deborah as she had hoped it would. The futility of it made her suffering seem even worse. The power of secrecy (surrounding the abuse) infuriated her now whereas previously it had made her feel utterly impotent.

She veered between thinking that her mother must have known about it (how could she not have?) to finding this intolerable (why did she do nothing to stop it?), and she was unable to trust her; indeed, she had had considerable difficulty in making trusting relationships during much of her adult life and then seemed to go out of her way to develop close friendships (possibly as substitute attachment experiences). Whereas her friendships with women were based on reciprocity, her relationships with men – both personal and professional – were much less so and she often felt intimidated and bullied by them. Her birth father's rejection of her and her sister following his remarriage appears to have contributed to her sense that men did not really cherish her unconditionally but had an ulterior motive (sex or power) in relating to her. It was quite a revelation to her that Giles could accept and not reject her just because she sometimes dissented to making love.

Explaining and understanding and working through the contradictory and ambivalent feelings about her abuse and mother's failure to protect her seemed gradually to lead to some resolution of her past and current dilemmas and, at follow-up, eighteen months after psychotherapy ended, Jane remained well, was happy in her relationship with Giles, was less anxious about sex and more self-assertive. She was planning to visit her sister and mother and, with her sister's support, intended to confront her mother about her abuse and 'find out some anwers to lots of questions I still have'.

The therapist's style

The therapist was a woman (MT) with considerable experience both in working with child and adult victims of sexual abuse, and of working in marital and family therapy using a variety of related techniques. The establishment of an empathic, warm rapport created an essential context in which Jane could 're-tell' and 're-edit' the traumatic experiences of her childhood, and helped to explore possible connections with them and subsequent patterns of personal development and openness.

Jane already made warm relationships with women, so the working therapeutic alliance was established with little transference distortion. Transference responses were not the focus of the therapeutic work and the shared task of resolving the effects of early abuse defined the therapeutic process.

With the use of cognitive and behavioural techniques and encouragement to feel more in control of her sexuality, Jane was helped to reconstruct a more satisfactory sexual relationship with her partner, free from the tyranny of the repetitive patterns emanating from the abuse and its context. The therapist's knowledge of the psychological consequences of such abuse enabled her to identify the patterns of traumatic sexualisation, powerlessness, stigmatisation and betrayal, and through the development of trust to begin to reverse them.

Breaking the power of secrecy, including sharing her experience with Giles (and her sister and prospectively her mother), helped Jane to create a new reality.

REFERENCES

Anderson, H., Goolishian, H. and Winderman, L. (1986) 'Problem determined systems towards transformation in family therapy', *Journal of Strategic and Systemic Therapies* 5: 14–9.

Bentovim, A. (1992) *Trauma Organised Systems – Physical and Sexual Abuse in Families*, London: Karnac.

Bentovim, A. and Davenport, M. (1992) 'Resolving the trauma organised system of sexual abuse by confronting the abuser', *Journal of Family Therapy* 14: 51–68.

Bentovim, A., Elton, A., Hildebrand, J., Tranter, M. and Vizard, E. (1988) *Child Sexual Abuse within the Family: Assessment and Treatment*, Bristol: John Wright.

Bentovim, A. and Kinston, W. (1991) 'Focal family therapy – joining systems theory with psychodynamic understanding', pp. 284–324 in A. S. Gurman and D. P. Kniskern (eds) *Handbook for Family Therapy*, vol. 2, New York: Basic Books.

Bruckner, D. F. and Johnson, P.E. (1987) 'Treatment for adult male victims of childhood sexual abuse, social case work', *Journal of Contemporary Social Work* 68: 81–7.

Cole, C. H. and Barney, E. E. (1987) 'Safeguards and the therapeutic window: a group treatment strategy for adult incest survivors', *American Journal of Orthopsychiatry* 57: 601–9.

Draucker, C. B. (1992) *Counselling Survivors of Childhood Sexual Abuse*, London: Sage.

Ellenson, G. S. (1990) 'Detecting a history of incest: a predictive syndrome (social case work)', *Journal of Contemporary Social Work* 66: 525–32.

Finkelhor, D. (1979) *Sexually Victimised Children*, New York: Free Press.

Finkelhor, D. and Browne, A. (1985) 'The traumatic impact of child sexual abuse: a conceptualisation', *American Journal of Orthopsychiatry* 55: 530–41.

Finkelhor, D. and Russell, D. (1984) 'Women as perpetrators: review of the evidence', pp. 171–87 in D. Finkelhor (ed.) *Child Sexual Abuse: New Theory and Research*, New York: Free Press.

Goldner, V., Penn, P., Scheinberg, M. and Walker, G. (1990) 'Love and violence: gender paradoxes in volatile attachments', *Family Process* 29: 343–65.

Green, R. and Money, J. (1961) 'Effeminacy in prepubertal boys', *Paediatrics* 27: 286–91.

Haugard, J. and Repucci, N. D. (1988) *The Sexual Abuse of Children*, London: Jossey-Bass.

Herman, J. L. (1981) *Father–daughter Incest*, Cambridge, MA: Harvard University Press.

Jehu, D. (1988) *Beyond Sexual Abuse*, Chichester: Wiley.

Kinsey, A. C., Pomeroy, W. B., Martin, C. E. and Gebhard, P. H. (1953) *Sexual Behaviour in the Human Female*, Philadelphia: Saunders.

Landis, J. (1956) 'Experiences of 500 children with adult sexual deviances', *Psychiatric Quarterly Supplement* 30: 91–109.

Madonna, P., Scoyk, S. and Jones, D. (1991) 'Family interaction within incest and non-incest families', *American Journal of Psychiatry* 148: 46–9.

Masson, J. M. (1989) *Against Therapy*, London: Collins.

Monck, E., Bentovim, A., Goodall, G., Hyde, C., Lwin, R. and Sharlande, E. (1993) *Child Sexual Abuse: A Descriptive and Treatment Study*, London: HMSO.

Mullen, P. E., Romans-Clarkson, S., Walton, D. A. and Herbison, G. P. (1989) 'Impact of sexual and physical abuse on women's mental health', *Lancet* 1: 841–5.

Oppenheimer, R., Howells, K., Palmer, R. L. and Chaloner, D. A. (1985) 'Adverse sexual experience in childhood and clinical eating disorders: a preliminary description', *Journal of Psychosomatic Research* 19: 357–61.

Peters, S. D. (1986) 'Prevalence', pp. 15–59 in D. Finkelhor (ed.) *A Source Book of Child Sexual Abuse*, Beverly Hills, CA: Sage.

Stoller, R. J. (1968) *Sex and Gender: On the Development of Masculinity and Femininity*, London: Hogarth Press.

Struve, J. (1990) 'Dancing with the patriarchy: the politics of sexual abuse', pp. 13–46 in M. Hunter (ed.) *The Sexually Abused Male*, vol. 1, Lexington, MA: Lexington Books.

Tranter, M. (1992) 'A study of women who abuse', Paper given to conference on Female Abusers, Westminster Hall, London.

Watkins, W. and Bentovim, A. (1992) 'The sexual abuse of male children and adolescents: a review of current research', *Journal of Child Psychology and Psychiatry* 33: 197–248.

White, M. (1989) 'The externalising of the problem and the reauthoring of lives and relationship', *Dulwich Centre Newsletter*, Adelaide: Dulwich Centre Publications.

Chapter 24

Sexual contact between psychotherapists and their patients

Tanya Garrett

LITERATURE SURVEY

Until relatively recently the issue of the sexual abuse of patients in psychotherapy had received little attention in the theoretical and research literature. It is now an established area of attention in the United States, but it is only within the past year or so that the issue has been taken up in the United Kingdom.

It is clear from North American research that sexual contact between psychotherapists and their patients is a significant problem, but that, like rape and child sexual abuse, it is under-reported.

In the United States, half the money for malpractice cases is spent on complaints regarding sexual intimacy (Pope 1991a). About 13 per cent of allegations of professional misconduct handled by the American Psychological Association (APA) insurance trust in 1981, and 18 per cent of the complaints to the APA Ethics Committee in 1982 involved sexual offences. Yet suits and complains are rarely filed, only in about 4 per cent of cases, and only half of these are completed (Bouhoutsos 1983).

The issue of therapist–patient sexual contact can be traced back over many centuries to its prohibition in the Hippocratic Oath (Bouhoutsos 1983). In more recent times, indirectly in their ethics codes the British professions have maintained this proscription by referring to, for example, the need for professional conduct which does not damage the interests of clients, or public confidence in the profession (British Psychological Society 1991). North American professions have, however, explicitly prohibited sexual contact with patients in their Codes of Conduct, and one has even produced a Position Paper on the subject (Sreenivassan 1989).

The taboo on sexual contact between psychotherapists and their patients has been raised and challenged in recent years in the context of growing sexual freedom in society (Siassi and Thomas 1973), and by articles in the popular press (Sinclair 1991). The last few decades have seen an increasing acceptance of physical and emotional intimacy between psychotherapists and their patients under the guise of humanistic approaches to psychotherapy, and a few psychotherapists have even openly advocated sexual relationships between psychotherapists and their patients (McCartney 1966; Shepard 1971).

The process of data collection in this field has been problematic. Butler and Zelen (1977) were threatened with expulsion from a professional organisation when they suggested research into the field of psychotherapist–patient sexual intimacy, and when early research was allowed, the results were suppressed (Forer 1968, cited in Bouhoutsos 1983). Not until the 1970s, at least in the United States, was concerted attention given to the problem (Bouhoutsos 1983), with a proliferation of research and theoretical papers.

Epidemiology

Until 1992, no systematic information was available in the United Kingdom for any professional or lay group of psychotherapists on their sexual contact with patients, or their attitudes towards it.

Generally speaking, the research in North America has yielded no differences in any epidemiological respect between the main psychotherapy professions of psychology, psychiatry and social work. It would therefore be reasonable to consider the surveys of different professions as a whole. No empirical evidence is available to date to indicate the extent of sexual contact between other professionals and lay psychotherapists and counsellors, and their patients.

Most surveys have found that, overall, something under 10 per cent of professional psychotherapists have had sexual intercourse with their patients. Kardener et al. (1976) indicate a figure of 6–7 per cent; Pope et al. (1979), 7 per cent; and Pope et al. (1986), 6.5 per cent. Pope et al. (1987) have more recently found significantly lower rates of sexual contact with patients than previous studies: only 1.9 per cent reported having had sex with a patient. Although Holroyd and Brodsky (1980) found that 3.2 per cent of respondents to their survey had had sexual intercourse with a patient, another 4.6 per cent engaged in other types of sexual behaviour.

As one might expect, there are large differences between male and female psychotherapists in this respect. When the overall figures are broken down by gender of psychotherapist, the percentage of male psychotherapists who engage in sexual intercourse with patients rises to around 10 per cent, and it becomes clear that women offenders form only a tiny minority of the total number. For example, Gartrell et al. (1986) surveyed US psychiatrists and found that 7.1 per cent of male and 3.1 per cent of female psychiatrists had had sex with patients. Other surveys indicate figures of 3 per cent and 12 per cent for women and men respectively (Pope et al. 1979); and 2.5 per cent and 9.4 per cent (Pope et al. 1987); and 0.6 per cent and 5.5 per cent whilst psychotherapy was ongoing (Holroyd and Brodsky 1977). The latter study found that

8.1 per cent of men and 1 per cent of women had ever had sex with patients.

The research suggests that a slightly higher number of psychotherapists have had 'erotic' non-intercourse contact with their patients. Somewhere between 3 and 13 per cent of psychotherapists fall into this category (Kardener *et al.* 1976; Pope *et al.* 1987).

Overall, according to recent research, it would appear that the rate of psychotherapist–patient sexual involvement is declining in the United States (Pope 1990).

The vast majority of North American psychotherapists have indicated in surveys that they believe sex with patients to be unacceptable. For example, Pope *et al.* (1987) found that 95 per cent of respondents believed that sexual contact with a patient is unethical, and about half believed that becoming sexually involved with a former patient is unethical. A similar result was achieved by Borys and Pope (1989).

In the light of these factors, sexual contact between psychotherapists and their patients must therefore be viewed within the broader context of gender and therefore power issues in psychotherapy. In particular, these power imbalances are demonstrated by the lack of mutuality evidenced in sexual contacts between psychotherapists and their patients or, in Claman's (1987) terms, in that the psychotherapist remains sole recipient of the mirroring and idealising in the 'relationship'.

In terms of what distinguishes offenders from non-offenders, it is clear that whilst offenders are more likely to advocate and use non-erotic touching of patients, they do not differ on most demographic variables from psychotherapists who do not have sex with their patients (Holroyd and Brodsky 1980).

There is, however, some evidence to suggest that psychotherapists who have had personal psychotherapy, or who had sexual contact with educators during professional training, may be more likely to develop sexual liaisons with their patients. Gartrell *et al.* (1986) surveyed US psychiatrists, and found that offenders were more likely to have had personal psychotherapy. This is the only study to look at this area, and the robustness of the association requires further testing.

Pope *et al.* (1986) argue that educator–student sex is a model for later psychotherapist–patient sex. For female respondents engaging in sexual contact with educators as a student was related to later sexual contact as professionals with patients, a figure of 23 per cent as compared with 6 per cent who had not had sexual contact with educators. For male respondents, the sample was too small to test the relationship. In summary, many psychotherapists who have sexual relationships with their patients were themselves sexually involved with their own teachers, supervisors or psychotherapists (Folman 1991; Pope 1989).

The earliest information about the characteristics of psychotherapists who become involved with their patients was provided by Dahlberg (1970), based on cases of psychotherapists who had had sexual relationships with their patients, whom he had treated. Usually, psychotherapists were over forty, ten to twenty-five years older than the patient; and always male. In those cases where sufficient information was available, the psychotherapist was having severe marital problems. Most psychotherapists practising at that time, Dahlberg points out, would be fairly unusual in their withdrawn-ness and introspection, studiousness and passivity, shyness and intellec-tualism. Having thus been unpopular with women, psychotherapists suddenly find themselves in the unusual position of having their female patients attracted to them, and thus, a fantasy fulfilled.

Gonsoriek (1987) gives information derived from the accounts of patients who have used the Minneapolis Walk-in Counselling Centre for clients who allege sexual involvement with psychotherapists. These psychotherapists were a diverse group, ranging from the uninformed (usually para- or non-professionals with little or no training in the area of boundaries and standards of care: an example of this would be the untrained 'hypnotherapist' who had sexually abused nine patients, described by Hoencamp (1990)), through those who are psychologically healthy or mildly neurotic (usually the largest category, whose behaviour is related to life stresses), the more severely neurotic or socially isolated, to those with impulsive, sociopathic or narcissistic character disorders, and psychotic or borderline personalities.

Butler and Zelen (1977) interviewed twenty offender volunteers, both psychologists and psychiatrists. Of these, 90 per cent had been vulnerable, needy and lonely in relation to marital problems at the time of the sexual contact with patients. Some psychotherapists saw themselves as domineer-ing and controlling (15 per cent): this would be supported by a case reported by Hoencamp (1990), but most (60 per cent) saw themselves as in a paternal relationship with the passive and submissive patient. Most experienced conflicts, fears and guilt.

In terms of the motivation for initiating sexual contact with a patient, Sonne and Pope (1991) conclude that psychotherapist–patient sexual intimacy usually involves anger (battering the patient, emotionally abusing the patient or recommending activity which will harm the patient, but are ostensibly intended for the patient's benefit), power (viewing the patient in almost exclusively sexual terms, substituting the patient for a significant figure in the psychotherapist's life, attraction to pathology, authoritarian orientation, and being attracted to a physically immobilised patient) and sadism (pleasure in causing pain and sexualised humiliation). Most studies agree that power need motivates psychotherapists who have sexual contact with their patients (Bouhoutsos 1983).

In a study of an in-patient facility, Averill *et al.* (1989) found that there were two main groups of care staff who became sexually involved with patients. First, a collection of younger, exploitative individuals, and secondly, a group of older, middle-aged, isolated staff who were experiencing personal problems which triggered longings for nurturing. Both groups appear to have considered their own needs and issues at the expense of those of their patients.

It is important to note that psychotherapists who have sexual contact with one patient are at a high risk of re-offending: about 33 per cent do so, and may abuse up to twelve patients, according to a study conducted by Gartrell *et al.* (1986). Earlier studies suggest higher figures: Holroyd and Brodsky (1977) found that 80 per cent of those who had sexual contact with patients in their study had done so with more than one patient. This would accord with the 75 per cent of psychiatrists who had been sexually involved with more than one patient in a study conducted at around the same time (Butler and Zelen 1977).

Dahlberg (1970) argues that the psychotherapist who becomes sexually involved with patients is usually a shy individual who does so against a background in psychotherapy sessions of having women attracted to him and informing him of this. When psychotherapist and patient become sexually involved, the psychotherapist is acting out a fantasy of 'being young, attractive and having beautiful girls throwing themselves at you without having to take the chance of being rejected by being the one who makes the first move' (Dahlberg 1970: 119). That is, there is a fantasy of masculine omnipotence by virtue of being in a position of power as a psychotherapist and a man, in sexual terms; as well as being older than the patient. Thus, Dahlberg concludes, sexual involvement with patients would be much less common in female psychotherapists.

Claman (1987) suggests that the research evidence shows that many sexually abusive psychotherapists fit a pattern of narcissistic disturbance of the self; such psychotherapists harbour from their childhood unfulfilled longings to be mirrored and needs to merge with others. When sexual contact occurs, these needs are mirrored by the patient, who functions as a self-object. Such a pattern would fit the research finding that abusing psychotherapists' relationship patterns tend to be problematic (Zelen 1985), and could go some way towards explaining the intractable nature of this problem.

Characteristics of patients who become sexually involved with psychotherapists

The literature describing the patients who become sexually involved with their psychotherapists has identified a variety of patient characteristics. Belote (cited in Bouhoutsos 1983) found female patients who had been sexually involved with their psychotherapists to be vulnerable and high on traditional feminine attributes such as other-directedness, poor self-image, low self-actualisation and little acceptance of their own aggression. Averill *et al*. (1989) found that in their in-patient sample the typical patients who had become sexually involved with their psychotherapists were those with borderline personality disorders, a history of childhood sexual abuse (about 32 per cent – Pope and Vetter 1991) and/or rape (about 10 per cent – Pope and Vetter 1991). They were usually involved in extended treatment with maximum opportunities for transference.

On the basis that psychotherapist–patient sex involves boundary violations, it has been argued that such violations are most likely to be evoked by patients with borderline personality disorder (Gutheil 1989) because of their rage towards the psychotherapist, their neediness and dependency, their confusion of the self/other boundary, and their manipulativeness and strong feelings of entitlement. These dynamics evoke powerful counter-dynamics in the psychotherapist, which can easily lead to boundary violations. However, it is here important to caution against locating the blame for psychotherapist–patient sex exclusively with the patient, particularly as Gutheil (1989) asserts that the majority of the patients who wrongly accuse psychotherapists of sexual abuse fall within this category. Cases of false accusation should not detract from the substantial numbers of psychotherapists who have behaved in a sexually abusive manner towards their patients.

Most patients who become sexually involved with their psychotherapists are female, and a numerically small, but none the less significant minority are minors – 5 per cent in a study by Pope and Vetter (1991). When Bajit and Pope (1989) looked at cases of psychotherapist sex with child patients, 81 examples emerged. Of these 56 per cent were girls, 44 per cent were boys. The ages ranged from three to seventeen, mean 13.75, with a standard deviation of 4.12.

Pope and Bouhoutsos (1986) suggest that three major categories of patients emerge from the literature: a low-risk group who, although they are highly stressed, are essentially healthy; a middle-risk group with a history of previous relationship problems and who may be personality-disordered; and a high-risk group with a history of hospitalisation, suicide attempts, major psychiatric illness and substance abuse problems. A high percentage of the women in the latter group had also experienced childhood sexual abuse.

Certainly, the patient who enters psychotherapy after being sexually involved with one psychotherapist is at considerable risk of sexual involvement with her new psychotherapist (Folman 1991; Gartrell *et al*. 1987). However, whether this is a result of patient or psychotherapist factors remains unclear.

When does sexual contact with patients occur?

In around three-quarters of cases, psychotherapists begin a sexual relationship with their patients after termination of psychotherapy. Figures vary from 69 per cent (Gartrell *et al*. 1986) to 77 per cent (Pope and Vetter 1991). Around 18 per cent of sexual contacts occur in sessions, and 17 per cent concurrent with psychotherapy, but outside sessions (Gartrell *et al*. 1986).

Does psychotherapist–patient sexual contact get reported – and what happens when it does?

Most authors agree that sexual abuse by psychotherapists is vastly under-reported. In a study of psychologists who had treated patients who had been sexually involved with a previous psychotherapist, Pope and Vetter (1991) found that only 12 per cent of the patients filed complaints.

Although Levenson (1986) argues that professionals have an ethical obligation to intervene and to report their knowledge of unethical practice by a colleague, when Gartrell *et al*. (1986) looked at the reporting practices of psychiatrists who knew of sexual misconduct by colleagues, only 8 per cent of cases were reported, but the majority favoured mandatory reporting of such cases.

One recent report in the literature describes a case of sexual abuse of two thirteen-year-old children by a nurse who had been convicted and sentenced through the criminal justice system. The case was referred to the UKCC, where judgement was first deferred (during which time he committed further offences) and, following reprimands, the nurse was subsequently allowed to remain on the register and practice as a nurse. This case was reported by Long (1992), who criticises the UKCC for its failure to protect the public.

How many sexually abusive psychotherapists admit their behaviour or seek help?

In the two studies available in this area, a relatively high percentage (41 per cent) sought 'consultation' (Gartrell *et al*. 1986), and Butler and Zelen (1977) found a similar figure of 40 per cent who had sought help from a colleague.

UNDERSTANDING SEXUAL CONTACT IN PSYCHOTHERAPY

The relationship between sexual attraction towards patients and sexual contact with them

Freud's prohibition on kissing, other preliminaries, and sexual contact with patients has had, Pope and Bouhoutsos (1986) argue, the un-intended consequence of psychotherapists becoming suspicious of any warm feelings towards their patients, thus intensifying anxiety around psychotherapist–patient sex and inhibiting full recognition of the problem and of attempts to address it.

It is important to recognise that sexual attraction towards patients is very common, at least among psychologists; in surveys, well over half of the psychologists (more frequently men) responding admit sexual attraction towards and sexual fantasies about their patients (Pope *et al.* 1986; Pope *et al.* 1987). This can give rise to anxiety; most psychologists, whilst admitting to sexual attraction towards their patients, are concerned about this (Pope *et al.* 1986), and a substantial minority believe it to be unethical (Pope *et al.* 1987). Reluctance to acknowledge and discuss the issue may well be contributing to our difficulty in confronting the reality of the sexual abuse of patients by psychotherapists (Pope 1990), especially in the United Kingdom. We may thus be reluctant to address sexual feelings for patients in professional training courses, and in this way may miss the opportunity to prevent psychotherapist–patient sexual contact from developing (Pope 1989). So our anxiety may directly contribute to the occurrence of sexual contact between psychotherapists and their patients.

Why do most psychotherapists refrain from sexual contact with their patients?

Pope *et al.* (1986) asked participants in their survey why they did not engage in sexual contact with patients. The reasons were usually to do with ethics, values and professionalism, as well as the belief that it would be counter-therapeutic. Other motives, however, touched on issues such as the psychotherapist already being in a relationship, fear of damage to oneself as psychotherapist, fears around one's reputation or of censure, either generally or on the patient's part, in terms of retaliation.

Why do some psychotherapists engage in sexual contact with their patients?

Herman *et al.* (1987) report that 2 per cent of psychiatrists believed that sexual contact with a patient could be indicated to enhance self-esteem, as a corrective emotional experience, to treat a grief reaction, or to change a patient's sexual orientation. Slightly more, 4.5 per cent, believed that it could be useful in treating a sexual difficulty, and 4 per cent believed it could be appropriate if the patient and psychotherapist are in love. Gechtman (1989) shows that 10 per cent of social workers believed that sex with a psychotherapist may be beneficial to the patient, and Gartrell *et al.* (1986) found that most sexually abusing psychotherapists thought that the patient's experience of psychotherapist–patient sex was positive. Pope and Bajt (1988) found that in 9 per cent of cases, psychologists had argued that they had engaged in sexual relations with a patient for the treatment and welfare of that patient.

Butler and Zelen's (1977) postal survey yielded twenty psychotherapists, both psychologists and psychiatrists, who had had sexual contact with their patients and who volunteered to be interviewed. Among them, 90 per cent reported being vulnerable, needy and/or lonely as a result of relationship difficulties when the sexual contact occurred. Some psychotherapists saw themselves as domineering and controlling (15 per cent), but most (60 per cent) saw themselves as in a paternal relationship with the passive and submissive patient; 45 per cent admitted to rationalising in order to permit otherwise unacceptable behaviour during psychotherapy. Most experienced conflicts, fears and guilt.

The use of touch in psychotherapy

The psychoanalytic tradition has always maintained a taboo on physical contact with patients, on the grounds that touching introduces reality into the therapeutic relationship and consequently gratification and tension reduction, which would both render problematic the identification and understanding of transference material, diminish the range and depth of the material and reduce motivation to engage in psychotherapy. There is a recognition, however, that other therapeutic approaches which concern themselves with the patient's reality may not consider touch to be problematic in certain circumstances.

Even within psychoanalysis, there is, however, disagreement. Touch is viewed by some as acceptable in the case of patients with certain presenting problems, such as delusions, or to provide a corrective emotional experience, or dependent on the theoretical approach of the clinician. Sponitz (1972, cited in Goodman and Teicher 1988) captures the debate in asserting that the use of touch in psychotherapy should be contingent on whether it would contribute a maturational quality to the therapeutic relationship.

Most of the literature concurs that touch should be used judiciously and with caution (Edwards 1981). This is particularly true because there are many different types of touch (Edwards 1981), which can be anything from nurturing to aggressive, prompting to sexual. Particularly for more damaged patients, touch may result in a loss of inhibition, or may be experienced as a sexual promise which, when unfulfilled, can make the patient feel betrayed and abandoned. It is also important to consider the power dynamics of psychotherapy and consequently how the patient may perceive being touched by the (powerful) psychotherapist. Furthermore, it is possible that whereas a psychotherapist may not touch a patient with sexual intentions or implications, the client may either perceive it as such or have sexual feelings towards the psychotherapist.

The American Psychological Association adopted the following statement regarding physical contact with patients: 'permissible physical touching is defined as that conduct which is based upon the exercise of professional judgement, and which, implicitly, comports with accepted standards of professional conduct' (1982, cited in Goodman and Teicher 1988: 492).

The research evidence supports the view that touch should either be avoided, or used with extreme caution, and advocacy of the use of touch in psychotherapy should be treated somewhat suspiciously. Pattison's (1973) findings on the effects of touch on patients and the therapeutic relationship were that patients who were touched engaged in more self-exploration, and touch had no effects on their perception of the relationship with the psychotherapist, suggesting that touch in psychotherapy may be extremely helpful to the therapeutic process.

However, some research has demonstrated a relationship between touching patients and sexual contact with them. For example, a survey by Kardener et al. (1976) showed that the freer a physician is with non-erotic physical contact, the more statistically likely they are also to engage in erotic practices with patients. Holroyd and Brodsky (1980) found that psychotherapists who had sex with patients advocated and used non-erotic contact with opposite-sex patients more often than other psychotherapists. Those who had non-intercourse sexual contact, however, did not differ from other psychotherapists in their use of non-erotic touching. So, 'the differential application of non-erotic hugging, kissing and touching to opposite sex patients but not to same sex patients is viewed as a sex-biased psychotherapy practice at high risk for leading to sexual intercourse with patients' (Holroyd and Brodsky 1980: 807).

Holroyd and Brodsky (1977), in a survey of psychologists' attitudes towards erotic and non-erotic physical contact with patients, found male psychotherapists to be more likely to see benefits in non-erotic contact for opposite-sex patients. In this context, it is relevant to note that the use of physical contact with patients is a relatively common practice in psychotherapy. Results of a survey by Pope et al. (1987) show that a quarter of respondents had kissed a patient and 44.5 per cent hugged clients rarely, with 41.7 per cent doing so more frequently. Most were prepared to shake their client's hand and most did not consider this to be unethical. Holroyd and Brodsky (1977) found that 27 per cent of their respondents engaged in non-erotic physical contact, mostly humanistically orientated psychotherapists. In general physicians, more female practitioners than male believe in and use non-erotic touch with patients (Perry 1976).

The effects on patients of sexual contact with their psychotherapist

Systematically gathered empirical data regarding the effects of psychotherapist–patient sex have only recently become available. Traditionally, these relationships have been assumed to be harmful to patients (Marmor 1972), but some writers have more recently argued that such contact may be beneficial (for example, McCartney 1966).

Taylor and Wagner's (1976) review of every available case in the literature of psychotherapist–patient sexual contact (thirty-four in all) showed that the majority had negative or mixed effects on the patient, but 21 per cent reportedly had positive effects. However, this conclusion must be interpreted in the light of the psychotherapist's motivation, and the findings (Holroyd and Bouhoutsos 1985) that (1) psychologists who reported that no harm occurred to patients as a result of sexual encounters with their psychotherapists are twice as likely themselves to have had sex with a patient than are psychologists generally, and (2) psychologists who have been sexually intimate with patients are less likely to report adverse effects of sexual intimacy, either for patients or for psychotherapy.

In a survey of psychologists who had treated patients who had been sexually intimate with a previous psychotherapist, Pope and Vetter (1991) found that harm had occurred in 90 per cent of cases overall. Harm also occurred in 80 per cent of the cases in which psychotherapists engaged in sex with a patient after termination of psychotherapy. Butler and Zelen conclude on the basis of interviews with psychotherapists who had had sexual contact with their patients, that 'it was not a therapeutic experience for either patient or therapist' (1977: 145).

There is only one report in the literature which attempts to study as close to experimentally as possible the effects of psychotherapist–patient sex. Feldman-Sumner and Jones (1984) compared women who had had sex with psychotherapists, women who had had sex with other health-care practitioners and women who had had sex with their health professional. The first group had a greater mistrust of and anger towards men and psychotherapists, and a greater number of psychological and psychosomatic symptoms than the third group. The first two groups did not differ in terms of the psychological impact of the sexual contacts. Severity of impacts was significantly related to the magnitude of psychological and somatic symptoms prior to treatment, prior sexual victimisation and the marital status of the psychotherapist/health care practitioner.

As a result of their work with victims of psychotherapist sexual abuse, and of growing anecdotal reports in the literature (for example, Schoener et al. 1984) of the damaging effects of psychotherapist–patient sexual contact, Pope and Bouhoutsos (1986) have developed the concept of the 'therapist–patient sex syndrome', which includes ambivalence and guilt (Schoener et al. 1984), feelings of isolation and emptiness and cognitive dysfunction (Vinson 1984, cited in Pope and Bouhoutsos 1986), identity and boundary disturbance and inability to trust (Schoener et al. 1984; Voth 1972), sexual confusion, lability of mood and suppressed rage (Schoener et al. 1984) and increased suicidal risk (D'Addario 1977, cited in Pope and Bouhoutsos 1986; Pope and Vetter 1991). Patients' symptoms are increased (D'Addario 1977, cited in Pope and Bouhoutsos 1986: Voth 1972) and hospitalisation is frequently necessary (Pope and Vetter 1991;

Voth 1972), as well as the development of disturbances in interpersonal relationships (Bouhoutsos *et al.* 1983: Voth 1972).

RECENT UK RESEARCH

An anonymous, confidential postal survey was undertaken at random of a thousand clinical psychologist members of the Division of Clinical Psychology of the British Psychological Society. A questionnaire was sent to subjects to gain epidemiological information about respondents' personal and professional circumstances, to ascertain their use of physical and sexual contact with patients, and to assess their experience of sexual contact between them as students and educators and with personal psychotherapists where applicable. Finally, questions were included about experience of treating patients who had had sexual contact with previous psychotherapists and knowledge of clinical psychologists who have become sexually involved with patients. Space was provided for further comments. The development of the questionnaire was informed by previous research in the United States.

A 58 per cent response rate (580 questionnaires) was received. For the purposes of this chapter, data are presented on 300 respondents. Many respondents did not answer some questions. The data given here exclude these non-responses; thus, for much of the data, percentages will not, when totalled, reach 100 per cent.

Among respondents 62 per cent were female and 36 per cent were male. Their mean age was thirty-nine years (range 25–77: s.d., 8.41) and the mean length of post-qualification practice as a clinical psychologist was eleven years (range 0–40: s.d., 7.74). Most respondents were married (60 per cent) or in a stable relationship (21 per cent). Many (13 per cent) were single and 4 per cent were separated or divorced, only 1 per cent describing themselves as widowed. The majority of subjects described themselves as heterosexual (96 per cent), with 2 per cent stating that they were bisexual and 1.7 per cent homosexual.

The most commonly cited influences on theoretical orientation were behavioural-cognitive-dynamic, in that order (11 per cent), or combinations thereof: cognitive-behavioural-psychodynamic (5 per cent) and psychodynamic-cognitive-behavioural (4 per cent). Just under 6 per cent of the sample identified their orientation as behavioural-cognitive-systemic, and 5 per cent as cognitive-behavioural-systemic.

Subjects gave their main area of clinical work (Table 24.1) and their main work setting (Table 24.2).

Respondents spent a mean fourteen hours per week in face-to-face patient contact (range 0–40: s.d. 7.21) and had a mean 14 per cent of patients in long-term psychotherapy (range 0–100: s.d. 22.42). Most respondents worked on a short-term basis with patients: 66 per cent of

Table 24.1 Respondents' main area of clinical work (percentages)

Adults	51.5
Children and young people	14.0
Learning difficulties	15.6
Elderly	5.3
Physical health	3.0
Neuropsychology	4.0
Other	3.7

Table 24.2 Respondents' main work settings (percentages)

National Health Service	89.7
Private practice	3.0
Social services	1.3
Voluntary agencies	0.3
Other	4.0

subjects' patients were in short-term psychotherapy (range 0–100: s.d. 30.61). A narrow majority of subjects had not undertaken personal psychotherapy (56 per cent), but a substantial minority had done so (43 per cent). Of these, women were more likely to undertake personal psychotherapy than men.

Most respondents (56.5 per cent) reported having been sexually attracted to a patient, but 42.9 per cent said that this had never happened to them. Male subjects were more likely to report experiencing sexual attraction towards patients. Of the subjects 87 per cent expressed current unconcern about the attraction, whereas 13 per cent were concerned.

Attitudes towards, and incidence of, sexual contact with patients

Although 3 per cent of the sample did not respond when asked whether they believed that patients could ever benefit from sexual contact with a psychotherapist, 3.7 per cent responded positively to this question, with 93 per cent responding negatively. Of the sample 4 per cent admitted to having engaged in what they regarded as sexual contact with current or discharged patients; 2 per cent had had sexual intercourse with a patient; and 2 per cent had engaged in other forms of erotic contact. One per cent of subjects did not respond to this question; 58 per cent of these psychologists were male, and 42 per cent were female. The male psychologists had exclusively engaged in sexual relations with female patients, and of the female psychologists, 20 per cent had had sexual contact with female patients and 80 per cent with male patients.

They were divided equally in terms of marital status between married, single and in a stable relationship. Most were heterosexual (67 per cent), a quarter were homosexual, and 8 per cent were bisexual. Of those psychologists who said that they had engaged in sexual contact with a patient, 83 per cent had done so with only one patient. For 17 per cent of these individuals, sexual contact had occurred with three patients. All of the psychologists were mainly employed in the NHS.

Of the psychologists who identified themselves as bisexual, it was a female psychologist who had had sexual contact with a male patient; of the heterosexual psychologists, 75 per cent were male having sexual contact with a female patient. Of those psychologists who identified themselves as homosexual, half were female psychologist–female patient contacts and half were female psychologist–male patient sexual involvements.

The most frequent number of occasions on which respondents had had sexual relations with patients was one (42 per cent). One individual reported three occasions, one reported four occasions, and one, ten occasions. One-third of those psychologists who had had sexual contact with patients did not respond to this question.

Over half (58 per cent) had not engaged in sexual contact with a current patient, one-third had done so with one current patient, and one individual reported sexual contact with three current patients. Fifty per cent of the sub-sample had had sexual relations with one discharged patient, and one individual had done so with three discharged patients. When those psychologists who had engaged in sexual relations with current patients were asked the circumstances in which this occurred, one did not respond, 40 per cent stated that it had happened only during psychotherapy sessions, and 40 per cent both within and outside psychotherapy sessions.

Only one of these psychologists had not disclosed their sexual involvement with patients before completing the questionnaire. Most (25 per cent) had disclosed to a colleague and friend/partner, and 17 per cent had disclosed to a colleague, manager and friend/partner. Each of the other psychologists had disclosed to, respectively, a personal psychotherapist; an unspecified individual; a colleague and a personal psychotherapist; a colleague, supervisor and friend/partner; a colleague, manager, friend/partner and personal psychotherapist; and colleague, manager, supervisor, friend/partner and unspecified individual.

The most recent patient with whom respondents had had sexual contact

When subjects were asked to consider the most recent patient with whom they had had sexual relations (if there had been more than one), 58 per cent reported that this patient had been female. One-third reported that the patient had been male, and one individual did not respond to this question. The patient's age was given by all but one subject. The mean age of patients was thirty-four years (range 19–41; s.d. 6.63).

All respondents who answered the question (92 per cent) stated that their sexual contact with the patient had been consenting and did not involve the infliction of pain on the patient. Among respondents 58 per cent considered the sexual involvement to be mutually initiated and one-third stated that the patient had initiated it. None of the subjects believed that they had exclusively initiated the sexual contact. One-third of these sexual contacts had been once-only encounters. A quarter had endured for more than five years and 17 per cent had lasted between three and eleven months. A further 17 per cent had lasted less than three months.

Most psychologists (67 per cent) reported that they had no current contact whatsoever with the patient. Eight per cent of subjects had continued social, but no sexual or psychotherapeutic contact with the patient; 8 per cent had continued therapeutic and sexual contact with the patient; and 8 per cent were married to or in a committed relationship with the patient. Although 58 per cent expressed concerns now about this sexual contact with a patient, one-third were unconcerned.

Attitudes towards, and incidence of, trainer–trainee sexual contact

Just over 22 per cent of respondents believed that trainees could benefit from sexual contact with a lecturer or supervisor, but 7 per cent did not respond to this question. Nine percent had had sexual contact as an undergraduate with a lecturer or tutor, and 8 per cent with a lecturer/tutor or supervisor, as a trainee clinical psychologist. Two per cent of those psychologists who had engaged in personal psychotherapy had had sexual involvement with their psychotherapist. Five per cent of lecturers/supervisors had had sexual contact with their trainees/undergraduates. These individuals were more likely to be male.

Information about treatment of victims of sexual abuse by psychotherapists

Twenty-two per cent of respondents had treated victims of psychotherapist–patient sex. None of these psychologists rated the effects of the sexual involvement as positive: 94 per cent believed that it had negative effects on the patient and 6 per cent viewed the effects as 'mixed'. Sixty per cent had treated one patient who had been sexually involved with a psychotherapist. The rest had treated two and five patients. Private sector psychotherapists (17 per cent) were the most commonly cited therapists who had been sexually involved with respondents' patients. Psychiatrists and 'other' psychotherapists (for example, GPs) each accounted for 16 per cent respectively of cases. Clinical psychologists, social workers and nurses made up 14 per cent each of the cases. Counsellors accounted for 4 per cent and voluntary agency psychotherapists and unknown psychotherapists had been sexually involved with patients in 3 per cent of cases.

Most of these psychotherapists (41 per cent) had not been reported to their employer, professional body, and so on, and respondents were uncertain in this respect about 28 per cent, whereas 31 per cent had been reported in some way.

Knowledge through sources other than patients or clinical psychologists who have had sexual involvement with patients

Over 40 per cent of respondents knew of clinical psychologists who had been sexually involved with patients. Most (63 per cent) knew of one such psychologist, but 30 per cent knew of two, 6 per cent knew of three and 2 per cent knew of four. Over half (52 per cent) were reported to their employer, or the British Psychological Society, 27 per cent were not reported, and for 18 per cent of offenders, respondents were uncertain whether or not they had been reported.

Well over half (61 per cent) of these psychologists known to respondents had been sexually involved with only one patient, and 39 per cent had been involved with more than one. Of respondents who knew of sexually abusive psychologists 14 per cent had taken action to report the colleague.

DISCUSSION AND RECOMMENDATIONS

If under-reporting of personal sexual contact with patients occurred here, responses to other questions may compensate for this. That is, respondents' treatment of patients who were sexually involved with previous psychotherapists, and their knowledge through other sources of clinical psychologists who had sexual contact with their patients, are alternative avenues to this information. However, there is inevitable overlap between respondents in knowledge of such psychologists, so no absolute figures may be concluded from this information.

However, the percentages of respondents who had treated patients who were sexually involved with their psychotherapists, and who knew of clinical psychologists who had engaged in sexual contact with their patients are substantial (22 per cent and 40 per cent respectively). The responses to these questions also demonstrate that many psychotherapists engage in multiple sexual contacts with patients, and that previous research findings documenting the negative effects of such sexual contact on patients, as perceived by treating psychotherapists, are supported. The questionnaire was insufficiently sophisticated to distinguish between those subjects who had themselves sexually abused patients, and those who had not, in order to control for the phenomenon of offenders reporting more positive effects on patients of sexual contact with psychotherapists.

Over half (58 per cent) of the patients with whom respondents had had sexual contact were discharged at the onset of the sexual contact. It might be argued that in these cases there are less pressing ethical problems, or even that there should be no ethical objection to such sexual contacts. This is clearly an area which could be investigated in future research but the fact that US studies have found that such contact causes harm to the patient, as well as the suggestion that psychotherapists may at times discharge a patient specifically in order to engage in a sexual relationship with them, thus giving little priority to the therapeutic needs of the patient, should be sufficient to cause psychotherapists to exercise extreme caution in this area.

It may be reasonable for the present to draw some broad conclusions from these results about the overall rate of psychotherapist–patient sexual contact in Britain, but further research is clearly required to establish whether any inter-professional differences exist in this respect. In view of the widespread practice of counselling and psychotherapy by non-professionals, and of the lack of regulation of this activity in the United Kingdom, research is required to define any differences which may exist between professional and non-professional groups in this respect. It is impossible to conclude from these results whether the British picture, as the North American, is that of a declining rate of sexual contact between psychologists and their patients: clearly, this is an area where further research could begin to contribute.

This study demonstrates that sexual contact with patients by clinical psychologists and other psychotherapists does occur in Britain and is largely perceived to be damaging to patients. Action could be taken to prevent and address the problem as follows:

1 Sexual contact with current and discharged patients should be explicitly prohibited in professional Codes of Conduct.
2 Consideration should be given to the treatment of offending psycho-therapists, and evaluated rehabilitation programmes should be considered by professional bodies.
3 Since most psychotherapists in a recent study had received little or no training about sexual attraction to patients (Pope *et al.* 1986), the issues of attraction to patients and sexual contact with them should be addressed in professional training courses (Thoreson 1986).
4 Folman (1991) suggests that concepts of transference, counter-transference and boundaries are fundamental for trainees to develop an understanding of attraction and intimacy between psychotherapists and their patients. Gutheil (1989) argues that training should equip psychotherapists with a knowledge of transference, with its power to produce flattering attitudes in the patient, and of counter-transference, with its potential to trigger the feeling that the psychotherapist and only the psychotherapist can save the patient. Such issues may also be raised with psychotherapy trainees in supervision.
5 A presentation of the research-based literature in the area of dual relationships as well as discussion of ethical implications of sexual contact with patients (Borys and Pope 1989) can serve to raise awareness

in training. Educational programmes for psychotherapists should aim to provide a supportive environment within which students and educators can consider their own impulses which might tempt them into unethical dual relationships (Borys and Pope 1989).

6 The recognition that inherent in the role and abilities of psychotherapists are the roots of a narcissistic disturbance (Claman 1987) leads to an understanding of the need for psychotherapists to examine personal motivation and background, particularly in training and supervision.

7 Educational establishments should take preventive and remedial action to address the problem of student/educator sexual contact (Garrett and Thomas-Peter 1992). Organisationally, the appropriate procedures should be followed, and written guidelines and standards could usefully be formed concerning dual relationships between educators and students, and procedures could be developed for avoiding conflicts of interest in monitoring and enforcing such standards.

REFERENCES

Averill, S. C., Beale, D., Benfer, B., Collins, D. T., Kennedy, L., Myers, J., Pope, D., Rosen, I. and Zoble, E. (1989) 'Preventing staff–patient sexual relationships', *Bulletin of the Menninger Clinic* 53: 384–93.

Bajit, T. R. and Pope, K. S. (1989) 'Therapist–patient sexual intimacy involving children and adolescents', *American Psychologist* 44(2): 455.

Borys, D. S. and Pope, K. S. (1989) 'Dual relationships between therapist and client: a national study of psychologists, psychiatrists and social workers', *Professional Psychology: Research and Practice* 20: 283–93.

Bouhoutsos, J., (1983) 'Sexual intimacy between psychotherapists and clients: policy implications for the future', in L. Walker (ed.) *Women and Mental Health Policy*, Beverly Hills, CA: Sage.

British Psychological Society (1991) *Code of Conduct for Psychologists*, Leicester: BPS.

Butler, S. and Zelen, S. L. (1977) 'Sexual intimacies between therapists and patients', *Psychotherapy: Theory, Research and Practice* 14: 139–45.

Claman, J. (1987) 'Mirror hunger in the psychodynamics of sexually abusing therapists', *The American Journal of Psychoanalysis* 47: 35–40.

Dahlberg, C. (1970) 'Sexual contact between patient and therapist', *Contemporary Psychoanalysis* 6: 107–24.

Edwards, D. J. A. (1981) 'The role of touch in interpersonal relations: implications for psychotherapy', *South African Journal of Psychology* 11(1): 29–37.

Feldman-Sumner, S. and Jones, G. (1984) 'Psychological impacts of sexual contact between therapists or other healthcare practitioners and their clients', *Journal of Consulting and Clinical Psychology* 52: 1054–61.

Folman, R. Z. (1991) 'Therapist–patient sex: attraction and boundary problems', *Psychotherapy* 28(1): 168–73.

Garrett, T. and Thomas-Peter, B. A. (1992) 'Sexual harassment', *The Psychologist* 5(7): 319–21.

Gartrell, N., Herman, J., Olarte, S., Feldstein, M. and Localio, R. (1986) 'Psychiatrist–patient sexual contact: results of a national survey, 1: Prevalence', *American Journal of Psychiatry* 143(9): 1126–131.

Gartrell, N., Herman, J., Olarte, S., Feldstein, M. and Localio, R. (1987) 'Reporting practices of psychiatrists who knew of sexual misconduct by colleagues', *American Journal of Orthopsychiatry* 57: 287–95.

Gechtman, L. (1989) 'Sexual contact between social workers and their clients', pp. 27–38 in G. O. Gabbard (ed.) *Sexual Exploitation in Professional Relationships*, Washington, DC: American Psychiatric Press.

Gonsoriek, J. C. (1987) 'Intervening with psychotherapists who sexually exploit clients', pp. 417–27 in P. A. Keller and S. R. Heyman (eds) *Innovations in Clinical Practice: A Sourcebook*, vol. 6, Sarasota, FL: Professional Resource Exchange.

Goodman, M. and Teicher, A. (1988) 'To touch or not to touch?' *Psychotherapy* 25(4): 492–500.

Gutheil, T. (1989) 'Borderline personality disorder, boundary violations and therapist–patient sex: medicolegal pitfalls', *American Journal of Psychiatry* 146(5): 597–602.

Herman, J. L., Gartrell, N., Olarte, S., Feldman, M. and Localio, R. (1987) 'Psychiatrist–patient sexual contact: results of a national survey, II: Psychiatrists' attitudes', *American Journal of Psychiatry* 144(2): 164–9.

Hoencamp, E. (1990) 'Sexual abuse and the abuse of hypnosis in the therapeutic relationship', *International Journal of Clinical and Experimental Hypnosis* 38(4): 283–97.

Holroyd, J. C. and Bouhoutsos, J. C. (1985) 'Biassed reporting of therapist–patient sexual intimacy', *Professional Psychology* 16: 701–9.

Holroyd, J. C. and Brodsky, A. M. (1977) 'Psychologists' attitudes and practices regarding erotic and nonerotic physical contact with patients', *American Psychologist* 32: 843–9.

—— (1980) 'Does touching patients lead to sexual intercourse?' *Professional Psychology* 11: 807–11.

Kardener, S., Fuller, M. and Mensh, I. (1976) 'A survey of physicians' attitudes and practices regarding erotic and nonerotic contact with patients', *American Journal of Psychiatry* 130: 1077–81.

Levenson, J. L. (1986) 'When a colleague practises unethically: guidelines for intervention', *Journal of Counselling and Development* 64: 315–17.

Long, T. (1992) '"To protect the public and ensure justice is done": an examination of the Philip Donnelly case', *Journal of Advanced Nursing* 17: 5–9.

McCartney, J. (1966) 'Overt transference', *Journal of Sex Research* 2: 227–37.

Marmor, J. (1972) 'Sexual acting out in psychotherapy', *American Journal of Psychoanalysis* 32: 3–8.

Pattison, J. E. (1973) 'Effects of touch on self-exploration and the therapeutic relationship', *Journal of Consulting and Clinical Psychology* 40(2): 170–5.

Perry, J. A. (1976) 'Physicians' erotic and nonerotic physical involvement with patients', *American Journal of Psychiatry* 133(7): 838–40.

Pope, K. S. (1989) 'Sexual intimacies between psychologists and their students and supervisees: research, standards and professional liability', *Independent Practitioner* 9(2): 33–41.

—— (1990) 'Therapist–patient sexual involvement: a review of the research', *Clinical Psychology Review* 10: 477–90.

—— (1991a) 'Unanswered questions about rehabilitating therapist–patient sex offenders', *Independent Practitioner* 18(2): 5–7.

—— (1991b) 'Rehabilitation plans and expert testimony for therapists who have been sexually involved with a patient', *Independent Practitioner* 22(3): 31–9.

Pope, K. S. and Bajt, T. C. (1988) 'When laws and values conflict: a dilemma for psychologists', *American Psychologist* 43: 828.

Pope, K. S. and Bouhoutsos, J. C. (1986) *Sexual Intimacy between Therapists and Patients*, New York: Praeger.

Pope, K. S., Keith-Spiegel, P. and Tabachnik, B. G. (1986) 'Sexual attraction to clients: the human therapist and the (sometimes) inhuman training system', *American Psychologist* 41(2): 147–158.

Pope, K. S., Levenson, H. and Schover, L. R. (1979) 'Sexual intimacy in psychology training: results and implications of a national survey', *American Psychologist* 34(8): 682–9.

Pope, K. S., Tabachnik, B. G. and Keith-Spiegel, P. (1987) 'Ethics of practice: the beliefs and behaviours of psychologists as therapists', *American Psychologist* 42(11): 993–1006.

Pope, K. S., and Vetter, V. A. (1991) 'Prior therapist–patient sexual involvement among patients seen by psychologists', *Psychology* 38(3): 429–38.

Schoener, G., Milgrom, J. H. and Gonsoriek, J. (1984) 'Sexual exploitation of clients by therapists', *Women and Therapy* 3: 63–9.

Shepard, M. (1971) *The Love Treatment: Sexual Intimacy between Patients and Psychotherapists*, New York: Wyden.

Siassi, I. and Thomas, M. (1973) 'Physicians and the new sexual freedom', *American Journal of Psychiatry* 130: 1256–57.

Sinclair, J. (1991) 'Article on sexual exploitation of clients by therapists', *Everywoman* (July): 27.

Sonne, J. L. and Pope, K. S. (1991) 'Treating victims of therapist–patient sexual involvement', *Psychotherapy* 28(1): 174–87.

Sreenivassan, U. (1989) 'Sexual exploitation of patients: the position of the Canadian Psychiatric Association', *Canadian Journal of Psychiatry* 34: 234–5.

Taylor, B. J. and Wagner, N. N. (1976) 'Sex between therapists and clients: a review and analysis', *Professional Psychiatry* 7: 593–601.

Thoreson, R. (1986) 'Training issues for professionals in distress', pp. 47–50 in R. R. Kilburg, P. E. Nathan and R. W. Thoreson (eds) *Professionals in Distress*, Washington, DC: American Psychological Association.

Vinson, J. S. (1987) 'Use of complaint procedures in cases of therapist–patient sexual contact', *Professional Psychology: Research and Practice* 18(2): 159–64.

Voth, H. (1972) 'Love affair between doctor and patient', *American Journal of Psychotherapy* 26: 394–400.

Zelen, S. L. (1985) 'Sexualisation of therapeutic relationships: the dual vulnerability of patient and therapist', *Psychotherapy* 22(2): 178–85.

FURTHER INFORMATION

**POPAN (Prevention of
Professional Abuse Network)**
Flat 1
20 Daleham Gardens
Hampstead
London NW3 5DA
Tel.: 071 794 3177

Chapter 25

An approach to the treatment of Post-Traumatic Stress Disorders (PTSD)

Nachman Alon and Talia Levine Bar-Yoseph

'NORMAL' RESPONSES TO EXTRAORDINARILY STRESSFUL SITUATIONS

Disastrous situations, whether naturally occurring (such as earthquakes, fires, floods and storms) or man-made (war, torture, violence, rape, child abuse), cause extreme disruption to the victims' lives. Individuals, families, groups and even whole communities experience, or are threatened with, major material, physical and/or psychological loss (Drabek 1986). This may shatter the fundamental *mental schemata* which constitute one's sense of personal, functional and interpersonal continuity and without which life is intolerable. The 'basic schemata' are the beliefs in one's invulnerability, in the trustworthiness of some people and in the predictability, manageability and meaning of the world (Horowitz 1986; Omer 1991; Omer and Alon 1994; Antonowski 1990). Such an experience evokes extreme mental anguish, as well as bodily disruption: hyper-arousal and increased sympathetic nervous system activity and reactivity to stimulation. These are evidenced by an increased EEG, alpha activity, heart and respiratory rate, and by disturbed sleep patterns (Kaplan and Sadock 1991). They may have to do with alternations in dopamine and norepinephrine levels as well as of endogenous opioids in the brain (Kolb 1987; Van der Kolk 1988).

If one's sense of personal continuity is to heal, the body has to resume balanced functioning, and the mental anguish has gradually to be processed and integrated into one's perceived world, through a pendular alternation between protective emotional numbness and constriction of interest and activity on the one hand, and painful re-experiencing of the event(s) through flashbacks, dreams and memories on the other (Horowitz 1986). Completion and integration are achieved when life before the trauma, the traumatic event itself, its meaning, the responses to it and life after, are perceived as parts of a meaningful continuum, rather than as fragmented, disconnected segments. *Personal continuity* is thus restored through cognitive and emotional working through; *functional continuity* is restored through relevant external action; while *interpersonal continuity* is restored by mutual support, trust and flexibility. Normally, advance in any one continuity facilitates advances in others, in a 'ripple effect' manner.

PTSD: FAILURES OF ADAPTATION

The Diagnostic and Statistical Manual of Mental Disorders (DSM-III-R) (American Psychiatric Association 1987) defines PTSD as follows:

(a) The person has experienced an event that is outside the range of usual human experience and that would be markedly distressing to almost anyone.

(b) The traumatic event is persistently re-experienced in at least one of the following ways:

    1 Recurrent and intrusive, distressing recollections of the event (in young children, repetitive play in which themes or aspects of the trauma are expressed).

    2 Recurrent distressing dreams of the event.

    3 Sudden acting or feeling as if the traumatic event were recurring (includes a sense of reliving the experience, illusions, hallucinations and dissociative (flashback) episodes, even those that occur upon awakening or intoxication).

    4 Intense psychological distress at exposure to events that symbolise or resemble an aspect of the traumatic event, including anniversaries of the trauma.

(c) Persistent avoidance of stimuli associated with the trauma, or numbing of general responsiveness (not present before the trauma) as indicated by at least three of the following:

    1 Efforts to avoid thoughts or feelings associated with the trauma.

    2 Efforts to avoid activities or situations that arouse recollections of the trauma.

    3 Inability to recall an important aspect of the trauma (psychogenic amnesia).

    4 Markedly diminished interest in significant activities (in young children, loss of recently acquired developmental skills such as toilet training or language skills).

    5 Feelings of detachment or estrangement from others.

    6 Restricted range of affect, e.g., unable to have loving feelings.

    7 Sense of a foreshortened future, e.g., does not expect to have a career, marriage or children, or a long life.

(d) Persistent symptoms of increased arousal (not present before the trauma), as indicated by at least two of the following:

    1 Difficulty falling or staying asleep.

    2 Irritability or outbursts of anger.

    3 Difficulty concentrating.

4 Hyper-vigilance.

5 Exaggerated startle response.

6 Physiologic reactivity upon exposure to events that symbolise or resemble an aspect of the traumatic event (e.g., a woman who was raped in a lift breaks out in sweat when entering any lift).

(e) Duration of the disturbance (symptoms in b, c and d above) of at least one month.

Onset of symptoms more than six months after the trauma is considered delayed onset. Duration for more than six months becomes chronic, and it has to do with self-aggravating family and work processes and interactions which fixate around issues of reciprocal helplessness, anger and blame (Alon 1985; Solomon *et al.* 1992). Family members may also become seriously and chronically affected by the original PTSD. The numbing aspect of PTSD is closely related to dissociative disorders and to unresolved grief disorders. In fact, it is often hypothesised that dissociative disorders, notably multiple personality disorder, have their origins in childhood trauma (Kluft 1984). PTSD may often be misdiagnosed, and inappropriately treated as factitious disorder, malingering, adjustment reaction, borderline personality disorder, schizophrenia, depression, panic disorder and generalised anxiety disorder (Kaplan and Sadock 1991).

VULNERABILITY FACTORS

The main factors determining the occurrence, duration and severity of an acute PTSD are the duration and intensity of the stressful situation (Kleber and Brom 1992). Personality factors, however, determine mainly the specific manifestation the acute PTSD will hold (Horowitz 1986) and the occurrence of a chronicity (Bernat 1991). Children and old people, as well as the economically and socially deprived, have more difficulty coping with PTSD (Kaplan and Sadock 1991). Previous traumatisation, such as child abuse or recent sudden loss, traumatic family background (for example, a family of Holocaust survivors) and previous psychological problems, as in hospitalisation or crises, are factors which predispose to acute or recurrent PTSD (Solomon 1989), while personality factors such as low perceived sense of control, lack of trust and low ego strength predispose one to difficulties in recovering from the trauma and to chronicity (Bernat 1991). Psychodynamic factors may also have a role in specific PTSD patterns, like the battered woman syndrome (Young and Gerson 1992). Child abuse may also bring about specific psychodynamic and developmental problems (Suffridge 1992). PTSD symptomatology may present even in people who have never sought help (Figley 1978; Solomon 1989).

The physical and human environment – health, physical resources, competence of leadership, availability and quality of leadership and of social support, clarity of information, roles and responsibilities, previous training and preparation, as well as early recognition of and intervention in PTSD – may be crucial, both for the prevention and overcoming of traumatic experiences (Omer and Alon 1994; Kleber and Brom 1992).

PSYCHOTHERAPY: THE CONTINUITY PRINCIPLE

Omer (1991) defined a unifying psychotherapeutic principle in treating PTSD as having the goal, whether with the individual, family, group or community, and at all stages of the problem cycle, of restoring the sense of personal, functional and interpersonal continuity that had been disrupted as the result of the traumatic experiences. Several forms of psychotherapy of PTSD conform to this principle, and it seems that most psychotherapists intuitively choose to work with it in emergency situations regardless of their habitual therapeutic approach. We will illustrate therapies of different stages of PTSD, all based on these principles.

MODELS OF PSYCHOTHERAPY OF THE ACUTE PHASE

Several models have been proposed for the treatment of acute PTSD (Ochberg 1991):

1 Individual psychotherapy. Among the influential models are Horowitz's (1986) brief psychodynamic psychotherapy and Ochberg's (1991) holistic model.
2 Behaviour therapy, based on trauma desensitization: exploration of the trauma, relaxation training with or without biofeedback, desensitization (Kleber and Brom 1992).
3 Cognitive-behaviour therapy.
4 Family therapy (Figley 1988), in which objectives are conjointly set, the problem is framed and then therapeutically reframed, and a family 'healing theory' is developed.
5 Self-help groups.
6 Group therapy (Rozynko and Dondershine 1991).
7 Milieu therapy (Solomon et al. 1992).

Treatment of the acute PTSD

The military front treatment of 'combat reaction', originally described by Salmon (1919), which is the most prevalent mode of treatment in many armies (Solomon and Benbenishty 1986) is based on *immediacy* – that is, treating the soldier as soon as possible after impact; *proximity* – as close as possible to the battlefield and to the unit; and *expectancy* – namely, communicating a systematic and clear expectancy for recovery and for a rapid resumption of functioning in the original unit. All may be conceived of as aspects of the continuity principle. The superiority of this 'harsh' approach to more 'soft', rear psychotherapies is well documented (Solomon and Benbenishty 1986). The basic principles apply to all forms of crisis intervention. Let us illustrate.

Case no. 1 – field treatment of an acute PTSD

In the 1973 war between Egypt and Israel a reserve officer, a psychotherapist in civilian life, was commanding a mechanised combat unit at the front line. A troop-carrier approached under light fire, and its commander, who had heard there was a psychologist around, sought the psychotherapist's help in dealing with 'a soldier who has collapsed'. The psychotherapist found the soldier lying on the floor of the vehicle, hyper-ventilating, mumbling, sweating and weeping. The crew members were standing around watching anxiously, neglecting their duties in spite of the bullet fire outside. Rapid inquiry revealed that the soldier had shown growing tension for several days. He had not eaten, slept or drunk anything except coffee. He had been smoking profusely, and had gradually become withdrawn. The psychotherapist assumed that the disruption the soldier had experienced had also become disruptive for the functioning of the whole crew. Intervention should therefore relate to the group as well as to the identified patient. A benevolent yet authoritative stance was indicated for this stressed, confused group. The commander was told emphatically to resume fighting, and to put all soldiers on duty except for two, who were to stay with the psychotherapist in order 'to learn what to do, so as to replace the psychotherapist later'. He then turned to the 'patient', starting with simple and basic questions, which grasped the soldier's attention and also helped in controlling hyper-ventilation by forcing him to talk. A simple relaxation exercise followed. The 'helper soldiers' were then told to make their friend eat and drink, while the psychotherapist continued to make the soldier talk. The 'patient' spoke of how anxious he was about his family, how difficult he found the mounting tension, how lonely and helpless he felt as his withdrawal progressed, and how affected he was by his unit's apparent helplessness with his situation. He was assured that this was a normal, universal reaction to threat, aggravated by dehydration, hunger, caffeine and nicotine, and that he would quickly recover now that his body was recovering and his mates were tending to him. After instructing the commander not to evacuate this soldier, but rather to keep him busy with much support, the psychotherapist left. Both the soldier and the crew showed an improvement on the two visits the psychotherapist made over the next three hours. Follow-up six months later showed that the intervention had allowed the soldier to resume functioning with no further problems. Maintaining the interpersonal and functional continuity by keeping the soldier with his unit rather than evacuating him were crucial in restoring well-being.

Case no. 2 – an acute family PTSD following a terrorist assault

A psychotherapist was asked to help a family whose apartment house had been attacked in a terrorist assault, resulting in several deaths and injuries. The family members – father, mother, and two sons aged six and nine – narrowly escaped, losing one another in the process. They all responded reasonably well in the following few days, until a financial crisis unrelated to the trauma occurred in the mother's family, shook the delicate balance and brought about a fully fledged PTSD to all members of the family: incessant terror, sleep disturbance, inability to resume, and avoidance of, previous study, work, domestic routines and staying alone; over-alertness, as extreme as watching the windows for hours on end looking for terrorists; and depression over the family crisis.

The first session was held in the home of the wife's family of origin. As the complex financial and social situation became clear, the psychotherapist contacted the municipal social services and secured their intervention in helping the family. Having thus achieved some peace of mind, the family held a de-briefing session in which each member recounted his or her action during and after the assault. The combined picture, which was vividly depicted in diagrams, and broadened as a result of the psychotherapist's questions to include thoughts and emotions, revealed everyone's courage and resourcefulness and delighted all, especially the proud parents.

The psychotherapist's next step was ostensibly to treat the children in this family, while indirectly helping the parents by asking them 'to serve as co-therapists and coaches for the children between sessions', thus fostering not only vicarious learning but also the resumption of habitual roles. Then freedom of movement at home was re-established by conjointly making a hierarchy of fear of the rooms, ranging from 'the most horrible, unbearable, devastating fear not to be tackled before next week' to the 'tiniest, bearable, comfortable fear that was almost no real problem to overcome'. On the door of the 'worst room', a conjointly made sign reading, 'The room of terrible fear! No entrance until next week!', and depicting a trembling Mickey Mouse, was drawn. The children were 'trained' to 'rush from the room in panic' to their parents' room, singing the 'Song of Fear', a humorously lamenting, wailing song improvised by the psychotherapist. In the following weeks they were taught self-hypnosis for relaxation and better sleep (proven by the spontaneous use of self-hypnosis for analgesia for toothache done by one of the children); then they were desensitised to the place in the house in which they had met the terrorists. This was done by playing ball near the site in such a way that the children would spontaneously run after it when it was missed. The family was then helped to resume work and study. The over-protective attitude of the father's employers, which made the father all the more depressed, had to be tackled so that the father would assume more, not less, responsibility. When the father started work again (also with a view to dealing more effectively with the family problem), the mother regained her competence at home and with the children. Each of the (ten) psychotherapy sessions would usually start with the joint family-and-psychotherapist lunch under the pretext that the psychotherapist came from a distant city and needed some refreshment. This was meant to reinforce family routine and cohesion. Since psychotherapy was overtly done with the children only, an open discussion of the parents' problems was quite limited. However, indirect discussions about children, about trauma and its implications, about the parents' image in the children's eyes, all served as an indirect suggestive psychotherapy for the parents. A two-year follow-up showed satisfactory adjustment.

An approach to treating the acute phase

Assessment

1 Assess the identified patient(s) and the family/group/community for numbing/intrusive symptoms (disruptions in personal continuity) as well as for disruptions in functioning and in relationships.
2 Assess whether others, such as family members, have been, or potentially are, affected by the problem. If psychotherapy is indicated, help with appropriate consultation/referral. When possible, give preference to working with the family/group to working with individuals.
3 Give special attention to areas of even minimal functioning: re-establishing continuities is best done on the basis of existing strengths and resources (including human resources).
4 Remember that the severity of symptoms by no means predicts the prognosis and outcome of psychotherapy.
5 The manner of appraisal should imply that the focus of attention is not 'personality-and-developmentally' focused but 'circumstances-and-present-and-future' orientated.

Milieu therapy

As far as possible, utilise and activate available material: human and organisational resources. Every person, every event can become 'therapeutic', if utilised to help the patient advance in the direction of bridging over some breach.

Communication

Establish communication on a simple level. Deal with down-to-earth matters before going to more complex issues. With the agitated or dissociated patient, the first goal is to capture their attention by whatever means, including touch.

Restoring personal continuity

(a) *Basic needs*: If necessary, allow for a medical check and for drinking, eating and sleeping. See to it that appropriate clothing, personal hygiene and other basic needs are taken care of. These actions are as therapeutic as any others, and should be a part of your therapeutic plan.

(b) *Orientation*: Orient the patient as to what has happened and what is happening now, including who you are, where he/she is and why, for how long, and so on.

(c) *Meaning*: Reframe the situation as being a 'normal, transitory process of adaptation'. Use positive expectancies without under-estimating difficulties and problems. Ascribing meaning to what has happened is vital (Figley 1988).

Processing the traumatic event(s)

(a) *Telling the story*: Have the patient(s) tell the story of the trauma repeatedly until the need to talk is exhausted and until a clear and full picture is obtained. Fill in memory gaps. Help them make an adaptive 'theory' of what has happened (Figley 1988).

(b) *Acknowledging emotions*: While recovering the facts of the event(s), name and discuss the accompanying emotions then and now, especially fear, anger, grief and guilt. If the patient finds it difficult to identify emotions and/or talk about them, make informed guesses about the emotional aspects of the event; for example, 'Most people would feel terribly guilty in this situation – how was it for you?' – so that the patient will still have a name for the emotions and will acknowledge and accept them.

(c) *Dealing with emotions*: Actively help the patient maintain a bearable level of emotional arousal (Horowitz 1986; Brown and Fromm 1986), by:

    1 Alternating between distancing tactics like exercise and acting, on the one hand, and introspection and exposure, on the other; emphasising either the observing ego or the experiencing ego stance. Useful techniques include helping the patient either to project memories on a TV screen for distancing, or to 'walk into the screen' for accessing emotions.

    2 Gradually allowing the patient to move from observing to experiencing mode, thus increasing the dose of bearable pain.

    3 When guilt is 'excessive' and normalisation does not decrease it, accept it and suggest symbolic reparatory ritual steps.

(d) *Overall psychotherapy structure*:

    1 At this stage of psychotherapy, the frequency of such 'loaded' sessions should be as high as three to four 90-minute sessions per week.

    2 Repeat the cycle in subsequent sessions until the gains are repeated and stabilised.

    3 A full-blown emotional abreaction, believed in the past to be the treatment of choice, may overwhelm the patient and unnecessarily re-traumatise them. It should therefore be avoided (Brown and Fromm 1986).

    4 Terminate the cycle only when the patient can comfortably discuss the events. The best indication for that stage is bodily and emotional exhaustion.

(e) *Hypnosis*: Hypnosis is an extremely useful modality for the treatment of acute PTSD, due to its power directly to stabilise bodily problems such as hyper-arousal, for relaxation and for the flexibility of thought and behaviour it fosters through suggestion and through the enhanced therapeutic rapport. The acute victim of PTSD is usually highly suggestible, and will respond favourably and promptly.

(f) *Pharmacotherapy*: At the acute phase, use pharmacotherapy only when stabilisation is not achieved by psychological interventions alone.

(g) *Functional continuity – action*: Make the patient act, even if on a very elementary level. Avoid doing things for them; preferably do things with them. Work to broaden the scope and complexity of functioning.

(h) *Interpersonal continuity – support*: Establish interpersonal support, preferably with significant others or other casualties; group work is very helpful in this respect. Mobilise whatever help you can get from others.

(i) *Psychotherapist's attitude*:

    1 In all your actions, assume a benevolent yet authoritative (not authoritarian!) stance. The patient needs clarity, structure and some confidence in you; sharing your doubts with them is not useful.

    2 When dealing with many casualties simultaneously, the psychotherapist should do only what others, less skilled, cannot do. The psychotherapist's time is better spent supervising others than in doing individual work.

Treating the delayed response

A delayed response may occur years, even decades, after the initial events. It may occur as a response to some stimulus which resembles or symbolises the original stimulus, or it may occur at a point of present trauma, crisis or loss. Psychotherapy has thus to deal simultaneously with both the present problem situation and the original, only partially resolved trauma. The intensity of the re-emergence of the original trauma may make it necessary to deal with this first, and to tackle the present situation only at a later time.

Case no. 3 – an acute delayed response

In 1985 Dan, a young veteran of the 1982 Lebanon war, was participating in a structured rehabilitation programme for the brain-injured in Israel. PTSD, if any, was considered to be of secondary importance in the overall serious sequelae of his head injury, which included loss of balance so severe that an urgent operation became essential. However, on arrival at hospital for the operation, he re-experienced the military field hospital in Lebanon in a hallucinatory manner with a tremendous sense of guilt and anxiety, grew extremely agitated, tore the medical equipment away and escaped from the hospital. He later announced his refusal to return to hospital, even if it cost him his health or possibly his life. A psychotherapist was called for consultation and after assessment proposed a four-hour marathon session 'to decrease re-experiencing the negative emotions from an unbearable to a bearable level, so as to enable Dan successfully to undergo the operation' – a minimalistic goal which Dan sceptically accepted.

During the marathon, the circumstances and stimuli that triggered the flashbacks were studied. Dan said that the sights and smells of the ward brought him back to that moment in the war when he had woken in hospital in severe pain from a prolonged state of unconsciousness. He could not account for the intense guilt he experienced.

He was then hypnotised and trained in projecting the memories onto a TV screen, 'to be detachedly and objectively observed while you are seated'. In this state he repeatedly watched the 'film' and became aware that each viewing brought new memories, and that emotions gradually and controllably intensified. At a certain moment, he became very agitated. He saw himself, wounded, confused and in severe pain, being carried into the hospital and noticing several casualties and corpses there. On further inquiry it became clear that when he was carried in this way, in a twilight state, he erroneously concluded that the casualties had all somehow been hit by his lorry, which in his mind had itself probably been hit by a shell and exploded. Therefore, 'he was the one to be blamed for the losses'. In defence against the mental pain he became totally amnesic to the experience, with only guilt reaching consciousness, as the flashback occurred. The psychotherapist and team now emphatically challenged this conclusion on purely logical grounds. If his lorry had exploded so violently, there was no chance of his surviving the explosion. 'His faulty conclusion was understandable in the light of his state, and in light of the human need to complete incomplete Gestalts, however irrational this may seem.' (The team believed this argument to be correct. No attempt at such persuasion could have been made had his guilt been more 'founded'.) Once Dan accepted this explanation, he experienced a tremendous relief from his guilt, was very exhausted and could enjoy profound relaxation.

Now he was ready for a desensitisation procedure. First, he learned to relax quickly and deeply. Then, while deeply relaxed, he watched alternately the war hospital and the real hospital on an imaginary TV set, having full control over the size, shape, colour and speed of the film, thus being able to control his level of anxiety. Throughout this stage suggestions were repeatedly made to the effect that he could *see* the real hospital and yet simultaneously *feel* deep comfort; 'You see the war hospital: it's in black and white, small, far away, double-speed film . . . a lot of "snow" . . . and yet your body stays deeply relaxed' – until the picture could be seen without much emotion. He then imagined being comfortably relaxed in a room in the 'real' hospital, enjoying the best of treatment and watching the shabby archive film showing the war hospital, remaining fully aware how real, friendly and caring was the real one, and how distant, far away, now unreal and 'just a memory' was the other.

He was then trained to use the mere thought of the 'real' hospital as a trigger for relaxation, and the war hospital memories as a trigger for distancing using the TV technique. After a four-hour session, he felt he could cope with the operation, and in fact did that successfully the following day.

In this case we see how personal historical continuity was damaged by loss of memory, by an unconscious thought process and the ensuing guilt which became a 'mental foreign body'. Once the personal breach was bridged over, the breach in functioning – in this case, taking care of his health – could be repaired. Considerable attention was paid to finding a balance between the need for distancing and the need for experiencing. Abreaction was actively avoided.

In another case, however, the psychotherapist chose to have the patient abreact rather than process the trauma in the manner described above. The patient in question was a young woman who, during military service, re-experienced a catastrophic childhood event in which severe family loss and a life-threatening injury took place. In spite of an overt initial alleviation of symptomatology, a separation a few months later evoked a depressive crisis, and the patient refused psychological help on the grounds that 'such help only deepens pain'. The crisis was overcome only with massive support and the formation of another relationship. In this particular case, abreaction seems to have unwittingly caused sensitisation rather than inoculation. She was exposed in psychotherapy to an overdose of pain that was beyond her ability to process. Distancing manoeuvres, as essential to psychotherapy as exposure moves (Horowitz 1986), were missing and the psychotherapy was not protective enough. This prevented her from recovering personal continuity.

TREATMENT OF CHRONIC PTSD

War and Holocaust may have far-reaching characterological and developmental effects which may turn chronic; for example, loss of modes of relatedness, pathological self-representations and impaired affective regulation (Brown and Fromm 1986). Chronicity is the outcome of a long process of ever-widening, intra- and interpersonal interacting vicious circles. For example, hyper-arousal and intrusion of memories interrupt sleep, inverting the habitual day/night cycles and causing fatigue, loss of concentration, irritability and deterioration in functioning; others react by benevolently taking responsibilities from the victim's shoulders, thus deepening the sense of helplessness, even victimisation; irritability further aggravates interpersonal friction and suspicion. Mutual self-fulfilling prophecies and rigid labelling are established. Both intra-personal and interpersonal patterns fixate and may perpetuate the situation indefinitely. Establishing a therapeutic alliance becomes very difficult, and at times only a cautious, indirect, one-down therapeutic approach can prevent an early drop-out (Alon 1985). Often only broad-spectrum, multifaceted, rehabilitative, educational and consultative teamwork can be of help (Ochberg 1991). Medication may be essential. In spite of intensive work in the field, clinical outcome research is still less than encouraging (Solomon *et al.* 1992).

Case no. 4 – a circumscribed chronic PTSD

Ruth, a forty-year-old married woman psychotherapist, a mother of two, attended a workshop on guided imagery. During a relaxation exercise she spontaneously experienced a fleeting distressing fantasy. She was a small child, walking in a field, and a tall, mean-looking man blocked her way. She came out of relaxation feeling very distressed, and sought professional help. More work revealed that as a child, she had been subjected to sexual abuse by an otherwise beloved uncle. Despite Ruth's initial unawareness of any connection, it soon became apparent that her lifelong history of unorgasmia and avoidance of sexuality, as well as her frequent nightmares and her emotional constriction in intimate relationships, originated with her childhood experiences, but these later became part of her relationships. Her husband had long ago unquestioningly accepted the scarcity of sex.

The first step in psychotherapy was to try to convince Ruth to have conjoint couples therapy. This she flatly and rigidly rejected, being afraid lest this would cause her husband, whom she conceived of as a very moralistic person, to reject her. She agreed, however, to share the problem with him privately, gradually and indirectly, as an attempt to counteract the 'conspiracy of silence'. No harm was done. In fact, to her relief, she discovered that although her husband responded at first with mild criticism of her 'over-reacting', he then became increasingly understanding and supportive on discovering that she did not withdraw resignedly from conversation. Instruction for pleasuring and sensate focusing (Kaplan 1974) turned the couple's attention away from the highly loaded field of sex into the more relaxed field of intimacy. Simultaneously, the traumatic experiences were clarified. Her guilt over her compliance to the man was counteracted, but as it did not fully subside, she was encouraged to take reparatory steps. With a great sense of mission, she volunteered to do psychotherapy in a drop-in clinic for child abuse victims, and this alleviated much of the remaining guilt. The emotional deadlock (being unable to get angry at the abusing uncle because of her love for him, and being unable fully to love him because of the resentment) was partially resolved by reframing her attitude to her uncle as 'loving the *person*, yet hating the particular *deeds*'. Under hypnosis she was then told, 'Watch little Ruth in distress with the eyes of the adult, experienced, empathic woman. . . . Knowing little Ruth better than anyone else in the world, you are able to help the little girl in the way most appropriate for her.' At that point she felt tremendous anger toward the perpetrator. In her fantasy, she prevented him by force from harming the little girl, then comforted her and established herself as an 'inner guard and counsellor' for little Ruth. An interactional 'beneficious' (as opposed to 'vicious') circle gradually evolved (Alon 1985) and enabled the couple to lead their own successful version of sex therapy. Consultation at this stage was aimed at problem-solving and at further consultation for this 'private' psychotherapy. Desensitisation to the traumatic events was then successfully achieved by controlled exposure.

In this particular case, personal continuity was enhanced by recovering memories and feelings, and by re-establishing a sense of trust via a fantasised relationship between the inner child and an inner parent. The interpersonal continuity was re-established by opening communication with the spouse and by indirectly engaging him in psychotherapy, whereas functional continuity was achieved by indirect, behaviourally orientated sex therapy.

Case no. 5 – chronic PTSD: individual treatment

Gad, a thirty-five-year-old married technician, reserve veteran and survivor of a massive bombardment in the 1982 war, was hospitalised in 1985.

He was diagnosed as suffering from atypical psychosis, and intensively treated with anti-psychotic drugs. Previously an industrious worker, Gad had started avoiding work after the war because of somatic complaints. He began to consume alcohol as a tranquilliser, to have sudden temper tantrums and depressive episodes, severe conflicts with treating agencies and occasional hallucination-like re-experiencing of his war memories. The situation at home became difficult. His wife gave up her job in order to help him and then grew bitter and frustrated when no change occurred. Hospitalisation complicated things further, not only by isolating Gad and damaging his self-esteem, but also by adding the adverse effects of medication.

The consultant suggested an alternative diagnosis of PTSD, and recommended release from the hospital and treatment at the out-patient clinic. The couple were relieved and hopeful. They were told that their problem was a well-known phenomenon, that most people would respond similarly to the difficult circumstances of war and its aftermath, and that although the situation was not easy to treat, it was far from hopeless, and that with determination and hard work it would improve. Stabilisation was declared to be the first goal. For several weeks, complaints were treated with antidepressant medication and hypno-behavioural methods (Brown and Fromm 1986) – relaxation and exercise for sleep, cognitive-behavioural strategies for irritability and sleep deprivation – for the reversal of the day/night sleep patterns. Couples counselling improved the home situation to some extent, as did the fact that Gad's wife resumed work. However, Gad's perfectionist, rigid and masochistic attitudes remained a source of vulnerability.

At the time, an experimental project for the treatment of chronic PTSD casualties of the Lebanon war was initiated by the Military Mental Health Authorities (Bleich et al. 1992; Solomon et al. 1992). Gad decided to volunteer.

Case no. 6 – a comprehensive milieu treatment

The project, which Gad had joined, took place three years after the Lebanon war. The forty-five veterans with chronic PTSD who volunteered for the project were treated in a military installation for thirty days, by three platoon teams, each consisting of two psychotherapists with past military experience and behavioural training, a physical-fitness instructor with experience in rehabilitation, and two squad leaders. The basic assumptions of the project were that PTSD was based on avoidance and therefore behavioural exposure and coping skills training were the treatments of choice (Solomon et al. 1992).

The project schedule was tight: an early wake-up, playful morning swimming, physical education activities ranging from judo to competitive football, a group session dealing mainly with everyday events and their meaning, coping skills group training, another physical fitness lesson, individual sessions, social events, basic military retraining and a self-help group. Each soldier made his own personal behaviourally defined goals, so as to make progress measurable. *Esprit de corps* developed very rapidly. The interest shown by the military and the enthusiasm of the psycho-therapists and participants alike was, for many, a corrective emotional experience. Spouses were trained in assertiveness, dealing with anger, child-rearing and so on. After the project ended, self-help couples groups continued to meet regularly for two years.

In spite of much enthusiasm among participants and staff, and in spite of marked improvement among individuals, research outcome was less encouraging. It seemed that patients were worse off at the end of the project on the intrusion dimension. In retrospect, stressing the here-and-now and avoiding dealing with the traumata, as well as ex-posing the patients to the military rather than to their natural civilian environment, constituted a breach of the continuity principle (Bleich *et al.* 1992).

Returning to case no. 5

Gad's depression deepened in the first two weeks of the project. The group took great pains to help him, and the concern shown was invaluable to him. Despite depression, he functioned adequately in the group, due to much encouraging and friendly pressure. It seemed that restoring func-tional and interpersonal continuities 'compensated', so to speak, for not dealing with the trauma. Towards the end of the project his energy and good mood rose considerably and, for the first time in three years, he was able to enjoy himself. However, his personal goals – notably, returning to work – were only partially met.

A few months after the project ended, Gad had another depressive episode after a quarrel at work. The self-help group organised a three-week home hospitalisation which helped him recover and take decisions about his career. He decided to retire on medical grounds, collect his pension and become the house caretaker, while his wife worked and provided income. This decision meant for him an end to the tyranny of macho values and the start of a new freedom. The plan was implemented with success, and in a five-year follow-up both spouses defined their present situation as 'happy'.

Dos and don'ts in treating chronic PTSD

Assessment

Assess bodily, intra-personal, interpersonal and organisational forces and vicious cycles that maintain the problems. Assess areas of undisturbed functioning and identify actual and potential support resources. Look for characterological problems and pre-morbid factors. Assess whether other family members need help.

Pharmacotherapy

Pharmacotherapy may be essential in counteracting chronic hyper-arousal. Imipramine (Tofranil) and phenelzine (Nardil) are most often reported to be useful in the treatment of PTSD. Preliminary studies reported on the effectiveness of clonidine (Catapres), propranolol (Inderal), benzodiazepines, lithium and carbamazepine (Tegretol) (Kaplan and Sadock 1991). Complement this treatment with self-hypnosis and/or biofeedback.

Stages of psychotherapy

(Brown and Fromm 1986; Alon 1985) The proposed stages should be flexibly applied. The more rigid the patient, the more useful will adherence to them be. We suggest that going from one stage to the next will be done only when the previous one has been stabilised.

1 *Establish a working alliance*. Chronic patients often appear 'resistant' due to their disillusionment with treatments, suspicion, criticism and anger. 'Resistance' is lessened when the psychotherapist (a) accepts the problem as 'normal in the difficult situation in which you have been', and (b) poses only modest, concrete goals, rejecting requests for more ambitious ones on the grounds that they have only limited power in the face of 'such a history of frustration, pain and misunderstandings'. Educating the patient and the family about PTSD is very important at this stage.
2 *Block vicious cycles and stabilise the symptom-picture*. Relief of symptoms and interpersonal frictions (functional and interpersonal continuity) at this stage takes precedence over more emotional aspects (personal continuity). Once relief is achieved, the patient will willingly go into more meaningful areas. Pay special attention to problems arising from avoidance. Target symptoms may be sleep disturbances, autonomic hyper-arousal, temper tantrums, flashbacks and/or behavioural avoidance. Preferred tools are relaxation training; physical exercise; desensitisation and exposure; coping skills (such as anger control); cognitive-behavioural tools (such as the modification of catastrophic self-talk); paradoxical interventions ('Do all you can *not* to fall asleep; instead, write down every thought so that we can cope with the sleep-preventing thinking' often leads to a good night's sleep); distraction; and directive family interventions ('I would like you to have a conjoint family dinner three times this week, so that we can better evaluate aspects of family

climate') for re-establishing family roles and routines. Self-monitoring is important in engaging the patient as a member of the therapeutic team. 'Disguising' intervention as 'diagnostic procedures' increases the likelihood of co-operation: readiness for risk-taking and commitment is higher at 'diagnosis' than at actual psychotherapy. After all, what could one resist in a diagnostic procedure?

3 *Activate 'beneficious cycles' that promote exploration and development of hitherto blocked functioning, so that change will become self-reinforcing.* Complement these cycles with skills such as assertiveness, friendship training and so on. Look for behaviours that will stimulate significant others to respond favourably, such as re-introducing the patient to long-avoided activities with the children. Often it is easier to induce significant, less damaged, others to activate such cycles than to help the avoidant, anxious patient to initiate change.

4 *Deal with the trauma in a controlled manner*, alternating between distancing and re-experiencing as suggested above. With patients who are reluctant to tackle the trauma, hold this stage until the end of the next stage.

5 *Deal with the more generalised personality and thinking patterns* – tendencies of dependency, avoidance, victimisation, somatisation and so on. At this stage the psychotherapist can deal more openly with hitherto untackled issues.

6 *Deal with long-standing psychodynamic issues when necessary.* Always be prepared for a prolonged psychotherapy, and for unexpected relapses and conflicts, especially at times of stress. Expect anniversary reactions, which may call for emergency interventions.

Teamwork

The need for co-operation with physicians, treating agencies, rehabilitation workers, law agencies, schools, vocational placement workers and other relevant people cannot be over-estimated. Without such teamwork the likelihood of getting to a therapeutic dead end becomes very high.

Relations between patient and psychotherapist

PTSD chronic patients may appear 'resistant' and 'uncooperative'. It may take considerable patience and flexibility to overcome counter-transferential reactions such as disappointment, resentment, blaming and fatigue. These have to be expected and handled, otherwise negative vicious cycles can easily occur in psychotherapy. These patients are often unaware of the positive aspects of their life, and do not volunteer positive feedback to the psychotherapist. One should therefore look for independent, 'objective' measures of therapeutic advance, to check against devaluing remarks.

A prevalent response towards patients' relapses is the assumption that the patient does not really *want* to change, or that 'What he *really* wants is compensation', and so on. This imputation of negative unconscious motivation is counter-productive. It is more appropriate to assume that the demands posed by psychotherapy were perceived by the patient as being beyond their powers, that the perceived disruption in continuity looked too deep to be bridged by that specific therapeutic move. In such cases it may be advisable to declare the relapse to be due to the psychotherapist's mistake ('I wrongly assumed that you could take more, having under-estimated your vulnerability') and either lower the demands or switch to another continuity.

Other relationship problems may include over-dependency, attempts at crossing boundaries of psychotherapy (for example, by protracted night telephone calls at times of crisis) and attempts to turn the psychotherapist into an ally in struggles with institutions on economic or practical matters. Keeping the fine balance between the necessary involvement and the no less necessary therapeutic distance becomes a special challenge, as is all the work with traumatic patients.

ACKNOWLEDGEMENT

The authors wish to thank Maggie Ridgewell for her valuable editorial assistance.

REFERENCES

Alon, N. (1985) 'An Ericksonian approach to the treatment of chronic post traumatic patients', pp. 307–26 in J. K. Zeig (ed.) *Ericksonian Psychotherapy*, vol. 2, New York: Brunner/Mazel.

American Psychiatric Association (1987) *Diagnostic and Statistical Manual of Mental Disorders (DSM-III-R)* (3rd edn, revised), Washington, DC: American Psychiatric Association.

Antonowski, A. (1990) 'Pathways leading to successful coping and health', pp. 31–63 in M. Rosenbaum (ed.) *Learned Resourcefulness*, New York: Springer Verlag.

Bernat, I. (1991) 'Pre-morbid personality factors in sustaining and recovering from combat stress reaction: their prediction value among Israeli combat soldiers in the 1982 Israel–Lebanon war', *Psychologia, Israeli Journal of Psychology* 2(2): 162–70.

Bleich, A., Shalev, A., Shoham, S., Solomon, Z. and Kotler, M. (1992) 'PTSD: theoretical and practical considerations reflected through Koach – an innovative treatment project', *Journal of Traumatic Stress*, 5(2): 265–72.

Brown, D. P. and Fromm, E. (1986) *Hypnotherapy and Hypnoanalysis*, Hillsdale, NJ: Lawrence Erlbaum.

Drabek, T. E. (1986) *Human Systems Responses to Disaster: An Inventory of Sociological Findings*, New York: Springer Verlag.

Figley, C. R. (1978) *Stress Reactions among Vietnam Veterans: Theory, Research and Treatment*, New York: Brunner/Mazel.

—— (1988) 'Post-traumatic family therapy', pp. 83–109 in F. M. Ochberg (ed.) *Post Traumatic Therapy and Victims of Violence*, New York: Brunner/Mazel.

Horowitz, M. J. (1986) *Stress Response Syndromes*, New York: Jason Aronson.

Kaplan, H. I. and Sadock, B. J. (1991) *Synopsis of Psychiatry*, Baltimore, MD: Williams & Wilkins.

Kaplan, S. H. (1974) *The New Sex Therapy*, New York: Penguin.

Kleber, R. J. and Brom, D. (1992) *Coping with Stress: Theory, Prevention and Treatment*, Amsterdam: Swets & Zillinger.

Kluft, R. P. (1984) 'An introduction to multiple personality disorder', *Psychiatric Annals* 14: 19–24.

—— (1985) 'Hypnotherapy of childhood multiple personality disorder', *American Journal of Clinical Hypnosis* 27: 201–10.

Kolb, L. C. (1987) 'A neuropsychological hypothesis explaining post traumatic stress disorders', *Psychiatry* 144: 989–95.

Lindey, J. D., Macleod, J., Spitz, L., Green, B. and Grace, M. (1988) *Vietnam: A Casebook*, New York: Brunner/Mazel.

Ochberg, F. M. (1991) 'Post-traumatic therapy', *Psychotherapy* 28(1): 5–15.

Omer, H. (1991) 'Massive trauma: the role of emergency teams', *Sihot-Dialogue: Israeli Journal of Psychotherapy* 5(3): 157–70.

Omer, H. and Alon, N. (1994) 'The continuity principle: a unified approach to treatment and management in disaster and trauma', *American Journal of Community Psychology* (in press).

Rozynko, V. and Dondershine, H. E. (1991) 'Trauma focus group therapy for Vietnam veterans', *Psychotherapy* 28(1): 157–62.

Salmon, T. W. (1919) 'The war neuroses and their lessons', *Journal of Medicine* 59.

Solomon, Z. (1989) 'A three-year prospective study of post-traumatic stress disorder in Israeli combat veterans', *Journal of Traumatic Stress* 2: 59–73.

Solomon, Z. and Benbenishty, R. (1986) 'The role of proximity, immediacy and expectancy in frontline treatment of combat stress reactions among Israelis in the Lebanon war', *American Journal of Psychiatry* 143(5): 613–17.

Solomon, Z., Bleich, A., Shoham, S., Nardi, C. and Kotler, M. (1992) 'The Koach project for treatment of combat-related PTSD: rationale, aims and methodology', *Journal of Traumatic Stress* 5(2): 175–93.

Suffridge, D. R. (1992) 'Survivors of child maltreatment: diagnostic formulations and therapeutic process', *Psychotherapy* 28(1): 67–75.

Van der Kolk, B. A. (1988) 'The biological response to psychic trauma', pp. 25–38 in F. M. Ochberg (ed.) *Post Traumatic Therapy and Victims of Violence*, New York: Brunner/Mazel.

Young, G. H. and Gerson, S. (1992) 'New psychoanalytic perspectives in masochism and spouse abuse', *Psychotherapy* 28(1): 30–8.

Chapter 26

Forensic psychotherapy

Estela V. Welldon

Crimes are directed against society; at any rate, this is what society believes. It is open to doubt whether that perception is accurate but, whether true or not, society has involved itself in the secret, sordid, domestic, run-of-the-mill situations which are the stuff of forensic psychotherapy. It is unfortunate that the focus of attention is most frequently placed exclusively on the offence and on the punishment of the offender. Any psychodynamic understanding of the offender and of their delinquent actions as a result of their own self-destructive internal and compulsive needs is automatically equated by society with their acquittal. This is an understandable but serious error.

The form of psychotherapy involved in forensic psychotherapy is different from other forms precisely because society is, willy-nilly, involved. Forensic psychotherapy has gone beyond the special relationship between patient and psychotherapist. It is a triangular situation – patient, psychotherapist, society. As Bluglass points out, 'The role of the forensic psychiatrist in confronting and trying to reconcile the differences between the interests of the law and those of psychiatry is a crucial and important one' (1990: 7).

Society, the state, authority is there looking over the end of the bed and making judgements. Analytical psychotherapy does not welcome this extra dimension in an already fraught and difficult task. But there is no option if the forensic psychotherapist is to help the patient; and of course the extra dimension is involved if the psychotherapist is to play a part in elucidating and resolving some of the painful problems with which society struggles, for the most part ineffectually.

Forensic psychotherapy is a new discipline. It is the offspring of forensic psychiatry and psychoanalytical psychotherapy. Its aim is the psychodynamic understanding of the offender and their consequent treatment, regardless of the seriousness of the offence. It involves understanding the unconscious motivations in the criminal mind which underlie the offences. This is not to condone the crime or excuse the criminal. On the contrary, the object is to help the offender and thereby to save society from further crime. One of the problems in achieving this object is that the offender attacks, through their actions, the outside world – society – which is immediately affected. Hence, concerns are rarely focused on the internal world of the offender. It is time to re-focus our concerns, at least in part. The more we understand about the criminal mind, the more we can take positive preventive action. This, in turn, could lead to better management and the implementation of more cost-effective treatment of patients.

The term 'forensic psychotherapy' has now been validated and legitimised. It is included, for example, in the final report of the Reed Committee (1992), the *Review of Health and Social Services for Mentally Disordered Offenders*.

This chapter will deal exclusively with the basic facts of forensic psychotherapy as it is practised in a National Health Service out-patient clinic, namely the Portman Clinic, where I have been working for over twenty years. Other settings such as special hospitals, medium secure units and therapeutic communities, though of great and increasing importance and relevance, are not directly addressed here, although the principles obtain in these institutions too.

The United Kingdom has from a very early stage been in the forefront of forensic psychotherapy and, within the United Kingdom, the Portman Clinic has been the leader. The history of the clinic (Rumney 1981) goes back to 1931, when a small group of men and women met in London and established an association to promote a better way of dealing with criminals than putting them in prison. It was later called the Association for the Scientific Treatment of Delinquency and Crime, a title proposed by an eminent psychoanalyst, Dr Glover, who became its first chairman (Cordess 1992a). Much later, in 1991, the original aims of the Portman Clinic were adopted by the newly established International Association for Forensic Psychotherapy. A year earlier, in 1990, the first course on forensic psychotherapy, sponsored by the British Post Graduate Medical Federation (University of London) in association with the Portman Clinic, began to train national and international professionals in the techniques of this special branch of psychotherapy. Williams (1991) describes the difficulties encountered in the successful bridging of both disciplines.

If forensic psychotherapy is the handling of three interacting positions – the psychotherapist's, the patient's and society's criminal justice system (de Smit 1992) – it follows that treatment of the forensic patient population should ideally be carried out within the National Health Service, and not within the private sector. Forensic psychotherapy has to be considered in the overall context of health care for people involved in the criminal justice process. Its aims, however, are not identical to those of the criminal justice system. There is an inevitable, and indeed necessary, conflict of values (Harding 1992). Evaluations should ideally be conducted independently, according to criteria which correspond to health-based values (Reed Report 1992).

A discipline such as this needs explanation. If we can understand the relationship between the offender and society we shall be making progress in research into the causes and prevention of crime. This is one of the tasks to which the Portman Clinic has been dedicated from its earliest days. For example, society instinctively views sexual offenders and their victims in distinct and reflex ways. Whereas the treatment of victims is encouraged and everyone is concerned about their welfare, the same does not apply to the perpetrators who are believed to be the products of 'evil forces'. Lip-service is paid to the fact that victims could easily become perpetrators, but emotional responses tend to be biased. The split is in full operation. Victims are left without the benefit of a full understanding, since generally it is expected and assumed that they are devoid of any negative, hostile feelings. The healthy expression of those feelings is not allowed and this suppression easily leads to revenge.

Another relevant stereotype is that in which women are victims and men perpetrators. When men are sexual abusers all sorts of different agencies, social and medical, intervene and very soon the police are called in. By contrast, the female 'offender' finds it very difficult to get a hearing (Welldon 1988/1992). Nobody wants to hear about her predicament, and nobody takes her too seriously. This happens even in group therapy where she finds that other patients minimise her problems. This reaction proves very anti-therapeutic, and if the psychotherapist is not ready to interpret this total denial for them, these women will never gain any insight into their problems, let alone be able to change themselves. The difficulties in acknowledging a woman's abusing power in motherhood ('they don't do those awful things') could be the result of massive denial, as a way of dealing with this unpalatable truth. Until recently, a lack of legislation on female perversion reflected society's total denial of it. The woman is thereby seen as a part-object, or just a receptacle of a man's perverse designs. The apparent idealisation of mothers prevalent in society contains a denigrating counterpart.

These are amongst the reasons for regretting that society has been slow to recognise the limited but significant contribution which forensic psychotherapists can make to the achievement of a dynamic understanding of the causes of delinquent and criminal behaviour. A major cross-disciplinary effort should be make to understand and eradicate at least some of the more correctable reasons for crime in our society. This involves political scientists, sociologists and community leaders as well as forensic workers. An imaginative effort is required to promote discussion and to educate the general public. Forensic psychotherapists can and must play a crucial role in this, but the main burden must fall on those in the media and in politics who have special skills of communication.

A crucial point about the discipline of forensic psychotherapy is that it is a team effort. The full meaning of this phrase will emerge from the discussion which follows, but at the outset it needs to be stated that this is not an heroic action by the psychotherapist alone. The action begins with the referral agencies, which include the courts of justice. But court or no court, there is no getting away from the fact that the offender's actions are blatantly carried out against society or those principles society values, and which we all share. Accordingly, a wide range of people are inescapably involved.

It is crucial to recognise that successful treatment rests not only with the professional psychotherapist but also with a team of helpers, including psychologists, social workers, administration and the clerical staff. In the sixty years of the Portman's experience the rapport of our patients to the clinic itself, and not just to their psychotherapist, has become basic to our approach.

For the general public it is, no doubt, society which matters most; but for the professional forensic psychotherapist the prime consideration must be the patient. If forensic psychotherapy is concerned above all with the patient, it must be scarcely less concerned with the 'treater' and their training. Why? Because, if they are not properly trained, the members of the team are bound to feel confused and overwhelmed by all the dimensions involved, many of which are unpleasant and stressful. The importance of the development of this discipline in the United Kingdom as an evolving species (Adshead 1991) is our main concern. If the treater is not trained and equipped with insight into their own internal world and their own motivations, they may unwittingly react to a situation as if they were a normal member of the public. This is a very natural reaction, but unfortunately it is an abdication of responsibility: it is unprofessional.

REFERRAL OF PATIENTS AND NATURE OF THE OFFENCES

Patients are referred to the Portman Clinic and other forensic psycho-therapists by various sources: external and self-referral. External sources include general psychiatric hospitals, general practitioners, probation officers, courts and other institutions. In some cases the public knowledge of a patient's sexual and/or criminal offence is very wide, as a result of that person having appeared in court – often with associated press reports. Usually, self-referrals are patients whose 'bizarre', unlawful sexual behaviour is unknown to anyone except themselves and their victims. They come to the clinic of their own free will. A very important characteristic in determining the prognosis and motivation for treatment is an intense sense of shame and despondency about the activities in which they are involved. This is reciprocated by society's response in judging and condemning them when their behaviour is detected regardless of their own feelings about their criminal actions. Both offender and society feel bewildered and unable to comprehend the motivations or symbolism attached to their deviant actions.

The criminal action is the central fact. Sometimes it has the capacity to become explosive, violent and uncontrollable, with attendant profound consequences for society. At times, it is the equivalent of a neurotic symptom. Pfäfflin (1993) describes the symptom as a constructive and healthy reaction. He adds that it is conservative, meaning that the patient needs it and keeps it until it can be properly understood and then he can give it up. At other times, it is the expression of more severe psycho-pathology; it is secretive, completely encapsulated and split from the rest of the patient's personality, which acts as a defence against a psychotic illness (Hopper 1991); at still other times, it is calculated and associated with professional, careerist criminality. The criminal action always appears understandable as an action against society, and yet at the same time it is a self-destructive act, with harmful effects for the offender. This aspect of criminality associated with unconscious guilt has been examined by Freud (1915), Glover (1960) and Tuovinen (1973), amongst others.

The action may be characterised by a manic defence, created against the acknowledgement or recognition of a masked chronic depression. Alternatively, it may include compulsion, impulsivity, inability to inter-sperse thought before action and, as mentioned earlier, a total failure to understand it.

The forensic patient is unable to think before the action occurs because they are not mentally equipped to make the necessary links (Bion 1959). Their thinking process is not functioning in their particular area of perversity, which is often encapsulated from the rest of their personality. This therefore is the work of psychotherapy; but at times the patient's tendency to make sadistic attacks on their own capacity for thought and reflection is projected and directed against the psychotherapist's capacity to think and reflect, and it is then that the psychotherapist feels confused, numbed and unable to make any useful interpretations.

Most forensic patients have deeply disturbed backgrounds. Some have criminal records and a very low self-esteem often covered by a façade of cockiness and arrogance; their impulse control is minimal, and they are suspicious and filled with hatred towards people in authority. Some rebellious and violent ex-convicts have long histories of crime against property and persons. Others may refer themselves, and in these cases are often insecure, inadequate and ashamed people. They enact their pathological sexual deviancy, such as exhibitionism, paedophilia or voyeurism, in a very secretive manner so that only their victims know about their behaviour. Some patients have a great capacity for expressing anger, yet seem shy and awkward in showing tenderness or love to anybody.

Often, forensic patients are deviant both sexually and socially. Some sexual deviations present themselves as criminal activities by definition, although some patients who indulge in these actions may never have been caught. This is a secret or secretive population who apparently lead normal lives, sometimes in both work and domestic situations. However, the links between criminal actions such as 'breaking and entering' and sexual deviations are not always obvious, at least not until the unconscious motivation is revealed. This connection has been noticed by many psycho-analytical authors, such as Zilboorg (1955), Glover (1944) and Limentani (1984).

ON THE LINKS BETWEEN CRIMINAL ACTIONS AND SEXUAL DEVIATIONS

Example 1

I will illustrate this point with a clinical vignette. A patient of twenty-eight was referred years ago by his employers, a City bank. This was, in itself, a revelation that a City bank could be so perceptive of the possibility of unconscious motivations. They had experienced a sense of bewilderment at this puzzling offence. He was the bank's 'bike' man, responsible for carrying money from and to different places. In the course of his work, he had been detected stealing spanners from other bikes' boxes. Alarm grew greatly when police found evidence of his having previously stolen 3,000 spanners. At the interview with me he tried unsuccessfully to make sense of his unlawful actions by explaining that he was a handyman and that the price of tools was subject to inflation. Obviously, such a clumsy and inadequate explanation pointed to other motivations. In describing his actions, he talked with a great deal of embarrassment mixed with excitement. In his own words:

> I'm on my bike. Suddenly I see another bike being parked and I feel taken over by an extreme curiosity to look at its box. I know this is wrong but cannot help myself. I start sweating. I feel my heart pumping and I just have to do it. I have to take the tools. Then I feel at peace, a great sense of relief surrounds me. I feel great. On my way home I start feeling confused, ashamed and guilty. I don't know any longer what to do with yet another spanner and I take it to the garage where I keep them all.

His statement is similar to that of a person suffering from sexual perversion, showing the same quality of urgency, the identical cycle which involves growing sexual anxiety, the fight against it, eventually giving in and succumbing to the action, the sexual relief, and the subsequent sense of shame and guilt.

This was a young, well-groomed man who was still living with his mother, a domineering, narcissistic woman who had never allowed him to lead his own life. When the police came to get him, her first reaction was: 'What shall I do if you take him away? I can't be on my own!' Apart from his mother he had never had any relationship of any sort and lived in complete isolation.

Our psychiatric court report briefly indicated that this man's criminal offences were the expression of his tremendous sense of social and sexual inadequacy which, in turn, were the product of a deprived and depraved early childhood. His father had been absent in the war and his mother had a severe narcissistic borderline personality. The magistrate not only found the report but also the recommendation useful. The patient was recommended to seek treatment in group psychotherapy, which, if accepted, was to be implemented immediately. The work of psychotherapy consisted of his growing awareness of the unconscious links between the sexual symbolisms and the enactment of his irresistible impulses. This unravelling made it possible for the patient to free himself from these urges.

ON OVERLAPPING OF SEXUAL PREDICAMENTS AND HIDDEN VIOLENCE

Example 2

Sometimes sexual predicaments and hidden violence overlap, as, for example, in the following brief case history. A young man of twenty-three first came to treatment because of fears of being homosexual. After a year of individual psychotherapy he left treatment having overcome that particular problem. A few years later he was back; this time, because he had experienced sudden, and unexpectedly violent, fantasies against all women, but particularly his mother, and later his girlfriend. He had achieved an intimate situation with his girlfriend but felt the urge to hurt her. In an obvious attempt to do so, he had had a one-night stand with another girl. In the following group session he described to us a recent dream. In this he had his fist inside a woman's vagina and was punching it vigorously. When he began to enjoy this process he became aware he was disintegrating: first the hand began to dissolve and later the whole body was annihilated. This dream represented his fears of being destroyed by a woman if he became close to her. His fear of homosexuality had been a protection – replaced later by a deeper fear, expressed through violent fantasies – against women who, he felt, had previously damaged him, indeed almost emasculated him.

ON THE DIFFERENT AIMS OF MALE AND FEMALE PERVERSIONS

As a clinician I have observed that the main difference between a male and female perverse action lies in the aim. Whereas in men the act is aimed at an outside part-object, in women it is usually against themselves, either against their bodies or against objects which they see as their own creations; that is, their babies. In both cases, bodies and babies are treated as part-objects (Welldon 1988/1992).

Example 3

A patient who was a practising prostitute was referred for a psychiatric assessment because of violent behaviour directed towards her second child. She had been a victim of paternal sexual abuse. Her first pregnancy came as a surprise to her. Still, she felt the need to go ahead with it, because in this way she was taking out insurance against a dread of being alone. The child could become utterly dependent on her and totally under her control. When this first child arrived, she was overcome by feelings of repulsion and revulsion against her baby. She felt ready to kick it, and after reflection she decided that in order to overcome these horrid feelings she would fix in her mind the idea of the baby being part of herself. Some days she would choose her right arm as being the baby, and at other times it would be one of her legs. In this way she felt able to master her impulses to beat up her first child. Later, with her second baby she asserted, 'There is no more room in my body for a second one. All has been used up by the first one.'

Example 4

Another woman patient was referred because of exhibitionism. She told me that her compulsion to 'flash' occurred when she became attached to a person whom she invested with idealised 'maternal' qualities. She wanted to get closer, to be noticed and to be taken care of by that particular person but she also wanted a shocked response from her 'victims'. She carefully planned the 'appropriate' clothing to wear when she was to meet that person. Usually she wore an overcoat covering only a little vest in order to respond readily to her urge. She knew this was wrong and that she would be rejected but she could not stop herself. She had a most deprived early history of being sexually abused by her mother and her siblings. It is interesting to note that, even when her exhibitionism could superficially appear to be the equivalent of her male counterpart's, this is not so. It is a well-known fact that male exhibitionists have the compulsion to 'flash' only to children and women – and women who are unknown to them – while my patient had suffered from this compulsion only with other women with whom she felt a close attachment. This is yet another remarkable difference between the genders.

In short, the sources of referral are various and the type of people who become patients even more so. But, if understanding is to occur, all patients must be treated according to a rigorous professional code in which the offender is understood whilst the crime is not condoned. This process must begin with a comprehensive assessment of the patient.

THE PSYCHODYNAMIC ASSESSMENT

The patient should be clear from the outset about the reasons for the assessment interviews. This is particularly important since the procedure could easily be taken as yet another legalistic encounter. If the purpose is the writing of a psychiatric court report this should be made clear from the start. All interviews should embody the utmost honesty. If treatment is recommended the patient should be told the length of the waiting list – especially if it is a long one – and should be informed that the assessment process may involve three or four meetings. Forensic patients usually complain and are sarcastic about the fact that an 'assessment' or psychiatric court report has been made within a mere twenty minutes of meeting a psychiatrist. They should not be allowed to get away with this caricature of a professional assessment by making sure that the allocated time is adequate for the purposes of a psychiatric report. The 'structuring of time' as coined by Cox (1978/1992b: 338) is a vital frame in forensic psychotherapy, and it is quite different as practised by forensic psychiatrists, who should be ready to be summoned at any time. Instead, forensic psychotherapists are aware that patients can only rely on those psychotherapists who keep strict timing for their sessions.

In the initial period of treatment, beginning with the first interview, it is especially important to follow firm guidelines. Never make a patient wait beyond the appointment time – neither earlier nor later; earlier will be felt as seduction, later as a sense of neglect, repeating the experience of 'nobody caring'. These diagnostic meetings should be conducted at irregular intervals in order to avoid the intensity of the emergence of transference. The meetings are not as structured as psychotherapy sessions: there is some flexibility but the timing is always to be preserved rigorously. The approach needs judiciously to combine silence and direct questioning so that the patient can feel allowed to talk freely about difficult and, at times, painful predicaments while also being expected to give, in answer to questions, more details for further clarification.

The clinician must not let the patient involve him/her in anti-therapeutic manoeuvring, such as laughing at a patient's joke. Frequently, such jokes are made at the expense of the patient's own self-esteem, with overtones of self-contempt and denigration of themselves: 'Nobody takes me seriously.'

Patients often try to engage the clinician in a jocular response. It is a serious mistake, into which inexperienced psychotherapists fall, to appear friendly and non-judgemental. No sooner has the psychotherapist laughed than a sudden realisation emerges that they are laughing *at* the patient and not *with* the patient.

During the assessment sessions, there are often attempts to re-create the original injurious, traumatic situation as experienced by the patient. Frequently, this will have been experienced as being treated as a 'part-object', and becomes vividly alive in the transference.

A sense of boundaries is crucial, amongst many other layers of need, to establish a sense of differentiation, in which 'them' and 'us' create a sense of order and justice which can be rightly acknowledged. This is one reason why patients powerfully resent the 'do-gooders'. In their eyes the 'do-gooders' try to proselytise, to infantilise, to make them believe 'we are all the same', a statement which is felt to be hypocritical, and based on double standards.

Summary of general approach in the psychodynamic assessment:

- The patient should be clear about the purpose of the meeting.
- This should be obtained in one to three sessions, at irregular intervals.
- Exact timing.
- Never engage in jocular response to the patient's 'jokes'.
- Keep a straightforward approach, neither too cold nor too friendly.
- Make it clear that information is needed for accuracy of the evaluation process.
- Listen to the patient's predicaments but if patient feels 'stuck' ask direct questions.

The psychodynamic meaning of the offence could be diagnosed as:

1 Neurotic symptoms.
2 Defence against psychotic breakdown, completely encapsulated and split from the rest of the personality.
3 'Careerist'-orientated.
4 Acting out as defined by Limentani (1989): an expression of the person's fantasy life and its motivation is at first unconscious, as a means of relieving increasing and unbearable sexual anxiety, and as a form of communication of anti-social acts.

THE CIRCUMSTANCES OF ASSESSMENT

Setting and surroundings are important – especially since the forensic patient has usually had previous experience of the judicial system, having been caught, detected and judged. In his dealings with the psychotherapist, he is likely to feel judged, charged, persecuted and subject to prejudice. If the diagnostician is not well trained, a new confrontation could easily be experienced by the prospective patient as a further condemnation of their illegal action. At times the action is symptomatic, in which the person knows it is wrong but finds themselves unable to resist it. At other times the action is an enactment which the person is not willing to admit is odd or wrong. This action has sometimes been unconsciously committed, in an attempt to obtain a response from society to the predicament of the individual offender; the action takes over, and society focuses its attention on the action and not on the person who has committed it, until, of course, it comes to condemnation.

Therefore, it is of basic importance to 'see' and to 'acknowledge' the person in their totality. For example, it is important that letters regarding all appointments are properly and formally addressed to 'Mr' or 'Mrs'. The same attitude should prevail when the patient arrives at the clinic where they are to be seen. The building should be accessible, the atmosphere warm and the attitude welcoming from the moment the patient faces the receptionist. Patients should be treated with dignity – surnames only, for example – and everything reasonable done to give them enough self-respect to face the complexities of their first diagnostic consultation with an unknown consultant. It is worth remembering that someone who has been referred for a psychiatric court report, fresh from involvement with police inquiries concerning offences, is frightened about having to face yet another figure of authority who is expected to be ready to judge and condemn.

Because of their fears of intimacy in the one-to-one situation these patients form a strong transference to the clinic as an institution. The institution treating them can become as important as, or more important than the psychotherapist themselves. A safe and containing atmosphere in which the patients feel secure and acknowledged from the moment of their arrival is essential. In short, the assessment is to be carried out like any other assessment but, if anything, with even more care and sensitivity.

Institutional setting

Forensic patients are very much in need of three structures – fellow patients, psychotherapist and institution – and family (if they have one). All are deeply related in their mental representations, which constitute a process of triangulation.

An important function provided by the institution is that of containment. It reinforces a sense of boundaries and so acts as a container for all tensions involved and allows the emergence of trust and a collective awareness of, and sensitivity to, the recrudescence of violence, reducing its likelihood.

At times of crisis, when for many reasons staff members are unable to fulfil these tasks properly, a breakdown of the system is likely – with serious consequences for all, including the patients.

Cordess (1992b) has described the application of family therapy to work with psychotic offenders and their family victims in a regional secure unit.

The topic of forensic psychotherapy and its contribution to forensic psychiatry in an institutional setting has been described by Cox (1983). The failure of psychotherapy to thrive specifically within the British special hospitals is critically examined by Pilgrim (1987).

TRANSFERENCE

It is necessary to understand the personality traits of forensic patients since they lead directly into an understanding of the transference and counter-transference phenomena, which appear from the beginning of the assessment and during the psychodynamic treatment.

An early and severe emotional deprivation is usually found in the psychogenesis of both sexes, which may include a history of neglect, abandonment, symbiotic relationship with mother, humiliation of gender identity, physical abuse, sexual abuse, wrong gender assignment at birth, cross-dressing during infancy. All the above may occur, either singly or in any combination. However, the commonest case is the victim of both seduction and neglect. There has frequently been an absence of acknowledgement of generational differences, especially in cases of incest with children being 'forced' to fulfil parental roles and victims becoming perpetrators, leading to the three-generational process.

These adult patients have experienced – as infants – a sense of having been messed about in crucial circumstances in which both psychological and biological survival were at stake. In other words, they were *actually* – in reality, not only in fantasy – at the mercy of others. These traumatic, continuous and inconsistent attitudes towards them have effectively interfered with the process of individuation and separation. There is a basic lack of trust towards the significant carer, which accompanies them all through their lives. From this early ill-treatment we can deduce some psychopathological features which will be understood in the light of the early background:

1 Need to be in control, which is apparent from the moment they are first seen and also during treatment.
2 Early experiences of deprivation and subjection to seductiveness make them vulnerable to anything which in any way is reminiscent of the original experiences.
3 A desire for revenge expressed in sadomasochism as an unconscious need to inflict harm.

4 Erotisation or sexualisation of the action.
5 Manic defence against depression.

There are very elaborate and sophisticated unconscious mechanisms which these patients have built up in themselves, which operate as a 'self-survival kit': this is 'turned on' automatically in situations of extreme vulnerability when they experience being psychically naked or 'stripped'. They use over-sexualisation in the same way, as a means to deal with an enormous sense of inadequacy and of inner insecurity. They themselves become the part-objects to be readily available and easily exploited, abused, seduced. Of course, this is no longer a unilateral, one-way system as happened when they were infants at the mercy of their parents or carers. Now, to the whole world, they appear to be adults, but, actually, much of their internal world belongs to much earlier phases of their emotional development in which an enormous sense of helplessness was acquired, and much revenge has been harboured for a long time. The one-way system has become a two-way system which is in constant dynamic activity. And here the psycho-therapist's work has to be defined. It is obvious that all these different survival mechanisms and ways of functioning will appear intermittently when the defences are down. Then alarm and the old feelings re-emerge and put the person concerned on the alert. Defence mechanisms go in waves, and when a situation of closeness is about to be achieved the person withdraws in horror. Such people loathe any new scenario which might involve or develop into trust. Thus the person could appear as a tyrannical and despotic paternal figure, who is only there to satisfy their own whims.

COUNTER-TRANSFERENCE

The forensic psychotherapist should feel safe and securely contained in caring and unobtrusive surroundings. Institutions should provide such structures, to protect the psychotherapists from the inherent anxiety produced by working with forensic patients. These patients act out sadistic and intrusive attacks on psychotherapists and on their treatment in many different ways, including on their capacity to think; this leaves psychotherapists confused and unable to offer adequate interpretations.

Money matters are important both in concrete and in symbolic terms. This is obvious with patients whose day-to-day living is provided by their own or close associates' delinquent or perverse actions. A frequent problem is the offer or 'pushing' of a gift which could at times render the psychotherapist a receiver of stolen goods.

The psychotherapists' inner knowledge that the state is paying for their professional services becomes invaluable while working with this patient population, since they are also aware of this basic fact. It reinforces both parties in the contractual agreement on which the psychotherapy is based.

The psychotherapists are debarred from blackmail, and the patients feel neither exploited nor able to exploit anybody about money matters. 'The forensic psychotherapist spends much of his time and energy waiting and witnessing, while his patients try to unravel that vitally important nodal point of experience "between the acting of a dreadful thing/And the first motion"' (Cox 1992a: 255).

The psychotherapist must listen to the patient carefully, without interrupting, however difficult or painful the material may be. Some supposedly 'unusual' or 'rare' predicaments are not that unusual: the so-called rarity is often due to the clinician's inability to listen because of the psychic pain involved. This is frequently the case with incestuous relationships. It is important to be aware of how our own feelings may be the origin, for example, of the under-recording of female perversions – such as female paedophilia and maternal incest. Patients may be ready to talk about these urges, but diagnosticians generally are not ready to listen to them. The requirement of personal psychotherapy for future treaters is of basic importance – in order to be able to discern what belongs to the treater's internal world and what to the patient. Most of these patients' material can disturb profoundly because at times it feels like dealing with dynamite. Sometimes, if unprepared, the psychotherapist could easily become irate, as if they are being 'taken for a ride', and indeed the patient often tries to be in total control of the situation. In other instances, patients succeed in making their psychotherapists become their true partners in their specific perversions. Here is a brief history of a case which illustrates the point.

Example 5

A patient came for a diagnostic interview because of his compulsive masochistic needs. These involved the hiring of prostitutes for the purpose of actively ill-treating him in a way which sexually excited him. In the course of the interview, the psychotherapist found to her horror that she had become actively engaged in a dialogue in which she began to scream at the top of her voice. She realised that every time she tried to say something to the patient he asked her to repeat it 'just a bit louder, because I'm hard of hearing'. One of the reasons the psychotherapist became aware of her own response was that at the time the patient was relating an incident in which he had secured the services of a nurse to function as a sadistic prostitute. The nurse symbolised the caring profession, which had been corrupted.

Alternatively, the treater may feel flattered by the fact that whatever positive change may have been achieved, the patients may ascribe it to the practitioner's own professional efforts. However, the flattery won't last for long; it will soon be replaced by complaints and dissatisfaction about relapses or re-offending assumed to be due to the practitioner's inefficiency and lack of 'skills', just as before the 'cure' of the problem had to do with their excellence.

In other words, there is a constant switch between idealisation and denigration. This happens because psychopathological predicaments and offending behaviour are the result of a deep, chronic, hidden depression. This turns into a manic and at times bizarrely funny acting out. There is so much pain underneath that the patient barely manages at times to confront it. They try at all costs to avoid their real feelings. The psychotherapist could easily be caught in the counter-transference process, assuming an omnipotent role in the patient's actions regardless of whether they are law-abiding or not.

SELECTION CRITERIA FOR PSYCHOTHERAPY

It is important here to make a basic distinction between offenders who are mentally disordered and those who are not. Some offenders have a professional orientation towards their criminal activities. For example, they calculate the consequences, even going so far as to engage in a cost-benefit planning of their actions, involving such matters as how many months or years in prison they are prepared to risk. In other words, such offenders may not differ in important psychological traits from careerists generally. These two seemingly different categories do at times overlap or succeed each other. It is not unusual to find patients who have been criminal 'careerists' for a number of years but who, on reaching their thirties, begin to question the validity of what they are doing and express a deep interest in seeking professional help to change their lifestyles.

The psychodynamic assessment requires a wider understanding of all other factors concerning that particular person, their psychological growth, their family – taking it back at least three generations – their own subculture, and other circumstances. The psychotherapist needs to investigate the 'crimes' in detail, especially the sequence of events leading up to the action as well as the offender's reaction to it. This can give clues to early traumatic experiences, and to the unconscious ways through which an individual tries to resolve conflicts resulting from these experiences. In this way, even during the evaluation itself, the psychotherapist is able slowly to uncover layers of primitive defences and the motivations behind them – enabling us to learn about the offender's capacity or incapacity for psychodynamic treatment, as well as initiating a process whereby the offender might acquire insight into the nature of their crimes.

It is important to record how the patient interacts with the clinician and the changes observed during the series of meetings. At times it is useful to make a 'trial' interpretation to elicit the patient's capacity to make use of it, and their capacity for insight. In order to assess treatability for psychotherapy accurately in these patients, we must modify terms and concepts from those used in assessing neurotic patients. For example, when the criminal action is committed clumsily, the person is especially susceptible to detection. The criminal action has become the equivalent of the neurotic symptom. The offender may also express fears of a custodial sentence, which may in their own terms denote motivation for treatment. This could signal that it is the appropriate time to start treatment, since the patient is susceptible, however much under implied duress. They are now ready to own their psychopathology, and this may denote an incipient sense of capacity for insight. From this therapeutic standpoint, it is not unfortunate that a patient has to face persecution, but what is unfortunate is that just when they are ready for treatment they may instead have to face punishment. The patient may actually acquire a criminal record for the first time while in treatment or on the waiting list. Ironically, the very success of our treatment may produce this result. It is when the patient who has hitherto escaped detection starts to acquire some insight into themselves, they become clumsy and are detected.

The relapse in delinquent and criminal behaviour is frequently found during the first long holidays in psychotherapy. This is associated with feelings of having been abandoned by their psychotherapists at times of need. Gallwey points out that this occurrence as

> The uncovering of areas of deprivation and unfulfilled dependency can produce enormous pressure on both therapist and patient, with a speedy move into delinquent acting out, or even violence, when the patient feels let down or abandoned within the therapy. The least hazardous tactic is to contain the individual in a way which minimises the reinforcement of delinquent strategies.

(1992: 359)

Delinquent adolescents also require innovative modifications of the traditional psychoanalytical therapeutic approach, as emphasised by du Bois (1992) and Scannell (1992).

It is vital to look closely at particular psychopathologies and needs, and to see if the selection criteria could be improved, either for group or individual psychotherapy. For example, given that the patients concerned present serious personality disorders and are unable to form relationships, it is obvious that some are more suitable than others for group treatment. It is important to assess certain factors in their personalities, family structure and living circumstances. For instance, the root family influence is crucial.

INDIVIDUAL ANALYTICAL PSYCHOTHERAPY

Patients who have never experienced satisfactory relationships in early life – for example, those who come from very large families with financial deprivation and emotional overcrowding – are likely to do better in individual treatment than in group treatment. Patients who are adopted or fostered react in quite different fashions, depending on whether they join a new group in which all members were 'born' simultaneously, or one with previous history and traditions. In the latter, they feel 'on trial' and closely observed by others, who are perceived as the 'old', 'legitimate', 'real' children.

Sometimes patients present themselves as 'perfect', 'ideal' patients for group therapy, but it transpires that they are rather good actors, often having been exposed previously to similar experiences in therapeutic prisons or communities. Indeed, they become good helpers but get little for themselves. This does not mean that they should not be treated in groups, but they warrant special consideration and might be treated more effectively in one-to-one psychotherapy.

Assessment of patients' present living circumstances is crucial. There are those who could benefit from group therapy but are involved in the criminal world. If they open up and talk of their own or their spouse's criminal activities, the confidentiality rule is impossible to sustain.

Example 6

Extreme secretiveness is sometimes a contraindication. For example, John, who came to the clinic because of frotteurism, was a shy, awkward married man with children who had never confessed to anyone about this perversion, and had even refused to give his address. At the first session when he admitted to his problem, the group's reaction seemed one of anxiety, covered by laughter. Everyone tried to minimise his symptom to such an extent that he felt humiliated, whereupon he became very flushed and left, never to return.

GROUP PSYCHOTHERAPY

Patients who have been subjected to an intense, suffocating relationship with one parent are suitable candidates for group therapy. Groups provide them with a much warmer and less threatening atmosphere than they can usually find in one-to-one psychotherapy, in which their sense of authority would be so intense. They can also share their experience with their peers. Often these people are still subjugated by an over-possessive mother, who will not allow them to develop any independence or individuation. Others have left home only to find themselves extremely isolated. In the group, with the help of fellow patients, they begin to express openly some rebellious, anti-authority feelings and eventually some self-assertion.

Bion (1967/1984) says that communication develops into a capacity not only for toleration by the self of its own psychic qualities, but also as a part of the social capacity of the individual. 'This development, of great importance in group dynamics, has received virtually no attention; its absence would make even scientific communication impossible' (p. 118).

Violent behaviour seems better contained and even better understood within the framework of group therapy. Freud points out that the mechanism of identification is a basic one in group formation, and he elaborates that identification not only helps to further positive feelings within the group, but also helps in limiting aggressiveness – since there is a general tendency to spare those with whom one is identified. The presence of other participants, who may notice hostility before it is expressed openly (often against the psychotherapist), gives the group a capacity to confront violent behaviour and to deal with it openly and honestly. Multiple transference provides patients with the possibility of more than just one target (as in one-to-one psychotherapy) for their anger, which they find highly reassuring.

This patient population presents a worthwhile challenge given the potential benefits of group analytical treatment for such 'anti-social' and 'asocial' people. All share an intense sense of shame and despondency about the activities in which they are involved. Group treatment often proves to be the most appropriate method of treatment if we use adequate selection criteria, are careful about the composition of the group and employ a modified technique keeping in mind the patients' particular psychopathology. The price paid for effectiveness is to give up rigid ideological psychotherapeutic principles.

Example 7

Gaining of insight and its communication are often not straightforward in working with destructive patients. A clear example of this occurred in a group session in which a member notorious for his criminal activities, which were at the service of the enhancement of his false self, told the other group members of changes he had experienced.

Herbert said, 'I am very worried about myself. I've recently noticed that when I'm about to embark on conning other people I lose my cool. For example, the other day when I went to the bank to pass some forged cheques I got scared. My heart began to pound, I got all sweaty in my hands, I avoided eye contact with the cashier. In other words, I was giving myself away.'

Another member asked, 'Do you think this *consciousness* has anything to do with this group?' Everybody showed much interest in this statement. (The term had never been used before.)

To which he replied, 'Yes. It has all happened since I came here and I am very scared.' This was an important change which had to do with his criminal activity changing from ego-syntonic to ego-dystonic. In other words, his capacity to corrupt his ego integrity was no longer so easily available, due to the formation of a new ego which had been internalised from the group, with an accompanying capacity for reflection. Perverse mechanisms in other patients were readily available. The group was split in two: some accepted this as a healthy development but others were not as generous with their response because of extreme envy.

So Adam, another member, said, 'I am extremely worried about you and the effect this group has on you if this means that you are becoming more ineffectual as a thief. Perhaps you ought to do something about that – I don't know whether you ought to leave the group or what, but be sure that the group is not affecting your skills as a thief.'

Other group members reacted to this statement in a very angry fashion, calling it cynical. They pointed out that, after all, Herbert had come to psychotherapy in order to deal with his criminal actions.

But Adam was merciless with his manic reaction, saying while laughing: 'He's not coming here to deal with his thieving problems, he's coming here because, as the doctor has remarked on many occasions, of his sense of emptiness, his deadness and his looking for excitement. So, first he'll have to know about this boredom. In the meantime he has to be careful not to get caught.'

Separation anxieties can easily produce most dangerous acting out. Psychotherapists' holidays are very distressing for group members since they feel neglected, abandoned and uncared for, just as they did when they were infants. There are often, however, signals in the sessions leading up to holidays that 'something is going on'. It is important to detect and recognise these clues, for they form part of this constellation or syndrome responsible for 'acting out' behaviour. It may be seen as a resistance to the therapeutic process (Welldon 1984).

The amount of fear, rejection and humiliation which such patients experience when confronted with their 'secrets' in a group therapy session is difficult to convey. It is not unusual for them to deal with their enormous fears of being rejected by conjuring up an image of a nagging or possessive mother who has been experienced as both frightening and rather contemptuous. They will tend to agree with one another, thus creating an atmosphere of unhealthy solidarity, with the main object of assigning that image to the psychotherapist. The psychotherapist may be trapped into situations, such as becoming a sadistic policeman who, every time they talk about their problems, will try to moralise, condemn, or put them away; or a nagging mother, who will use the group to question every patient in a persistent and repetitive way about their illegal actions, expecting them to conform to society's norms. Hence the psychotherapist has to be skilful in dealing with such interactions between patients from the outset. If collusion appears, this will create further anxieties because patients are aware that covering up brings frustrations when the psychotherapist does not intervene properly by offering adequate interpretations. Unless unhealthy expectations can be interpreted quickly as part of transference interpretations, the psychotherapist and their expertise are likely to be immobilised.

Psychotherapy aims to provide the patient with the necessary understanding of their chosen symbolisms, and the part that the affect plays in them, but in the instance of the forensic patient this is especially relevant since this anxiety is only relieved by bizarre actions, of whose unconscious mechanisms they are aware. If they are able to gain the relevant insight, they might then interpose the thought between the urge and the action. This new link is created to overcome or to prevent succumbing to the acting out. In Bion's words, 'a capacity to think would diminish the sense of frustration intrinsic to appreciation of the gap between a wish and its fulfilment' (1967/1984: 113).

This process is highly accelerated in group psychotherapy when a group member, whose particular psychopathology is driven by a compulsive need to alleviate the increasing tension, is confronted by other group members at different stages and that member's condition is understood in some of its intricacies. At this point the rest of the group does the thinking. The learning by experience then is multiplied not only by the actual number of group members but also by their own growing process of maturation, which intrinsically involves the development of their own capacity to think.

Example 8

A patient came because of her compulsive shoplifting. She was an extremely intelligent person who, to start with, could not apprehend the complicated mechanisms involved in her self-destructive behaviour, despite her deep motivation for important inner change. Eventually she began to learn of her rage against her partner, and her desire for revenge which pervaded the acting out, that took place after angry rows with him because of her inability to tolerate frustration. It was only when she learned about it in transferential terms that she told the other group members how she had been able to resist the temptation to steal a beautiful garment in the most propitious circumstances. In her thinking she had been able to replace authority – loved/hated parents/therapist/husband – by her peer-group members. In this way she thought of what her fellow patients' actions and feelings would be after her shoplifting. She had first said to herself: 'I want this jacket very badly, and it will make me feel great.' Immediately, she recoiled from that urge by thinking of the 'afterwards': the group process involving both peer group and authority. Then she proceeded: 'I know that what I most want in my life is peace of mind and this will never be achieved by this theft, because I'm doing it in order to take revenge. As a matter of fact, the opposite will happen. Afterwards, I will feel full of shame and self-disgust.'

She had been able to interpose this thought before the action, using both her newly gained insight and the group as an auxiliary ego which stopped her, this time, from committing the action. After she had appropriately left her psychotherapy, the hope she created lived on for a long time as other members of the group talked of how deeply affected they were by her experience and how much help they had gained from her capacity to learn. Her urge to steal had to do with the aggrandisement of her false self – in order to reinforce her omnipotence versus her despondency; her discovery about herself needed to be communicated to the other members, because it constituted an important dimension of her recognition of her own true self.

Group analytical therapy may often be the best form of treatment not only for some severely disturbed perverse patients, but especially so for sexual abusers and sexually abused patients. Secrecy is the key issue in incest. It has prevailed not only in the one-to-one situation but also through collusion in the dynamics of the family situation. This being so, group analytical psychotherapy becomes the chosen treatment for these patients. The family-social microcosm which occurs in group therapy affords them a much better understanding of their problems since they are so deeply related to violence and anti-social actions that occur within the family dynamics.

This is very different to a one-to-one situation in which these patients tend to feel unique, and usually succeed in making the psychotherapist feel not only protective but also possessive about them. In some cases, this can even provoke feelings of collusion in the psychotherapist, who could easily feel cornered or blackmailed by the confidentiality clause. At other times, the psychotherapist might feel either as the consenting child or as the seductive parent in the incest situation. Either way psychotherapy – meaning internal change – is in real jeopardy.

The group setting will not allow this transferential–counter-transferential process to take place. Group members must open up and overcome the taboo of secrecy. This is because trust must lie with the peers and not only with the psychotherapist.

Sometimes these patients present problems related to violence and secrecy in the family, as in the case of incest where the fathers or mothers – yes, mothers too – have been the perpetrators of the sexual abuse. Alternatively, in the case of adult women, an undetected early history of incest accounts for a wide spectrum of problems, from chronic psycho-somatic symptoms to a very high incidence of prostitution. These are unconsciously related to those early traumatic events, which underlie the present unconscious motivations for their predicaments.

For example, I have seen female patients with a history of early incest who, while entering group analytical psychotherapy, behave from the very start as 'ideal assistants' to the psychotherapist. Even those who had previously never been familiar with the unconscious processes seem to discover immediately appropriate ways to 'help' the psychotherapist-mother-father keep the group-family together. Fellow patients often react with surprise and bewilderment, and later with competitiveness. When interpretations are made to the effect that the newcomer is repeating a pathological pattern learned early in life, fellow patients seem relieved by this understanding, but it is then the turn of the newcomer to be filled with rage at this interpretation. After all, she is 'doing her best'; why is she being so 'harshly criticised'?

Secrecy, especially in paternal incest, is at the core of the situation; each member of the family is involved, whether 'knowing' or 'unknowing', but nobody talks about it. Indeed, when paternal incest has occurred it is irrelevant whether mother acknowledges the possibility of incest or not. Had she been able to acknowledge it in the first place, incest would never have happened. Incest is committed in an effort to create ties to 'keep the family together'. Nobody 'knows' about it, or rather nobody acknowledges it.

By treating in a group the victims and perpetrators of incest and, for that matter, also both genders as perpetrators and victims, there are unexpected qualities of containment and insight to be gained which could be virtually impossible in a one-to-one situation. Also, perpetrators become deeply aware of the vast consequences of their actions when confronted by other members who correspond to their victims' mirror reflections, and they grasp how unable they are to see themselves as separate human beings, but only as parts of their parental figures. For example, each member experiences a powerful sense of belonging to the group. Expressions of self-assertion, emotional growth, independence and individuation are some of the characteristics that patients acquire during the treatment period, in which they see others and themselves developing into individuals with respected self-esteem acknowledged by others and by themselves. At times they are not only allowed but encouraged to express openly anger and frustration which has been kept hidden for long periods of time. This encouragement comes especially from other 'old' members who have gone through similar predicaments.

Workers of all sorts involved in cases of incest frequently find it difficult to maintain a detached, professional stance. They tend to take sides, usually becoming emotionally bound to the victims. Additionally, or alternatively, they feel punitive towards the perpetrators. In their distress, they lose their understanding of the dynamics of what is happening. For example, they sometimes become so indignant that they fail to see that victims who become perpetrators experience a conscious or unconscious desire to avenge the pain inflicted upon them. These victim-perpetrators believe they are creating a situation in which justice is satisfied. Actually, however, they are identifying with their aggressors. In somewhat similar ways, the professional workers often identify with the victims.

According to Davies (1992), the network could easily become corrupt, hence the therapeutic task is first to recognise the splits operating with the staff members before this could reach the patient population.

There is a strong tendency for the workers in incest cases to re-enact within their professional network the splits, denials and projections which are so characteristic of the experience of family members caught up in the dynamics of incest. In such circumstances, we professionals would do well to listen to one another, thus allowing healthy interactions in a different context. This could lead to better integration of professional workers dealing with members of a family involved in incest. So, in a sense, the patients could usefully become role models for the psychotherapists.

ACKNOWLEDGEMENTS

The author owes a great debt to Dr Limentani, one of her earliest mentors, for his valuable contribution to this chapter. She wishes to thank Dr Chris Cordess for his useful suggestions, and is grateful to Kate Brophy for her expert secretarial help.

REFERENCES

Adshead, G. (1991) 'The forensic psychiatrist: dying breed or evolving species?' *Psychiatric Bulletin/British Journal of Psychiatry* 15: 410–12.

Bion, W. R. (1959) 'Attacks on linking', *International Journal of Psychoanalysis* 40(5 and 6): 308–15.

—— (1984) *Second Thoughts*, London: Karnac (originally published 1967).

Bluglass, R. (1990) 'The scope of forensic psychiatry', *Journal of Forensic Psychiatry* 1(1): 7.

Bois, R. du (1992) 'Adolescent delinquents: psychodynamics and therapeutic approach', pp. 353–9 in *Proceedings of the 17th International Congress of the International Academy of Law and Mental Health*, Leuven, Belgium.

Cordess, C. (1992a) 'Pioneers in forensic psychiatry: Edward Glover. Psychoanalysis and crime – a fragile legacy', *Journal of Forensic Psychiatry* 3(3): 509–30.

—— (1992b) 'Family therapy with psychotic offenders and family victims in a forensic psychiatric secure unit', *Proceedings of the 17th International Congress of the International Academy of Law and Mental Health*, Leuven, Belgium.

Cox, M. (1983) 'The contribution of dynamic psychotherapy to forensic psychiatry and vice versa', *International Journal of Law and Psychiatry* 6: 89–99.

—— (1992a) 'Forensic psychiatry and forensic psychotherapy', p. 255 in M. Cox (ed.) *Shakespeare Comes to Broadmoor*, London and Philadelphia: Jessica Kingsley Publishers.

—— (1992b) 'Forensic psychotherapy: an emergent discipline', p. 338 in *Proceedings of the 17th International Congress of the International Academy of Law and Mental Health*, Leuven, Belgium (first published 1978).

Davies, R. (1992) 'The corrupt network', *1st International Congress of the International Association of Forensic Psychotherapy*, London.

Freud, S. (1915) 'Some character-types met with in psychoanalytic work', *Standard Edition*, vol. 14: 311–33.

Gallwey, P. (1992) 'Social maladjustment', pp. 359–81 in J. Holmes (ed.) *Textbook of Psychotherapy in Psychiatric Practice*, London: Churchill Livingstone.

Glover, E. (1944) *Mental Abnormality and Crime*, London: Macmillan.

—— (1960) *The Roots of Crime*, London: Imago.

Harding, T. (1992) 'Research and evaluation in forensic psychotherapy', *1st International Conference of the International Association of Forensic Psychotherapy*, London.

Hopper, E. (1991) 'Encapsulation as a defence against the fear of annihilation', *International Journal of Psychoanalysis* 72(4): 607–24.

Limentani, A. (1984) 'Toward a unified conception of the origins of sexual and social deviancy in young persons', *International Journal of Psychoanalytical Psychotherapy* 10: 383–401.

—— (1989) *Between Freud and Klein*, London: Free Association Books.

Pfäfflin, F. (1993) 'What is in a symptom? A conservative approach in the therapy of sex offenders', *Journal of Offender Rehabilitation, Department of Sex Research*, Psychiatric Clinic, Universitätskrankenhaus Eppendorf, Hamburg (in press).

Pilgrim, D. (1987) 'Psychotherapy in British special hospitals: a case of failure to thrive', *Free Associations* 11: 59–72.

Reed Report (1992) *Report of the Academic Advisory Group 1992*, London: Department of Health/Home Office.

Rumney, D. (1981) 'The history of the Portman Clinic', Unpublished monograph.

Scannell, T. (1992) 'Infant psychiatric principles in working with adolescents', *1st International Congress of the 1st International Association of Forensic Psychotherapy*, London.

Smit, B. de (1992) 'The end of beginning is the beginning of the end: the structure of the initial interview in forensic psychiatry'. *Proceedings of the 17th International Congress of the International Academy of Law and Mental Health*, Leuven, Belgium.

Tuovinen, M. (1973) 'Crime as an attempt at intrapsychic adaptation', Monograph, University of Oulu, Finland.

Welldon, E. (1984) 'The application of group analytic psychotherapy to those with sexual perversions', pp. 96–108 in T. Lear (ed.) *Spheres of Group Analysis*, Naas, Co. Kildare: Leicester Leader.

—— (1992) *Mother, Madonna, Whore: The Idealisation and Denigration of Motherhood*, New York: Guilford Press (original work published 1988 by Free Association Books, London).

Williams, T. (1991) 'Forensic psychotherapy: symbiosis or impossibility', Address given at 17th International Congress of the International Academy of Law and Mental Health, Leuven, Belgium.

Zilboorg, G. (1955) *The Psychology of the Criminal Act and Punishment*, London: Hogarth Press and Institute of Psycho-Analysis.

For further information see also the material on Grendon Underwood Prison referenced in Table 18.1 (page 316).

Chapter 27

Psychotherapy with the dying and the bereaved

Colin Murray Parkes and Charlotte Sills

A great deal of research has taken place in recent years into the problems occasioned by the loss by death of a loved person. This has clearly demonstrated that bereavement can cause serious damage to physical and mental health. It has also shown that bereavements, like other stressful situations in life, are opportunities for personal growth and maturation.

We are now beginning to understand why it is that some people emerge from the stress of bereavement stronger and wiser, while others develop lasting problems. The identification of these causal sequences not only facilitates the treatment of pathology, it also opens the door to prevention. At times of bereavement we have the opportunity to identify people who are at risk before they become mentally or physically ill and to reduce the risk by appropriate action. Random allocation studies by Raphael in Australia (1977) and by Parkes in the United Kingdom (1981) have demonstrated the reduction in pathology which can result from preventive intervention programmes offered to 'high-risk' bereaved. They provide clear evidence that the right kind of counselling, given to the right people at the right time, can be effective; and they fully justify the establishment of counselling services for the bereaved. Most bereavement counsellors in the United Kingdom are not professional psychotherapists; they are volunteers who have received a short course of basic training and a period of supervised probation before becoming fully accredited. The evidence of Parkes's study (1981) indicates that this degree of expertise is quite sufficient to enable them to reduce bereavement risk in a majority of bereaved people.

Psychotherapists who choose to do so can provide valuable support to such services by assisting in the selection, training and supervision of counsellors and by treating the minority of bereaved people who 'fall through the net', either because they fail to respond to counselling or because it is apparent from the start that their problems are of such gravity or complexity that it is unreasonable to expect a lay counsellor to take them on. Normally, a person who has suffered a major bereavement would be expected, after a short period of shock and numbness, to experience strong feelings of grief, anger, fear and anxiety which diminish over the course of one or two years. Bereavement can be said to be proceeding abnormally if there is significant disruption in this process, either by the non-emergence of these signs with, instead, some manifestation of physical or behavioural dysfunction; or by the chronic persistence of some symptom or symptoms. The decision whether to refer these people to a psychiatrist or a lay psychotherapist will depend on the nature of the problem as well as the help available. Bereavement can precipitate almost any mental illness, including schizophrenia or psychotic depression; it can increase the risk of suicide and violence, including murder. In these cases referral to a psychiatrist is imperative. In most other cases, a lay psychotherapist would be an appropriate referral.

In this chapter we shall not discuss the role of the psychotherapist in the selection, training and support of counsellors, nor shall we describe the process of bereavement counselling. These topics have been well covered elsewhere (for instance, Parkes 1986; Worden 1983). Rather, we shall focus on the psychopathology and treatment of the complications of bereavement, that group of conditions which are intimately related to the process of grieving and to the attachments which precede it.

Of course the human brain's capacity to anticipate events means that many people start to grieve before the object of their attachment is dead. Illness such as cancer, AIDS and multiple sclerosis evoke severe grief in patients and their families, and it is sometimes appropriate for psychotherapists to become involved before the patient dies. Frequently psychotherapeutic support can be offered in the context of hospices, the best of which function as therapeutic communities, in which psychosocial and spiritual help is available to families facing death. Through their Home Care Services they also reach out to the wider community of care.

For this reason we have included a brief section covering the needs of dying patients and their families. Space will not permit detailed exposition of the full range of special problems associated with these diseases, which are covered in specialist texts.

PSYCHOPATHOLOGY

Although bereavement is full of complexity, the feature which distinguishes most people who require psychotherapy at this time is the persistence of distressing symptoms or behaviour beyond the time when it would normally be expected to decline. We believe that this persistence usually results from the establishment of patterns which, once set up, perpetuate the condition.

Sometimes these patterns are established at the time of the bereavement. More often they are manifestations of patterns of coping with life that have been laid down long before.

It can be useful to think of human behaviour as occurring in cycles of experience. A cycle starts with the receiving of a stream of incoming stimuli which, after preliminary processing in the brain, are identified as *perceptions*. These, taken together, lead to conscious awareness that a particular situation exists. It is at this stage that emotions may be aroused as the individual *appraises* the situation and becomes *aware* of its implications. If the situation is appraised as problematic it will give rise to a *plan* to deal with the problem. This leads to *action*, the effects of which are then *reviewed* to determine whether or not the problem remains. If it does not, the behavioural sequence will end and the individual becomes free to pay attention to other stimuli. If the problem is not resolved, it is reappraised and another plan considered. This sequence is repeated in many different ways. At any time, the individual is primed to pay attention to some sensations rather than others. This creates a hierarchy which is partly determined by long-established or in-born assumptions – for instance, that certain stimuli are potential indicators of danger. It is also determined by how needs have been met in the past and by long-term plans.

An example of this cycle in a newly bereaved widow (Figure 27.1) might start with her returning to an empty house. The unaccustomed absence would constitute a perception which, on appraisal, would remind her, 'My husband is missing' and give rise to a plan, 'I must search for him', which, on being put into action, leads to the classic searching behaviour of the bereaved. On reappraisal, the failure to locate the dead husband taken in conjunction with the cognitive awareness that he cannot be recovered, presses the widow towards an alternative plan. She begins to accept the permanence of the loss and is motivated to seek other ways of meeting needs for security, friendship and all the other needs that are met by relationships. Bereavement is the process of repeating such cycles in order to test reality and adjust the inner assumptive world to the new situation.

Within this larger cycle of adjustment are a myriad of smaller cycles as the person pays attention to all the demands of the current life, as well as thoughts, memories and other triggers which occur and cause the expression of feeling.

The cycle can be blocked or diverted at any stage, as indicated in Figure 27.1.

1 Some people may deny that the death has occurred. This can be done by withdrawing from society, blocking attempts by family and friends to discuss the loss, shutting away photographs or other reminders of the dead person and leaving undone any job which would formerly have been the responsibility of the dead person. In this way she avoids painful *stimuli* which would lead to an appraisal of the situation. Thus she fails to go through the individual loops of grieving which are the work of the overall cycle of coming to terms with life as it now is.

2 Many people interrupt the cycle at *appraisal*. They will acknowledge the

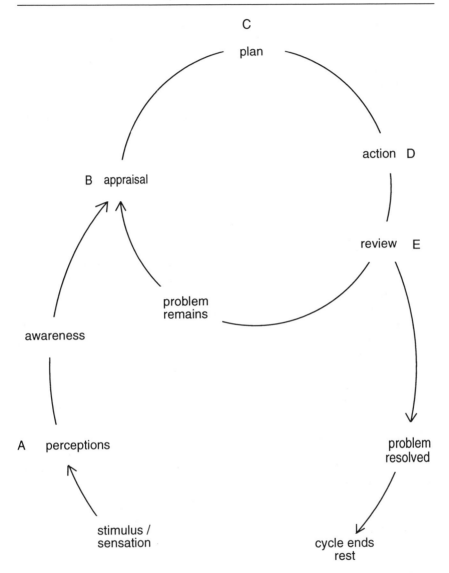

Figure 27.1 The cycle of experience

fact of death but deny its implication. They behave and feel as if their spouse were near to hand, refuse to make plans and continue to behave as if nothing has happened. The sensation is felt and correctly identified but, perhaps because of learned helplessness, an appraisal takes place in which the enormity of the change is ignored and feelings repressed.

3 For some, grief is not simply a reaction, but a sign of love. Those who have a continued sense of obligation, perhaps because they feel guilty for some failure or lack of love, may find it difficult to stop the grieving process. Far from avoiding reminders of their loss they may seek them out. This kind of self-punitive grieving may persist because it is difficult to make restitution for a wrong once a person is dead. The *plan* reached by the bereaved is calculated to perpetuate the painful duty of grieving rather than to resolve it.

4 For other people, the difficulty lies at the action stage. They may become busy with 'things to do'. This distracts the person from reminders for a time but leaves basic assumptions unchanged. Again, however, the 'mistake' was at the planning stage.

5 An example of a failure to *review* is a wife who continues to search for her husband in all his old haunts long after it should be obvious that he is not to be found. The review is not providing the correct feedback which would make her change her plan.

The way in which a person tends to interrupt the grief cycle is largely determined by pre-established patterns. Our ways of functioning grow out of our innate natural behaviour, moderated by the responses we get from the environment. This learning starts early.

Learned patterns of behaviour are established in every area of life, as the child received responses for thinking, deciding, being powerful, expressing feelings and so on. All of these patterns can affect the course of bereavement if they cause an interruption to the cycle. Those people who have learned how to deny knowledge as a way of facing stress may refuse to accept the evidence of their common sense. Those who have learned to be silent in distress may repress their grief. Those who have learned not to trust their own experience may have difficulty appraising the situation. Some have never learned to make decisions or take responsibility for their lives. All this will affect bereavement.

Each of these learned patterns can lead to an 'alternative cycle' – prematurely or unsatisfactorily closed, so that the need to grieve and to adjust is denied and the person repeats over and over the unsuccessful pattern in an attempt to achieve peace. There is thus both the natural response to the stimulus and simultaneously the defence against it in the learned response.

An example of such a fixed cycle or Gestalt (Zinker 1977) is in Figure 27.2. Here at 'appraisal' the person, whose belief about herself is that she

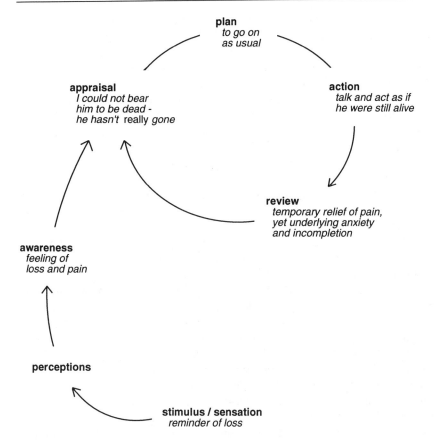

Figure 27.2 An interrupted cycle

could not survive such loss, decides 'He hasn't gone'. She forms a plan therefore to live her life as usual. At the review stage she experiences some relief at the temporary avoidance of the unpleasant truth. Yet there is, of course, still something unresolved and incomplete. Therefore she recycles this apparently satisfactory plan. She does not acknowledge the loss at appraisal, and therefore avoids the 'plan' to grieve. Somehow the bereaved person must be helped to interrupt the fixed pattern and find that healthy cycle which, though painful, will lead to resolution.

Probably the patterns which will be most significant in relation to problems with bereavement are those which are developed around attachment. Research into the relationship between pathological grief and attachment mechanisms shows that the constellation of feelings and behaviour which the child develops during the first two years of life not only influence the risk of pathological reactions but also determine the pattern that these will take (Parkes 1991; Bowlby 1988).

Grief is itself a component of the repertoire of attachment mechanisms which are inborn but modified by learning from their inception in infancy. These mechanisms include behaviours which maintain the attachment between the child and its primary carer – smiling, babbling, clinging and following – and behaviours which come into play following undue separation or when the child is frightened or distressed (crying and searching). These latter patterns, because they are essential to survival, tend to take priority over most other behavioural tendencies and to be accompanied by strong emotions. In the normal course of events they soon bring about the reunion which is their biological aim, proximity is restored and the behaviour is switched off leaving the child free to respond to other demands of lower hierarchical importance. But in the event of a lasting separation the response may persist for great lengths of time. It is this response that is grief.

Even when crying and searching do not lead to reunion they eventually die down, which psychologists cite as an example of 'extinction by non-reinforcement'. But these behavioural tendencies are easily switched on again by any reminder of the loss and, in the early stages, by any train of thought which leads back to the lost person. Hence the recurrent 'pangs' of grief that are so painful during the early stages of bereavement.

Human beings gradually learn that separations are seldom permanent and that alternative sources of support and security are available. They also learn that, to an increasing extent, they can stand on their own two feet. This enables them to tolerate longer and longer periods of separation and, eventually, to detach themselves from their parents and to make new attachments.

Research into early child development (Ainsworth 1991) has shown clearly how easily these learned behaviours are influenced by parents. Three patterns have emerged as likely to give rise to later problems. Each of them is a type of insecure attachment which easily becomes self-perpetuating.

1 *Anxious dependent pattern*. In order to survive, a child must learn what to fear. Young children are, therefore, extremely sensitive to the fears of their parents. A mother who is abnormally fearful, who gives out messages to her child that he won't survive unless he stays close to mother, will soon find that her child tends to cling and to become very intolerant of separation. Once established, this pattern becomes difficult to eradicate. In adult life a tendency to cling often evokes the very behaviour it is intended to prevent – rejection. Rejection then increases fear and evokes more clinging, a vicious circle (or cycle) which includes both anxiety and dependence.

2 *The avoidant pattern*. Some parents find it very hard to tolerate closeness. When their children cling to them they back away and may

even punish the child. The child eventually learns that clinging is dangerous and inhibits this kind of behaviour. This pattern causes children to avoid, as far as possible, situations in which they will be tempted to cling or to cry, and they become compulsively independent.

Of course, a person who has learned to avoid painful situations has no way of discovering that avoidance is no longer necessary. In later life their relationships are seriously compromised and there is a real danger that they will pass on their problems to their children because of their intolerance of closeness.

3 *The inconsistent pattern.* Both of the above patterns are adaptive in the sense that they enable the child to adapt to the demands of a particular type of parenting. But what of the parent who has no consistent style of parenting, who is responsive at one time and unresponsive at another? Mothers who suffer from recurrent depression or who frequently get to the end of their tether may swing between occasions when they are warm, caring parents who respond rapidly or appropriately to their child's smiles and tears to occasions when they are withdrawn or irritable and may be downright punitive in response to the same behaviour. The child ends up quite unable to know how to cope, and helpless in the face of any situation which evokes the need for attachment.

These are precisely the conditions which give rise to what Seligman calls 'learned helplessness' and which he has postulated as a major cause for depression in later life (1975). Faced with any threat the child withdraws into a state of numb inaction, lacking any hope that there could be a way of handling the situation, so that the situation remains unresolved and may even be aggravated. Once again a vicious circle has been established.

Bereavement is one of those life situations which makes demands upon the coping abilities of all who undergo it. It evokes powerful attachment behaviour and we cannot be surprised if people whose attachments have followed the patterns described above respond in ways which can be regarded as pathological:

(a) Anxious, dependent persons respond severely to loss. They exhibit intense separation anxiety with a tendency to panic. They may cling intensely and angrily to their children or to anyone else who is at hand, including their psychotherapist. Such behaviour, as we have seen, may evoke rejection and plunge them still deeper into chronic grief, anxiety state or panic syndrome.

(b) Avoidant persons tend to deny their need to grieve. A variety of avoidant strategies may be adopted ranging from hectic hyper-activity which enables people, by keeping busy, to drive all thoughts of loss out of their minds, to deliberate concealment of photographs or other mementoes which might remind them of the lost person and evoke a pang of grief. Others will direct their attention into a search for the lost person, half-convincing themselves that there has been a mistake and the person is not dead after all. Others seek for a scapegoat who can be punished for the death, as if this would resolve the problem and magically restore the dead person to life. In all of these cases grief is inhibited or delayed, but remains potentially waiting to be activated so that a considerable amount of mental activity needs to be devoted to the maintenance of avoidance.

(c) Persons with inconsistent patterns tend to withdraw into a state of helplessness and hopelessness following bereavement with many of the classical features of depression. Negative cognitions dominate thinking and suicide may be a real risk, although some are so helpless that they cannot even bring themselves to act upon the impulse.

COMPLICATING CIRCUMSTANCES

Thus far we have focused attention on the vulnerability of the bereaved person, but we also need to recognise that there are some bereavements that are more traumatic than others and which themselves increase the risk of pathology regardless of the personal vulnerability of the bereaved. These include the unexpected and untimely death of a spouse or child, deaths for which the bereaved feel responsible, horrific circumstances as when the survivor was a witness to mutilation, mass disasters, bereavement by suicide and bereavement by murder or manslaughter. Each of these has special aspects which lie beyond the scope of this chapter.

What they have in common is a tendency to overwhelm normal coping mechanisms. Traumatic bereavements evoke an alarm response, high levels of anxiety with hyper-vigilance and a tendency to startle. These are triggered and maintained by reminders of the loss, the memories of which remain extremely vivid, to be relived repeatedly both during waking hours (as flashbacks), and during sleep (as nightmares).

Global defences are called into operation in order to cope with these intensely painful reactions. Sufferers often shut themselves up at home avoiding anything which threatens to 'bring home' the reality of what has happened. There is a general psychic numbing or depersonalisation limiting the expression of any strong emotion, and a tendency to foster the illusion that the dead person is still near at hand. The bereaved, while recognising at one level the reality of the loss, will simultaneously say, 'I can't believe it is true'. This sense of incomprehension may persist for years, and itself reflects the difficulty which they experience in making appropriate modifications to their internal world or 'doing the grief work'.

These are the symptoms of post-traumatic stress disorder, and they have received much prominence in recent years since the syndrome was included in the *American Diagnostic and Statistical Manual* (DSM-III-R).

They are widely accepted as sufficient grounds for compensation in courts of law.

Of course, these various types of vulnerability and reaction seldom occur in pure form. It is often the case that people are vulnerable for more than one reason. Parents may evoke fear *and* punish closeness, people who are already insecurely attached may suffer traumatic bereavement. The outcome will often be a mixed picture in which anxiety, depression and avoidance coexist.

THE TREATMENT OF PATHOLOGICAL REACTIONS TO BEREAVEMENT

The above analysis of the roots of psychopathology in the bereaved may have left the reader somewhat apprehensive. How can we hope to deal with life situations which are both urgent and complex? There is a real danger that we, as well as our clients, will feel overwhelmed.

The truth is, of course, that neither we nor our clients can cope with more than a few things at a time. It may, and indeed will, be useful for us to attempt an overall view of the situation, and much of our first meeting with the client will be devoted to this kind of wide-ranging discussion but, just as the microscopist must switch back and forth between wide and narrow focus so the psychotherapist must switch between broad perspectives and the immediate problems and reactions which are occupying the client's attention at this time.

The basic assumption which underlies our psychotherapy with the bereaved is that reality-testing is worth doing however painful this may be. In other words, the bereaved have a life left to live and it is worth helping them to re-appraise this life situation in the face of this new reality.

There are, of course, exceptions to this rule. Perhaps our client is so sick that it would be kinder to encourage denial. This may be the case in a late-stage cancer patient who is in blissful ignorance of the prognosis or in a person with organic brain damage who cannot remember, from one day to the next, that their partner is dead.

With these exceptions it seems that the majority of people will make a better adjustment to life and, in the long term, will find it easier to recognise their potentialities if they bring their internal models of the world, their assumptions about the life space that impinges upon them, into line with reality. But the role of the psychotherapist is not to force people to face reality. Reality is brutal enough without our shaking it in our client's face. Rather, we must establish a secure base from which it becomes possible for the client to explore the real world. In this respect the psychotherapist is performing the same role as a good parent. We try to develop a relationship of trust which encourages clients to discover both their own strength and the extent to which they can trust us. We respect their strength without expecting the impossible, and we hope that they will learn to trust in our genuine concern for their welfare without expecting us to take control of their lives and to protect them from dangers which do not exist.

This may sound trite, but there are powerful reasons why many psychotherapists inculcate very different attitudes which do harm rather than good. These include attitudes derived from medicine in which a 'patient' is seen as sick and therefore weak, the passive recipient of the doctor's treatment. Family and friends are de-skilled by this vision and back off instead of remaining closely involved, and psychotherapists adopt authoritarian attitudes which undermine the patient's self-respect and encourage excessive expectations of and reliance on the psychotherapist.

Another, linked problem is the understandable tendency for psychotherapists to blame their clients for being dependent. '*Love*' is good, 'dependency' is bad and the client seen as 'dependent' is likely to be a nuisance. This is most likely to occur at times when, for one reason or another, the client is feeling insecure. They cling to the psychotherapist who, instead of providing support, backs away and admonishes the client. The situation is much like that of the mother who, returning from hospital with a second baby, finds herself faced with a clingy, angry first child. If she recognises the child's need for attachment and gives a little extra attention to the child the clinging will soon subside. If, on the other hand, she pushes the child away and punishes clinging she will aggravate the problems and set up a vicious circle which may become intractable.

It is often hard to handle excessive clinging. Such clients make excessive demands on our time and patience. The problem is what we and the client can do about it. The sensitive psychotherapist has an opportunity to show concern for the client not by giving in to their demands for extra time at the end of the session, for instance, but by indicating our sympathy for the pain which they suffer and expressing our confidence in their ability to come through despite it.

Equally difficult to handle is the pseudo-autonomy of the anxiously avoidant client. Compelled as children to 'stand on their own two feet' even when they 'hadn't got a leg to stand on' they back away from any interaction which might expose their underlying need for succour. We need to be most careful not to intrude or violate their personal space, but, at the same time, we must be on the lookout for ways of making contact which will minimally reduce their lonely isolation. The compulsively self-reliant are trapped in a hole in the snow; they can best be rescued by a thaw rather than a blow-torch.

In our view the only psychotherapy which has any chance of success is a specialised form of supportive psychotherapy which combines respect for our clients' strength with recognition of their fear, while simultaneously encouraging increasing autonomy and rewarding all progress, however slow, towards self-realisation.

SHORT-TERM PSYCHOTHERAPY

The establishment of basic trust in oneself and others can be a slow process, but this is not usually the case. Bereavements and other life crises are a test of strength and one which almost everyone, often to their surprise, will pass.

Bereavements also evoke support, not just from psychotherapists, but also from family and friends. In this context, although the psychotherapist may have to provide fairly frequent support in the early stages, the frequency of interviews can soon be reduced and an expectation of increasing autonomy adopted.

Regular interviews at fixed intervals are inappropriate, and it is much more consonant with the client's needs to reduce the frequency and duration of interviews as time passes. As we have implied above, the death of a loved person initiates countless cycles, behavioural and learning sequences between the initial discovery of the death and the steady state of homeostasis which can arise when the bereaved person has learned what it means to be a widow (or whatever other new roles and status are possible) and developed the new skills necessary to fill these new roles. Problems can arise in the course of any of these sequences, and it is one of the aims of psychotherapy to try to unravel them. While people are describing themselves to us, they are also describing themselves to themselves. Insight gives power, either to make different plans from a new point of view or to interrupt a recurrent cycling and move on.

The act of 'telling the story' is, therefore, psychotherapeutic, and there are many bereaved people who only need one thorough assessment interview in order to achieve sufficient insight to continue without further help. There are many others who will get all the help they need from a short series of meetings and only a small minority who need more than six sessions. Twelve sessions is long-term psychotherapy.

People with psychiatric problems after bereavement mostly perceive the world as a dangerous place. Many of them have little trust in themselves and/or little trust in others. It may be possible to achieve insight without building up a therapeutic relationship (the success of the one-off intervention and of bibliotherapy is evidence of that), but for most patients psychotherapy will be much easier if a relationship of trust has been established.

In therapy we have the opportunity to explore the nature of the attachment to the psychotherapist and to question the assumptions which are made about it. Clients have sufficient experience of relationships to realise that people are not all alike, but their ways of relating to others are likely to have created the very situations which they dread and to confirm them in a negative view of others and self. It is most reassuring to discover one situation in which this does not happen.

A CONSULTANT PSYCHIATRIST'S VIEW OF PSYCHOTHERAPY

A major issue is the extent to which the psychotherapist should actively steer the conversation towards problem areas. Working in settings in which long-term psychotherapy is seldom possible (NHS clients), one of the authors (CMP) has developed an interactive style and a structured approach to psychotherapy which differs from the approach adopted by many psychoanalysts. He does not believe that it works in *every* case and there are still a few patients who need to be referred for longer-term psychotherapy elsewhere, but it does seem to meet the needs of most clients and is cost-effective.

The approach starts in the form of a questionnaire (Parkes 1993) which clients are invited to fill in before the initial interview. This was initiated for research purposes, but turned out to be so useful that it is now used in every case, bereaved or not. It involves recalling and thinking about the client's past and present relationships and life patterns in a detailed way.

At the first meeting Parkes takes a psychiatric history using a loosely structured format. Having read and digested the referral letter and tried to figure out the reason for referral, he invites the patient to tell him what they would like from him. This leads on to a discussion of their present state and of the events which preceded it.

Bereaved people usually want to plunge into an account of the bereavement and subsequent events and feelings – all of which they are encouraged to do. He then invites them to 'tell me a little about your background' and draws a geneogram of the family while they tell him a little about each member. This leads naturally into an account of their childhood and later life up to the bereavement, with further additions being made to the geneogram (which remains the most used 'ready reference' to the background). Parkes may or may not go through the questionnaire with the patient at the first session (depending on the time available), and this sometimes makes a good starting point for the second interview. Finally, he attempts to sum up the situation as he sees it, and invites the patient to tell him if they agree or disagree with his formulation. Psychotherapist and client then develop a plan for further therapy if this seems indicated. Often this takes the form of an offer of 'a few more meetings in order to continue what we have started to do today'.

Parkes usually starts the second meeting by inviting the patient to tell him what they felt about the first. This often steers them towards issues that were not covered in the first meeting or to 'second thoughts' reflecting the fears and fantasies which patients have about psychotherapy.

Thereafter the second meeting is much less structured than the first. Issues which were not touched upon in the first session may be explored in more depth. In this and in subsequent meetings patients who have been avoiding problems often begin to feel secure enough to share them and the feelings which they evoke. Over the first few meetings a trajectory develops which makes it possible to plan for the ending of psychotherapy.

Parkes does not use contracts except in those cases where the attachment which the patient has made means that they are going to grieve for him. In these cases he sets up a fixed number of three or four further meetings (or more if the psychotherapy has been very long-term) and reminds the patient at the start of each meeting of the number of meetings left. This is usually sufficient to ensure that they will anticipate ending and do the grief work.

Because self-defeating patterns or *vicious circles* are a common cause of psychopathology, their accurate identification and termination is an important part of treatment. They often cause psychotherapy to get 'stuck' and, at such times, Parkes tends to play an active role in spelling out what he thinks is happening. Sometimes it is necessary to challenge the patient. This is particularly important in self-punitive grieving when the patient is attempting to atone by endless mourning.

The frequency of visits is reduced progressively over time. Thus the second visit may take place a week after the first, the third two weeks later and the fourth a month after that. Parkes is fairly flexible (or tries to be), but avoids the expectation of regular psychotherapy in most (not all) cases. This reduces problems at ending.

A PSYCHOTHERAPIST'S VIEW

Sills' approach differs in some respects from that of Parkes, largely as a result of the difference in the method of referral, the context of the work and the expectations of the clients. Otherwise, the work proceeds in a similar way.

Usually, the first contact is with the bereaved person herself. Sometimes this has been recommended by a GP or friend. Sometimes it is simply that the person is experiencing herself as functioning poorly or as being depressed and she has decided to come for help. The symptoms are rarely as acute as those which would necessitate a psychiatric referral. The setting is not in a hospital where people expect to 'receive treatment', and frequently they do not know what to expect from psychotherapy.

The first session is one of assessment and exploration. If the person seems to be showing signs of some severe psychiatric condition which requires medical intervention, arrangements are made for the assessment and possible involvement of a psychiatrist. Otherwise the focus is on making contact and listening to the story. In cases where the client identifies a bereavement as being the source of the problems, it is possible then to discuss a contract. Sometimes, simply the provision of information about what is to be expected during bereavement and help in planning the setting up of appropriate support is all that is needed.

Sometimes, however, it is clear that the bereaved is stuck in a more complex, fixed pattern of response which requires identifying and changing. The aim of the psychotherapy would be to establish or re-establish grieving as soon as possible. In this case, a short number of sessions would be agreed, with a specific focus. The psychotherapist would be quite explicit that bereavement would be the agenda and that the work would be likely to be difficult or painful.

With the client's agreement to this contract, the work continues. Session 2 would be likely to start with exploring the client's reactions and thoughts since session 1. Then, and in subsequent sessions, the client is invited to tell her story and her history in some depth. The psychotherapist looks for signs of where in the normal cycle of grieving the client may be blocking. Historical patterns of attachment and patterns of coping with stress are identified – including those which are manifested in the consulting room; the short-term psychotherapy is thus similar in focus, if not in style, to Davanloo (1992). Usually, beliefs are identified at the appraisal stage, of the cycle, which substantially hinders the person's ability to go forward. These beliefs may include 'I can't survive alone', 'The world is a dangerous place', or 'If I start to feel, I'll die'. Then a survival plan has been formed – for instance, to become ill in order to be looked after, to keep away from people or to keep busy. People tend at first to be unaware of these plans but begin to become aware of them in the session.

With the assumption that the client is likely to have become fixed in some self-perpetuating cycle, the aim is to intervene in any way that interrupts the maladaptive system and gives the opportunity to continue grieving. Insight and phenomenological understanding of such patterns can go some way to changing them. Work in the sessions can also help. Interventions such as work with dreams, conversations with the dead person in the imagination – with the use of an empty chair, the planning and execution of rituals, bringing of mementoes and photographs may all be used.

As termination of the sessions is approached and addressed, the psychotherapist hopes to facilitate their ending in such a way that the bereaved person can have a complete cycle – including feeling and expressing emotions, thinking over the significance, making a plan for the future in terms of setting up appropriate support, saying goodbye and leaving.

Sometimes longer-term psychotherapy is offered. There are three circumstances where this is likely. The first is when the client himself is not aware that his problems may be due to a bereavement. It is only the psychotherapist's hunch that this may be the case. She may offer that hypothesis and even receive some tentative agreement from the client, yet it is clear that this is not at all obvious to him. In this case it would seem necessary and more respectful that the initial contract be for exploring 'to see whether psychotherapy can be of any help'. The second circumstance is when the client and psychotherapist begin to identify patterns of coping with life, long before any connection is made with the loss of a specific person. Frequently again, that loss will be associated to an earlier loss or losses which need to be addressed. When this has been identified, a further contract can be made to focus on this work.

Both the above situations concern a client whose history reveals difficult patterns of coping with pain and change, but an overall level of functioning which is within the normal range. A third category of client is one in which there has been a significantly unsatisfactory way of life even before the bereavement. The client may report an excessively withdrawn life with only one close person, or a pattern of intense and unstable relationships, inability to keep employment and so on. With these clients, longer-term psychotherapy is offered (perhaps an open-ended contract). It is not unusual for a client, even at the first interview, to identify that while the present crisis is the precipitating one, they are unsatisfied with their way of being in the world. One such example was Laura, who developed symptoms of agoraphobia after her mother's death, but said that she had been agoraphobic ten years earlier while her children had been little. In both cases the phobia had served to divert her from her real feelings, and she wanted to change her way of handling life.

With other people it is during the process of identifying the patterns that this connection is made, and they express a desire to understand more and to deal with the past experiences of attachment and loss. Patricia was a thirty-five-year-old accountant, who developed problems after the death of her aunt. She found herself unable to function at work and also developed a distressing symptom of not being able to look at herself in the mirror. During the course of the first sessions she revealed a pattern of developing loose attachments to unavailable men whom she then resented and left. Her aunt, it seemed, had been the only person who had ever been faithful to her. She had very few close friends and no women friends. She realised that several sudden losses in her early childhood were affecting her present life in many ways and chose to commit herself to an open-ended psychotherapy contract.

In situations like these, bereavement therapy becomes 'ordinary' psychotherapy and proceeds at its own pace.

AN EXAMPLE OF SHORT-TERM PSYCHOTHERAPY

In the first session, John, fifty-two, told the story of his bereavement. He had been a model husband, taking care of his wife during her long and debilitating illness. After she died he lost no time in joining various voluntary groups to offer help to the disabled. Four nights a week he spent collecting people in his car and driving them around. At the weekend he helped with a centre for disabled people. He said it helped to keep busy. However, he had become seriously depressed. He refused to be involved with the local bereavement service, saying that 'it does no good to dwell'. According to him, he had lost the light of his life but he had had thirty wonderful years with her and now he was going to help those less fortunate than himself.

He saw a doctor for his depression, who persuaded him to have 'a couple of sessions' with a psychotherapist. At session 3, John began to admit that the last few years of his wife's life had been terrible for him. She had been in pain and suffered physical symptoms which he found not only distressing but revolting. Also she had become increasingly irritable. He had only admitted to himself that he would like to run away from the situation, then in guilt and self-loathing had sworn to 'stay with her to the end'. He began to see how in helping the disabled he was still 'staying with her'. When it was suggested that his reaction to the illness had been very normal he experienced palpable relief. Then he made the link to his childhood. His father had left home when he was six, and for the first year or so he had been sure that his mother would die of sadness if he left her alone. He remembered wishing guiltily that he could go out to play with the other children. John realised how much he wanted to talk about it all, and readily agreed to approach the bereavement service for counselling.

PSYCHOTHERAPY BEFORE BEREAVEMENT

Although in temporal terms, the care of the family in which someone is dying begins before bereavement, we have postponed discussion to this point because we have found it easier to conceptualise the grief of the dying patient after a full consideration of the less complex grief of the bereaved.

A major problem for families faced with life-threatening illness is uncertainty. The cycle of response described above assumed that reality-testing is possible, facts can be established and plans made. The client's internal model of the world can be revised to bring it into line with the world which now exists. Illness such as cancer and AIDS regularly face patients and their families with long periods of uncertainty. Sometimes the doctors themselves are unsure of the likely outcome, and other times doctors may have a strong expectation that a person will soon die but fail to communicate this on the assumption that 'ignorance is bliss'. At other times the medical authorities think that they have told the truth but the recipient has not understood or absorbed the message. Even so, as the disease progresses it becomes increasingly difficult to deny that something is wrong, and the patient and family enter a state in which planning is no longer possible.

Planlessness, as we have seen, gives rise to helplessness and helplessness to depression which will only be relieved when the true prognosis is declared. 'Thank goodness I know' is often the first reaction of a patient who has been given a bad prognosis; the reaction is one of relief.

Psychotherapists who work in a hospital or palliative care teams can do much to train and support staff in the arts of communication. Although we are not normally expected to break bad news, we are very likely to become involved when, for one reason or another, communication has broken down. We are then asked to take over the treatment of someone whose emotional disturbance results from their inability to escape from the cycle in which they are blocked at the planning stage. Nor can they leave this cycle for another because of the high salience of any situation which involves a possible danger to life.

In each situation we can be of great help if we provide people with opportunities to share their thoughts and feelings about the illness. We may be surprised to find that we are the only ones to invite questions; medical staff and family members may be afraid to 'rock the boat', and tend to skirt around sensitive issues of diagnosis and prognosis leaving the patient feeling that everybody is afraid of the truth.

Conversely, the psychotherapist who indicates that there is nothing that they are afraid to discuss and who accompanies that message by non-verbal reassurance (with a touch of the hand or a hug) will relieve anxiety whether or not the patient chooses to respond to the invitation to share their fears. In our experience, people seldom ask questions if they don't want answers. We should always tell the truth if we know it. If we are asked questions we cannot answer, we should not be afraid to admit our ignorance. If there are others who are better informed, we should make sure that the person has a chance to ask them. If nobody knows the answer, we must acknowledge the difficulty with which the patient is faced.

One way of dealing with uncertainty is to develop contingency plans: 'If the pain is caused by a recurrence of my cancer I shall do such and such, if not then I shall go back to work.' Even though a plan cannot be put into operation until the situation is clear, the very possession of plans for all eventualities reduces the need for endless cycling and frees the person to pay attention to other issues.

In the later stages of a terminal illness there may be very little time left. Awareness of that fact can 'concentrate the mind', and a great deal of psychodynamic progress may take place in a short space of time. Issues that have been avoided for years and secrets that have been concealed arise, and unresolved problems may be brought out of the cupboard and re-appraised. In the face of terminal illness long-standing ambivalence may be forgotten, and family members who have been avoiding one another may take advantage of a last chance to come together. This can make time spent in psychotherapy with dying people most rewarding and the psychotherapy is often an inspiration to the psychotherapist as well as the client.

Of course the problems of vulnerability that were discussed above affect the dying as well as the bereaved. Particular problems arise when it is a compulsively self-reliant person who is dying. Such people find it very hard to ask for help. They will deny pain or other symptoms rather than 'becoming a burden', and it takes considerable sensitivity to recognise that their bravado is a thin disguise for considerable insecurity.

Rather than accept the fact that their illness is worse such patients will often blame their symptoms on the drugs or other treatments which they have received. It is easier to blame the doctors and nurses than to admit the truth. Other patients adopt a combative attitude to everyone, as if by taking on the doctors they could conquer death itself. Anger is a part of grief, and we should not be surprised when patients take it out on the people around them. This can create problems in management, and it is not uncommon for the psychologist or psychiatrist to be called in, in the hope that we will make the patient behave. Occasionally staff may respond to unreasonable behaviour by themselves acting in angry or rejecting ways. This is likely further to undermine the patient's security and may aggravate the problem. It follows that the psychotherapist's role in this setting is as much concerned with reassuring and increasing the understanding and tolerance of staff as it is with the treatment of psychiatric disorders in patients. This can best be done by involving members of the caring team in psychotherapy and/or by providing detailed feedback to staff of our interactions with patients and their families.

Most psychiatrists and psychologists who serve palliative care teams are not in a position to provide intensive daily psychotherapy but attend on a weekly or less frequent basis and may be too overstretched for this. Yet there is a special urgency in the provision of care to a patient who may only have a few days to live or family members who have little time left to resolve their relationship difficulties with a dying person.

This is a further reason for involving the caring team. Strict rules of confidentiality are inappropriate in this setting, and, unless the client prohibits disclosure, it is better to assume that information and opinion can be shared within the team.

It also means that we may have to take a more active role in focusing psychotherapy on important issues and using medication to get rapid control of severe anxiety or depression than would normally be the case. We just don't have time to wait for long-term psychotherapies to take effect.

Serious illnesses have complex effects on the lives of those who suffer them, and we should seldom assume that we know better than our patients what they need from us. We may expect dying patients to be concerned about their own death, but there are many patients who are much more concerned about the welfare of a pet, the disposal of a flat or the limitations imposed by their illness. Even those who express a fear of dying will often qualify it by pointing out that it is not being dead that they fear but the process of dying. Fears of pain, fears of mutilation, fears of becoming a burden to others, fears of losing control of bodily functions, all of these are issues involving illness and its effects which are associated in people's minds with dying. They are the outcome of a 'horror comic' view of death rather than of the quiet slipping away which, in good circumstances of care, is the usual reality. Once such fears have been expressed it is usually possible to provide reassurance.

One elderly patient said, 'I wish you could tell people how good it is to die of cancer.' What she meant was that, since we all have to die of something, cancer is not a bad way to go. She had had time to wind up her affairs, say goodbye to her family and friends, and was now peacefully subsiding. Her pain had been successfully controlled and all of the passions and stresses of life seemed to be ebbing away. She had lost all of her appetites including her appetite for life itself, but this did not mean that she was suffering. 'Life,' she said, 'is like a good meal, when you've had enough you don't want a second helping.' It is not unreasonable to expect that those who are being well cared for will achieve this kind of quietness.

Those with a tendency to anxious, clinging attachments may respond well to the 'tender loving care' which they receive when very ill but badly if it is a partner who is dying. In the latter case their own need to succour may make it difficult for them to care for the patient at home and admission to a hospice or other in-patient unit may be needed in order to relieve stress in the family. In cases of this kind a full family assessment is important. If there are children it is very likely that they too will need extra support before and after the patient's death, but we should not assume that the outlook is bad. As indicated above, there is nothing like a bereavement to enable people to discover their own strength.

Similarly, people who have always viewed the world as a dangerous place will have their worst fears realised when faced with a terminal illness, but they may then find that, having faced the worst, they have nothing left to fear. The aim of psychotherapy in such cases is not to conceal the truth but to convey our own confidence that, however bad things may be, the patient or relative involved will cope. In a paradoxical way people who have always feared death may find the reality less fearful than they had imagined, they may then cope better than they or their family had expected and in doing so, become heroes. In our society opportunities for heroism are few, and those individuals who rise to the occasion by transcending their fears reassure others as well as themselves. As psychotherapists we cannot expect such transcendence to happen, we can only try to foster situations in which it is possible by adapting a matter-of-fact and accepting attitude which implies that an extraordinary situation can become quite ordinary. We neither play down the seriousness of what is happening nor do we add to the stress by excessive shows of pity or dramatisation.

It is sometimes said that psychotherapists who work with the dying have got to come to terms with their own death. This is a tall order since none of us can know until we get there whether or not we have 'come to terms' with anything of the kind. Having said that, it is reasonable to expect a psychotherapist to have a realistic view of what the passage to death is like and to have some sort of philosophy of life or religious faith which enables us to stay engaged with people who are in panic at the prospect. In the final analysis, if we can find meaning in life, then it is not unreasonable to assume that there must be meaning in death.

As in the preceding section we have not here been able to do more than to sketch out some basic principles and to highlight some of the major issues that will arise in our attempts to offer psychotherapy to the dying and the bereaved. We hope that we have said enough to encourage a few of our readers to read more widely and to enter a field of service which many find daunting but which can be so rewarding that we end up feeling that it is we who have benefited from the psychotherapy, for, in the end, we are all dying, yet somehow we can find a greater sense of living.

REFERENCES

Ainsworth, M. D. S. (1991) 'Attachments and other affectional bonds across the life cycle', pp. 33–51 in C. M. Parkes, J. Stevenson-Hinde and P. Marris (eds) *Attachment across the Life Cycle*, London and New York: Routledge.

Bowlby, J. (1988) *Attachment and Loss: III, Loss, Sadness and Depression*, London: Hogarth Press.

Davanloo, H. (1992) 'A method of short-term dynamic psychotherapy', pp. 43–71 in H. Davanloo (ed.) *Short-term Psychotherapy*, London and New Jersey: Jason Aronson.

Parkes, C. M. (1981) 'Evaluation of a bereavement service', *Journal of Preventive Psychiatry* 1: 179–88.

—— (1986) *Bereavement Studies of Grief in Adult Life* (2nd edn), London: Tavistock. Also Harmondsworth: Pelican; and New York: International Universities Press.

—— (1991) 'Attachment, bonding and psychiatric problems after bereavement in adult life', pp. 268–92 in C. M. Parkes, J. Stevenson-Hinde and P. Marris (eds) *Attachment across the Life Cycle*, London and New York: Routledge.

—— (1993) *Assessment Questionnaire*, London: St Christopher's Hospice.*

Raphael, D. (1977) 'Preventive intervention with the recently bereaved', *Archives of General Psychiatry* 34: 1450–5.

Seligman, M. E. P. (1975) *Helplessness: On Depression, Development and Death*, New York: Freeman.

Worden, J. W. (1983) *Grief Counselling and Grief Therapy*, London and New York: Tavistock.

Zinker, J. (1977) *Creative Process in Gestalt Therapy*, New York: Vintage.

* Available from Dr C. M. Parkes at St Christopher's Hospice, 51–59 Lawrie Park Road, London SE26 6DZ, at cost price.

Structure of the United Kingdom Council for Psychotherapy and list of its member organisations

Michael Pokorny

Registration of psychotherapists was recommended by Sir John Foster in the Report named after him (HMSO (1971)). A working party began in 1975 and reported in 1978, but its proposals led to no further action. In 1981 Graham Bright, MP, in association with others, introduced a Private Member's Bill to the House of Commons to regulate the practice of psychotherapy. It failed at second reading.

In 1982 the British Association for Counselling organised a symposium at Rugby. A working party was formed and led a second symposium at Rugby. Run on a shoestring, the so-called Rugby Psychotherapy Conference laid the foundation for the founding in 1989 of the United Kingdom Standing Conference for Psychotherapy. UKSCP had a federal structure in which different approaches and groupings of psychotherapy sorted themselves into eight Sections. In addition, there was a category of Special Member for the statutory bodies of direct relevance, and the British Association for Counselling were given a special category of their own as 'Friends of Conference', which they have continued to enjoy. Later a category of Institutional Member was added. The advent of the Register of Psychotherapists gave rise to the need for a change of name to the United Kingdom Council for Psychotherapy in 1993. UKCP is an organisation of organisations. There is no individual membership. Each member organisation may nominate two delegates to the Conference, and every position within Conference may only be held by a delegate. The gateway into the UKCP is the Section which is appropriate to the form of psychotherapy that an aspiring organisation represents or teaches. The Sections are the arbiters of their own branch of psychotherapy, and the Section criteria are open to scrutiny and acceptance or veto by the other Sections of the Council. This ensures that the criteria of any Section are sensible and within reasonable conformity with the other Sections. The central authority is the Governing Board which is composed of one representative from each of the eight Sections, one representative from each of the Special members and not more than two representatives of the Institutional members. There are also five officers and four elected members

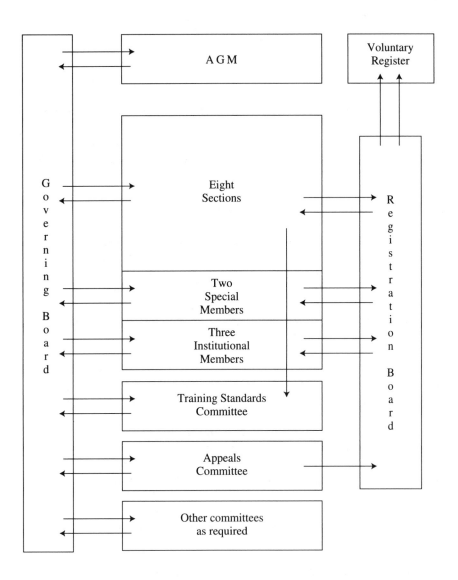

Figure A1 The United Kingdom Council for Psychotherapy

of the Governing Board. All elections are annual and there are strict limits on the tenure of office. Committees of the Governing Board are set up each year as needed. Every year at the annual meeting the Governing Board reports to the delegates of the member organisations and decisions are taken by a two-thirds majority vote. Separate from this, and not answerable to either the Governing Board or the annual meeting, is the Registration Board. Composed of delegates appointed by the Sections and the Special and Institutional members it is responsible for the Register. Only delegates of organisations recognised by their Section as a training or accrediting organisation are eligible to serve on the Registration Board.

Complaints against a registered psychotherapist are, first, the responsibility of the organisation to which that psychotherapist belongs. If the procedure there is not satisfactory the complaint goes to the Section to which the organisation belongs. Only if that also fails to resolve matters can the Governing Board become involved. Registration is through the Sections and the organisations and is not done on an individual basis. That is because the Register is voluntary. A statutory register would be managed quite differently and on an individual basis; any complaints would go to the disciplinary committee of the register.

Figure A1 shows the structure of the United Kingdom Council for Psychotherapy, and a list of its member organisations for 1995 follows. The United Kingdom Council for Psychotherapy is at:

167–169 Great Portland Street
London W1N 5FB
Tel.: 0171 436 3002

The current Chair is Professor Digby Tantam

UNITED KINGDOM COUNCIL FOR PSYCHOTHERAPY: LIST OF MEMBER ORGANISATIONS, 1995

Association of Cognitive Analytic Therapists (ACAT)
Association of Child Psychotherapists (ACP)
Association for Family Therapy (AFT)
Association for Group and Individual Psychotherapy (AGIP)
Association of Humanistic Psychology Practitioners (AHPP)
Association of Jungian Analysts (AJA)
Association for Neuro-Linguistic Programming (ANLP)
Arbours Association (ARBS)
Association of University Teachers of Psychiatry (AUTP)
British Association for Behavioural and Cognitive Psychotherapy (BABCP)
British Association of Psychotherapists (BAP)
British Association for Sexual and Marital Therapy (BASMT)
Bath Centre for Psychotherapy and Counselling (BCPC)
British Psychodrama Association (BPDA)

The Gerda Boyesen Training Centre (BTC)
Chiron Centre for Holistic Psychotherapy (CCHP)
Centre for Counselling and Psychotherapy Education (CCPE)
Centre for Freudian Analysis and Research (CFAR)
Centre for Personal Construct Psychology (CPCP)
Centre for Psychoanalytical Psychotherapy (CPP)
Cambridge Society for Psychotherapy (CSP)
Centre for the Study of Psychotherapy (University of Kent) (CSPK)
Forum for Advancement of Educational Therapy and Therapeutic Teaching (FAETT)
The Family Institute, Cardiff (FIC)
The Gestalt Centre, London (GCL)
Guildford Centre and Society for Psychotherapy (GCSP)
Gestalt Psychotherapy Training Institute (GPTI)
Guild of Psychotherapists (GUILD)
Hallam Institute of Psychotherapy (HIP)
Institute for Arts in Therapy and Education (IATE)
Institute of Family Therapy (IFT)
Institute of Group Analysis (IGA)
The Independent Group of Analytical Psychologists (IGAP)
Institute of Psychotherapy and Counselling (WPF) (IPC)
Institute of Psychosynthesis, London (IPS)
Institute of Psychotherapy and Social Studies (IPSS)
ISA Centre for Attachment-Based Psychoanalytic Psychotherapy (ISA)
Institute of Transactional Analysis (ITA)
Kensington Consultation Centre (KCC)
Karuna Institute (KI)
London Association of Primal Psychotherapists (LAPP)
London Centre for Psychotherapy (LCP)
Minster Centre (MC)
The Metanoia Trust (MET)
Northern Association for Analytical Psychotherapy (NAAP)
The National Register of Hypnotherapists and Psychotherapists (NRHP)
National School of Hypnosis and Psychotherapy (NSHAP)
North Staffs. Association for Psychotherapy (NSTAF)
North West Institute for Dynamic Psychotherapy (NWIDP)
The Oxford Centre for Human Relations (OCHRE)
Philadelphia Association (PA)
Psychosynthesis and Education Trust (PET)
Regent's College School of Psychotherapy and Counselling (RCSPC)
Society of Analytical Psychology (SAP)
The Sherwood Psychotherapy Training Institute (SHPTI)
Severnside Institute for Psychotherapy (SIP)
South Trent Training in Dynamic Psychotherapy (STTDP)

Tavistock Marital Studies Institute (TMSI)
University of Liverpool Diploma in Psychotherapy (ULDP)
University of Leicester Diploma in Psychodynamic Studies (ULDPS)
West Midlands Institute of Psychotherapy (WMIP)
The Women's Therapy Centre (WTC)
Yorkshire Association for Psychodynamic Psychotherapy (YAPP)

Appendix B

The United Kingdom Council for Psychotherapy
Ethical guidelines

ETHICAL RELATIONSHIPS IN THE CONTEXT OF PSYCHOTHERAPY

Petrūska Clarkson (Ethics Committee, British Association for Psychoanalytic and Psychodynamic Supervision) and Lesley Murdin (Ethics Committee, UKCP and Deputy Head of Training, Westminster Pastoral Foundation

These remarks are a contextualisation which we as individual professionals thought valuable and necessary as a brief frame for consideration in reading the ethical guidelines of the UKCP. This piece is *not* to be taken as official or representing the views of the various committees on which we serve. Extensive discussion is available elsewhere (P. Clarkson and L. Murdin, 1995, in press, 'Ethical relationships: the context of psychotherapy'.

The primary task of therapy is the restoration of relationship with oneself, with others, with the world. The work of the psychotherapist is conducted through relationship. Like all other relationships, it is vulnerable to the ills of exploitation or defensive practice, reductionism or betrayal, dependency or deprivation, invasion or bystanding, rigidity or lack of boundaries constellated in the delicate fabric woven from the interaction of at least two people. Because of its particular intimacy, it may be even more vulnerable.

Ethical guidelines exist as changing and developing articulations of the best moral thinking of a professional group at any particular time. Changing circumstances, special situations and exceptions as well as case law influence, shape and also change practice. Theoretical developments take place. Political/cultural currents and world events affect sensibilities in addition to challenging certainties.

The first principle in considering ethical relationships in psychotherapy is to maintain healthy and effective working relationships. Where there appear to be difficulties, the principle should be to work towards restoring the interrupted or disturbed relationship between therapist and patient if at all possible in the first place. Many problems could be prevented from the beginning if a client or patient openly discussed his or her discomforts with the therapist, giving him or her the opportunity to change, explain, seek supervision or other help as needed. Supervisors, mediators or independent consultants could perhaps effectively be involved at a next stage.

Only when such attempts at reconciliation and mutual understanding have demonstrably failed, should there be recourse to formal complaints procedures. Psychotherapy is about love and hate and cannot avoid entanglement with the most profound of human emotions. In many cases discussion, working through, insight into the complex dynamics of the therapy can resolve apparent irrevocable breakdowns. There are certain exceptions – as always – particularly in cases where sexual behaviour takes place. Sexual relationships are always wrong.

Most codes of ethics assume that their purpose is primarily to protect clients from the wrongdoing of therapists. That certainly is their major purpose. We might also consider the need of therapists for protection and help. Therapists may sometimes be particularly vulnerable to displaced feelings of vengeance or retaliation for the same complex reasons that doctors who go to help earthquake victims may be attacked. Transference theory also teaches us that clients (and others) may see us in illusional and, at times, delusional ways as the need arises for them. This is also open to misinterpretation – as well as therapeutic transformation – from both sides.

It is our hope that, as the primary function of ethical codes becomes more educational and protective of the therapeutic relationship, the policing and punitive function may in time become less important.

1 INTRODUCTION

1.1   The purpose of a Code of Ethics is to define general principles and to establish standards of professional conduct for psychotherapists in their work and to inform and protect those members of the public who seek their services. Each organisation will include and elaborate upon the following principles in its Code of Ethics.

1.2   All psychotherapists are expected to approach their work with the aim of alleviating suffering and promoting the well-being of their clients. Psychotherapists should endeavour to use their abilities and skills to their client's best advantage without prejudice and with due recognition of the value and dignity of every human being.

1.3   All psychotherapists on the UKCP Register are required to adhere to the Codes of Ethics and Practice of their own organisations which will be consistent with the following statements and which will have been approved by the appropriate UKCP Section.

2 CODES OF ETHICS

2.1   Each Member Organisation of UKCP must have published a Code of Ethics approved by the appropriate UKCP Section and appropriate for the practitioners of that particular organisation and their clients. The Code of Ethics will include and elaborate upon the following ten points to which attention is drawn here. All psychotherapists on the UKCP Register are required to adhere to the Codes of Ethics of their own organisations.

2.2   *Qualifications*: Psychotherapists are required to disclose their qualifications when requested and not claim, or imply, qualifications that they do not have.

2.3   *Terms, Conditions and Methods of Practice*: Psychotherapists are required to disclose on request their terms, conditions and, where appropriate, methods of practice at the outset of psychotherapy.

2.4   *Confidentiality*: Psychotherapists are required to preserve confidentiality and to disclose, if requested, the limits of confidentiality and circumstances under which it might be broken to specific third parties.

2.5   *Professional Relationship*: Psychotherapists should consider the client's best interest when making appropriate contact with the client's GP, relevant psychiatric services, or other relevant professionals, with the client's knowledge. Psychotherapists should be aware of their own limitations.

2.6   *Relationship with Clients*: Psychotherapists are required to maintain appropriate boundaries with their clients and to take care not to exploit their clients, current or past, in any way, financially, sexually or emotionally.

2.7   *Research*: Psychotherapists are required to clarify with clients the nature, purpose, and conditions of any research in which the clients are to be involved and to ensure that informed and verifiable consent is given before commencement.

2.8   *Publication*: Psychotherapists are required to safeguard the welfare and anonymity of clients when any form of publication of clinical material is being considered and to obtain their consent whenever possible.

2.9   *Practitioner Competence*: Psychotherapists are required to maintain their ability to perform competently and to take necessary steps to do so.

2.10 *Indemnity Insurance*: Psychotherapists are required to ensure that their professional work is adequately covered by appropriate indemnity insurance.

2.11 Detrimental behaviour

2.11.i Psychotherapists are required to refrain from any behaviour that may be detrimental to the profession, to colleagues or to trainees.

2.11.ii Psychotherapists are required to take appropriate action in accordance with Clause 5.8 with regard to the behaviour of a colleague which may be detrimental to the profession, to colleagues or to trainees.

3 ADVERTISING

3.1 Member organisations of UKCP are required to restrict promotion of their work to a description of the type of psychotherapy which they provide.

3.2 Psychotherapists are required to distinguish carefully between self-descriptions as in a list and advertising seeking enquiries.

4 CODE OF PRACTICE

4.1 Each Member Organisation of UKCP will have published a Code of Practice approved by the appropriate UKCP Section and appropriate for the practitioners of that particular organisation and their clients. The purpose of Codes of Practice is to clarify and expand upon the general principles established in the Code of Ethics of the organisation and the practical application of those principles. All psychotherapists on the UKCP Register will be required to adhere to the Codes of Practice of their own organisations.

5 COMPLAINTS PROCEDURE

5.1 Each Member Organisation of UKCP must have published a Complaints Procedure, including information about the acceptability or otherwise of a complaint made by a third party against a practitioner, approved by the appropriate UKCP Section and appropriate for the practitioners of that particular organisation and their clients. The purpose of a Complaints Procedure is to ensure that practitioners and their clients have clear information about the procedure and processes involved in dealing with complaints. All psychotherapists on the UKCP Register are required to adhere to the Complaints Procedure of their own organisations.

5.2 *Making a Complaint*: A client wishing to complain shall be advised to contact the Member Organisation.

5.3 *Receiving a Complaint*: A Member Organisation receiving a complaint against one of its psychotherapists shall ensure that the therapist is informed immediately and that both complainant and therapist are aware of the Complaints Procedure.

5.4.i.   *Appeals*: After the completion of the Complaints Procedure within an organisation, an appeal may be made to the Section on grounds of improper procedure.

5.4.ii   *Reference to UKCP Governing Board*: Appeals not resolved by the Section or those where the Section cannot appropriately hear the appeal shall be referred to the Governing Board of UKCP.

5.5   *Reports to UKCP Section*: Where a complaint is upheld the Section shall be informed by the organisation.

5.6   *Report to the UKCP Registration Board*: Member Organisations are required to report to the UKCP Registration Board the names of members who have been suspended or expelled.

5.7   *Complaints Upheld, and Convictions*: Psychotherapists are required to inform their Member Organisations if any complaint is upheld against them in another Member Organisation, if they are convicted of any notifiable criminal offence or if successful civil proceedings are brought against them in relation to their work as psychotherapists.

5.8   *Conduct of Colleagues*: Psychotherapists concerned that a colleague's conduct may be unprofessional should initiate the Complaints Procedure of the relevant Member Organisation.

5.9   The resignation of a member of an organisation shall not be allowed to impede the progress of any investigation as long as the alleged offence took place during that person's membership.

6 SANCTIONS

6.1   Psychotherapists who are suspended by, or expelled from, a Member Organisation are automatically deleted from the UKCP Register.

7 MONITORING COMPLAINTS

7.1   Member Organisations shall report to the Registration Board annually concerning the number of complaints received, the nature of the complaints and their disposition.

7.2   The Registration Board shall report annually to the Governing Board on the adequacy of Member Organisations' disciplinary procedures.

GUIDELINES FOR INCORPORATION WITHIN CODES OF PRACTICE FOR TRAINING ORGANISATIONS AND TRAINEES

This document should be read in conjunction with the Training Requirements document of UKCP and the Codes and Ethics of each individual organisation. There is a pre-supposition that the training requirements are being fulfilled.

Each training organisation is required to conduct its training in such a way as to address the needs and best interests of its trainees and of their clients. Trainees in turn are required to act in the best interests of their clients and to abide by the requirements of their training organisation.

Each organisation is advised to seek legal advice regarding its Code of Practice.

Each training organisation must therefore have a Code of Practice which incorporates the following minimum requirements:

1 Pre-course information

1.1 All prospective trainees will be fully informed of the nature and requirements of the course including its philosophy, objectives, assessment criteria and requirements for satisfactory completion.

2 Teaching

2.1 The detailed syllabus, objectives, methodology and assessment criteria for this part of the course will be clearly set out and given to all trainees.

2.2 All teachers training psychotherapists will be governed by a Code of Ethics and Practice appropriate to their work.

2.3 Teachers will respect the diversity of trainees and not discriminate on grounds of difference.

2.4 Teachers will not exploit their trainees sexually, financially or in any other relationship.

3 Clinical work

3.1 The interests of clients and trainees will be considered in establishing clinical requirements.

3.2 Requirements will be clearly set out and given to all trainees at the outset of the training.

3.3 Organisations will help trainees to make clients' interests paramount and to maintain appropriate confidentiality.

3.4 Trainees' work with clients presented for training purposes will always be closely supervised.

4 Personal and financial involvement

4.1 All prospective trainees will be clearly informed of the requirements of the course.

4.2 The degree of confidentiality will be clear. There will be safeguards to protect the confidentiality of trainees' personal material.

4.3 Training organisations will arrange for trainees to have a personal tutor and will specify the extent to which the tutor may be involved in assessment.

4.4 If an organisation wishes to change its training requirements, there must be reasonable respect for existing arrangements.

4.5 All responsibilities of costs and fees and the possibility for increases in costs during the course of training will be explicit at the outset.

5 Supervision

5.1 Organisations will ensure that supervisors are abiding by an appropriate Code of Ethics and Practice.

6 Assessment

6.1 Organisations will clearly inform trainees in writing at the outset of training of the criteria and process of assessment.

6.2 The process will be as open as possible.

6.3 Assessment processes will accord with the UKCP Training Requirement.

7 Complaints

7.1 Each organisation will clearly set out and publish a complaints procedure.

8 Appeals

8.1 Each organisation will clearly set out and publish an appeals procedure.

8.2 If a trainee or training committee is not satisfied with the organisation's internal process, complaints may be referred to the appropriate Section of UKCP and, if necessary, ultimately to the Governing Board of UKCP.

Name index

Subject index